PATRIOTS

A. J. LANGGUTH

A TOUCHSTONE BOOK
PUBLISHED BY SIMON & SCHUSTER INC.
NEW YORK   ·   LONDON   ·   TORONTO   ·   SYDNEY   ·   TOKYO

The Men Who Started
the American Revolution

Touchstone
Simon & Schuster Building
Rockefeller Center
1230 Avenue of the Americas
New York, New York 10020
Copyright © 1988 by A. J. Langguth
All rights reserved
including the right of reproduction
in whole or in part in any form
First Touchstone Edition, 1989
TOUCHSTONE and colophon are registered trademarks
of Simon & Schuster Inc.
Designed by Edith Fowler
Illustration research: Natalie Goldstein
Manufactured in the United States of America

10 9 8 7 6 5 4 3 2
10 9 8 7 6 5 4 3 2 1 Pbk.

Library of Congress Cataloging in Publication data
Langguth, A. J., date.
  Patriots/A. J. Langguth.
    p.   cm.
  Bibliography: p.
  Includes index.
    1. United States—History—Revolution, 1775–1783. I. Title.
E208.L27 1988
973.3—dc 19   87-26586
                                                                CIP

ISBN 0-671-52375-9
ISBN 0-671-67562-1 Pbk.

Pages 4-5:
"The Generals at Yorktown," by James Peale
Colonial Williamsburg Foundation

FOR
DORIS LANGGUTH
(1906–1988)

Contents

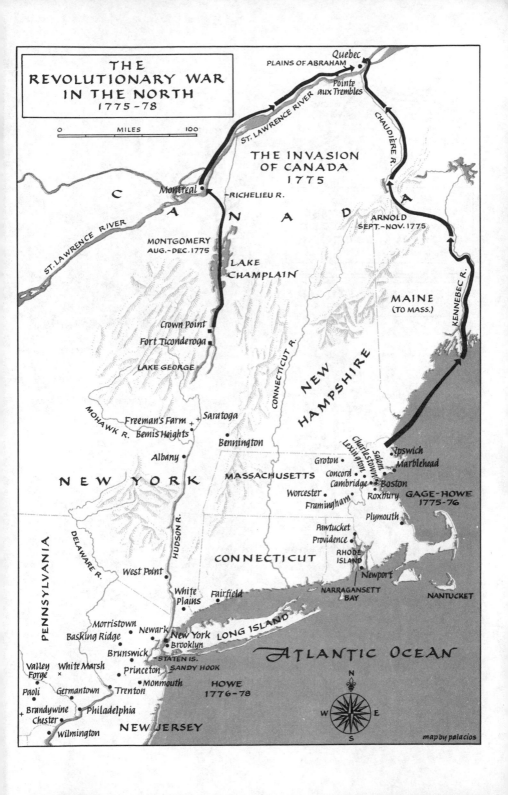

THE
REVOLUTIONARY WAR
IN THE NORTH
1775-78

0 MILES 100

Quebec
PLAINS OF ABRAHAM
Pointe
aux Trembles
ST. LAWRENCE RIVER
CHAUDIÈRE R.

THE INVASION
OF CANADA
1775

C   A   N   A   D   A

Montreal
RICHELIEU R.

ARNOLD
SEPT.–NOV. 1775

MONTGOMERY
AUG.–DEC. 1775

LAKE
CHAMPLAIN

MAINE
(TO MASS.)

KENNEBEC R.

ST. LAWRENCE RIVER

Crown Point
Fort Ticonderoga
LAKE GEORGE

NEW
HAMPSHIRE

CONNECTICUT R.

MOHAWK R.   Freeman's Farm   + Saratoga
Bemis Heights

Bennington

Albany

NEW   YORK

MASSACHUSETTS

Groton

Worcester
Framingham

Ipswich
Marblehead
Salem
Charlestown
Lexington
Concord
Cambridge   Boston
Roxbury   GAGE–HOWE
1775-76

Plymouth

Pawtucket
Providence

RHODE
ISLAND

Newport

NARRAGANSETT
BAY

NANTUCKET

HUDSON R.

DELAWARE R.

West Point

White
Plains   Fairfield

CONNECTICUT

PENNSYLVANIA

Morristown
Basking Ridge   Newark
Brunswick
Princeton   STATEN IS.
Monmouth
Valley   White Marsh
Forge
Paoli   Germantown   Trenton
Brandywine   Philadelphia
Chester
Wilmington

NEW   JERSEY

New York
Brooklyn   LONG ISLAND

SANDY HOOK

HOWE
1776-78

ATLANTIC OCEAN

N
W   E
S

map by palacios

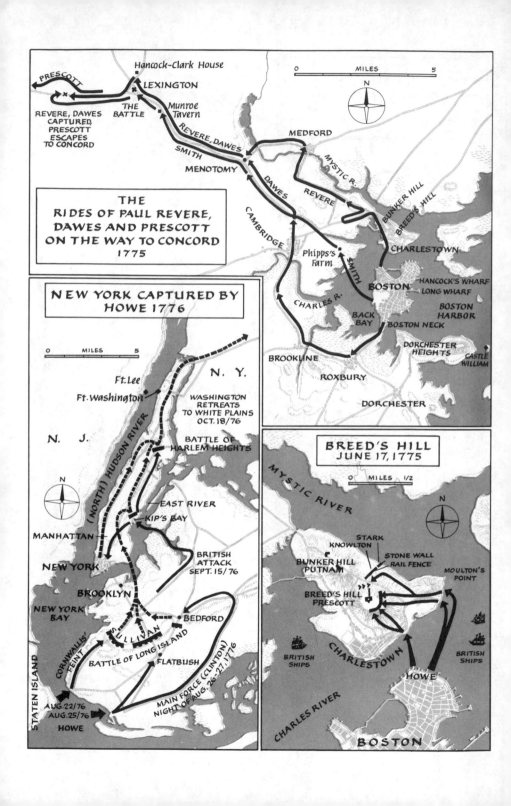

THE RIDES OF PAUL REVERE, DAWES AND PRESCOTT ON THE WAY TO CONCORD 1775

Hancock-Clark House
LEXINGTON
PRESCOTT
REVERE, DAWES CAPTURED, PRESCOTT ESCAPES TO CONCORD
THE BATTLE
Munroe Tavern
REVERE, DAWES
SMITH
MENOTOMY
DAWES
REVERE
CAMBRIDGE
MEDFORD
MYSTIC R.
BUNKER HILL
BREED'S HILL
CHARLESTOWN
Phipps's Farm
SMITH
BOSTON
HANCOCK'S WHARF
LONG WHARF
Charles R.
BACK BAY
BOSTON NECK
BOSTON HARBOR
DORCHESTER HEIGHTS
CASTLE WILLIAM
BROOKLINE
ROXBURY
DORCHESTER

MILES 0 5
N

NEW YORK CAPTURED BY HOWE 1776

MILES 0 5
N. Y.
Ft. Lee
Ft. Washington
WASHINGTON RETREATS TO WHITE PLAINS OCT. 18/76
BATTLE OF HARLEM HEIGHTS
N. J.
(NORTH) HUDSON RIVER
EAST RIVER
KIP'S BAY
MANHATTAN
BRITISH ATTACK SEPT. 15/76
NEW YORK
BROOKLYN
NEW YORK BAY
BEDFORD
SULLIVAN
CORNWALLIS' FEINT
BATTLE OF LONG ISLAND
FLATBUSH
MAIN FORCE (CLINTON) NIGHT OF AUG. 26-27, 1776
STATEN ISLAND
AUG. 22/76
AUG. 25/76
HOWE

BREED'S HILL JUNE 17, 1775

MILES 0 1/2
N
MYSTIC RIVER
STARK
KNOWLTON
STONE WALL
RAIL FENCE
BUNKER HILL
PUTNAM
MOULTON'S POINT
BREED'S HILL
PRESCOTT
CHARLESTOWN
BRITISH SHIPS
BRITISH SHIPS
HOWE
CHARLES RIVER
BOSTON

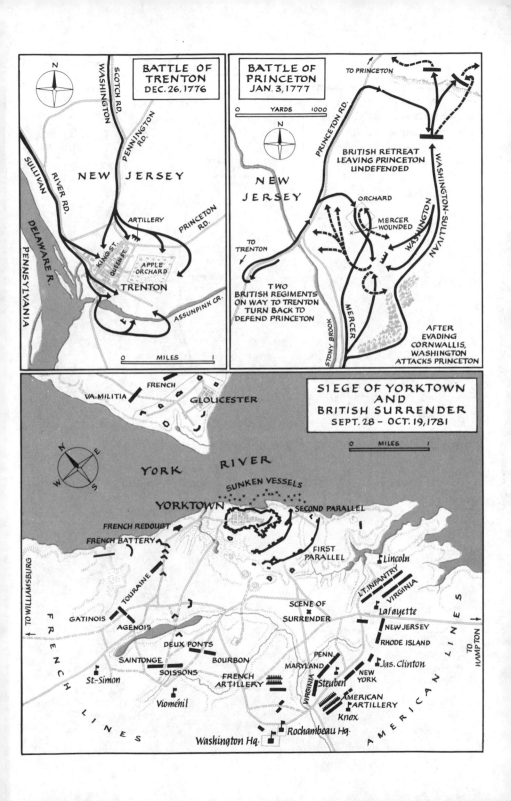

BATTLE OF TRENTON
DEC. 26, 1776

N

SCOTCH RD.

WASHINGTON

PENNINGTON RD.

NEW JERSEY

RIVER RD.

SULLIVAN

ARTILLERY

DELAWARE R.

PENNSYLVANIA

KING ST.

QUEEN ST.

APPLE ORCHARD

PRINCETON RD.

TRENTON

ASSUNPINK CR.

0 MILES 1

BATTLE OF PRINCETON
JAN. 3, 1777

0 YARDS 1000

N

TO PRINCETON

PRINCETON RD.

BRITISH RETREAT LEAVING PRINCETON UNDEFENDED

NEW JERSEY

ORCHARD

MERCER WOUNDED

WASHINGTON-SULLIVAN

WASHINGTON

TO TRENTON

TWO BRITISH REGIMENTS ON WAY TO TRENTON TURN BACK TO DEFEND PRINCETON

MERCER

STONY BROOK

AFTER EVADING CORNWALLIS, WASHINGTON ATTACKS PRINCETON

SIEGE OF YORKTOWN AND BRITISH SURRENDER
SEPT. 28 – OCT. 19, 1781

FRENCH

VA. MILITIA

GLOUCESTER

YORK RIVER

N

SUNKEN VESSELS

YORKTOWN

SECOND PARALLEL

FRENCH REDOUBT

FRENCH BATTERY

FIRST PARALLEL

Lincoln

TO WILLIAMSBURG

TOURAINE

LT. INFANTRY

VIRGINIA

GATINOIS

SCENE OF SURRENDER

Lafayette

AGENOIS

NEW JERSEY

DEUX PONTS

RHODE ISLAND

FRENCH LINES

SAINTONGE

BOURBON

PENN.

Jas. Clinton

SOISSONS

MARYLAND

NEW YORK

St.-Simon

FRENCH ARTILLERY

VIRGINIA

Steuben

Vioménil

AMERICAN ARTILLERY

Knox

AMERICAN LINES

TO HAMPTON

Washington Hq.

Rochambeau Hq.

0 MILES 1

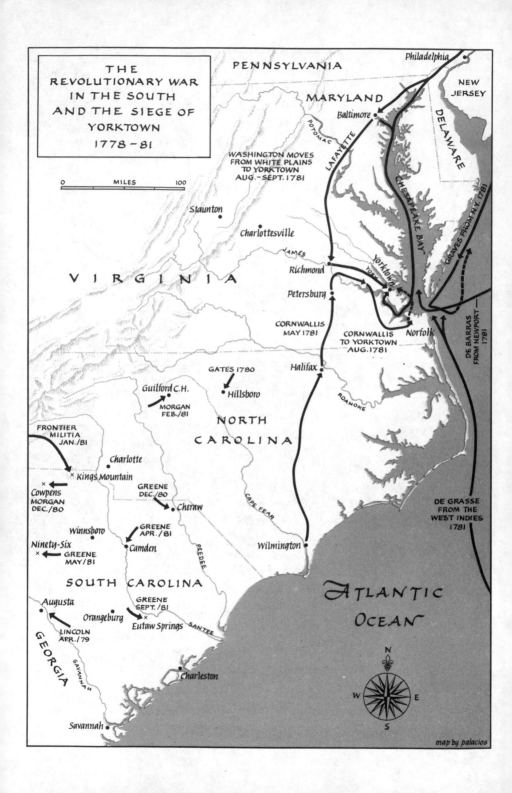

THE
REVOLUTIONARY WAR
IN THE SOUTH
AND THE SIEGE OF
YORKTOWN
1778 – 81

0 MILES 100

PENNSYLVANIA

Philadelphia

MARYLAND

NEW JERSEY

DELAWARE

Baltimore

POTOMAC

LAFAYETTE

WASHINGTON MOVES
FROM WHITE PLAINS
TO YORKTOWN
AUG.–SEPT. 1781

Staunton

Charlottesville

CHESAPEAKE BAY

JAMES

GRAVES FROM N.Y. 1781

Richmond

VIRGINIA

Yorktown

YORK

Petersburg

CORNWALLIS
MAY 1781

CORNWALLIS
TO YORKTOWN
AUG. 1781

Norfolk

DE BARRAS
FROM NEWPORT
1781

GATES 1780

Halifax

ROANOKE

Guilford C.H.

Hillsboro

MORGAN
FEB./81

NORTH
CAROLINA

FRONTIER
MILITIA
JAN./81

Charlotte

× Kings Mountain

GREENE
DEC./80

CAPE FEAR

×
Cowpens
MORGAN
DEC./80

Winnsboro

GREENE
APR./81

Cheraw

Ninety-Six
× ← GREENE
MAY/81

Camden

PEEDEE

DE GRASSE
FROM THE
WEST INDIES
1781

Wilmington

SOUTH CAROLINA

Augusta

Orangeburg

GREENE
SEPT./81
×
Eutaw Springs

SANTEE

ATLANTIC
OCEAN

LINCOLN
APR./79

GEORGIA

SAVANNAH

Charleston

Savannah

N
W   E
S

map by palacios

Otis
1761-62

JOHN ADAMS, a twenty-five-year-old lawyer from the country, looked around Boston's Town House and was dazzled by its splendor. Adams had never been to London, but he was sure that nothing in the House of Commons could be more imposing than the sight of five judges in scarlet robes and luminous white wigs, seated in front of a marble fireplace. On the wall were portraits of two former British kings, Charles II and James II, which had been sent from London years before. They had been stored in an attic until a recently installed governor of Massachusetts, Francis Bernard, had discovered them and had them cleaned and mounted in magnificent gold frames. Adams was aware that both kings were autocrats and he suspected that giving them such a place of honor showed Bernard's political bias. But he thought them beautiful, worthy of Rubens or Vandyke.

Adams had come on this overcast morning in February 1761 to see the climax to a political drama that had been unfolding for months. Normally, the day's proceedings would have been routine: a new king had recently taken the throne in England, and a document called the writ of assistance had to be approved once again by the colony's Superior Court. But the writ was in fact a general search warrant, and it represented a serious economic threat around Boston Harbor. When ships sailed past the islands in the channel and came to anchor at one of Boston's long wooden wharves, they were often smuggling illegal goods along with their legitimate cargo. Molasses was especially popular, since it could be shipped legally only from British ports. Some sixty distillers around Massachusetts turned the molasses into millions of gallons of rum each year, and the traders who supplied them bought a better quality at French and Dutch ports in the West Indies and avoided the British taxes. Over the past twenty years, Bostonians had suffered economic depressions, and they were worried now that London's attempt to enforce the customs law might set off more hard times. That would affect not only the merchants but also the men who built the ships and sailed them, the distillers and shopkeepers, the artisans who supplied silver buckles and candlesticks, even the town's hundreds of teenage apprentices in their leather aprons.

The persistent war between England and the French and their Indian allies had provided an economic boom for a few profiteers, but the peace that now seemed assured might bring inflation and greater debt. Boston's wealthiest merchants enjoyed a cushion against a depression; five hundred of the sixteen thousand residents owned nearly fifty percent of the town's assets. But one out of three adult men had no property or even a regular job, and they hung about the wharves taking whatever work they found or signing on as sailors. Some were forced to leave the capital altogether for one of the smaller communities—Salem, Gloucester, Marblehead.

British law already gave the crown's tax collectors permission to search a ship while it lay at anchor in the bay, although few had ever been zealous about making the effort. Some of those appointed were Londoners who never bothered to come to America. Others could be bribed. Britain spent eight thousand pounds each year on salaries for the customs service and collected two thousand pounds in taxes. But the writs that were to be reauthorized were more menacing because they allowed officials to break into a man's warehouse or even his home to find contraband. Disruptions during the war with the French had prevented the writs from being widely used, but now, with Britain moving to enforce the law, merchants in Boston and Salem had responded by challenging the writs' legality and had hired two prominent lawyers to argue the case before the Massachusetts Bay Colony's highest court.

This public aspect of the dispute was what had drawn Adams to the Town House. But, like most observers, he knew there were also personal resentments that could affect the case's outcome. At the center was Thomas Hutchinson. Despite his lack of training as a lawyer, Hutchinson had been appointed by Governor Bernard three months earlier to replace the chief justice who had died. For thirty years, Massachusetts lawyers had been struggling to win respectability for their calling, and many were disgusted that their profession's highest honor had gone to a man who was reading elementary law texts at night to prepare for court. John Adams was a self-conscious young man, desperately ambitious, and he had come to the capital from the town of Braintree to make his reputation. He thought he understood why Hutchinson had been named to the high court. The previous chief justice had expressed doubts that the writs were legal. Hutchinson was known to support them. But the significance of his appointment went far beyond that.

John Adams came from an honest and hard-working but not particularly distinguished family, and he was contemptuous of the idea that a man's place in society should be determined by his lineage. And in Boston, few men represented entrenched privilege more clearly than Thomas Hutchinson. The Hutchinsons had been successful businessmen for generations, and Thomas had been brought up to be a member of Boston's ruling class, although he had to contend with problems within the family. His father suffered from nervous disorders that kept him shut up in his house for weeks and from chronic insomnia, and he had lost two favorite sons and a daughter to smallpox and consumption.

By the time Thomas Hutchinson entered Harvard College,

two months before his twelfth birthday, his character was already formed. His one lapse—he had used a Greek trot to translate a Latin lesson—had caused his tutor to remark, "*A non te expectare,*" I did not expect it of you. Thomas would remember that rebuke for the rest of his life. He loved history best and wept at the account of Charles I's beheading.

At college, Thomas began his business career by trading several hundred pounds of fish his father had given him. By graduation, he had built that capital into nearly five hundred pounds sterling. When he married, at twenty-three, Thomas had become an imposing young man, six feet tall. His seventeen-year-old bride was the daughter of a man whose family had been the Hutchinsons' business partners for four generations. Though Thomas was normally aloof, it was a good marriage. He would remark that the intimacy he found with Peggy Hutchinson was proof that he had a soul.

Hutchinson turned naturally to public service and in 1737, at the age of twenty-six, was elected to the Massachusetts House of Representatives, ignoring his father, who warned him, "Depend on it, if you serve your country faithfully, you will be reproached and reviled for doing it." More than Thomas cared to recognize, he had inherited the spirit of his great-great-grandmother Anne Hutchinson, who had been banished to Rhode Island in 1637 as a religious zealot. He might be temperate and rational in his religion, but in a political cause he could be stubborn to the point of foolhardiness. Hutchinson used his mastery of economics to defend Boston's aristocrats against challenges from a growing party of workers and shopkeepers. When Boston went through periods of inflation, Hutchinson antagonized much of the town by advocating hard-money policies, and in 1749 he had led a move to base the colony's currency on silver. The economic contractions that followed turned his name into a curse among the town's working people. When his house caught fire, crowds gathered, shouting, "Let it burn!"

Hutchinson remained within a close circle of family and prosperous friends. He considered it contemptible to seek a wider popularity and described the multitude as "foreign seamen, servants, Negroes and other persons of mean and vile condition." When his conservative fiscal policies cost him his seat in the House, the governor had named him to the Council, the more aristocratic upper body. Hutchinson's career was destined to continue at that higher level. He built a summer house on a hundred acres in Milton, eight miles from Boston, and visitors from abroad assured him they had never seen a finer view than the one from his hilltop.

In 1754, Peggy Hutchinson died at the end of her twelfth pregnancy. Hutchinson had always believed that religion—like sound money—was essential to a well-ordered society, but his faith was no consolation to him now. He buried his wife and moved to Milton with his four children and his new daughter, another Peggy, who had survived.

When Hutchinson returned to public life, he served first as an aide to the royal governor, then as his lieutenant. His ambition revived, and he fought successfully to preside over the Council. He was also a judge of probate, a justice of common pleas and governor of Castle William, the royal fortress in Boston Harbor. His hobby was collecting documents, letters and journals, and he planned to publish his version of the history of the Massachusetts Bay Colony.

In Boston's many taverns, men had not forgiven Hutchinson for his consistent support of the rich and powerful and were troubled by the way he was consolidating his authority. They called him "Summa Potestatis," the supreme power, or simply "Summa." Now he had added the position of chief justice to his collection.

Hutchinson's appointment had annoyed John Adams, but it was far more disturbing to a thirty-five-year-old lawyer named James Otis. When the chief justice died in September, Otis had called on Thomas Hutchinson to ask his help in getting an appointment to the court for his father, the speaker of the Massachusetts House of Representatives. A previous governor had promised Speaker Otis a place on the Superior Court, and the younger Otis wanted Hutchinson to use his influence with Governor Bernard to secure it.

Otis had gone to the Hutchinson mansion in Boston's North End, one of the town's most beautiful houses. Most Bostonians knew that the Hutchinson family looked down on the Otises, but

James Otis, who was quick-tempered and haughty, had put aside his pride to make the call. Hutchinson, approaching fifty, was slender and fair, with the assurance of privilege. Otis was plump, with a round face and a short neck, but his eyes were keen and he exuded energy. Although he had studied law, the one book he had published was a study of Latin poetry.

Otis had put his appeal diffidently. If Mr. Hutchinson himself had any interest in serving on the high court, he would not say another word about his father. Hutchinson swore later that he had told Otis candidly that he had considered the appointment but that he wasn't sure he would accept if Bernard offered it to him. Otis had left convinced that Hutchinson had said he would turn it down.

Soon after, Otis had called directly on Governor Bernard. The town of Boston was almost an island, linked to the mainland by a narrow road called Boston Neck, and as Otis was riding his horse toward the governor's mansion he saw Thomas Hutchinson coming the other way in a carriage, apparently returning from his own audience with the governor. Then there were other disturbing portents about the appointment. Some of Boston's established merchants were openly questioning whether Speaker Otis was qualified to sit on the Superior Court. Over the years, he had done many favors for the colony's conservative governors, but his career had begun fifteen years earlier, in rougher times, when election officials sometimes reached into the hat that doubled as a ballot box and threw out all of the opposition votes.

Speaker Otis' first bill in the House had set a bounty on Indian scalps—one hundred English pounds for males twelve years or older, fifty pounds for women. And although the Otises were an established New England family, Speaker Otis had worked as a shoemaker in his youth. Since two thirds of the members of the Massachusetts House listed "farmer" as their primary occupation, that was no disgrace, and Otis had gone on to become a prosperous lawyer. But he had always regretted his lack of a classical education and had made sure that James went to Harvard College and then to study law under Jeremiah Gridley, the colony's finest legal scholar.

Memories among Boston's aristocracy were long and unforgiving. Conservative merchants were arguing that Speaker Otis was backed by the same men they had been fighting for years—Boston's retailers, innkeepers, others of the lower classes. Thomas Hutchinson had told friends that Otis had become speaker of the House only because he had done "little low dirty things" that no reputable person would stoop to doing.

Two months passed after James Otis' appeal to Hutchinson until, in mid-November, Governor Bernard told Hutchinson that he wanted him as chief justice. Hutchinson warned him that he might be courting trouble by disappointing the Otises, and he added that around town James Otis was threatening violence if his father was not chosen. But Bernard offered Hutchinson the job and added that whatever his answer, he did not intend to appoint Speaker Otis.

Hutchinson accepted. For years, the king's ministers in London had passed him over for the governorship, and he had served under three governors from England. It seemed unlikely that he would ever hold the highest title, although he had several consolations beyond his judgeships. As lieutenant governor, Hutchinson was already the colony's deputy executive. As president of the Council, he was its ranking legislator. Now he would hold the highest judicial post.

When he heard about the appointment, James Otis was enraged. Aside from the insult to his father, Otis believed that Hutchinson would hold two titles too many. Montesquieu's *The Spirit of Laws* had been published a dozen years earlier, and Otis had been impressed by its argument for separating the three branches of government. But now, because Otis had tried to get the post for his father, his criticism of Hutchinson's expanding power could be dismissed as coming from a disgruntled loser. And Hutchinson's friends did soon accuse Otis of making wild threats against the colony's government. They said he had vowed to set the province in flames, though he himself might perish in the fire. Everyone knew that Otis was proud of his Latin scholarship, and his antagonists clinched their charge by quoting a line from Virgil that Otis was supposed to be repeating: *"Flectere si nequeo superos, Acheronta movebo."* (If heaven I cannot bend, then hell I'll stir.) Otis' political allies called the allegation a lie. They said no one would become frenzied over such a trivial setback. But in Boston's small world, Otis was well known. John Adams, who was eager to learn from other men's success, had been studying Otis carefully and admired his agile mind. But he had also watched Otis' quick temper cause him to stutter and had seen Otis' muscles twitch even when he was sitting still. Everything about Otis' tense brilliance made the reports of his threats entirely plausible.

James Otis' energy and his unpredictable moods had been apparent even when he was growing up. Pressed into playing the violin for friends who wanted to dance, he had thrown it down and run off to the garden, shouting, "So fiddled Orpheus and danced the brutes!" He had entered Harvard in 1739, at fourteen, young but not as remarkable as Hutchinson's going before he was twelve. He had frittered away his first two years but then began coming home on vacations to Barnstable and locking himself up with his books. He spent seven years at Harvard, earned the traditional master's degree and was in no hurry to start working. He spent a year and a half reading the classics at home before he began to study law.

James Otis' apprenticeship with Jeremiah Gridley seemed to harness his mercurial temperament, and at last he gave his father reason to be proud, a welcome development at a time when the Otises' neighbors accused James's younger brother of getting their black nanny pregnant. Gridley also had a classical bent, and the young man's years with him were congenial except for the assignments in Sir Edward Coke's impenetrable volumes. After his apprenticeship, Otis set up practice briefly in Plymouth, but he tired of small-town life and moved to Boston. Soon he was collecting the largest fees in the province. But money didn't drive James Otis, and he often didn't bother to hide his indifference.

Each year on November 5, gangs from North and South Boston paraded through the streets in a ceremony called Pope's Day. It was an American version of England's Guy Fawkes Day, commemorating the Gunpowder Plot of 1605, when a band of Catholics had tried to blow up King James I and the Parliament with him. In New England, the occasion had become the excuse for a brawl; an almanac summed it up, "Powder plot is not forgot. 'Twill be observed by many a sot." Each gang carried a large effigy of the Pope, and the two parades collided in an explosion of rocks and fists. After one such melee, Otis was hired by men charged with breaking windows and doing other damage. In court, he defended the tradition and argued that a few youths had simply gone on a spree with no malice and doing little harm. Otis won an acquittal and refused a fee.

At the age of thirty, he made a love match with Ruth Cunningham, a reserved, pretty woman entirely committed to the conservative principles of her merchant father. She brought with her a handsome dowry, which Otis immediately put in trust as an inheritance for their children.

By the time Otis went to Hutchinson on behalf of his father, he held a well-paid post as the king's advocate general in the Vice-Admiralty Court at Boston. But he refused to argue for the crown's customs officers in the writs-of-assistance case, and when the merchants asked for his help in opposing them Otis responded enthusiastically. "In such a cause," he said, "I despise all fees." Before Hutchinson joined the Superior Court late in December 1760, James Otis resigned his royal commission to prepare for the legal battle of his life, and John Adams had come to court to witness the result.

Jeremiah Gridley, Otis' tutor in the law, was acting as the king's attorney, and he opened the case with the crown's arguments. He admitted that the writs had provoked widespread antagonism by infringing on the common rights of Englishmen, but he defended the principle of a search warrant. How could a state protect itself against foreign enemies or subversives at home? Which was more important, protecting the liberty of an individual or collecting the taxes efficiently? Gathering public money must take precedence.

Many in the audience were not convinced, remembering the case of a man named Ware, who had acquired a writ from a customs official who casually endorsed it over to him. When a justice ordered a constable to bring Ware to court for profane swearing on the Sabbath, Ware had listened to the charge and then asked the judge if he was finished. "Yes," said the judge. "Very well, then," said Ware, "I will show you a little of my power. I command you to permit me to search your house for uncustomed goods." Ware tore up the judge's house from attic to cellar. When he finished, he started all over again at the constable's house.

Gridley returned to his seat, and Otis' co-counsel, Oxenbridge Thacher, spoke. Thacher had briefly studied divinity, because he was ambitious and clergymen ranked at the top of
Massachusetts society. When his voice proved too weak to reach
beyond the pulpit, he had turned to law, launching his career by
taking the divorce cases his fellow lawyers shunned. But Thacher
had begun to distrust Hutchinson's growing power, and now his
voice was echoing through the colony. Hutchinson had mocked
his new attachment to the workingmen's faction by remarking
that Thacher had not been born a plebeian but seemed determined
to die one. Thacher's opposition to the writs had dismayed the
conservatives more than anything James Otis had said, since they
couldn't discredit him as a vengeful troublemaker.

In his opening statement, Thacher argued that simply because
the writs were being freely issued in London was no reason for
Massachusetts courts to do the same. He denounced the fact that
one writ could be used over and over as a wanton exercise of
power. His argument might have carried the day. The writs were
unpopular, and not every judge took the same pride Hutchinson
did in flouting public opinion. But then, in wig and black gown,
James Otis stood up to speak, and something profound changed
in America.

To John Adams, Otis rose in the hall like a flame of fire. He
seemed to overflow with dates, events, legal precedents, classical
allusions. His erudition swept everything before him. Although
he treated Gridley with great respect, Otis took on each of his
arguments and demolished it. Adams thought that Gridley—who
was merely doing his duty for the crown—seemed to be exulting
in his pupil's triumph.

What was Otis' argument? He claimed to be doing nothing
more than applying a lesson from the textbooks. Coke's compila-
tion of English law in the previous century had often challenged
the king's power and called upon judges to nullify any act that
went against an Englishman's common rights, or against reason,
or was repugnant or impossible to enforce. Otis took Coke as his
authority and made a strong case that any law was void if it violated England's constitution. But a newcomer to the law like
Hutchinson, who had not pored over Coke's commentaries, accepted Gridley's version of more recent history. For Hutchinson,

Britain's Glorious Revolution of 1688 had not only deposed James II but also left Parliament the empire's supreme authority. The British constitution was now only and whatever Parliament said it was.

But Otis soared beyond that argument. Every man lived in a state of nature, he said. Every man was his own sovereign, subject to laws engraved on his heart and revealed to him by his Maker. No other creature on earth could legitimately challenge a man's right to his life, his liberty and his property. That principle, that unalterable law, took precedence—here Otis was answering Gridley directly—even over the survival of the state. Then Otis issued a guarded warning to the new king: The writs of assistance represented the sort of destructive and arbitrary use of power that had cost one king his head and another his throne.

Otis turned to the subject of English liberty, particularly freedom at home. "A man's house is his castle," he said, and if a man behaves quietly there he must be as well protected as a prince. As John Adams listened and made notes, he found his attitude toward England changing. Otis' argument was making him see the mother country as not only powerful but also haughty. This writs case could be merely the beginning. Britain's politicians might be intending to impose complete control over the colonies' finances and politics. From now on, every action from Parliament and the king's ministers had to be weighed carefully to see what motive lay behind it.

Otis had spoken for more than four hours. When he finished, John Adams wanted to rush out and take up arms against the writs, and he was sure every man in the packed hall was ready to join him. The court adjourned with Thomas Hutchinson sensing that his fellow judges might have been stampeded along with Otis' audience. During their conference, some judges began talking of compromise. One reported that in England writs were now being issued only in specific cases and after very detailed information about possible smuggling. Hutchinson was concerned that any tightening of the procedures might lead to an informant's name being made public, which would stop men from coming forward to report smugglers. No one else had heard of that change in the law, and the judge remembered only that he had read about it in

London Magazine. Hutchinson used the uncertainty to buy time and agreed to write to England for clarification. Receiving an answer could take months. Meanwhile, the court held off its ruling until the following year.

Throughout Massachusetts, however, it was clear that James Otis had won his case. When he appeared at Boston's next Town Meeting, he was greeted with loud applause. Three months later, the town voted overwhelmingly to send him to the House of Representatives. It dismayed Hutchinson that Bostonians seemed to agree that Otis had acted out of a sincere concern for liberty rather than from spite, and around Massachusetts other conservatives sensed that a dangerous new adversary was arising. John Adams was dining with prominent lawyers in Worcester when he heard one of the king's loyalists, Timothy Ruggles, say, "Out of this election will arise a damned faction, which will shake this province to its foundation."

James Otis' opponents weren't the only ones who worried about sending such an explosive man to a deliberative body. As Otis took his seat in the House after the election of May 1761, a friend who would be sitting nearby approached him with a warning: "Mr. Otis, you have great abilities but are too warm, too impetuous. Your opponents, though they cannot meet you in argument, will get the advantage by interrupting you and putting you in a passion."

Otis said, "Well, if you see me growing warm, give me a hint and I'll command myself."

A dispute soon arose and Otis murmured that he intended to speak. Remember, his friend said, don't get irritated. Otis took the floor and was crushing the opposition when Timothy Ruggles interrupted him. Otis flushed and intensified his attack. From behind him, his friend pulled lightly on his coat. Otis turned with a scowl but checked himself and softened his tone.

He had barely resumed when another man, Choate of Ipswich, interrupted. Once more, Otis began to flare up. The friend pulled on his coat a little harder. This time, Otis turned around and said, "Let me alone! Do you take me for a schoolboy?" And he proceeded to devastate the conservative opposition.

House members learned that when Otis was out of control even past loyalties couldn't restrain him. On an occasion when he and Oxenbridge Thacher took opposite sides, the younger Otis became so abusive that Thacher had to ask the elder Otis, the House speaker, for protection. In court, Otis went out of his way to attack the judges who would be hearing his cases. Finally, Hutchinson's brother-in-law, Judge Peter Oliver, complained to John Adams that Otis had slandered the entire judiciary. Adams had his own reservations about Otis, but he pointed out that he had many fine talents.

"If Bedlamism is a talent," said Oliver, "he has that in perfection."

The early 1760s were supplying a wealth of controversies to keep Otis agitated. He blocked the conservatives who wanted to punish counterfeiting with the death penalty, and he succeeded in ousting William Bollan from his job as the Massachusetts agent in England, the man paid to look after the colony's interests. Otis admitted that he didn't much care who held the post; he simply hated to see Hutchinson win at anything. In a light mood, he proposed a law charging with high treason any man who believed in "certain imaginary beings called devils." His motive wasn't religious. At home, Otis did not hold family prayers, and, in a time when gentlemen were expected to attend church, he had never joined a congregation.

By the time the job of London agent went to a draper named Jasper Mauduit, Otis was as determined to thwart Governor Bernard as Hutchinson. He was overheard describing Bernard as a bigot and a plantation governor interested only in filling his own pockets. When those insults appeared anonymously in print, the governor knew who was responsible. Bernard had redeemed himself with Otis' father by letting him disburse all the patronage in Barnstable County, and Speaker Otis hadn't hesitated to pick off the two best judgeships for himself. That peace offering had also appeased James Otis long enough for him to back a grant of land that Bernard coveted. But no sooner was one hatchet buried than Otis was brandishing another. Thomas Hutchinson concluded that whenever Otis was annoyed by anyone, anywhere in the colony, he would take his revenge on Hutchinson.

The strain of his temperament told on Otis. During his second session in the House, he angrily resigned his seat and then asked for it back the next day. But even at his most erratic, he had a sure touch for language that touched Boston's heart, and he fought the conservatives effectively by contrasting himself with Hutchinson and his circle.

"I know it is the maxim of some," Otis wrote in an antigovernment weekly, the *Boston Gazette*, "that the common people in this town live too well; however . . . I do not think they live half well enough."

Carpenters and bakers, along with the men who ran shops and taverns, had watched their incomes decline until their work was paying less than in their grandfathers' day. Meanwhile, the colony's benefits seemed to be flowing to the small circle of the lieutenant governor and his friends. At the beginning of 1762 Otis wrote, "My dear friends, fellow citizens and countrymen, I am forced to get my living by the labors of my hand and the sweat of my brow, as most of you are." He pledged to go on defying those men who owed "their grandeur and honors to grinding the faces of the poor and other arts of ill-gotten gain and power."

Thomas Hutchinson considered suing for libel.

By now, Otis found reasons to oppose almost any action by the governor or his lieutenant. Despite England's victory over France, Frenchmen in Newfoundland were continuing to threaten British fisheries. Governor Bernard intended to allocate a few hundred pounds to protect Britain's interests by sending an armed sloop up the coast. The conservative Council approved the project. But Otis and his allies saw a peril in bypassing the House on a revenue measure, and he drew up a protest. If the House gave up its right to raise revenue, he wrote, Massachusetts might as well be ruled by the king of France instead of George III. If either king could levy taxes without a House vote, the two kings would be equally arbitrary.

When Otis read his protest on the House floor, a conservative delegate objected to his reference to Britain's new monarch and shouted, "Treason! Treason!"

Otis defended his language, and it passed the House easily. But the governor also found the allusion to the king improper and sent the message back to the House to have the sentences expunged. Otis inserted a few diplomatic words expressing all due reverence for the king's sacred person but kept to his original point.

When the protest was back on the House floor, the man who had shouted "Treason!" listened to Otis' compromises and cried, "Erase them! Erase them!" A majority of the House agreed, and the provocative language was dropped. James Otis learned that his countrymen were not ready to attack the power of the British crown.

Samuel Adams, by John Singleton Copley

Adams
1762-63

IN LONDON, the new young king had been struggling since his coronation to gain for himself the kind of power James Otis was suggesting he already had. His subjects saw Prime Minister William Pitt as their true leader, since it was under his command that England had won the Seven Years' War, with its American phase known as the French and Indian War. When the prince assumed the throne as King George III in October 1760, he might have ensured a tranquil reign by keeping Pitt as his prime minister and contenting himself with being a royal figurehead.

At first, George seemed headed for that serenity. A Virginian wrote home from London that the only crisis facing the tall, fair young man with full lips and protruding gray eyes was the danger of being kissed to death by the ladies of his court. But in the House of Commons, one member was less sure. "The young man," said Charles Townshend, "is very obstinate."

Young George had come to the throne full of resentments. Power had been draining away from the crown to Parliament for seventy years, even before George's ancestors had come from Germany to found the Hanoverian dynasty and accelerate the monarchy's decline. The London court had regarded George I, his great-grandfather, and George II, his grandfather, as Teutonic oddities. When George I became Britain's king, he spoke no English, and his ministers had to speak to him in simple Latin. George I had questioned whether he was the father of his heir, Prince George Augustus, and as the young man grew up the two quarreled so violently that the king had his son arrested. When the king died abruptly of apoplexy, however, the prince became George II, but he spent much of his reign at Hanover and left ruling England to his wife, Caroline, and Sir Robert Walpole.

George II and Caroline had shared a distaste for their own son, Frederick. Then, soon after Caroline's death in 1737, Frederick's wife gave birth to a son so frail that he was baptized at once and was expected to die. Instead, the third George survived, grew into his large frame and showed from infancy that he had inherited his grandfather's bulging eyes. It was Frederick who died young, and George II began to take a bullying interest in his thirteen-year-old grandson. He chided him for his solitary nature and for days spent playing cards with his attendants. When the king tested him with a history question and the tense young man couldn't answer, George II slapped him. "You are only fit for reading the Bible to your mother," the king said.

The boy's widowed mother, Augusta, was being consoled by a Scotsman named John Stuart, third Earl of Bute, who had become the young prince's closest friend. He wrote to the earl about his most intimate worries—how badly he was racked by sexual desire, how eager he was to find a wife. The prince complained to Bute that Pitt treated them both like children: "He seems to forget the day will come when he must expect to be treated according to his deserts." Augusta wanted her son to reverse the crown's loss of power and encouraged him to be sensitive to slights and condescension. "Be a king!" she would tell her son. "George, be a king!"

One morning when George was twenty-two, he was summoned to the palace from an early gallop. An hour later, William Pitt arrived in his blue-and-silver carriage to tell him that his grandfather had died and he was now George III. The young man's first act as sovereign was to set out over a back road for Lord Bute's estate. George would try to be a king to please his mother, but he needed someone to show him how.

In the two years after the writs-of-assistance case, many of James Otis' countrymen tired of his insistent calls to oppose the royal governor and his circle. By the elections of 1763, Otis' allies had lost control of the Massachusetts House and were outnumbered two to one by Francis Bernard's faction. The peace treaty between Britain and France that same year had reminded Bostonians to be grateful for the victory over the French and the Indians. Thomas Hutchinson lectured his fellow citizens: God had delivered them from their foreign enemies, and the people shouldn't go on quarreling among themselves. Otis was not adjusting to the days of good feeling. Even his brother was calling him "Esquire Bluster," and among his Whig allies he was "Furio." As the new House session of 1763 began, Otis threatened once more to resign and once more changed his mind.

Much of the colony had lost interest in the factional bickering, though the conservatives were attempting to consolidate their control. Hutchinson and his group were supported by Francis Bernard, who wielded the king's patronage. Otis' political base depended on a shifting alliance of Boston's merchants, lawyers and workingmen. To organize and inspire them he could rely on the tireless efforts of an ally, Samuel Adams.

Samuel Adams, a cousin of John, was a politician in a day when the label was demeaning. His father had been one before him, though he had been a successful maltster, the merchant who steeped barley in water to prepare it for brewing. At the Old South Church Samuel's father had been known as Deacon Adams, a godly man devoted to the Congregational faith. But above all, the deacon had been committed to politics, and the crusade of his life was an economic scheme called the Land Bank.

In 1740, Massachusetts had sunk deep into depression. Farmers and workers had become indebted to merchants who had aggravated their distress by refusing to accept paper money in place of gold or silver. Deacon Adams, along with fellow members of Boston's Caucus Club, had thrown himself into the conflict. The Caucus, an alliance of tradesmen and artisans, had first been known as the "Caulkers" Club, since shipwrights were well represented, and that had evolved to "Corcas" and then "Caucus." For years the club had set the agenda for Boston's Town Meetings and decided who would be appointed to the various town offices. Deacon Adams and his comrades wanted to revive the economy by instituting a floating currency backed with their own real estate. The colony's richest merchants opposed this Land Bank, claiming that it would promote inflation and favor the debtors by cutting into the assets of those who lent money. Conservatives like Thomas Hutchinson demanded to be paid in gold and were hostile toward the Land Bankers. They called them "the idle and the extravagant," more often "the rabble." Deacon Adams' participation upset them because he was, by their definition, a gentleman.

When the Land Bank supporters won a healthy majority in the Massachusetts House, the conservatives turned to the governor for protection. He threatened to strip the offices and titles of any man who invested in the Land Bank, and he punished Deacon Adams, who had risked his sizable fortune in the people's cause, by removing him as justice of the peace. At the next election, however, the people gave the Land Bankers another overwhelming victory and sent Deacon Adams to the Council, the colony's upper house. The governor vetoed his appointment and wrote to London for action. In 1741, Parliament declared the Land Bank illegal and charged its directors with financial crimes. If the Massachusetts court had not intervened, Deacon Adams' enemies might have seized his property and sent him to jail.

That calamity had overlapped with another controversy in Boston, and both shaped the political opinions of young Samuel Adams. The deacon had enrolled his son in the Harvard class of 1740, paying his tuition in molasses and flour. In Cambridge, the greatest influence on the boy was George Whitefield, an evangelist who had arrived from England to lead a religious revival known as the Great Awakening. Samuel and many of his classmates responded to Whitefield's call for spartan piety and gave up their fashionable clothes for Puritan gray. The Great Awakening—and promptings from his devout mother—had led Samuel to consider becoming a clergyman.

After graduation, however, Samuel began to study law, but his mother didn't think that career was respectable enough and prevailed on him to quit. He returned to Harvard for a master's degree. By the time he graduated, in 1743, the colony's rich and powerful men had been denounced by the preachers of the Great Awakening for their lack of piety and by the Land Bankers for their greed. Samuel Adams was convinced on both counts. He argued in his final paper at Harvard that when the existence of the commonwealth was at stake it was lawful to resist even the highest civil authority. Deacon Adams had been crushed by superior forces, but his son didn't believe he had been proved wrong.

At twenty-one, Samuel Adams was apprenticed to Thomas Cushing, a wealthy trader and political ally of his father's. Cushing, who was called "Death's Head," had no trouble separating his trading practices from his liberal politics. Within a few months, however, he saw that Samuel Adams was not able to make that distinction. He let Samuel go, informing the deacon that he trained young men for business, not politics. Deacon Adams' next approach was to lend Samuel a thousand pounds to set himself up in business. Samuel immediately loaned a friend half of it. When the friend couldn't repay him, Deacon Adams took his son into his malt business.

The young man spent his middle twenties learning to be a maltster. Then, in 1748, Deacon Adams died, and Samuel was free. His father's will forgave the thousand-pound loan and left him the malt company, which ought to have ensured him a respectable place in Boston society. Instead, Samuel let the business slide away. He married the daughter of his clergyman at Old South Church and took his wife to live in the deteriorating house on Purchase Street with its fine view of the harbor and its pervasive smell of malt.

Samuel had also inherited debts from the Land Bank. At one point, he had to take out advertisements warning Boston's new sheriff, Stephen Greenleaf, not to try to sell his house at public auction. A narrow escape on that occasion taught Adams a tactical lesson: he had made Sheriff Greenleaf back down by threatening to sue and by intimidating potential buyers. As he later described his technique, one should always "put your adversary in the wrong. And keep him there."

In the early 1750s, Adams and a group of friends formed a secret club. Their newspaper, the *Independent Advertiser*, assailed the royal governor so persistently that conservatives called them "the Whippingpost Club." Samuel Adams had chosen austerity for himself because he thought materialism softened the character and sapped what he called "the good old New England spirit." But as the years passed and he had trouble maintaining his household, even friends began to wonder whether his indifference to money wasn't a flaw in his character. The newspaper expired, and after five pregnancies in six years of marriage his wife died, leaving Adams with a son and a daughter. By 1763, at the age of forty-one, he was still passionate about liberty and justice, even though his fellow Bostonians weren't paying him much attention.

Yet they had not lost their respect for Samuel Adams. Here was a man who lived by values that most of them honored only on the Sabbath. He had a good voice for the Sunday meeting and joined in singing the psalms. But the rest of the week he wasn't a bore or a scold, and men were glad to have him at their table. In his middle years, Adams was still solidly built, with pale skin and light-blue eyes. Settling in at a tavern, drinking little, talking well, he wore the same red suit and cheap gray wig, its hair pulled back and tied in a bow. When the weather turned cold, he added a shabby red cloak.

Samuel Adams was building a following apart from the Caucus or the political factions. As he mingled at the taverns, the lodges and the volunteer fire companies, he asked shopkeepers and shipworkers their opinions and seemed to take their answers seriously. He could explain political injustice to an illiterate sailor without condescending, and he had no use for Thomas Hutchinson's kind of social divisions. Adams sought out men who had spoken with a gentleman only to take his orders or abuse. His own ideas were unshakable, but he offered them in a tentative way that flattered his listeners. "I think . . ." Adams would begin, or "It seems to me . . ." He criticized such aristocrats as Hutchinson not as if he were a humble man who envied the lieutenant governor his wealth or position but as a moral superior.

Adams' politics were cast in theological terms: goodness meant the welfare of the most people, evil was tyranny by the few. He regarded the Massachusetts General Court—the House of Representatives and the Council—as the equal of Britain's Parliament.

An Englishman might find that idea preposterous. But if one considered America from the Atlantic to the Mississippi River, it was the size of Great Britain, France, Spain, Germany and Italy combined.

Although he circulated along the waterfront, Adams was not neglecting likely recruits from his alma mater. He sought out young Harvard graduates who were clever and idealistic, and among his cadre were two students of medicine: Joseph Warren, tall, handsome and fearless, and Benjamin Church, a deacon's son who wrote irreverent verses about his college tutors—"His matted wig of piss-burnt horse-hair made / Scarce covers half his greasy, shining head." Drawing men into his circle, Samuel Adams played on their love of America, their suspicions of the British and any other resentments he thought might win them over. He cultivated, too, his ambitious young second cousin from the town of Braintree, John Adams, working upon John's desire to be accepted by Boston's scholars, lawyers and the men who ran the Town Meeting.

Preaching his message left Samuel Adams no time for any job except one of Boston's sinecures. He had collected liquor taxes for the county for three years. Then, in 1756, he was elected one of the five general tax collectors. Bostonians knew they had made a shrewd choice. Each collector was required to post a personal bond to guarantee the delivery of his receipts. But when the colony was going through bad times, Samuel Adams would always defer the collections. If a smallpox epidemic ravaged Boston, he put them off again. His enemies accused him of skimming off public money to support even his frugal way of life, although no one offered any proof. It may have been a slander, but it was true that Boston wasn't getting its tax money. And its lenient collector was sinking into substantial debt.

Boston's conservatives had been trying to do away with the Town Meeting for nearly fifty years. Why, they asked, should rich men who came to vote be jammed into a crowded hall with the lower classes? Who could blame the colony's great merchants for their disgust when nearly destitute men stood up to claim the same privileges?

The conservative faction's last attempt to gain control of the town government had come three years before, in 1760, when it had set up the "New and Grand Corcas." The *Boston Gazette* had warned readers that this false caucus would try to buy votes and, failing that, would threaten workers with arrest or the loss of their jobs. The original Caucus had struck back at the conservatives by urging workmen to wash their hands and faces and put on their Sunday best so that they would look neat and clean at the next Meeting. The Caucus also instructed them to refuse any attempts at bribery and to vote in their self-interest. The conservatives lost that year, but the outcome was close enough for them to try again in 1763.

Before that election, the newspaper of the governor's party, the *Evening Post*, printed an exposé of the Caucus. It accused Samuel Adams and his allies of conducting their business behind locked doors and then inventing a few sham debates to entertain the rabble. But Boston's workmen had learned to trust the Caucus to look after them. Almost eleven hundred men turned out to vote, the greatest number in Boston's history. The Caucus was vindicated, and Samuel Adams held on to his slippery pole as tax collector. James Otis fared even better. The Tories and the *Evening Post* had been calling him a wild and envious man, a raccoon, "a filthy skunk," but his fellow citizens chose him to moderate their Meetings. He surprised everyone by using the forum to praise the new peace treaty with France and swear his abiding loyalty to England.

Otis' speech seemed to bury the recent ill-feeling, and calm in 1763 was agreeable to Thomas Hutchinson, who had been stealing time from his public duties to work on his history of the Bay Colony. Hutchinson was trying to write as he lived—avoiding emotion or interpretation, collecting facts and trusting them to speak for themselves. For him, one persisting scar from the recent controversies was the names that had been given to the colony's factions. The Caucus had succeeded in branding the governor and his friends as Tories, an unpopular label in Massachusetts. Hutchinson considered it equally misleading that his opponents called themselves Whigs or, worse, patriots. But those were small irritations. Surveying the political scene, Hutchinson ignored the underlying tensions in the colony and hoped instead that future problems would stem only from petty ambition. That was something he could understand. Men who were out of power always wanted to be in.

Governor Bernard understood Hutchinson's liking for money better than Samuel Adams' indifference to it. His annual salary totaled twelve hundred pounds, and he enjoyed other perquisites. He had ignored warnings that the people of Massachusetts might be difficult to manage when he had left his previous post as governor of New Jersey, and during his first years in Boston he seemed self-confident. He had all the signs of success—an Oxford education, a career in the law, a wellborn wife. Bostonians had no way of knowing how roughly life had treated Francis Bernard or that behind his placid facade he was full of trepidation.

His father, a clergyman, had died before he was three, and the Reverend Anthony Alsop, who came to Berkshire to replace him, married Francis' widowed mother when her year of mourning was over. But Bernard's mother died of smallpox a year later; his stepfather fled to Holland to escape a breach-of-promise suit, and Francis was left with an aunt. The suit was finally settled and Alsop returned to England, where he fell into his garden ditch and was drowned. Francis was thirteen.

Bernard studied at Christ Church, read law at the Middle Temple and married another orphan, who had a powerful uncle. He set out to found a family large enough to defy fate. His wife bore ten children who survived, but tragedy followed into the next generation. When his eldest son was admitted to Westminster, his friends celebrated by tossing the youth in the air on a blanket. He was dumped out, landed on his head and was severely injured.

It was Mrs. Bernard's uncle, Lord Barrington, the secretary of state for war in London, who arranged for Bernard to be appointed governor of New Jersey, and after two years he bettered his prospects with the move to Massachusetts. By 1763, Bernard was aligned firmly with the Tories. With no divisive issue looming on the horizon, the squabbling had become personal. Servants in the governor's house reported that he was stingy. The Tories mocked Samuel Adams as "Sammy the Maltster," and James Otis became "Jemmy" in the conservative *Evening Post*: "Jemmy is a

madman, Jemmy is an ass / Jemmy has a leaden head, and forehead spread with brass."

During 1763, a quiet interval, George III replaced William
Pitt with George Grenville as prime minister. Grenville's younger
sister was married to Pitt, but the brothers-in-law were estranged
and Grenville had never won Pitt's following. Although King
George had married and produced an heir, his court was finding
that the amiable young man now was impatient with any adviser
who dared to contradict him. Soon after Grenville's appointment,
the king was complaining, "When he has wearied me for two
hours, he looks at his watch to see if he may not tire me for an hour
more." At the end of each interview, the king spurred Grenville
on his way, "It is late. Good morrow, Mr. Greenville. Good morrow, Mr. Greenville." It was George's small revenge never to call
his prime minister by his right name.

Grenville was dull but also dogged. The war had left England with a deep debt, and he was determined to reduce it. He
began to entertain new ideas for raising revenue.

Patrick Henry opposing the Parsons' Cause in Hanover Court House

Henry

WHILE George Grenville was struggling with England's debt in the autumn of 1763, the Reverend James Maury of Fredericksville, Virginia, was worrying over his family's budget. Bostonians might have found Maury's preoccupation with money unbecoming in a minister, but Virginians had a less exalted opinion of their clergy. The Church of England had been the established religion from the time the colony was first settled, and the law required

1763-64

Virginians to take communion twice a year in an Anglican church, although their attendance was rarely enforced. Ministers of other denominations who went to the capital at Williamsburg for a dispensation would be licensed to preach, and the Presbyterians accepted that restriction. Baptists, Methodists and Quakers refused on principle and could expect to be jailed or fined. Sometimes they had their meetings broken up by the sheriff or by a

Church of England clergyman leading a band of hostile neighbors.

With the Anglican Church enjoying that monopoly, many of its parsons took their positions as sinecures and turned to worldly pleasure. They could be seen at horseraces and cock fights—not always sober—or playing backgammon, billiards and cards. They also went dancing. As one visitor put it, Virginians would dance or die. The current fancy was the jig, which had reached plantation ballrooms by way of the slave quarters.

The Reverend Maury neither gambled nor danced. He eked out a living for his wife and his eleven children by teaching school. In daily life, he also made use of his classical education in naming his slaves—Clio, Cato, Ajax and Cicero. One of his brightest pupils, Thomas Jefferson of Albemarle County, had joined Maury's classes in 1758, at the age of fifteen. Thomas' father had died the previous year and left the boy a comfortable estate, but Thomas noticed that Pastor Maury was hard pressed. He seemed harassed by a lack of money and that he often complained about a recent law called the Two Penny Act.

The act's very name reminded Virginia's clergymen that they were paid servants of the state. Throughout the colony, each town's officials—or vestrymen—hired a minister and set his salary. Since the vestry were usually large plantation owners, they paid in tobacco. In 1748, the Virginia House of Burgesses had fixed a parson's salary at sixteen thousand pounds of tobacco a year, and vestrymen who did not provide that amount could be sued for damages. After the king ratified the legislation, it had become a royal law that only the king himself could undo.

But with the next bad crop, the legislators regretted their generosity. In 1755, and again three years later, they meddled with the quota. Instead of granting a parson the full sixteen thousand pounds—worth about four hundred pounds sterling in 1758—the Burgesses compelled him to accept Virginia's depreciated paper money at the rate of twopence for every pound of tobacco. As a result, a clergyman was collecting only about one third of what the law had guaranteed him.

Virginia's parsons were not men to take consolation in the beatitudes; they sued. After one court awarded a parson double his regular pay in damages, the Reverend Maury filed a similar suit in the courthouse at Hanover, eighteen miles north of Richmond. The case took a year and a half to come to trial, but then, in November 1763, the proceedings couldn't have gone better for Maury and his fellow Anglicans. The court ruled that since the king had never agreed to repeal the law of 1748, the vestry had acted illegally in holding back two thirds of Maury's pay. A hearing to assess damages was set for December 1.

Parson Maury had clearly chosen well in his attorney—Peter Lyons, a charming Irishman who weighed three hundred pounds but was renowned for his refined courtroom manner. The arithmetic of the case hadn't been challenged, which meant that the damages hearing would be only a formality. A deputy sheriff named Thomas Johnson could expect a steep fine for not collecting the quota of tobacco due Parson Maury.

The hearing was only three weeks away, and Johnson had no hope of hiring a distinguished lawyer to represent him. In desperation, he turned to the judge's son, a young man who had recently taken up the law after failing at everything else. Would this untried lawyer accept fifteen shillings to do his best against Parson Maury and Peter Lyons? Patrick Henry said that he would.

Maury's former student, Thomas Jefferson, knew Patrick Henry but wasn't much impressed by him. They had met in December 1759, during a Christmas house party at the estate of Colonel Nathaniel West Dandridge. Jefferson had just finished his studies at Maury's school and was headed for William and Mary College in Williamsburg. Patrick Henry was between failures. He had tried farming, and twice he had tried keeping a store. The best that could be said of those attempts was that he had never been declared bankrupt. But at the colonel's party he was showing no sign of discouragement.

Thomas Jefferson, gangling and judgmental at sixteen, watched grudgingly as Patrick Henry made himself popular with the other guests. Although he was his elder by only seven years, Henry was married and a father and seemed much older to Thomas. That made his conduct all the more unseemly—being so passionate about dancing and so eager to please. Henry didn't seem interested in engaging young Jefferson in serious conversation, and Thomas found his manners somewhat coarse.

A few months later, though, Patrick Henry sought out Thomas on the William and Mary campus with astonishing news. Henry had been reading a lawbook at home between the hours he helped

out at his father-in-law's tavern. Now he had come to Williamsburg to ask the legal examiners to license him as a lawyer. One
had to admire his nerve. For generations, Virginia families had
sent their sons to London to study law at the Inns of Court. Young
men who couldn't afford that expense apprenticed themselves for
many months with an established lawyer. Here came Patrick
Henry announcing that he had borrowed a copy of *Coke upon
Littleton*—the text that James Otis had read and cursed for years.
After six weeks of glancing through it, Henry considered himself
qualified to open a law office.

Thomas didn't know then that Henry enjoyed playing the
rustic. From boyhood he had loved to hunt ducks and geese along
the Pamunky River, and at eleven and twelve, while other children
were anchored in school, he had roamed the countryside. Red-
haired and blue-eyed, he had grown into a boy who liked to exaggerate his rural accent. "Naiteral parts," he would say, "is better
than all the larnin' on yearth." But in his teens a different Patrick
emerged, tutored at home by his Scottish father and by his uncle,
the Reverend Patrick Henry, who taught him Latin and Greek
along with his catechism. By fifteen Patrick was lying on his bed
reading for hours, and the next year, when he was sent to work
at his first store, he discovered the joys of conversation. Customers
commented that the young clerk seemed beguiled by the thrust and
parry of any argument and determined not to let his job get in
the way of a good debate.

One day, stretched full length on a sack of salt, he was arguing with his friends when a customer entered the store and
asked, "Have you any salt, sir?"

Henry broke off talking only long enough to shake his head.
"Just sold the last peck."

Henry hadn't let Thomas Jefferson see his serious side or
Thomas had chosen to ignore it. Jefferson certainly didn't hold out
much hope for Henry's success with the examiners. A candidate
for the bar could pick the men to test him, and Thomas knew the
lawyers Henry had chosen. They included the Randolph brothers—Peyton, who had studied in London at the Inner Temple, and
John, who had studied at Gray's Inn. Another examiner, Robert
Carter Nicholas, was related to the "King" Carter who held three
hundred thousand acres of Virginia land. Most distinguished of all

was George Wythe, the lawyer with whom Jefferson hoped one day to serve his apprenticeship.

The four men did not sit as a board, and there were no written tests. Instead, each lawyer interviewed the applicant in his chambers. Afterward at least two of them had to agree to sign his license. As Patrick Henry went off on his rounds, his appearance tended to work against him. He was tall but rather stooped, and his forehead beetled noticeably. Early in life, his red hair had become a scant fringe, and in public he usually wore a wig. His clothes were cheap and he wore them carelessly. But Henry's eyes were lively under their long lashes, and he had a habit of paying close attention. His jaw was big, his teeth flashing, and his wide mouth always seemed ready to stretch into a grin. Combined with the flash to his eyes, the half-smile gave Henry a considerable appeal.

It was appeal wasted on George Wythe. He asked Henry a few questions, refused to sign his license and bowed him out of his office. John Randolph was also put off by the young man's lack of polish, but he sensed an original mind and let the examination stretch to several hours. Randolph saw that Henry knew nothing about municipal law, but when they took up natural law and general history his arguments were bold and strong. At one point, challenging his interpretation of the common law, Randolph said, "You defend your opinions well, sir, but now to the law and the testimony."

He led Henry to a shelf of books and paged through one of them. "You have never seen these books," Randolph said, "nor this principle of law. Yet you are right and I am wrong. And from this lesson you have given me—you must excuse me for saying it—I will never trust to appearance again."

Randolph added that if Patrick Henry's hard work matched his gifts, he could become a valuable member of the legal profession.

That may simply have been a gracious way of yielding to the inevitable, since Randolph seemed to believe that Henry had already obtained the necessary two signatures. In fact he had only one, extorted from kindly Robert Carter Nicholas after much importuning and Henry's solemn promise to study more law when he returned to Hanover. Thomas Jefferson said afterward that the Randolph brothers had signed Henry's license with as much reluctance as good manners permitted them to show. But he granted that while both men lamented Henry's ignorance, they agreed that he was a young man of genius.

License in hand, Henry began to build a lucrative practice in Hanover. Virginia had once considered barring all lawyers from the colony because so many of them were unskilled and money-hungry, and at the time Henry opened his office a law forbade lawyers from charging exorbitant fees. Lawyers like the Randolphs were winning respect for the profession, however, and over the next three years Henry carved out a place for himself by representing the poor and the dispossessed. His sympathy came naturally to Henry, who, marrying at eighteen, had been as poor as most of his clients. His bride, Sarah, had been no better off, and between the two sets of parents the newlyweds had received only a tiny farm at a spot called Pine Slash and half a dozen slaves to help them work it. When the house burned down, Henry had sold the slaves to finance one of his unprofitable stores. As a shopkeeper he had learned the perils of depending on tobacco for a living: he was never paid until the crop came in.

Yet Henry was willing to argue on behalf of the Two Penny Act and the profit it brought to Virginia's richest planters. Until Parson Maury sued, those tobacco growers had been selling one of their best crops in history at fifty shillings per hundredweight and paying off their debts to tradesmen and the clergy at a rate of sixteen shillings. But the Anglican parsons also represented a ruling class in the colony, which was enough to set Henry against them. The Great Awakening that spread over New England had also reached tiny Hanover, Virginia, and as Patrick was growing up his mother and grandfather had become New Lights, dissenters from the established church. They had taken Patrick to hear a prominent evangelist, Samuel Davies, who argued that freemen should never be taxed to support a religion they might abhor. The Anglicans found Davies' style of preaching tasteless and loud, but to Patrick the oratory was a revelation.

On the Monday morning of James Maury's hearing for damages, twenty fellow parsons appeared at the small brick courthouse in Hanover to await vindication. Wealthy planters from nearby counties, or parishes, had also come, dressed in velvet and with their hair fashionably powdered. The lesser planters wore home-spun, and the townspeople showed up in the sort of leather breeches and coarse linen shirts Patrick Henry wore when he wasn't in court. Today, he had put on a black robe and the court wig that improved his sallow appearance. On his way into the courthouse, he met his uncle and asked him not to attend the hearing. The Reverend Henry asked why.

"Because, sire," said Patrick Henry, "I fear that I shall be too much overawed by your presence to be able to do my duty to my clients. Besides, sire, I shall be obliged to say some hard things of the clergy, and I am very unwilling to give pain to your feelings."

His uncle advised Henry that speaking ill of the clergy would do more harm to him than to them. He didn't think his presence should matter—but since his nephew was asking him so earnestly to leave, Pastor Henry reined his horse about and rode home.

Inside the courtroom, Patrick's father, Colonel John Henry, took his seat as the presiding judge. He was one of the few men around Hanover who had been to college, and the judgeship had come to him by default. Many of his townsmen could barely write; women and slaves got no schooling at all. Judge Henry sent the sheriff out to summon twelve gentlemen to serve as jurors. When he returned, Parson Maury was indignant at the choices. Apparently the sheriff had gone to the one tavern where qualified gentlemen were known to congregate, but the first man had asked to be excused and the sheriff hadn't approached the others. He had gone instead to the town green, where another gentleman also begged off. Then, Parson Maury complained afterward, "he went out among the vulgar herd." Surveying the sheriff's candidates, Maury protested that they were neither men of substance nor loyal Anglicans. Patrick Henry insisted that they were all honest men and got them sworn in at once. The spectators knew the reason for his haste. Three jurors were New Lights, and one of them was also Patrick Henry's cousin.

After the acrimony over the jury, the trial itself opened tamely. Peter Lyons was entirely at his ease as he summed up the verdict from the previous month. Lyons spoke pleasantly to his opposing counsel and called him "young Pat."

Rising for the defense, Patrick Henry submitted a receipt to show that in 1758 Parson Maury had accepted one hundred and forty-four pounds as his year's salary. He said nothing else, and when he sat down the crowd was disappointed. Lyons concluded his argument by demonstrating that except for the discredited Two Penny Act, the parson would have received four hundred and fifty pounds. He called on the jury to award Maury three hundred British pounds in back pay for the year 1758. Pressing that claim, Lyons praised the Anglican clergy long and reverently.

When Henry's turn came, he got to his feet slowly, bowed to the bench and ambled over to the jurors. His first words came falteringly, and after Lyons' assured performance a lost cause looked doomed still further. Townspeople who liked Henry looked away from him, and the parsons on their bench were seen exchanging smiles. One onlooker thought that Judge Henry seemed ready to slide under his seat from shame.

Then Patrick Henry underwent a transformation. His mind seemed to turn on and generate heat until he began to glow. His shoulders straightened, and he looked for the first time as though he might be six feet tall. His movements had become graceful, even elegant, but when he turned his eyes on the jurors they saw lightning in them. One man swore afterward that Henry's voice had made his hair stand on end and his blood run cold.

Parson Maury was appalled by the beginning of Henry's harangue, which he considered only a barrage of irrelevant precedents aimed at confusing the jury. But then Patrick Henry went beyond all decency. He announced that a king and his people had a binding contract. The king was duty bound to protect the people, and they were pledged to obey him. The Two Penny Act of 1758 had been good and valid legislation. When King George II did not approve it, he had given evidence of misrule. Whenever that happened, a king ceased to be the father of his people and degenerated into a tyrant.

At that point, Peter Lyons rose from his chair. "The gentleman has spoken treason," Lyons said, "and I am astonished that your worships can hear it without emotion or any mark of dissatisfaction."

From around the room came murmurs of support: "Treason!" "Treason!"

The bench refused to interrupt. One juror nodded vigorously at Henry, who rounded now on the parsons. Was a clergyman supposed to set an example of selfishness? Should he want more than his brother outside the church? When a parson became grasp-

ing or worldly, was he serving God or serving himself? Shame on
greed! said Henry. But especially, shame on pulpit greed!

"We have heard a great deal," he went on, "about the benevo-
lence and holy zeal of our reverend clergy. But how is this mani-
fested? . . . Do they feed the hungry and clothe the naked? Oh,
no, gentlemen!

"These rapacious harpies would, were their power equal to
their will, snatch from the hearth of their honest parishioner his
last hoe-cake, from the widow and her orphan children her last
milch cow! The last bed—nay, the last blanket—from the lying-in
woman!"

That picture of a mother shivering as she gave birth set the
parsons to muttering among themselves. Then they rose from their
seats and filed out to the courtyard. Henry went on for almost an
hour. In conclusion, he pointed out that the jurors weren't obliged
to award any damages at all. But if they chose to do so, let the
damages be nominal. He suggested a farthing.

After Peter Lyons had spoken again, the jurors went out to
deliberate. A moment later, they were back. They had decided
that to award a farthing would be insulting to Parson Maury. Instead, they awarded four times more—one penny.

There was uproar in the court. As the sheriff demanded order
and Lyons called for a retrial, spectators lifted Patrick Henry to
their shoulders and carried him out to the courtyard. There he
sought out James Maury and apologized for any offense he might
have given. This time, Henry's habit of deprecating himself may
have provoked him into going too far. Maury told a friend later
that Henry had admitted that his only reason for taking the case
was to make himself popular. You see, Maury added bitterly, that
here is a man who thinks the ready road to popularity is to trample
on religion and on the prerogatives of the king.

For the next few weeks Virginia's other parsons discussed
their options, but they wound up doing nothing. Within a year,
Patrick Henry added a hundred and sixty-four new clients to his
practice. He had defended the richest men in the colony and made
himself the people's hero. It was the same paradox James Otis had
discovered when he took the side of wealthy smugglers and became the most popular man in Boston. Otis and Henry had each
learned that it only increased their popularity to have gentlemen
opposing them with cries of "Treason!"

In London, George Grenville had concocted a plan for increasing Britain's revenues. The Seven Years' War had swelled the nation's debt to 130 million pounds, and now Grenville's advisers were arguing that to protect the colonies England must maintain an army of twenty thousand soldiers in America. Grenville cut their estimate in half, but the expense would still amount to another 220,000 pounds each year. From his service as chancellor of the exchequer, Grenville knew that the colonists could be cunning in evading taxes, but he believed that the time had come for them to bear a fair share of their own defense. In March 1764 he introduced a new schedule of taxes in the House of Commons. The most important was the Sugar Act, which cut the duty on foreign molasses from sixpence a gallon to threepence. But, for the first time, it would be rigorously collected.

The attractive idea of taxing the colonies had glimmered before. In 1759, William Pitt, the Great Commoner, had been annoyed that some colonial legislatures were being slow to appropriate funds for the war and had asked the governor of Virginia what he thought about levying a direct tax that would bypass them. When the governor wrote back that such a tax was sure to set off a protest, Pitt had dropped the idea. Even earlier, direct taxes had been recommended to Sir Robert Walpole at a time when his popularity was lagging. Walpole had also rejected the thought. "What!" he had said. "I have old England against me, and do you think I will have New England likewise?" He had offered to bequeath the plan to any successor with more courage than he had. Walpole had been willing to overlook America's rampant smuggling because he calculated that England always got back whatever money the colonies earned, by way of the British goods they had to import. "This is taxing them more agreeably to their own constitution," Walpole had said, "and ours."

When reports of Grenville's new taxes reached America, the first resistance came from the king's own party. Governor Bernard warned Parliament that even threepence on molasses was too much. He said that the merchants were predicting that the new tax would kill commerce in Massachusetts.

Grenville rejected the American protests. Smugglers already paid as much as a penny and a half per gallon on molasses to bribe tax collectors to overlook their shipments. Even with that expense, their trade was flourishing. The merchants could certainly afford another penny and a half to make their business legitimate and assist the mother country. The Massachusetts agent in London, Jasper Mauduit, argued that a tax of one penny would cause no protest and would even generate more revenue than the higher one. But Grenville was convinced of his figures, and Parliament went along without debate. Members added a warning that England might later defray its expenses in America by levying certain stamp duties.

The king's appointees in America had protested the Sugar Act, but among the patriots the law confirmed their worst predictions, and James Otis and Samuel Adams had found their cause. The idea of Britain levying taxes to raise money represented a shocking reversal of policy. In the past, taxes had been used only to regulate trade in ways that favored Britain, but Otis published a pamphlet, *Rights of the Colonies Asserted and Proved*, arguing that Parliament had no right to tax the colonies at all—not on their trade, not on what they produced.

Boston's Town Meeting asked Samuel Adams to draft instructions for the town's four delegates in the House of Representatives, and on May 24, 1764, the people gathered in Faneuil Hall to hear the result. From his battles with Sheriff Greenleaf, Adams had learned that a grievance must never look narrow or selfish. In fighting the Land Bank judgment against his estate, Adams had warned the town that his case was not isolated; the precedent would threaten every Bostonian's house. Now, in opposing the Sugar Act, he wanted to persuade the colony's farmers that the danger was not limited to the merchants of Boston, who had never been popular in rural Massachusetts. The farmers must see that a tax on molasses could easily extend to their crops as well. "For if our trade may be taxed, why not our lands? Why not the produce of our lands and, in short, everything we possess or make use of?" James Otis had argued that since the colonies had no delegates in the Parliament, they could not be taxed. Taxation without representation was tyranny. Samuel Adams put the point another way: Parliament had no right to tax the colonies without their consent.

But the farmers didn't see that they were threatened, and Adams' alarm went largely unheeded. The slogan "No taxation without representation" was forceful but disingenuous. Most of the patriot politicians, including Adams, had never wanted the colonies to send members to Parliament. Benjamin Franklin, as Pennsylvania's agent in London, had proposed seating Americans in the House of Commons ten years earlier, and Grenville now seemed agreeable to the idea, but Adams realized that a handful of colonial members in the House of Commons would be swamped in every vote. And the Town Meeting would be surrendering its authority. With the delegates so far from home, instructions sent from Boston would always be late and incomplete.

In the Massachusetts House, James Otis drew up a letter to Jasper Mauduit that followed Adams' outline. The London agent was to seek repeal of the Sugar Act and prevent the passage of a proposed law called the Stamp Act. The House also voted to send copies of Otis' letter to legislatures in the other colonies and ask them to join the protest. Francis Bernard and Thomas Hutchinson worried that a concerted action by the colonies was likely to bring together every demagogue on the American continent. To stop the letters from being sent, the governor shut down the session. "Perhaps I may be too suspicious," Bernard wrote to London. "A little time will show whether I am or not."

But Otis' letter was widely circulated, delegates from other colonies began arriving in Boston with their own protests, and their meetings provoked the reaction Bernard had feared. The majority of Americans might be untroubled by the new taxes, but clusters of men in each colony seemed to be as agitated as James Otis. When Rhode Island's delegates saw that their petition was weaker than New York's, they went home to draft a harsher one.

Meanwhile, Grenville was moving on two fronts. His office answered the Otis letter by admitting that perhaps there shouldn't be taxation without representation but pointing out that the Americans were being treated no differently from the 75 percent of adult male Englishmen who couldn't vote for one reason or another, usually because they didn't own sufficient property. Grenville insisted that those men—and the colonists—were in fact represented because each member of Parliament voted in the interests of the entire empire and not simply for his borough. In case that argument didn't silence them, Grenville called in the American agents who lived in London. He said that America must contribute to her own defense, and he wouldn't hear any argument against Parliament's inherent right to impose taxes.

"I am not, however, set upon this tax," Grenville assured them. If the colonies could agree on a better solution, he would be pleased to consider it. Benjamin Franklin of Pennsylvania suggested that the financing of the French and Indian War had worked well enough. Let England say how much money it needed and let America decide how to raise it. But Franklin admitted that he couldn't guarantee that each colony would agree to contribute its share.

In the end, Grenville went to Parliament in early February 1765 and introduced taxes he described as "the easiest, the most equal and the most certain that can be chosen." He would require that the colonists buy a stamp for every American newspaper, legal document or license and bond. They would also need stamps for any pamphlet, almanac, college diploma, deck of cards or pair of dice. The proposal's very sweep guaranteed that no individual taxpayer would be overburdened. And because the richer colonies transacted more business than the poorer ones, they would pay more in taxes. To reduce tax evasion and bribes, only a few collectors would be licensed to issue the stamped paper and receive money for it.

Few voices in the House of Commons protested Grenville's plan. One member who knew the colonies very well did oppose it, but he couldn't convince his colleagues. Colonel Isaac Barré had returned from the French and Indian War with a disfiguring wound in one cheek and high admiration for America's fighting men. Barré ridiculed the suggestion that the colonists somehow owed England a debt. Rather, he said, the behavior of Britain's officials toward Americans "on many occasions has caused the blood of those sons of liberty to recoil within them."

In using the phrase "sons of liberty," Barré hadn't meant to imply that the colonists were disloyal to Britain or the king. It was simply a familiar term for men who were determined to defend their freedom. But the political stresses of 1765 gave Barré's phrase a new luster, and when reports of his speech reached America hundreds of men in each colony were proud to learn that they were being called Sons of Liberty.

Stamp master in effigy

Riots

DURING the early morning hours of August 14, 1765, a stately elm across from Boylston Market in Boston was festooned with several curious objects. By 5 A.M. on that Wednesday, many Bostonians had heard about the decorations and were hurrying to see the tree for themselves. Hanging from one branch they found an effigy of Andrew Oliver, who was the recently appointed stamp master for Massachusetts Bay and Thomas Hutchinson's brother-in-law.

1765

Nearby hung a boot. Everyone understood that it was a symbol for Lord Bute, who the colonists feared was exercising a sinister influence over young King George. The figure of a devil popped from the boot with a copy of the Stamp Act in his hand. Oliver's effigy was marked with his initials, and a couplet was pinned to the left arm: *What greater joy did New England see*
Than a stampman hanging on a tree.

Beneath the figure was a warning: "He that takes this down is an enemy to his country."

Andrew Oliver had been married to a sister of Hutchinson's wife for more than thirty years, and he shared the lieutenant governor's keen sense of self-interest. Oliver had argued against the Stamp Act, not because it was wrong but because it would be unpopular. Once the act had passed and he was named the tax collector, however, he began to see benefits in it. The stamp master would draw a handsome salary.

During the spring of 1765, a prevailing calm had suggested that the usual dissenters had been exaggerating the public's antagonism to the act. James Otis claimed that "one single act of Parliament had set people a-thinking in six months more than they had ever done in their whole lives before." But the public silence over the Stamp Act was so profound that by April the king's supporters were assuring his ministers in London that the people would go along quietly. That response emboldened Andrew Oliver, and when the stamp master from Connecticut passed through Boston on his way from London, Oliver accompanied him on the ride out of town. His courtesy provoked an angry article in the *Boston Gazette*, and now there was this display hanging from the hundred-year-old tree on High Street.

As the crowd around the elm grew larger, its leaders began a boisterous charade. Every farmer or shopkeeper who brought his goods to market had to flop down before the tree and have his wares stamped by the dummy on the tree. When Samuel Adams came out to take a look, some Tories suspected that he wasn't seeing the display for the first time. One of them approached as Adams stared up at the branches and asked him whether he knew whom the effigy was supposed to represent. Adams was giving nothing away. He said he didn't know and wanted to look into the matter.

As the morning wore on, Governor Bernard heard about the disturbance and urged his Council to take action. Most of the councilmen argued that it was only a prank and Bernard should ignore it. But Thomas Hutchinson, as chief justice, sent out Sheriff Greenleaf with orders to cut the effigy down. Greenleaf was soon back to report that he couldn't do it. The throng at the tree was too large. He would be risking his own life and the lives of his men.

By late afternoon, Bernard was still calling upon the province's councilmen to act, and they were trying to shame the sheriff into

British tax stamp

doing something. The immediate problem was solved at dusk when the protest leaders cut down the figure of Oliver and nailed it to a board, which four men hoisted to their shoulders. Behind them, forty or fifty tradesmen led a march through the street, followed by several hundred townspeople. As they passed his office, Bernard heard them giving three cheers and he thought they sounded defiant. The procession continued down to a brick building that Andrew Oliver had constructed along the waterfront. The crowd was sure that Oliver meant it to be his stamp office, and they went to work destroying it. That took half an hour.

Sheriff Greenleaf was worried enough about the safety of Oliver and his family to persuade them to leave their house. They had barely retreated through their back garden when the crowd came streaming up Fort Hill. There, in front of Oliver's windows, men with knives beheaded his effigy. They set a great bonfire on the hill and burned the figure along with whatever scraps of wood they had brought from the building they had just torn down.

Until that point, reputable businessmen in the group, disguised in rough trousers and jackets, had managed to keep the crowd orderly. But when those men went home to their suppers, tempers around the bonfire were still running hot. Ebenezer Mackintosh, a South End cobbler, was well known for the gang he raised each Pope's Day, and he led a charge against Oliver's house.

Rioters broke open Oliver's stables and were about to drag his chaise and coach to the bonfire when a few onlookers spoke against it. Instead, the mob burned only the coach's door and several cushions. Then they raced to the bottom of Oliver's garden and began ripping down a fifteen-foot fence. Once inside the garden, they stripped all the fruit from the trees, broke off the branches and tore down a gazebo. When men began to smash windows at the back of the main house, it was not idle vandalism. Window glass had to be imported from England and was expensive to replace.

The mob's leaders wanted to search the neighborhood for the family, but a quick-witted friend headed them off, insisting that Oliver had taken his family to safety at Castle William in Boston Harbor. By then, men were inside the house and heading for the cellars, where they helped themselves to the stores of liquor. Upstairs, rioters found the family's looking glass, which was reputed to be the largest in North America. They left it in shards and went on to break furniture and scatter the Oliver silverplate throughout the house. The patriots insisted later that no one made off with anything valuable.

At his office, Governor Bernard demanded that the militia send out drummers to beat an alarm. His officers told him that it was impossible—the drummers were part of the mob. Sometime before midnight, Thomas Hutchinson collared Sheriff Greenleaf and demanded that they go together to Oliver's house and force the rioters to disperse. All his life Hutchinson had been giving orders, but tonight he had barely begun to speak to the crowd when a shout went up: "To your arms, my boys!" Hutchinson and Greenleaf were pelted with stones and forced to retreat. The dismantling of Oliver's house went on for another hour.

The next morning, Bostonians were talking about nothing else. In the *Boston Gazette*, anonymously written articles treated the destruction lightheartedly, but Governor Bernard was offering a hundred-pound reward for the apprehension of the demonstration's leaders. He was also promising amnesty to anyone in the mob who came forward with information, an offer that could prove embarrassing to Samuel Adams and his friends. They may not have intended that Oliver's house be destroyed; that was probably a boozy afterthought by the mob. But otherwise, the entire protest had followed the patriots' script as surely as any Town Meeting had ever done.

Samuel Adams' legions did not all come from the Caucus. The Loyal Nine was a social club that met in Boston's Hanover Square, and its members included several distillers, a jeweler and a sea captain. One of the nine, Henry Bass, was Samuel Adams' cousin, and Adams was always a welcome guest at their meetings. He also had friends among the Masons, although he preferred smaller and more political groups; even a Tory like Andrew Oliver could be a Mason. To rally support against the Stamp Act, Adams had been speaking with workers from the docks and the ropewalks—those covered arcades where rope was braided—and at the Green Dragon Tavern in Union Street, the tavern in Salvation Alley and the Bunch of Grapes in King Street. These were the same men, or their sons, who had supported Deacon Adams and the Land Bank, and their resentment against the Hutchinsons and the Olivers was greater even than their outrage against the stamps. On Wednesday night, these new Sons of Liberty had supplied the muscle, but the planning had come from the second floor of Chase and Speakman's distillery in Hanover Square, not far from the elm where the effigies were hung. In their drawing rooms, the Tories laughed at the patriots for meeting in taverns and distilleries. They claimed that the rabble depended on barrels of rum to give them courage, and they took to calling Samuel Adams "Sam the Publican."

Adams' political sense warned him that his opponents must not be allowed to make a martyr out of Andrew Oliver. The parade and the bonfire could be excused as legitimate protests by an oppressed people. But he sensed that the ransacking of Oliver's house

had provoked deep misgivings, even among his allies. Not that rioting was a novelty in America. During the years of bad crops, Virginia and Maryland had seen tobacco revolts, and in the midst of a
food shortage the people of Massachusetts had risen up to stop the
exporting of meat and grain. Bostonians had razed whorehouses,
and about thirty years earlier they had blackened their faces and
gone out one night to burn down a barn that was blocking a proposed public road.

But everyone understood that the violence against Oliver's
property had been more serious. Boston's leading citizens had seen
a spark of anarchy and were determined to snuff it out. On Thursday, they called on Oliver and told him that he must appease the
mob by resigning as stamp master. Oliver replied that he resented
their lack of support when he had stood "a single man against a
whole people for thirty-six hours."

At about nine o'clock that evening, a crowd of men and
women gathered again outside Oliver's house and shouted slogans
about liberty and property. Oliver gathered his family around him
and sent out a note. He said later that his message had promised
only that he would delay taking office as stamp master until he had
informed London about the public outcry over the act.

The crowd heard a different promise—that Oliver would send
his resignation to London by the next ship. Since he seemed to be
capitulating, they retreated to Oliver's gate, sent up three cheers
and hurried along to Thomas Hutchinson's house. Hutchinson had
counseled London against the Stamp Act, but his attempt the night
before to quell the rioting made it easy to believe that he supported
the tax.

Hutchinson heard the fists beating on his door and the voices
demanding that he come out onto his balcony and swear that he
had not endorsed the act. His courage—or pride—would always prevent the lieutenant governor from bowing to the will of a mob.
Hutchinson braced for the worst and gave no answer. Before any
ransacking could begin, a neighbor called from his window that he
had seen the family in their carriage, heading for the country house
in Milton. With that news, the spirit seemed to go out of the
crowd and it reluctantly dispersed.

The rest of the week passed quietly. Possibly, the Sons of
Liberty were planning more demonstrations. At least rumors kept

circulating of different plots and their targets. Hutchinson was inclined to blame the discontent less on the politicians than on several of the town's clergymen, and the Tories quoted James Otis as calling Boston's rebellious ministers his "black regiment." One of the most notorious was Jonathan Mayhew, an incendiary preacher who attacked the doctrine of the Trinity and called the organized clergy the greatest enemies of true religion.

Francis Bernard was convinced that Mayhew had joined with Samuel Adams and James Otis. But Bernard's information was wrong. In his religion Mayhew might be a Nonconformist, a Dissenter, and he did describe himself as a friend of liberty, but before August was out Mayhew would find that he did not qualify as a Son of Liberty.

The Reverend Mayhew took his text on Sunday, August 25, 1765, from Galatians: "I would they were even cut off which trouble you, for brethren ye have been called unto liberty." Thomas Hutchinson noticed that Mayhew ended his message there because the next verse went on to warn about limitations on liberty.

The next night, bonfires blazed again in King Street, and whistles and horns filled the air. Governor Bernard heard a large crowd gathering in the streets and crying, "Liberty and property!" and he reflected sourly that the mob always shouted those words when it intended to pull down a house. Once again the mob's leader was Ebenezer Mackintosh from the South End. Tonight, however, his motives were less clear than they had been twelve days ago.

An official at the Vice-Admiralty Court, William Story, had been accumulating depositions that accused several Boston merchants of being smugglers. In this morning's newspaper, Story had published an advertisement denying that he had sent those incriminating documents to England, but some members of the mob didn't believe him and they tore up his living quarters, along with much of the Admiralty's archives. Other men headed in the direction of the home of the comptroller of customs, Benjamin Hallowell. In a day when laborers might be earning less than sixty pounds a year, Hallowell had spent more than two thousand pounds on a new house. The mob ripped off his windows and doors, drank his wine cellar dry and carried off his official papers.

If Mackintosh had only been obliging a few merchants by destroying the evidence against them, the night's rampage might have ended there. Instead, the mob's two flanks joined forces and set out to wreak the greatest civil violence North America had ever experienced.

Only that morning, Thomas Hutchinson had returned to Boston from his Milton country estate. By afternoon, he was hearing rumors that a mob was being raised again. He even knew it would attack officers from the Custom House and the Admiralty office. Hutchinson's friends assured him that he would be spared. They said his courage the last time in standing up to rocks and insults had won the mob's respect. For some reason, Hutchinson believed them.

Now he was at supper. Since the night was warm, he had dressed informally in a woolen jacket over his waistcoat. Around him at the table were his sister-in-law, Grizell Sanford, who had raised his children since his wife's death; his sons Thomas Junior and Elisha, graduates of Harvard who were training to become merchants; Sarah, a daughter who was reaching marriageable age; Billy, Hutchinson's youngest son; and Peggy, her father's favorite, eleven years old and already acting as his secretary.

As the family ate, a friend burst in to warn them that the mob was heading their way. Hutchinson sent the children from the house and bolted the doors and shutters as he had done before. He was determined to wait out the assault alone. But Sarah came running back to say that she wouldn't leave unless he came away with her. Hutchinson couldn't resist, and they hurried together to a neighbor's house. Stories circulating in town had Hutchinson not only encouraging Parliament to pass the Stamp Act but actually drawing up the law here in his mansion on Garden Court Street. A few minutes after he escaped, the mob fell upon the Hutchinson house in a fever of hatred.

One of Hutchinson's sons was near enough to the axes splitting the front door to hear a cry on the night air: "Damn him! He is upstairs! We'll have him!"

Some men ran at once to the top of the house, others swarmed into the graceful drawing room. Still more headed for the stores of liquor in the cellar. This time, merely tearing off wainscoting and breaking windows would not be enough to satisfy the mob. Instead, men shattered the inner doors and beat down the walls between the rooms. Standing at the upper windows, they slit open mattresses and buried the lawn beneath a summer blizzard of feathers. They climbed the roof to swarm over a cupola, and even though the job took two hours, they finally sent it crashing down.

Word reached Hutchinson in his hiding place that the crowd had picked up his scent, and he wound his way through neighboring yards and gardens to a house even farther away. He stayed there until 4 A.M. By then, the mansion he had inherited, one of the finest in Massachusetts, was a splintered shell. Near dawn, men were still crouched on the roof, prying up slate and boards. Only daylight stopped them from razing the house's outer walls to the ground. Around the battered frame, every fruit tree had been broken to a stump and every shrub crushed back to the earth.

Out of the ruins came a trail of dinner plates and family portraits, books and children's clothes. A strongbox had been broken open and nine hundred pounds taken. The manuscript pages of Hutchinson's history of Massachusetts had been strewn in the mud, along with the rare documents he had spent a lifetime collecting.

The next morning, Hutchinson's fellow justices in their red robes had already taken their places when he appeared in court. He was wearing what he had fled in and, because overnight the weather had turned abruptly cold, a few borrowed bits of clothing. Whether he had calculated the effect or not, the sight of this patrician man in his middle fifties, pale after his sleepless night and fitted out in other men's clothes because his own lay trampled in the street, affected everyone in the court. Even Josiah Quincy, a twenty-one-year-old who was reading law with Oxenbridge Thacher and who had recently joined Samuel Adams' Sons of Liberty, pitied the lieutenant governor. "Such a man in such a station," Quincy described Hutchinson in his diary, "thus habited, with tears starting from his eyes and a countenance which strongly told the inward anguish of his soul."

Rising to speak, Hutchinson rejected any suggestion that he was appealing for sympathy. He had come to court, he said, only because there wouldn't have been a quorum without him. But Hutchinson went on to demonstrate that the patriot leaders had no monopoly on eloquence.

"Some apology is necessary for my dress," he said. "Indeed, I had no other. Destitute of everything: no other shirt, no other garment but what I have on, and not one in my family in a better situation than myself."

He wanted to absolve himself, but with no suggestion that his spirit had been crushed. "I am not obliged to give an answer to all the questions that may be put to me by every lawless person, yet I call on God as my witness—and I would not, for a thousand worlds, call my Maker to witness a falsehood—I say I call my Maker to witness that I never, in New England or Old, in Great Britain or America, neither directly nor indirectly, was aiding, assisting or supporting—in the least promoting or encouraging—what is commonly called the Stamp Act but, on the contrary, did all in my power, and strove as much as in me lay, to prevent it.

"This is not declared through timidity, for I have nothing to fear. They can only take away my life, which is of but little value when deprived of all its comforts, all that was dear to me . . ."

Hutchinson said he hoped the people would see how easy it was to spread false reports against the innocent. But violence was wrong, even against the guilty. "I hope all will see how easily the people may be deluded, inflamed and carried away with madness against an innocent man.

"I pray God give us better hearts!"

The sacking of Hutchinson's house had filled Jonathan Mayhew with remorse. He wrote at once to assure Hutchinson that he abhorred violence from his very soul, and he told friends that he would rather lose a hand than encourage such an outrage. But, like many Bostonians, Mayhew saw nothing improper about the demonstration two weeks earlier. His error had been in preaching liberty when his audience was so apprehensive about the threat to their freedoms. In the future, Mayhew said, he would try to calm his sensitive congregation rather than excite it.

Samuel Adams and his cohorts might not be feeling that same guilt, but they recognized a grievous tactical error. As Hutchinson was addressing the court, Adams at a Town Meeting heard Bostonians condemn the latest rioting, and he voted with them to help the sheriff keep order during the coming nights. When Hutchinson was told about the vote, he noted that the loudest lamentations were coming from the very men who had destroyed his house.

Many Bostonians knew that Samuel Adams gathered his circle together every Saturday afternoon to edit Monday's edition of the *Boston Gazette*, and they took the newspaper's account of the second demonstration as a change in strategy. The report could have been dictated by Thomas Hutchinson: "Such horrid scenes of villainy as were perpetrated last Monday night it is certain were never seen before in this town, and it is hoped never will again." The participants were "rude fellows" who went about "heating themselves with liquor" before they vented their "hellish fury" on the lieutenant governor's house. But the article also drew the same distinction that Mayhew had made. "Most people seem disposed to discriminate between the assembly on the 14th of the month and *their* transactions, and the unbridled licentiousness of this mob." To underscore that point, Samuel Adams wrote to Richard Jackson, who had replaced Mauduit as the colony's London agent, exonerating the law-abiding people of Boston from any blame. The second riot had been perpetrated by "vagabond strangers" interested only in plunder.

Adams didn't try to explain the presence on both nights of Ebenezer Mackintosh, the twenty-eight-year-old shoemaker from the South End. Mackintosh's ancestors had come from Scotland as indentured workers more than a hundred years before, supplying cheap labor for a Massachusetts ironworks. As freemen in later generations, however, the family hadn't found the New World hospitable. When Ebenezer was fourteen, his father, Moses, had been warned out of Boston, which meant that the town was publicly relieving itself of any obligation to help him if he became destitute or sick. He took the boy to the community of Wrentham, which tolerated Moses for eight years and then gave him another warning out.

By that time, Ebenezer was already working in Boston as a shoemaker in Ward 12, the section of the South End where the gallows stood. When Sheriff Greenleaf recruited him for a volunteer fire company, Ebenezer persuaded the other firemen to form a gang for Pope's Day. Slightly built, with a sandy complexion, Mackintosh had learned to read and he liked to memorize verse, but his quick temper put him at the center of every brawl.

The Tories considered Mackintosh only a tool of the patriots, and Peter Oliver admitted to a grudging admiration for him. His clashes on Pope's Day had made him a well-known figure around Boston, and Bernard's inquiry quickly identified Mackintosh as the leader at Hutchinson's house. Sheriff Greenleaf was sent out with a warrant to arrest him.

When he spotted Mackintosh in King Street, the sheriff summoned up his nerve and took him to jail. Very soon, a group of gentlemen sought out Greenleaf and delivered a potent threat. Although the Town Meeting had voted to send out patrols to prevent any further rioting, no man would agree to go that night unless Ebenezer Mackintosh was set free. Greenleaf returned to the Council to report that ultimatum.

Hutchinson listened to the sheriff's story. "And did you discharge him?"

"Yes," said Greenleaf.

"Then you have not done your duty."

Bernard raised to three hundred pounds the bounty for identifying the mob's leader. Hutchinson was not surprised when the reward went unclaimed. He guessed that the shoemaker was threatening to implicate the men who had planned the demonstration. And if Hutchinson had seen a letter from Henry Bass of the Loyal Nine, it would have confirmed his suspicions. Samuel Adams' cousin wrote: "We do everything to keep . . . the affair private, and are not a little pleased to hear that Mackintosh has the credit of the whole affair."

At first, the example of the mob's assault on Andrew Oliver seemed to be spreading. Newspapers in other provinces praised Boston's patriots, and in Newport, Rhode Island, local Sons of Liberty built effigies of their stamp master. He resigned within the week. In New York and New Jersey, stamp masters were also pressured into giving up their posts, and the nominees of other colonies fell into line until only Georgia's stamp man was allowed to take up his duties unmolested. But after the attack against Hutchinson, patriot leaders outside Massachusetts agreed with Samuel Adams that more violence would only harm their cause.

Even if the Stamp Act were eventually repealed, the Sons of

Liberty pledged that they would guard against any further abuses by Parliament. Christopher Gadsden of Charleston, South Carolina, had mobilized his social club against the Stamp Act, and he caught the mood of the patriots when he said that the Grenville Ministry "must have thought us Americans all a parcel of apes, and very tame apes, too."

> St—p!   ft—p!   ft—p!   No!
>
> *Tuefday-Morning, December* 17, 1765.
>
> **THE True-born Sons of Li-**
> berty, are defired to meet under LIBERTY-
> TREE, at XII o'Clock, THIS DAY, to hear the
> the public Refignation, under Oath, of ANDREW
> OLIVER, Efq; Diftributor of Stamps for the Province
> of the *Maffachufetts-Bay*.
>
>   A Refignation ? YES.

Sons of Liberty broadside

Politics
1765

WHILE Samuel Adams was sounding the alarm in Boston against taxes on sugar and stamps, Patrick Henry in Virginia also had been gliding toward politics. The two years since he had triumphed over the parsons had been the best time of Henry's life. Thomas Jefferson, who was now midway through his own rigorous law training with George Wythe, preferred to believe that Henry was far too lazy to succeed as a lawyer and that he spent all of his time in the woods hunting deer. But Henry had built up a healthy practice. He was being called—mostly around Hanover—"the Orator of Nature," and in the fall of 1764 he went to Williamsburg as the lawyer for Colonel Nathaniel Dandridge, his host at the Christmas house party five years before. On Dandridge's behalf, Henry was challenging the seat of James Littlepage in the House of Burgesses. Littlepage was charged with having used undue influence during the last election, when he had gone about the county knocking on doors and pledging to change the regulations over tobacco warehouses. In Virginia, candidates were expected to behave like gentlemen and refrain from asking for votes or making campaign promises. Littlepage was also accused of buying drinks for a man named Grubbs.

That last charge smacked of hypocrisy. On election day, Virginians stepped forward one at a time at the polls and named their choices out loud. Grubbs had come reeling over the courthouse green, bawling out his promise to vote for anyone who would give him another dram. Littlepage's men had reached him first. But, like every other candidate, Dandridge had also provided refreshments that day. A man running for office set out near the polls several barrels of rum and neat whiskey, along with applejack and beer. Any candidate who didn't offer a few drinks was considered too stingy or lacking in respect for his neighbors to deserve their votes. Several years earlier, a planter named George Washington had been rejected for failing to provide decent drink and a roast pig. Washington learned from that defeat, and the next time he ran he bought a quart and a half of liquor for each of his 361 supporters and won his seat in the Burgesses.

When members of the Committee on Privileges and Elections saw Henry's coarse clothes, they treated him with a casualness just short of contempt. As he presented Dandridge's case, however, their mood changed. They agreed that he put the case brilliantly, but they found Dandridge's complaint frivolous and vexatious and ordered him to pay all costs.

The next year, with agitation over the Stamp Act spreading through the colony, Henry decided to run for his own seat in the Burgesses. His impatience made him skip over the usual path of serving first on a county court. When the House member from Louisa County resigned to become coroner, Henry hoped to vault directly to the Burgesses. He still lived in Hanover County, but he bought land in nearby Louisa to make himself eligible. Henry spent more than eight pounds sterling to get elected—seven pounds to buy twenty-eight gallons of rum, the rest for carrying it to the polls.

As he entered the House in May 1765, Patrick Henry was not a typical member. His colleagues owned an average of eighteen hundred acres—to Henry's six hundred acres of poor land—and held forty slaves. Usually their holdings were inherited. Half of the

House leadership had been to college, most often William and Mary. But Boston's division between Whigs and Tories was blurred in Williamsburg. Some of the one hundred and sixteen Burgesses who always supported the crown were called the Old Field Nags. Younger and more rebellious members were the High-Blooded Colts. Members of both groups might be from established Tidewater families, while others were called "Qo'hees," came from the upper counties and wore buckskin to House sessions. Yet at home on their plantations, men from both factions spent their days out of doors and on horseback. They were often land poor, and they could be receptive to a democratic argument.

Even so, the House had its own established hierarchy, and within three days of taking his seat Patrick Henry was affronting its leaders. One of them, John Robinson, was both the speaker and the colony's treasurer, and he had come up with a plan for a Public Loan Office. No one knew then that Robinson had been lending public money to his friends and that the Loan Office was his way of covering those illegal debts. But, alerted by an instinct, Henry listened dubiously to the argument that the office should extend credit to wealthy men who were momentarily strapped for cash. At the end, he rose to make his maiden speech.

"What, sir?" he asked. "Is it proposed then to reclaim the spendthrift from his dissipation and extravagance by filling his pockets with money?"

The members ignored his objection and approved the Loan Office.

A few days later, Patrick Henry confronted the leadership again. Over the past year, the Burgesses had drafted earnest petitions against the Stamp Act. Now, with the current session ending and many members already returned home, word reached Williamsburg that the stamp duties would take effect in November. Only thirty-nine of the one hundred and sixteen members were still in the House as Henry scribbled out a set of resolutions on the blank page of an old lawbook. It was his twenty-ninth birthday, and he intended to celebrate with a speech.

Henry first presented four resolutions that followed along the lines of Virginia's earlier protests, although they were framed in much sharper language: The settlers had brought to Virginia all of the liberties of the people of Great Britain. The two royal charters granted by King James I had conferred on the colonists the same privileges as if they had been born in England and still lived there. Taxes must be levied on a people only by men they had chosen to represent them. This right of legislating their own affairs always had been recognized by Britain's kings and her people. Henry then added a fifth resolution: Only a colony's legislature could tax its citizens, and any attempt to transfer that power to another group would destroy freedom in Britain as well as in America.

For the House leadership, Henry's offense was less in what he was saying than in his presuming, after only nine days in the Burgesses, to say anything at all. Thomas Jefferson was in the House lobby the next day to listen while Henry defended his resolutions, and what he heard made him revise his first impressions of Patrick Henry's provincialism. Jefferson recalled years later that he would sometimes close his eyes as Henry spoke and, when he opened them again, could not remember a single word; he was left with only the impact of the speech, which was dazzling.

As Henry spoke, tempers in the chamber began to boil. The Old Field Nags were particularly incensed by Henry's fifth resolution, which seemed to deny that Parliament ever had a right to tax the colonies. And in arguing his case, Henry had let himself be swept to the farthest boundaries of his position. Jefferson was listening when Henry warned Britain's king against his unreasonable tax.

"Tarquin and Caesar had each his Brutus," Henry said, speaking in a steady voice, "Charles the First his Cromwell, and George the Third—"

At that point, Speaker Robinson interrupted with a cry of "Treason! Treason!"

By now, the accusation was no novelty to Henry. He looked to the Speaker as he improvised an ending for his threat. "—may profit by their example!" And he added, "If this be treason, make the most of it!"

A Frenchman visiting Williamsburg that day was standing with Jefferson in the outer hallway, and he recalled that after Henry alluded to Caesar and Charles I he apologized for any affront he might have given the members and pledged his last drop of blood to the king.

Arrayed against Henry and his resolutions were Speaker Robinson and three of Henry's examiners from two years ago, Peyton Randolph, George Wythe and Robert Carter Nicholas. They argued that since the House was still waiting for a reply from London to the earlier petitions, they shouldn't alienate the king's ministers with Henry's blunt language. But despite their prestige and seniority, Henry's resolutions passed that afternoon, each by a narrow margin and the fifth one by the single vote of twenty to nineteen. Jefferson was still hovering by the door when Peyton Randolph came, fat and petulant, from the floor. "By God," Randolph said, "I would have given five hundred guineas for a single vote."

Even though Randolph and the rest of Henry's opponents were cautious men, they differed from Thomas Hutchinson in Boston. Privately Hutchinson might express reservations about the Stamp Act, but once it was passed it became law to him. In Virginia, even the most conservative Burgesses intended to go on protesting the act; they merely didn't want to be lumbered with Patrick Henry's provocative language.

Henry left the capital that night, his battle won and his reputation made. But the next day, when Thomas Jefferson went back to the House, he saw Peter Randolph, Peyton's cousin, searching through old records for a precedent that would let the Burgesses expunge their vote. He found it. When the members convened that afternoon, they reconsidered Henry's fifth resolution and defeated it.

By that time Henry's resolutions were already circulating, and they soon found their way into the newspapers. In less than a month, the *Newport Mercury* had printed them all, along with a sixth that branded as an enemy to Virginia anyone who defended Parliament's right to impose taxes.

In early July 1765, Henry's resolutions reached Boston, where the patriots read them with admiration and a sense of shame for having let Thomas Hutchinson persuade them to soften their own letter to Parliament.

Oxenbridge Thacher's wife had died of smallpox the year before. Now, though Thacher was only forty-five, it looked as though he would not recover from his own inoculation, and he sent for John Adams to take over some of his legal business. Adams, when he arrived, asked whether Thacher had seen the Virginia Resolves.

"Oh, yes," said Thacher. "They are men! They are noble spirits! It kills me to think of the lethargy and stupidity that prevails here. I long to be out. I will go out! I will go into court and make a speech, which shall be read after my death as my dying testimony against their infernal tyranny!"

Thacher's agitation troubled Adams and he changed the subject. But he thought to himself that it was only because Thacher was confined to his bed that he could think Bostonians were apathetic. When Thacher died a few days later, the town held a special election for the House. A rich young merchant named John Hancock was a likely candidate, but the voters chose Samuel Adams.

In late September 1765, a month after the rioting, Governor Bernard convened the legislature to warn that the Stamp Act would be enforced. House members were still chastened by the mob's rampage, but the Virginia Resolves had made them bold, and they were determined to stick by their plan to hold a protest meeting of all the colonies. Aware that it would be a historic occasion, the patriots were calling it the Stamp Act congress.

Francis Bernard was not sure how to cope with this latest challenge to his authority. The governor's popularity had been dropping rapidly, and his hunger for money to support his large family, combined with a taste for luxury, made it easy for the patriots to paint Bernard as Hutchinson's partner in greed. Before the riots, Bernard had seen himself very differently—good-natured, canny, unruffled. When a visitor from London asked how he dared walk through Boston without a bodyguard, Bernard had assured him that the people of Massachusetts were not bloodthirsty, and he had been advising London that the colonists were jealous of their liberties but remained loyal to the crown. Bernard had said that by indulging their sense of independence he could keep them calm. But now the riots had proved him wrong, and he was drafting a plan to put down the unrest.

Bernard thought the answer was to send American representatives to Parliament. He calculated that twenty members from the colonies and ten from the West Indies should be enough to pacify the people. Then, mulling over his proposal, he raised the figures to thirty and fifteen. Even those higher numbers would be a cheap price to pay for tranquillity. But in the meantime, Bernard was living under constant stress. The spies he had planted among the patriots represented his only security, and they were unreliable. Twice he sent away his papers and valuables because he expected a mob to descend on him.

These days when he wrote to London, Bernard lamented Britain's folly of levying taxes before she had sent troops to tighten her control over the colonies. He complained that because of threats from the mob, he was governor only in name. "The dignity of Great Britain will require an absolute submission," Bernard wrote, "and these people are not at this time disposed to give it." Where Hutchinson had prayed for better hearts, Bernard was more pragmatic: "God give us better times."

For the governor, any rays of light were faint ones. Bernard tried to convince the Lords of Trade in London that his position wasn't strong enough to let him oppose the Stamp Act congress, which had been called for October 1, 1765, in New York. But he was pleased to report that two of the three delegates from Massachusetts were friends of his government and that they would agree to nothing improper. Bernard even hoped that the congress might recommend submitting to the Stamp Act for the time being. If so, even the bothersome Massachusetts House would have to go along. And yet, he warned, rioting in Boston could break out again at any time.

From London, the king's ministers offered Bernard one hundred regular British soldiers to protect Castle William in the bay. The governor declined them. They wouldn't be enough to provide security, he said, and the sight of the troops might only inflame the mob. Lord Barrington arranged to send Bernard a letter of recall, which the governor could use at his discretion. Bernard assured his patron that he was ready to leave Massachusetts for any other royal post—except in the West Indies. He thought his complexion was too fair to expose to the Caribbean sun.

Just before the Stamp Act congress convened in New York, the first stamped paper arrived in Boston Harbor. The stamp was shaped like a badge, with "America" lettered at its top. Around a Tudor rose ran the motto of the Order of the Garter, *Honi soit qui mal y pense*—Shame to him who thinks evil of it. In large letters across the bottom was the value of the stamp in shillings and pence. A town council's documents would cost one shilling, a bail bond twice that amount. When Bernard asked the House what it wanted him to do with the paper, the members replied that the stamps

were none of their business. The governor had the paper sent to
Castle William under guard of the British warships in the harbor.

Governor Bernard's two trustworthy delegates to the Stamp
Act congress were Timothy Ruggles and Oliver Partridge from
the western counties. James Otis was to be the third representative,
but for months his behavior had been so erratic and contradictory
that even the governor sometimes could take comfort from one of
his speeches. Had Otis written a tract last year against England's
right to tax the colonies? Now he was publishing another defending that right. In the first pamphlet, Otis had spoken out against
slavery: the law of nature made all men free, whether they were
white or black. Did Otis free his own slave? He did not.

Falling into melancholia, Otis would curse the day he ever became a Whig. Then, exhilarated by the cheers of a Town Meeting,
he would challenge George Grenville to come to America and
meet him in hand-to-hand combat on the floor of the Massachusetts
House. And what had been Otis' reaction to Patrick Henry's resolutions? He called them treasonable.

Despite Otis' rudeness to him, Oxenbridge Thacher had usually
been able to pull him back into the patriot ranks. But now Thacher
was dead. Only steady attacks from the Tories—especially some
nasty verses by a customs official named Samuel Waterhouse—had
convinced the Sons of Liberty to return Otis to the House of Representatives. Once installed, though, he had been railing against
Francis Bernard as harshly as ever. What James Otis would do at
the Stamp Act congress, no one wanted to predict.

Twenty-seven men responded to the invitation from the Massachusetts House and traveled to New York for the congress. The
governors of Virginia, North Carolina and Georgia refused to convene their legislatures to select delegates. In New Jersey and Delaware the governors also balked, but their assemblymen met all the
same and chose delegates from among themselves. The legislators
of New Hampshire declined to send anyone but volunteered in
advance to sign whatever statement might come out of the meeting.

The congress was giving its delegates a rare chance for free
discussion among the colonies. Parliament had established mail ser-

vice in America as early as 1710, but postage rates were exorbitant, and a letter from Boston to Philadelphia never arrived in less than a week. New Yorkers could keep in close touch with eastern New Jersey, and Pennsylvania, Delaware and western New Jersey sent letters and parcels along the Delaware River, but the people of South Carolina felt more isolated from the northern colonies than from the West Indies.

As its first decision, the congress passed a vote that would have heartened Francis Bernard. James Otis had put himself forward as chairman, but his notoriety disturbed the other delegates and they turned instead to Timothy Ruggles. The invitation from Massachusetts had called for a statement from this congress that was loyal and humble, and nothing about Otis suggested either quality.

Setting to work, the delegates found themselves facing one central issue. They all agreed that Britain had no right to meddle in the internal affairs of her colonies. Parliament couldn't take away basic rights—trial by jury was one—and it couldn't raise money by taxing commerce within the colonies. But most delegates granted that Parliament could regulate the colonies' trade. Otherwise, of what use were her colonies to Britain? The congress had to decide whether to list Parliament's rights or simply spell out those it did not have.

The wrangling went on for twelve days, with a break for the Sabbath. Christopher Gadsden of South Carolina argued against acknowledging Parliament's authority in any way. This congress, Gadsden said, was leading him to believe that "there ought to be no New England men, no New Yorker, known on the continent, but all of us Americans."

The final statement came close to what Gadsden had wanted. Among its thirteen resolutions, the language of the twelfth was the most vivid, calling for those full liberties that were vital to the "prosperity and happiness of these colonies." Representatives from New York, Connecticut and South Carolina hadn't been authorized to sign any statement until their colonies had a chance to approve it, and at first Otis said he wouldn't sign, either. But after another delegate brought Otis around, Timothy Ruggles became one of the two individual members who refused to sign. Thomas McKean from Delaware kept badgering him to give his reasons. Finally Ruggles said that the statement went against his conscience. McKean continued to berate him until Ruggles, twenty years older and more than six feet tall, challenged him, "Young man, you shall hear from me tomorrow."

Instead of dueling, however, Ruggles rose before dawn and slipped away from New York. Back in Boston, the House scolded him for not following its instructions, but James Otis' behavior was even less pleasing to the patriots. Before he left New York, Otis was heard to say that if the government in London didn't send troops to Massachusetts very soon, the people would be "cutting one another's throats from one end to the other of it." Governor Bernard picked up that story and passed it along gleefully to his friends in Britain. But on October 25, 1765, the same day that the Stamp Act congress adjourned, the Massachusetts House passed its own resolutions, as combative as Patrick Henry's, insisting that the colonists were "unalienably entitled to those essential rights in common with all men."

When James Otis got back to Boston, he was no longer in a conciliatory mood. Reporting on the congress to the Town Meeting, he became so vituperative against Thomas Hutchinson that his audience seemed sorry Hutchinson no longer had a house left to destroy. But then John Adams heard that Otis had told a customs officer that of course Parliament had the right to tax the colonies and only a damned fool would deny it.

As Pope's Day, the fifth of November, approached, Boston seemed ripe for more violence. According to the gossip, the mob's leaders had drawn up a list of fifteen wealthy men whose houses they could plunder, and Samuel Adams recognized that a potent political asset might degenerate into a gang of thieves. Since he knew both Ebenezer Mackintosh and Samuel Swift, the leader of the North End gang, Adams brought them together to fuse their traditional rival marches into one patriotic crusade.

For a street fighter, Swift had a curious background. Fifty years old, he had graduated from Harvard five years before Samuel Adams, and he too had studied briefly for the clergy. Swift turned instead to law, and he maintained a steady practice and a circle of friends that included Thomas Hutchinson. The lieutenant governor knew exactly how the mob was run these days. Swift and Mackintosh controlled the rabble. The Loyal Nine—along with other groups of distillers, carpenters and master masons—tried to control Swift and Mackintosh. But behind the scenes the influential merchants among the patriots, such men as William Molineux and Solomon Davis, took over on important matters. They scheduled a Town Meeting to provide a stage for James Otis, whom Hutchinson was calling "the distracted demagogue of Boston."

To seal the new friendship between the rival gangs, the Whig merchants underwrote a huge banquet called the Union Feast, which gave gang members from North and South Boston a chance to celebrate liberty with unlimited drinks. One popular toast wished any friend of the Stamp Act "a perpetual itching without the benefit of scratching." When Pope's Day arrived, the gangs paraded in orderly ranks, led by Mackintosh and Swift in magnificent uniforms of blue and red and hats laced with gold. Small canes rested on their left arms as they delivered orders to their assistants through speaking trumpets. Blacks had been kept from the march, and there was not a weapon or a club to be seen. At Mackintosh's side was a colonel in the Massachusetts militia, who praised the gangs for their discipline and assured the crowd that the shoemaker held one of the highest posts in government. Samuel Adams and the Sons of Liberty couldn't yet claim an army, but they were reminding Boston that they had their own shock troops.

As Boston's traditional politics continued to unravel, Samuel Adams' life was becoming more stable. Not only had Boston voters sent him to the House of Representatives, but he had taken a second wife, Elizabeth Wells, the daughter of one of Deacon Adams' closest friends. Although some twenty years younger than Samuel, she was proving to be an exemplary wife—intelligent, amiable, a kindly stepmother to his children. She also knew the secret of running a household on next to nothing, which continued to be her husband's annual income. The mother of Adams' first wife tried to lighten the young bride's routine by presenting her with a slave named Surry. When Adams immediately set her free, she chose to stay on in the house as a servant.

Adams' increasing prominence had led the Tories to look harder at his laxity as a tax collector. An audit revealed that he had been especially lenient during the fire of 1760, which destroyed one tenth of Boston, and during another smallpox epidemic. His deficit had risen to seven thousand pounds. At the next election, Adams suggested that the job pass to other hands, but his townsmen recognized that no one else was likely to be so obligingly slipshod and insisted on his reelection. For the moment, Adams seemed to be safe.

In the House of Representatives, members were finding him indispensable for his hard work and his genius for compromise. Whenever he was appointed to a committee—and within weeks he had been named to all of the important ones—Adams would appear with a complete set of resolutions on whatever subject was being debated. Having framed the discussion on his own terms, he was then ready to give way amiably on the small details. Thomas Hutchinson recognized the way Adams was manipulating the House and blamed him for its new belligerence.

When the Stamp Act took effect, on November 1, 1765, Hutchinson decided that the protests of Adams, Patrick Henry and the Sons of Liberty had alarmed every family from Canada to Pensacola. Tories like Peter Oliver told the story of a country gentleman whose servant refused to go out to the barn one dark night because he was afraid. "Afraid of what?" his master demanded. "Me 'fraid Massah Tamp Act he catch me," said the servant.

The Massachusetts House asked Samuel Adams to write a new protest against the act, and the town of Braintree chose John Adams to frame a similar letter. Samuel assured his cousin that the assignment would get him better known and promote his law practice, but John Adams was less sure. Since a standoff over the stamps was developing—the people wouldn't buy them, and Governor Bernard wouldn't recognize any legal papers without them—the courts were sure to be shut down. John Adams took the crisis as a personal affront and poured out his anguish to his diary. "I have had poverty to struggle with—envy and jealousy and malice of enemies to encounter, no friends or but few to assist me," he wrote, and now, just as he was beginning to succeed, along came the Stamp Act to ruin him, and incidentally to destroy America as well.

His only consolation was Samuel Adams' invitation to meet with the patriot leaders. For almost three years, John Adams had been tantalized by gossip about the Caucus Club, which held its meetings in the attic of Tom Dawes, an officer in Boston's militia. John had heard that Dawes would take down a movable partition in order to give the whole group room enough to assemble.

"There," Adams told his diary, "they smoke tobacco till you cannot see from one end of the garret to the other." He assumed that they also drank flip, a drink made with an egg beaten in sweetened ale, set by the fireplace and stirred until it was thick. At last his cousin was giving him the chance to see for himself, and the prospect appealed to John Adams immensely, especially since membership in the Caucus was considered good for business.

When the night arrived, John Adams was impressed by the genial familiarity of the members and their politeness to him, a stranger. But the private faces of these public men held few surprises. Around the hearth, James Otis would blaze with rage and then fall into despondency. Thomas Cushing was diligent in gathering intelligence about the Tories, but even among these allies he remained silent, even secretive. Samuel Adams urged his colleagues to approach political matters delicately, but whenever a matter of principle became involved he turned stiff and inflexible. John Adams saw that Samuel wasn't versed in the law; after all, he wasn't a lawyer. But he felt that Samuel had the most thorough understanding of liberty and the deepest and most radical love of it. John Adams left the meeting pleased with his cousin.

A month after the Stamp Act took effect, Andrew Oliver had still not officially resigned his commission as stamp master. Throughout the colonies, other officials were giving up the post, and on December 16, 1765, the *Boston Gazette* published an anonymous letter accusing Oliver of plotting to keep the office. That evening the Loyal Nine gathered at a distillery in Hanover Square. A few hours later, as Oliver was preparing for bed, his servant was handed a letter ordering Oliver to appear at noon the next day under the elm where his effigy had first hung. Over the last few months the patriots had named it the Liberty Tree and were calling the area around its trunk Liberty Hall.

If Oliver showed up, the note concluded, he would be treated with the greatest politeness. "If not . . . !"

The night was stormy, but by dawn the town was covered with broadsides from the press of Edes and Gill. "St - - p! St - - p! St - - p! no," they read and invited all Sons of Liberty to gather at the Liberty Tree to hear Oliver's statement. The leaflets ended, "A Resignation? Yes."

Since both Hutchinson and Bernard were at their country houses, Oliver couldn't reach them for advice. He sent a friend to ask Ebenezer Mackintosh whether he could spare himself a drenching on this rainy morning and offer his resignation at Town House instead. The shoemaker refused, and Oliver's friends warned him that if he didn't appear he might set off another riot. As a result, Andrew Oliver began the half-mile trek to the Liberty Tree, with Mackintosh leading the procession. When they arrived, they found that two thousand people had braved the downpour to witness this moment.

Standing under the bough where his effigy had hung four months ago, Oliver read his resignation. He said he detested the Stamp Act and hoped that now he would no longer be considered an enemy but only another man. His humiliation complete, the crowd gave Oliver three cheers and sent him home.

Even before that public drama, Oliver's refusal to accept the stamps had left Governor Bernard in a quandary. Every other official was edging away from the issue and trying to force the decision on him. Bernard had expected that the Sons of Liberty would close down both the harbor and the courts by boycotting any activity that required stamps, but they had devised a more artful response, one that wouldn't bring commerce to a standstill. They ignored the law and went on with life exactly as before.

Tory shipowners faced a harder choice. They didn't want to defy Parliament, but neither did they want their houses leveled by the Sons of Liberty. When they came to Bernard for permission to load their vessels, he referred them to his attorney general, who in turn announced that the rheumatism in his right arm had become so severe that he couldn't attend to any business at all. The impasse was resolved when customs officials heard that a mob was ready to storm their offices. On December 17, 1765, the Custom House opened again and cleared all the ships in the harbor. Their owners did not require stamps.

That night Samuel Adams joined the Sons of Liberty at a banquet to celebrate.

Now that they had opened the harbor, the patriots turned to the courts. The morning after the banquet, the Sons of Liberty called a special meeting in Faneuil Hall to ask Francis Bernard and his Council to let the courts resume their business. Not long before, Bernard had received a disturbing letter from the king's ministers in London. They had assumed that the revolt had arisen only among the ignorant lower classes, and the letter expressed their surprise at his administration's "total languor and want of energy" in putting down the challenge. To placate London and yet save his residence from the torch, Bernard realized that he had to shift the responsibility for the courts. He called a meeting of his Council members to inform them that he was leaving entirely in their hands the decision to open the courts.

Meanwhile, Samuel Adams was busy explaining the issue to men at the taverns and along the docks. Late on a winter afternoon, he stopped by the Hancock countinghouse, the office of the young merchant he had defeated for the House. John Hancock was sitting by the fire with several Boston officials, talking about Adams' petition to open the courts. After the round of formal greetings, Hancock invited Adams to take a pinch from his gold snuffbox. It was engraved with a likeness of George III, a gift from the young king when Hancock had visited London during the coronation.

Getting to business, Adams reminded the group of the seriousness of this cause. "If we approve that petition tomorrow"—he pulled his draft from a side pocket—"we must choose a committee of our best legal men to present and enforce it. It is useless to petition the governor and Council unless we have some emphasis behind it."

Hancock and his friends agreed with that evaluation, and John Adams soon learned, to his trepidation, that he had been chosen to supply that emphasis by speaking before the Council. He came prepared with a page of notes headed "Right," "Wrong" and "Remedy," but he abandoned his formal argument and simply charged that Parliament had no more right than a French legislature to tax the colonies. Jeremiah Gridley, the colony's patriarch of the bar, spoke next, and then James Otis, who began to weep and delivered his remarks with tears streaming down his cheeks. Since all three men were arguing points of law, Bernard and his Council saw a way out for themselves. They passed along the decision on whether to open the courts to the judges themselves.

The Probate Court of Suffolk County was currently in session, although Thomas Hutchinson, one of its judges, wouldn't consider conducting further court business without the stamps. Friends rode out to Milton to plead with him. They offered him three options: Bow to the will of the people. Quit his judgeship. Or leave the country. Ever since his house was destroyed, Hutchinson had been talking about spending some time in London, and now his friends were assuring him that his life was in danger. Hutchinson rode into Boston, expecting to find such turmoil that he would have to escape immediately to New Hampshire and book the next passage to England. Instead, the town was sullen but peaceful. Then, consulting with Governor Bernard, Hutchinson found another way to advance his family's fortunes. Even if he didn't go abroad, he could leave the court temporarily and let his brother take his place. Forster Hutchinson, thirteen years younger than Thomas, didn't share his brother's aversion to conducting court business without stamps. Following his example, courts around the province began to open again. By late January 1766, the Massachusetts House was supporting, by a vote of eighteen to five, a call to open all of them.

But as the moment approached for an open defiance of Parliament, travelers returning from England said that George Grenville's government had fallen and that Parliament might repeal the Stamp Act. The same Boston lawyers who had been demanding that Superior Court be opened on March 1, 1766, now wondered whether it was wise to be identified with the insurgents. Suddenly, James Otis wasn't willing to appear in court, and Thomas Hutchinson fabricated a reason to be out of Boston during the showdown. At last an old lawsuit was exhumed, one that had been held over for a year and didn't require stamps. It was tried, and the patriots claimed another victory. The court then adjourned, to let Parliament struggle with cutting the knot they were all tied into.

As they waited, merchants in New York were boycotting all English goods, and they were joined by the patriots of Boston. Rumors about the Stamp Act's repeal came before the boycott could become fully effective, but the patriots had evolved a strategy for punishing British arrogance in the future. Parliament might meet to undo the damage of the past year, but could Parliament repeal the new spirit in America?

John Hancock, by John Singleton Copley

Hancock
1765-68

IN THE SPRING of 1765, King George III fell ill with a sickness serious enough that his councillors urged Parliament to make some provision for his successor. The debate over that regency bill exposed the tensions between George Grenville on one side and Lord Bute and the king's mother on the other, and when the vote came, Grenville's side was defeated. By then, George III had recovered and was incensed by the affronts to his mother. Determined to have a new prime minister, the king put aside his antipathy for William Pitt and interviewed him for the post, but Pitt was ridden with gout and all but retired from public life. When he declined, George turned instead to Charles Watson-Wentworth, the Marquis of Rockingham. The marquis was an unprepossessing young man who led a faction that had opposed almost everything Grenville had introduced, including the Stamp Act.

Each ship from the colonies brought Rockingham fresh reports of demonstrations and riots against the act. The readers of London's conservative newspapers were indignant. One Tory wrote, "These yellow shades of men are by no means fit for a conflict with our troops." Another writer accused the Sons of Liberty of hypocrisy for upholding their own right to inflict violence on the customs officers but arguing that the king's forces had no right to retaliate. With the new prime minister, the opinions that counted most heavily came from his supporters among England's manufacturers and traders. They told him that America's threat to boycott their goods could worsen Britain's current recession, and they wanted the Stamp Act repealed.

Grenville and another House leader, Charles Townshend, were adamant that the Stamp Act remain. King George was insisting that Parliament uphold its right to tax. At best, he would agree to some sort of modification in the law. In that stalemate, who held the title of prime minister had become less important than who had the power to sway the Commons. After twelve months away from the House floor, William Pitt returned in January 1766 to avenge himself on George Grenville, a boyhood friend who was now a bitter enemy. Early in the debate, Pitt rose on his crutch and announced that every measure taken during Grenville's ministry had been entirely wrong.

As always, those first words came so quietly that Pitt couldn't be heard beyond the next bench. During his absence, he had been rumored to be gravely ill, perhaps mad. This day, men wondered whether he would have the strength to continue. They might have remembered that Pitt had always turned his infirmities to his advantage. Now he was recalling that "when the resolutions were taken in the House to tax America, I was ill in my bed." But, Pitt added, if he could have endured being carried to the House floor he would have come, just to testify against the Stamp Act. Today's debate over its repeal was more important than anything the House had faced since it confirmed the Bill of Rights nearly a hundred years ago. In this present case, said Pitt, the colonists shared the natural rights of mankind and the peculiar privileges of Englishmen.

Usually, Pitt seemed to appeal directly to each member, but now he was lifting his voice implacably: "The Americans are the sons, not the bastards, of England." He ridiculed Grenville's contention that the colonies were somehow already represented in Parliament as "the most contemptible that ever entered the head of a man." America's assemblies had always possessed a constitutional right to give and grant their own money. "They would have been slaves if they had not enjoyed it," Pitt said. He would never admit to the justice of taxing America internally, he added, until she enjoyed representation.

Springing up to defend his act, Grenville warned that the Stamp Act issue was only a pretext for the colonies to move toward independence. "Ungrateful people of America!" Grenville cried, and chided Pitt for remarks that would lead to revolution.

Stung by that challenge, Pitt stood, along with the other members who wished to speak, and the House members demanded that he be allowed to reply. "Mr. Pitt!" they shouted. "Go on!" Pitt mocked the House rule that would have stopped him from making a second address—"I do not speak twice; I only finish." Then, glancing at his notes, he launched his rebuttal. In private life, Pitt had always deplored laughter and taught his children that it was a sign of vulgarity. But in debate he relied upon the laughter his sarcasm could provoke.

"I have been charged," he began, "with giving birth to sedition in America. I rejoice that America has resisted. . . . The gentleman asks, When were the colonies emancipated? But I desire to know when they were made slaves. . . . In a good cause, on a sound bottom, the force of this country can crush America to atoms. I know the valor of your troops. I know the skill of your officers. But on this ground, on the Stamp Act, when so many here will think it is a crying injustice, I am one who will lift up my hands against it.

"In such a cause, your success would be hazardous. America, if she fell, would fall like a strong man. She would embrace the pillars of the State, and pull the Constitution along with her.

"Is this your boasted peace? To sheathe the sword, not in its scabbard, but in the bowels of your countrymen? . . . The Americans have not acted in all things with prudence and temper. They have been driven to madness by injustice. Will you punish them for the madness you have occasioned?

"Upon the whole," Pitt concluded, "I will beg leave to tell the House what is really my opinion. It is that the Stamp Act be repealed absolutely, totally and immediately."

Pitt carried the day. At 2:30 A.M. on February 22, 1766, in the presence of five hundred members, the House of Commons repealed the Stamp Act. But even his allies insisted on one compromise to reassure the king and his faction. They passed the Declaratory Act, an intentionally vague restatement of Parliament's right to make binding laws for the colonies. Over Pitt's objection, the act was adopted.

Rockingham's fragile Ministry soon collapsed. Once again, King George asked William Pitt to lead the government, and as an inducement the king elevated him to the title of Lord Chatham. Throughout Europe, men were astonished that the Great Commoner would think that moving to the House of Lords represented a promotion. "It argues a senselessness to glory," said the king of Poland, "to forfeit the name of Pitt for any title."

During the debate over repeal, Benjamin Franklin, Pennsylvania's agent in London, had gone to the Commons to answer questions about the mood in the colonies. He had been invited as a leading authority on the American character, and he reminded his audience of the immense goodwill that Americans had felt toward Britain only three years earlier. Franklin hoped to soothe those members who felt that the Sons of Liberty must be taught a lesson, and he assured the Commons that the colonists accepted the idea of taxes on their trade and objected only to taxing their internal affairs. Some Americans agreed with Franklin in making that distinction, but many did not. He hadn't been in America during the last two years or felt for himself the heat of a Stamp Act bonfire. Franklin added that he could foresee no resentment over the Declaratory Act, especially if it was never enforced.

A member asked whether British soldiers could enforce the Stamp Act. Franklin replied that they could not. "What are they to do? They cannot force a man to take stamps who chooses to do without them.

"They will not find a rebellion. They may indeed make one."

Almost three months after Parliament's vote, a copy of the repeal of the Stamp Act reached Boston in mid-May 1766. At 1 A.M. the following Monday, the patriots began their celebration by ringing bells in the church steeple nearest the Liberty Tree. The bells of Christ Church answered them from the North End, and by 2 A.M. the town resounded with gunfire, drums and singing. Boys climbed rooftops to hang out flags, and John Hancock, a part owner of the ship that brought the news, opened his house overlooking the Common and provided Madeira wine for the rounds of toasting. James Otis and the other patriots who lived around the Common did the same, and the result was the greatest party Boston had ever seen.

The Sons of Liberty had been planning the event for three weeks. They banned all bonfires except the ones they set, and they warned children, servants and the town's two thousand slaves to stay off the streets. By Monday evening, prosperous men had paid up the bills of Boston's debtors and cleared the jail. A local craftsman, Paul Revere, had engraved copperplates of a huge obelisk to rise beneath the Liberty Tree. It was lighted with two hundred and eighty lamps and inset with portraits of Rockingham, Pitt and other men who had spoken for the colonies. George III was also there, the only face shown in profile.

Hancock had ordered a stage for fireworks built in front of his house. At dusk, twelve rockets were set off near the workhouse and answered by a dozen from Hancock's party. The volleys went back and forth, outdoing each other in star bursts and fiery wheels. Somehow, during the exchange, the obelisk caught fire and was destroyed.

Gentlemen and ladies passed from one open house to the next until, at 11 P.M., a horizontal wheel of fireworks sent sixteen dozen blazing serpents hurtling through the night air. That was the signal that the festival was over and the Sons of Liberty expected people to go quietly to bed.

Throughout the celebration, the Tories had been watching dourly. "Every dirty fellow just risen from his kennel," one wrote afterward, "congratulated his neighbors on their glorious victory over England." Samuel Adams had also viewed the scene skeptically. The people of Boston seemed maddened with a new loyalty to Britain and their king. They thought the battle was over.

Because of Samuel Adams, John Hancock had presided over a night of bonfires, secure that a mob wouldn't attack his lavish house or his lovely gardens. Since Adams had defeated him for the House seat, Hancock had seemed to renounce politics. He had told friends that the Stamp Act would probably ruin him and yet the colonies must submit to it. But during the months of protest, Samuel Adams had drawn him into his circle of patriots, and soon

Hancock was making lists of the dozen Boston Tories who, he joked, should be beheaded for supporting the use of stamps. As the town prepared for another election on May 6, 1766, some of Adams' colleagues proposed backing a merchant named John Rowe for a House seat, but Adams turned his eyes toward Hancock's house and asked, "Is there not another John that may do better?" The patriots took the hint and gave John Hancock the victory.

Hancock, who was not yet thirty, had inherited the largest fortune in New England, which helped to explain why, despite his modest accomplishments, he had joined Samuel Adams' roster of exceptional young men. At the time of his birth in North Braintree, John's prospects had been less brilliant. His father and grandfather were clergymen, but that guaranteed them only respect, not riches. At the age of seven, John himself seemed destined for the clergy, until his father died, leaving a widow and three small children. John's merchant uncle, the very successful Thomas Hancock, and his stout, kindly wife, Lydia, were childless, and they took the thin and frail child into their home as a cherished foster son.

Because of his delicacy, John was kept out of school for a year and allowed to become acquainted with his new guardians and their extravagant household. Thomas Hancock's granite-faced mansion had been built to the plans of a London architect, with graceful black chimneys, a sloping tiled roof and fifty-four windows. Thomas Hancock ran four trading ships and instructed his captains to bring back luxurious furnishings—damasks, exotic plants, English wallpaper patterned with peacocks. From England had also come a black walnut clock that stood ten feet tall. For his gardens, Hancock imported peach and apricot trees from Bilbao, yews and holly from a London horticulturist. The holly vines arrived dead and some of the alien flower seeds never bloomed, but the five thousand pounds sterling that Hancock had spent on his house and grounds had produced a Boston showplace.

Thomas Hancock and his wife took an equal pride in their attractive foster child. At eight, John entered the Public Latin School, where the last hour of each day was devoted to a class in penmanship. At thirteen, he was enrolled at Harvard College. There he rose at 6 A.M. for chapel services and afterward a breakfast of biscuits, coffee and beer. At noon the students poured themselves drafts of cider from two pewter mugs set out amid the meat and vegetables. That indulgence toward alcohol, combined with the severe New England winters, bred habits that lasted a lifetime. When he became master of his uncle's house, John Hancock kept a gallon jug of hot rum punch on his sideboard day and night.

He had entered the Harvard class of 1754 ranked fifth among his classmates, which assured him better chambers, a front pew at chapel and first choice of food at the head table in the commons. But Hancock was demoted four notches when he and another boy engaged in the undergraduate sport of getting a Negro slave drunk; the college authorities said they had endangered the slave's life. Hancock's rank had been restored by the time he sailed out into the world, a slender young man who favored lavender suits when he went riding in a family carriage always painted yellow. The Hancock rigs, however expensive, could never be quite sleek enough to be fashionable. Ordering a new carriage from London, Thomas Hancock explained the problem: "You know, Mrs. Hancock is none of the shortest and smallest of folks, though I'd prefer as light a one as possible to her size."

Thomas Hancock sent his ward to Europe for a final polishing, and John was visiting London in the fall of 1760 when George III was installed as king. John Hancock was dazzled by the coronation ceremonies. Presented at court, he received from his sovereign—who was one year younger—the snuffbox he took back to Boston.

Returning home, Hancock set about learning his uncle's business. How Thomas Hancock had become rich so quickly had always puzzled some Bostonians. When he was not quite fourteen, Thomas had been apprenticed to a bookbinder in Cornhill Street. He stayed there for seven years and then opened his own bookshop in Ann Street. Within two years he was investing his profits in a load of goods bound for Albany, and that led naturally to importing—cloth, tea, books. But those small profits didn't explain how he had gone from apprentice to merchant in less than a decade. Thomas Hutchinson had heard a story that during those first years in trade Hancock had bought a diamond cheaply and sold it at a vast profit. But Hutchinson knew that the truth was more prosaic. Thomas Hancock was a smuggler.

His smuggling would have been unremarkable except for the scale on which he operated. To cut his risk, he took only temporary partners. With them he sent his ships with legal cargo to Surinam in Dutch Guiana and they returned with South American contraband. Hancock dealt in coarse cloth, ribbons, buckles, fans, all merchandise that could enter the colony legally only through Britain. He also dealt in hardware, pins, coal. And tea. From his own expertise, Hutchinson knew that Hancock bought cargoes of tea at St. Eustatius in the Dutch West Indies and shipped it to Boston in hogsheads marked as molasses. He also imported a few chests of tea from England to act as a cover for the smuggled barrels.

John Hancock began by waiting on customers at the store on the family pier, Hancock's Wharf. When his uncle died of apoplexy in 1764, everyone agreed that John had proved himself qualified to take over the empire. But they were curious how he would handle his new riches, some seventy thousand pounds or more. For the first months after his mourning, John became a busy host, caught up in a round of parties and balls. He was the most eligible bachelor in New England. But when someone claimed him, it was not a Boston merchant's daughter for marriage but Samuel Adams for politics.

On the day of Hancock's election to the House, John Adams was walking on the Common when he ran into his cousin. They had taken a few turns around the green when they came into view of the mansion that Hancock had inherited two years earlier. Pointing up at its stone façade, Samuel Adams remarked, "This town has done a wise thing today."

"What?" asked John Adams.

"They have made that young man's fortune their own."

Samuel Adams was fifteen years older than John Hancock, and these days he was looking older still. On both sides of the Atlantic the strain of the past year had told on many of the chief figures. King George was said to be unstable. Pitt's enemies claimed that his gout had moved to the brain. James Otis drank too much and raved on both sides of every issue. Thomas Hutchinson, perhaps warned by his father's example, had undertaken a strict regimen of diet and exercise. John Hancock, never robust, was sending to London for a variety of remedies. And Samuel Adams suffered from a perpetual tremor, sometimes so severe that he

Dorothy Quincy Hancock

could barely write because of the way his pen careened around the page.

And yet the mass of men remained tranquil. In his diary John Adams wrote that the repeal of the Stamp Act had hushed the popular clamor into silence. The Sons of Liberty seemed ready to disband. Governor Bernard spent much of the rest of 1766 trying to win compensation for Thomas Hutchinson and others who had suffered from the riots. But leaders in the House wanted to tie any payment to an amnesty for those men who had been arrested.

James Otis had persuaded the House to open a gallery for visitors, and for the first time in Massachusetts history those debates would be public.

Hutchinson was apprehensive when he heard himself described once again on the House floor as an unscrupulous man who lusted for power. He guessed that the charges were being repeated all over the colony. But he and Bernard were willing to accept the abuse—and agree to the amnesty—in order to get the reparations. Hutchinson had claimed losses of twenty-five hundred pounds sterling. An independent audit put the figure about seven hundred pounds higher, and the colony agreed to reimburse him. The riot's leaders who had been set free from Sheriff Greenleaf's jail had been lying low for months, but now they were walking boldly through the streets. Their amnesty prompted England to refuse the terms; by that time, however, Hutchinson had already been paid. Officially, the affair was ended.

But Samuel Adams and his dwindling band were determined that Boston remember the protests. On August 16, 1766, one year after the effigies appeared on the Liberty Tree, the Sons of Liberty staged an anniversary dinner under its branches. While the town's leading patriots toasted the king and Pitt, young apprentices and black seamen massed in the street and shouted the old slogans. The Tories continued to regard those men as rabble and scum, but Samuel Adams and the Sons of Liberty were impressing on them that they had shared in one of Boston's brightest moments.

When they opposed the Stamp Act, Lord Rockingham and Benjamin Franklin had unwittingly misled Parliament about the nature of the American protests. That was why, barely one year after the rioting, the king's ministers could provide Samuel Adams for the second time with the inflammatory issue he had been lacking. Adams' chief antagonist was another official trying to ease Britain's debts, but Charles Townshend was no humorless accountant like George Grenville. His rollicking speeches in the Commons usually came after a long and festive supper, and they had won Townshend the nickname "Champagne Charley." William Pitt—now Lord Chatham—considered Townshend a weak leader and was determined to see him gone. To prove himself, Townshend turned again to the idea of an American tax. But this time he would hold the colonists to their word. They had claimed that they objected only to taxes on their internal affairs. Townshend found that distinction ridiculous, but he would respect it. Fighting for his political life, he assured the Parliament that he knew "the mode by which a revenue may be drawn from America without offense." Few men in the Commons knew the Americans well enough to tell him that by the year 1767 that mode didn't exist.

Townshend proposed imposing external duties, those collected at the ports, on several of the commodities that Americans were required by law to import exclusively from England—paint, paper, lead and tea. William Pitt, Lord Chatham, was ailing again, but, alarmed by this new provocation, he called on George III and persuaded him to dismiss Townshend from the Exchequer. When the king cast about for a replacement, however, he could find none, and it was Chatham who left the government.

An effective propaganda campaign in London by the American Tories helped Townshend win support in Parliament. Governor Bernard, Thomas Hutchinson and Andrew Oliver had been supplying their British friends with inflammatory articles from the *Boston Gazette*, especially those about the amnesty for the Stamp Act rioters. Down the coast, New Yorkers had begun to balk at paying part of the expense for quartering British troops there, and the Massachusetts House was congratulating New York on that insubordination.

In that climate, Townshend's duties won passage easily. He could also earmark a portion of the new revenue to pay royal appointees for serving in America. For years, the patriots had thought that their only control over a haughty governor or judge was the fact that their legislature paid his salary. Townshend was removing that leverage. And to guarantee that the duties raised as much money as he had promised to Parliament, he was tightening control over America's slack customs procedures. Townshend appointed five new commissioners of customs and sent them to Boston with broad powers. Since colonial jurors rarely convicted a local merchant of smuggling, Townshend's acts set up new admiralty courts that could try smugglers without a jury. And the acts made it easier for customs officials to obtain writs of assistance.

In approving the Townshend Acts, Parliament was ignoring the way the Americans viewed their customs system. Rockingham's Ministry had listened to the colonies and cut the duties on molasses from threepence a gallon to one penny; since the old bribe and the new tax were identical, traders had lost any incentive to pay off the customs officials. But the veteran customs men London was sending to Boston would know even more lucrative ways to exploit their position. The punishment for violating the Sugar Act was seizure of a ship and its smuggled cargo. At customs, the trick was to pretend to be lax and then crack down abruptly and catch the merchants with large stores of contraband. In London, that increase in confiscated goods might look as though honest officials were finally doing their job. In Boston, shipowners and retailers knew the tactic was extortion.

This time when Samuel Adams sounded the alarm, he could expect a reaction from his province. He argued that Townshend's relatively small duties would soon give way to larger ones. They would be followed by British soldiers to enforce the law and strip America's legislatures of their power. Adams knew, though, that abstract predictions aroused less fear and resentment than pointing out specific men with royal titles. These new commissioners of customs, he wrote, were "the greatest political curses that could have been sent amongst us." Adams proposed a fitting reception for them. As it happened, the commissioners would be landing in Boston on Pope's Day. They should be taken into custody by Mackintosh's irregulars, marched to the Liberty Tree and shown the wisdom of resigning their commissions immediately.

Once again, Adams was more militant than his allies. James Otis was among the patriots who weren't willing to treat British representatives of the king as roughly as they had handled a fellow American like Andrew Oliver. In a long harangue at the Town Meeting, Otis upheld the king's right to appoint as many customs officials as he pleased. As for threats or riots, Otis said that "to insult and tear each other in pieces was to act like madmen."

The Pope's Day parade went off on schedule on November 5, 1767, and the commissioners entered Boston without incident. The head of this new board, Henry Hulton, even paused with the crowd to join in laughing at the figures of the Pope and twenty demons as they were carried past. Whatever his disappointment, Samuel Adams was a tactician. Today he was advising the patriots that not a hair of the commissioners should be touched. But he added, "The time is coming when they shall lick the dust and melt away."

For now, Adams would keep his forces leashed until the moment when all of Boston approved the next attack.

Three years had passed since the shortages in Samuel Adams' tax collecting had first been revealed, and during that time the Tories had come to hate and fear him. One conservative artist said that if wanted to draw the devil, he would get Sam Adams to sit for him. But, as Peter Oliver complained, Adams had ingratiated himself so shrewdly with the vulgar classes that he seemed invulnerable. All the same, the Tory press kept up its assault. One article called Samuel Adams a cur-dog—"very artful, loves babbling, especially when he gets into a very large room; has been taught to run into houses, to pick up money and run away with it directly to his kennel."

By March 1767, Bostonians had become enough disturbed about the tax deficits to examine the books of its five collectors. The other four men were also found to have money outstanding, but Samuel Adams' debts were three times the average. He owed a total of four thousand pounds. Thomas Hutchinson called that debt a "defalcation," and it would have meant public ruin for a less resourceful man. But, as the Tories watched in outrage, John Hancock rode in to save Adams by expanding his political patronage and guaranteeing control of the Town Meeting. As Peter Oliver put it, Hancock was already "as closely attached to the hindermost part of Mr. Adams as the rattles are affixed to the tail of the rattle snake."

After delays and lawsuits, the Town Meeting forgave much of Adams' debt and transferred the remainder to another man to collect. At last, Samuel Adams was free from a persistent embarrassment. "His power over weak minds," said Peter Oliver, "was truly surprising."

In May 1768, six months after the customs commissioners arrived from England, John Hancock's sloop the *Liberty* entered Boston Harbor with a cargo of wine from Madeira. Her captain told the customs men that the wine on board totaled twenty-five pipes, or casks, which was slightly over three thousand gallons but well below the ship's capacity. A month later, Thomas Kirk, the investigator charged with verifying the report, came forward to claim that during his inspection he had been shoved into a cabin and nailed inside by a gang of men led by another of Hancock's captains, John Marshall. While Kirk was held captive, other workers removed the stores of undeclared wine. When they were finished, Captain Marshall warned Kirk that his life and property depended on his silence. Now he was ignoring the threat and accusing Boston's wealthiest merchant of violating the Townshend Acts. Captain Marshall couldn't refute the story, since he had died, apparently of a heart attack, the day after the *Liberty* was unloaded.

For the first time, the customs officials thought they could crack down forcefully. A crown ship, the H.M.S. *Romney*, with fifty guns, had entered the harbor in May and dropped anchor six hundred feet from shore. Armed with Kirk's testimony and reassured by the gunship, the commissioners made their move. Near dusk, while many workers were leaving the docks, the commissioners boarded the *Liberty* and seized her as punishment for the false tax declaration.

Around the dock, the crowd's mood was ominous. Even before the boarding, resentment against the *Romney*'s British crew had been running high. On Sunday an officer had prevented a group of impressed men from jumping ship, and the *Romney*'s captain, John Corner, had been heard calling Boston "a blackguard town ruled by mobs." Now there were clearly enough men on the dock to retake Hancock's sloop and sail it to safety. Seeing the danger, the customs men signaled the *Romney* to send barges of troops armed with bayonets. As the patriots protested, the *Liberty* was towed out to the *Romney* and secured under her guns.

That provocation once again transformed the crowd on the wharf into a mob. Throwing stones and swinging clubs, it burst upon the customs officials. Joseph Harrison, a collector, was beaten badly. His son, Richard, a customs clerk, was dragged through the streets by his hair. Thomas Irving, inspector of imports and exports, escaped with his sword broken and his clothes ripped. John Hancock's Madeira, including an especially rich vintage he had ordered for his own table, disappeared from the pier.

About 10 P.M., the mob's leaders spotted Harrison's large pleasure boat at the wharf. Cheering, they dragged it to the Common and set it on fire. Moving across the open grass, the throng milled around the houses of Harrison and Benjamin Hallowell, the comptroller of customs, yowling and breaking windows. An Englishwoman staying with one of the commissioners thought the hideous noise sounded like attacking Indians. As she was packing her valuables and preparing to flee, she heard one of the leaders call out to the mob to stop its rampage. "We will defend our liberties and property by the strength of our arm and the help of our God. To your tents, O Israel."

The next morning was quiet, but the commissioners decided that they were no longer safe in Boston and sent a delegate to Governor Bernard. He authorized the customs officers and their families to leave the harbor in a barge and take refuge on the *Romney*. Three days later, the party moved to unassailable quarters at Castle William, three miles into the harbor. Thomas Hutchinson saw to their comfort at the castle, providing food and a steady stream of Tory dinner guests.

These days, the Liberty Tree had a towering pole rising up through its branches. On Tuesday at 10 A.M., banners were flying from the top of the pole, and despite wet and disagreeable weather so many people had gathered at the trunk that the entire assembly moved a half mile to larger quarters at Faneuil Hall. Every time meetings were moved from the tree, there would be a stirring parade through the center of town and past the governor's chambers.

At Faneuil Hall, the patriots made their protest legitimate by calling a Town Meeting for three o'clock that afternoon, and when even more people turned up than could fit inside, they moved to the lofty Old South Meeting House. The show of support for Hancock did not surprise John Adams. He calculated that a thousand Boston families depended for food every day of the year on Hancock's business. Add to that the new firemen's rig that Hancock had bought for the town and the thousand pounds sterling he had contributed to the Brattle Street Meeting House, and John Hancock was New England's most popular man.

As the town debated its next step at the Old South, the commissioners across the harbor at Castle William were piecing together rumors to send to General Thomas Gage, the British commander in New York. They had heard that one speaker told the Town Meeting that "he hoped, and believed, that they would one

and all resist, even unto blood" to defend Boston's liberty. If that
was Samuel Adams, he was finally saying aloud what he had been
too discreet to suggest even to his closest allies. A Tory innkeeper,
Richard Sylvester, claimed that on the day after the *Liberty* was
taken Samuel Adams challenged a band of patriots to join him in
an uprising: "If you are men, behave like men. Let us take up arms
immediately and be free and seize all the king's officers. We should
be joined with thirty thousand men from the country with their
knapsacks and bayonets fixed."

Even if Samuel Adams was aroused to that pitch, he failed
to sway his listeners at the Town Meeting. They voted instead to
send a delegation to the governor, accusing the *Romney* of ob-
structing their harbor and threatening them with famine.

With two other men, John Hancock left the Meeting to ask
Francis Bernard when he would receive the delegation. They
found that the governor had left for his house in Roxbury, and
the twenty-one delegates boarded eleven chaises and followed him
there. They were dressed according to their means, Hancock in
damask lined with silk, Samuel Adams in his worn plainspun. Heading the delegation was the oily Royall Tyler. Greeting him was
an equally unctuous Francis Bernard. The governor exerted himself
to charm the delegates he didn't know and had wine passed
around as he listened to their presentation. The delegates had become subdued in the governor's presence, and they raised no
objection when he said that he preferred to give his answer the
next day, in writing. Bowing them out, Bernard was impressed
with his own suave manners.

The next day his written answer came: since the *Romney*
was not his to command, he could not order it to leave Boston.
James Otis reported that response to the Town Meeting and mentioned the governor's graciousness. He truly believed, Otis said,
that Bernard wished the colony well. When Bernard's spies reported that rare compliment, the governor promptly passed it on
to the king's ministers in London. "Just at this time I am popular,"
Bernard wrote on June 16. "I do not expect to enjoy it a week."

He would enjoy it five days .

During the last session of the Massachusetts House, Otis and
Samuel Adams had suggested trying to unite the colonies by sending them a letter opposing the Townshend Acts. Most House mem-

bers had rejected the idea since London was sure to take the letter as a provocation, possibly even an invitation to another rebellious gathering like the Stamp Act congress. When the proposal was rejected two to one, Governor Bernard was delighted that two men wouldn't again be inflaming a whole continent.

But, like the Burgesses of Virginia, who were always impatient to leave Williamsburg for their plantations, Boston's farmers wanted to get back to their crops. Men from the country were inclined to be conservative, and Bernard watched his allies drift away from Boston while his enemies worked toward a majority. On February 4, 1768, the House appointed Samuel Adams, Otis, Thomas Cushing and Joseph Hawley to write a circular letter. A sparsely attended session approved the letter and sent it on to the other colonies.

The letter marked a shift in the patriots' argument. Adams and Otis now said that Parliament had no right to impose even external taxes if their sole purpose was to raise money. Levying taxes to pay the salaries of governors and judges had become a new violation of natural law. The letter stopped far short of rejecting Parliament's authority altogether. The patriots were still not ready to say that England couldn't use taxation to regulate trade. Instead, they recognized Parliament as the "supreme legislative power over the whole Empire." John Adams was surprised that his cousin would make that concession, and he blamed the vacillating Otis. Certainly Otis was willing to take credit for the letter. To a friend who asked about their progress, he replied, "They are nearly ready. I have written them all and handed them over to Sam Adams to quieuvicue them"—Otis' term for the editing.

During the months when America was debating the letter, King George was setting up a new impediment to reconciliation with the colonies. At the age of forty-one, Champagne Charley Townshend had died of a lingering fever, possibly typhoid. To replace him as chancellor of the exchequer, the king appointed Lord North, who regretted the repeal of the Stamp Act and believed that the colonies were on the brink of mutiny. Early in 1768, four months after North's appointment, the king authorized a new office, a secretary of state for colonial affairs. That post went to Lord Hillsborough, a man who thoroughly endorsed Lord North's policies. When Hillsborough received the Massachusetts circular letter, he took it at once to George III. Acting for the king, Hillsborough then, in April 1768, wrote to warn each colonial governor that his legislature must ignore the Massachusetts letter, "which will be treating it with the contempt it deserves." Hillsborough also told Francis Bernard that the Massachusetts House must either disavow the letter or Bernard must dissolve the House.

On June 21, five days after Governor Bernard congratulated himself on winning over Otis and the Town Meeting, he had to bring that peremptory message to the legislature. Having heard the king's demand, the representatives demanded to see Hillsborough's letter. By that time, Samuel Adams and the *Boston Gazette* had convinced the patriots that Bernard's letters to London did not reflect a fair picture of Boston's mood, and the House asked that Bernard also turn over his letters to Hillsborough. The governor responded as the patriots knew he would: "You may assure yourselves that I shall never make public my letters to his majesty's ministers, but upon my own motion and for my own reasons."

In that strained atmosphere, Otis took the House floor. "Who are these ministers?" he demanded. "The very frippery and foppery of France, the mere outsides of monkeys!" He added that the king appointed only boys as his ministers, and they had no education at all except for traveling through France, where they picked up slavish attitudes. Here Otis paused to congratulate himself and his allies: Not a person in England was capable of composing so elegant and so pure a piece of writing as the petitions that the House had passed during its last session. Then he moved on to accuse Parliament of being "a parcel of button-makers, pin-makers, horse jockeys, gamesters, pensioners, pimps and whoremasters." The public gallery was jammed and more men were listening at the doors as Otis began to praise Oliver Cromwell, not least for murdering a king. But however carried away, Otis stopped short of abusing George III. The speech was a two-hour violent rant, and Bernard collected it all from his spies and sent it off to London to let the Parliament know what sort of men he had to contend with.

Other arguments in the House that day were quieter but as determined. Why should this session undo a measure passed during the last one? By now, the circular letters had become a historical fact. They had appeared in newspapers. Many colonies had already answered them. It was up to the world to judge the merit of the House's position.

Samuel Adams composed the House's response to Governor Bernard. "We have now only to inform your Excellency that this House have voted not to rescind, as required, the resolution of the last House; and that upon a division on the question, there were 92 nays and 17 yeas." The members who had voted against rescinding the letter, Adams added, were moved by their duty to God, their king and their country, and their posterity. They ardently wished and humbly prayed that in the future the governor would be guided by those same principles.

Receiving the insolent message, Bernard immediately recognized its author. "Samuel Adams!" he had written about another example of Adams' work. "Every dip of his pen stings like a horned snake." The next day, he dissolved the House. The patriots had moved another square forward in a game being played without rules or precedent on both sides of the Atlantic.

The patriots took the number "92" as a new rallying cry. The names of the seventeen dissenters were posted at the Liberty Tree. In a letter written on July 4, 1768, John Dickinson of Pennsylvania sent Otis a song he had composed with Arthur Lee of Virginia. One couplet ran:

Then join hand in hand, brave Americans all,
By uniting we stand, by dividing we fall.

Besides the circular letter, Samuel Adams and the patriots had launched three other campaigns against the Townshend Acts. Their crusade for a heightened sense of public morality was proving the least effective. Adams relished his reputation as a Puritan, and he desired a future in which the gallant citizens of his colony would shun foppery and carousing. He had been distressed by the customs commissioners, who he thought were importing a touch of London high life to Boston. At the Peacock Tavern the drinking often went on until four in the morning, and after one revel Thomas Hutchinson had been amused to see the commissioners and their ladies nursing hangovers. One woman's rosy Nova Scotia complexion had turned so pale and sickly she might have been from South Carolina, and another bright and talkative wife had become noticeably taciturn. "Poor Paxton's usual refreshing nap after dinner," Hutchinson wrote to a friend, "was turned into a waking coma, more insensible with his eyes open than he used to be when they were shut." He added that he only wished that the same misery could be visited on James Otis, Samuel Adams, John Hancock, William Molineux and another fifty patriots he could name.

Samuel Adams was concerned that Hutchinson might get his wish and the patriots would succumb to sodden and worldly pastimes. At first the Whigs had boycotted the commissioners' parties, but slowly the attraction of fine clothes, gilded carriages and sumptuous banquets had eroded their high principles. Adams heard that Whig wives and Tory gentlemen were drinking punch together and dancing the minuet. When he complained that it was a "bad thing for Boston to have so many gay idle people in it," only the town's clergymen seemed to listen. The staunchest Sons of Liberty set up a "Liberty Assembly" that would permit dancing but exclude the commissioners and their Tory friends. Even so, it was one battle that Samuel Adams had been losing up to the moment the mob sent the commissioners fleeing to Castle William.

Another of his tactics was not rooted in Adams' morality but in his sense of expediency. He turned to exploiting the anti-Catholic sentiment that ran deep throughout the colony. Writing as "A Puritan" in the *Boston Gazette*, he claimed that popery was becoming even more of a threat to New England than the Townshend Acts, and he equated support for Bernard with allegiance to Rome. He divided towns by the way their delegates voted in the House— "Protestant" towns, Boston being the leading one, or such "popish" towns as Hatfield, Salem and Springfield. Adams was appealing to instincts firmly rooted in Boston. The first book that children in the colony read was the *New England Primer*, whose frontispiece showed the Pope being pierced with darts.

The most direct of Adams' campaigns worked best. From the time the acts took effect, November 20, 1767, many Bostonians had been boycotting luxury goods from Britain by signing a "nonimportation agreement." At the same time, they were trying to produce more of their own goods throughout the province. During the brief experiment of 1765, the patriots had seen that a boycott could pinch English nerves quickly and severely. Now stricter enforcement at the customs offices was drawing off hard currency from America, and bad times were spreading across the colonies. A ban on luxury imports was easy to maintain. As far away as Virginia, George Washington, the planter and retired colonel, welcomed the boycott because it gave his neighbors who were plagued by debt an acceptable excuse for cutting back on their lavish expenses.

The agreement drafted by Boston was relatively mild. By signing, a person promised to give a "constant preference" to those merchants who didn't import from London. New York's version was more stringent—a total boycott of the shops that continued to bring in British goods. To many patriots, those traders who didn't sign were traitors.

Andrew Oliver had signed the nonimportation agreement on behalf of the family firm, but his brother Peter noticed the signatures of porters and washerwomen among those who were agreeing not to import silks, velvets, coaches and chariots. The patriots were insisting that any banned goods that arrived at the port—including all ready-made apparel, furniture and loaf sugar—be crated up and returned to London. But Peter Oliver claimed that mobs sometimes gathered at the pier, made off with the imported finery and shipped back wood shavings, brickbats and rancid bacon. He also accused the patriot merchants of drawing on their experience as smugglers to evade the boycott. They signed the agreement but brought in the prohibited items anyway, he charged. A Tory newspaper began running the names of those double-dealers.

Throughout the maneuvering, the Tories believed that they held one trump card. When London's patience was finally exhausted, British troops would land in Boston, disband the Sons of Liberty, close the Town Meetings and crush the mob. Ever since the Stamp Act riots, Francis Bernard had been torn about calling for those troops. On the one hand, he was sure he had to have them to save his administration. But he knew that as soon as the town heard that troops were on their way, the mob would take vengeance against him. As Adams and Otis had suspected, Bernard was indeed trying to influence London against the patriots. In letters to the king's ministers, the governor poured out his fears at the same time that Samuel Adams was assuring Hillsborough that the Massachusetts circular letter had been respectful, not at all seditious, and that whoever told him otherwise was misinforming him. But in London, Bernard's dire warnings rang truer than Adams' bland reassurances.

Until troops could somehow be inveigled into the colony, there seemed to be no limit to the abuse Bernard would have to endure. One of Samuel Adams' trustiest lieutenants, Joseph Warren, published as scathing an attack on Bernard as the *Boston Gazette* had yet dared to print. Writing as "A True Patriot," the twenty-seven-year-old physician told the governor, "We have known for a long time your enmity to this province. We have had full proof of your cruelty to a loyal people. No age has, perhaps, furnished a more glaring instance of obstinate perseverance in the path of malice." For good measure, Dr. Warren summed up the governor as a man "totally abandoned to wickedness," concluding with a rhyme:

> *"If such men are by God appointed,*
> *The Devil may be the Lord's anointed."*

This time, Bernard was determined to be avenged. He went first to his Council, which advised him to take the matter to court or to the House. Bernard chose the House. His charge of libel was considered, but Bernard heard that during the night members had been subjected to the usual pressures, and the next morning the House dismissed his grievance. Freedom of the press was a great bulwark of the people's freedom, House members told the governor. "Although defaming a man, public or private, is certainly an outrage, yet the freedom of newspapers to tell lies on public men is so associated with their power to tell the truth that we think it impolitic to attempt by law to punish such lying."

Bernard went to court, but the patriots haunted grand-jury members wherever they went, and he was defeated again.

Reporting these humiliations to London, the governor was angry enough to be indiscreet. He criticized the fact that members were elected to the Council rather than appointed by the governor, which meant that they could not resist the will of the people. And he passed on a story that James Otis "behaves in the House like a madman; he abuses everyone in authority and especially the Council in the grossest terms."

The constant quarreling had caused men of both factions to question America's relationship with Britain. As Francis Bernard vacillated about his future, he told Lord Barrington that he must stay in Boston, because replacing a governor when the people grew rebellious only increased their ill-temper. Resigning would be nothing but humoring a willful child. That metaphor for the colonies had been appropriate for many years. In the past, even men who had never set foot on British shores called England "home." A kindly king had been regarded as father to his grateful children.

But what happened when those children left home to live far away? When he opposed the Stamp Act, John Hancock pointed out that he already paid more taxes than anyone in Britain; he was a full-grown and independent man. Samuel Adams had inherited his father's name and adopted his principles. If Adams could replace his father, what need did he have for a substitute in London? Another Junior, James Otis, was coping with a father who remained half captive to George III, and the younger Otis' rebellion against one or another of those fathers led him to curse and repent, to cut his bonds and then, weeping, bind himself up again.

Thomas Hutchinson had inscribed the flyleaf of his diary with a verse from Isaiah: "I have nourished children and brought them up, and even they have revolted from me." Even after the *Liberty* had been seized Hutchinson wrote to London, "My hopes of tranquility have been confined to one plan—that we should be convinced the Parliament will not give up their authority; and then find by experience that it is exercised in the same gentle, tender manner that a parent exercises his authority over his children."

But a dutiful son like Hutchinson could never appreciate that Americans were no longer children and would not pretend to be. The metaphor had been outgrown. Thousands of citizens in the colonies had been swept into the struggle and had become Sons of Liberty rather than sons of a living king across the sea.

In London, politicians were sure they knew how to deal with their offspring. "America must fear you—before she can love you," Lord North told Parliament. Repeal the Townshend Acts? "I hope we shall never think of it, till we see America prostrate at our feet."

Occupation

WITH THE *Liberty* rioting as his excuse, Francis Bernard asked his Council, early in July 1768, to recommend that he request troops from the crown. The Council members knew he was trying to pass an unpopular decision to them and replied that they preferred not to be knocked on the head. Neither did he, said Bernard. He wouldn't act alone, but if they agreed to share the blame he would make the request. In his letters to London, the governor hinted

View of Boston and British warships landing their troops, September 30, 1768, by Paul Revere

1768-69

broadly that he needed soldiers, but he also passed along a spy's report that a leading Son of Liberty was saying that the man who requested British troops would certainly be put to death.

When the rumors multiplied, a joint delegation from the House and the Council was sent to ask Bernard what he was doing behind their backs. Reporting the call to General Thomas Gage, Britain's commander in New York, Bernard said that the delegates had been polite and had apologized for asking the question. He had given them a technically truthful answer: he had not asked for troops. But he assured Gage that the fact that he wasn't requesting troops didn't mean they weren't wanted. "I must beg that you keep this letter to yourself as much as you can," the governor ended, ". . . for obvious reasons."

During that anxious interlude, Bernard hoped that Gage and his deputy, Lieutenant Colonel William Dalrymple, would somehow rescue him on their own initiative. It was no use. Gage was not going to send soldiers to Boston without an official appeal from the governor, and the Council continued to advise Bernard that he didn't need them. Bernard might have passed a more tranquil summer had he known what was going on across the Atlantic. Lord Hillsborough had been sufficiently alarmed by reports from the customs commissioners about the hostility in Boston that, even before the *Liberty* affair, he had directed General Gage to send at least one regiment from Halifax to Boston. That order took weeks to arrive in New York, and as Bernard's letters grew more urgent Hillsborough ordered two regiments based in Ireland to set sail for Boston at once.

The patriots in the Massachusetts House were writing openly to London while their governor was being furtive. One of Bernard's spies reported an exchange between Otis and Samuel Adams when Otis asked what Adams intended to do with a recent letter to Hillsborough. Adams said that he intended to publish it in the *Boston Gazette* the next Monday.

"Do you think it proper to publish it so soon that he may receive a printed copy before the original comes to his hand?" Otis asked.

"What signifies that?" Adams answered. "You know it was designed for the people and not for the minister."

Otis twitted him. "You are so fond of your own drafts that you can't wait for the publication of them to a proper time."

But Adams was not in a mood for teasing. "I am clerk of this House," he said, "and I will make what use of the papers I please."

Even after Governor Bernard got word that troops were coming, he denied that he had received any official notification. But he verified the rumor of their arrival to friends, hoping that a slow confirmation of the news would give the calmer voices among the patriots a chance to prevail. When an English officer arrived from Halifax to make arrangements for his troops, however, all of Boston knew by nightfall what lay ahead. The Sons of Liberty called a Town Meeting for September 12, 1768, and at the top of Beacon Hill they rigged a makeshift alarm—a turpentine barrel on a tall pole. The Tories believed that when the troopships were sighted in the harbor, the barrel would be set aflame and, if Otis and Adams had their way, that would ignite the population.

Francis Bernard viewed the barrel as a more personal provocation. He had received a false report that Adams was promising that when it was lighted thirty thousand men from the countryside would storm Boston, seize Bernard and Hutchinson, plunder the town treasury and fly their own flag from the Liberty Tree.

By the time of the Town Meeting, Otis had become the chief incendiary of the Boston mob again. Two days before, he and Samuel Adams had met at Joseph Warren's house to draft the agenda for the meeting. Now, with Faneuil Hall packed to the walls, the first order of business was a motion to haul down the turpentine barrel. The Meeting ruled it should stay. Next, Otis and Adams argued that the king could not impose an English army on the Massachusetts Bay Colony without the consent of the colony's representatives. A committee had already asked Bernard to call an emergency session of the House and the Council. The governor had replied that because of the House's refusal to rescind its circular letter, only the king could reconvene the session.

Samuel Adams had foreseen that response and was ready with two other daring forays. First, Boston patriots would invite their counterparts in other Massachusetts towns to a convention in ten days' time. Such a meeting would flout the governor's ban against assemblies and let the colony make a concerted plan before the English regiments arrived. Adams also suggested that the citizens of Boston be armed with muskets from the town's armory.

Expecting that his listeners would balk at that open declaration of disloyalty to Britain, Adams had prepared an excuse for them. At his instigation, other patriots arose to warn that a new war with France was imminent. The town's stock of arms had been taken from their storehouses a few days earlier on the pretext of cleaning them. Now, the patriots argued, they should be distributed so that the people could protect themselves against their enemies. Around the hall, men exchanged knowing looks. James Otis declared that the speakers and the audience "understood one another very well." No one doubted who the invaders would be. But for the moment the Town Meeting voted against passing out muskets and musket balls. Gesturing to a cache at his feet, Otis said, "There are the arms. When an attempt is made against your liberties, they will be delivered."

During the interlude between that Town Meeting and the convention that was called for Boston, Samuel Adams and his allies strained to goad the colony into resistance. Three days after the Town Meeting, Sheriff Greenleaf screwed up his courage and hauled down the turpentine barrel. It was empty. But Samuel Adams' exhortations were resounding as never before. "We will destroy every soldier that dares put his foot on shore," he was quoted as saying. "His Majesty has no right to send troops here to invade the country, and I look upon them as foreign enemies."

Companies of the town's militia began to march in drill formation and to practice firing their muskets. But no answering shots were being heard from the countryside. Only eastern Connecticut seemed ready to follow Boston's lead; the town of Lebanon, which had demonstrated against the Stamp Act, now pledged to support Boston's resistance "at the expense of our lives and fortunes." More common, though, was the response from Hatfield, deep in western Massachusetts. There the Tory farmers scoffed at the transparency of alarms against the French. If France posed a real threat, shouldn't Boston be welcoming the assistance of British troops? On Monday, September 19, Governor Bernard finally made public the orders bringing troops from Halifax and Ireland. Samuel Adams' convention opened the following Thursday, but only seventy delegates appeared. As the warships drew closer, many Sons of Liberty found their resolve waning, and James Otis stayed away from the convention for its first three days.

With Otis absent, Thomas Cushing was named the convention's speaker. He set the tone by announcing that the meeting's only purpose was to "bring together some prudent people who would be able to check the violent designs of others." Samuel Adams was elected clerk, but without Otis' oratory he couldn't move the stolid delegates from the farms. When Otis finally appeared he was too late to alter the prevailing mood.

Samuel Adams had tested the tide, and now he swam with it. As clerk, he saw to it that not a line of the Town Meeting's defiance appeared in the convention's published conclusions. Writing on behalf of the delegates, he called them "plain, honest men" and asked George III to regard their meeting as "a fresh token of the loyalty of our respective towns to his Majesty."

When the convention had been in session for just one week, British men-of-war were spotted off the Massachusetts coast. The delegates voted to adjourn. Or, as John Mein, the Tory printer, described the scene, they "broke up and rushed out of town like a herd of scalded hogs." On that same afternoon, September 29, 1768, the ships drew near the harbor, approaching cautiously, unsure of their reception. The next day the fleet moved into siege formation, surrounded Boston from the northeast and pointed its guns at the town.

This was the moment the Tories had awaited through three humiliating years. At Castle William, the customs commissioners set off skyrockets and sang choruses of "Yankee Doodle":

> *"Yankee Doodle came to town,*
> *a-riding on a pony.*
> *He stuck a feather in his hat*
> *and called him macaroni. . . ."*

Sung to an old air, the verses had evolved during the French and Indian War. By 1758 the British were referring to the New England militia as the Yankee companies. "Macaroni" was London slang for a fop, and for Samuel Adams, dreaming of a new Sparta, it was a galling serenade—this celebration of dancing and wenching and extravagant fashion.

> *"Yankee Doodle, keep it up!*
> *Yankee Doodle, dandy!*
> *Mind the music, and the step,*
> *and with the girls be handy!"*

For Francis Bernard, the arrival of the soldiers was three years overdue, but they presented fresh problems. He wanted one regiment quartered in town, with a back-up regiment on call at Castle William. But his Council refused to provide housing in town, preferring to restrict all of the troops to the Castle. Bernard wanted to prove to the English commander, Colonel Dalrymple, how restricted his authority was these days, and he arranged to ferry Council members to the Castle, where Dalrymple could meet with them in person. The colonel's approach was mild. He said that his orders called for maintaining a regiment in the town, but he could assure the Council that his men would be well-behaved. He hoped that he would be among friends in Boston, and his troops would act in that same way.

The Council would have none of it. Members pointed out that since Castle William was considered within the town limits, Dalrymple would be obeying his orders if he kept the troops there. The meeting broke up in a less friendly spirit. The colonel appealed again to Bernard, but the governor had retreated into the aggrieved helplessness that had become his only defense. General Gage had heard about the tumultuous Town Meeting and had sent word that both regiments should go ashore. Dalrymple was concerned that each day's delay in landing his soldiers gave the Sons more time to plot their resistance.

But when the day came, no one resisted. At noon on Saturday, October 1, 1768, with drums and fifes setting the pace, British soldiers in their bright-red coats and black three-cornered hats marched up King Street. Many of the drummers were black men, wearing yellow coats and the high white bearskin caps of the grenadiers. The officers were adorned with silver armor at the neck and the chest, crimson sashes at the shoulder and swords at the waist. Sergeants marched with halberds, the long-handled battle axes.

For nearly four hours, the British paraded through the town, past Town House and the Old Granary Burying Ground, until at last they assembled on the cow pasture that Bostonians called their Common. The ranks included nine companies each from the Fourteenth and Twenty-ninth Regiments, one company of artillery and an eighty-four-man unit from the Fifty-ninth Regiment—a total of a thousand men. Paul Revere, the silversmith, stood on the sidelines, angered by the British insolence. But the soldiers could afford to be arrogant. Each soldier had been issued sixteen rounds of powder and ball, and Boston's arms remained stacked in Faneuil Hall.

Samuel Adams had lost.

Andrew Oliver's small grandson watched the redcoats land and ran home happily. Now, the child announced, the mob wouldn't tear down any more houses. His grandfather said that the sight of the troops on the Common allowed him to sleep easy in his bed. The *Boston Gazette* still promised that the people would not be awed into being taxed without their consent. And Samuel Adams could write, "I am *in* fashion and *out* of fashion as the whim goes. I will stand alone." But Adams' only immediate revenge was to take John Adams' young son to the Common and try to instill in the child a patriotic loathing of the redcoats parading there.

To the Tories, the few threats of defiance rang hollow. Before the troops had landed, General Gage had described the patriots as "a people who have ever been very bold in council but never remarkable for their feats of action." Boston's cowed acceptance of the two regiments was proving him right. Mather Byles, the foremost Tory clergyman in Boston, met a group of patriots in the mall and taunted them with a pun: "Well, gentlemen, you have been exerting yourselves for some time, and I congratulate you now that your grievances are red-dressed." In New York, the local Sons of Liberty derided Boston's collapse as evidence of "the ridiculous puff and bombast for which our Eastern brethren have always been too famous."

Thomas Hutchinson was not so sure that Adams and his crowd had been routed. Calling the Massachusetts convention had been a bold stroke, and, if it hadn't given Samuel Adams all he had asked, the meeting itself had been the most open step yet toward revolution. But for now the general opinion in England was that Americans could not endure the smell of gunpowder.

For lack of better quarters, the Twenty-ninth Regiment pitched its tents on Boston Common. Dalrymple led the Fourteenth to Faneuil Hall and forced town officials to open one door. Inside was a bonus: before bedding down for the night, Dalrymple's men commandeered the four hundred arms still on display from the Town Meeting. The next morning, Francis Bernard opened Town House to the troops, including the room where the House of Representatives usually sat. James Otis warned that the stench from the troops in the House chamber might be infectious and urged that members meet elsewhere.

With winter approaching, the troops needed warmer lodging. Officers began to rent quarters in town, but some of their men solved the problem by deserting. Within two weeks, seventy men were gone, and Dalrymple was offering a reward of ten guineas to the soldier who would point out any man urging him to defect. Private Richard Ames of the Fourteenth was caught and shot on the Common as a warning to the others, and the execution shocked those Bostonians who were accustomed to the laxer discipline of their own militia. Dalrymple hoped his strictness would prevent more desertions and any further friction with the town. Public lashings on a soldier's bare back with a cat-o'-nine-tails became a regular event.

Even the threat of reprisal couldn't curb natural hostilities. One drunken British captain came upon a group of slaves one night in late October. "Go home," he shouted, "and cut your masters throats." He was hauled before a justice of the peace, and the town watchmen were ordered to keep Negroes off the streets late at night.

Boston's antagonism gave the British troops reason to welcome the reinforcements London had promised. In mid-November, ships carrying the Sixty-fourth and Sixty-fifth Regiments finally arrived in the harbor after being blown off course as far as the West Indies. By that time, Colonel Dalrymple had rented enough warehouses to accommodate his men, and one leading patriot, William Molineux, was letting his property on Wheelright's Wharf for twenty-five pounds sterling a month. A detachment of the fresh troops went to Castle William. The rest quietly took other lodgings in the town, and married officers found suitable rooms for their families. The customs officials returned from their exile at the Castle and took up their normal duties. Some even bought houses near Boston. The gala dances started up again.

But in England, political life was roiling. America's nonimportation agreements were choking off lucrative trade and throwing thousands of men out of work. Benjamin Franklin heard of rioting all over the country and saw for himself hordes of men storming through London streets. Prompted by letters from Governor Bernard and other Tories, Parliament was ready to take action against the lawless colonials, and George III pledged himself to enforce any measures Parliament might adopt. The Duke of Bedford, urging that England punish the instigators of the Boston riots, exhumed a law from the reign of Henry VIII that would permit Parliament to bring men like James Otis and Samuel Adams to England, where juries would convict them and judges would order them hanged. Early in 1769, Hillsborough wrote to Francis Bernard to inform him that the king wanted evidence sent to him of any treason committed within the colony since December 30, 1767.

For eight years, the word "treason" had been flung about loosely in legislatures and courtrooms. Now the Tories had to produce evidence that would convince a British attorney general to prosecute. Thomas Hutchinson forwarded to London an affidavit from Richard Sylvester that accused Samuel Adams of open calls to rebellion against the English troops. Sylvester claimed that on one occasion Adams had spoken treason to seven men in the South End. Another time, he had called on Sylvester at his house and preached treason there: "We will take up arms and spend our last drop of blood before the king and Parliament shall impose on us."

Sylvester also gave evidence against Dr. Benjamin Church. In the *Boston Gazette*, Church had called Governor Bernard "Fop, witling, favorite stampman, tyrant tool. / Or all those mighty names in one, thou fool!' According to Sylvester, Dr. Church was urging the patriots to seize both Bernard and Hutchinson and confiscate their papers to learn what lies against the people of Boston they were sending to London.

As proof, the Sylvester affidavit was scant and somewhat tainted. Many of the alleged statements did reflect Samuel Adams' prejudices—"The times were never better in Rome than when they had no king and were a free state, and as this is a great empire we shall soon have it in our power to give laws to England." But since Sylvester was not a prominent Son of Liberty, why had Samuel Adams been calling regularly at his parlor? Still, that was the extent of the case against Adams, and the Boston Tories hoped it would be enough to get him shipped off to London, along with James Otis and John Hancock. Tories joked that when Samuel Adams passed the ropemakers' galleries these days, he "shuddered at the sight of hemp."

In London, however, the attorney general reviewed the evidence, ruled that Samuel Adams and the rest had come "within a hair's breadth" of treason, but declined to prosecute them.

That refusal, combined with the growing pressure from the nation's afflicted merchants, began to change Parliament's mood. Arguments for restoring harmony with the colonies were once again being heard. Samuel Adams had never lost faith in the power of the nonimportation agreement, and now merchants throughout London were urging Parliament to recall Governor Bernard. From Hillsborough they won a pledge that Bernard not only would be replaced but would never again be appointed to any post in any colony. In March 1769, Hillsborough wrote to Bernard to inform him that it was he, not Samuel Adams, who would be boarding a ship headed for London. Officially, Bernard was being recalled only to report in person to the king on conditions. As consolation for the loss of his post, he would receive the title of baronet.

Bernard was not fated to leave Massachusetts peaceably. Before Hillsborough's instructions could reach Boston, a ship from London brought a new calamity for him. Bernard's confidential letters to Hillsborough over the past months had come home again to America.

William Beckford was among those members of Parliament who were friendly to the patriots. He had invoked a House of Commons rule that permitted any member to read and make copies of all ministry correspondence. Beckford delivered the copies of Bernard's letters to a London agent for the patriots, who dispatched six of them to America, most of them dating from November 1768, as well as one from General Gage to Lord Hillsborough. In his letters, Bernard had castigated the town of Boston and the Council for refusing to house the troops promptly and pressed again for changes in the charter to make the Council more responsive to the king and his governor. The Sons of Liberty read those letters in public, and there was a ferocious outcry. The

Council immediately voted to print them as soon as the patriots could prepare an essay refuting them.

Francis Bernard became fearful all over again. When his letters were printed, he warned London, they would be sent throughout the province to stir up the people, "and I fear it will have the worst effects."

Bernard's fears always proved more reliable than his hopes. Writing home, a British officer stationed in Boston said: "His doubles and turnings have been so many that he has altogether lost his road and brought himself into great contempt."

The spring opening of the Massachusetts legislature was delayed because the patriots objected to a British cannon that was aimed directly at the House chambers. The English officer in charge declined to move it. For a week, the House refused to transact business in the face of such a threat, and Bernard ordered the House session moved to Cambridge. Amid much angry protest, the House members met at Harvard College. There, Francis Bernard was told, someone had cut the heart out of his official portrait.

The legislature finally convened, and Adams and Otis introduced a petition that Bernard be recalled. They charged that in opposing the patriots Bernard had opposed the king's true interests, had misinterpreted conditions in Boston and had given the province "what is technically known as a black eye." The hundred and nine House members present on June 27, 1769, passed the resolution unanimously.

Bernard had received the summons to London, but in his opening statement to the legislature he hadn't announced his departure. The baronetcy, however, was too good to keep secret, and the *Boston Gazette* was soon reporting the news with a barrage of mockery. No story about the governor failed to give him full due as "Sir Francis Bernard, of Nettleham, Bart."

As he prepared to leave, Bernard asked the hostile legislature to pay him a year's salary in advance. The members turned him down and reminded him that during a smallpox epidemic he had charged the victims rent for their quarantine at Castle William. Now the patriots demanded that Bernard reimburse the colony at the same rate for the nights he had sheltered the customs commissioners there.

Bernard wasn't likely to find much sympathy in London. To ingratiate himself with his patron, he had arranged to have a native American artifact delivered to Lord Barrington. But when it arrived in London, his lordship's thanks had been chilly.

"I have been considering that the admirable canoe you were so good as to give me will be useless here," Barrington wrote. "Nobody can navigate it or will venture to go into it. Let me beg of you to give it to some other friend."

On July 31, 1769, Francis Bernard boarded a warship, the *Rippon*, while his wife and large family stayed behind to close the houses. For a day the *Rippon* lay becalmed just outside Boston Harbor, and the governor couldn't miss the festivities that were accompanying his departure. The Union Jack was run up the pole at the Liberty Tree, and banners flew from Hancock's Wharf. Throughout the day he heard church bells and militia cannon. At night the *Rippon* still couldn't sail, and its passengers saw a huge bonfire on Fort Hill, where Andrew Oliver's effigy had burned four years before.

If Bernard had left Massachusetts on that same day in 1765, his administration might have been judged a success. Apart from the blunder of appointing Hutchinson as chief justice, and an enthusiasm for money that opened him to scorn, he had brought a few small gifts that might have served him well in calmer times. Hutchinson had claimed he was a charming storyteller with an anecdote for every occasion. Bernard may not have been able to recite all of Shakespeare by heart, as he sometimes boasted, but no one would ever challenge him to prove it, and his appreciation of literature was genuine. He had promoted the fortunes of Harvard College and had drawn the designs for Harvard Hall. He was more kindly than not, more affable than many of his opponents. But he lacked the will or the sense to understand the nature of the battle. He had consistently underestimated the appeal of the patriots, sure that the people's goodwill or his own deft maneuvering would keep the population civil. Bernard was an orphan who wanted above all to be loved, and in Boston he had come against the one heart that would never love him.

When Francis Bernard boarded the *Rippon*, it had just returned from taking the soldiers of the Sixty-fifth Regiment to

Halifax. Since Boston had been quiet throughout the winter and the spring, General Gage had decided he could withdraw those troops and now the other regiment from Ireland, the Sixty-fourth. The second transfer was held up briefly when Samuel Adams persuaded the Massachusetts House to pass a resolution unanimously that no law—not merely no tax law—was binding on a colony unless its own legislature passed it. Thomas Hutchinson heard that Adams had told a Town Meeting, "Independent we are, and independent we shall be." That sounded ominous enough for the officers in Boston to hold up the sailing of the Sixty-fourth.

Half of the English garrison was gone, relieved to be escaping from Boston. There had been no serious outbreak, but Samuel Adams had seen to it that the hostility from the town was unrelenting. The disappointment of the Massachusetts convention had taught him that he had to recruit his allies from other Northern towns and not from the rural areas of his own province. In the fall of 1768, Adams and his allies in New York began a news service devoted to reporting the misbehavior of the British troops in Boston. Their "Journal of the Times" reached south to newspapers in Georgia and across the ocean to London's *Gentleman's Magazine*. John Adams was among those who went every Sunday evening to join in preparing copy with Samuel Adams, James Otis, William Davis and John Gill. He called it "working the political engine," and he found cooking up each week's anecdotes a curious business. The journal was a melange of sexual scandal and outright fabrication edited by his cousin Samuel, the province's most puritanical and high-minded politician. News of rape abounded in the journal, and no woman was pictured as being safe from the English troops, who were usually called "bloody-backed rascals" for their red coats. It did the soldiers no good to respond that Boston women were so easy and willing that rape would have represented wasted effort. One soldier claimed that this Yankee war would be the first in history to produce more births than deaths.

But according to the "Journal," when the British weren't raping, they were seducing. One story reported that an outraged citizen "the other morning discovered a soldier in bed with a favorite grand-daughter." When they weren't seducing, they were beating small boys in the street, carousing until dawn and profaning the Sabbath with gunfire and horseraces on the Common. Thomas Hutchinson read those stories and decided that Samuel

Adams and his host of writers were a half dozen of the most wicked fellows on the globe. "They stick at nothing," he complained, and no denial of one story would stop the concocting of another. Worse, Hutchinson detected signs that the campaign was stirring up previously cool heads in New York and Philadelphia.

Throughout much of his life, Hutchinson had wanted to be governor. Now, when the job was worse than worthless, his wish was being granted against his will. He had asked to stay on merely as chief justice, but London ordered him to assume Bernard's duties as well. Since no announcement had been made about Bernard remaining in England, Hutchinson's title would be acting governor. But with the *Boston Gazette* stepping up its attacks, that distinction didn't make his job easier. The provocations between soldiers and the town weren't all invented, nor were they all one-sided. Bostonians were accustomed to their own watchmen who demanded that anyone on the street at night identify himself, but now English sentinels were posted at public buildings around town to make the challenge. Many Bostonians couldn't bring themselves to answer "Who goes there?" with the traditional password of "Friend." They answered rudely or said nothing.

Their most vulgar retorts, however, wouldn't have shocked these troops. The Twenty-ninth Regiment was made up of rough men primed for a fight. Even the acting governor admitted that they were "bad fellows." They jostled any Bostonian off the sidewalk or, if they thought they could get away with it, gave him a sharp dig in the ribs with the butt of a bayonet. The soldiers disrupted the town's daily routine by parading through the streets and disturbed church services on Sunday by changing the guard. At Meeting times the band struck up a mocking rendition of "Yankee Doodle." The English commander agreed to change the parade schedule and quiet the band, but John Adams found no relief. One regiment exercised directly in front of his house, and he was awakened each morning by an ear-piercing fife. The sight of the redcoats also convinced him that Britain's determination to subjugate the colony was too strong to challenge.

Reflecting on the differences in the patriot leaders, John Adams compared them to religious figures. Samuel Adams was like

John Calvin, if Calvin could be imagined in a tavern. He was "cool, abstemious, polished." James Otis was more like Martin Luther—"rough, hasty and loved good cheer." But John Adams considered Otis unstable and was watching him these days with alarm. Opening the legislative session in Cambridge, Otis had inspired the Harvard students who flocked to hear him. They were moved to tears when Otis proclaimed that the first and noblest of duties was to serve one's country, even to die for it. But privately he couldn't stop talking, compulsively, nonsensically, obscenely. Adams mourned for him and for his effect on the patriots' cause. And then Otis was fiercely struck down.

Through their contacts in London, the patriots received another packet of official correspondence, including letters from the customs commissioners to the Treasury in London. In them Otis was accused of treason. To a man who still proclaimed his loyalty to the king, the accusation was intolerable. On September 4, 1769, the *Boston Gazette* carried Otis' paid advertisement assailing four of the commissioners. As a deliberate insult, he used only their first names as he asked Lord Hillsborough and the Board of Trade in London "to pay no kind of regard to any of the abusive representations of me or my country that may be transmitted by the said Henry, Charles, William and John or their confederates; for they are no more worthy of credit than those of Sir Francis Bernard, of Nettleham, Bart., or any of his cabal." Otis had filed a defamation suit against Sir Francis, but he sought personal apologies from the men still in Boston. He went twice to see one commissioner, John Robinson, and left dissatisfied each time. Now, after calling all four "superlative blockheads" in print, Otis once again invoked natural law, this time against libel: "If Robinson misrepresents me, I have a natural right, if I can get no other satisfaction, to break his head."

The next day, a Tuesday, Otis heard that Robinson had bought a stout walking stick. He went to the same store and demanded an identical one. Armed with it, he set out that evening for the British Coffee House, near the Custom House. He knew it was hostile territory, and when he entered he met the usual crowd of Tories, including captains from both British regiments, along with John Mein, the acerbic publisher, and William Browne, one of the seventeen representatives who had voted the previous year to rescind the Massachusetts circular letter.

John Robinson entered the tavern, saw that Otis had no sword, and went at once to the back, where he unbuckled his own and set it down. He returned to confront Otis in the public room.

Otis spoke first. "I demand satisfaction of you, sir."

Robinson asked what satisfaction Otis would prefer.

"A gentleman's satisfaction." Gentlemen could fight only with their fists. Dueling with swords was against the law.

Robinson said, "I am ready to do it."

But as they moved for the door, Robinson reached out to give Otis' nose a scornful tweak. Otis blocked Robinson with his cane. Robinson raised his own, and for a moment they were dueling with their walking sticks. Then onlookers took away the canes, and they began pummeling each other with their fists.

John Gridley, a nephew of the well-known lawyer, was walking in King Street and had paused by the open door when he heard Otis' challenge. As the two men fought, Robinson's friends began to push Otis and hold his arms. Gridley shouted that it was a dirty thing to treat a man that way, and he rushed in between Otis and Robinson. Someone grabbed Gridley by the shoulder. He pulled away and seized Robinson by the collar. When the commissioner drew back, his coat was torn down to its pockets. A man standing on a bench struck Gridley twice on the head with a weapon, and he was blinded by his own blood. Flailing about, Gridley took a blow on his right hand that broke his wrist. He heard men shouting "Kill him!" and knew they meant Otis.

Gridley was pushed out of the coffeehouse. Fighting his way back inside, he picked up a walking stick from the floor. A lamp had been broken or snuffed out, but one witness saw men holding Otis while Robinson struck him in the face. Another blow had laid open the bone of Otis' forehead. Benjamin Hallowell, the comptroller, succeeded in separating the two men. Gridley reached Otis and tried to defend him with his good left hand. But the fight was over. Otis went off to have his wounds dressed.

Painful as the set-to had been for Otis, it was a grim blessing to the patriots. From that night on, Otis' mad extravagances could be blamed on his martyrdom. John Adams knew better. Passing an evening with Otis two weeks after the attack, he found him, if anything, more cheerful and subdued and consequently better company than he had been for months. But Boston's sympathies lay with Otis. The *Boston Gazette* announced that the brawl had been an assassination attempt. Otis endorsed that interpretation and sued Robinson for three thousand pounds in damages, charging him with "very unfair play." A month after the attack, Robinson married a Boston merchant's daughter and sailed for England, leaving his father-in-law to see the case through court. Years later, although Otis refused a cash settlement, Robinson was ordered to pay all costs.

Of the chief Tory figures, William Browne fared the worst. Many patriots were convinced that he had struck the blow that broke Gridley's wrist, and they became more hostile to him than to Robinson. Browne was forced to hide the next day in a back room of the coffeehouse until late in the afternoon, when the patriots found him and bore him to Faneuil Hall for a preliminary hearing. Two thousand spectators jammed the hall, and when James Murray, a justice considered friendly to Browne, arrived, they pushed him back each time he tried to enter. Finally, amid jeers and boos—to which Murray responded with courtly bows—he was permitted inside.

The judges held Browne on charges of assault. When no one would stand his bail, Justice Murray announced that he did not approve of Gridley's beating but would post the bond. When Murray made his way to the door, someone snatched off his wig and other men tried to trip him. His friends shielded the bald-headed justice as he moved toward his house, followed by men bearing his wig on a pole. As Murray disappeared inside, some men in the mob remembered that John Mein had also been at the coffeehouse the previous night. They rushed to his bookstore and to the shop where he printed his Tory newspaper. At each place the mob's leaders smeared Mein's signs with a mixture of excrement and urine, which they called "Hillsborough's paint."

While those upheavals were going on in Boston, a fourteen-year-old merchant's apprentice sat at his desk in the West Indies, praying to be delivered from a life of trade. Alexander Hamilton was a small and slender boy with no prospects for the glory he craved. His beautiful mother, Rachel, had been pressed into marriage at sixteen with a rich cotton farmer from Copenhagen, but within a few years he had charged her with adultery. Under the Danish laws that governed the island of St. Croix, he had her jailed. Upon her release, Rachel Lavien or Levine or Lawein—her planter husband had been careless about the spelling of his name— left him with their small son, Peter, and went to live with her mother. Two years after the separation, when Rachel was in her early twenties, she met James Hamilton, who was ten years older. The handsome fourth son of a Scottish laird, he had come to make his fortune on the island.

In England, divorce took an act of Parliament, but in the West Indies people were more inclined to shrug away formalities. Hamilton lived with Rachel Lavien long enough to give her two sons and fritter away her small inheritance. He drifted away, but Rachel remained an attractive and popular woman despite her two fatherless children. James was ten when Hamilton left, Alexander two years younger. Rachel opened a small store, and Alexander helped her to run it until her death five years later. Rachel's family did what they could for the boys. James was apprenticed to a carpenter. Alexander was sent to help a thriving island merchant.

At school Alexander had enjoyed his brief exposure to the classics. He spoke French well and went regularly to a Jewish schoolmistress who taught him the Decalogue in Hebrew. He wanted to become a great captain of war, but he was stuck forever behind a desk. Alexander poured out his frustrations in November 1769 in a letter to his favorite cousin, Ned Stevens, who had gone to New York to study medicine.

"For to confess my weakness, Ned," Alexander wrote, "my ambition is prevalent, so that I contemn the groveling condition of a clerk, or the like, to which the future condemns me and would willingly risk my life, though not my character, to exalt my station."

Alexander Hamilton knew how absurd his self-pity might sound in New York, and he asked his cousin not to mock him. "I shall conclude by saying, I wish there was a war."

"The Bloody Massacre," by Paul Revere   METROPOLITAN MUSEUM OF ART

Massacre
1770

SAMUEL ADAMS was hardening the lines. When more cargo from London arrived in early October 1769, the organizers of the non-importation agreement demanded that it be locked up until the agreement expired on New Year's Day. Later that month, Adams also persuaded a special Town Meeting that any merchant who had continued to import goods should be considered an enemy of the people. Someone protested that several men who had rejected the agreement were now ready to sign it. For such men it was too late, Adams said. "God perhaps might possibly forgive them, but I and the rest of the people never could."

Adams had come prepared with a list of those he wanted stigmatized, and high on the list was the Tory publisher John Mein. For the past three months Mein had been printing the names of patriot merchants who claimed to support the agreement as they went on importing and selling the forbidden goods. Adams disliked seeing those lists, because he was more concerned with defending patriot reputations than with punishing a few back-sliders. One firm that Mein didn't name was Thomas Hutchinson's, which was building a secret stockpile of tea against the day it could be sold openly. Hutchinson handled those transactions himself and wrote to London in code.

What Mein spared Hutchinson he gave double to John Hancock. In Mein's *Chronicle* James Otis was dismissed as "Muddle-head," but Hancock was "Johnny Dupe, Esq., alias the Milch-cow," for the way the patriots were milking him. The Tories often said that Samuel Adams might write the letters but John Hancock paid the postage. The mockery had spread far enough to rankle Hancock, and Mein elaborated on it. Hancock was "a good-natured young man with long ears—a silly conceited grin on his countenance—a fool's cap on his head." The *Chronicle* said that Hancock also wore a blindfold so that he couldn't see who was rifling his pockets.

Two days after that attack appeared, Mein and his partner, John Fleeming, set out along King Street for Mein's print shop. Both men had begun to carry guns since Mein was named an enemy of the town. Now twenty men surrounded them, including the hot-tempered William Molineux and a merchant named Edward Davis. The patriots began to shout at Mein, and Davis poked Mein in the ribs with his cane.

Mein pulled out his pistol and cocked it and, with Fleeming at his side, backed up King Street, shouting that he would shoot the first man who touched him. The crowd pursued him but kept out of range of his weapon. "Knock him down!" some cried, and "Kill him!" With bits of brick flying, Mein and Fleeming reached the British sentries at the Main Guard station near Town House. Those soldiers let the two men slip to safety behind them. Mein would have escaped injury altogether except for Thomas Marshall, a tailor, who had picked up a heavy shovel during the flight up King Street. Marshall delivered a blow that gashed Mein's shoulder. In the melee Fleeming's pistol discharged, but no one was injured.

As a crowd of two hundred clamored outside the guardhouse, Mein sent a message to Hutchinson, demanding that the law come to his aid, but meanwhile Molineux and Samuel Adams went to a justice of the peace and applied for a warrant to arrest Mein for firing his pistol during a peaceable assembly. They were accusing the wrong man, but the justice issued the warrant. When they showed up with it at the guardhouse, Mein hid in the attic while Adams and the others searched for him. After they had left, Mein borrowed a British uniform and escaped to Colonel Dalrymple's house.

The episode had proved to both sides how severely limited Thomas Hutchinson's new authority was. Despite prodding by Mein, who remained in hiding, the acting governor did not call out British soldiers to protect him. Hutchinson's Council refused to authorize the use of British troops to put down a disturbance. On Pope's Day John Mein snuck aboard a British ship, and he sailed for London ten days later. Reflecting on the mob that had milled in front of his guardhouse, Colonel Dalrymple realized that the crisis he had been expecting was coming on very fast.

When the nonimportation agreement ended officially, on New Year's Day, 1770, Thomas Hutchinson and his two sons were eager to begin turning a profit. But the boycott's organizers wanted to punish those who had been stockpiling goods, and they ruled that nothing should go on sale before the time it took a ship to sail to London and return. Hutchinson's sons rejected that new restriction. They broke off the locks that the Committee of Inspection had fastened to the doors of their warehouses and moved the tea to a hiding place.

Faced with that defiance, Samuel Adams arranged a mass meeting at Faneuil Hall. The patriots voted unanimously to have William Molineux lead a delegation ordering merchants to obey the extension. The first trader they approached, William Jackson, barred his doors, and the delegation shouted at him for a while but went away.

Jackson had heard that the Hutchinsons might capitulate and turn over their tea, and he hurried to their house, where Thomas Junior, thirty years old, and Elisha, twenty-five, lived with their father. The Hutchinsons agreed to hold firm. The next morning they sent away the wagons that the patriots had brought to collect the tea. Back at Faneuil Hall, James Otis spoke. No one could understand him. William Molineux was determined to lead a demonstration to Hutchinson's house, but Otis, John Hancock and other prominent patriots refused to join him. The acting governor now represented the king; any appearance of coercion could mark the patriots as traitors. Emotion ran high until Molineux leaped up, announced he was leaving and hinted at suicide. Thomas Young, a patriot doctor, cried out, "Stop, Mr. Molineux! Stop, Mr. Molineux! For the love of God, stop, Mr. Molineux! Gentlemen, if Mr. Molineux leaves us, we are forever undone! This day is the last dawn of liberty we ever shall see."

Molineux returned, and Otis and Adams agreed to join a committee that would go to the Hutchinsons. A thousand men and boys followed as they marched to the North End. From a window, Hutchinson asked the leaders what they wanted. Molineux said, "It is not you but your sons we desire to see."

One of the sons came to stand beside his father at the window. Hutchinson invoked the king's authority and warned the crowd to leave. No one moved. Hutchinson chided Otis for lending himself to an illegal assembly. The acting governor said that he could make out six or seven of the men who had helped to tear down his house four and a half years before. "Gentlemen," Hutchinson said, "when I was attacked before, I was a private person. I am now the representative of the greatest monarch on earth, whose majesty you affront in thus treating my person."

At that the delegation backed away. But after they left, Hutchinson encountered more resistance. He wanted to use troops to disband Samuel Adams' irregular assemblies in Faneuil Hall, but the Council continued to refuse. When they saw Hutchinson's helplessness, his fellow Tories persuaded him to give in. Hutchinson capitulated completely. The next morning he sent word to Faneuil Hall that he would see that his sons turned over their tea, along with any money they had received from that already sold. It was the bitterest moment of Hutchinson's political life. Even the destruction of his house, he wrote afterward, had not distressed him as much.

The patriots began taking even bolder measures against traders who refused to bow to them. They pointed a large wooden hand labeled "Importer!" at offending shops. One of them belonged to Theophilus Lillie, who had refused to join the boycott, saying, "I'd rather be a slave under one master than under a hundred or more. At least, with one, I might be able to please him."

Despite that refusal, Lillie was regarded as a harmless man, but his neighbor, Ebenezer Richardson, was a known informer for the Custom House. When the crowd caught Richardson trying to pull down the wooden hand pointing at Lillie, they attacked him with stones and dirt. Disappearing into his house, Richardson swore to the patriot leaders, "By the eternal God, I'll make it too hot for you before night."

One of the patriots, Thomas Knox, shouted after him, "Come out, you damn son of a bitch! I'll have your heart out! Your liver out!"

Richardson came to his door and tried to run off a swarm of boys. Leave, he said, or he would make a lane through them. The boys answered that King Street was a public place and they wouldn't go. Thomas Hutchinson heard of the disturbance and gave Sheriff Greenleaf a direct order to break up the crowd. Greenleaf said he didn't think it was safe to try.

Back inside with his family, Richardson saw a stone hurtle through a window and strike his wife. He went upstairs, rested his musket barrel on a windowsill and fired down into the crowd. A boy of eleven, Christopher Snider, was just bending to pick up a rock when a cluster of small pellets tore into his chest.

At the sound of the shot, the bell of the church on Hanover Street began to toll, and from all over Boston men rushed to Richardson's house. Trapped upstairs, he held off the crowd with a cutlass. "Damn their blood," he said. "I don't care what I've done."

Richardson might have been lynched, although—for all their loud oaths—the patriots had never killed anyone. Molineux persuaded the crowd to bring Richardson before a justice of the peace. At Faneuil Hall, he was charged with firing at Snider with swanshot. That evening the boy died.

Over the weekend, Samuel Adams and his colleagues organized the largest funeral the American continent had ever seen. Snowdrifts from a blizzard on Saturday did not stop their procession late Monday afternoon from the Liberty Tree to the

Old Granary Burying Ground. First five hundred schoolchildren marched two by two. Some carried banners that read in Latin, "Innocence itself is nowhere safe!" Then came six young men bearing the coffin, followed by family and friends and two thousand citizens of Boston.

Thomas Hutchinson watched unmoved. "The boy that was killed was the son of a poor German," he wrote, disturbed by the way the town was being manipulated. "A grand funeral was, however, judged very proper for him."

Four days later, toward noon on Friday, March 2, 1770, William Green was working out of doors with a group of men who were braiding hemp for John Gray. As one of Boston's largest ropemakers, Gray hired unskilled workmen by the day, and when soldiers from the British regiments wanted to pick up extra money they would spend off-duty hours at the ropewalks. These days work was scarce, and Bostonians resented the competition.

Patrick Walker of the Twenty-ninth Regiment was approaching the walk when William Green hailed him: "Soldier, do you want work?"

"Yes, I do, faith," said Walker.

"Well, then," said Green, "go and clean out my shithouse."

"Empty it yourself," the soldier said.

After a few curses, Private Walker swore by the Holy Ghost that he would be avenged. He rushed at Green and the other ropemakers, but they made short work of him. Nicholas Ferriter knocked him down. John Wilson snatched up a bare cutlass that had fallen out of Walker's coat. Humiliated, Walker fled to his barracks.

It was a minor incident compared with the night John Mein was driven up King Street or Ebenezer Richardson's shooting of Christopher Snider. But it wasn't over.

At the barracks, Patrick Walker recruited eight or nine fellow troopers, and within twenty minutes they were back at Gray's ropeworks, armed with clubs. They searched out Green and his friends and demanded to know why they had roughed up Walker. As their answer the ropemakers shouted for reinforcements and threw the soldiers off the premises.

John Hill, an elderly justice of the peace, had presided over many hearings for unruly British soldiers. He was watching now from a nearby window as the British troopers returned, this time in a gang of forty men. Hill called to a tall Negro drummer who was leading them, "You black rascal! What have you to do with white people's quarrels?"

"I suppose," the drummer replied, "I may look on."

Hill came outside and ordered everyone to go home. Instead, the soldiers rushed at a group of ropemakers who were gathered around a tar barrel and beat them with clubs. But the workmen had their own weapons—the heavy wooden slats they used for twisting rope. Once again, the soldiers were forced to run back to the barracks. Justice Hill prevailed on the Bostonians not to follow after them.

The next day, Saturday, another fracas at another ropeworks, MacNeil's, ended the same way. Three grenadiers from the Twenty-ninth Regiment were routed, one of them with a fractured skull. A worker suspected that another British soldier had followed him to his boardinghouse, and he asked his landlord, a barber named Benjamin Burdick, to look out the window. Burdick said he saw a soldier loitering near the house.

That night one of the regiment's sergeants missed roll call, and stories spread through the British ranks that he had been murdered in town. The missing man was later found alive, but not before his commanding officer, Lieutenant Colonel Maurice Carr, had used the incident as an excuse for a surprise raid on the Gray ropewalk. Carr may have been looking for a cache of weapons or hoping to intimidate Gray. All he accomplished, however, was to provoke Gray to protest directly to Colonel Dalrymple.

Gray and Dalrymple compared notes. Later on, William Green's words to Private Walker would be changed in court transcripts to "clean my necessary house" or "clean my little-house." But the ropemaker and the colonel agreed that their accounts of the incident tallied and that William Green had been offensive. Gray agreed to fire him the next morning and to warn his other workers not to be insolent to the British troops. On his side, Colonel Dalrymple pledged to do everything he could to keep his men away from the ropewalks.

But at Benjamin Burdick's house the same British soldier had come back to stand watch. Burdick went out to ask him what he was doing.

"I'm pumping shit," the soldier answered.

"March off!" said Burdick.

"Damn you!" said the soldier.

Burdick began to strike him with a stick, and the soldier ran away.

From all over town, stories like that one were sweeping the Main Guard—the troop headquarters—and threats of retaliation from the British were reaching the patriots at Faneuil Hall. Even before William Green's run-in with Walker, one patriot claimed to have heard four soldiers of the Twenty-ninth Regiment saying that a great many men would eat their dinners on Monday who wouldn't be eating them on Tuesday. A British soldier appeared at the door of a Bostonian named Amos Thayer to tell Thayer's sister that she must keep him at home because there would be a great deal of bloodshed before Tuesday. Another patriot heard a teenage British fifer say he hoped to God the soldiers would burn the town down.

On Monday morning, March 5, Thomas Hutchinson laid before the Council a letter from Colonel Carr complaining about the town's mood. Council members replied that the people would never be satisfied until the troops were removed. Royall Tyler added that the customs commissioners had to go, too.

The day had been cold but clear. A foot of snow covered the town, and along King Street the snow had frozen. Boston did not have streetlamps like London's, and at night the only light shone through windows or from the moon. By 7 P.M., small bands of patriots armed with clubs had begun patrolling the streets.

John Gillespie had come out for a drink with friends, and on his way to a South End tavern he saw fifty men in those roving patrols. Gillespie had been drinking about an hour when a friend came to the tavern to say that three hundred men had gathered at the Liberty Tree with clubs and sticks to assail the British soldiers. Meanwhile, at the Brick Church in the North End, a man boosted a small boy through an open window and told him to climb to the belfry and start ringing the bell. By 8:30 P.M. bells were ringing all over Boston. Gillespie was sure there must be a fire. Ever since a devastating blaze ten years before, whenever men heard bells at night they ran for leather bags to carry water and for the pumps mounted on wheels that they called fire engines.

The tavern's owner assured Gillespie that it wasn't a fire. It was to collect the mob. Gillespie was walking home when two fire engines were pulled past him. He asked again whether there was a fire. No, the men answered, they were for fighting the soldiers.

William Davies, a sergeant major in the Fourteenth Regiment, saw men tearing up an outdoor butcher stall for clubs. They were shouting, "Now for the bloody-back rascals!" When they added, "Murder!" and "Kill the dogs!" Sergeant Davies slipped over to a friend's house and exchanged his red uniform for civilian clothes.

Crowds seemed to be streaming toward the ropewalks and toward the British barracks. Only a few apprentices had gone to King Street, where the Main Guard stood just south of Town House and about forty yards from the customs office. At customs, Private Hugh White of the Twenty-ninth was on duty in the sentry box. The apprentices had gathered there when one of them, young Edward Garrick of Piemont's wigmaking shop, spotted a British officer named John Goldfinch passing the sentry post. Garrick began jeering at him.

"There goes the fellow that won't pay my master for dressing his hair," he cried.

Goldfinch ignored him.

But even after the officer had disappeared the boy kept it up. Goldfinch was cheap, Garrick said. He wouldn't pay Piemont the money he owed him.

Now Private White rose to the bait. Of course his captain would pay his debts, White said. Captain Goldfinch was a gentleman.

There were no gentlemen in that regiment, said Garrick.

Hugh White stepped out of the small sentry box and into the street. "Let me see your face," he said.

Garrick did not flinch. "I am not ashamed to show my face."

White swung his musket and struck Garrick a blow on the side of his head with its butt. Dazed and reeling, the young man ran to the doorway of a shop and began to yell for help. White followed and hit him again.

The eight or nine other apprentices in the street taunted White when he returned, muttering and cursing, to his post. "Bloody back!" the boys called. "Lousy rascal!" "Damned rascally scoundrel lobster son of a bitch!"

The shouts began to attract a crowd.

Around town, the encounters between soldiers and citizens were increasing. As three armed soldiers passed a Bostonian, Robert Pierpoint, one jabbed him with the handle of his bayonet. When Pierpoint protested, the others said he soon would hear more from them. Samuel Adams' cousin Henry Bass watched a party of soldiers coming out of Draper's Alley, a covered passageway that led to a barracks. The soldiers had drawn their cutlasses and were swinging them as they strode along, ripping clothes and nicking shoulders. A man called to them, "Gentlemen, what is the matter?"

They answered, "You will see by and by."

On either side, a few men were trying to defuse the looming explosion. With the bells clanging and packs of boys racing through the streets, one civilian asked a group of British officers, "Why don't you keep your soldiers in the barracks?" They claimed they were doing their best. The Bostonian persisted. "Are the inhabitants to be knocked down in the street? Are they to be murdered in this manner? You know," he went on, "that our country and our town has been badly used. We did not send for you. We will not have you here. We will . . ." The rest was lost in the roar from a crowd that had collected around him.

The officers went on answering politely. A portion of the crowd was mollified and shouting, "Home! Home!" But others yelled, "The Main Guard!" and men went rushing toward King Street.

British officers like Captain Goldfinch were also trying to dampen tempers. Goldfinch was not aware of the blows Private White had struck to defend his honor, and at the end of Draper's Alley he found a band of redcoats trying to swat away snowballs from the crowd with a shovel. Goldfinch worked his way through to the soldiers and ordered them back to Murray's Barracks. They withdrew under a barrage of snowballs and insults: "Cowards!" "Afraid to fight!"

A merchant, Richard Palmes, stopped a band of officers to say that he was surprised to see soldiers out of their barracks after 8 P.M.

"Pray, do you mean to teach us our duty?" one officer demanded.

Palmes's answer was tactful: "I do not. Only to remind you of it."

Snowballs and curses had gone on falling as he spoke, and the officers had to stoop to avoid them. One gestured to the crowd and asked Palmes, "Why do you not go to your homes?"

Palmes turned to the townspeople. "Gentlemen, hear what the officers say. You had better go home."

Some drifted away, others took up the cry, "To the Main Guard!" Shouting and pounding on walls, they raced to King Street. There Edward Garrick was pointing to Hugh White in his sentry box and bawling, "This is the son of a bitch that knocked me down!"

The throng pressed in on White, hurling icicles at him, along with chunks of ice pried from the street. Private White shouted that he could not leave his post. If they did not stop, he said, he would have to call the main guard and the crowd would take the consequences. A civilian wearing a red cloak also pleaded for a halt, but the men and the boys retreated only for a moment. As the pelting went on, White fixed his bayonet and let everyone see that he was loading his musket.

Henry Knox, a heavyset Boston bookseller, approached White and urged him not to fire. If he did, he would die for it.

"Damn them," said White. "If they molest me, I will fire."

Jonathan Austin, a law clerk for John Adams, had been drawn to King Street by the bells and tried with no success to send the crowd home. Ice was bursting around Private White's head when he pounded on the door of the Custom House. Inside, no one would open it. White heard a chorus of shouts from the crowd: "Kill him! Kill him!" "Knock him down!" "Fire, damn you, fire! You dare not fire!"

A town watchman assured White that his tormentors were mere boys and the sentry had nothing to fear from them. But White could see the size of the mob flocking to King Street. As he ducked from shards of ice, he shouted for help, "Turn out, Main Guard!"

That cry mingled with another call. "Town born," the civilians were shouting to their fellow Bostonians, "turn out! Town born, turn out!"

At the main guardhouse, the officer of the day got word of the danger Private White was facing. Forty years old, his face pitted with smallpox scars, Captain Thomas Preston was an Irish officer respected for his solid judgment. He was also a musician who had performed regularly at Francis Bernard's amateur musicales. Now he paced up and down for almost half an hour trying to decide what to do. Captain Preston understood that the law didn't give him the right to march out his troops and disperse a crowd unless a civilian authority called on him to do it. Tonight, no justice of the peace was likely to brave the mob and come forward. And yet Private White was alone, one sentry facing men and boys armed with clubs and ice more deadly than rocks. In this crisis, Captain Preston could not rely on his officer of the guard, Lieutenant James Basset. Through family connections Basset had been commissioned at the age of twelve, and he was barely twenty years old, completely inexperienced, and shaking.

"What shall I do in this case?" Basset asked Preston.

The captain decided that his first duty was to Private White. "Take out six or seven of the men," Preston said, "and let them go to the assistance of the sentry."

Basset put together a relief party of one corporal and six grenadiers who included the tallest men in the regiment. Three of the six had fought the previous week at the ropewalks. Shedding their cumbersome watchcoats, they prepared to set off, but Preston knew he couldn't trust the command to the corporal or even to his lieutenant. Basset stayed behind, and Preston and his column moved off, bayonets fixed but muskets empty.

Marching toward Private White, the soldiers brandished their bayonets to ward off anyone from coming too close. As they passed one Bostonian, he felt a blade brush his hat. But the men of the column, although they were tense, weren't eager to fight. When another Bostonian, Nathaniel Fosdick, found them bearing down on him, he snapped, "Why are you pushing at me?"

"Damn your blood," said a soldier. "Stand out of our way."

"I will not," said Fosdick. "I am doing no harm to any man, and I will not stand aside for anyone."

The column of soldiers broke to either side and moved around him.

The relief party reached Hugh White's sentry box, and Henry Knox cautioned Captain Preston as he had done with White. Approaching Preston as his men were loading their muskets, Knox seized him by the coat. "For God's sake, take care of your men. If they fire," Knox said again, "you die."

Preston answered that he was aware of that. He brushed Knox aside and ordered Private White to join the relief column. As he left the box, the crowd didn't try to stop him. With White safe, Preston turned his men around and ordered them to march back to the Main Guard. But the mob had become too dense for the soldiers to move, and all at once the fury that had been growing for eighteen months erupted on King Street.

"Damn you, you sons of bitches, fire!" someone shouted from the crowd. "You can't kill us all."

Preston formed his men in a semicircle next to a corner of the Custom House. They stood three feet apart as men from the crowd pressed within inches of their bayonets.

Richard Palmes still hoped to avert a calamity but had armed himself with a club. He went up to Captain Preston to ask whether his men's guns were loaded. Preston said that they were, with powder and ball.

Palmes said, "I hope you do not intend they shall fire upon the inhabitants."

"By no means, by no means," Preston said, and he pointed out that since he was standing directly in front of the musket barrels, he would be the first to fall if the guns were fired. Giving an order to fire under those circumstances, Preston told Palmes, would prove that he was no officer.

Not everyone was reassured. A young woman who was a neighbor of Private White's approached him, but he pushed her toward the corner. "Go home," he said, "or you'll be killed."

As men kept the soldiers hemmed in, a rumor spread that James Murray was hurrying toward the scene. He was the justice of the peace who had stood bail for William Browne after the assault on James Otis. A voice cried, "Here comes Murray with the Riot Act!" If it was true, Murray would be bringing Preston the authority he needed to disperse the crowd. Under province law, a civilian official could invoke the king's name to tell a gathering of fifty men, armed or not, to disband within one hour. The penalties for not obeying included the seizure of land, flogging, even prison. On this night, Bostonians would not be read the Riot Act. The figure drawing nearer was bombarded with snowballs and sent running down Pudding Lane.

The mob knew that without a civil authority the redcoats were helpless. Samuel Gray, one of the ropemakers who had fought on the day Patrick Walker was insulted, had rushed to King Street vowing to knock a few heads. A little drunk, he clapped an apprehensive friend on the back and told him, "They dare not fire." Around him sticks and ice flew through the air, and men were yelling, "Damn you, you rascals, fire!" "You dare not fire!" "Fire and be damned!"

A Tory had worked his way behind Preston's men and took up the cry in a different spirit. "Fire!" he urged the soldiers. "By God, I'll stand by you whilst I have a drop of blood! Fire!"

It was the one word everyone was shouting—those who heard the bells and still thought the town might be burning, those goading the troops for their impotence, the Tory who wanted the British soldiers to avenge his politics. Everyone—except Captain Preston— was shouting, "Fire!"

A stick flew through the air and struck Private Hugh Montgomery of the relief column. He fell, and as he scrambled back to his feet a voice rang out above the others: "Damn you, fire!"

Montgomery cocked his musket and shot into the crowd. Richard Palmes, standing nearby, hit Montgomery's arm and then aimed a blow directly at Captain Preston's head. But Palmes slipped on the ice and only hit Preston's arm. Montgomery prodded him away with his bayonet.

That first shot hit no one. The crowd had pulled back, and for a few seconds there was silence. Then Preston moved behind his troops. He didn't order them to fire, but he didn't give the command to recover—to cease fire. Without any order from their captain, the British soldiers began to shoot.

Private Matthew Kilroy, one of the brawlers at the ropewalks, fired with no apparent aim. Yet he struck Samuel Gray directly in the head and opened a hole as big as a man's fist. Gray, who had just called, "My lads, they will not fire," died instantly.

Another volley from the soldiers, and two bullets tore into the broad chest of Crispus Attucks. Dark-skinned, Indian or mulatto, Attucks stood six feet two inches and towered over most British soldiers, who rarely reached five feet ten. Two decades before, at the age of twenty-seven, Attucks had run away from his master. Now, nearing fifty and a leader by his age and size, he had come to King Street at the head of a band of Boston sailors. Gasping, Attucks fell to the street in front of the relief column.

A civilian shouted that the crowd should advance in order to stop the soldiers from firing again. It was a fatal misjudgment. As men pressed nearer, the British fired from even closer range. James Caldwell, a sailor, was struck by a bullet that passed through his body, and he took a second wound in the shoulder.

Robert Paterson's trousers had been grazed when Ebenezer Richardson fired from his window twelve days before. Now as he raised his right hand a bullet struck him in the wrist.

Patrick Carr, an Irishman living in Boston, had started for King Street with a small cutlass fastened under his coat, but his neighbors persuaded him to leave it at home. The blade would not have helped him. He was struck by a bullet that tore away his backbone to the hip.

Edward Payne, a merchant living in King Street across from the Custom House, had gone out earlier to see whether there was a fire. Coming home to tell his wife she had nothing to fear, Payne lingered at his doorway, watching as the crowd grew. A bullet caught him in the right arm.

Ebenezer Mackintosh's brother-in-law, Samuel Maverick, was racing away from the shooting when a bullet ricocheted and caught him in the chest. Dying, Maverick fell to the street. He was seventeen.

At first, with the smoke, the pushing and the din, no one could be sure what had happened. Many in the crowd couldn't believe that the soldiers had been firing real shot and not merely trying to scare them with powder. Some thought that a few men had fainted from fright. Others decided that men had run away and that what was left in the street were only the greatcoats they had shed as they ran. The confusion explained why seventeen-year-old Christopher Monk could not persuade anyone that he had been hit in the chest. Monk had come armed with a bat that he used for street

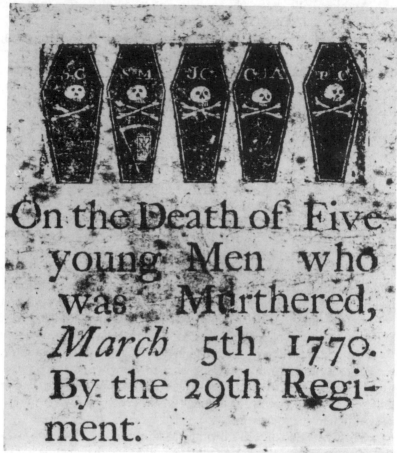

Sons of Liberty broadside

games, and now he felt himself lurching. Idly, his friend James Brewer asked whether he was wounded.

"Yes," said Kit Monk.

"You are only frightened," Brewer assured him.

But a man named John Hickling had felt the gaping wound in Samuel Gray's head, and, as the powder blew away, others in the crowd began to realize what had happened. Men who had withdrawn now edged forward warily to care for the wounded. The soldiers reloaded and cocked their muskets.

Captain Preston rushed down the firing line, pushing the

musket barrels toward the night sky. "Stop firing!" he ordered. Furiously, he demanded to know why his men had fired. They said that they had heard the word "Fire!" and thought it had come from him. At once, Preston understood the enormity of what had happened.

Benjamin Burdick, who had run a British soldier off his property, inspected the body of Crispus Attucks and then walked directly to the line of soldiers and peered at them in the moonlight.

"I want to see some faces that I may swear to another day," Burdick said.

Captain Preston, with the prospect of a murder trial vivid before him, said, "Perhaps, sir, you may."

Abigail Adams in 1763, the year before her marriage

Trial

JOHN ADAMS had joined a club of fellow lawyers, and on the fifth of March they were meeting in the South End when the alarm bells began to clang. The club members assumed that the town was on fire, snatched up their hats and cloaks and ran off to help fight the flames. Only when he was in the street did Adams learn that British soldiers had fired into a crowd. Adams and his wife had lost an infant daughter only a few weeks before and were awaiting the birth

John Adams, about 1764

1770

of another child, and he hurried home to be with his family. The route took him past a company of British troops with muskets on their shoulders and bayonets fixed. The soldiers had left a narrow path for a man of Adams' stocky build, but he pushed forward, ignoring the soldiers' menacing expressions as if they were a row of marble statues. By the time he reached his house in Cold Lane, the town seemed to be calming down for the night.

At thirty-four, John Adams was nearing the age James Otis had been when he argued against the writs of assistance, but Adams was aware that he had not made the same impact on the province. Both men had come from rural backgrounds. Like Speaker Otis, Adams' father had once been a shoemaker before he became a farmer. But differences in the two boys' characters had shown up early. The young Otis had loved the classics. John Adams had found studying Latin so dull that he went to his father one day and asked to be excused from it.

"Well, John," his father said, "if Latin grammar does not suit you, you may try ditching. Perhaps that will. My meadow yonder needs a ditch."

Exhilarated by his escape, the boy threw himself into the digging. Within minutes, he realized that a shovel weighed more than a textbook. That first morning was the longest he had ever endured, and he rejoiced when the day finally ended. After the second morning, he wanted to tell his father that he had made a mistake, but pride wouldn't let him. By nightfall, John asked to return to Latin. In August 1751, at fifteen, John entered Harvard College.

During graduation ceremonies four years later, Harvard's president singled out John as a first-rate scholar, and a minister from Worcester hired him as Latin master for his grammar school. Nothing about the job appealed to the young man except the pay. An escort came for him with a horse, and, before he was twenty, John Adams went off to become a provincial schoolteacher.

His class quickly saw through Adams' teaching method. He picked the brighter boys and told them to teach their classmates while he wrote voluminously at his desk. He was considered pious, and the other masters supposed that he was composing sermons. But Adams was writing to his former classmates, mourning the end of their days at Harvard.

Some days he passed the time by imagining himself a dictator, with his students as famous generals and distinguished politicians. Then he remembered that his generals were three feet tall and many of his politicians still wore infant petticoats. Very soon he was considering routes of escape. He rejected the ministry because he thought a congregation's first requirement in choosing a preacher was not piety, integrity, good sense or learning; it was stupidity. Medicine was possible, and he thought of making his name as a surgeon. The army took personal wealth or a rich patron. Yet military service had one great appeal: he could find out whether he was a hero or a coward.

Adams dipped into lawbooks, went to court to hear the colony's better lawyers, and became drawn to the bar. He saw its shortcomings, all the hours lost on meaningless writs and indictments, but the law seemed a quick, sure road to prosperity, and he apprenticed himself to a leading lawyer.

During the next two years, Adams taught during the day and studied law at night. Over meals, his tutor was something of a freethinker, interested in debating religion more than the law. John Adams, with a prickly disposition, enjoyed their debates, and other learned men also engaged him in friendly arguments that exposed him to theories of equality and liberty. Adams, conservative by nature, contended that some persons could never enjoy complete suffrage—women and children, idiots and madmen, criminals and debtors. But he was listening and learning. Most of all, he was watching himself and the impression he was making.

Although he lived in a province that banned the theater, Adams treated life as though it were a drama going on around him. In his diary he recreated each day's scenes and dialogue, then stood apart and criticized the figure he cut on Worcester's stage. Almost always it was a poor one. He was sharp-tongued when he should have been bland, he wrote. Insipid when he should have been witty. With women, he was tongue-tied and awkward. Worst of all, he was sure he was irredeemably lazy. Why couldn't he be like Mr. Benjamin Franklin of Philadelphia, whom the best people in Worcester considered an industrious genius? But then, should he be worrying so much about fame? No! Man's true goals must be piety and virtue.

Nothing seemed to come easily for John Adams, and being admitted to the bar at Braintree became another ordeal when his law tutor did not go along to present him to the court. Jeremiah Gridley came to his rescue, offering to shepherd him through the formalities. Then Gridley said, "Mr. Adams, permit me to give you a little advice. In the first place, pursue the law itself, rather than the gain of it." And, he added, don't marry early.

When that last advice made John Adams smile, Gridley asked whether he was engaged.

Adams said he was perfectly disengaged. But he couldn't vouch for how long he'd remain so.

Gridley smiled in resignation. "An early marriage will probably put an end to your studies and will certainly involve you in expense." He looked at his watch. "You have detained me here the whole forenoon and I must go to court."

But John Adams followed Gridley's advice. He threw himself into more study even though he couldn't always find the volumes he wanted. "No books," he wrote during a low moment, "no time, no friends." His studies might not make him rich, but they were a way of gaining respect. Adams wanted to end the casual insolence of colleagues like Robert Treat Paine, who once challenged him during an argument to cite the source of his opinion.

Adams said, "Vinnius."

"Vinnius!" said Robert Paine. "You can't understand a page of Vinnius!"

He had no right to say that to me, John Adams complained to his diary. He knows nothing of me at all. "For the future, let me act the part of a critical spy upon him, not that of an open unsuspicious friend."

His diary had become John Adams' one intimate. He could dissect in its pages each new personality entering his life. Hannah Quincy, for example, usually managed to lead their banter to some provocative question about the relation between a husband and a wife. John Adams found Hannah more thoughtful than most young women and noted with approval that she was always reading. More often, though, he analyzed himself: "I have not conversed enough with the world to behave rightly." People always seemed to be laughing at him. Adams talked with Robert Paine about Greek, which made Paine laugh. He told Samuel Quincy that he wanted to be a great man, which made Quincy laugh. He lectured young women on the folly of love, which made everyone laugh. Meanwhile he was neglecting his true duty. "Reputation ought to be the perpetual subject of my thoughts and of my behavior. How shall I gain a reputation!"

Over the next half-dozen years, Adams became known as a competent lawyer, an acceptance that brought him neither riches nor fame. He lamented that never had a man conducted so much business—Yankees were litigious—for so little profit. At the same time, he continued to examine the available young women of the colony. He came close to proposing to Hannah Quincy, but finally chose Abigail Smith, daughter of a Congregational minister and born to the Puritan aristocracy. Abigail's father had given her and her two sisters the freedom to read and think at a time when learning for a woman was unfashionable. Daughters of wealthy families were taught only to read and write, add and subtract, and possibly play a musical instrument. Hannah Quincy and James Otis' witty sister, Mercy, were exceptions. Abigail Smith had been too delicate to attend even a dame school. But she read—poetry, fiction, *The Spectator* from London—and wrote long letters to her friends, who disguised themselves with names like "Calliope," "Aspasia" and "Aurelia." Over their four-year courtship, Abigail became "Diana" in her letters to Adams, who was "Lysander."

Adams, now twenty-eight, argued himself out of any doubts about marrying Abigail by entering a list of her virtues in his diary: "Tender feeling, sensible, friendly, a friend. Not an impudent, not an indelicate, not a disagreeable word or action. Prudent, modest, delicate, soft, sensible, obliging, active." But at nineteen, Abigail was perplexed by the difference between the suitor she knew, ardent, kindly, sensitive, and her friends' impression of him as stiff and formidable. It troubled her that her friends—and sometimes she herself—felt ill at ease with him. Abigail, though, had learned how to deal with Adams when he became pompous. Once he complained to her that she was too free in crossing her legs when she sat. "A gentleman," Abigail replied, "has no business to concern himself about the legs of a lady."

If the world found him haughty or ill-tempered, Abigail Smith knew better. She saw the man of the diary, not the drawing room, and agreed to marry him. Her choice baffled her father's congregation. John Adams, with a bland face that could have been carved from suet, was not distinguished enough in family or prospects to deserve a fine-featured beauty like their preacher's daughter. The resentment grew until Abigail's father based his first sermon after the wedding on a verse from Luke: "For John came neither eating bread nor drinking wine, and ye say, he hath a devil."

John Adams did have a devil. It was his ambition. As the patriot cause spread, he had drafted Braintree's brief against obeying the Stamp Act and had published well-received essays in the newspapers. But at the next election for selectmen from Braintree he was passed over, and he poured out his mortification to his diary.

With marriage, however, Adams' entries were less self-lacerating. He became more assured socially, although his politics remained in flux. When Joseph Warren urged him to take an active part in the Boston Town Meeting, Adams replied that those public appearances were the path to madness; Warren knew he meant James Otis. And Adams detested the Boston mob.

When the patriot fervor waned in the later years of the 1760s, John Adams had pulled further from the fray. He did refuse a high post in the Admiralty Court because of his Whig principles, and the sight of British troops on Boston Common never stopped enraging him. But most of the time Adams was back to providing for his family. At Salem he defended a man charged with fathering a bastard and managed an acquittal after his client testified in court, "I fucked once, but I minded my pullbacks. I swear I did not get her with child."

In August 1769, Adams had accepted a dinner invitation from three hundred and fifty Sons of Liberty in Dorchester to mark the fourth anniversary of the Stamp Act protest. Adams knew that James Otis and Samuel Adams promoted the celebration hoping to revive the flagging patriot spirit. John Adams went only as an onlooker. His pleasure in the lawyers' club was being marred in that same period by Otis and his dervish moods. "He talks so much," Adams wrote in his diary, "and takes up so much of our time, and fills it with trash, obsceneness, profaneness, nonsense and distraction that we have no [time] left for rational amusements or inquiries."

That had been John Adams' life on the eve of the shootings in Boston. He remained convinced that moral laws made men equal and independent, but thought he was realistic about the physical and mental differences among them. Adams' self-appraisal had led him to decide that the supreme urges of the human race were a need for fame and a love of power.

The morning after the fatal shootings on King Street, John Adams was sitting in his office near the steps of Town House when James Forrest knocked at his door. Born in Ireland, Forrest was a successful merchant and a staunch Tory. With tears pouring down his cheeks, he said he had come with a very solemn message from a very unfortunate man. Adams, who knew Forrest slightly,

Thomas Hutchinson

watched his florid weeping and recalled that he was often called the Irish Infant. His message was from Captain Preston, who was in prison and needed legal counsel but could get none.

Adams didn't know that it was Thomas Hutchinson who had recommended him to Preston, along with another young patriot lawyer, Josiah Quincy. The previous night Hutchinson had acquitted himself well, hurrying at first report to the site of the shooting. Once there, he found the noise from the crowd so loud that he couldn't question Captain Preston. With Bostonians pressing in on them, the acting governor went to the balcony of Town House and promised that justice would be done. "The law shall have its course!" Hutchinson cried. "I will live and die by the law!"

After the people had gone home, Hutchinson had stayed on for most of the night, sending out justices of the peace to take depositions from eyewitnesses. By 3 A.M. Captain Preston had agreed to surrender, and the long night ended as he was led to jail.

The patriots could only speculate about why Hutchinson would recommend Quincy and John Adams. Perhaps if either of them refused, it might be taken as proof that the patriots put their politics above justice, and yet if they accepted, their prestige might wane among the Sons of Liberty. Or Hutchinson may simply have observed John Adams in court and believed he was the best lawyer for so difficult a case. After the *Liberty* affair, the customs officers had sued John Hancock for smuggling, and Hancock had hired John Adams to defend him. The case had become painful drudgery for Adams as it dragged on throughout the winter, but at last the government had dropped its charges.

So it wasn't necessarily a Tory trick that Forrest was standing before him, telling him that Josiah Quincy had said he would represent Preston and his men only if Adams would join the defense.

Forrest must understand, Adams told him, that this case would be as important as any ever tried in any court or country of the world. An accused person with his life at stake should have the counsel of his choice. But Captain Preston must expect from Adams no art or sophistry or prevarication, nothing more than fact, evidence and what the law would justify.

Forrest assured him that Captain Preston desired nothing more. From all that he had heard of John Adams, Preston had said, he could trust his life to him. "And," Forrest added, "as God Almighty is my judge, I believe him to be an innocent man."

"That," John Adams reminded him, "must be ascertained by his trial, and if he cannot have a fair trial of that issue without my assistance, without hesitation he shall have it."

Forrest offered him a single guinea as retainer and Adams accepted it. Money was not the issue.

As John Adams took on Preston's defense, Samuel Adams was savoring the sweetest moment in a lifetime of political agitating. He and the other patriots were referring to the killings the previous night as "the Boston Massacre," and today thousands of men were crowding into Faneuil Hall, echoing Adams' demand of the past two years: the British troops must leave Boston. At Town House, Thomas Hutchinson had to push his way through a delegation of Boston selectmen in order to meet with his Council. The Council members proved to be divided, but several members urged Hutchinson to order the troops out of town. He refused. The selectmen were admitted to the chamber and told Hutchinson of their fears. When they finished, he repeated that he did not have the power to order Colonel Dalrymple to remove his forces to Castle William.

Faced with that impasse, the meeting at Faneuil Hall sent a messenger to tell the selectmen to return there. Samuel Adams had organized a committee that would call on the acting governor and impress the people's will on him even more urgently. The crowd at the hall had now reached three thousand, though the number of legal voters in Boston was only half that number. This time, Samuel Adams decided against sending other men to do his bidding. He and John Hancock and other leaders would confront Hutchinson directly. Hutchinson braced for the encounter by asking both Colonel Dalrymple and Colonel Carr to remain at his side.

The delegates were shown in. They took off their gold-laced hats from large white wigs and placed them on the table in front of them. When they had laid down their ultimatum, they retired to a nearby room while Hutchinson once again canvassed his Council. Now all but two members were urging him to give in. Hutchinson remained adamant. At that point, Colonel Dalrymple proposed a compromise. Since the Twenty-ninth Regiment was especially obnoxious to the Bostonians, and since the orders for that regiment originally called for them to be billeted at Castle William, Dalrymple was prepared to move them there while he awaited instructions from General Gage in New York.

When the town's committee filed back into the chamber, Hutchinson repeated that he lacked authority over the troops but intimated that one regiment, the Twenty-ninth, might be removed. Then Samuel Adams, confronting his lifetime adversary not by letter or through the newspapers but face to face, gave his answer:

"If you have the power to remove one regiment," Adams said, "you have the power to remove both. It is at your peril if you refuse. The meeting is composed of three thousand people. They are becoming impatient. A thousand men are already arrived from the neighborhood, and the whole country is in motion. Night is approaching. An immediate answer is expected.

"Both regiments or none!"

The room fell silent. Hutchinson tried to recover his bargaining position. You alone, he told the delegation, have the power to calm the people, and you must use it.

No, said Deacon William Philips, even if we got down on our knees before them, it would have no effect.

Know then, said Hutchinson, that if there is further violence or an attempt to drive the troops out of Boston, everyone who advised or abetted that effort will be guilty of high treason.

Hutchinson stood, ending the interview, but Colonel Dalrymple stopped him. Wouldn't Hutchinson agree to meet again with his Council that afternoon?

"I can do nothing further," Hutchinson said, moving toward the door.

But Dalrymple repeated his request, and several Council members seconded him. Hutchinson agreed to another meeting that afternoon.

During a break for noontime dinner, Dalrymple sought out Hutchinson's advisers with a further compromise. If, instead of issuing a direct order, the acting governor would simply express a desire that the troops be removed from town, Dalrymple would oblige him.

At 3 P.M. a regular Town Meeting was convened at Faneuil Hall. The numbers again were so great that the session was moved to the Old South Meeting-house. Even there the overflow filled Cornhill Street. Samuel Adams read out Hutchinson's concessions about one regiment, but his own answer had circulated among the audience beforehand, and they roared, "Both regiments or none!"

Hutchinson had watched the meeting move from Faneuil Hall past the doors of Town House to the Old South. When he convened the afternoon session, he knew he was alone with his decision. Samuel Adams had come back for the kill, and he noted with relish that Hutchinson's knees were trembling as he received news of the vote at the Town Meeting. Once more, the Boston delegation was asked to wait while Hutchinson met with his Council. Now even the two who had supported him in the morning had turned against his position. This current crisis, they warned Hutchinson, was not provoked by the sort of people who pulled down your house five years ago. This time, the rebellion is led by some of the very best men among us—wealthy men, religious men. Thomas Hutchinson took their remarks as proof that the whole bloody affair on King Street had been plotted by a clique of patriots as a callous way of getting the troops out of Boston. But even if they were making a confession, their admission didn't ease his dilemma.

Hutchinson was assured that if the British troops stayed on, ten thousand men from throughout the province would march on Boston and annihilate them. Boston's charter, its property, its future, all would be lost. Hutchinson asked the Council members to reconsider. They would not. Even his kinsman Andrew Oliver told him to yield.

At last, Hutchinson gave in.

Colonel Dalrymple tried to console him. "What else could you do?" he asked.

Hutchinson said, "Retire to the Castle and remain there until the people come to their senses."

"And take the troops with you," said their commander.

Three days after the shootings on King Street, funerals were held for the victims. Every shop in Boston was closed, and church bells tolled across the countryside. The procession for young Snider had been immense; this day's march was even greater—ten thousand people, perhaps twelve thousand. The bodies of Crispus Attucks and James Caldwell, who had no house in town, had been placed in Faneuil Hall. Samuel Maverick was taken from his mother's house in Union Street, Samuel Gray from his brother's house in Royal Exchange Lane. The four hearses met in King Street. There they were joined by the coaches of Boston's leading citizens. Behind that came a column of men six abreast and stretching for blocks through the town. The file proceeded to the Liberty Tree and then to the Old Granary Burying Ground, where the four bodies were lowered into a common grave. Curiosity had brought out even Hutchinson's supporters. The loyalist clergyman Mather Byles watched the cortege and rephrased to a companion the question that Theophilus Lillie had raised two weeks before: "They call me a brainless Tory. But tell me, my young friend, which is better—to be ruled by one tyrant three thousand miles away, or by three thousand tyrants not one mile away?"

Since the news circulated that the regiments would be removed, Boston had been calm. But two days after the funeral the troops still had not been evacuated, and at another Town Meeting Samuel Adams pointed out that since it had taken only forty-eight hours to land the soldiers in Boston, there was no excuse for any further delay.

In New York, General Gage had been late in getting Colonel Dalrymple's request for instructions and approved the transfer thinking that the troops had already gone to the Castle. When he learned a few days later that they were still in Boston, he urged Dalrymple to make every effort to keep at least the Fourteenth Regiment in town. But his directive didn't arrive until the end of March, and by that time the troops had been marched to the wharf—with William Molineux at their side to guard against any outburst from the town—and ferried through the harbor to Castle William. In London, Lord North began to refer sarcastically to the Twenty-ninth and the Fourteenth as "Sam Adams's two regiments."

The deaths of March 5 were soon enshrined in patriot mythology. Henry Pelham, a young half brother of the artist John Copley, produced a partisan engraving of the shootings. Set against the serene buildings of Boston, the redcoats were shown opening fire at point-blank range while distressed but orderly citizens gathered up their dead. He labeled the Custom House "Butcher's Hall." When he sent off his work to the printers, it was intercepted by Paul Revere, the silversmith, who based an engraving of his own on it. Revere never claimed to be an original artist and often borrowed ideas or characters. His version beat Pelham's to the public by two weeks and became a great success. In the minds of patriots throughout the colonies, it confirmed the wanton nature of the killings. Pelham urged Revere to reflect upon his dishonorable action, but the engraving was already going up on walls throughout the province.

The patriots were shrewd in exploiting their victory. British officers were allowed to walk through the town unmolested, and even though Josiah Quincy's father tried to dissuade him from defending the accused soldiers, Samuel Adams gave no sign that he disapproved of his two young friends accepting the assignment. Indeed, Quincy could assure his father that he had taken on the case only after he had been urged forward by an Adams, a Hancock, a Molineux, a Warren and five more of the leading patriots.

Samuel Adams preferred that the trial begin promptly, while memories were fresh and emotion ran high. But when two judges fell ill Hutchinson refused to appoint temporary replacements for them, and it was early September, six months after the shootings, before Captain Preston and his men were arraigned. Each pleaded not guilty.

"How wilt thou be tried?" the clerk asked.

"By God and my country," the men answered, a formality that meant they were requesting a jury trial. A murder case could not be heard by only a judge.

"God send thee a good deliverance," was the clerk's ritual response.

The court adjourned and it was not until October 24, 1770, that John Adams rose to defend Captain Preston. His men had petitioned that since they had only followed Preston's orders, they should all be tried together. It was unfair, they said, that he, as a gentleman, should have a better chance to save his life than the poor men obliged to obey him. But Preston was being tried alone. John Adams and Josiah Quincy—joined by a Tory attorney, Richard Auchmuty—were taking one challenge at a time. First they would prove that Preston gave no order to fire. Then they would consider where that left the defense of his troops.

The Tories feared that the jury would be packed with Sons of Liberty, but those patriots who had encouraged Quincy to act for the defense also wanted to make this trial a model of province justice. After nineteen challenges, Preston's lawyers seated seven jurors, only two from Boston. Another five Tories were quickly empaneled. One had been overheard to say that if he had to sit to all eternity he would never convict Preston. But by the time his vow had reached the courtroom, the clerk had already given the jury the usual admonition, "Good men and true, stand together and harken to your evidence."

Captain Preston had reason for optimism aside from a tame jury. Assurance had come from England that even if he or his men were convicted, Acting Governor Hutchinson should not impose their sentences until he had heard directly from the king. And around Boston temperatures were cooling. The people continued to call the shootings a massacre rather than—in Colonel Dalrymple's words—a scuffle, but their fever had broken over the long summer. There was even speculation that the local court might issue a complete reprieve for the defendants, apart from whatever George III might do for them.

The courtroom in Queen Street held about sixty spectators. Most of the places were taken by British military men, sitting stolidly and waiting to see how the town would treat their comrades. By the standard of the day, the trial would be a slow one. After seating the jury, the crown had time for only eight witnesses, and Captain Preston's became the first criminal trial in Massachusetts history to run more than one day. Accompanied by a guard from both defense and prosecution, the jurors were locked up overnight in the house of Boston's jailer.

Josiah Quincy's older brother, Samuel, had once been a Son of Liberty but had been won over to the Tories. Now, as one of the crown's prosecutors, he opened the argument against Preston. He set out to establish that even if Preston had not given the order to fire the first shot, he had had sufficient time to call, "Recover" before the volley began. One witness swore to that. But the testimony soon became as chaotic as the night itself. One unpersuasive witness said he had heard Preston shout, "Damn your bloods, fire again, let the consequence be what it will." Benjamin Burdick, who had peered into the faces of the men to prepare himself for this trial, now admitted for the first time that he had been carrying a sword and had been prepared to cut off the head of any soldier who stabbed him with a bayonet. John Adams' law clerk testified for the prosecution, but lamely. He had heard no orders—not to prime, not to load, not to fire.

The crown rested late in the second day, and John Adams opened his defense. From the bench, Justice Peter Oliver sent an apologetic note to Thomas Hutchinson: "I know you think you would have finished the cause in half the time, and I know it would not have taken half a day at the Old Bailey, but we must conform to the times." The defense, however, was moving its witnesses quickly. Twenty-two testified on the third day alone. Since the law forbade the accused to take the stand, Preston did not speak in his own defense. His best witness was Richard Palmes, the merchant and Son of Liberty, who said that Preston had been facing him and that he had had his hand on Preston's shoulder when the shout came to fire. Although Palmes couldn't entirely rule out the possibility that Preston had given the command, John Adams thought that his was the most relevant testimony so far.

Three black witnesses also bolstered Preston's defense. Andrew, a slave who belonged to a Son of Liberty named Oliver Wendell, told about Crispus Attucks swinging his stick, first at Preston, then at Private Hugh Montgomery. Andrew was sure that the voice that called, "Fire" had come from a point beyond where Preston was standing. Then Oliver Wendell affirmed that Andrew had lived with him for ten years and that his reputation for integrity was good. Jack, a Boston doctor's slave, testified to the provocation of the snowballs. Newton Prince, a pastry cook and a freeman from the West Indies, said he had been watching Captain Preston and had heard him give no order to fire.

With a break for the Sabbath, the court was done in six days. On October 31, 1770, Captain Preston wrote triumphantly to General Gage about the previous day's verdict: "I take the liberty of wishing you joy of the complete victory obtained over the knaves and foolish villains of Boston." The jury had found him not guilty. True, Preston observed, the prosecution had been weak. But he praised all three of his lawyers for their great skill and cleverness. What the captain hadn't done, in his rush from jail, was pause and thank his lawyers in person. John Adams noted the lapse in his diary.

As the trial of the remaining soldiers proceeded in early December, Colonel Dalrymple wrote to General Gage to complain about their defense. This time, Dalrymple said, the lawyers were holding back much evidence, and he was right.

Josiah Quincy, at the age of twenty-six, was at least as wholeheartedly devoted to the law as John Adams, and he was determined to win the case. An older brother had died of tuberculosis, and there were signs of erosion in Josiah's frail body, but he was a handsome and smiling young man who radiated goodwill to everyone except Thomas Hutchinson. For years, Quincy had been denouncing Hutchinson's administration, and, as chief justice, Hutchinson had retaliated by denying Josiah the long robes of a barrister; instead, he had to plead his cases in street clothes.

To save his clients, Quincy now wanted to put the town of Boston on trial. Despite his own devotion to the patriots' cause, he hoped to show—in far greater detail than John Adams had permitted during Preston's trial—the provocations the British troops had been responding to. Samuel Adams hadn't attended the captain's trial, but he was in court this time to see that at least the soldiers who had fired were punished. From his spectator's seat, Adams took notes and sent advice to the prosecution. The case would be damaged, perhaps fatally, if Josiah Quincy called witnesses to prove that there had been a premeditated plot to drive the soldiers out of Boston.

When John Adams heard that Quincy intended to do just that, he moved to quash it. If Quincy put the town on trial, Adams said, he would quit the case. The threat worked. Quincy canceled some witnesses and scheduled others in their place. Even with that shift of tactics, a parade of men testified to the violence of the attack, first against the sentry and then against the file of soldiers. The slave Andrew was called again to testify to Crispus Attucks' assault on one of the British privates. Samuel Adams listened glumly, aware that Andrew's testimony was having a significant effect, especially when Oliver Wendell, a man of undeniable honor, vouched again for his slave's truthfulness. It was small consolation for Adams to reflect that no man knew less of the real character of a servant than his master.

· There was worse to come. Dr. John Jeffries, a Harvard classmate of Josiah Quincy, had been treating Patrick Carr for his wounds until, four days after the shootings, the Irish boy died. Jeffries had questioned his dying patient often about the circumstances of the fatal night, and each time the boy had given the same answers. "I asked him," Dr. Jeffries testified, "whether he thought the soldiers would fire." Carr answered that he had thought they would fire much earlier. Jeffries asked whether he thought the soldiers had been abused a great deal. Carr said he thought they had been.

On and on the patriots' young martyr defended his assailants from beyond the grave. Yes, the soldiers would have been injured if they hadn't fired—Carr had heard many voices crying, "Kill them." Did they fire in self-defense or purposely to kill civilians? In self-defense. And, in a final poignant moment, Carr told the doctor that he did not blame the man, whoever he was, who had shot him.

It was all hearsay evidence, but when Josiah Quincy put the next question, "Was he apprehensive of his danger?," it became admissible. Colony law permitted unsworn testimony from someone who knew he was dying: no man facing the ultimate judgment would use his last breath to lie. Samuel Adams' rebuttal from the sidelines pointed out that Carr, an Irishman, had probably died a Roman Catholic. Protestant Boston could make up its own mind how much his last words were worth.

John Adams offered the final summation. Samuel Adams had been arguing that a few harsh words from the crowd didn't give the soldiers license to kill. John Adams had never shared his cousin's tolerance for mobs, even when they were supporting his cause. For the sake of those jurors who had never heard a Boston mob, John Adams tried to recreate one. A whistle from one boy in the street was no formidable thing, he admitted. But a mob's whistling, along with its shouting, became a most hideous shriek—almost as terrible as an Indian war whoop. John Adams used his summation to remind his audience that, under the law, everyone who had joined in an illegal assembly was guilty of every crime a mob might commit. But to pacify the Sons of Liberty, Adams claimed that an insurrection was always due directly to despotism from the government.

Adams spoke until the court adjourned at 5 P.M. Continuing the next morning, he showed how a man could seem to be direct and forthright and yet serve the patriots' cause. "We have been entertained with a great variety of phrases to avoid calling this sort of people a mob," John Adams said. "Some call them shavers, some call them geniuses. The plain English is, gentlemen, most probably a motley rabble of saucy boys, Negroes and mulattoes, Irish teagues and outlandish jack tars. And why should we scruple to call such a set of people a mob, I can't conceive, unless the name is too respectable for them. The sun is not about to stand still or go out, nor the rivers to dry up, because there was a mob in Boston on the fifth of March that attacked a party of soldiers."

But then, he added, "Soldiers quartered in a populous town will always occasion two mobs where they prevent one. They are wretched conservators of the peace."

Robert Treat Paine, John Adams' longtime rival at the bar, summed up for the crown. Tired and sick, Paine made an uninspired case, rousing himself only when he turned one of Adams' arguments back on him by claiming that if one soldier was guilty, all must be found guilty. Paine did not point out that three of the six privates who marched out on the line—Matthew Kilroy, William Warren and John Carroll—had been among the brawlers at the ropeworks.

The jurors were out for two and a half hours. When they filed back into the courtroom, the clerk asked, "Gentlemen of the jury, are you all agreed in your verdict?"

"Yes," the twelve men answered.

"Who shall speak for you?"

"Our foreman." He was Joseph Mayo, a captain in the Roxbury militia.

The clerk directed the first of the defendants, the group's corporal, to identify himself. "William Wemms, hold up your hand. Gentlemen of the jury, look upon the prisoner," the clerk said. "How say you, is William Wemms guilty of all or either of the felonies or murders whereof he stands indicted, or not guilty?"

"Not guilty," said Mayo.

The clerk addressed the entire jury. "Harken to your verdict as the court hath recorded it. You upon your oath do say that William Wemms is not guilty."

The process was repeated with Privates James Hartigan, William McCauley, Hugh White, William Warren and John Carroll, all not guilty. But the jury had also decided that the soldiers had fired before it was absolutely necessary to their defense. Since Matthew Kilroy and Hugh Montgomery were the two soldiers whom witnesses had seen firing, Mayo's verdict for them was different: "Not guilty of murder, but guilty of manslaughter."

Those two men were held for sentencing, and the others were released. They walked into the streets of the town, and there—the patriots were proud to note—they were undisturbed.

Nine days later, John Adams was back in court to hear Kilroy and Montgomery sentenced. They were asked whether there was a reason they should be spared the death penalty. Each man pleaded the benefit of clergy, a remnant of medieval law that provided that defendants who could prove they were clergymen might insist on being tried by an ecclesiastical tribunal. Usually, the church's punishments were far less severe than those of a secular court. Since the law dated from the time when the clergy were the only literate class, a man could establish his status merely by reading Psalm 51, verse 1. It came to be called "the neck verse." By claiming the benefit, the two soldiers would escape with only branding by fire. Thomas Hutchinson had been asked to spare them even that punishment, but he and Colonel Dalrymple decided that the law should take its course. Still claiming that they were innocent, Kilroy and Montgomery held out their right hands, and Sheriff Greenleaf seared their thumbs.

Dalrymple shipped the two convicted privates and the acquitted men to join their regiment. In May the Twenty-ninth had been transferred from Castle William to forts in New Jersey, and now the colonel decided to send his men by boat. If he allowed them to march south, he suspected that they would all desert.

As the soldiers prepared to sail, Hugh Montgomery confessed to one of his lawyers that on the night of March 5, after being knocked down, he had been the one who shouted, "Damn you, fire!"

The outcome of the trials pained Samuel Adams. Writing as "Vindex" in the *Boston Gazette*, he launched a series of articles to persuade the town that justice had not been done. Adams' pseudonym provoked Thomas Hutchinson to make a despairing joke: "As it is the custom now for people to give their children two or three names, I could wish he would add 'Malignus' and 'Invidus' to make his names a little more significant." Adams was especially aggrieved by speculation in London newspapers that the Boston mob had planned to murder the sentry that night in order to plunder the king's coffers, which were kept at the Custom House. The Tories could not have riled Adams more than by accusing the patriots of greed. He also objected to the way Judge Oliver had dwelled on testimony about a man in a red cloak who had been seen haranguing the crowd on the night of the shootings. His wasn't the only red cloak in Boston, but it was the most notorious.

Despite his attempt to retry the case in the newspaper, there was no question that Samuel Adams' cause had suffered in the nine months since the shooting. At the height of the drama, Adams had humiliated Thomas Hutchinson. By the end of March, Hutchinson had sent his resignation to Lord Hillsborough in London. The job of governor, Hutchinson wrote, demanded a man of greater powers than his. He asked only to be allowed to resume the post of chief justice. But his letter was late in arriving. In the meantime, Francis Bernard had lobbied to have Hutchinson named as his replacement. When Hutchinson's resignation finally reached London, Hillsborough wrote to assure him that no one had ever given London more satisfaction than he. If Hutchinson accepted the governorship, he would never regret it. Against his instincts, Hutchinson let himself be persuaded. Two days after the jury returned its verdict on the British soldiers, Lord Hillsborough sent Hutchinson his commission as governor, along with a guarantee of an annual salary of fifteen hundred pounds sterling, paid directly by the crown.

Hillsborough explained that a governor would no longer be dependent on the spiteful moods of the Massachusetts legislature. From now on, his salary would be absolutely secure. It would come out of taxes raised on the sale of tea.

Patriots dumping tea into Boston Harbor   GRANGER COLLECTION

Tea
1771-73

For Samuel Adams, the year 1771 opened with Thomas Hutchinson entrenched as never before and with troubling defections from his own ranks. For months he had been unable to confide in James Otis, who, whenever he became overwrought, sought out Hutchinson with tearful apologies: "I meant well but am now convinced that I was mistaken. Cursed be the day I was born." Sane or raving, Otis professed a reverence for England and a respect for Parliament that embarrassed patriots like Adams and William Molineux. Even before the Massacre trials, Adams had decided that he must strike Otis from the list of Boston candidates for the legislature. Otis had been incensed, and when John Adams agreed to serve in the House for the first time, Otis railed at him about Samuel Adams' treachery and called John a damned fool. With the passing months, Otis' behavior became more bizarre. At night he broke windows in Town House. By day he stood at his own window, firing a gun into the air. At last James Otis was bound hand and foot and trundled into a cart. His family drove him to a farm outside Boston, where they hoped his disordered mind would find peace.

Engineering John Adams' election to the House may have been Samuel Adams' proof to his cousin that his reputation among the patriots wouldn't suffer from defending Preston and the British soldiers. John Adams took no cheer from his election, but saw it instead as one more portent of doom. He had built his practice until he had more clients than any other lawyer in Boston. Being plunged further into the political maelstrom would mean ruin for his family and, given his precarious health, death to him. At home, when he informed his wife of this latest honor, Abigail Adams burst into tears.

To punish the town of Boston, Thomas Hutchinson had ordered the legislature moved again to Cambridge; John Adams joined in condemning the move. And despite signs of favor from the patriots, Adams was insulted on the street for his role in the recent trial. One February night his nerves broke. "Never in more misery in my whole life," Adams wrote the next day. "God grant I may never see such another night." He resolved to leave Boston. At the end of the legislative term two months later, he took his family back to Braintree. He would divide his time between the law and his farm. "Farewell, politics," he wrote.

For Samuel Adams, another loss was even more alarming: John Hancock was starting to slip away. Hancock had long been skittish, and after the Massacre he was threatening to renounce his House seat because he was dissatisfied with the recent vote. He had received only 511 of the 513 votes cast. Samuel Adams urged him to change his mind, reminding him that one of the two negative votes had been Hancock's own.

Adams' letter was a studied blend of flattery and challenge. "You say you have been spoken ill of. What then?" Would Hancock resign because of one contemptible person, who had perhaps been bribed to vote against him? Adams signed his note "Your affectionate friend and brother." It had its effect; Hancock stayed in the House.

But during a brief return to lucidity, James Otis appeared in Boston, arguing that the governor had the right to convene the legislature anyplace he chose. Hancock also took up that position, against the two Adamses. Nothing done by a man as wealthy as Hancock went unscrutinized. Hutchinson wrote to London of a falling out between Hancock and Samuel Adams. "Some of my friends blow the coals," Hutchinson wrote, "and I hope to see a good effect." Lord Hillsborough told Hutchinson that, on command from the highest authority, he should promote John Hancock at every occasion.

Hutchinson's own career had been built on patronage, and he hoped to win Hancock over with similar honors. First he named him colonel of the cadets, although that appointment was scarcely a bribe. Hancock certainly loved the finery of the uniforms, but it was his dedication to the cadets over the past six years that had led them to elect him unanimously as their colonel. Hutchinson was simply ratifying a popular choice. But if Hancock also wanted to be promoted from the House to the Council, this might be the time.

Samuel Adams watched those overtures carefully, even though much of what was separating him from Hancock was beyond his control. His wealthy friend was ailing, tired, ready to compromise, and for Samuel Adams compromise meant surrender. The wrangle over the location of the legislature went on for months, with Adams making it one more test of the limits of royal authority. Hancock and the House speaker, Thomas Cushing, were prepared to be more flexible, and they suggested that the House ask Hutchinson to move the legislature back to Boston only because of the inconvenience in traveling to Cambridge. Samuel Adams had the votes to defeat that face-saving motion.

Before the next session, Hancock and Cushing called on Hutchinson to ask what his terms were for returning the House to Boston. Hutchinson said he could not agree to any undercutting of the king's authority. His visitors explained that they would accept his condition but that Samuel Adams would oppose them. Hutchinson took heart from this proof of a rift among the patriots and warned them against Adams' cunning.

Late in May 1772, Hancock was able to persuade the House to make a moderate request for the return to Boston. The governor replied with equal moderation, and the move was made. During that same session, the House elected Hancock to the Council. In the new spirit of unity, Hutchinson said he would approve him. Here was John Hancock's reward. For more than a year he had demonstrated his independence, scored a victory over Samuel Adams and warned Adams not to take him for granted. Now that he had proved his point, he refused Hutchinson's bribe and declined a seat on the Council.

Samuel Adams had learned his lesson. He reached out his hand and Hancock accepted it, commissioning John Singleton Copley to paint two portraits, one of himself, one of Adams. When Hancock hung the pictures in his parlor, the Tories recognized that New England's greatest fortune was pledged again to their defeat.

At about noon on a June day in 1772, Captain Benjamin Lindsey sailed his sloop out of the harbor at Newport, Rhode Island, with another ship chasing him. It was the *Gaspee*, which had been sent to Narragansett Bay that spring to cut down on smuggling. From the time the *Gaspee* arrived, its commander, Lieutenant William Dudingston, had been battling Newport's captains and crews. The local merchants complained that Dudingston was stopping every kind of vessel, even small boats heading to market. Whenever Dudingston was challenged, he refused to show his authorization papers, and when he uncovered smuggled goods he ordered them shipped to Boston, even though the law required that the shipowner be tried in the colony where his goods were confiscated.

Protests had become so loud that Rhode Island's governor sent his sheriff to summon Dudingston and demand to see his authorization. Dudingston was as obstinate on land as he had been aboard the *Gaspee*, and his commander, Rear Admiral Montagu, upheld his bad manners. From Boston, Montagu wrote to the governor, calling his challenge to Dudingston insolent and warning him never to send his sheriff aboard a king's ship on such a ridiculous errand. Admiral Montagu added that he had heard rumors that the people of Newport were talking about fitting out an armed vessel and using it to rescue any ship the *Gaspee* detained. Let them try it, Montagu warned, and they would be hanged as pirates.

On this day, Lieutenant Dudingston was trying to maneuver the *Gaspee* so that he could board Captain Lindsey's sloop. But, some seven miles below Providence, Lindsey hove about at the end of Namquit Point, and Dudingston ran the *Gaspee* aground as he tried to change course. Captain Lindsey continued up the river, arriving about sunset at Providence, where he spread the happy news of the *Gaspee*'s distress. The seamen knew that it would be well after midnight before the tides could lift Dudingston's schooner free.

John Brown, a respected Providence merchant, decided that this was the town's chance to be rid of Dudingston's harassment. He sent one of his shipmasters to collect eight of the largest longboats in the harbor, each with five sets of oars. The boats were taken out to Fenner's Wharf with their oars and rowlocks well muffled.

As the shops were closing, a man marched down the main street of Providence, beating a drum. He directed anyone who wanted to help destroy the troublesome ship to a house on the wharf. Ephraim Bowen, nineteen years old, heard the call. At 9 P.M., with his father's gun and his own powder horn and bullets, he went to the meeting spot. The room was already filled. Some men were going to the kitchen next door to cast their bullets. At ten o'clock the group crossed the wharf and boarded the longboats. Each boat had a sea captain to guide it.

Silently, the protesters rowed the boats into a line and moved toward the *Gaspee*. They got within sixty yards of their target before a sentinel called, "Who goes there?" They gave no answer. A minute later, Lieutenant Dudingston, in shirtsleeves but with a pistol in his hand, mounted the starboard gunwale and called, "Who comes there?"

The second time, Captain Abraham Whipple shouted back, "I am the sheriff of the county of Kent, God damn you! I have got a warrant to apprehend you, God damn you! So, surrender, God damn you!"

A man standing in the boat with Ephraim Bowen said, "Eph, reach me your gun and I can kill that fellow." Bowen handed him the gun, and before Captain Whipple had finished his cursing the man fired through the darkness at Lieutenant Dudingston and exclaimed, "I have killed the rascal!"

In less than a minute after the challenge, the boats were alongside the *Gaspee* and the colonists were boarding without a fight. At the sight of their wounded commander, the crew on deck melted away.

A medical student in the raiding party, John Mawney, grasped a rope from the *Gaspee*'s bow and tried to swing himself on deck.

The rope slipped and he fell to his waist in water. When he recovered and boarded the schooner, Mawney found his friends tying the hands of the crew with tar-coated string. John Brown saw him and beckoned him to the deck. Brown told him not to mention any names but to go immediately into the cabin. There was a man bleeding to death inside.

Mawney entered the cabin. Lieutenant Dudingston was sitting huddled under a thin white blanket with blood pouring from his wound. Mawney saw that a musket ball had ripped open the lieutenant's groin, five inches below his navel. He feared that the femoral artery had been severed, and he undid his waistcoat, took his shirt by the collar and began tearing it for bandages.

Dudingston stopped him. "Pray, sir, don't tear your clothes. There is linen in that trunk."

Mawney called on one of the raiding party to break open the trunk and start to tear linen and to scrape lint. The other man tried, but the linen was too new and stiff to raise lint from it. Mawney had pressed the heel of his left hand against Dudingston's wound, and he directed his helper to slip his hand underneath Mawney's own and press hard to keep the blood stanched. With that, Mawney tore the linen into compresses, stacked them six deep and told the other man to raise his hand. Mawney slapped the compresses into the gaping wound, wrapped another strip firmly around Dudingston's thigh and pulled it tight.

As Mawney worked, other voices were calling to him. Finally the cabin door was forced open, and men from the raiding party rushed in to destroy Dudingston's liquor supply. Mawney broke each bottle under the heels of his boots while others in the party carried Lieutenant Dudingston out of the cabin to one of the longboats. The rebel leaders told the *Gaspee*'s crew to collect their clothes and other belongings, put them onto the boats and set out for shore. One of the raiding boats stayed behind to set the *Gaspee* on fire. From a distance, the Rhode Islanders watched it burn down to the water line. Dudingston was put ashore at Pawtuxet, along with five men and a blanket for carrying him.

Almost everyone understood that since a king's officer had been badly wounded and a king's ship destroyed, secrecy was essential. Yet the next morning one young raider, Justin Jacobs, was found standing on the Great Bridge in Providence, wearing Lieutenant Dudingston's gold-laced beaver hat and telling everyone about the exploit. Other men from the expedition told him to take off the hat and shut up.

Rhode Island's deputy governor, Darius Sessions, called on Lieutenant Dudingston that same day to make amends on behalf of the colony. He offered anything—money, surgeons, transfer to another place. The lieutenant asked that his men be collected and sent to Newport or Boston. But he refused to tell Sessions what had happened. Dudingston had let his ship be taken away from him, and if he lived he faced a court-martial. But if he died, Dudingston wanted the night's humiliation to die with him.

When Thomas Hutchinson heard about the burning of the *Gaspee*, he said that if so flagrant an insult to England was ignored, all friends of the government would despair. But this indignity would surely rouse the British lion, which Hutchinson thought had been asleep these past four or five years. He decided that executing a few of the raiders would be the only effective way to prevent further attacks. At its last session, Parliament had extended the death penalty until a man could now be hanged for destroying so much as an oar on one of the king's boats.

The alarm quickly reached London. The attorney general called the burning five times as serious as the Stamp Act protests. But revenge would not be easy. Hillsborough ordered Admiral Montagu to go to Rhode Island and arrest the raiders. Then, within a week, Hillsborough resigned as secretary of state for the American Department, and William Legge, second Earl of Dartmouth, replaced him. The change held up Montagu's mission.

With London in confusion, the Rhode Island patriots sought the expert counsel of Samuel Adams. A group of men, including the deputy governor, wrote to ask him what to do next. Adams agreed with Thomas Hutchinson that the *Gaspee*'s burning should open some eyes. But Adams wrote that it was the American colonists, not the British, who had been "too long dozing upon the brink of ruin." The *Gaspee* affair should unite them again. Colonists must realize that an attack on one province was an attack on them all.

After pondering further, Adams wrote to Darius Sessions again: "I have long feared this unhappy contest between Great Britain and America would end in rivers of blood. Should that be the case, America, I think, may wash her hands in innocence." Still,

Adams said, that dreadful calamity should be prevented if at all possible. He urged Sessions to dissuade Rhode Island's governor from cooperating with the royal commission being established to investigate the burning. The governor's participation would only make the inquiry legitimate. And Rhode Island should draft a circular letter to tell the other colonies its side of the affair.

For the Tories, the episode was winding down to an unsatisfactory end. The official inquiry established that many of the raiders seemed to be gentlemen, although no specific names were cited. Lieutenant Dudingston recovered from his wound and tried to send a gold buckle to the man who had saved his life. It went unclaimed. Admiral Montagu's solution for quelling the lawless people of Rhode Island was to ask London to send him warships.

Ever since the collapse of the nonimportation agreements, Samuel Adams had been casting about for a new way to bolster patriot spirits. Reviving the circular letter was his best inspiration. On behalf of the town of Boston, he drafted a pamphlet that attacked Hutchinson for accepting his governor's salary directly from the crown. Each town in the colony was asked to endorse it. At first Thomas Hutchinson scoffed at the pamphlet as a puny weapon. Even in Boston, the governor wrote, the Whigs had not been able to revive their mob, and now they were trying to correspond with towns around Massachusetts, "which is such a foolish scheme that they must necessarily make themselves ridiculous."

For once, Tory optimism did not seem misplaced. James Warren reported to Samuel Adams from Plymouth about the neighboring towns he had been canvassing. "They are dead," Warren said, "and the dead can't be raised without a miracle."

"*Nil desperandum,*" Samuel Adams chided him. Never despair. "That is a motto for you and for me. All are not dead; and where there is a spark of patriotic fire, we will rekindle it."

What did it matter that the Tories were laughing at their efforts? Samuel Adams said he knew they would, but gradually his faith in the tactic was justified. Endorsements of Boston's position began to come in from the western towns—from South Hadley, Petersham, Leicester and Lenox; from Essex, Lynn, Marblehead. Even from Plymouth, where James Warren had lost hope. From Framingham and Medford. From Concord. Until more than a third of the two hundred and sixty towns in the province were allying themselves with Samuel Adams' position.

On March 12, 1773, the House of Burgesses in Virginia named eleven members to maintain a correspondence with the sister colonies. Four months after Samuel Adams had linked the towns of Massachusetts, the colony of Virginia was expanding his plan into a full-fledged network across America. It was made only of paper, but Adams had forged a union.

One day in London, Benjamin Franklin was reviewing America's affairs with a British friend. Franklin still expected a reconciliation between Britain and the colonies, and he had been angered when the Ministry in London sent troops to Boston. The other man told Franklin he was wrong. All the errors of recent years, he said, had been urged on Hillsborough and now Dartmouth by high-ranking American officials. Franklin claimed not to believe it. To convince him, the friend returned a few days later with a stack of letters.

They had been written between 1768 and 1771 to Thomas Whatley, one of the chief authors of the Stamp Act. Fourteen were from Thomas Hutchinson, and several had come from Andrew Oliver at the time he accepted the post of stamp master. Other Tories had also written frankly and unguardedly to keep Whatley informed of events in the colony. Hutchinson's correspondence offered nothing that he hadn't already said publicly many times, but when Franklin saw six of his letters he grasped their value at once. He got permission to send the originals to Boston, but the man who had provided them made certain stipulations: Whatley's name was to be erased from each letter; no copies were to be made in America; and the letters were to be shown only to a few patriot leaders and then returned to England. Franklin insisted that his only motive in sending off the packet was to ease the bad feeling between the Americans and the London Ministry. The letters reached Thomas Cushing, the Massachusetts House speaker, at the end of March 1773.

History was repeating itself; the patriots remembered the time, four years earlier, when Francis Bernard's letters had helped to destroy him. But then Edes and Gill had been able to publish them. Cushing wrote to Franklin that if Hutchinson's letters were to prove equally damaging, they must be released. Franklin consulted with his friend and replied that the letters still couldn't be copied or published, but they could be kept in America for as long as they were useful, and they could be shown to anyone.

Rural life had palled quickly for John Adams, and he had returned to politics. Making the rounds of Superior Court, he took along Hutchinson's letters and let them be read in the towns beyond Boston. As early as 1768 Samuel Adams had been suggesting that Hutchinson was engaged in a secret correspondence aimed at destroying America's liberties. Now, although Adams didn't have evidence, he had raw material that could be passed off as proof. But because of the restrictions on the letters, Adams didn't believe they were proving useful, and he felt it was his duty to resolve the dilemma.

Over the next month, the patriots hinted that the letters would bring many dark things to light. The *Massachusetts Spy*, a new Whig newspaper underwritten largely by John Hancock, reported on June 3, 1773, that the amazing discoveries in the letters would make tyrants tremble. A week later, Samuel Adams announced that copies of the letters had arrived in Boston independently of those that Franklin had sent. To buttress that claim, John Hancock swore on the House floor that someone had passed this second set of letters to him on Boston Common. No one was fooled, least of all Benjamin Franklin. The copies were a ruse, he said, concocted to let the House break its pledge to him.

On June 15 the letters were published and went on sale, and Americans learned no more than what Hutchinson had said six months earlier during a debate with the legislature—that he believed that a colony because of its distance from the parent state could not enjoy every liberty of the citizens at home. But somehow that same point became far more sinister in a private letter, and Hutchinson was burned in effigy as far away as Philadelphia.

Writing as "Novanglus" in the *Boston Gazette*, John Adams denounced the governor as a vile serpent. In arguing for any abridgement of English liberties in America, Adams wrote, Hutchinson must surely be mad. Josiah Quincy, ignoring his earlier defense of the British soldiers, spoke now of their victims. He called

Hutchinson "the man against whom the blood of our slaughtered brethren cries from the ground."

Governor Hutchinson stood by helplessly as his letters were woven with those of other Tories into irrefutable proof of a conspiracy. Throughout America he was being accused of promoting views that he had never expressed, and his explanation of the limits on colonial freedom became, to readers, a call for England to deprive America of all her rights. That last slander, Hutchinson decided, was as though the patriots had accused King David of saying, "There is no God." But what court could clear his name? The Massachusetts House was demanding that Hutchinson and his lieutenant governor, Andrew Oliver, be removed from their posts. That petition would go to the Privy Council in London, and Hutchinson could hope that its members would absolve him of the patriots' charges, but the investigation might take months.

Hutchinson wrote to Lord Dartmouth, asking for a leave of six to nine months. If necessary, he would sail to England during that time to defend his reputation. But he was sixty-two years old and prone to seasickness, and he hoped to be spared the voyage. As he waited for a response, communication with England seemed to be slower than ever. The summer passed without Hutchinson receiving word on either the Massachusetts petition or his request for a leave. Cursed on every side in a colony he still loved, the governor waited for instructions.

One afternoon in the last days of the nonimportation agreement, John Adams had dined at John Hancock's mansion along with the two patriot doctors, Joseph Warren and Benjamin Church. When a green tea was served, John Adams hoped to himself that it had come from Holland, not Britain. But at Hancock's table one could never be sure.

By late in 1773, John Hancock had imported four hundred chests of British tea, well over a million pounds. Despite the patriots' ban, tea had remained a lucrative business in Boston. Thomas Hutchinson had secretly invested almost all of his ready capital, some four thousand British pounds, in the stock of the East India Company. He estimated that Americans drank six and a half million pounds of tea each year. In London, tea merchants thought the figure was more like half that amount, but it was impossible to know since nine tenths of America's tea came in illegally. New York was another leading port for smuggled tea, and the customs officer there was told that if he wasn't overly diligent, he might expect thousands of pounds sterling each year from appreciative merchants. Thomas Hutchinson's salary as governor was only a fraction of those New York bribes, but his pay was linked to the tax on tea in Massachusetts.

When George III retained the tea duties in 1770, it was less to raise income than to insist upon his right to levy a tax on the Americans. Townshend's act had imposed the small import duty of threepence for every pound of tea, but it had also removed all duties in England from tea shipped to America. As a result, during the calm that followed the Boston Massacre legal tea from Britain cost less than smuggled tea.

But in 1771 the East India Company, once second only to the Bank of England among Britain's financial institutions, was near bankruptcy. To recover, the company raised the price of tea to three shillings a pound; tea in Holland cost only two shillings. Overnight, smuggling became profitable again. Then, in May 1773, Parliament offered the East India Company further relief by changing the law once more. In the past, the company had been required to sell its tea at a public auction. English traders bid on it and then exported it to merchants in America. Now the East India Company would be permitted to handle both shipping and sales. That would greatly lower the price, but English and American traders like John Hancock would be stripped of a great source of their revenue. The new system would benefit only those few men who were licensed by East India's monopoly to handle sales in the colonies. In Boston, five men comprised that favored group, including Thomas Hutchinson's two sons and a son-in-law. The governor swore, falsely, that he had done nothing to win the commissions for them.

This time, Bostonians were alarmed, even without prompting from Samuel Adams, that the new method for selling tea could be applied to other commodities. Throughout the colonies, men realized that other British companies might adopt a similar approach. Then all trade would disappear and Americans would be reduced to fur trappers and lumberjacks.

Each colony had its own idea for fighting the menace. In Philadelphia, John Dickinson, whose letters as a "Pennsylvania Farmer" had helped to repeal the Stamp Act, denounced the past record of the East India Company. "They have levied war," Dickinson wrote, "excited rebellions, dethroned princes and sacrificed millions for the sake of gain." An elderly citizen wrote to a Philadelphia newspaper to remind readers that years before, when tea was less popular, people had seemed both healthier and happier. A patriot physician in Boston agreed with him. He said that the introduction of tea to Europe from China in 1610 was responsible for spasms, vapors, apoplexy, palsy, dropsy, rheumatism and nervous fevers.

More colonists, however, were saying they would back a boycott of tea when the patriots also agreed to give up rum, and no one could be sure that the same threats from the days of the Stamp Act would work this time. In October 1773, four cargo ships laden with tea—the *Dartmouth*, the *Eleanor*, the *Beaver* and the *William*—set out for Boston. On November 2 the North End Caucus met and voted "that the tea shipped by the East India Company shall not be landed." Once again, the patriots, led by John Hancock and Samuel Adams, rallied at the Liberty Tree and demanded that the five new representatives of East India appear and resign their commissions. When they didn't obey, William Molineux took a delegation to their houses. But Hutchinson's son-in-law dismissed him curtly.

Clearly this crisis was beyond the powers of the Boston mob. Throughout November, Hancock presided over Town Meetings, and each time Faneuil Hall was packed. But Benjamin Faneuil himself, another of the five East India agents, ignored a threatening letter slipped under his door. Far away from the public meetings, Samuel Adams and his trusted colleagues were preparing a more adventurous plan. "One cannot foresee events," Adams wrote to a friend in London, "but from all observations I am able to make, my next letter will not be upon a trifling subject."

On Sunday, November 28, the *Dartmouth* arrived in Boston Harbor, carrying one hundred and fourteen chests of tea. Before dawn the next morning, a notice went up on trees and fences all over town: "Friends, Brethren, Countrymen—That worst of plagues, the detested tea shipped for this port by the East India

Company, is now arrived in this harbor. The hour of destruction, or manly opposition to the machinations of tyranny, stares you in the face. . . ."

The poster called upon every friend of his country to hurry to Faneuil Hall upon the ringing of the bells at 9 A.M. It had become a ritual that the crowd would assemble first at Faneuil Hall. When that proved too small, the populace would be marched through the streets to the Old South Meeting-house. Thomas Hutchinson could anticipate every maneuver. He was sure Samuel Adams had never been in greater glory.

The audience on Monday morning exceeded five, even six, thousand. Bostonians were ignoring the restrictions that had limited the size of the Town Meetings. I may not own enough property to qualify to vote, men said, but my sons will, and I am entitled to protect their future. The crowd voted unanimously to approve the proposition "that the tea should be returned to the place from whence it came, at all events." The meeting also appointed a committee of twenty-five, including Henry Bass and the silversmith Paul Revere, to keep watch night and day at Griffin's Wharf to make sure no tea was unloaded. The meeting stood adjourned until 9 A.M. the next day. The East India Company's five agents had become alarmed by the mounting hostility, and before sundown they withdrew to Castle William.

Tuesday morning, Thomas Hutchinson watched every prosperous merchant in Boston flock to the Old South Meeting-house. He still could not believe that they would press ahead in such madness, and he sent Sheriff Greenleaf to the meeting with a proclamation. Once inside the hall, Greenleaf asked for permission to read it. The crowd wasn't in a mood for another lecture from Hutchinson, but Samuel Adams spoke on the sheriff's behalf and he was allowed to proceed: "I warn, exhort and require you, and each of you, thus unlawfully assembled to disperse, and to surcease all further unlawful proceedings, at your utmost peril."

When Greenleaf finished, the crowd gave a loud hiss, and Adams revealed the full fury of his hatred for Thomas Hutchinson. "He? He?" Adams demanded. "Is he that shadow of a man, scarce able to support his withered carcass or his hoary head! Is he a representative of *majesty?*"

The meeting voted against dispersing. Hutchinson, who was being informed of events in the hall, noted with sour admiration that no irregular or eccentric motion had been permitted from the floor. It all seemed planned by a few persons, the governor decided. Perhaps even by a single man.

One of the *Dartmouth*'s owners, a twenty-three-year-old Quaker named Francis Rotch, had come from his home on Nantucket to negotiate on behalf of his ship. The *Dartmouth* had arrived with other cargo besides tea, which the crew had been allowed to unload. At the Town Meeting, Rotch readily agreed to send his chests of tea back to England. But because his ship already had been entered at the Custom House, he couldn't get clearance for its return trip until he paid the tea duty. And that duty couldn't be collected until the tea had been unloaded. If he tried to run his ship out of the harbor without a pass, the British authorities would be justified in sinking the *Dartmouth* or confiscating its load. Increasing Rotch's bind, the law gave him only twenty days to pay the tax or leave port. But he couldn't sail without a pass.

With the days racing toward a confrontation on December 17, the *Eleanor* arrived at the harbor. The patriots ordered the second ship to join the *Dartmouth* at Griffin's Wharf so that they needn't keep a separate watch. Five days later, the brig *Beaver* approached port, but smallpox had broken out during the voyage, and the ship was moored at an outlying island for scrubbing and fumigating. An announcement came from New York that the local tea agents had refused all responsibility for any tea sent there, and a letter from Philadelphia said its agents had resigned outright. The letter also jeered at those Boston merchants who had violated nonimportation agreements in the past and asked whether they could be trusted in the current crisis.

On December 11, Samuel Adams summoned Francis Rotch before a town committee to ask why he had not honored his pledge to return the tea to England. Rotch claimed that it was impossible to get a pass. Samuel Adams advised him to try anyway. "The ship must go," said Adams. "The people of Boston and the neighboring towns absolutely require and expect it." Adams himself and the two doctors, Warren and Church, would be among a committee of ten who would accompany Rotch to the Custom House. They would be on hand merely to witness his request, Adams said.

Making his plea to the customs collector four days later,

Francis Rotch saw the presence of the patriots differently. They were compelling him, he told Joseph Harrison, to demand a clearance for the *Dartmouth* with the tea still on board. The collector was unmoved. Rotch could have the pass only after his tea was unloaded. That was December 15. Rotch had two days before His Majesty's warships, the *Active* and the *King Fisher*, would resolve his dilemma for him.

The patriots didn't need handbills to draw a crowd on the morning of Thursday, December 16. Boston's male population, along with two thousand onlookers from neighboring towns, were either jammed into the Old South or ignoring a cold rain and standing in the street, straining to hear at the windows. The patriots had learned that the fourth ship, the *William*, had been destroyed when it ran aground on Cape Cod, but that its cargo had been saved. The *Beaver* had been fumigated and had entered the port. There were now three tea ships at Griffin's Wharf.

Rotch was told he must make one last appeal. He must go to the governor and ask Hutchinson for a pass out of Boston Harbor. Hutchinson was seven miles away at his country house in Milton. To allow Rotch ample time for the trip, the meeting adjourned until 3 P.M.

Hutchinson was braced for a showdown. He had written to Lord Dartmouth a day or two earlier that this was surely the time to put down Boston's anarchy. The governor had researched legal precedents and found that provincial law prevented him from issuing a pass to a ship that had not been cleared by customs. Hutchinson believed that he had always upheld the law, even against the mob. Now he had the security not only of the law, but also of harbor guns from the king's Navy. The only compromise he offered Rotch was that Admiral Montagu could tow the *Dartmouth* to Castle William. There, like the stamped paper of eight years ago, the tea could be stored until a more tranquil time.

Rotch protested that the mob would then turn its rage on him. He refused.

At that, Hutchinson made his denial official. To issue a pass would be to abet a violation of the Acts of Trade. Francis Rotch was left to ride back to Boston and report his failure to the Meeting.

The town had met again at three. When Rotch didn't appear,

the leaders used the free time to invite speakers from neighboring towns to report on the way their communities were giving up tea altogether. That testimony provoked a resolution that any drinking of tea was pernicious, and towns were advised to appoint committees of inspectors to prevent its use.

After two hours of speeches, the crowd was restless and calling to dissolve the meeting. But in the Long Room over the Edes and Gill printing office, Samuel Adams had plotted his response to the governor's certain refusal. He had consulted with Hancock, Molineux, Dr. Joseph Warren, Dr. Benjamin Church and a few dozen other patriots. The Meeting was persuaded to agree to an hour's extension.

The Old South was lighted with candles when Francis Rotch returned to Boston shortly before the new deadline. He told his audience that the governor had denied his pass. A cry went up, "A mob! A mob!" But the louder cries for order prevailed. Two more questions were put to Rotch: Would he order his ship back to England with its cargo of tea? No, said Rotch, that would ruin him. Would he unload the tea? Yes, but only if the authorities insisted upon it and if he had no other way to protect himself.

Samuel Adams rose from his chair and said, "This meeting can do nothing more to save the country."

That was the signal. First came a war whoop from the gallery. Then suddenly forty or fifty men who had been lurking at the church door burst inside. They were dressed as Indians and were sounding their own war call. The Old South exploded. Three blocks away, families could hear the shouts—"The Mohawks are come!" "Hurrah for Griffin's Wharf!" And, from those men who knew the plan, "Boston harbor a teapot tonight!"

The meeting broke up with Hancock calling above the tumult, "Let every man do what is right in his own eyes."

James Brewer, who made shipping gear, had volunteered his house near the wharf as a gathering place. As his friends arrived, his wife blackened their faces with burnt cork and sent them along to the pier. Paul Revere's Masonic Lodge usually met at the Green Dragon tavern, but the evening meeting had been canceled for lack of members, and Revere himself was headed for the harbor. The rebels disguised as Mohawks at the Old South had spent all afternoon in Benjamin Edes' parlor, painting their faces and guarding the door. Even Edes' son, Peter, was confined to another room, where he made quantities of rum punch for them. As they waited for night, the Mohawks consumed several bowls.

George Robert Twelvetrees Hewes, a shoemaker in his early thirties, went to a blacksmith's shop on Boylston's Wharf to daub grime on his face. Hewes was among the tradesmen John Hancock invited each year for a glass of Madeira on New Year's Day. Standing with James Caldwell near the Custom House the night of the Massacre, Hewes had caught Caldwell in his arms when he was felled. From the day Hewes first turned up at the Liberty Tree as a young shoemaker, people had made the same joke: Ah, they said, here is a man staking his awl for the good cause. Tonight Hewes was ready to do it again.

When he had darkened his face, Hewes went to a friend's house and borrowed a blanket. This was not the first night that colonists had smeared their faces. Nine years earlier, a crew rescuing a ship impounded in Rhode Island had taken that precaution. But this time the patriot leaders hoped to pass themselves off as Mohawks from Narragansett. They wrapped themselves in blankets, swathed their heads and carried a hatchet or an ax along with their pistols. They spoke in low grunts they thought approximated an Indian dialect. Only some of the group appeared in full disguise. Others did the best they could and, as the crowd grew, still more flocked to the pier with no disguise at all.

Walking together from a house on the wharf, two patriots passed a British officer who thought they were Indians and reached for his sword. One of the Mohawks drew a pistol, pointed it at the officer's chest and said, "The path is wide enough for us all."

After a steady drizzle throughout the day, the night had turned clear, and the moon shone brightly over the wharf. Leaders divided the volunteers into three ranks, each with about fifty men and a commander and a boatswain. George Hewes was so short that he had nailed another heel on his boot to persuade the army to accept him during the French and Indian War, and he was so frail that he had almost died from his smallpox inoculation. But, for this night's proceedings, he had one indispensable talent: he was renowned for the power of his whistle. Since talking was discouraged, Hewes was named boatswain to whistle orders for Captain Lendall Pitts. His cadre was made up of apprentices, carpenters, blacksmiths and bricklayers, all dressed in their oldest clothes and some sporting red woolen caps.

Low tide was just ending and the water had started to rise when the boarding parties jumped on the decks of the *Dartmouth* and the *Eleanor*. The *Beaver* was at anchor off the wharf, and it was hauled alongside on a rope by the third group. On all three boats, the work went forward in the way that Captain Pitts was directing his group.

After Pitts led his men aboard, he sent an aide with a polite message to the cabin of the first mate. Pitts asked for a few lights and the keys to the hold so that his men would damage the ship as little as possible. The patriots were pleased and relieved to hear that the mate was reacting like a gentleman. He surrendered the keys at once and sent his cabin boy for a bunch of candles. From the wharf, sailors were helping the Mohawks attach block and tackle to the chests of tea and hoist them from the hold. The silence was so total that the first blows of the hatchets on the chests could be heard far into Boston.

Some of the younger men wanted to follow the example of the *Gaspee* and set the ships on fire. They were dissuaded because a fire could spread to the town. Only the tea was to be destroyed. The Mohawks were in a jubilant spirit as they broke open each chest, shoveled the tea over the ship's rail into the water and threw the chest after it. One young man murmured, "What a cup of tea we're making for the fishes."

At anchor a few hundred yards away, the British naval squadron watched the steady and methodical destruction. Lamps and torches added to the moonlight and made Griffin's Wharf as bright as it had been at noon. On Atkinson Street at the foot of the wharf, the British commander, Admiral Montagu, surveyed the scene from a Tory's house. The Mohawks didn't know that the admiral had no orders to stop them. Reviewing his options, Montagu decided that opening fire would kill a number of bystanders. In fact, the crowd on the wharf had become so dense that onlookers were getting underfoot whenever the Mohawk leaders tried to pass between the ships. But the patriots thought retaliation could come at any moment, and the men were axing and shoveling furiously. Tea was piling so high on top of the water that some of it was falling back onto the deck and had to be shoveled out all over again. The younger men were thinking that they had never worked harder in their lives.

As George Hewes shoveled, he noticed the odd behavior of

a man named Charles O'Conner. O'Conner had made an incision in his coat's lining and was filling it with tea. When O'Conner saw Hewes reporting him to Captain Pitts, he made a run for the wharf. The other men sent up the cry "East Indian!" and Hewes grabbed him by the skirts of his coat and pulled him back on deck.

As they scuffled, O'Conner cursed him and said he would complain to the governor.

Hewes showed him a fist. "You had better make your will first!"

A band of men stripped O'Conner of his coat and kicked at him as he fled for the wharf.

By nine o'clock, the last of three hundred and forty-two chests of tea had been emptied into the harbor. The work had taken less than three hours. Hewes's scuffle with O'Conner had alerted the Mohawk leaders, who didn't want anyone to profit from the raid or be identified by telltale signs of tea. They directed each man to take off his shoes and shake them out over the railing. Then they ordered that the decks be swept clean of wood scraps and other debris and called up the first mate of each ship to testify that nothing but the chests had been damaged. As the Mohawks swarmed ashore, Captain Pitts was appointed their commander in chief. He formed them into ranks and marched them into town with their axes and tomahawks on their shoulders. A fifer played at their side. Everyone felt exhilarated, exhausted and content.

As they passed the house on Atkinson Street, Admiral Montagu threw open the window and hailed them. "Well, boys, you have had a fine, pleasant evening for your Indian caper, haven't you? But mind, you have got to pay the fiddler yet!"

Lendall Pitts shouted back, "Oh, never mind! Never mind, Squire! Just come out here, if you please, and we'll settle the bill in two minutes."

The men roared. The fifer piped a derisive tootle. Montagu slammed the window shut.

With the return home came an inevitable letdown. George Hewes burst in upon his wife, Sally, and regaled her with the whole adventure. "Well, George," she said when he had finished, "did you bring me home a lot of it?" Hewes was reminded again that his wife was more a tea-drinker than she was a Whig.

A young Boston woman named Betsy Palmer had just become a mother, and she was rocking her baby when she heard her gate open. She thought it was her husband returning from his club, and she opened the door to the parlor. There stood three Indians.

Mrs. Palmer screamed and started to faint until one of the Indians stepped forward and said in her husband's voice, "Don't be frightened, Betsy, it is I. We have only been making a little saltwater tea."

After the tea was dumped, Henry Purkitt and Edward Dolbin, two eighteen-year-old apprentices, had hurried back to Essex Street and their cots at the house of Samuel Peck, a barrelmaker. At 1 A.M. they heard Peck stealing in. The next morning they saw smudges of red paint behind his ears and were sure he had been one of their chieftains.

Samuel Sprague had smeared his face with soot from a chimney and boarded a ship, where he had recognized his master, a stonemason. At the shop the next day, neither man said anything about what they had done. The young Mohawks apprenticed to Tories had to be even more guarded. Robert Sessions, who worked for a lumber merchant, had been spotted at the scene, and the next day he slipped out of town. Ebenezer Mackintosh had come into Boston for the excitement, but he still knew too much, and patriot leaders persuaded him to travel north. In time, he became a shoemaker for a village in the Green Mountains.

Since the Mohawk chieftains had communicated only with grunts and gestures, there was intense speculation about who they had been. When George Hewes saw a flash of ruffles beneath one of the cloaks, he was convinced that the man was John Hancock. Hewes was also sure that Samuel Adams was on the scene. But in both cases he was mistaken. Hancock may have owned an undisclosed part interest in one of the ships, and Samuel Adams tended to think that his most valuable service was not on the front lines.

The next day, Boston's harbor looked less like a teapot and more like a vast dank beach. Shaped into dunes, the tea lay upon the water and clogged the sea lanes. Sailors had to row out to churn the sodden heaps and push them farther out to sea. As far away as Dorchester, tea was found spread like hay in long lines where the wind had carried it. But while the town was clearing away the traces, the patriots were eager to share news of their escapade with the other colonies. After only a few hours' sleep, Paul Revere volunteered to saddle his mare and carry a letter first to New York, then to Philadelphia. He set out on Friday morning, reached New York the next Tuesday evening and then sat up all night talking with his hosts. The message Revere carried was decidedly rosy. "We are in perfect jubilee," it began. "Not a Tory in the whole community can find the least fault with the proceedings." Revere took a ferry to New Jersey at dawn and rode to Trenton for another boat across the Delaware River to Pennsylvania. He had averaged sixty-three miles a day by the time he returned home with heartening news. The Sons of Liberty in both cities vowed to stand with Boston, whatever the consequences. Revere also reported that New York's merchants had been afraid that the tea headed to them would also be destroyed and had made a pact with the local Sons of Liberty to send it back to England. At that news, bells rang out all over Boston.

The account that Paul Revere carried south had been correct. Boston's Tories did admit that the whole affair had been conducted as correctly as a crime could be. Anonymous Mohawks even sent a lock the next day to one of the ship captains as a replacement for one they had broken. It was also true that the more moderate Whigs seemed to endorse the dumping. John Adams, who had denounced the Boston mob so eloquently, wrote in his diary, "There is a dignity, a majesty, a sublimity, in this last effort of the patriots that I greatly admire."

At the Green Dragon the Masons sang,

> "Rally, Mohawks! Bring out your axes
> And tell King George, we'll pay no taxes."

But throughout the other colonies, the Tories and the undecided colonists were astonished and outraged. Trying to mollify them, the patriots were describing the event as a party, even though at least ten thousand pounds sterling in private property had been destroyed. First had come the harrowing phrase "the Boston Massacre." Now there was the cozy "Boston Tea Party." Whatever the label, Thomas Hutchinson saw it as one more riot. He had been sure that Hancock and the other merchants would never put themselves in the position of having to pay for the tea. Because that was what they surely must do.

In London, news of the destruction was received incredulously. Lord Dartmouth hadn't even been informed that the East

India Company had shipped the tea. Now its dumping appalled even America's oldest friends. William Pitt, Lord Chatham, was certain the destruction had been criminal. He saw it as "no real kindness to the Americans to adopt their passions and wild pretensions." Benjamin Franklin termed it an act of violent injustice and recommended that the town of Boston immediately reimburse the shipowners.

By the time Franklin's advice reached Samuel Adams, South Carolina was reporting that its tea agents had resigned and the tea was rotting in cellars. From Philadelphia, Adams heard that a throng of five thousand people had persuaded the town's agents to resign. Events had moved more quickly than Franklin could have foreseen, and when his call for restitution reached Boston, Samuel Adams was curt.

"Franklin may be a good philosopher," Adams said, "but he is a bungling politician."

In London that winter, Benjamin Franklin was being assailed in ways that tested his philosophy. Attempting to act as a mediator, he was antagonizing both London and America. When he had agreed to serve as agent for the Massachusetts House as well as for Pennsylvania, his assistant, Arthur Lee, had assured Samuel Adams that Franklin was a mere hireling of the British Ministry. On the other side, Lord Hillsborough had become convinced that Franklin was abetting the colonies in their treason and refused to see him. When Dartmouth became minister, Thomas Hutchinson tried to turn him against Franklin as well.

London had been gossiping for weeks about who had supplied Boston with the Whatley letters. Franklin had managed to keep clear of the speculation. But in December William Whatley accused John Temple, a former customs commissioner, of stealing his father's letters, and the two men fought an inept duel. On Christmas Day, 1773, Franklin felt obliged to acknowledge his role. A month later he was called before the Privy Council, which was meeting to consider the demand from the Massachusetts House that Thomas Hutchinson and Andrew Oliver be removed from office.

For the occasion, Franklin appeared in an old-fashioned full wig and wearing his best suit of figured velvet. The man who would be questioning him, Solicitor General Alexander Wedder-burn, was no friend of America. He had once glanced through a copy of Samuel Adams' pamphlet on the rights of the colonies. "It told them of a hundred rights of which they had never heard before," he said, "and a hundred grievances which they had never before felt." Wedderburn had once caused a scandal in Edinburgh by abusing a judge in open court, and the British officials who packed the hall were primed for a similar performance.

With Franklin standing before him, Wedderburn began by praising Governor Hutchinson as a distinguished jurist and a scholar of proved integrity. Now, he said, the governor was the victim of thieves who had stolen his private letters in an attempt to ruin him. And the reason was clear—it was because Hutchinson had put a stop to the scheme of Dr. Franklin's clients to inflame their own colony and then the other twelve. That was their true motive for seeking Hutchinson's removal.

Wedderburn then turned to the letters. "Nothing then will acquit Dr. Franklin of the charge of obtaining them by fraudulent or corrupt means, for the most malignant of purposes," he declared as the galleries burst into applause.

Franklin had decided ahead of time on his strategy. Although he was sixty-eight years old, he would stand impassively during the entire tirade, which was running on for almost an hour. Whatever the provocation, he would not change his expression.

Wedderburn went on to say that it was Franklin, not Hutchinson, who should be stripped of his office. "I hope, my lords," he added, "you will mark and brand this man for the honor of this country, of Europe and of mankind." From this time on, men would hide their papers from Franklin and lock up their desks. Henceforth men would consider it libelous to be called "a man of letters."

As he endured the insults, Franklin was baffled. Why hadn't the Ministry seen the advantage of blaming Hutchinson and his allies for the frictions of the last decade? Then Britain could have changed her policy with no loss of dignity and could have restored harmony with America. Instead, Wedderburn chose to pillory him.

In its ruling, the Privy Council held that Thomas Hutchinson's letters were not at all reprehensible and called the petition for his removal scandalous. As Wedderburn greeted his admirers in the Council's anteroom, Franklin went home alone. The next day he received a letter telling him he had been dismissed as deputy post-master general for America. He also heard that William Whatley was suing him to collect any profits from the edition of letters the patriots had printed and sold. At first Franklin thought of sailing for home, but friends persuaded him he still had a role to play in London. His position was hazardous, but he decided that the worst thing that could befall him was prison.

All the same, Franklin added, he preferred to avoid that eventuality. Prison was expensive and vexing and dangerous to one's health.

Port Act
1774

WHEN Lieutenant General Thomas Gage traveled to London to explain the Americans to Lord North, he could draw upon his experience with the New Jersey woman he had married. The colonists would be lions, he said, as long as the British went on being lambs. But if Britain took resolute measures, the Americans would prove very weak. Send four regiments to Boston; that should end the problem. Although he had just come from America, General Gage said he was ready to turn around and direct those regiments himself.

New Yorkers might have found his belligerence out of character. To them, Gage had seemed distinguished for having a viscount as his father, for his patience, and for the dull conversation at his table. Some who knew them both thought Gage bore a striking resemblance to Samuel Adams, except that he lacked Adams' firmness. But his show of militancy was not altogether new. He had tried to force Francis Bernard to request British troops in 1768, and at least two years before that he had recommended that Boston be subdued by having two regiments stationed there.

Lord North sized up Gage as honest and determined, and George III, who hated disagreements, concurred. Fourteen years after ascending to the throne, George had turned out to be even more obstinate than Charles Townshend had predicted. Now, in Lord North and Thomas Gage, he had a pliant prime minister and a general who was telling him what he wanted to hear.

As a result, Solicitor General Wedderburn and Attorney General Thurlow drew up a bill to punish Boston properly. Rumors arose that Lord Dartmouth opposed it. Certainly Pitt, Lord Chatham, did. He called the measure wicked and cruel. Even North was said to have some doubts. But in London the anger over the deliberate insult to England in dumping the tea pushed the bill toward victory. In mid-March 1774 Lord North introduced it in Parliament, and several days later he rose to defend it. The bill, called the Port Act, would transfer the Boston customs office to Plymouth. From that day forward, no vessel would be permitted to enter Boston Harbor. Only boats carrying fuel or supplies for the town would be admitted, and even those would have to stop for inspection at Marblehead. The province's government would be moved to Salem. Boston as a great port and political center would be destroyed.

One member of Commons warned that only armed strength could enforce such oppressive acts.

"If a military force is necessary," North replied, "I shall not hesitate for a moment to enforce a due obedience to the laws of this country." The bill did not provide for lifting the penalties if Bostonians agreed to pay the East India Company for its tea. As North explained, "Obedience, not indemnification, will be the test of the Bostonians."

For all his resolve, North's was a temperate voice during the debate. One member of Parliament said that the town of Boston ought to be knocked about the ears and destroyed. Isaac Barré, who had named the Sons of Liberty, now supported Lord North, although members laughed when he exclaimed, "Boston ought to be punished. She is your eldest son!"

William Bollan, representing Massachusetts, asked to speak, but the House voted 170 to 40 against hearing him. Lord North said it would only mean listening to the colonies deny again that Parliament had the right to tax them. There was no enthusiasm, either, for one member's advice that it was time to give up the colonies altogether because they were becoming more a burden than an asset. North's opposition didn't even press for a formal vote. Edward Gibbon, working on his book about the collapse of ancient Rome, was one member who supported North. He wrote to a friend that the Port Act had passed unanimously because it seemed so mild. From the throne, George III jeered at the opposition's weakness, although he understood the stakes. "The die is now cast," the king told North. "The colonies must either submit or triumph."

The London merchants who traded with Boston remained convinced that the town would pay for the ruined tea. Forming a committee, they met with Lord North to guarantee the East India Company sixteen thousand pounds sterling—six or seven thousand pounds above the tea's value—if North would give them six months to negotiate with Boston before he closed the port. North asked whether they would answer for Boston's behavior if more tea was shipped there. The merchants knew better than that; on March 7 another load of tea had arrived in Boston and had been dumped almost casually into the sea. Lord North advised the merchants to return to their countinghouses and leave politics to him.

Their ease in passing the Port Act emboldened North's ministers to propose changes in the Massachusetts charter that Francis Bernard had once urged. One new bill would allow the king to name the governor's Council, rather than letting the colony's House select its members. The governor would be given sole power to appoint sheriffs and judges in the lower courts. In the greatest swipe at the patriots, each community would be limited to one Town Meeting a year and then only to elect its municipal officers. Whenever Samuel Adams wanted to call a special meeting, he would have to get the governor's permission. That last change reflected the ministers' ignorance of the realities of Boston. Hutchinson's attempt to disband a meeting had been hissed down. Lord Dartmouth seemed to understand the situation better than the other ministers, and he supported only the change in naming the Council. The other provisions were enacted over his protest.

The sweep of the new acts shocked those friends of America

who hadn't condoned the Tea Party. Isaac Barré attacked a provision that would prevent the colonies from holding their own trials of government officials in America. He had supported the Port Act, Barré said, only as "a bad way of doing right." With this bill, he told Parliament, "you are becoming the aggressors."

On April 9, 1774, Lord Dartmouth instructed Thomas Gage to leave for Boston at once in His Majesty's ship the *Lively*, to replace Thomas Hutchinson as governor. The king's dignity still required a full and absolute submission, Dartmouth said, but once that was given, the colony would regain its full privileges. Gage should use mild and gentle persuasion in winning the people of Boston over to the new laws.

General Gage had lobbied for the job. He arrived in Boston sixteen days before the Port Act would go into effect on June 1. Since no welcoming committee awaited him at the harbor, Gage joined Thomas Hutchinson at Castle William until festivities could be arranged. The Bostonians who might have turned out from courtesy to greet the man who was delivering them from Hutchinson were otherwise occupied. They were attending a Town Meeting, listening to Samuel Adams and the other patriots attack the Port Act. News of its passage had reached Boston four days earlier, and it was being denounced as intolerable.

The Tea Party had been a tonic for Samuel Adams, but he expected retribution and had been busy throughout the spring. For the last four years the anniversary of the Boston Massacre had been marked by a major oration in front of a massive crowd. Adams had always chosen the speakers. In 1772, when John Adams was still resisting a more active role in the cause, he had declined the honor. He was thirty-seven, he had told his diary, and too old. That year Joseph Warren had accepted the invitation. In March 1773 it was the other doctor, Benjamin Church. But the Tea Party had made it essential to have the most popular patriot of all, and if that man lacked the fluency of his predecessors Samuel Adams was happy to draft appropriate phrases for him. Adams' daughter Hannah watched as John Hancock came each day to consult with her father, but she was told she must never mention their collaboration. At 10 A.M. on March 5, 1774, at the Old South, John Hancock had delivered Samuel Adams' speech.

Throughout the month of March, Thomas Hutchinson's future had continued in limbo. In February he had booked passage on one of the large ships headed for London. Hutchinson intended to negotiate with the Ministry for a substantial pension and then sail back to America as a private citizen and devote himself to his history of Massachusetts. His children would stay behind to look after the trade that he considered an inheritance for his sons and a dowry for Peggy, who was now twenty-one. But when Peggy wouldn't hear of his making the trip alone, Hutchinson relented and booked a place for her.

On March 3, Hutchinson's lieutenant governor, brother-in-law and dearest friend, Andrew Oliver, had died from a bilious attack, and his death put an end to Hutchinson's travel plans. He couldn't leave the province with no lieutenant to take command. Nor could he expect any widespread mourning in Massachusetts over Oliver's death. Instead, the Boston mob had followed Oliver's hearse and had given three cheers when the onetime stamp master was lowered into his grave. At the burial grounds, men were overheard saying that they would like to put on that same show for their governor.

General Gage's arrival in May meant that Hutchinson could finally board the *Minerva* on the morning of June 1, 1774, the day the Port Act took effect in Boston. Just before his departure, dozens of merchants, lawyers, Episcopal clergymen and neighbors from Milton bestowed warm and affectionate tributes on him. Samuel Adams said that the testimonials came from obscure and insignificant people, mere law clerks, but that parting shot couldn't dull Hutchinson's pleasure at the outpouring of goodwill. Elisha Hutchinson had also insisted on going to England with his father and his sister, even though making the journey meant leaving his pregnant wife at home. It turned out to be a wise decision, since the passage was short but unusually rough and both Thomas Hutchinson and Peggy were continually seasick. They had barely landed, traveled from Dover to London and notified the Ministry of their arrival when Hutchinson received a note from Lord Dartmouth asking him to call that same afternoon.

At 1 P.M. on July 1, the two men met for the first time. After they had talked for an hour, Dartmouth suggested that the governor meet the king. Hutchinson protested that he was still weak from the voyage and not dressed for court. Dartmouth insisted. The king wouldn't be having another reception for some days. But after Hutchinson agreed to go, Dartmouth then took so long over his own toilette that the public audience had ended by the time they reached St. James's Palace.

All the same, Hutchinson was admitted to the royal presence. In the privacy of his chambers, the king—contrary to custom, Thomas Hutchinson noted happily—permitted his American visitor the privilege of kissing his hand. From his first question, George III was extremely amiable. "How do you, Mr. Hutchinson, after your voyage?"

"Much reduced, sir, by seasickness," Hutchinson replied. "And unfit, upon that account, as well as my New England dress, to appear before Your Majesty."

Dartmouth explained that since Hutchinson had just come ashore, he had assured him that his appearance would give no offense. The king graciously agreed.

George asked how the people had responded to Parliament's recent acts. Hutchinson explained that when he sailed he had known only about the shutting of the port and that had been extremely alarming to the people.

Dartmouth told the king that Governor Hutchinson had received a paper praising his conduct from merchants, clergy and lawyers. He showed it to George.

"I do not see how it could be otherwise," the king said. "I am sure his conduct has been universally approved of here by people of all parties."

Hutchinson said, "I am very happy in Your Majesty's favorable opinion of it."

"I am entirely satisfied with it," said the king. "I am well acquainted with the difficulties you have encountered and with the abuse and injury offered you. Nothing could be more cruel than the treatment you met with in betraying your private letters."

Hutchinson assured the king that in his letters he had tried to avoid dealing in personalities.

George asked, "Could you ever find, Mr. Hutchinson, how those letters came to New England?"

"Dr. Franklin, may it please Your Majesty, has made a public declaration that he sent them," Hutchinson replied. Speaker Cushing said he had shown them to only six people.

"Did he tell you who were the persons?" the king asked.

"Yes, sir." Hutchinson named the six but added that Cushing's list did not include the two Mr. Adamses.

"I have heard of one Mr. Adams," the king said. "But who is the other?"

"He is a lawyer, sir." Hutchinson could have volunteered much more about John Adams.

"Brother to the other?"

"No, sir, a relation." Hutchinson explained that John Adams had been a member of the House but was not currently, that he had been elected to the Council but had been refused a seat by the governor.

The king said he thought the episode of the letters had been strange and wondered aloud where Benjamin Franklin might be at the moment. Then, apparently still musing, the king asked, "In such abuse, Mr. Hutchinson, as you have met with, I suppose there must have been personal malevolence as well as party rage?"

For Hutchinson, the size of his pension could depend on his answer to that innocent question. It was vital that the king appreciate how much he had endured in his service. The upheaval in Massachusetts must not come to look like petty bickering among colonials. "It has been my good fortune, sir," Hutchinson began cautiously, "to escape any charge against me in my private character." Then he explained respectfully to George that the attacks had come only over what the king had required him to do.

George did not drop his line of pursuit. "I see they threatened to pitch and feather you."

Since Hutchinson was there to instruct the king, he would be thorough. "Tar and feather, may it please Your Majesty. But I don't remember that ever I was threatened with it."

Lord Dartmouth stepped in to protect the king from seeming to be wrong, since being contradicted could excite George to near-madness.

"What guard had you, Mr. Hutchinson?" the king then inquired.

It was not the time for Hutchinson to tell about his flights to Milton or the armed forces at Castle William. "I depended, sir, on the protection of Heaven. I had no other guard." He added that he had hoped the mob meant only to intimidate him. "By discovering that I was afraid, I should encourage them to go on."

"Pray," George asked, "what does Hancock do now? How will the late affair affect him?"

"I don't know to what particular affair Your Majesty refers."

"Oh! A late affair in the city," the king said vaguely. "His bills are being refused." He turned to Dartmouth, who this time couldn't help him.

Hutchinson recalled that there had been a minor flap between Hancock and a London merchant. "Mr. Hancock, sir," Hutchinson went on, since the king seemed intrigued, "had a very large fortune left to him by his uncle, and I believe his political engagements have taken off his attention from his private affairs."

"Then there's Mr. Cushing," said the king. "I remember his name a long time. Is he not a great man of the party?"

"He has been many years speaker. But a speaker, sir, is not always the person of the greatest influence." Hutchinson said it was Mr. Samuel Adams who was considered the opposer of government in New England.

"What gave him his importance?" the king asked.

"A great pretended zeal for liberty," Hutchinson answered, "and a most inflexible natural temper."

After some minutes while the king tried to puzzle out who the Congregationalists were and what they stood for, he changed the subject. "Pray, Mr. Hutchinson, does population greatly increase in your province?"

"Very rapidly, sir. I used to think that Dr. Franklin, who has taken much pains in his calculations, carried it too far when he supposed the inhabitants of America, from their natural increase, doubled their number in twenty-five years, but I rather think now that he did not." Massachusetts seemed to have doubled in that time, Hutchinson said, and there weren't enough settlers from Europe to account for the increase.

George took him up on that point. "Why do not foreigners come to your province as well as to the Southern governments?"

"I take it, sir, that our long cold winters discourage them. The Southern colonies are more temperate."

The king asked why Massachusetts raised no wheat, and Hutchinson explained that the mid-July heat tended to shrivel the wheat, and straw became musty and black. The people lived on coarser breads mixed from rye and corn.

"What's corn?" asked the king.

Hutchinson explained and added that some colonists preferred rye to wheat since it stayed moister.

"That's very strange." That was George's way of dismissing what he didn't understand. Returning to the more familiar ground of politics, he said he thought that New Yorkers were nearest to Boston in their opposition to the government.

"Does Your Majesty think nearer than Pennsylvania?"

"Why," the king granted, "I can't say that they do, of late. Rhode Island, Mr. Hutchinson, is a strange form of government."

Hutchinson agreed. "They approach, sir, the nearest to a democracy of any of your colonies," he said disapprovingly.

The talk turned to Indians.

"It looks, sir," Hutchinson ventured, "as if in a few years the Indians would be extinct in all parts of the continent."

"To what is that owing?" asked the king.

Hutchinson said he thought it was partly because they were dispirited "at their low despicable condition among Europeans who have taken possession of their country and treat them as an inferior race of beings." But the governor also blamed "the immoderate use of spiritous liquors."

The interview was running down. The king asked after Hutchinson's family and advised him to stay home for a few days to recover his health. With that, George withdrew.

Thomas Hutchinson had been standing in the royal presence for almost two hours, and Lord Dartmouth worried that he might be tired.

"So gracious a reception has made me insensible of it," the governor assured him. It had been one of the great days of Thomas Hutchinson's life, and he hurried to a notebook before he forgot any of it.

General Thomas Gage left Castle William after three days and entered Boston to the welcome of cannon fire from the king's ships in the bay and a coldly correct ceremony. Rumors were circulating that he had come to arrest the patriot leaders, and yet John Hancock, as commander of the cadets, was leading the general's escort. Gage's commission from George III was read out in the Council chamber, and the general was sworn in as Thomas Hutchinson's successor. A reception followed at Faneuil Hall, with many toasts to the king and a hiss when Hutchinson's good health was proposed.

Lord Dartmouth's orders to Gage had been specific. The king wanted the ringleaders of the tea affair caught and punished. But, thousands of miles from London, Gage began to draw back from his brave words at the Ministry. All of America was receiving word of the Port Act and the other "Intolerable Acts," and patriot newspapers were printing their texts with a thick black border. In towns around Boston, hangmen climbed up on their scaffolds to set copies of the acts on fire. Gage debated the wisdom of trying to enforce the Port Act by shutting down the trade in Boston's harbor, but he consulted with naval officers and customs officials, who reminded him of his duty. On May 26 he told the legislators that on June 1 they would start meeting in Salem. He received the House's list of newly elected Council members and vetoed thirteen of them, including John Adams. On June 1, 1774, he closed Boston Harbor.

Samuel Adams was determined to prevent Lord North from isolating Boston. He wrote to Arthur Lee in London that it was a "flagrant injustice" and "barbarous." Even in the evil history of Constantinople he found nothing to match it. As chairman of the Overseers for the Poor, Adams collected food to prepare for the inevitable shortages. In another circular letter he called on citizens of every colony to ask themselves "whether you consider Boston now as suffering in the common cause." That phrase touched the conscience of the continent, and one by one Committees of Correspondence pledged their complete support. In Virginia, the Burgesses declared June 1 a day of fasting and prayer, and Joseph Warren reported that a new group was being formed that would pledge to halt all trade with Britain until the Port Act was repealed. It would be called the Solemn League and Covenant.

For some months, Samuel Adams also had been floating the idea of a general congress of the colonies, a meeting that would be longer and more ambitious than the hurried gathering at the time of the Stamp Act. Writing under a pen name in the *Boston Gazette* the previous September, Adams had not only proposed the congress but also set out its agenda. Acting as independent but united states, the delegates should draw up a bill of rights, publish it around the world, and then send an ambassador to represent them at the British court. But, speaking for Boston, Adams couldn't be that radical. Instead, he reassured the moderate or timid colonists that no one in Massachusetts wanted to break with England.

When New York's Committee of Correspondence publicly proposed a meeting of all the colonies, Adams began to intensify his efforts. On June 7, 1774, the Massachusetts legislature convened in Salem. Adams was delayed. Ever since Gage had announced that he would soon be joined by four regiments, the Tory leaders had become brash again; now they taunted the patriots that their firebrand was afraid to show himself without the protection of the Boston mob. There was a rumor that Adams and Hancock had been arrested and would be shipped to England for trial. That was the mood in Salem when a Tory took a seat at the desk reserved for Samuel Adams as clerk of the House. Other Tories gathered around him there.

Adams appeared at last and made his way through the crowds at the door of the hall. Looking about, he saw that his place had been taken, and the man in a gold-laced coat showed no sign of moving. Adams stared at him and then addressed Thomas Cushing in a clear, firm voice. "Mr. Speaker, where is the place for your clerk?"

Everyone looked first to Adams, then to his chair. Cushing motioned him to it.

"Sir," said Samuel Adams, "my company will not be pleasant to the gentlemen who occupy it. I trust they will remove to another part of the House."

The Tories surrendered their beachhead. Adams had proved that though Salem might not be Boston it wasn't Newgate Prison.

During the first days of the session, Adams and his confidants lobbied discreetly on behalf of their secret plan. They knew that a supposed patriot named Daniel Leonard was reporting regularly to General Gage. To trick him, Adams' group pretended they were considering a payment to the East India Company for its tea. But on the first evening of the session Adams met with his nucleus of five men, and by the third night he had more than thirty members sworn to his side. To get commitments from a majority of the House took another week. On June 17, Adams struck.

Before he rose to speak, he instructed the doorkeeper to lock the House. None of the one hundred and twenty members present were to be let out, and no one else was to be let in. When he was sure no Tory could escape to General Gage, Adams introduced his resolution: Five delegates—James Bowdoin, Thomas Cushing, Robert Treat Paine, John Adams and himself—would meet with representatives from the legislatures of the twelve other colonies. The meeting would take place on September 1, 1774, at Philadelphia or any other site that was deemed suitable.

There was an immediate clamor, and some members demanded to leave the hall at once. Adams took the key from the doorkeeper and put it into his own pocket.

A vote was called, but before it could be taken a Tory member claimed to have become ill. When he was allowed to leave the chamber, he went directly to General Gage. This was Gage's first test, and he wanted to meet it firmly. He sent his secretary to dissolve the House. But the door had been locked again, and the key was still in Samuel Adams' pocket. A page was permitted to enter the hall to tell Speaker Cushing that Gage's secretary had brought a message from the governor. The page returned to say that the House chose to keep its door bolted.

The excitement was bringing out the people of Salem, and they filled the hallway and the stairs leading to the locked chamber. For lack of any other audience, Gage's secretary read out his order to them.

Behind the locked door, the House was acting with nervous speed to endorse Adams' plan. Only twelve members voted against sending the delegation. Since Gage was sure to refuse treasury money for the expedition, members voted to charge each town in the province a fee based on its last tax rolls. That should raise about five hundred pounds. After resolutions calling for the relief of Boston and a boycott of British goods, House members unlocked their door and obeyed the governor's order to dissolve their session.

Britain's Fourth and Forty-third Regiments landed at Long Wharf in mid-June 1774. The Fifth Regiment and then the Thirty-eighth arrived, then the Royal Welsh Fusiliers and companies of marines, until General Gage had an army of four thousand well-equipped men at his command to subdue a town of seventeen thousand. They camped on Boston Common. Most stores on the wharf had shut down, and men who could afford it were sending their families to the outlying towns. Real-estate values throughout Boston were dropping daily, and unemployment was rising. Sympathetic farmers and fishermen from the countryside sent carts of dried fish and corn, but Boston was suffering as Parliament had intended. Tories watched the suffering and decided to attack the patriots on their own territory. This time it was the conservatives who collected signatures to petition for a Town Meeting.

Because they had no jobs, even more men than usual could attend on June 27. After Samuel Adams was elected moderator, the crowd made its usual march from Faneuil Hall to the Old South, where a Tory offered a sweeping resolution. Boston should censure the conduct of its Committee of Correspondence, and the committee itself should be annihilated. Facing that challenge, Adams did not want to be trapped behind the moderator's desk. He announced that if the committee's conduct was going to be debated he would surrender his place, and Thomas Cushing agreed to take it. Adams went down to the floor of the Old South to hear out his enemies. The debate continued until dark and resumed at ten the next morning. When Adams chose to answer, his manner was less impassioned than earnest, speaking to the thousands of men as he had spoken to many of them individually along the wharves and at the Green Dragon.

"A Grecian philosopher," Adams said, "who was lying asleep upon the grass, was aroused by the bite of some animal upon the palm of his hand. He closed his hand suddenly as he awoke and found that he had caught a field mouse. As he was examining the little animal who dared to attack him, it unexpectedly bit him a second time, and it made its escape.

"Now, fellow citizens, what think you was the reflection he made upon this trifling circumstance? It was this: that there is no animal, however weak and contemptible, which cannot defend its own liberty, if it will only *fight* for it."

Almost fifty-two, Adams could have been the father of many of his lieutenants and the grandfather of some of the Mohawk apprentices at the Tea Party. For thirty years the people of Boston had watched him disdain money.

"For myself," Adams said, "I have been wont to converse with Poverty. And however disagreeable a companion she may be thought to be by the affluent and luxurious, who were never acquainted with her, I can live happily with her the remainder of my days, if I can thereby contribute to the redemption of my country.

"Our oppressors cannot force us into submission by reducing us to a state of starvation. We can subsist independently of all the world. The real wants and necessities of man are few."

If all others fail us, Adams concluded with a practical touch, we can live as our ancestors did, on the clams and mussels that abound off these Massachusetts shores.

When the Tory motion was put to a vote, the Meeting overwhelmingly struck it down. In its place, the town called on the Committee of Correspondence to persevere with its usual firmness. When his informants brought this news to General Gage, the new governor interpreted the vote much as his predecessor would have done. The better sort of people, he assured Lord Dartmouth, had tried to pay for the tea and to disband the Committee of Correspondence, but they had been outvoted by the lower class.

In another respect, however, Gage's perception differed from Hutchinson's. When the Ministry in London had suggested that Hutchinson buy Samuel Adams off with an honor or a pension, the governor had replied that such efforts would be worse than useless. Adams would use any new position as a better platform for further attacks. As for money, Adams had said, "A guinea has never glistened in my eye." All the same, bribery was a time-honored way of converting an enemy to a friend, and General Gage decided to try it. He sent a Colonel Fenton to call on Adams, empowered to bestow on him whatever rewards would end his opposition to the government. The figure might be one thousand pounds sterling for life for Adams and the same amount for his son.

Adams listened politely, even with a show of interest.

General Gage's advice was that Adams should not displease His Majesty further, Fenton continued. Mr. Adams should remember the penalties of the act of Henry VIII, which allowed political enemies to be sent for trial in England. He could avoid that peril by changing his course, and in the process make his peace with the king.

When Colonel Fenton had finished, he waited for Adams to name his terms. Instead, Adams rose from his chair and said, "Sir, I trust I have long since made my peace with the King of Kings. No personal consideration shall induce me to abandon the righteous cause of my country."

Showing the colonel to the door, Adams gave him a message

for his commander. "Tell General Gage it is the advice of Samuel
Adams to him no longer to insult the feelings of an exasperated
people."

    Virginia's day of fasting and prayer to protest the closing of
Boston's harbor was another sign that leadership in the House of
Burgesses was being wrested from the older members by younger
men—Patrick Henry, Richard Henry Lee, Thomas Jefferson. When
they first learned of Boston's plight, they shut themselves up in
the legislative library and rummaged through precedents to support their call for a day of mortification. They then asked the Burgesses' treasurer, who had a reputation for piety, to move their
resolution, and it passed unopposed.

    The same group, including Lee's brother, Francis Lightfoot
Lee, was meeting regularly now in the Apollo Room of the Raleigh Tavern, down the road from the Burgesses in Williamsburg.
Discussing how they should respond to the crisis in Boston, they
had come to agree with Patrick Henry: "United we stand, divided
we fall." They scheduled a convention for August 1, 1774, to pick
delegates for the meeting in Philadelphia.

    For the occasion, Thomas Jefferson had prepared an essay
called *A Summary View of the Rights of British America.* Jefferson was a little past thirty now, but his document rang with youthful energy. At a time when the king was still being toasted and
America's troubles were being blamed on his wicked or indifferent
ministers, Jefferson's pamphlet denounced George III directly for
a host of civil crimes. He even accused him of forcing slavery
upon the colonies—a practice, Jefferson added, that insulted the
rights of human nature. He ended his essay by urging the king
to be honest. Do your duty, he told George III, and mankind will
forgive you even your failures.

    Jefferson's vehemence might have been better received in
Williamsburg if he had been on hand to defend his position. Instead, he fell ill with dysentery on his way to the capital and sent
two copies ahead with his allies Patrick Henry and Peyton Randolph. Jefferson thought that Henry had probably been too lazy
to read the essay. Randolph, Jefferson's cousin, placed his copy on
the meeting table for the other delegates to look over. Although
they appreciated Jefferson's skill with language—"Let those flatter

who fear; it is not an American art"—his essay went further than the majority were prepared to go. The convention chose seven men to send to Philadelphia, some from the liberal faction, some from the moderate, all highly regarded in the Burgesses. Peyton Randolph got the most votes, with one hundred and four. Then Richard Henry Lee and George Washington. Patrick Henry drew eighty-nine votes. The final three were Richard Bland, Benjamin Harrison and Edmund Pendleton. Jefferson, with fifty-one votes, was not chosen.

The Virginia convention also provided its delegates with instructions. All British imports were to end on November 1, 1774. That included any newly purchased slaves. If London did not lift its punitive measures against Boston within one year, all American exports to Britain would stop, including tobacco.

As the delegates left for home, the newly elected representatives prepared for their trip to Philadelphia. Patrick Henry met Edmund Pendleton at George Washington's plantation, Mount Vernon, where they spent the night and lingered on for a noon dinner before leaving to cross the Potomac and stay overnight in Maryland. Washington, who had won a reputation for youthful bravery during the French and Indian War, had married an amiable widow with a tidy fortune behind her. As the men set out, Martha Washington bade goodbye to her guests. "I hope you will all stand firm," she said. "I know George will."

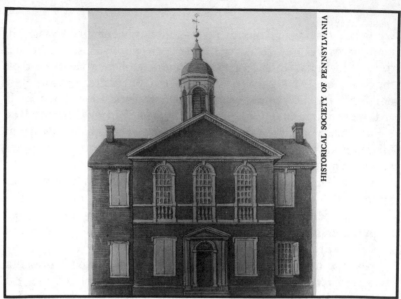

Carpenters' Hall, Philadelphia

Congress
1774-75

SAMUEL ADAMS may have helped to reconcile Bostonians to their own deprivations, but his speech at the Town Meeting also reminded them that if he was going to represent them properly in Philadelphia he needed some polish. About a week before he was due to leave for the Congress, Adams and his family were eating their evening meal when someone knocked at the door. Their visitor turned out to be one of Boston's most popular tailors, and he asked permission to measure Mr. Adams for a suit of clothes. Adams' wife and daughter tried to pry from him the name of the person who had sent him, but he said he was not at liberty to tell. The tailor took the measurements and left. The family had barely returned to the table when there was another knock. This time Boston's leading hatter wanted to establish the size of Mr. Adams' head. He was soon followed by a shoemaker and then by other craftsmen, all taking measurements, all refusing to say who had sent them.

A few days later, a large trunk addressed to Mr. Samuel Adams appeared at the family's front door. Inside were a full suit of clothes, two pairs of fine shoes, a set of silver shoe buckles, sets of gold knee buckles and gold sleeve buttons, six pairs of silk hose and the same number of good cotton ones, a goldheaded cane, a cocked hat and a new red cloak. Cane and buttons were stamped with the insignia of the Sons of Liberty.

Other friends were coming forward more openly. They put up a barn in place of Adams' old and decayed structure and made repairs on his house. One sympathizer asked diffidently whether it might not be said that Mr. Adams' finances were rather low.

Adams answered that it was true. But he said being poor was a matter of indifference to him so long as his *poor* abilities were of any service to the public.

At that the other man pressed on him a purse with fifteen or twenty johannes, a Portuguese gold coin that was worth more than three pounds sterling. Virginia had voted to pay its delegates half of one for each day's service.

When the day came for the Massachusetts delegates to leave, James Bowdoin could not go because of sickness in his family. Samuel Adams, John Adams and Robert Treat Paine met at Thomas Cushing's house and rode together to a dinner in their honor at Watertown. There the delegates said goodbye to fifty of their allies, including Samuel Adams, Jr., who had recently become a doctor. They left Watertown after the meal, but because the day was very hot they pushed on only as far as Framingham. Boston had sent them out in a lavish style that matched Samuel Adams' new wardrobe—a coach and four, preceded by two white servants, armed and on horseback, and four blacks behind them, all in livery, two riding horses and two as footmen.

As the party passed through Connecticut over the next days, every town rang its bells and shot off its cannon. Cheering men, women and children crowded the doorways, and John Adams, who was not entirely averse to pomp, reflected that no governor, no general of any army, had ever been treated to such ceremony. At Hartford they met Silas Deane, one of Connecticut's delegates, who gave the Massachusetts delegates a briefing on the New Yorkers they would be meeting: which were merchants and which were lawyers, who was the most popular—that was Philip Livingston—and how they were related by marriage. At each stop along their route to Philadelphia, the Massachusetts group were meeting patriots who were new to them and ready to debate all over again the arguments in James Otis' pamphlets of ten years ago.

This was John Adams' first trip out of his own colony, and he was flooded with impressions. In New Haven he saw a watermelon so red it looked painted. In New York the colonists had erected a solid lead statue of King George III on horseback, gilded and mounted on a towering marble pedestal. Adams had to admit that New York's streets were more elegant, its houses grander, than those he had left behind. Everything seemed to have been decorated, even the red brick buildings that Bostonians left unpainted.

Reaching New York had taken five days, and the Massachusetts party rested there. On Sunday the church services seemed old-fashioned to them, too much drawling and quavering from the clergymen. But they were treated to the most sumptuous breakfast John Adams had ever seen—richly designed plates, large silver coffee urns and teapots, luxurious napkins, perfect toast and butter and, afterward, luscious peaches and pears and plums and muskmelon.

At each stop, the Massachusetts representatives were hearing more speculation about this delegate or that. It was indispensable gossip for men who would be meeting fifty strangers on whom their lives depended. John Alsop of the New York delegation was said to be goodhearted but not very able. James Duane was probably sensible, but to John Adams his squinting eye made him look a bit sly. Talking with Philip Livingston was impossible, since he was all rough bluster. Livingston was sure that if there was a breach with England the colonies would immediately make war among themselves. And besides, he demanded, what about the fact that Massachusetts had once hanged Quakers? John Adams found reasoning with him as futile as talking logic to an avalanche.

After four days in New York, the town's luxuries were beginning to cloy. All this dining and drinking coffee in houses around the city might be pleasant enough, John Adams told his diary, but it was keeping the Bostonians from seeing the worthy things—the college, the churches, the printers and the bookshops.

As for the people: "With all the opulence and splendor of this city, there is very little good breeding to be found. We have been treated with an assiduous respect. But I have not seen one real gentleman, one well-bred man, since I came to town." Adams concluded that New Yorkers had no modesty, no interest in another person's opinion. They talked very loud, very fast and all at the same time. "If they ask you a question, before you can utter three words of your answer, they will break out upon you again—and talk away."

The Massachusetts delegates reached Philadelphia on Friday, August 29. Although they rode into town dusty and weary, they couldn't resist heading for the City Tavern, which had been open for only a few months but already had the reputation of being the best public house in America, as good as anything London had to offer. They mingled there with a host of Philadelphians and met Christopher Gadsden of South Carolina. Delegates from the other colonies were also making their first judgments of the Bostonians, and some of the wealthier saw through Samuel Adams' new finery and pronounced him a dangerous man with nothing to lose. Dr. Benjamin Rush of Philadelphia shared a coach with John Adams and found him cold and reserved.

Joseph Galloway, who was also from Pennsylvania, was dubious about the ulterior aims of the Bostonians. He sounded them out over dinner and reported his impressions to the governor of New Jersey, William Franklin. William was the illegitimate son of Benjamin Franklin, and he had received his post at the age of twenty-seven, before his father's influence at court had dropped so precipitously. As governor, William seemed to favor the loyalists. Now from Galloway he heard that while the Boston delegates might appear moderate, they were throwing out hints that suggested otherwise.

The author of the "Pennsylvania Farmer" letters, John Dickinson, called on the Bostonians and complained of his gout. He would not be joining the Congress just yet. Dickinson first seemed a shadow to John Adams, as pale as ashes, but, looking more closely, Adams decided that Dickinson would last many more years. Thomas Lynch, Jr., of South Carolina invited the Massachusetts party to dine at his lodgings with his wife and daughter, and although the heat was oppressive the afternoon was a great success.

At one point, Lynch praised a brief speech that Colonel George Washington had made before the Virginia convention. John Adams asked, "Who is Colonel Washington and what was his speech?"

Lynch explained that Washington had become famous during the French and Indian War and had fought in the battle at which General Braddock fell. As for his speech, the Virginians had been arguing over what to do if the Bostonians began to fight the British. As the arguments raged, Washington had risen to say, "I will raise a thousand men, subsist them at my own expense and march myself at their head for the relief of Boston." It was the most eloquent speech that Lynch had ever heard.

That sort of anecdote—touched up or even fabricated as Lynch's story had been—was lending a celebrity to certain delegates even before the first session. And yet, John Adams had been brooding for weeks over how few outstanding leaders the colonies seemed likely to produce. "We have not men fit for the times," he complained to his diary. "We are deficient in genius, in education, in travel, in fortune—in everything." All the same, Peyton Randolph, Thomas Jefferson's cousin, was being admired for the way he could be open and cordial. Patrick Henry's reputation as a modern Demosthenes had preceded him. And when a man seemed to show special strength and persistence in the cause—Gadsden of South Carolina or Charles Thomson of Philadelphia—he was likely to be introduced as the Samuel Adams of his colony.

By September 1, 1774, not enough members had arrived in Philadelphia, and the opening was held over until the following Monday. As they waited, Silas Deane wrote home to ask his wife to assure their friends that the delegates were in high spirits, sobered only when they remembered that millions of eyes—and all of posterity—were watching their conduct.

When Monday came, the delegates first assembled at their informal headquarters, the City Tavern. As speaker of the Pennsylvania House, Joseph Galloway had offered the House chamber to the Congress and was quite insistent that it meet there. But within his own delegation Galloway was suspected of being too moderate, and others opposed his suggestion and led the delegates instead to Carpenters' Hall. There they found a white-paneled room, not large but beautifully proportioned, together with a library and a long hall where delegates might stroll and caucus, all overlooking a quiet square. In the first vote of the Continental Congress, a great majority decided to make the tradesmen's building their home.

Here in Philadelphia, the political labels of the past decade suddenly seemed inadequate and even misleading. Presumably all of the delegates were Whigs and patriots. Why else would they be here? But men like Galloway were clearly less impassioned than Patrick Henry or the two Adamses. Such tepid delegates sounded like "halfway patriots" or conservatives. The new division didn't show up in the selection of a chairman, since no one opposed the nomination of Peyton Randolph. He had presided over the Virginia Burgesses, and here the delegates decided to call him their president.

After having lost on where the Congress should meet, the conservatives suffered a second setback when it was time to choose a secretary.

During the selection of delegates for Pennsylvania, Charles Thomson's reputation as his colony's Samuel Adams had ruined his chances. A cheerful businessman in his midforties, Thomson struck some hesitant men as too popular among the poor and ill-educated, and he had used debating tricks that even Samuel Adams might have questioned. After the Port Act, Thomson had been speaking on behalf of Boston when he was drowned out by shouts from the conservatives. He had retaliated by seeming to faint and being carried from the hall. But just before the Congress was due to meet in Philadelphia, Thomson, a widower, had married John Dickinson's wealthy cousin. Even that connection hadn't reassured the halfway patriots, and they had passed him over as a delegate. Now his friends rallied and got Thomson elected as the Congress's secretary, and he was called back from his honeymoon to take up his duties.

Although twenty-two of the fifty-six delegates were lawyers, there hadn't yet been any of the quibbling that John Adams considered the bane of his profession. One crucial question to resolve, however, did not turn on personalities, and the Congress had to confront it early. Should each of the twelve colonies—Georgia had declined to send delegates—have one vote or should votes be allotted to colonies on the basis of their population or wealth?

The delegates expected the governor of Rhode Island to argue that each colony, whatever its size, was taking the same risk in op-

posing Britain and each should have the same vote. John Jay of
New York would probably counter that a colony with twice the
population of many others shouldn't have its vote cut in half. But
a rancorous debate might end the Congress before it began, and no
one wanted to be the first to speak. Finally a delegate did arise, and
Charles Thomson felt sorry for him. He was probably a Presbyte-
rian minister, dressed in drab gray with an unpowdered and unfashionable wig, and clearly out of his depth.

"We are here met in a time of great difficulty and distress,"
the man began.

Delegates were only starting to recognize one another, and
they were asking their neighbors, "Who is speaking?" It was Patrick Henry of Virginia. Henry was arguing that it would be a
great injustice for a small colony to have the same weight as a large
one. He was in the middle of his speech when the first day of the
Continental Congress came to an end.

The next day, Henry resumed his argument. Overnight, John
Adams had also been fretting that five small colonies, each with
one hundred thousand people, might outvote four colonies with
five hundred thousand each. On the other hand, how could they
possibly get accurate figures about either population or a colony's
volume of trade on such short notice? Charles Thomson had decided that as secretary he should record only the final vote, not the
discussion that led up to it. He simply listened as Patrick Henry
spoke. But writing was as natural as breathing for John Adams,
who set down Henry's flowing argument in a burst of notes:

"Government is dissolved. Fleets and armies and the present
state of things show that Government is dissolved. Where are your
landmarks? Your boundaries of colonies? We are in a state of nature, sir."

Henry urged that ten thousand Virginians must outweigh a
thousand residents in another colony. But if he was overruled, he
said, he was willing to submit to the majority. Mostly, he wanted
the delegates to appreciate their new circumstances. "The distinc-
tions between Virginians, Pennsylvanians, New Yorkers and New
Englanders are no more.

"I am not a Virginian but an American."

Henry's declaration was appealing and visionary, but it didn't
carry the day. Two fellow delegates from Virginia, Richard Henry
Lee and Richard Bland, made the same point that had worried John

Adams: the delegates lacked the data to weight the votes. The Congress, deciding that this first decision would not be irrevocably binding, agreed to give each colony one vote. The first debate had reminded the delegates of the staying power of some speakers, and they also voted that from then on no man could speak twice on the same subject without express permission.

The next obstacle they faced was religious and potentially even more divisive. On Monday, Thomas Cushing had moved that each session open with a prayer. Jay of New York and Rutledge of South Carolina had opposed the idea. The delegates came from so many faiths—Episcopalians, Anabaptists, Presbyterians, Congregationalists and Quakers—that there was no way they could all worship together.

Samuel Adams was known to be as pious as any man in the hall and more strict, and he impressed the delegates by announcing that he was no bigot, that he could hear a prayer from any virtuous gentleman so long as he was also a friend to his country. He himself was a stranger in Philadelphia, but he had heard that Mr. Duché was such a man. Adams moved that he read prayers to the Congress the next morning.

When the session ended, Peyton Randolph went to see Jacob Duché, the assistant rector at an Episcopal church. The clergyman said that if his health permitted he would be there. Overnight, reports reached Philadelphia that General Gage had bombarded Boston and several people had been killed. When the Reverend Duché arrived the next morning, he read the Thirty-fifth Psalm, "Plead my cause, O Lord, with them that strive with me . . ." and the delegates felt they were hearing a message from Heaven. Duché then prayed extemporaneously for ten minutes on behalf of Boston. Even Quakers wept, and Congregationalists declared that they had never heard better preaching.

On Wednesday the delegates learned that Boston had not been shelled. General Gage had merely sent troops to the armory at Cambridge to seize the gunpowder stored there. That action was provocative, but no blood had been spilled, and the Congress could settle down to its business.

A committee had been formed to spell out the grievances with Britain and suggestions for resolving them. Nothing that was said was new to John Adams. It was the old debate over natural rights, constitutional rights, laws at the pleasure of a king or by the power of an elected Parliament. For years, every patriot in Boston had read and heard them. But as Adams took down each argument, he was reassured about the quality of the delegates. They were better than he had first thought. Richard Lee wanted to rest their case on its broadest defense—natural law. Joseph Galloway said he had looked for laws in nature and had never found any there. "Power," said Galloway, "results from the real property of the society." John Adams couldn't endorse that argument, and yet Galloway was buttressing it with allusions to Greece and Rome and Macedonia. Writing at night to his wife in Braintree, Adams praised the delegates in Philadelphia as the greatest men upon the continent. They made him blush, he said, for the sordid, venal herd of public officials in Massachusetts.

The Congress was now meeting in committees rather than in general session. Delegates worked from nine each morning until three in the afternoon, adjourned for a lavish dinner at four and sat again until six or seven, drinking claret or burgundy and going over the day's debates one last time. John Adams was eating and drinking as never before—jellies, sweetmeats, trifles, curds and creams, whipped sillabubs, Parmesan cheese, almonds and raisins, and washed down with strong punch and rich red wines. He did vow, however, that he would drink only beer and porter in Philadelphia. New Englanders found the local cider far inferior to what they enjoyed at home.

Amid the good living, the business of the Congress was inching forward. Late in September, Richard Lee made a motion for the nonimportation of goods from England. Earlier, John Adams had been called upon to defend the conduct of John Hancock and other Boston merchants during the last agreement. This time, the boycott must be more sweeping. A first proposal suggested that no goods be imported after December 1, and no goods exported either. But Virginia had tobacco inventories to clear, and the delegates were determined to preserve a united front. They agreed that the ban on exports should not go into effect for one year.

Samuel Adams knew the suspicions that the Massachusetts delegation aroused, and so far he had let Christopher Gadsden, Richard Lee and the other Southerners take the lead while he consulted with them from the shadows. Then, just as adjournment seemed possible, the halfway patriots offered a resolution that would unravel the past month's work. Joseph Galloway objected to the nonimportation agreements and put forward his own plan. Galloway assured the delegates that he was as much a friend of liberty as existed, but "we must come upon terms with Great Britain." Not exporting to England meant throwing tens of thousands of people out of work. His proposal called instead for an American Grand Council that would represent every province. Britain's Parliament would validate its statutes, and the king would appoint its leader—Galloway called him a Resident General.

Samuel Adams and his allies had not come three hundred miles to doom America to second-class citizenship. But James Duane of New York seconded Galloway's motion and so did John Jay. Richard Henry Lee protested that he couldn't possibly agree to such a plan without consulting his constituents. Patrick Henry said the Congress would be saving the people from a corrupt House of Commons only to turn them over to an American legislature that Britain was sure to bribe. By one vote, however, the colonies agreed to go on debating Galloway's plan, and Charles Thomson entered the proposal in his minutes.

Samuel Adams was no longer a stranger in Philadelphia, and the opposition he organized to Galloway was different from Richard Henry Lee's and Patrick Henry's. The crowds around Carpenters' Hall soon heard that a faction led by Joseph Galloway was bent on selling out their liberties. Galloway headed a powerful Quaker bloc, and yet he began to fear being attacked by a mob in his own home precincts. As the crowd clamored, Adams dined with men whose support he needed. After one pleasant session, Colonel George Washington wrote home that he had consulted with the New England delegates and was convinced that they weren't aiming for independence.

Galloway's proposal did not come up again, and sometime later it was erased from the minutes. Galloway knew that Adams had engineered his defeat. "He eats little," Galloway said of him, "drinks little, sleeps little, thinks much, and is most decisive and indefatigible in the pursuit of his objects."

The Congress disbanded on October 24 after seven intense weeks, and the exhausted delegates were happy to be heading home. Patrick Henry had urged that they keep their deliberations secret, and that vow, along with the uncertain delivery of mail, had kept them doubly separated from their wives and families. John Adams had learned the cost of being locked up with so many voluble men, and he complained to Abigail that if a proposition was presented that three and two made five, the result was two days of speeches on logic and rhetoric, law, history, politics and mathematics, before at last the resolution passed unanimously. Samuel Adams' wife wrote to tell him that Tories were flocking to Boston from the countryside to seek protection under General Gage's guns. Elizabeth Adams, who shared her husband's politics, said the Tories' arrival had turned the town into a den of thieves, a cage of every unclean mind.

His political allies also had kept Adams informed of events at home. Dr. Benjamin Church wrote to say that he was doing his duty to keep the public alert, and Joseph Warren was proving himself worthy of his teacher. Following Adams' instructions, Dr. Warren drew up a set of resolutions called the Suffolk Resolves and got them passed at a county meeting. They declared that the Port Act needn't be obeyed and called on the people to prepare for a defensive war against England whenever Boston sounded the alarm. In Philadelphia, Joseph Galloway recognized the Suffolk Resolves as a declaration of war, but they were presented to the Congress so reassuringly that rejecting them would be disowning Boston in its hour of distress. Passing the resolutions consoled Samuel Adams for the delays and loopholes added to the trade boycott.

The delegates were leaving Philadelphia with affectionate regret. John Adams had come to know Patrick Henry better after they spent an evening working together on a petition to the king. Henry had told Adams about his lack of education, how he had read Virgil and Livy at fifteen but had never looked into a Latin book since. His father had died about that same time, Henry said, and he had been struggling through life ever since. Recording that tale in his diary, John Adams gave no sign that he had been touched by Patrick Henry any more than Thomas Jefferson had ever been. Adams was dryly amused, though, by Henry's highflown ideas and his praise for exalted minds, by which he seemed to be including his own. And yet Patrick Henry was clearly an ally against men like Galloway and Jay, and they had parted that evening as brothers.

In Boston, General Gage was sending mixed signals both to London and to his own edgy men. Just before the Continental Congress met, Gage had estimated privately to Francis Bernard's patron, Lord Barrington, that in a war with England the colonies could be vanquished in a year or two. His optimism was well received in London. But less than a month later Gage wrote to Thomas Hutchinson, recommending that he show the letter to Lord Dartmouth and urging that the Intolerable Acts be suspended, since it would take no fewer than twenty thousand men to crush an uprising. That disagreeable prospect had barely been digested when the Ministry received word that the Continental Congress had adopted the bellicose Suffolk Resolves. Now war, which had been considered so unlikely just weeks before, started to seem possible, even imminent. And leading Britain's troops was a general whose vacillations had discredited him with his superiors.

Gage's September 1 raid against the public store of gunpowder at Cambridge had contributed to his pessimism. Although the British soldiers had commandeered three hundred barrels of powder, the price had been a storm of protest. The rumors that had reached the Congress in Philadelphia had been even more inflated throughout Massachusetts, where men had heard that six colonists had been killed and that Boston was in flames. Within a day, tens of thousands of farmers from miles around Boston laid down their plows and were marching to the town. Two or three thousand reached Cambridge, where they found that the reports were untrue. Heading for home, they advised men on the road to turn back. But their spontaneous outpouring had been a warning to Gage.

These days, the general seemed to lack the will to carry out the orders he had helped shape. Gage was striving to prevent incidents in the streets, and his troops complained acidly when he refused to let them wear sidearms around Boston. They called him "the Old Woman" and claimed that he sided with the town in any dispute. British troops were deserting freely, caught only when they were rash enough to show themselves in the marketplace. By January 1775, discontent in the ranks had spread so far that soldiers said one cannon in the center of Boston was reserved as a signal against mutiny. If it was fired, all the men who chose to stick by Thomas Gage were to hurry there with their weapons.

The petitions from the Continental Congress were being ignored by everyone in London, with the significant exception of William Pitt. Lord Chatham ended a long retirement to tell the House of Lords that he had read Thucydides and had studied the greatest statesmen of history, but that for solid reasoning, sagacious force and wise conclusions no nation had ever done better than the Congress at Philadelphia. "When your lordships look at the papers transmitted from America," he said, "when you consider their decency, firmness and wisdom, you cannot but respect their cause and wish to make it your own."

Chatham made a politic bow to the British armed forces before he made his next point. The troops, he said, had his warmest love. All the same, "you may call them an army of safety and of guard. But they are in truth an army of impotence and contempt, and to make the folly equal to the disgrace, they are an army of irritation and vexation."

In Commons as Pitt and in Lords as Chatham, he had given Parliament consistent advice for ten years, and it had been consistently rejected. Now the House of Lords defeated by a vote of 68 to 18 his motion to withdraw the troops from Boston. Less than two weeks later, he returned to urge that the vindictive measures of the previous April be repealed and that Parliament renounce forever its right to tax the colonies. In the House of Commons, Edmund Burke argued the same point on grounds of simple expediency: an abstract right to tax was not worth the consequences that seemed to lie ahead. In his letters Lord Chatham was putting the case as starkly as he could: "We shall be forced ultimately to retract. Let us retract while we can, not when we must."

Retract? Never! said John Montagu, fourth Earl of Sandwich. He called the Americans raw, undisciplined, cowardly men, and he said he hoped they would not field forty or fifty thousand soldiers but two hundred thousand. It would make conquering them all the easier. Large majorities in both houses showed that Parliament believed Montagu.

As Samuel Adams and his Massachusetts colleagues were meeting in Philadelphia, the colony's towns had elected delegates to a new Massachusetts Provincial Congress after the dissolution of the House by General Gage. Convening in Salem, with Hancock as president, the delegates launched the colony's first government independent of the British king. They ordered money held back from the royal collections and channeled into their own accounts. They set up elite units within the militia—companies of fifty privates who were instructed to be ready to move at the shortest notice. And they established Committees of Safety to oversee those shock troops, who were calling themselves Minute Men.

On January 27, 1775, Lord Dartmouth sent explicit orders for General Gage to arrest the principal rebels in the Massachusetts Provincial Congress. The Americans couldn't mount much resistance now, and any conflict with them should come before their rebellion had a chance to ripen. John Hancock certainly qualified under Dartmouth's definition as a leading actor, and yet Gage did not move against him. Hancock went on living in Boston, with his aunt, Lydia Hancock, and her young protégée, Dorothy Quincy, a cousin of Josiah and Hannah Quincy. Aunt Lydia had been determined for years that her nephew should marry Dorothy.

When Boston's Tories decided that General Gage didn't seem to know whom to arrest, they attempted to enlighten him. They tossed leaflets into British camps and barracks telling the soldiers what was expected of them if a rebellion broke out: "You will put the above persons to the sword, destroy their houses and plunder the effects!" Samuel Adams headed the list of fifteen names, along with Hancock, Thomas Cushing, Josiah Quincy and Dr. Benjamin Church. John Adams was somehow omitted, and William Molineux frustrated them by dying in bed before he could be stabbed. The Tory note had a postscript—"Don't forget those trumpeters of sedition, the printers, Edes and Gill, and Thomas."

As Gage weighed his next step, the time came around for the fifth annual commemoration of the Boston Massacre of March 1770. Samuel Adams was again chairman of the committee to pick an orator, and this year, with British troops swarming over Boston, the choice was especially delicate. Threats were being made against any man who gave the address, and when Dr. Joseph Warren, who had spoken three years earlier, heard about them, he asked Adams to choose him again.

On the Monday of the oration, Samuel Adams, John Hancock, Dr. Benjamin Church and other leaders took their places on the raised platform of the Old South. Immediately, about forty British soldiers crowded into the doorway, and Adams called out an invitation for them to take seats at the front. Soldiers and civilians waited nervously more than an hour for Warren to arrive. Men in the audience were looking quizzically around the hall when a one-horse carriage approached the drugstore across the street and Dr. Warren hurried inside, followed by a servant with a large bundle. When Warren appeared again, he was wearing a toga in the style of Cicero. He crossed the street, entered Old South and climbed into its pulpit, which had been draped in black.

After his dramatic entrance, Warren's speech seemed muted. Gesturing with a white handkerchief in his right hand, he seemed to be avoiding any phrases that might offend the soldiers in the front rows, and with good reason. A number of officers were outraged that General Gage hadn't seized the chief rebels and were vowing to do it themselves. Their strategy called for an army ensign to throw a raw egg at Joseph Warren in the pulpit. That signal would set off his fellow soldiers, who would rush forward and arrest Adams, Hancock and possibly several others.

When Warren's speech ended, there was applause from the patriots and groaning from the soldiers and the Tories, but Dr. Warren had committed no flagrant offense.

Samuel Adams got to his feet determined to correct that oversight. Speaking on behalf of the town, he wanted to thank Dr. Warren for his elegant and spirited oration. Then he provoked the British troops. There would be another oration next year, Adams announced, to commemorate the bloody massacre of the fifth of March, 1770. At the words "bloody massacre" the soldiers began to hiss, and some officers cried loudly, "Oh, fie! Fie!"

In the galleries, the patriots heard their shout as "Oh, fire! Fire!" They swarmed out windows to the roof and clambered down gutters to the street. At the same time, the Forty-third Regiment was returning from an exercise and marching near the Old South. Its drums threw the crowd into even greater panic. Inside the hall, Samuel Adams restored order and found a way to put the patriots in the right. If it were not for their restraint, he claimed later, no British soldier would have left the Old South alive.

When the aborted British plot was revealed, the patriots dwelled on one detail, whether or not it was true. The egg hadn't been thrown on cue because the soldier who was supposed to throw it had slipped and fallen on his way inside the hall, dislocating his knee and breaking the egg.

General Gage had inherited informers from Thomas Hutchinson, and Samuel Adams' circle suspected that someone high in their council was betraying them, but they had not unmasked him. For routine intelligence, Gage depended upon British soldiers who put on civilian clothes and rode out to reconnoiter. About the time Adams was organizing the memorial at the Old South, Gage had sent out two officers to scout the lay of the land between Boston and Concord, where the patriots were said to be storing arms. Sometime during the spring, Gage would have to march his troops there and confiscate them.

Ensign D'Bernicre and Captain Brown set out on their scouting dressed in brown outfits with red handkerchiefs knotted at the neck. It was D'Bernicre's first trip out of Boston, and he found Cambridge with its brick college buildings a pretty town. So far, no one on the road seemed to be taking notice of them, and the two soldiers traveled on to Watertown, which was considered a large town in America, but which D'Bernicre thought would be a village in England. The two spies stopped for dinner at a tavern owned by a patriot, expecting their disguises to shield them through the meal.

A black woman came politely to their table, took their order and returned with their food. But as they ate, they noticed that she kept eyeing them. Then she slipped out of the tavern. When she returned, the scouts thought they had better be a little friendlier.

It's very fine country around here, one said.

So it is, the woman answered, and we have got brave fellows to defend it. If you go farther up the road, you'll find that it is so.

That warning disconcerted the soldiers. Throwing down money for their bill, they made their escape, but outside the inn they learned that the woman had told even more to Captain Brown's servant, John. She had recognized the captain from five years earlier in Boston, and she had guessed that his errand now was to draw a map of the countryside.

The two soldiers consulted. Being picked for this mission had been an honor and they had left a number of jealous rivals behind in their regiment. If they went back now, they'd look foolish. There was no choice but to push on.

Over the rest of the journey, they fared no better. Finally, in a house in Marlborough, they were trapped by patriots and asked their host, a Mr. Barnet, what was likely to happen if they were captured. He seemed reluctant to answer. When they pressed him, Barnet said that he knew his townsmen very well, and that they should expect the worst. They slipped out a back door, left their horses and walked the thirty-two miles to safety through snow.

Their commander didn't consider the mission a failure. After several more expeditions, Gage thought that he had the military intelligence he needed: The town of Concord lay between hills that commanded it entirely. The town was spread out over a wide area, and a river with two bridges ran through its center. The houses were not close together. Tory informants said the town had fourteen pieces of cannon—ten of iron, four of brass. The Lexington road was open for six miles on the way to Concord, but some of it was lined with houses. And for troops marching down it, there was one patch that could be somewhat dangerous.

The British soldiers who hadn't got their hands on John Hancock were venting their frustration on his property. In the weeks after the memorial service, Hancock returned to preside over Massachusetts' renegade Provincial Congress, which was now meeting at Concord. The Continental Congress seemed likely to meet again in Philadelphia later in the spring, and Hancock was voted a delegate to that second session. Meanwhile, British soldiers hacked at the fences of his mansion on the Common with their swords and lobbed rocks through the windows. One night he went outside to put a stop to the destruction, but the soldiers refused to leave. They told him that since both the house and the stables would soon be theirs, they could do as they pleased.

General Gage's attitude toward John Hancock remained unclear. As winter approached, he had enlisted Hancock's help in finding barracks for his men. But then, even though he couldn't bring himself to arrest Hancock, Gage had stripped him of his title as commander of the cadets. The corps had disbanded in protest.

At last, life in Boston became too perilous for Lydia Hancock.

She loaded up her carriage and set off for the Lexington parsonage where John Hancock had grown up. Mrs. Hancock's niece and her husband, the Reverend Jonas Clark, occupied the manse, and they warmly received their aunt and her young friend, Dorothy Quincy.

John Hancock was now thirty-eight, and his aunt was impatient for him to marry. Years before, when he had visited London as a young man, reports had filtered back to Lydia Hancock about a compliant chambermaid, and later there had been rumors about a middle-aged mistress, Dorcas Griffith, who ran a grog shop near Hancock's Wharf. That arrangement, if it existed, was entirely commercial. Mrs. Griffith welcomed upstairs any man with her price, including contingents of British soldiers. During those same years, Hancock had also called on Sally Jackson, the daughter of a respectable Boston family. But Hancock had sent her a letter ending the courtship, and soon afterward Miss Jackson married a Boston selectman named Henderson Inches.

Given the latitude of his tastes, John Hancock may well have been ready to marry Dorothy Quincy from the Sunday when he was first captivated by a glimpse of her shapely small foot as she stepped out of church. But despite his aunt's connivance, the romance seemed stalled. For about four years Lydia Hancock had brought the couple into almost daily contact while she fended off all other suitors. Her nephew was handsome, stalwart, certainly rich, without question the most popular man of his day. Since the Provincial Congress was meeting only a few miles from Lexington at Concord, Hancock could still visit Miss Quincy regularly. Her twenty-seventh birthday was approaching when she allowed herself to be evacuated from Boston.

Virginia's delegates to the Continental Congress returned home from Philadelphia with widely different predictions for the future. Richard Henry Lee was sure that their appeals to England, combined with the threat of a trade embargo, would lead to the king's ministers to send back their capitulation by the next ship. Patrick Henry was less hopeful, but he seemed to be in the minority. Virginia's Revolutionary Convention met at St. John's Church in Richmond on March 20, 1775, to approve what had been accomplished in Philadelphia, and the prevailing mood was self-satisfaction. The colony's patriots were sure that Britain would bend.

The convention had been under way three days when Patrick

Henry shattered their complacency. He proposed to prepare the Virginia militia to defend the colony in case of war, and Thomas Jefferson was forced to admire Henry's foresight, although he still found the man something of a trial. Jefferson had been pleased to receive reports from Philadelphia that the committees there had considered Henry's writing inadequate. But at this meeting in Richmond, Jefferson had to grant that Henry's nerve was leaving the rest of them behind.

George Washington and the Lee brothers were with Jefferson at the church on the fine spring day when Henry waited in the third pew to defend his proposal. Peyton Randolph was presiding from the pulpit. The church windows had been opened, and since the hundred and twenty delegates filled most of the seats, the windows were crowded with spectators.

Preparing to speak, Patrick Henry felt his heart begin to pound, and the longer he waited the hotter his brow became. Few of the spectators knew that Henry's tension was not entirely political. His wife, Sarah, the mother of his three daughters and three sons, was stricken with an affliction the family was trying to keep quiet. She had gone mad, and she threatened so often to kill herself that at last she had to be tied into a straitjacket.

When Henry was recognized, he began by praising the honor of those men who held a different opinion. But, he went on, "this is no time for ceremony. The question before the House is of awful moment to this country." He said that if he did not speak he would consider himself guilty of treason to his country. Do not be lulled by an occasional smile from London, he added. Do not let yourself be betrayed with a kiss. Ask instead why British armies have come to your shores.

"Has Great Britain any enemy in this quarter of the world to call for all this accumulation of navies and armies? No, sir, she has none. They are meant for us; they can be meant for no other. They are sent over to find and rivet upon us those chains which the British Ministry has been so long forging. And what have we to oppose them? Shall we try argument? Sir, we have been trying that for the last ten years.

"Sir," said Henry, addressing Peyton Randolph in the pulpit, "we have done everything that could be done to avert the storm which is now coming on. We have petitioned; we have remonstrated; we have supplicated; we have prostrated ourselves before the throne and have implored its interposition to arrest the tyrannical hands of the Ministry and Parliament. Our petitions have been slighted; our remonstrances have produced additional violence and insult; our supplications have been disregarded; and we have been spurned, with contempt, from the foot of the throne."

Henry had begun calmly, but as his voice rose, tendons in his neck were standing out white and rigid. He said that if the colonists wished to be free, they must fight. "I repeat, sir, we must fight! An appeal to arms and to the God of Hosts is all that is left to us.

"They tell us, sir, that we are weak—unable to cope with so formidable an adversary. But when shall we be stronger? Will it be next week, or next year? Will it be when we are totally disarmed, and when a British guard shall be stationed in every house?"

They were not weak, Henry said. "Three millions of people, armed in the holy cause of liberty, and in such a country as that which we possess, are invincible to any force which our enemy can send against us." Besides that, they had no choice. "The war is inevitable. And let it come! I repeat, sir: Let it come!"

As Patrick Henry turned his eyes around the church, men leaned forward in their seats. "Gentlemen may cry peace, peace—but there is no peace. The war is actually begun! The next gale that sweeps from the north will bring to our ears the clash of resounding arms! Our brethren are already in the field! Why should we idle here? What is it that gentlemen wish? What would they have?"

Patrick Henry's shoulders sank. He crossed his wrists as though he were the one in a straitjacket. "Is life so dear," he asked, "or peace so sweet, as to be purchased at the price of chains and slavery?" He paused, raised his eyes and lifted up his hands, still held together. "Forbid it, Almighty God!" Henry turned to stare at the men who opposed him. Slowly, he bowed his body down. "I know not what course others may take." He rose and straightened to his full height, and his next words came from between clenched teeth: "But as for me, give me liberty—" He paused to let the word die away. His left hand fell to his side. His right hand formed a fist as though he held a dagger, and he struck that fist to his heart. "—or give me death."

There was no applause, only silence.

Lexington

ONE SATURDAY midnight in the middle of April 1775, Paul Revere suspected that General Gage was finally going to move against the patriot leaders. All the boats from the men-of-war in the harbor had been hauled to shore and repaired, and the grenadiers and the light infantry regiments had been taken off their regular duties. Because of the exodus of patriots from Boston and the Provincial Congress meeting in Concord, Revere found few leaders

Battle at Lexington

1775

left in town to inform. Even Isaiah Thomas, the editor of the *Massachusetts Spy*, had packed up his press, his wife and their children and was heading for Watertown. Of the inner circle, only the two doctors had remained behind—Benjamin Church and Joseph Warren. Dr. Warren's medical students were pleading with him not to make night calls, because they were sure he would be ambushed. But Warren was fearless, and Samuel Adams trusted him above his other young lieutenants. After his wife died two years earlier, Warren had turned over his four children to their grandmother and thrown himself headlong into the cause. When he heard British soldiers and their Tory sympathizers assuring one another that the colonials would always back down, he said, "These fellows say we won't fight. By heavens, I hope I shall die up to my knees in blood."

Paul Revere had stayed in Boston to serve as messenger when he was needed. After five months as a widower, he had married again. Although he was nearing his fortieth birthday and was raising five children, the eldest in her teens, he wasn't ready to surrender his duties to younger men.

Revere's family had come more recently to America than the Adamses or the Hutchinsons. Like the Faneuils and the Bowdoins, his father had been a Protestant Huguenot driven out of Catholic France. After several years in Massachusetts, Apollos Rivoire had changed his name to Paul Revere—"Merely on account that the bumpkins pronounce it easier," he said—and had passed that name on to his son. The Reveres lived one block from Thomas Hutchinson, but the social distance was unbreachable. Young Paul had been sent to the crowded North Writing School rather than to North Latin. Instead of studying at Harvard, he learned his father's trade of silversmith.

When the demand for silver goods flagged during bad times, the younger Revere made false teeth. That was always a reliable business in a town where a European traveler noted that Boston girls often had lost half their teeth before they were twenty. Advertising in the *Boston Gazette*, Revere pointed out that a lack of teeth affected not only a person's appearance but also one's ability to speak in public, and he promised to supply teeth that would pass for nature's.

Revere was a veteran of the French and Indian War, a strong, swarthy man who was quick to smile with his own fine teeth and who never powdered his hair or wore a wig. Modeling himself after Samuel Adams, he provided a valuable link between the wealthier party leaders and the town's craftsmen.

Joseph Warren was six years younger than Paul Revere, but Revere regarded him as both his leader and his friend. On this April Saturday night, Revere took his news of the British preparations directly to Warren's house, which had become the patriots' headquarters. Warren agreed that Gage was probably headed for Concord to arrest Samuel Adams and John Hancock and to seize any arms stored there.

On Sunday morning, Revere rode to the Lexington parsonage where Hancock had grown up. The Provincial Congress had adjourned the day before, and he found Adams and Hancock visiting there. They asked Revere to alert Concord, five miles to the west. Within hours, Concord's men and boys were hiding their cannon and their flour. Sacks of bullets they stowed in the outlying swamps.

Returning to Boston, Paul Revere passed through Charlestown, where he met with William Conant, of the town's Committee of Safety, to devise a set of signals since they couldn't be sure which way Gage would march his troops. He could send them out along Boston Neck, the isthmus that connected the town with the mainland. But that route would be so conspicuous that he would have no hope of surprising Concord's militia. Going by land also meant either making a great curve all around Back Bay or heading west to Waltham, north to Lexington and then on to Concord.

The fact that Gage had prepared the boats suggested he would exercise his better option. Boston had enjoyed its mildest winter in memory; the Charles River had not frozen over, and now April was balmy. The general could ferry his troops across the Charles, land in East Cambridge and march almost directly to Menotomy and then to Lexington. Going by land would mean a march of twenty-one miles; taking the river route could cut off five of them.

By keeping watch in Boston, Paul Revere could know within minutes which route Gage had chosen. But how would he get that information to Concord? The British had posted a guard on Boston Neck, and slipping across the Charles in a boat on a night of such tight security might be difficult. Revere told William Conant that he or an ally would go to Christ's Church in Boston and flash a message to the patriots in Charlestown. If no one could get out of Boston, Conant's men would be able to forward the alarm to Concord. They should watch the steeple across the Charles. One lantern would mean that Gage's troops were coming by land, two that they were being rowed across the water.

As he prepared for his most ambitious foray out of Boston, Gage was determined to preserve absolute secrecy. He was ready to commit twenty-one companies of his tallest and best-armed grenadiers and infantrymen. Since companies averaged twenty-eight men, the general would be sending out nearly six hundred soldiers. That should be enough, since the rebels wouldn't dare take up arms against His Majesty's troops. He confided his battle plan to only two persons, his wife and Hugh, Earl Percy. Young and charming Lord Percy had been camping out on the Common near John Hancock's house. Because he was an earl and attractive, he had often been invited in for dinner, and Dorothy Quincy had been especially taken with Percy's commanding voice as he drilled his men each daybreak. Gage ordered Percy and his Fifth Regiment to be ready in the unlikely event that reserves should be needed.

Gage was entrusting the mission itself to Lieutenant Colonel Francis Smith, a heavy young officer who, ten days earlier on another spying expedition, had encountered the same black serving woman who had recognized Captain Brown. At Watertown, wearing his civilian disguise, Smith had tried to disarm her by asking where he and his companion could find employment.

The woman had looked him over. "Smith, you will find employment enough for you and all Gage's men in a few months."

Since D'Bernicre and Brown hadn't mentioned their own humiliation, Colonel Smith was not prepared for that answer. He complained to the landlord about the woman's sauciness and then sent his private to continue the mission while he stumbled through the bushes back to camp. Smith had vowed that if he ever returned with his regiment, he would kill the wench.

On Tuesday evening, April 18, Gage's select British companies were ordered to gather at a rendezvous point, walking there in small numbers to avoid arousing suspicion. If challenged about their purpose, they were to answer, "Patrol." Colonel Smith still had not been officially informed of the destination, but if he had not guessed it he was the only person in Boston who hadn't. One Boston matron employed the wife of a British soldier as her maid, and when his sergeant couldn't locate the soldier he came to the woman in confidence. Should she see him, would she please tell him to report at eight o'clock that evening at the bottom of the

Common, equipped for an expedition? As soon as the sergeant left, the woman relayed his message to Dr. Benjamin Church. Around the town's stables, British officers readied their horses and talked about tomorrow and the hell there would be to pay. Hearing them, a stableboy ran to Paul Revere, who said, "You are the third person who has brought me the same information."

Hugh Percy had come to Boston a principled Whig, but despite John Hancock's hospitality he soon found himself loathing these colonials who showed him every courtesy while plotting to betray him. "The people here are a set of sly, artful, hypocritical rascals, cruel and cowardly," Percy wrote home after two months in America. "I must own that I cannot but despise them completely."

As dusk fell on the night of the operation, Lord Percy walked undetected among the townfolk as they watched the soldiers lining up on the Common. A man at his elbow said, "The British troops will miss their aim."

"What aim?" Percy asked.

"Why," said the man, "the cannon at Concord."

Percy hurried back to tell Gage their target had been discovered. But by that time the operation had already begun. The general could only hope to bottle up the news by forbidding anyone to leave Boston.

As the troops climbed into boats to be ferried across the Charles, Joseph Warren asked Paul Revere to leave at once for Lexington and warn Hancock and Samuel Adams that they were about to be arrested. Revere should try to get out of Boston on the river. Dr. Warren had already sent another messenger, William Dawes, to attempt to reach the parsonage by the overland route.

Before he set out, Revere went to the house of Robert Newman across the street from Christ's Church. Newman, the church's twenty-three-year-old sexton, had agreed to hang the one or two lanterns in the steeple. But there was a complication. Newman's mother rented rooms, and his house was filled with British soldiers. Newman had pretended to go to bed early, slipped out an upper window, dropped to the street and waited for Paul Revere at the church. With a vestryman standing guard outside, Newman took two lanterns from a closet and climbed to the highest window in the belfry.

He lighted his lanterns and hung them only long enough for the watchman in Charlestown to catch a glimpse. He didn't want to alert any British officers at the harbor. The *Somerset*, a man-of-war with sixty-four guns, had moved to the mouth of the Charles to protect the British soldiers as they were rowed across. After extinguishing the lanterns, Newman lowered himself out a back window of the church, climbed to the roof of his mother's house and went back to bed.

The first signal had been sent. Now Paul Revere had to reach Lexington—even Concord, if he could—with the details he and Warren had been collecting. He went to his own house in North Square to put on his heavy riding boots. He had made dozens of rides in the patriot cause but never one as dangerous as this. In his excitement, he forgot two necessities—his spurs and the cloth he normally used to muffle the sound of the oars if he was able to launch his rowboat.

Two men were waiting at the riverside to row Revere across the Charles in a boat he had been hiding throughout the winter. When they discovered that Revere had forgotten the cloth, one led them to his sweetheart's house and gave a whistle. The girl came to the window. When she heard their problem, she stripped off her petticoat and threw it down. The flannel was still warm when it was passed to Paul Revere.

Since the *Somerset* was guarding the river's mouth, the men had to row east to reach the old Battery at Charlestown. From there Revere was to go on alone. Conant and his men had spotted the signal from the steeple, but they said that the road to Concord was now filled with British officers, who were acting casually, as though they were not on patrol. But one had already asked a patriot for directions to Clark's tavern. Apparently their information was faulty and they didn't know that Jonas Clark was a clergyman. The question was more evidence, though, that Gage's men intended to seize Adams and Hancock.

Revere thought he might be able to slip past the patrol. He asked for a horse, and one of Charlestown's wealthiest merchants, John Larkin, volunteered his best animal. Getting from Joseph Warren's house to Larkin's stable had taken one hour. Lexington was twelve miles to the north and west. At 11 P.M. Paul Revere set off to warn Massachusetts' two most notorious rebels that the redcoats were coming after them.

William Dawes, the messenger who had already set out overland, was a twenty-three-year-old shoemaker who had won Joseph Warren's respect by smuggling out two of Boston's cannon from under General Gage's nose. For Billy Dawes the blockade of Boston was a lark, and he enjoyed seeing how often he could slip past the British guard at Boston Neck. His allegiance to the patriots was personal; he had once knocked down a British soldier for insulting his wife. After that, Dawes had moved his family to Worcester, and although General Gage had prohibited gold from leaving the town, Dawes had devised a way to smuggle out his reserves. He began to wear cloth-covered buttons on his waistcoat instead of brass ones. When the British guards had tired of joking about his eccentricity, Dawes began sliding gold coins inside the cloth.

By now he knew most of the guards at the Neck. Sometimes he played drunk, which usually got him past the checkpoint. This night, he hung about and waited until a squad of soldiers marched to the gate on a routine patrol. The guard was a friend, and when the soldiers passed out of Boston, Dawes trailed after them and headed for Lexington. He had started earlier than Paul Revere, but his route was five miles longer and he faced the same British patrols assigned to keep any patriot from getting through to sound the alarm.

Like Boston, Charlestown was surrounded by water—the harbor to the east, the Charles River to the south and west. Paul Revere rode through town, past Breed's Hill and Bunker Hill, and across another slender neck of land that General Gage had not attempted to close off. Revere passed over it and onto a stretch of marsh and scrub brush. He intended to head west for the same direct route Billy Dawes was taking. The alternative was a swerving river road to Menotomy. There the two roads joined and, except for one bend near the Munroe Tavern, led directly to Lexington.

Revere's ride took him past a spot along the road where a slave named Mark had been hanged twenty years earlier for poisoning his owner with arsenic. Still in chains, the rotted skeleton had been left as a warning to other slaves, and to Paul Revere it had become a marker on the way to Lexington. The moon was shining brightly. Revere was almost past the desolate moor when he spotted two British officers on horseback in the shadow of a tree. By the time he saw them, he was close enough to make out their holsters. One started toward Revere, the other rode farther up the road to cut him off. Instead, Revere wheeled his horse smartly and went at full gallop for the narrower Mistick road. John Larkin's horse was quicker and surer than the officer's heavy parade horse, and when Revere had gone three hundred yards he was sure he could stay ahead. The British horse got mired down in clay, and Revere was alone and heading for Lexington.

He rode without stopping until he reached the town of Mistick, where he woke up the captain of the Minute Men. All of the towns had drummers trained to beat an alarm and men to ring the steeple bells. In Mistick, a cry went up, "The regulars are out!" The Minute Men grabbed their muskets and sent their wives and children with any money or jewels to hide in the swamp. From Mistick on, Revere began to shout an alarm in front of each house along the road to Lexington.

By Arlington, he was back on the main road and galloping along easily. Even with the detour, the trip from Charlestown had taken just under an hour, and it was a little before midnight when Revere reined in his horse at Jonas Clark's neat two-story parsonage. Sergeant William Munroe, who owned the tavern down the road, was considered the militia's most alert noncommissioned man, and he had taken charge of the seven-member guard at the house.

Paul Revere told him that he must go inside.

Sergeant Munroe replied that the family and their guests had retired for the night. If he let Revere in, the noise would disturb them.

"Noise!" Paul Revere said. "You'll have noise enough before long! The regulars are coming out!"

He rapped loudly on the door.

The Reverend Clark opened an upstairs window and demanded to know what was going on.

Revere said he must see John Hancock.

In the dark the clergyman didn't recognize him and said he couldn't let strangers into his house. But John Hancock, in bed but not asleep, recognized Paul Revere's voice. Opening his window, he called cheerfully, "Come in, Revere! We are not afraid of *you*."

The British troops had waded ashore and were huddling, chilled and wet, at Phipps's farm on the western bank of the Charles as they waited for their marching orders from Colonel Smith. In the dark, their boots and trouser legs soaked and muddy, the men tried to puzzle out the reason they hadn't moved for an hour.

Even when dry, British uniforms had been designed for splendor, not comfort. Under the bright-scarlet coats heavy with linings and piping and brass buttons, other garments also constricted the troops—tight white or red waistcoats above knee breeches cut close enough to chafe. Wide belts cinching in at the waist. Stiff collars rubbing against the neck. Cumbersome hats jammed down on temples they had greased and powdered white. When they passed in review, the effect could be magnificent. But on a march the British soldier was trussed and bound. With provisions and arms, he lugged about one hundred and twenty-five pounds on his back.

A little before 1 A.M.—almost two hours from the time they had landed—food for the day's march was brought ashore and passed out. Most of the men had packed their own provisions, and they threw the army rations away.

The Minute Men at Lexington had been storing gunpowder and musket balls all winter for a morning like this. The town had also bought a drum, and veterans of the French and Indian War had taught a boy of sixteen named William Diamond to beat out battle calls. As their captain the Minute Men had elected John Parker, who had once fought against the French as a ranger and was now a big-boned forty-five-year-old farmer with seven small children. He had alerted his men the previous afternoon when he got the first report of unusual British patrols along the Lexington road. Most of the militia had spent the evening at Buckman's Tavern near the town's green, awaiting Parker's orders. After Paul Revere confirmed that British regulars were on their way, Captain Parker told his men to fall in on the green. It was about 1 A.M.

Lexington's Minute Men were hardly formidable. Only seven hundred and fifty-five people, five of them slaves, lived in the town, along with four hundred cows. Since gunpowder was too expensive and scarce to waste on target practice, the men had been summoned to the green only once or twice before. The oldest of Parker's men was sixty-three, but that was not odd, because, with the French and Indian War over for eleven years, all the men with military experience were older than the usual fighting age. Of the seventy-seven Minute Men who answered Captain Parker's first call, fifty-five were more than thirty, and father-and-son teams were commonplace. At that first muster, six families had furnished twenty-nine of the men. One quarter of them were related to either Captain Parker or his wife.

When Parker told his men that Britain's best-trained and best-equipped forces were on their way to Lexington, few greeted the news with bravado. The men voted to disband, go to their homes and lie low. They would do nothing to provoke the British soldiers.

Then, sometime during the next four hours, that obvious and sane decision was reversed.

At Jonas Clark's parsonage, not far from the green, the household was awake and active. Billy Dawes had joined Paul Revere there, and after a brief rest they rode off to warn the Minute Men of Concord. John Hancock had dressed and was busy cleaning a sidearm. He knew that his proper place was out on the green with the Lexington Minute Men. When the Reverend Clark couldn't dissuade him, Samuel Adams reminded him that fighting was not their business. Why risk giving the British the triumph of capturing them? Adams' message was underscored by a verse the British troops had adopted lately to keep cadence as they marched:

> *"As for their King, John Hancock*
> *And Adams, if they're taken,*
> *Their heads for signs shall hang up high*
> *Upon that hill called Beacon."*

With a show of reluctance, Hancock agreed that Adams was right and had his chaise prepared for their escape. But before they could get away, another dispute arose. Dorothy Quincy, who had left her father in Boston, announced that she would be returning to his side the next day.

"No, madam," said Hancock. "You shall not return as long as there is a British bayonet left in Boston!"

Miss Quincy snapped, "Recollect, Mr. Hancock, I am not under your authority yet. I shall go to my father's house tomorrow!"

Lydia Hancock reasoned with the young woman, and Dorothy agreed to remain outside Boston for the time.

Riding away from the parsonage, Paul Revere and Billy Dawes came upon Samuel Prescott, a young doctor from Concord, who was heading home after an evening with his Lexington sweetheart. When Prescott heard where they were going, he volunteered to go along. He said the people of Concord knew he was a devoted Son of Liberty, and they would take his warning more seriously than an alarm sounded by strangers.

The three men had ridden halfway down the five-mile road when Dawes and Prescott stopped at a house to wake its owner. As he cantered two hundred yards ahead, Paul Revere spotted British officers hiding under a tree, just like the two men who had almost intercepted him earlier. Revere called to his companions, but it was too late. Four officers descended on them with pistols drawn.

"God damn you, stop!" one said. "If you go an inch further, you are a dead man."

Prescott turned sharply, and all three Americans tried to escape. But the officers kept them in their sights and shouted that they would blow their brains out if they didn't turn off into a nearby pasture. Billy Dawes took advantage of the darkness to flap his leather breeches and yell, "Haloo, boys! I've got two of them!" His call confused everyone, and Dawes whipped his horse around and dashed down the road. A little farther, though, he pulled up short in his excitement and his horse threw him. Dawes's ride was over for the night.

In the pasture, the British had prepared a makeshift jail. As they were forcing Revere into it, Samuel Prescott wheeled about, jumped his horse over a low stone wall and sped down the road to Concord. Revere spied a grove not far away and made for that.

Just as he reached it, six officers emerged from the shadows, seized his bridle, put pistols to his chest and ordered him to dismount. One of the officers asked what town Revere had come from and when he had left it. He seemed surprised by the answers. "Sir," he said, "may I crave your name?"

"My name is Revere."

"What? Paul Revere?"

"Yes."

As more proof of his fame, the other soldiers began to curse him and his exploits as a messenger. But the officer told him not to be afraid. No one would hurt him.

Revere thought he saw a way of turning his capture to good use. He assured the soldiers that they weren't going to achieve their goal that night.

The spokesman protested that they were only out looking for some deserters down the road.

Revere said he knew what they were after. But since he had already alarmed the countryside along their route, they would find five hundred men waiting in Concord. In fact, one man had told him there'd be fifteen hundred.

A major from the Fifth Regiment stepped forward, clapped a pistol to Revere's head and said if he didn't tell the truth, he'd blow his brains out.

When Revere repeated his story, the officers withdrew a few paces and murmured among themselves. When they returned, they ordered Revere to get back on his horse but they took away his reins. "God, sir," said the major, "you are not to ride with reins, I assure you." He passed them to an officer on Revere's right.

The patrol had picked up four other men suspected of being messengers. The British formed a circle around them and started toward Lexington at a good pace.

"We are now going to your friends," the major warned Revere, "and if you attempt to run, or we are insulted, we will blow your brains out."

Revere said the major could do as he pleased.

As he rode, Revere was harassed. "Damned rebel," the British called him and warned that he was in a critical situation. His reins were turned over to a sergeant with instructions that if Revere tried to run he should be killed. They were about half a mile from Lexington when a gun went off in the distance.

What was that for? the major asked Revere.

To alarm the country, Revere said.

The prisoners had become an impediment to the British. The major ordered the girths and the bridles cut on the horses of the other four suspects and told them they were free to walk home. Revere asked to be set loose with them. The major refused, but as they heard another round from the alarm guns in Lexington he admitted that if there was shooting ahead he couldn't afford to be burdened with Revere.

He called a halt and asked a sergeant whether his small horse was tired. When the sergeant said it was, the major ordered Revere to alight and the sergeant mounted John Larkin's fine animal. The British rode off, leaving Revere alone. To avoid being picked up again, he moved into a field. He was weighed down by his riding boots, but he began picking his way back to Lexington. Joseph Warren had directed him to warn John Hancock and Samuel Adams. Revere had accomplished that mission. If Concord was going to be alerted on this night, Samuel Prescott would have to do it.

With John Parker of the Lexington Minute Men facing the gravest decision of his life, the two most famous patriots in America were only steps away. Dorothy Quincy heard John Hancock slip away to consult with the militia on the green. Captain Parker never said afterward that either Hancock or Samuel Adams had persuaded him to reverse his decision to send his men home, and yet something changed his order, because at about 5 A.M. William Diamond again beat on his drum, and the Minute Men reassembled on Lexington Green. When they heard reports of the British advancing, some of them slipped away in the darkness. But others arrived to replace them. Captain Parker's thirty-eight men were strung across the green in one thin line, with enough men left to start a second file behind them. When the British regulars approached, the Lexington Minute Men were to stand fast, not firing, but not cowering. That mild show of defiance could be taken as a compromise. Or a provocation.

Paul Revere reached the parsonage a second time just as John Hancock's chaise was being loaded for his flight. He and Samuel Adams were leaving the women behind. Even if the British officers recognized John Hancock's aunt and Miss Quincy, they wouldn't harm them. Adams and Hancock were taking shelter with a clergyman's widow at Woburn. Revere was to join them, as well as Hancock's clerk, John Lowell, and Sergeant Munroe from the Lexington militia. At the door Hancock protested once more. He assured his audience, "If I had my musket, I would never turn my back on those troops."

They had traveled about a mile when Hancock remembered that a trunk he had left behind in John Lowell's room at Buckman's Tavern was filled with papers that would incriminate other patriots. Lowell and Revere agreed to retrieve it. Once again, Revere rode across the green. Captain Parker now had about sixty Minute Men arrayed in front of him. But Dorothy Quincy, who was examining the formation from the parsonage, could see how badly armed they were.

Hancock's trunk was on the tavern's upper floor. From the window, Revere looked down the road and watched the British troops drawing near. Their commander was Major John Pitcairn of the Marines, who was known in Boston as an agreeable and honest man who went to church on Sundays and swore blue oaths the rest of the week. Close by was the major who had captured Revere. With Lowell's help, Revere got the trunk downstairs and into a carriage. Pitcairn had brought his troops to a halt as he and his officers rode toward Captain Parker.

Riding past the scene, Revere heard Parker telling his Minute Men to let the troops march by and not molest them unless they acted first. Moving off the green, Revere headed for Woburn to deliver the trunk. He was facing away from the green when he heard a shot and turned his head. But he could see only smoke rising in front of the British soldiers. Then a great shout went up, and every British gun seemed to be firing.

The British major who had captured Paul Revere—his name was Mitchell—had raced back to report to Colonel Smith what Revere had told him on the Lexington road; the colonel had taken his information seriously. Revere had said there were at least five hundred men marshaling to meet the British, perhaps three times that number. Since it had been close to 4 A.M., Colonel Smith sent back to General Gage for the reinforcements he had been promised—Lord Percy leading eight hundred more men. Now Revere's threat was confirmed by the alarm guns Colonel Smith could hear across the countryside and by the bells pealing in every church steeple.

General Gage had specifically instructed Smith to secure, early on, the two bridges entering Concord. The colonel decided he must reach them before the rebels could surround them and stop him from crossing. That was why Major Pitcairn had ridden ahead with his six infantry companies at the moment Paul Revere was recovering John Hancock's trunk. Pitcairn had no intention of confronting Lexington's militia. But to get to the bridges he had to march his troops directly across the town's green, a two-acre triangular patch that divided the road into two branches.

As the British drew nearer, they heard William Diamond's drumming, but Major Pitcairn was the first to see the small number of Minute Men on the green. He ordered his men not to fire. He intended simply to advance, surround Captain Parker's few men and persuade them to throw down their arms. But Pitcairn was a Marine officer and only a volunteer on this operation. The light infantry marched in quick time toward the green, shouting curses.

Pitcairn approached the Minute Men and bawled, "Disperse, ye villains, ye rebels! Disperse! Lay down your arms! Why don't you lay down your arms and disperse?"

By that time, Captain Parker's militia totaled seventy-seven. As Pitcairn appeared, Parker called to them to show restraint. Lexington's Minute Men had made their statement. They had stood fast on the green and met the British Army. When Pitcairn came nearer, Parker called to his men to hold their fire and disband. Some began to amble off the green, carrying their muskets. They were not obeying Pitcairn's command to throw down their arms, but they were breaking ranks and walking away. There were exceptions; Jonas Parker, the captain's elderly cousin, threw his hat filled with musket balls on the ground between his feet and prepared to fight all by himself.

Otherwise, the crisis seemed to be passing. Major Pitcairn was now shouting to his own troops, "Soldiers, don't fire. Keep your ranks. Form and surround them."

In his carriage headed for Woburn, Samuel Adams heard the first sounds of gunfire. "Oh, what a glorious morning is this!" he exclaimed to John Hancock.

Adams knew from his answer that Hancock thought he was talking about the fair spring dawn, and he explained. "I mean," he said, "what a glorious morning for America."

Old Jonas Parker, who had vowed never to run from British guns, fell from a musket ball. He tried to fire from the ground, but a British soldier ran him through with a bayonet. As Captain Parker's men moved off the green, the British soldiers fired at them. A shot either from behind a stone wall or from a window at Buckman's Tavern—in the confusion no one could be sure—had touched off the onslaught, and in an instant the British professionals were beyond any attempt by their officers to control them. At most a handful of Parker's militia fired at the British, and that was only after the infantry was already pumping shot into the backs of fleeing Minute Men. When the smoke cleared, eight Americans lay dead on the green.

Most of the men the troops killed had not defended themselves. Now the British were breaking into houses along the green, looking for the Minute Men. When Colonel Smith caught up with his men, he was appalled. Turning to a lieutenant, Smith said, "Do you know where a drummer is?" The officer found one, who began to beat the tattoo to lay down arms. Hearing it above the din triggered a response that no amount of shouting had achieved. The British troops stopped firing.

Lydia Hancock was leaning out of an upper window at the parsonage and saw the slaughter on the green. She heard a whiz close to her ear. "What's that?" she asked. Her family told her that it was a bullet and she had better be more careful.

Once Colonel Smith had restored order and chastised his men for the breakdown in discipline, he sent them marching off the green with their fifes and drums, headed for the stores of ammunition at Concord. They were leaving behind the eight corpses and nine wounded Minute Men. The only British casualty was one private, lightly hit.

The town came out to see what had happened. Weeping, Lydia Hancock helped to dress the Clark children. Dorothy Quincy and Jonas Clark hid money, watches and other valuables in a potato bin and in the attic. They had watched as the British stormed neighboring houses and knew that when the troops had finished in Concord their return to Boston would lead them through Lexington again.

John Hancock sent his carriage back for the two women, with a note telling them where to meet him. He remembered a fine salmon that had been intended for dinner and instructed them to bring it. The women joined Hancock and Samuel Adams at Woburn, and the salmon was cooked, but before they could eat it a man burst in and told them the British were coming.

A slave led Adams and Hancock to a nearby wood, where they waited until they decided the report was false. Unsettled now, the party moved on by horse cart to a house in Billerica. There John Hancock finally had his dinner—salt pork and cold potatoes, served on a wooden tray.

At headquarters, General Gage had been awakened at 5 A.M. by Colonel Smith's courier. Anticipating Smith's call for reinforcements, Gage had instructed Lord Percy and his men to be dressed, armed and on the parade ground at four. But Gage's orders had been left at the house of the brigade's major, who was out. When he came home, his servant failed to tell him about his commander's message. The major, along with the entire brigade, was still asleep at 5 A.M.

It was already 7:30 before the troops were roused and ready to march. Then Percy was held up waiting for the Marine battalion, whose sealed orders had been sent in care of Major Pitcairn. The major had already left for Concord, and for hours no one at his headquarters thought to open them.

At 9 A.M. the relief column marched out Boston Neck and down the overland route that Billy Dawes had traveled ten hours before. With more than six hundred men and two cannon, Percy took along the regimental band. It played "Yankee Doodle" to humiliate the townspeople as they looked on from their doorways. As the British column passed near the Public Latin School, a loyalist teacher, John Lovell, who had taught John Hancock, turned to his class and said, "*Deponite libros*." (Lay down your books.) Samuel Adams was not the only one to grasp the day's significance. "War's begun," Lovell said, "and school's done."

With Paul Revere captured and Billy Dawes thrown from his horse, it was Samuel Prescott who reached Concord to sound the alarm. Between 1 and 2 A.M., bells began to ring, and the Concord militia gathered at Wright's Tavern. With a population of fifteen hundred, Concord was twice the size of Lexington, and the number of Minute Men who turned out was three times as large as Captain Parker's force. At daybreak a scout returned to say that there had been gunfire at Lexington but he didn't know whether the British had fired gunpowder as a warning or had loaded their weapons with ball. The two hundred and fifty men of the militia caucused and decided not to wait for the British to carry the battle to them. Led by their major, John Buttrick, they started down the Lexington road, with fifes and drums to set the pace.

They had gone a little more than a mile on the narrow road when they sighted Colonel Smith's troops coming toward them. The Minute Men halted and waited until the British were within five hundred yards. Then, as the British officers watched in surprise, Major Buttrick called for an about-face and marched his men, fife and drum still sounding at their side, back toward Concord, as if they were an advance escort for the British troops. Colonel Smith's men were also accompanied by fife and drum, and martial music filled the air as the two contingents marched.

Near the approach to the town, a high ridge ran along the road. Colonel Smith saw that the ridge posed a tactical danger and sent infantrymen to take command of it. The late-straggling militia who had been watching from those heights now drifted back to town. Not a shot had been fired. Sticking to the road, the British grenadiers entered Concord at 8 A.M., sixteen miles and eleven hours from their starting point in Boston.

The morning of April 19 was cold and windy, though bright, and the cherry trees were in bud. As the Minute Men slipped away from the British troops, they debated hurriedly about their next course of action. The Reverend William Emerson called for resistance: "Let us stand our ground. If we die, let us die here." Others had more respect for the odds, and the Minute Men faded back until they reached a hill from which they could see militia from the neighboring country pouring toward Concord.

Colonel Smith's men secured both bridges, the North and the South, and then he sent his infantry companies to search the town for gunpowder, arms and hoarded food. One company went ahead two miles looking for a cannon that had been buried that morning.

As the British troops spread out, the Minute Men consolidated their forces in the hills and organized the arrivals streaming in.

In the town, the grenadiers conducted only a routine search. After their dressing-down at Lexington, they were subdued. The treasurer of the provincial congress, Henry Gardner, had left a chest of documents in his room at the inn in the care of a young woman. She told the soldiers that it was hers and demanded that they leave. At gunpoint, Major Pitcairn made the jailkeeper show where the town cannon had been buried, then ordered his men to dig it up and disable it.

General Gage had instructed his troops to pay for whatever they might need. When the wife of a militia officer refused to accept money for food and drink, several soldiers tossed coins into her lap. Tucking them into her pocket, she said, "This is the price of blood." As the privates continued to look for weapons, their commanders sat in chairs on the lawns. To those in Concord, who had not heard details of the shooting at Lexington, Pitcairn seemed to be an amiable if scrawny figure, although he made a casual vow of vengeance. Stirring a brandy-and-water with his finger, he said he hoped he'd be stirring damned Yankee blood that same way before nightfall.

While Smith's officers ordered breakfasts of meat and potatoes, trouble was mounting at the North Bridge. By midmorning, Captain Walter Sloane Laurie, along with three British companies, twenty-eight men to a company, was charged with securing the bridge against the Americans gathering two hundred yards away. Laurie's men were estimating that behind a nearby hill a thousand Minute Men might be waiting; the number was closer to four hundred. Still, when two of Laurie's companies were ordered to climb a nearby hill he was left to hold the bridge with only one company, barely more than two dozen soldiers.

For a time, twenty-eight British infantrymen looked warily in the direction of hundreds of concealed Americans. The Minute Men seemed content to let the British control the bridge until they noticed smoke rising from the town.

Smith's grenadiers were destroying the few armaments they had found. They hacked down the town's Liberty Pole and set it on fire, and they burned gun carriages and entrenching tools. From their lookout on the hill, the Minute Men saw smoke from the bonfires and concluded that the British were burning their houses.

One Concord lieutenant asked his men, "Will you let them burn the town down?"

Their officers told them to get ready to move. They were to hold fire until the British soldiers at the bridge fired, then they were to fire as fast as they could. The Minute Men loaded their guns and started to march.

Captain Laurie not only had few troops but had deployed them badly, keeping them at the far end of the bridge with their backs to the river as they faced the rebels. The two British companies on the nearby hill saw the militia advancing and scrambled down to join Laurie at the entrance to the bridge. With only a narrow footbridge for his escape, the captain had about eighty men to face four hundred grim farmers armed with muskets.

The Minute Men were three hundred yards away when Captain Laurie asked a young lieutenant whether he should inform Colonel Smith of the danger. By all means, the lieutenant agreed. The men swarming toward them looked very determined. Smith was less than half a mile away. As Laurie backed his men hastily across the bridge, a messenger returned to say that Smith himself would be leading the reinforcements.

For Captain Laurie, the news was calamitous. The fat colonel would slow down his troops. As the Minute Men strode toward Laurie two by two, he told his soldiers to tear up the planks at their end of the bridge.

The commander of the Concord militia at the bridge, Major Buttrick, called out to the British to stop the destruction. The Minute Men were so close by that time that Laurie's soldiers had to obey. Laurie ordered them into columns for street fighting. It was a new technique for the infantry—the front rank was supposed to fire, then turn about-face and march to the rear to reload while the next rank fired. Street fighting might have been an orderly way to retreat through an English city, but Laurie's men were surrounded by open meadows. Worse, they didn't understand the tactic very well.

What each British soldier could depend upon was his musket, a four-and-a-half-foot weapon called Brown Bess. A man didn't need to be a sharpshooter. All he had to do was get within a hundred and twenty-five yards, point it and pull the trigger. Fired from much farther away, the three-quarter-inch balls simply fell to the ground. Given that range, a man had little time to aim. The emphasis was on volume. A well-trained company could fire, load and fire again fifteen times in four minutes. Though it might not have required a keen eye, steady hands were essential. To load, a soldier bit off the end of a paper cartridge that held the powder and the ball, shook some powder into the firing pan and closed the lid. He then rested the butt of his musket on the ground, poured the rest of the powder and the ball down the barrel and rammed in a wad of paper to hold the shot in place.

When he pulled the trigger, the firing cock fell, the flint struck steel and the spark ignited the powder in the firing pan. Fire flashed from the touchhole into the charge, and the ball was sent flying. That was the way Brown Bess worked—when the powder wasn't too damp to catch the spark and the touchhole wasn't too badly clogged.

In the end, none of it mattered—neither the strategy nor the weapons. Captain Laurie never gave an order to fire. Just the same, as had happened in Boston, a musket went off. Two or three more shots followed. The British infantrymen may have fired on their own initiative or they may have fired as a warning. The first bullets only roiled the surface of the river.

But they set off a volley from twenty British muskets. The Americans hadn't believed that the British regulars meant to do anything more than frighten them with harmless bursts of powder. "God damn it!" a militia captain shouted. "They are firing ball!"

Two militia officers were struck dead, and the fifer from the town of Acton was wounded. Since the British had opened fire, Major Buttrick gave the order the Minute Men had been waiting for. "Fire, fellow soldiers! For God's sake, fire!"

Advancing and firing as fast as they could, the Americans drove Laurie's men onto the riverbank at the end of the bridge. Their aim was deadly. Few of their weapons were as new or as efficient as Brown Bess, but the Minute Men had been shooting a weapon, often the same one they were using now, since they were old enough to walk. Some had even brought the long guns they used for duck hunting. The British soldiers may have been equipped and trained by a great world power, but this morning at the North Bridge the Minute Men were more effective. In that first round, they killed three men and wounded four of the eight British officers.

Captain Laurie's men broke and ran for the center of town.

On the way, they came upon Colonel Smith plodding to their rescue. Smith had never had much enthusiasm for this entire operation. Hearing of the rout, he marched his grenadiers back to Concord. It was 10:30 A.M. As Smith debated his next move, Minute Men were rushing to Concord from every farm within the sound of the shots. The alarm bells spread from town to town, and when they reached Watertown, Joseph Palmer, who had mixed saltwater tea at Boston Harbor, saddled up his wife's horse and rode to the battle. At Sudbury, Deacon Josiah Haynes had risen at dawn, and he had run and walked the eight miles to Concord's other bridge. Once there, Haynes, who was seventy-nine, chafed at the caution of the militia commander: "If you don't go and drive them British from that bridge, I shall call you a coward."

Colonel Smith didn't know that a series of bungles had delayed Lord Percy and the reinforcements. He waited nervously for ninety minutes as scouts brought him reports of the hundreds of farmers flocking into the hills around Concord. Smith retained one bargaining chip by staying in town. Despite the confusion over the smoking bonfires, his men hadn't set fire to any houses, and Smith assumed that the militia would not turn their town square into a battlefield. Yet the number of Americans surrounding him kept growing, until at last Smith felt that he couldn't wait for Percy. At noon he ordered his troops to march back down the road to Lexington.

As the British soldiers waited and listened to every rumor, their anxiety had risen. One story was particularly harrowing. Not satisfied with their slaughter at the bridge, the Minute Men were supposed to be scalping their wounded victims. It was a nightmarish vision for veterans of the French and Indian War, and for the younger men who had only heard of such atrocities. In this case, there was a trace of fact to the story. A feeble-minded young man from the countryside had been hurrying across the bridge to join the Minute Men and had come upon a wounded British soldier. Before anyone could stop him, he had split the soldier's head with a tomahawk.

At Lexington, the dead had been cleared from the green. John Parker ordered William Diamond to beat his drum as the order for survivors to fall in, and although some Minute Men were bandaged and aching, they answered Parker's call. Six hours after losing one third of their ranks to the British onslaught, Captain Parker's men were on the road to Concord.

The British were now withdrawing from Concord with surprising ease. Because General Gage had conceived the mission as routine, he hadn't sent along a military doctor. While Colonel Smith had fretted about his next move, injured British troops had been taken to local doctors around Concord, who agreed to dress their wounds. Soldiers who couldn't walk were hoisted onto horses, and chaises were commandeered for those who couldn't ride. With no drums or martial airs, Colonel Smith led his limping troops out of Concord. The Minute Men seemed content to watch them go. The British moved quietly along toward a bend in the road called Meriam's Corner.

Here the road to Lexington veered right, joining with another road, from Bedford. As the British were marching down the Lexington road, Concord's Minute Men and their new reserves had cut across the meadows and reached Meriam's Corner before them. Lining up behind houses and barns, behind trees and stone fences, they waited.

Nearby, a narrow bridge stretched across a brook. Colonel Smith's light infantry came down from the ridges where they had been surveying the road and bunched together to cross over. At that moment, with the British troops trapped in a slow and unprotected file, shots burst on them from every fence and tree trunk. The Americans were not fighting by the accepted rules of war. They were sniping at their enemies and picking them off. To Colonel Smith and his men, this was not warfare, it was murder. Within minutes, the road at Meriam's Corner was bright with blood.

At first the British fought back in the classic manner they had been taught. Standing their ground, they tried to return shot for shot. But they were exposed under the noon sun, their attackers mere fleeting shadows. As they pushed past the Corner, the British commanders realized that this was no isolated ambush. The Minute Men had launched their own variation of street fighting. They fired, rushed ahead behind walls or the embankment, reloading as they ran, and popped up ready to fire again two dozen yards down the road. Their crossfire kept Colonel Smith and his men pinned to the road, and they faced fifteen more miles to Boston.

As he came up the road from Lexington, Captain Parker heard the British soldiers rushing toward him, and he ordered his men to take cover. The Lexington Minute Men began to avenge the comrades killed that morning. Once again, the British had no idea how many enemy were lurking along the road. One officer was sure, from the amount of gunfire, that there must be five thousand. When the shooting intensified, the British troops broke and ran under the barrage, leaving their dead and wounded on the road. They paused only for Colonel Smith, who had been struck in the leg. His men pushed him up on a horse, but he made so visible a target that he slipped back to the ground to hobble along as best he could. Major Pitcairn was thrown from his horse, which ran across the fields toward the Minute Men. Whenever a British soldier fired now, it was aimlessly. Once in a while a British shot did hit home, and Deacon Haynes was killed as he reloaded his musket. Two of Captain Parker's Minute Men died.

One British regular came out of a house where he had been searching for snipers and ran into James Hayward of the Acton militia. The British soldier pointed his musket and said, "You're a dead man."

Hayward raised his weapon and answered, "So are you."

They fired together.

For Colonel Smith's men the mission had now lasted more than fifteen hours. Wounded, exhausted, short of ammunition, stumbling under the weight of their uniforms, they ignored their commanders as they ran toward Lexington. Finally, a line of officers managed to get in front of them. They turned, facing their men with bayonets drawn. If you run another step, the officers warned, you will die. The soldiers were coerced into loose ranks and marched dazed and ragged to Lexington. At two-thirty that afternoon, they once again entered Lexington and learned that they were saved. Lord Percy's reinforcements had arrived.

Hugh Percy was shrewder at strategy than Colonel Smith. His men had towed two cannon from Boston, and Percy had put one on each of the hills overlooking Lexington. He had halted his forces well short of the green, at about where Major Pitcairn had left the infantry to ride ahead and tell John Parker's Minute Men to throw down their arms. From the hills, Percy's men could watch the Americans bob up from behind walls and fences. Whenever a group formed, a cannon shot sent them running.

Percy wanted only to get Smith's men and his own back to Boston with the fewest casualties. The infantrymen had fallen panting to the ground after their dash down the Lexington road. Percy let them rest there for half an hour while he shot his cannon to discourage the Minute Men from approaching. It was quarter to four before Percy and some eighteen hundred soldiers began their retreat. A third of them were wounded or so badly shaken by the American barrage that they were useless.

In their hiding places, the Minute Men rested. A new commander had come to take charge, Major General William Heath, who had been appointed in February by the Provincial Congress. Heath, a farmer stouter than Colonel Smith, was a devoted reader of military tactics with a long service in the militia. His extensive study of past battles counted for less now than the Minute Men's instinctive strategy of finding cover and picking off the enemy whenever he showed himself. As the British organized their retreat, the Americans got ready to repeat what they had been doing successfully since noon.

This time, the British were not caught by surprise. Lord Percy ordered three houses near the green burned to the ground so that no snipers could harass the men at the rear of his column. Along the route, the British were told to storm houses from which gunfire was coming, kill the snipers and burn the houses.

As the retreat began and the Americans fired from behind trees and fences, Percy's enraged men forced their way into every suspicious house and shot any man they found there. The British excused their behavior by saying they were being unfairly provoked. Why wouldn't the Americans make one open, manly attack? Instead, they went on skulking like dastards behind their hedges. Sometimes a rebel yelled, "King Hancock forever!"

British flankers were plundering the houses they were supposed to be searching, and the Minute Men chased them faster and sniped with greater determination. As sunset approached, Percy realized that he had to use the last hour of light to get his men to Boston, and he had to decide which route to take. He knew that if he went by way of Cambridge, he couldn't cross the Charles because General Heath had sent Minute Men to take up planks of the only bridge. The other route would take Percy to Charlestown. Once there, his men would be protected by the guns of the *Somerset*. Heath anticipated Percy's choice. Mustering a band of Minute Men, he ordered them to come out into the open and hold the Charlestown road. But one shot from Percy's cannon sent them back into hiding.

The Minute Men had a final chance to engage Percy. Fifteen miles north of Boston, Colonel Timothy Pickering of the Salem militia had heard within three hours about the shooting at Lexington. Pickering had convinced himself that Colonel Smith probably had taken his troops back to Boston immediately afterward and that they were already in their camp by this time. Pickering's men had pleaded with him to set out for Lexington all the same. He had refused. At last the townspeople had compelled him at least to try to intercept the British on their return march. But Pickering's heart was not in the attempt. He held up his men repeatedly while he waited for messengers. The well-trained troops from Salem and Marblehead were outraged when they heard at nightfall that the British had reached safety in Charlestown only thirty minutes ahead of them.

The British troops had traveled about fifteen miles since noon. American losses had been heavy, but the figures told the story: Forty-nine Americans killed compared to seventy-three British soldiers. Thirty-nine Americans wounded against one hundred and seventy-four British casualties. Five Americans and twenty-six British soldiers missing. The ratio of casualties was even more damning for Colonel Smith. Twenty percent of the British officers and men who had taken part in the day's operation had been killed, wounded or taken prisoner. A few had run away.

The day had been shameful for most of the British commanders from General Gage down. Only Hugh Percy had played a bad hand to a draw. For a few Americans, the outcome was also damaging. Colonel Pickering did not live down his hesitation. General Heath hadn't won the full victory that his numbers and the terrain might have assured him. But Dr. Joseph Warren, the most uncompromising of the younger theorists, had become a warrior. The next day the Minute Men were praising the nerve

A LIST of the Names of the PROVINCIALS who were Killed and Wounded in the late Engagement with His Majesty's Troops at *Concord*, &c.

KILLED.

Of *Lexington*.

* Mr. Robert Munroe,
* Mr. Jonas Parker,
* Mr. Samuel Hadley,
* Mr. Jona⁵ Harrington,
* Mr. Caleb Harrington,
* Mr. Isaac Muzzy,
* Mr. John Brown,
Mr. John Raymond,
Mr. Nathaniel Wyman,
Mr. Jedediah Munroe.

Of *Menotomy*.

Mr. Jason Russel,
Mr. Jabez Wyman,
Mr. Jason Winship,

Of *Sudbury*.

Deacon Haynes,
Mr. —— Reed.

Of *Concord*.

Capt. James Miles.

Of *Bedford*.

Capt. Jonathan Willison.

Of *Acton*.

Capt. Davis,
Mr. —— Hosmer,
Mr. James Howard.

Of *Woburn*.

* Mr. Azael Porter.
Mr. Daniel Thompson.

Of *Charlestown*.

Mr. James Miller,
Capt. William Barber's Son.

Of *Brookline*.

Isaac Gardner, Esq;

Of *Cambridge*.

Mr. John Hicks,
Mr. Moses Richardson,
Mr. William Massey.

Of *Medford*.

Mr. Henry Putnam.

Of *Lynn*.

Mr. Abednego Ramsdell,
Mr. Daniel Townsend,
Mr. William Flint,
Mr. Thomas Hadley.

Of *Danvers*.

Mr. Henry Jacobs,
Mr. Samuel Cook,
Mr. Ebenezer Goldthwait,
Mr. George Southwick,
Mr. Benjamin Daland, jun.
Mr. Jotham Webb,
Mr. Perley Putnam.

Of *Salem*.

Mr. Benjamin Peirce.

WOUNDED.

Of *Lexington*.

Mr. John Robbins,
Mr. John Tidd,
Mr. Solomon Peirce,
Mr. Thomas Winship,
Mr. Nathaniel Farmer,
Mr. Joseph Comee,
Mr. Ebenezer Munroe,
Mr. Francis Brown,
Prince Easterbrooks,
(A Negro Man.

Of *Framingham*.

Mr. —— Hemenway.

Of *Bedford*.

Mr. John Lane.

Of *Woburn*.

Mr. George Reed,
Mr. Jacob Bacon.

Of *Medford*.

Mr. William Polly

Of *Lynn*.

Joshua Felt,
Mr. Timothy Munroe.

Of *Danvers*.

Mr. Nathan Putnam,
Mr. Dennis Wallis.

Of *Beverly*.

Mr. Nathaniel Cleaves.

MISSING.

Of *Menotomy*.

Mr. Samuel Frost,
Mr. Seth Russell.

Those distinguished with this Mark [*] were killed by the first Fire of the Regulars

Sold in Queen Street.

PUBLISHED BY S.G. DRAKE 17 BROMFIELD STREET BOSTON.   HELIOTYPE

Roster of Americans killed and wounded at Lexington and Concord with which he had charged in to treat the wounded, even as musket balls burst around him and once grazed his wig. Overnight, Samuel Adams' protégé became an American hero.

The fighting along the Lexington road had created a new army for Joseph Warren to deal with. General Gage's four thousand men were now trapped in Boston while reports about the bloodshed at Lexington and Concord were bringing thousands of patriots to the scene. On behalf of the Committee of Safety, Warren wrote an account of the events of April 19, asking all available men to come to Cambridge and enlist in an American army. He language was urgent:

"Our all is at stake. Death and devastation are the instant consequences of delay. Every moment is infinitely precious. An hour lost may deluge your country in blood and entail perpetual slavery upon the few of your posterity who may survive the carnage."

He set up a headquarters in Cambridge at Harvard Yard. General Artemus Ward arrived at the head of the Shrewsbury militia to take charge. General Heath's command had lasted one day. The appeal from Dr. Warren reached far across the countryside. Israel Putnam, a lieutenant colonel in the Connecticut militia, got the summons at his farm in Pomfret. Colonel Putnam, known as "Old Put," had already endeared himself to the patriots by driving a herd of sheep into Boston to ease the food shortage. Now, without stopping to change clothes, he left his plow and rode the eighteen hours to Cambridge. Elsewhere in Connecticut, the commander of the New Haven guard was wrangling with the town selectmen. They were reluctant to release their powder and ball to the militia on the basis of the rumors out of Lexington, but Captain Benedict Arnold assured them that if they delayed him any longer he would break the lock on the powder house and take whatever his men needed.

Within a day, Joseph Warren was surrounded by a throng of twenty thousand men, impulsive soldiers who had been drawn by the emergency. They had turned out the year before because of reports of an attack on Boston but within hours had drifted back to their farms. This time, Warren was better prepared to harness his volunteers. Keeping General Gage's troops penned up in Boston would take fewer than half of the men who had answered his call. He drew up a quick plan for enlisting eight thousand men for seven months' duty or a shorter period should the crisis be ended sooner. Warren's first version of the order of battle would have reduced the rank of some local militia officers, and he knew that would offend them. He divided the new army into companies of fifty men, allowing him to name more officers.

Other complications weren't so easily resolved. Colonel Pickering, Salem's reluctant commander, thought over the events of a day in which the Americans had killed or wounded two hundred and forty-seven British soldiers and decided that war was not inevitable. Pickering announced that the Americans could still work out a settlement with General Gage. When the other officers ignored him and went on preparing for war, Colonel Pickering led most of his men back to Salem.

Two days after the battle, Dr. Benjamin Church surprised the Committee of Safety in Cambridge by saying he intended to go into Boston the next morning. By now, the patriots had heard about Church's courage under fire and considered him almost equal to Joseph Warren. Church had shown Paul Revere blood on his stockings and told him it had come from a dying man as Church was leading the militia forward. For such a well-known patriot to try to slip into Boston now seemed foolhardy.

"Are you serious, Dr. Church?" Warren asked him. "They will hang you if they catch you in Boston!"

Since Church was determined to go, the committee asked him to bring back medicine for the wounded Minute Men. But Church didn't return to Cambridge until Sunday. He explained to Revere that he had been arrested and taken to General Gage's headquarters. He was held there, Church said, and finally released. Back in Cambridge, Church was eager to aid the cause. He agreed to write an account of the battles at Lexington and Concord, and his version gave an accurate description of the British troop movements on April 18 and 19. It incorporated the most grisly rumors of British atrocities—unarmed old men shot in their houses, women driven into the street just after giving birth. As Church's narrative circulated in newspapers throughout the colonies, his stories were improved—now the new mothers were naked when they were forced out of doors. Dr. Church's report was taken as one more proof of his commitment to the patriot cause.

Forty-one days after the first shot at Lexington, the London *Chronicle* printed a detailed story of the day's events. It was entirely favorable to the Americans and included a note from Arthur Lee, the London agent for Massachusetts. Lee said he had received sworn statements from witnesses who confirmed that the British had fired first. The affidavits were on file with the Lord Mayor should any reader care to consult them. General Gage's side of the affair arrived ten days later. Although it differed in emphasis, it confirmed that the unthinkable had happened, that Americans had fired back at His Majesty's troops. At first, Lord Dartmouth had not commented. Then Gage's version arrived, and Dartmouth tried to play down the battle's significance. But, having misjudged American resistance in the past, he seemed unlikely to be staying on in his post, especially since George III was clearly digging in for a showdown. America, the king told Dartmouth, was either a colony or an enemy.

Benedict Arnold

Arnold
1775

CAPTAIN Benedict Arnold's lineage in America was long and illustrious. His great-grandfather had succeeded Roger Williams as the president of Rhode Island Colony. By the time Benedict's father moved to Connecticut in the 1730s, however, the family's fortunes were slipping, and he became a barrelmaker. When Benedict was a child, his father was already drinking heavily.

The boy was not large—he never grew taller than five-foot seven—but strong and fearless. He was dark, with striking blue eyes and a quick, cold smile. Benedict's teachers remembered him as mischievous but bright and inventive, and his mother had no trouble in apprenticing him to her Lathrop relatives, two brothers from Yale College who had become druggists in Norwich.

Benedict found life at the pharmacy tame. When he could escape to the local mill, he rode the waterwheel like a bronco, soaring high in the air, holding tight as it dunked him under the water. That kind of daring made him famous around Norwich. It is not true that he stole young birds from the nest and maimed them or that he strewed glass shards near the school. His neighbors traded those stories only much later.

When Benedict was fourteen, the sheriff caught him stealing tar barrels from a shipyard for an election-day bonfire, and the husky boy stripped off his jacket and challenged the sheriff to settle the matter with his fists. A year later, Benedict ran off to join the British Army in the French and Indian War. He got as far as Hartford before his mother appealed to her minister, who had the boy sent home. The next year he succeeded and reached the battle over Fort Ticonderoga. But when he grew bored with military discipline, he deserted with a pocketful of parched corn and slipped back to Connecticut and his job at the drugstore. The British advertised in the *New York Gazette*, offering forty shillings for information leading to his arrest. When a British officer came through Norwich looking for deserters, Benedict's friends hid him in a cellar.

His apprenticeship ended at twenty-one, and the Lathrop brothers helped him open a shop in New Haven where he sold drugs, books and sundries imported from London. For his sign Benedict chose a Latin motto: *Sibi totique*—For himself and for all. Benedict's mother died and then his father, whose drinking had eventually made him a public embarrassment. Benedict spent his inheritance on a trip to London to buy stationery, drugs and rare books—the Bible in Hebrew, copies of *Tom Jones*. A year or two after he returned, he had acquired his own warehouse and partnerships in merchant vessels. Sailing up and down the coast, he traded in livestock and timber. John Hancock may have inherited his fortune, and Benedict Arnold made his own, but both fortunes were built on smuggling.

With his growing prosperity, Arnold became acceptable to the old families of New Haven. He bought a fine white house set off with luxuriant shrubbery on Water Street, where his only sister, tall, blond, gentle Hannah, acted as his hostess. Arnold had kept a jealous eye on Hannah from the time their parents died, and when she fell in love, he set out to end the romance. The man was French, Catholic and a dancing master, and Arnold ordered him to stay away from his sister. One day he looked through a window and caught the couple together in the sitting room. He sent a friend to rap loudly on the door. When the dancing master leaped out through the window, Arnold chased him, firing pistol shots at his heels. Hannah subsided into spinsterhood.

His success seemed to offer Arnold more scope for indulging his bad temper. When he was on a trading voyage to the Bay of Honduras, a British captain, Croskie, sent a note inviting him for the evening. Arnold was tired and didn't acknowledge the invitation. He intended to apologize the next morning, but Croskie found him first. "You are a damned Yankee," he told Arnold, "destitute of good manners."

Arnold removed a glove, bowed and returned to his own ship. Duels were forbidden in New England, but this was the West Indies. The next morning he arrived in a small boat at an island in the bay with his second and a surgeon. Captain Croskie appeared, followed by a band of natives. Arnold sent them away at gunpoint. Croskie fired first and missed. Arnold then grazed him. "I give you warning," he said as Croskie's wound was being dressed, "if you miss this time, I will kill you."

The British captain apologized.

Arnold almost lost one of his ships to confiscation when he was twenty-five. A sailor, Peter Boole, tried to blackmail him over contraband from the Indies. Arnold refused to pay, and Boole informed the customs agents. Soon afterward, Arnold caught him and beat him badly. When Boole threatened to sue, Arnold collected a gang of men who considered informing a heinous crime. They inflicted forty lashes on Boole and ran him out of town. Boole continued to press for justice until two judges awarded him a mere fifty shillings in damages. The judges were burned in effigy, and a torchlight parade was staged in Benedict Arnold's honor. Only six months after the Stamp Act riots, Arnold had found a way to turn the antigovernment sentiment to his own uses.

With his powerful build and his Caribbean tan, Arnold was popular with New Haven's young women. At twenty-five, he fell passionately in love with Margaret Mansfield, the daughter of New Haven's sheriff. They had their first son within a year of their marriage, and two more not long afterward. His shipping business sometimes faltered, London merchants hounded him for bills, and his wife grew estranged and would not answer his letters while he was away at sea. One winter he returned to find that Peggy

Arnold had heard that her husband had contracted a venereal disease in the islands and would not let him touch her.

One consolation was his membership in the Governor's Foot Guards, a unit made up of the most prominent young men in New Haven. When Arnold was named its captain, he was as proud as John Hancock had been of leading Boston's cadets, and he celebrated in the same way. He ordered his tailor to run up a scarlet coat, which he wore with white breeches and white stockings.

By the time of the Boston Port Act, Arnold was drilling his men regularly on the New Haven green. He had recruited about sixty of them, including many students from Yale. When news of the slaughter at Lexington reached New Haven, about noon the next day, Arnold bullied the selectmen into opening the powder magazine, but an officer asked him to delay his march to Massachusetts until orders could be issued. Captain Arnold wasn't prepared to wait. "None but Almighty God," he said, "shall prevent my marching."

All the same, sending the local guardsmen away from home required a written agreement, and before they left Arnold and his men signed a pledge to conduct themselves decently and inoffensively. They also agreed to avoid every vice, including gambling, swearing and drunkenness. Officers were not permitted to strike their men, but an unruly private could be expelled for being unworthy of serving in such a glorious cause.

Captain Arnold reached Cambridge and took as his headquarters the mansion of a Tory who had fled to Boston. His smart apparel and the uniforms of his men stood out among the dusty farm clothes of the other troops, and when the Americans wanted to return the body of a British officer who had been taken prisoner at Lexington and died of his wounds, Captain Arnold's men were chosen as the honor guard. But he was not content with ceremonial duties. The captain went before Dr. Joseph Warren and the Committee of Safety with a plan. He said that he knew Fort Ticonderoga, although he didn't reveal his desertion there. He proposed to lead a band of Americans to seize the fort from the British. The idea was daring but not original. Months before, Samuel Adams had anticipated what the British strategy might be when war came. He concluded that General Gage would try to cut off New England from the south and the west by sending troops down through Lake Champlain, Lake George and the Hudson River to

the town of New York. As Gage was dispatching scouts to Concord, Adams had sent John Brown, a Pittsfield lawyer, to Canada
to gauge Canadian attitudes toward an American revolt. Brown
was also told to gather information about the condition of the forts
since the French and Indian War. Three weeks before the battle
of Lexington, he had returned to say that if the king's troops provoked a battle, Fort Ticonderoga should be seized at once. In
fact, Brown had assigned the task to a group of New Hampshire
farmers who were already waging a running battle against New
Yorkers in a property dispute. Those men from New Hampshire,
led by a giant named Ethan Allen, called themselves the Green
Mountain Boys.

Joseph Warren and his committee knew nothing about Ethan
Allen and were enthusiastic about Benedict Arnold's suggestion.
Dr. Warren's army was less than two weeks old and needed Ticonderoga's cannon, mortars and howitzers. On May 3, the committee named Benedict Arnold a colonel in the new American Army
and authorized him to go to western Massachusetts and recruit
four hundred men for his expedition. Three days later, Colonel
Arnold heard in Stockbridge that a band of men had set off to
take Ticonderoga. Arnold had only a few officers with him and
no troops, but he resolved to overtake the ragtag upstarts from
New Hampshire and make them yield to his official commission.
He left his officers behind to drum up an army and hurried after
the trail of the Green Mountain Boys.

What Ethan Allen and Benedict Arnold had in common was
audacity. When Ethan was two years old, his father had moved
the family to a rough frontier farm in the New Hampshire Grants
lands. By the age of ten the boy was fending off wolves and rat-
tlesnakes, but his only schoolbooks were the family Bible and
Plutarch's *Lives*. When he was about sixteen, he was sent to the
town of Salisbury, where his family hoped that tutoring from a
local clergyman could make him acceptable to Yale. Then Ethan's
father died, and he was called home. From that time on he knew
that he was smart—smart enough, he thought, to see through ortho-
dox Christianity—but he apologized often for his shaky command
of grammar and spelling.

Before he turned twenty, he went off to fight the Marquis
de Montcalm during the French and Indian War. In the course

of that long struggle, a talented French military engineer named de Lotbinière built a star-shaped fortress of stone, earth and timber near the southern end of Lake Champlain. Across the lake the new fortress faced a bluff, and a little to the south Lake George emptied into a channel that flowed through a gorge into Champlain. As a result, whoever held the fort controlled the one southward passage out of Champlain, leading toward the Hudson River by way of Lake George, and on to Albany. The Frenchman had called his fort Carillon because of the loud splash of nearby rapids. For the same reason, the Indians called the spot Cheonderoga, which meant "noisy." Jeffrey Amherst took the base for the British in 1759, and his men called it Ticonderoga. The Americans called it Fort Ti.

When the French and Indian War finally ended, an irksome border war arose. New Yorkers claimed to hold deeds to the land Ethan Allen and his neighbors had been farming for years. Allen was chosen to represent them in court, but when he lost, the people of Bennington and its outlying areas dispensed with further legal pleas. Whenever a New York sheriff appeared in the disputed area, he was roughed up and sent home. Ethan Allen formed his own permanent posse in the early 1770s, with a man named Seth Warner as his captain. By New Year's Day 1772, the Green Mountain Boys were holding formal drills and passing in review like a professional army.

New York's governor called the Boys riotous trespassers and offered a twenty-pound reward for Allen's arrest. As the disturbances grew, the bounty went up to a hundred and fifty pounds. Allen resented the charge of trespassing, but the accusations of riotous behavior helped to keep his more timid opponents at bay. He proved it by betting his Boys that he could ride into Albany, drink a bowl of punch at the busiest tavern in town and return unharmed.

Allen reached the town, entered a crowded tavern and called for the punch. As he was sipping it, people flocked to the tavern to watch the noted outlaw. The county sheriff went with them. Allen finished the bowl, walked deliberately to the door and climbed back on his horse. The sheriff decided that the reward still wasn't large enough to risk an arrest. Ethan Allen rode off with a cry, "Huzzah for the Green Mountains!"

Allen and his Boys didn't expect the British crown to support them in their struggle with New York, and the dispute had left Allen with a passion for liberty. Lexington to him was only another proof of Britain's desire to enslave all of America. In a vote of confidence at the Catamount Tavern in Bennington, the Green Mountain Boys elected Allen their commander for the assault on Fort Ti. He withdrew to plan his campaign, and the Boys readied themselves by getting drunk.

They were deep in their preparations when Benedict Arnold arrived at the tavern. Colonel Arnold, resplendent as ever, announced that he had come to lead the charge against Ticonderoga. The Boys laughed. Arnold produced his commission from the Massachusetts Committee of Safety. To show how impressed they were, the Boys climbed on the tables and danced, flapping their coattails at him. One of their number spelled out their message: If Ethan Allen was replaced, the Boys would stay home. Amid mockery and shouts, Colonel Arnold was taken to meet Allen. Hours passed, heads cleared, and the Boys learned that their mission would now have two commanders. One of them had an army of two hundred and fifty men, the other had a piece of paper signed in Cambridge, Massachusetts.

The Boys reached the shore at Lake George well before dawn, but neither of their leaders had remembered that the water here was a mile wide, and no one had boats. It was nearly daybreak before they had rounded up enough small craft to row eighty-three men across the water to the fort's high walls. The Boys crept to the fortress gate. It was open. The sentry on duty was asleep. At the prospect of such an easy victory, the Boys began to whoop, which roused the sentry. He aimed his weapon, thought better of it and ran away. Ticonderoga had been built as a garrison for four hundred men, but during the dozen peacetime years the British had let it deteriorate and kept it severely undermanned.

A British lieutenant, Jocelyn Feltham, who heard the triumphant shouts ringing over the battlements, jumped from bed, threw open his door and ran into an immense man. Another, very dapper man was standing beside him. By what authority have you stormed this fort? Lieutenant Feltham demanded.

"In the name of the Great Jehovah and the Continental Congress!" roared Ethan Allen.

When they pressed on to the commander's quarters, Allen's eloquence failed him. Waving his sword above his head, he shouted over and over, "Come out, you old rat!"

Captain William Delaplace appeared, nearly speechless. "Damn you," he said, "what—what—does this mean?"

Allen assured the captain that the Green Mountain Boys had already disarmed his men; there had been only forty-two of them. At that news, Captain Delaplace held out the hilt of his sword in surrender.

It was then that the battle for Ticonderoga began in earnest. The Boys had discovered stores of rum. As they reinforced their high spirits, they ran through the fort, grabbing what they could from the British soldiers. Since Ethan Allen didn't try to stop them, Benedict Arnold raised his voice above the din to declare that military law strictly forbade looting. Several Boys spat at Colonel Arnold's feet.

One American had found a trinket, and its British owner was trailing after him, pleading to have it back. Colonel Arnold wrested it away and returned it. The Boy loaded a musket and pressed it hard against Arnold's chest. Admit, he demanded, that Ethan Allen was the leader here.

Benedict Arnold stared contemptuously at the man and said he was the official commander appointed by the authority of Massachusetts Bay and to him the Green Mountain Boys were behaving like drunken outlaws. The man lowered his weapon.

Four days later, fifty men recruited by Benedict Arnold's officers arrived on the scene, and Arnold took formal command of the fort, with its one hundred and twenty iron cannon, two brass cannon, fifty swivels, two 10-inch mortars, ten tons of musket balls, three cartloads of flints, thirty gun carriages and ten cases of powder.

Since their escape from Lexington, Samuel Adams and John Hancock had kept moving, but the stealth and the isolation were taking a toll of Hancock's nerves. From Worcester he wrote to the colony's Committee of Safety asking, What were they to do next? Where were the rest of the delegates who would be going to the second session of the Continental Congress in Philadelphia—Thomas Cushing, Robert Treat Paine, John Adams? Hancock craved news and was full of advice. Seize Castle William! Stop up the port! "Boston *must* be entered; the troops must be sent away. Our friends are valuable, but the country must be saved." Hancock added that he and Adams needed some sign of support from their countrymen. Where was the escort that would prove that they were the first citizens of the colony and not criminals on the run? "We travel rather as deserters, which I will not submit to."

A few days later, Lydia Hancock, along with Dorothy Quincy, joined her nephew at Worcester, and the party left for New York. At Fairfield, Connecticut, Hancock entrusted his aunt and Miss Quincy to the sheriff, Thaddeus Burr. After Hancock and Adams set out for Philadelphia, Burr welcomed another house guest to his mansion, his nephew Aaron.

The young man was a precocious nineteen. When he was an infant, his mother's death had launched Aaron Burr on a lifelong quest for affection, and he was helped along by his remarkable looks. He was slight but with a large head, a wide mouth and deep-set hazel eyes that many women found irresistible. He had come to understand early that every time a woman fell in love with him and he rejected her, however gently, he had made another enemy. All the same, he kept their letters. Some were from ladies, some from less than ladies, but Aaron cherished them all. His father, who died when Aaron was young, had been president of the College of New Jersey and had raised the money for Nassau Hall, the first building erected when the college moved to Prince Town. Aaron had applied for the freshman class when he was eleven years old and looked nine, but the college had rejected him. Two years later he was admitted as a sophomore. He had studied law and had eloped. The couple was caught at a ferry crossing and Burr was ducked in the water by the young woman's brothers. Now he was caught up in the politics exploding around him.

That commitment didn't stop Burr from a few days' flirtation with Dorothy Quincy. He enjoyed listening to his own deft flattery, and Lydia Hancock watched as he and Dolly Quincy talked together with obvious fascination. Miss Quincy discovered that Burr not only was pleasingly handsome but also had been left pleasantly rich. He may not have had John Hancock's holdings—few men did—but young Burr could support a wife in comfort. To her irritation, however, Dolly Quincy was never left alone with him. Lydia Hancock was always at her side. When Burr cut his visit short, Dolly Quincy knew whom to blame.

Her fiancé was also being diverted during his journey to Philadelphia. New York had provided a reception fit for a king, and Hancock described the scene to Miss Quincy in detail while assuring her that such displays were distasteful to him. Within three miles of the town he had been met by a grenadier company, a militia regiment, men in carriages and on horseback and thousands of people following in the road on foot and raising the greatest cloud of dust Hancock had ever seen. A mile outside New York, men stopped his carriage, freed the horses and insisted on using their own muscle to pull him into town. Hancock told Miss Quincy that he had protested against that excessive display and prevailed on them to return his horses. But he let her know that "in short, no person could possibly be more noticed than myself."

At King's Bridge, just north of New York, Hancock and Samuel Adams had joined the other Massachusetts delegates, and although Miss Quincy wouldn't know it from Hancock's letter, all five men had been included in the tumultuous welcome. It was Samuel Adams, riding in Hancock's phaeton, who had put a stop to pulling the carriage by hand. He thought the spectacle would be humiliating and said he wouldn't permit his fellow citizens to degrade themselves to the level of beasts.

By the time the delegates reached Philadelphia, Samuel Adams no longer cut much of a figure. His fine apparel had been abandoned when he fled Lexington, and he had only the clothes on his back. He needed a new outfit for this second session of the Congress, but he had almost no money of his own and he questioned the ethics of charging his clothes to the colony. In the end, politics prevailed. He decided that he must not disgrace Massachusetts, and Massachusetts should pay the bill, which it readily did.

No gentlemanly attire could deceive the conservative delegates as they convened on May 10, 1775, this time in Pennsylvania's State House. They suspected that Adams hoped to use the bloodshed at Lexington to provoke Congress into declaring America independent from Britain. If they were right, Adams stood nearly alone in that goal. Benjamin Franklin had come home from London and was there as one of Philadelphia's delegates. But Franklin's resolutions were mild ones—offering official thanks to Lord Chatham, to Edmund Burke, to all the members of both houses who had championed America's cause. Otherwise, to the dismay of John Adams, Franklin spent most of the proceedings fast asleep in his chair.

The session was barely launched when Samuel Adams' emissary, John Brown, showed up with news that Ticonderoga had been captured, along with its hoard of weapons. Ethan Allen was even talking about attacking Montreal and Quebec. The report disconcerted most delegates in Philadelphia. They first passed a resolution that Allen and Benedict Arnold take charge of the Ticonderoga artillery but make an inventory so that everything could be returned to Britain when harmony was restored. That order was soon countermanded. In fact, some delegates detected a slight shift in this session toward Samuel Adams' more combative position. For the first time, Georgia had sent a delegation to Philadelphia. Joseph Galloway of Pennsylvania had retired. George Washington of Virginia was attending every session in his colonel's uniform.

John Adams, before he had come to Philadelphia, had toured Dr. Warren's headquarters at Cambridge and had found confusion and shortages. He had retraced the march to Lexington and talked with townspeople along the route. Now he offered the Congress a comprehensive military plan. First, he urged the delegates to protect the patriots still living in Boston, who might be robbed, even killed, given the temper of the British soldiers. Adams recommended that each colony seize all British officials and hold them—humanely and generously—as hostage for Boston's patriots. Each colony should then set up its own new government, and the Continental Congress should declare independence and offer to negotiate peace terms with Britain. Adams also wanted to warn the British that if fighting continued, America would seek alliance with France, Spain or any other European power. At the same time, Congress should consider Warren's volunteers in Cambridge as a Continental Army, appoint a commanding general for them and underwrite their pay and costs.

Presenting that package, John Adams saw horror and detestation on many faces around the hall, particularly from some Pennsylvania delegates. He wasn't wrong this time to think he was unpopular. The delegates advocating reconciliation were determined to resist him, although the Congress had no trouble rejecting an unsatisfactory peace proposal from Lord North. John Dickinson, the "Pennsylvania Farmer," who had joined the Congress, introduced a resolution asking the king to open negotiations that would heal the breach. Samuel Adams, who tried to avoid public speeches, was content to let his cousin lead the attack against Dickinson.

Charles Thomson, the Congress's secretary, wanted to prevent a break between the Bostonians and the Pennsylvanians. He had confided to John Adams that Dickinson and his family were under great pressure from the Quakers. Dickinson's mother had warned him, "Johnny, you will be hanged, your estate will be forfeited and confiscated, you will leave your excellent wife a widow and your charming children orphans, beggars and infamous." Hearing that made Adams appreciate more than ever the support he was getting from his own wife and family.

After Adams' speech opposing reconciliation, Adams was called from the hall. John Dickinson grabbed his hat and followed him into the courtyard. "What is the reason, Mr. Adams," Dickinson asked, "that you New England men oppose our measures of reconciliation? Look ye! If you don't concur with us in our pacific system, I and a number of us will break off from you in New England, and we will carry on the opposition by ourselves in our own way."

Adams considered it a rude lecture, but he knew Dickinson had the votes. For once, even Samuel Adams was advocating a moderate public position. Although he promised his friends "one of the grandest revolutions the world has ever yet seen," he also reminded them that he had learned to wait until the fruit was ripe before he tried to gather it. John Adams accepted that argument reluctantly and voted for Dickinson's resolution. But in his diary he denounced the latest petition to the king as an embarrassing imbecility. He made his disgust more widely known a little later in a letter to Boston that described Dickinson as "a great fortune and piddling genius who has given a silly cast to our whole doings."

While his cousin was emerging as a leader in this new session of the Congress, Samuel Adams learned of the loss of another protégé. Josiah Quincy had been near death when he went to London to sound out British opinion and had died on shipboard during the return trip. The loss struck Samuel Adams hard. One of Quincy's last letters to his wife expressed the devotion that

Adams kindled in his young followers. "The character of your Mr. Samuel Adams runs very high here," Quincy had written from London. "I find many who consider him the first politician in the world."

John Hancock had taken his reception in New York and Philadelphia as proof that he was the world's foremost politician, and during this second session he received two more tributes. From Boston, General Gage issued a general pardon for all Americans who had taken part in the rebellion so far, but made two exceptions—Samuel Adams and John Hancock.

That mark of British disfavor enhanced Hancock's standing among the most militant delegates. And it did not estrange the Southerners who found Samuel Adams somewhat underbred but appreciated Hancock's congenial style. They knew that Hancock, like themselves, had something substantial to risk.

Peyton Randolph had been reelected president of the Congress but was called back to Virginia to preside over the Burgesses. Thomas Jefferson had ridden to Philadelphia to take Randolph's place in the Virginia delegation, but that still left the president's chair open. On May 24, 1775, both factions in the Congress tried to win over Henry Middleton of South Carolina by electing him to the position. Middleton declined because of ill-health, and in a mild assertion of their independent spirit the delegates chose John Hancock. Conducting Hancock to the president's chair, Benjamin Harrison of Virginia told him, "We will show Britain how much we value her proscriptions."

Samuel Adams knew the difference between supplying an Ebenezer Mackintosh with epaulets and creating a real army for America. He confessed that he knew nothing of military matters and had strong misgivings about any standing army. He much preferred fighting England with militia drawn from the various colonies. That way, no ambitious general could impose a military dictatorship on America.

But by early June he recognized that concerted military action was inevitable. Dr. Benjamin Church came to Philadelphia with petitions from Joseph Warren and the Massachusetts Provincial Congress for guidance in setting up a civil government there. The colony was acknowledging the authority of the Continental Congress and forcing its delegates to exercise a power they had been shrinking from. The petitions also urged the Congress to take command of the army, which was now almost six weeks old and still camping out around Cambridge.

With time, several aspects of John Adams' earlier plan had become outdated. General Gage was now letting anyone who chose to leave Boston to do so, which meant that no British hostages were required. The Pennsylvanians had prevailed, and a conciliatory resolution had been sent to London. Congress was waiting for a response. But the army at Cambridge remained a stubborn reality that the delegates in Philadelphia could no longer ignore. On June 7, 1775, the Congress advised Massachusetts to set up a temporary government. John Adams wanted to follow that unmistakable sign of separation from Britain by naming a commander for the troops at Cambridge. There were now three parties at the Congress—the patriots, the halfway patriots and a group of Southerners who would resent the selection of a New England general as commander in chief. They appeared to be committed to Colonel George Washington.

John Adams consulted with his cousin, but Samuel Adams seemed undecided about what to do. They both knew that John Hancock badly wanted to be asked to be commander in chief, but they weren't entirely sure why. Perhaps Hancock only wanted to be offered the honor and then would decline it. But what if he accepted? Beyond drilling his cadets on Boston Common, Hancock had no military experience.

John Adams had been sounding out other delegates, hoping to find a unanimous choice, but they had been reluctant to commit themselves. Early on June 14, John Adams invited Samuel Adams to walk with him in the State House yard for a little fresh air before the session began. He again laid out the troubling pieces to the puzzle. Samuel Adams agreed with his analysis but said only, "What shall we do?"

John Adams decided to force a showdown. He said he would move that morning that Congress adopt the army at Cambridge and appoint Colonel Washington as its commander. Samuel Adams had been protecting John Hancock's vanity for a decade. He listened to what his cousin was proposing but said nothing.

When the session convened, John Adams took the floor and reminded the Congress of the dangers in further delay. At any moment, the British Army might take advantage of the disarray in Cambridge and march out of Boston, spreading havoc across the countryside. Adams faced the president's chair as he spoke, and he saw John Hancock's pleasure at his preamble. Adams concluded with a motion that the Congress adopt the army at Cambridge and appoint a general for it. This was not the proper time to nominate that commander, Adams continued, since it might be a difficult choice. But he wouldn't hesitate to declare that he had one gentleman in mind for that vital position.

He was a gentleman from Virginia, John Adams said, and he watched with pleasure as John Hancock's expression began to change—first to mortification, then to bitter resentment. It was the triumph of Braintree over Beacon Hill. George Washington had been sitting near the door. At the hint that he might be the nominee, he made a quick exit to the library.

John Adams went on with his nominating speech: A gentleman whose skill and experience as an officer, whose independent fortune, great talents and excellent reputation would be approved by all America and unite the colonies better than any other person in the country.

Samuel Adams knew the consequences but rose to second the nomination. John Adams thought that President Hancock gave him a hard look.

In the debate that followed, no one denied that Colonel Washington possessed every virtue that John Adams claimed for him. But the entire army came from New England, and they seemed satisfied with General Artemas Ward. Wouldn't they resent a Southerner? Since the Congress wanted its army only to keep the British shut up in Boston, there seemed to be no urgency to the decision, and the subject was postponed to the following day.

But in Cambridge the army's leaders didn't know their mission was so limited. As John Adams went from delegate to delegate securing votes for George Washington, America's soldiers were preparing an ambitious surprise for the British and their king.

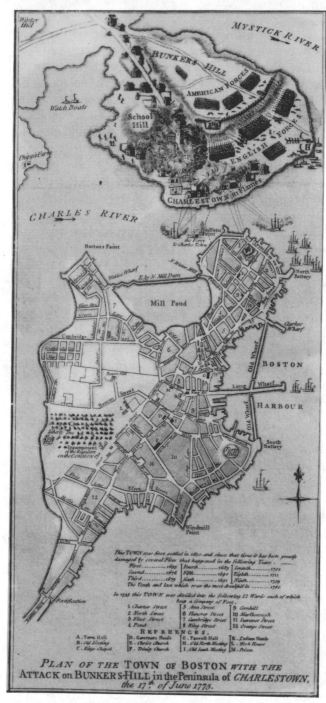

PLAN OF THE TOWN OF BOSTON WITH THE ATTACK on BUNKERS-HILL in the Peninsula of CHARLESTOWN, the 17ᵗʰ of June 1775.

Boston and the battle of Bunker Hill

Bunker Hill
1775

MAJOR GENERAL Henry Clinton was out reconnoitering for the British on the night of June 16, 1775, when he heard stirring on a hill overlooking Boston. Short and plump, somewhat fussy but well regarded in the king's army, Clinton was one of three major generals who had arrived less than three weeks earlier to shore up General Gage's command. Their orders had been signed long before Lexington, and the three—Clinton, William Howe and John Burgoyne—landed in America full of contempt for Gage's performance. When General Burgoyne was told that there were about five thousand British soldiers stationed in Boston, he had made a joke that circulated widely among both the loyalists and the patriots.

"What!" Burgoyne had jeered. "Ten thousand peasants keep five thousand king's troops shut up? Well, let *us* get in, and we'll soon find elbow room!"

The logical place to make that room was on the three crucial hills around Boston—Dorchester Heights, Bunker Hill and Breed's Hill, which looked down upon Charlestown's peninsula. The Americans could entrench themselves there and then fire down on the ships in the harbor or on the town itself. General Gage had been advised to secure one or all of the hills but had chosen instead to keep his men in Boston. With some accuracy, Lord Chatham had described Gage and his men to Parliament as "an impotent general and a dishonored army, trusting solely to the pickaxe and the spade for security against the just indignation of an injured and insulted people."

On this night, General Clinton heard the sound of pickaxes and spades from one of the hills above Charlestown and knew they didn't come from the British. Clinton rushed back to headquarters and urged Gage to land two divisions on the hills at daybreak. William Howe was also present and instantly agreed, although he was as torn as Gage in his allegiances. A large and florid man of forty-six, Howe had recently stood for Parliament as a Whig and had assured his constituents that he would never fight against the Americans. But when the king ordered him to Boston, Howe couldn't refuse. He had another incentive: as a dedicated gambler, he needed active-duty pay to clear his debts.

Howe and Clinton pressed Gage to take action, but he overruled them. Who could be sure what the Americans were up to? It was better to delay any decision until dawn.

When the sun came up, a lookout aboard the frigate *Lively* docked in the harbor spotted on Breed's Hill unmistakable signs of earthen walls that had been thrown up overnight. He sent word at once to his captain, and in the half-light the *Lively* opened fire. The battle of Breed's Hill had begun.

It had been intended as the battle of Bunker Hill. Early in June, a patriot visiting Boston had heard that the British planned to attack the Americans on June 18 at Roxbury and perhaps at Cambridge itself. Returning home to New Hampshire, the man passed his information to the Committee of Safety in Exeter, and its members had sent an express rider to warn Joseph Warren and the Massachusetts Provincial Congress.

Meanwhile, John Burgoyne had drafted a proclamation for

General Gage's signature ridiculing the rebels' claim of holding the British Army under siege in Boston. At fifty-three, Burgoyne was the eldest of the three generals sent to reinforce Gage, but also the most junior. He had spent much of his twenties and early thirties out of the Army. When he rejoined, he had made his reputation a dozen years earlier in the Portugal campaign when his cavalry took Valencia de Alcántara. Burgoyne always treated his soldiers well, and they responded by calling him "Gentleman Johnny." Like William Howe, Burgoyne had been elected to Parliament, but he had a greater distinction: shortly before he came to America, Burgoyne's play *Maid of the Oaks* was staged in London by David Garrick. Since he was too significant for his low rank under Gage, the king had agreed that Burgoyne either would receive a more appropriate command within six months or could return to London. The proclamation Burgoyne wrote for Gage showed a newcomer's ignorance of the political realities and a dramatist's partiality for fine language. It concluded by placing Boston under martial law.

Alarmed that Gage might be stirring at last, the Committee of Safety in Cambridge authorized the American Army to take control of Bunker Hill above Charlestown, along with the hills above Dorchester. The decision pleased Israel Putnam, who had been urging that a fort be built on Bunker Hill. One day he had attempted to provoke the British to fight by marching two thousand Connecticut troops up both Bunker and Breed's Hills. But Artemas Ward had believed that the new army, which was less than a month old, wasn't ready for a showdown and ordered Putnam to march his men down. They were allowed one war whoop, which the British ignored. Joseph Warren told Old Put that he admired his spirit, respected General Ward's prudence, needed them both and had to temper one with the other. Now Warren considered the Americans ready. On June 16 they would climb again to Bunker Hill and not march down.

The committee chose Colonel William Prescott to lead the operation. A popular veteran of the French wars, Prescott had showed such promise as a soldier that the British had offered him a military commission before he was twenty. Instead, he had spent the last thirty years farming until the Minute Men recruited him. When night fell, Colonel Prescott ordered his men to light their lanterns. With eight hundred and fifty men and about forty artillery gunners and their weapons, he marched down the Charlestown road toward Bunker Hill.

Along the route, Prescott's men passed Harvard College, where students had turned over Stoughton, Harvard and Massachusetts Halls as barracks for the makeshift army. To avoid damage, the college library had been moved to the town of Andover. The mild evening favored the expedition. Once past the college, the men marched beside orchards and farmland, kicking up billows of dust as they went. They crossed the stretch of clay and scrub that Paul Revere often traveled and went by the gibbet with the skeleton of Mark the slave.

A narrow bridge linked the Charlestown peninsula to the mainland. Beyond it, Bunker Hill rose abruptly from the marsh. Colonel Prescott called a halt and conferred with his officers. After a brief debate, Prescott marched his troops past Bunker Hill to the lower rise, Breed's Hill.

Prescott had made an aggressive choice. An American fort on Bunker Hill could have harassed Boston only slightly, and its position would have been largely defensive. Breed's Hill commanded the northern section of the town. But it also brought the Americans nearer the firepower of the British fleet.

With the delays and a need for stealth, it was nearly midnight before the soldiers reached a meadow on the top of Breed's Hill. For weeks the neighboring farmers hadn't dared send livestock to graze in such an exposed position, nor had they ventured up to mow the pastureland. Prescott's men moved through grass damp with dew and growing almost to their waists. Another veteran, Colonel Richard Gridley, inspected the land by starlight and staked out a redoubt. Prescott's men began digging. He ordered them not to speak and to muffle the sound of their shovels as best they could.

Prescott was building the fort on an angle, one hundred and thirty-six feet to each side. The southern corner pointed toward Boston, the eastern side faced the sea and looked down upon the large church and three hundred houses of Charlestown, which had been evacuated after Lexington. Digging by moonlight, afraid that the ships in the harbor might start shelling them at any moment, the nine hundred men worked swiftly. Prescott sent scouts to make sure the British hadn't been alerted by the sound of the shovels. They reported back that no one was stirring in Boston.

By 3:30 A.M., the fort of earth and timber was nearly done,

with ramparts five and six feet high. Colonel Gridley had provided a narrow entrance on the north side, but in his haste he hadn't thought of building bases for the artillery or openings for firing the guns. The men hadn't eaten since the previous noon and now were running low on water. They knew that with the first light they would face a barrage from four British ships firing a total of seventy-eight big guns. At Louisbourg years before, Prescott had seen mortar shells spread terror as they rolled forward with their fuses lighted. Most of his troops had never endured that sort of siege, and this defense they had thrown up in less than four hours was a rude one. But they had done what they could, and the ditch they had dug might protect them.

After firing its first shots, the *Lively* stopped shelling Breed's Hill and lowered a boat to send a message to General Gage. On the hill, Colonel Prescott used the sudden quiet for one last shoring up of his breastworks. In Boston, Gage convened his three major generals. They were still rankled by his delay the night before and impatient now to rout the Americans before they could dig in any deeper on the hill or receive reinforcements from Charlestown Neck. At dawn the generals could see black dots of men on top of the hill as they scurried around the pile of dirt they had raised. The rear of the fort seemed poorly defended, and Henry Clinton urged that they march troops up along the Mystic River and attack there.

The British ships had resumed firing, and cannonballs blazed through the air, raising dust clouds in the tall grass wherever they hit. Weighing his strategy, Gage decided not to take advice from Henry Clinton. The slope of Breed's Hill was gentle and the fortress barely more than a mound of earth. He could send his men on a forward charge straight up the hill.

Chatham's gibe about Gage's trusting to the spade had been especially stinging because the British Army despised digging in and huddling behind barricades. A direct assault would be more courageous and more satisfying. It was the gift Gage would give his troops.

He chose William Howe to lead the soldiers who would sweep the Americans down. Like Clinton, Howe had pressed for an instant response, yet now he would have to wait still longer, because the spot where he wanted to ferry his troops was too shallow for landing; high tide would not reach the site, called Moulton's Point, for nine or ten more hours. The landing would have to be put off until three in the afternoon. Howe tried to turn the delay into an advantage by having meat and bread prepared for his men. They were heading for a site barely two miles away, but General Howe loaded their knapsacks with supplies for three days.

Even though the British couldn't possibly lose, Thomas Gage remembered the lesson of Lexington and sent great numbers of his best men with Howe. Two thousand grenadiers and infantrymen would storm the hill, while battalions of marines on alert would wait for orders. As the troops got ready, Gage rode out to an advance headquarters for a closer look. With his lens, he watched the activity on Breed's Hill and then passed the glass to an aide, Abijah Willard.

Who was that tall man on the parapet who seemed to be in command? Gage asked. Willard studied the figure and announced that it was his brother-in-law, William Prescott.

"Will he fight?" Gage asked.

"I cannot answer for his men," Willard said, "but Prescott will fight you to the gates of hell."

Colonel Prescott had been using the hours of grace to prepare his troops for the bloodshed to come. They were deeply shocked when a cannonball tore off the head of a stocky farmboy named Asa Pollard as he was digging outside the fort. Prescott wanted to use this first casualty as a lesson. Bury him at once, he said; there would be no ceremony.

His men wouldn't agree to such callousness. They defied Prescott's order to return to work and gathered around Pollard's open grave while a clergyman offered prayers. The solemnity affected the survivors as Prescott had feared. Frightened men began wandering away and disappearing down the slope, headed for home.

When Israel Putnam showed up with a corpulent colonel named Samuel Gerrish at his side, he told Prescott to send the tools the men had been using back to a safe place. Prescott warned him that if he sent men off the hill, he would never see them again.

Putnam insisted. Every man of them will return, he said.

The colonel did as the general ordered, and a large party of men left with the tools. Not one came back.

Even before those defections, Prescott had appealed to headquarters for reinforcements, but his messenger found the army's leaders in Cambridge suffering from distress of their own. General Artemas Ward was prostrate with a gallbladder attack. He had already ordered part of General John Stark's New Hampshire regiment to join Prescott but was reluctant to part with any more men until the British response was clearer. There was nothing to stop Gage from ignoring Breed's Hill and charging into Cambridge to seize the patriots' food and ammunition.

General Ward agreed, however, to take Prescott's request to the Committee of Safety, which was in session. But its leading member, Dr. Joseph Warren, hadn't been able to sleep all night and was now lying down, trying to overcome a throbbing headache. Meeting without him, the committee was more willing to take risks than General Ward had been. The rest of General Stark's regiment was ordered to Breed's Hill, along with James Reed's men, who were also from New Hampshire. Stark was in Medford, about four miles away, when the order reached him. He lined up his troops and passed out what meager supplies he had—one cup of powder per soldier, fifteen musket balls, one flint. Since few of his men carried the same-caliber weapon, the balls had to be melted down and reshaped to their individual barrels. When that was done, they stuffed their ammunition into their pockets and rushed to the hill.

General Gage wasn't going to let the rebels slink down from the hills, barricade themselves in deserted houses in Charlestown and pick off his men as the snipers had done along the Lexington road. When a few shots came from the town, Gage ordered his artillery to bombard all of Charlestown's houses and its main church. They heated musket balls until they were red hot and also shot "carcasses"—hollow balls filled with burning pitch. By 2:30 P.M., the entire ghost town was in flames.

At Hancock's Wharf, General Howe's soldiers were massing to board the boats that would carry them to Moulton's Point. So many troops required more than one trip, and the twenty-eight barges each ferried fifty men, crossing while guns on the British ships gave them a heavy cover. As soon as the troops vaulted from the boats at Moulton's Point, the crews took up their long white oars for the return trip. When all of Howe's soldiers had been rowed to the shore, they were ready at last to assault Breed's Hill.

Since British soldiers expected words of encouragement before a battle, Howe had them called to attention.

"Gentlemen," he began, "I am very happy in having the honor of commanding so fine a band of men. I do not in the least doubt that you will behave like Englishmen and as becometh good soldiers."

He went on, "If the enemy will not come out of their entrenchments, we must drive them out at all events. Otherwise, the town of Boston will be set on fire by them. I shall not desire one of you to go a step farther than where I go myself at your head."

Howe reminded them that more than a hill was at stake. "Remember, gentlemen, we have no recourse to any other resources if we lose Boston but to go on board our ships, which will be very disagreeable to us all."

When John Stark and his troops reached Charlestown Neck, they found other reinforcements halted there because of the heavy bombardment from the *Lively* and other British guns in the harbor. General Stark sent Major Andrew McClary ahead to tell the reluctant officers that if they didn't intend to move they should stand aside and let the New Hampshiremen through. McClary stood nearly six and a half feet tall. A path was cleared instantly.

General Stark led his men out on the narrow spit of land while balls of nine and twelve pounds—even twenty-four—streamed through the sky and thudded or splashed around them. Stark moved very deliberately, and at his side a nervous aide named Henry Dearborn suggested that they might march faster to get out of the crossfire.

General Stark slowed still more and looked at him calmly. "Dearborn," he said, "one fresh man in action is worth ten fatigued men." They advanced at the same pace to the top of Bunker Hill, where Israel Putnam had taken up his post. Resting there as he waited for his rear columns to join him, General Stark was at the highest point in the series of ridges. Below him he could see the outlines of Prescott's fort and the British approaching across the water.

But Stark also saw on his left that the American position was badly exposed right down to the Mystic River. The gap gave the British an opening for a successful flanking attack. Stark gathered his men around him for short but urgent instructions. Give three cheers, he said, and then run to that rail fence about forty yards from Prescott's fort. The men were to patch up the fence and gather armloads of grass and hay to drape over its rails. The result would be a flimsy barricade that any cannonball, even a musket shot, could penetrate, but men could hide behind it, and it might look more substantial than it was.

Stark told the men to pile stones from the point where the fence ended straight down to the edge of the Mystic. Behind that wall, which was rough but more substantial than the fence, he posted his best men three deep. The newly commissioned American generals didn't share the British disdain for entrenchments or breastworks. General Israel Putnam said that the average American fighting man was more afraid of an injury to his legs than of one to his head. Get him behind a trench, he said, and an American would fight forever.

At the primitive fort on Breed's Hill, British shells continued to pound down on the American forces. When one ball burst the head of a lieutenant, Colonel Prescott was sprayed with the man's brains and blood. But amid the hours of din and fear he had been marshaling his forces calmly. As the British completed their landing, the American desertions had ended, and his men were taking up their positions. On Bunker Hill, Israel Putnam and Samuel Gerrish were readying fifteen hundred milling and disorganized men to fight.

By 3 P.M., smoke from the fires of Charlestown rose like a thundercloud around the fort. Through the haze, Colonel Prescott saw Joseph Warren riding toward him from Bunker Hill. Even before his headache Warren had felt a premonition, and the previous night he had mentioned it to Betsy Palmer, whose husband had joined the Tea Party and the battle at Lexington. Mrs. Palmer admired Dr. Warren above every other patriot and was especially taken with his handsome features and light-blue eyes. During dinner Warren had said, "Come, my little girl, drink a glass of wine with me for the last time, for I am going on the hill tomorrow and I shall never come off."

At the Committee of Safety that morning, Elbridge Gerry had tried to keep Warren from joining Colonel Prescott. "It would be madness for you to expose yourself," Gerry had said. "As surely as you go there, you will be slain." But at noon, with a book of poetry in his pocket, Warren borrowed a horse and a musket and sped out along Charlestown Neck.

Warren wore an expensive light-blue coat and a satin waistcoat fringed with lace. But his manner was somber, and the men already on Breed's Hill didn't smile at his appearance. Prescott came to Warren's side and greeted him by his new title. He had been named a major general, although his commission hadn't arrived.

I am happy to see you, General, Prescott said. I am relieved of command, and I will obey your orders.

"I have no command here, Colonel Prescott," Warren told him. "I have come to give what assistance I can and to let these damned rascals"—he gestured to the British gathering at the base of the hill—"see that the Yankees will fight."

Prescott persisted. I wish, then, you would look over the work we have thrown up and give your opinion, he said.

Warren said, "You are better acquainted with military matters than I am." He walked over to the fortress wall to see how it was constructed.

After the British ships had fired red-hot ball into Charlestown, soldiers went ashore and set the rest of the town on fire. The town became an inferno that couldn't possibly shelter more snipers to harass the British troops. With reinforcements landing downshore from his main force, General Howe now had twenty-two hundred men and was deploying them cleverly. Because of the hectic activity by John Stark's men, he knew that the Americans were vulnerable on their left flank. Howe sent his light-infantry companies down a path along the water's edge toward Stark's jerrybuilt stone wall. He ordered them to sweep away any opposition, climb the hill and storm the American fort from the rear. At the same time, other infantry companies, grenadiers and marines would attack the front, rushing the Americans and stabbing them with bayonets. Howe suspected that the Americans were badly equipped, but he didn't know how few bayonets they had. If the British got close enough for hand-to-hand combat, the Americans would be lost.

Howe's infantry marched out four abreast led by the Welsh Fusiliers and moving slowly toward Stark's stone wall and hayrack. The sun was hot, and the soldiers sweated in their woolen uniforms and under the weight of blankets, ammunition and the three-day rations strapped to their backs. They waded through grass above their knees and boosted themselves over the dozen low stone walls built to safeguard cattle. Whenever a wall or a fence broke the even line of their march, officers hurried over to correct the imperfection.

General John Burgoyne stood among the British guns bombarding the hill and was thrilled by the panorama unfolding before him. A roar of cannon and mortar filled his ears as he watched Howe's infantrymen make their way over the low fences and the other British wing climb steadily up Breed's Hill. Straight ahead of him, Charlestown was ablaze, the wooden church steeples rising over the rest like fiery pyramids. Behind him, Boston's rooftops swarmed with men and women who had come out to shudder at the spectacle or gloat over it. Burgoyne reflected that a defeat today could spell the loss of America to the British Empire.

With his men crouching behind their stones on the beach, John Stark knew exactly how little ammunition they had. Before Howe's men came into sight, Stark had made a mark in the river-bank about forty yards from their hiding place. Don't fire, he told them, until the British have reached that mark. Moving up to the men at the fence, who were peering out through holes in the hay, Stark calculated the rise to the ground and told them not to fire until they could see the enemy's half gaiters. Israel Putnam had come down briefly from Bunker Hill to repeat a well-known phrase spoken by a Prussian prince thirty years earlier: "Don't fire until you see the whites of their eyes."

The British plodded forward, unaware of what lay behind the stones they could see in the distance.

The fusiliers were the first to pass Stark's line. A row of muskets rose on the stone wall, and blasts of ball tore into the British ranks and cut them down. Before they could escape, ninety-six British soldiers were killed. The survivors quickly backed out of range. Behind the fusiliers, the infantrymen formed for their own charge and marched over the fallen bodies until they were also driven back by fire from the wall. Once more the British officers urged their men forward. Again they were mowed down. To John Stark, the dead seemed to be lying as thick as sheep in a fold. The water at the edge of the beach was running red, and British corpses were being lifted out on the tide.

There was no fourth attempt. The infantrymen were running back along the narrow strand to where they had landed. Some were trying to get into the landing boats, hoping to row to safety. Their officers were swearing and gesturing wildly with their swords to force the men back. General Howe's strategy had failed.

Howe's only choice was to send all of his remaining forces head on against Prescott's earthen fort. He decided to attack on three sides. The Forty-seventh Regiment and the Marine battalion would move to his left. The Fifth, Thirty-eighth and Forty-third Regiments would go to the center under Brigadier General Robert Pigot, who had helped to get the survivors of Lexington back safely to Charlestown. Howe would take the grenadiers and the Forty-second Regiment to the right. He would avoid the stone barricade that had been so lethal to the fusiliers, but his march would take him past the rail fence draped with hay.

Prescott and Stark had no joint battle plan. Each was fighting according to his own judgment. But Prescott had also urged his men to let the British get within close range before opening fire. Prescott had fewer than four hundred men in his fort and behind a sketchy breastwork. Stark had four to five hundred crouched behind the stones and the rail fence.

When Howe's men were within sixty yards of the fence, they halted to shoot. When the British stopped, the Americans opened fire from behind their curtain of hay and ripped through the British front line. Howe himself wasn't struck, but the Americans were determined to hit every officer on the hill. Whenever someone spotted a British insignia, he shouted, "There!" or "See that officer!" Two or three others then rested their gun barrels on the rail fence and took aim. "Let us have a shot at him!" Since they all opened fire at once, they could usually drop their target.

Inside the fort, dirt had been piled up three feet high and the best shot among Prescott's men climbed to the top of the mound. He stood there exposed while the men below him remained protected. One by one, he picked off his prey. As soon as he fired one musket, another loaded weapon was handed up to him. At last a grenadier took careful aim and brought him down, but not before

Prescott's lone marksman had killed or wounded twenty British regulars.

William Howe couldn't believe what was happening. It was a moment and an emotion he had never experienced. In the face of the most sustained fire his troops had ever confronted, they had broken and were running away through the high grass. Writhing and groaning among the dead, wounded British soldiers were trying to crawl from the line of fire. Howe saw his army in full retreat. Up and down the rail fence and inside the fortress, the Americans cheered loudly. Prescott and Stark moved among them, praising their skill and bravery but reminding them that the afternoon wasn't over.

General Howe needed about fifteen minutes to collect his troops and line them up for another charge. This time, General Pigot's men would storm the fort, and Howe's men would assault the rail fence. Once again, there was no fire from the Americans until the British were within a hundred feet. Then the Americans sprayed a hail of lead, driving the British front rank back into the men behind them. Three fourths—and as many as nine tenths—of each company fell to the ground. For the second time, Howe watched his army turn and run for their lives.

Despite their success, many American soldiers were feeling the same fear. A dozen men were helping to move the wounded to safety on Bunker Hill when only three or four could have done the job. Other Americans slipped away. When challenged, they claimed to have permission to go because they had been digging all night and firing all afternoon and were famished and parched and exhausted. One captain from Connecticut saw an American company retreating from the hill with its officers in the lead, and he ordered his own men to cock their muskets and drive the deserters back to Colonel Prescott.

But Prescott faced a shortage more serious than defections. If Howe asked his men to make a third charge, Prescott's troops had almost no powder left to drive them back.

Howe was weighing his next move. Some officers were begging him not to charge the American line again. His wounded were being carried to boats to be ferried back to Boston. Many of his dead still lay in front of the American fort, too near the rebel muskets to drag away. But Howe had reinforcements to draw upon. Henry Clinton had joined those troops who had only feinted at the left side of the fort while Howe led the main charge. Clinton's men hadn't taken many casualties, and if Howe chose to try again, he could count on them.

Colonel Prescott thought he also had available reinforcements among the hundreds of men wandering aimlessly on Bunker Hill. Israel Putnam was trying to get them into fighting ranks, but he was short of officers and even those he had weren't all willing to face a new attack. At the first sight of the redcoats advancing, Colonel Samuel Gerrish had trembled and cried, "Retreat! Retreat! Or you'll all be cut off!" His men had followed him to the safe side of the hill. Now Gerrish lay flat on the ground, fat and immobile, claiming he was too exhausted to go on. Putnam tried cajoling him and slapped some of Gerrish's more hysterical men with the flat of his sword. It was no use. Colonel Prescott's troops would not receive reinforcements.

Meantime, William Howe had made his choice. His drummers beat the tattoo to rally the men. Many were bleeding or bandaged, but again they formed a line twelve feet apart and moved toward the breastwork and the redoubt. Behind that front line, the British were massed in files that looked impossibly deep to the Americans inside the fort. The gallantry of the British in their beautiful, impractical uniforms—and memories of fighting alongside such men in past battles—stirred profound feelings among the Americans. One rebel from Ipswich thought they were too handsome to fire at. All the same, he raised his musket.

This time, pride or desperation kept Howe's ranks intact. As a man fell in front, the man behind him stepped over his body as though it were a log in the meadow and took his place. But once more the American fire was so accurate that the line could only move forward very slowly. At last a British captain, George Harris, got close enough to lead his grenadiers in a rush up the slope between the breastwork and the fort. Twice they had to fall back. On the third charge, a musket ball scraped the top of Harris' head. Four soldiers leaped forward to carry him out of range, but when three were hit Harris snapped, "For God's sake, let me die in peace." The men ignored him and got him to a boat for Boston.

Major Pitcairn, who had damned the Americans on the Lexington green, led a unit of marines up the hill. The burning houses at Charlestown were sending up waves of intense heat, the afternoon sun was unbearable, and the fire from the fort was worse than anything one of Pitcairn's young captains had imagined. When he complained of feeling hot, Pitcairn offered no sympathy. Soldiers must inure themselves to any hardship, he said. They shouldn't even recognize heat or cold. Pitcairn added that doing his duty took all of his attention.

Behind his walls, Colonel Prescott sent a series of messengers to the rear, appealing to General Putnam for reinforcements. Putnam, who was riding around Bunker Hill with entrenchment tools slung across his horse, could hear the battle roaring on the next hill but didn't join it. By now, Prescott and his men were out of ammunition. Some fired nails or other bits of metal they could pick up from the ground. Others tried to hold back the approaching line of bayonets by hurling rocks from the top of the fortress wall.

The American desperation goaded the British. Howe's men stormed the fort with cries of "Push on!" One last blaze of muskets cut into their ranks, but by then they were scrambling up the ditch and over the wall. Some Americans raised their heads to fire even as the British were on top of them. Prescott thought one more round of ammunition could have repelled them, but he didn't even have that. Bellowing with frustration and revenge, the British soldiers swarmed over the fort, stabbing with their bayonets. Through thick black smoke from the final rounds, the Americans groped along the walls for the single narrow exit at the rear of the fort. In the murk, the British didn't dare fire for fear of hitting their own men. Colonel Prescott was able to beat back the bayonets with his sword and retreat from his fortress with only slashes in his coat.

But as the Americans escaped from the fort, they found themselves trapped between British soldiers on both sides. The rebels behind the rail fence provided their only cover as they stumbled toward Bunker Hill with the British pursuing them. Thirty of John Stark's men managed to save one cannon, dragging it up the hill and down to Charlestown Neck. A fresh American regiment from Charlestown was firing to keep the British at bay. A few kegs of powder arrived from Portsmouth, and the Americans were covered long enough to gather up many of their wounded as they retreated. The British were exhausted and, with their dead strewn around them, not pressing their advantage. Every one of General Howe's aides was killed or wounded. Working his way to Howe's side, Henry Clinton thought he had never seen such confusion. British officers complained that even in victory their men weren't obeying them.

On Bunker Hill, Israel Putnam made the same report to Colonel Prescott about the Americans. Prescott knew that Putnam's disorganized reinforcements, only about six hundred yards from the battle site, might have given him a victory and reminded Putnam of his agreement to come to the fort's defense. "Why," Prescott demanded, "did you not support me, General, with your men?"

Putnam said, "I could not *drive* the dogs up."

But Prescott was in no mood for alibis. "If you could not *drive* them up," he said, mimicking Old Put, "you might have *led* them up."

The shooting had lasted less than an hour. Entering the fort in the final moments, Major Pitcairn was shot in the head by a black American named Salem Prince. The Committee of Safety had forbidden enlisting slaves into the army, but several freed blacks fought that day on the hill. Fatally wounded, Pitcairn fell into the arms of his son, who carried him to a boat, kissed him farewell and went back to fight. Henry Clinton led a force chasing after the Americans. He expected them to make a last stand on Bunker Hill, but by the time he got there the rebels had gone.

When he went out to make sure that the British had left the scene, Andrew McClary, the American major who had bulled his way through Charlestown Neck five hours earlier, was struck dead by a last random cannonball from the harbor. Outside the fort, a British soldier came upon the body of Joseph Warren lying in a trench. America's newest general was dead before he could receive formal notice of his commission. Warren had been one of the last men to leave the fort. When a bullet struck the back of his head, a reflex jerked his hand to the wound. But he had been killed instantly. The British soldier cursed his corpse and said Warren had done more mischief than anyone else in the colonies. Later, when General Gage heard the news, he agreed and said that Warren's death was worth five hundred men to him. On the hill, the soldier stripped Warren of his coat, his satin waistcoat and his white breeches with silver loops. Walter Sloane Laurie, the British

captain who had been forced to back his men across the North
Bridge at Concord, was also present. Laurie ordered a grave dug
and took pleasure in seeing Warren wrapped in a farmer's coat and
stuffed into the ground along with another dead rebel.

Dr. Warren had been Samuel Adams' most diligent student.
But he hadn't mastered the lesson of secrecy and had carried to
the hill letters from James Lovell in Boston that revealed information about British troop strength and deployment. Lovell's father
was the loyalist schoolmaster who had dismissed his class on the
morning Percy's troops marched on Lexington. His son was such
a dependable patriot that in 1771 Samuel Adams had chosen him as
the first orator to commemorate the Boston Massacre. Because of
Dr. Warren's indiscretion, James Lovell was arrested and locked
in the Boston jail.

A half hour after Prescott's men had been dislodged from the
fort, a British officer, Lieutenant John Dutton of the Thirty-eighth
Regiment, sat down on the grass. He suffered from gout and
wanted to change his stockings. Dutton's orderly saw two men
moving toward them, carrying muskets. He knew from the crude-
ness of their clothes that they weren't British soldiers and ran to
warn Dutton. The lieutenant scoffed at him. The Americans were
coming to surrender and give up their arms, Dutton said. After
all, an entire British unit was only fifty yards away. But the men
raised their weapons and shot the lieutenant and his servant dead.
John Dutton became the last British soldier to die that day on
Breed's Hill.

James Otis, in and out of asylums since 1771, had been passing
his days lethargically at his sister's house in Watertown. When he
heard rumors of war that morning, Otis roused himself, borrowed
a musket from a nearby farmer and set off to join in the excitement. His brain was still disordered, but he escaped the British
guns and returned home that evening about ten o'clock. He had
apparently spent the day with American snipers near Charlestown.

By now, any threats James Otis might have made fifteen years
ago were irrelevant. In the shadow of Breed's Hill, Otis had seen
the province in flames, but the best part of him had perished long
before the fire.

George Washington at the battle of Princeton, by Charles Willson Peale

Washington
1775

GEORGE WASHINGTON was still in Philadelphia when he heard reports of the battle on Breed's Hill. He had been confirmed by the Congress and was preparing to take up his command in Cambridge. From the casualty figures, he could tell that the British had paid an exorbitant price for their victory. A British colonel who was dying from his wounds had said, "A few such victories would ruin the Army." Another British veteran of the battle wrote home, "We have got a little elbow room, but I think we have paid too dearly for it." Nathanael Greene, an American commander from Rhode Island, said, "I wish we could sell them another hill at the same price."

Nearly one third of the British soldiers sent from Boston had been killed or wounded—more than eleven hundred casualties. British losses at the rail fence had run to seventy percent. And yet William Howe remained extremely popular with the men who had

survived his three assaults. The day after the battle, he congratulated them on their bravery. As they repaired their gear and cared
for the wounded, Howe's men went about their duties with good
humor.

For all the heroism on Breed's Hill, the American camp was
filled with accusations and reprisals. Colonel Prescott wanted
Israel Putnam court-martialed, but Putnam was too well liked for
that. General Artemas Ward was severely criticized for not be-
stirring himself during the engagement. Had he provided coherent
tactics, his men said, the Americans could have held the hill. When
the Congress debated whether to appoint George Washington as
commander in chief, some members had worried that they might
be slighting General Ward, given how esteemed he was by his
men. By the morning of June 18, three days after Washington was
unanimously elected, Ward's popularity was no longer an obstacle.

That same day, Washington wrote to his wife to inform her
of the honor being conferred upon him. He seemed eager to reassure her of his devotion: "I should enjoy more real happiness and
felicity in one month with you, at home, than I have the most
distant prospect of reaping abroad if my stay was to be seven times
seven years." Washington promised to return safely to her in the
fall. But he enclosed a will. He allowed himself more candor with
his favorite brother, John Augustine. "For a while," Washington
wrote, "I am embarked on a wide ocean, boundless in its prospect
and from whence, perhaps, no safe harbor is to be found."

One of Washington's traits that had impressed the Congress
in Philadelphia was his modesty. He seldom joined in their debates;
his education had been limited, and he wasn't a fluent speaker. He
asked his fellow Virginian Edmund Pendleton to draft his acceptance speech, but the tenor and sincerity of his words were his
own. He spoke as frankly to members of the Congress as he would
to his brother.

Washington said he was distressed that his abilities and his
military experience might not be adequate for the trust they were
conferring upon him. Still, he promised to exert his every power
in the glorious cause. But if—here Washington revealed a lifelong
dread—he failed, if his reputation lay in ruins, the Congress should

remember that he had warned them on this day that he wasn't equal to the command. In concluding, Washington refused the monthly salary that the Congress had voted for him. Instead, he promised to keep an exact account of his expenses and be reimbursed only for them.

His brief speech was favorably received. John Adams thought it was noble, particularly the part about renouncing his pay.

Washington's candor to the Congress had not been mere humility. At the age of forty-three, he was honest with himself. He knew that he was not a master of military strategy. He didn't disagree that he could perform better in this new post than either John Hancock or his rival from Virginia, Colonel William Byrd, but his country was asking him to defeat men who had given their lives to the art and science of war.

Washington had been raised for the ambiguous life of a Virginia gentleman with a limited fortune. He wasn't the eldest son in his family, nor had he been born to his father's first wife, who had died after giving Augustine Washington two sons and a daughter. Three years later, the widower married an orphan, Mary Ball, who was twenty-three and a little past the usual age for marriage. She gave birth to a boy on February 11, 1732, a date that would be moved forward to February 22 when the calendar was revised. That first son of Augustine's second family was named George to honor Mary Ball's guardian, a lawyer named George Eskridge. Three more sons and a daughter survived.

Augustine Washington prospered as a planter. He was no Byrd or Lee or Randolph, but he acquired more than ten thousand acres of land and fifty slaves. He sent his two older sons to his old school in England. He might have intended to provide the same education and social finishing for the sons of his second marriage, but he died when George was eleven, making a British education impossible. Although Augustine Washington's will favored his first family, George was not ignored. At twenty-one he was to inherit the family house at Ferry Farm, along with ten slaves and twenty-five hundred acres of not especially fertile land. Until that time, his property would be controlled by his mother. As a widow, however, Mary Ball Washington seemed to combine an enthusiasm for money with an indifference to the way it was managed. In her thirty-five years Mary Washington had lost both of her parents and her husband; now she was determined to cling to her oldest son. Under the terms of the will, she and her other children were to live with George at Ferry Farm. But within a year or two George began to mature rapidly and cast about for an avenue of escape.

The young man's Latin was sketchy and his spelling uncertain. He had grown into a remarkably fine horseman, however, and a fair shot. Early in his teens it was clear he would have an impressive physique and would stand well over six feet. His face was square, with a thrusting jaw and a florid fair skin that was often regarded as the English ideal. But what set George apart from other tall and robust Virginians was the intensity of his determination to better himself. He copied rules into a notebook that would guide him in making his way in the world. When speaking to men of quality, for example, he was not to look them full in the face. At meals, he shouldn't clean his teeth on the tablecloth. The easiest rule for George to observe was a warning against biting humor. Life with Mary Washington had left him a serious young man.

For a time, he considered becoming a lawyer and filled pages with drafts of legal papers. He also copied out several verses on true happiness from an author who defined it as a good estate on healthy soil and a quiet wife.

At the age of fourteen George tried to break away from Ferry Farm. His half brother Lawrence suggested that George could make his fortune by shipping out on a tobacco freighter and tried to cajole Mary Washington out of her opposition to the idea. Lawrence, who was twice George's age, had already sailed to the West Indies to fight in Admiral Edward Vernon's expedition against the Spanish fleet. Many of Vernon's men died of yellow fever, but Lawrence came back to Virginia with stories of adventure at sea and named his estate for his commander—Mount Vernon. Mary Washington's self-absorption was well known to her neighbors, and her coldness terrified their children. No appeal could move her now. George could not go to sea. But two years later, when he turned sixteen, she began allowing him to spend many of his days at Mount Vernon.

There George met Lawrence's brother-in-law, George William Fairfax, who was seven years older than George and living nearby at Belvoir, his family's plantation. Through the Fairfaxes, George Washington was introduced to a grander life than anything at Ferry Farm. At Belvoir he learned to play billiards and whist and became addicted to dancing. Lawrence Washington had become an amiable substitute for George's father and was already living a squire's life at Mount Vernon on land that included the four thousand acres his wife had brought him in marriage. To have a similar estate George would have to earn it—or marry it—for himself. Like many Virginians of his background, he ached to buy land, but that took money.

At Belvoir he came to know Lord Fairfax, an Oxford graduate in his midfifties, who had come to Virginia to look after his far-flung properties. Young Washington made an engaging companion for riding and hunting, and Fairfax asked him to travel beyond the Blue Ridge Mountains and help survey the Fairfax forest land there. At sixteen, George Washington took his first job, running lines for his lordship's estate.

Even for a hardy young man, frontier life was rigorous. During that first trip, George usually made terse entries in his diary—"Nothing remarkable happen'd"—but he recognized a joke when it was on him. The first night out, he had stripped off his clothes for bed, as though he were a house guest at Belvoir. But his bed was only matted straw with no sheets and a threadbare blanket heavy with lice and fleas. George jumped up in the dark, dressed again and settled down to sleep in his clothes like the more experienced surveyors. He wrote to a friend that most nights he bunked on a little hay or on a bearskin, along with a frontier family huddling together like dogs and cats. Happy, George said, was the man who got the berth nearest the fire. But he considered his pay generous—a doubloon a day. In time he earned enough to take a claim on four hundred and fifty-three acres of wild land in Frederick County.

When he returned to the luxuries of home, George found a disturbing surprise. George Fairfax had married a tall and lively eighteen-year-old named Sarah Carey. Everyone called her Sally. Washington had been susceptible to girls for some time. Schoolmates accustomed to his stolidity had remarked on the times he romped with one of the neighborhood girls. But Sally Fairfax was not one for romping. She was only two years older than he, but she was married and her husband would inherit lavishly. Sally wasn't beautiful, but her long face was alight with intelligence and humor and she moved with a mature grace. Her teasing overtures stirred George Washington profoundly.

For the next four years, Washington divided his time between surveying the countryside and weeks of indulgence at Mount Vernon and Belvoir. There always seemed to be a host of pretty girls on hand, not least Mrs. Fairfax. Washington acquired more land and was named a county surveyor. But he appeared doomed to fall in love easily and lucklessly. He wrote to one young woman in Fredericksburg three times and got no answer. As he took up his pen for a fourth attempt, he confessed to her that he was almost discouraged. Nearing his twenty-first birthday, Washington seemed to have inherited his mother's intense will and was on the way to harnessing it.

Then George's prospects improved abruptly for a distressing reason. Lawrence Washington's three children had died, and now he was suffering from a persistent cough that suggested tuberculosis. He sailed to the West Indies hoping that the sun would cure him. George went with him to Barbados while his wife stayed behind to tend their frail fourth infant. The trip mocked their expectations. Lawrence became worse and sailed on to Bermuda alone because George had contracted smallpox, a light case that left a few scars across his nose. On his return to Virginia, George found that he had also developed pleurisy. Meanwhile, Lawrence gave up his quest and came home to die.

The foresight of Lawrence's will reflected his recent losses. During his wife's lifetime she would live on at Mount Vernon as guardian for their surviving child. If that daughter also died, Mount Vernon and the rest of the estate passed to George upon the death of Lawrence's widow. Lawrence had been one of the four majors in Virginia's militia. As his heir, George sought that commission, and the Fairfax family helped him get it. Within six months, Lawrence's infant daughter had died and his widow had remarried and moved away. George Washington began to assume responsibility for Mount Vernon. He had become a prosperous gentleman farmer, complete with a gentleman's military rank.

Washington wanted his rank to be more than honorary. In 1753, at twenty-one, he volunteered for his first assignment, even though the mission seemed political rather than military. French forces had occupied a great thin curve from Canada to the Loui-

siana territory and were confining the British colonies to the Atlantic coast and out of the fertile Western lands. The British planned
to challenge the French claims by building a fort on the Ohio
River. But scouts reported that the French were constructing their
own forts from the Ohio north to Lake Erie. When Virginia's acting governor, Robert Dinwiddie, drafted a letter warning France
to stop its inroads into English territory, Major Washington volunteered to deliver it. The journey was arduous, nearly five hundred
miles each way, and Mary Washington took his departure for
abandonment. Years later, she continued to complain that his military service had given her no end of trouble.

    Traveling by canoe and horseback along icy rivers and snow-
bound trails, George Washington's party took fifty-two days to
reach the French camp. Washington delivered Dinwiddie's politely
phrased ultimatum, and a captain named La Force composed a reply for the French that was equally civil: "As to the summons you
send me to retire, I do not think myself obliged to obey it." But
after several French officers had drunk quantities of wine, they assured Washington privately that they intended to take the Ohio,
and by God they would do it.

    When Washington returned to Williamsburg with that re-
sponse, Dinwiddie insisted that he write a full account of the episode. Washington obeyed with grave misgivings and apologies for
his literary shortcomings. But Dinwiddie had the six-thousand-
word account published and circulated widely, even in London.
The House of Burgesses rewarded Washington with fifty pounds
for his performance, and Virginia decided to send its militia to hold
the Ohio country by reinforcing a British fort on the Monongahela
River. Washington, who had just turned twenty-two, was promoted to lieutenant colonel and named second in command for
the expedition.

    He marched west from Alexandria early in April 1754 with
two companies of men. Washington was an untried soldier, but he
looked imposing in the red coat and three-cornered hat of Virginia's militia officers. His youth caused him to accentuate his natural reserve. Washington thought a degree of distance was essential
in a leader of men and wasn't concerned if his troops considered
him aloof. Establishing his authority was especially important because he had doubts about the quality of the troops his officers had
scared up. They looked to him like drifters who would be hard to

control. Most of them hadn't seen any more warfare than he had, and their pay was bad—about eightpence a day. Their real incentive, which Washington understood, was the prospect of owning land. Dinwiddie had promised that the volunteers would divide the twenty thousand acres of rich frontier land that the French were contesting.

Washington brought along as his interpreter a young Dutchman who had accompanied him on the earlier mission. Jacob van Braam, who had been in America barely two years, made his living teaching French and fencing and had joined the Masonic lodge at Fredericksburg about the same time as Washington. Once again the march was grueling. The wagons at the outset covered eleven miles a day, but as they got farther into the wilderness Washington had to be content with little more than a mile. Rumors reached him that the French had already overrun the British garrison on the Monongahela, but Iroquois tribesmen along the route encouraged Washington to keep going. The twenty thousand warriors of the Six Nations Iroquois confederation held the balance between the French and the English, and for more than a century they had allied themselves with Britain. Washington took their advice and pressed on.

During the last week in May he reached the Great Meadows, a two-mile stretch of long grass and low bushes. As Washington rested his men there, a brave named Silverheels brought a message from his chief. Tanacharison, called the Half-King, knew where a band of French soldiers were encamped. Even though France and England were officially at peace, George Washington and the Half-King agreed to launch a surprise attack.

At 7 A.M. on May 28, forty of Washington's men and a dozen Iroquois braves caught thirty Frenchmen as they were getting dressed and making breakfast. The gunfire went on for less than fifteen minutes and killed ten of the French, including their commander, Coulon de Jumonville. As the rest tried to escape, they were blocked by the Half-King's braves with raised tomahawks. George Washington took ten prisoners and sent them under guard back to Virginia. His first taste of battle exhilarated him. He was still excited—though he tried to appear nonchalant—when he wrote about the engagement to his younger brother, John Augustine. Only one of his own men had been killed, Washington reported casually, and only two or three wounded. "I heard the bullets whistle," he added, with a bravado he would regret, "and, believe me, there is something charming in the sound."

George Washington had ordered the first shots of the French and Indian War.

He learned belatedly from his prisoners that the French party had been only a diplomatic mission, much like the one that had taken him to Captain La Force. All the same, Washington was promoted on the spot to full colonel and made commander of the entire Virginia contingent. But he had little time to bask in his success. A large French force led by Jumonville's brother was heading toward the Great Meadows for revenge. Washington threw up hasty defenses on the plain. With an accuracy bordering on wit, he named the result "Fort Necessity."

After a month with the young colonel, the Half-King concluded that Washington was good-natured but appallingly inexperienced and unwilling to take advice. Long before the news of the French retaliation, the chief had urged him to dig in at the meadow, but Washington hadn't listened. When he was forced to act, he had pitched his fort on ground with such poor drainage that the least rain would flood his trenches. Washington also cut the trees back only sixty yards from the southeast side of his fort, which brought the trenches within musket fire. The Half-King's Iroquois warriors began to fade away.

On July 3, during a rainstorm, the French struck. This time the battle lasted longer, about an hour, and Washington's green troops were clearly outfought. Thirty Americans were killed, including one of Washington's slaves, and another seventy were wounded. Unless he was willing to fight to the death, Washington had only one option. In the early hours of the fourth of July, 1754, he surrendered.

Jacob van Braam's translation of the French surrender document made its broad outlines sound favorable to Washington. He would be allowed to march his men out from Fort Necessity with all honors of war. The Americans could take only one cannon but all of their personal belongings. Two of Washington's captains would stay behind as hostages until the French prisoners from the earlier engagement were released in Virginia. Those generous terms carried a preamble, however. As rain continued to pour down, van Braam, whose knowledge of French was not infallible, stumbled through the text by candlelight under a leaking stockade roof. It claimed that the French raid had never been intended to disrupt the peace between France and England but only to avenge the assassination of a French officer. When he translated that phrase for Colonel Washington, van Braam rendered *"l'assassinat"* as "death." The error misled Washington about the magnitude of the confession he had just signed.

As Washington returned to Virginia, the Half-King gave his verdict on the battle. The French had been great cowards for not pressing their advantage, but the Americans had been fools. Other warriors from the Six Nations heard about the battle and agreed with him. Before Washington reached home, many of the tribes were turning away from the English, and by the year's end their warriors had either joined with the French or were staying neutral.

Washington's private journal was lost or stolen during his retreat. When it turned up in Europe, the French were already using his surrender terms to portray the British as murderers. A London magazine printed Washington's letter to his brother, and when King George II read that the young American commander had called the whistle of bullets charming he remarked, "He would not say so had he heard many." Among Britain's military officers, George Washington's name was becoming famous—as a byword for colonial incompetence.

In Williamsburg, Robert Dinwiddie, who had been the young colonel's patron, was separating himself from the defeat at Necessity. The authorities also refused to honor Washington's surrender terms and release the French prisoners. They said he had exceeded his authority. Youth and inexperience had contributed to Washington's defeat, but his bravery had been unmistakable, and the men who served under him valued it above an error in translation. Washington came back to Virginia under a haze, if not a cloud, but he was now a man to be taken seriously. He leased Mount Vernon from Lawrence's widow for fifteen thousand pounds of tobacco a year and took it as his country seat. He dined often at Belvoir, where Sally Fairfax remained charmingly impudent and instructed her seamstress to make shirts for him.

But Washington's military ambitions were effectively blocked. The new commander in chief for all royal forces in America openly criticized Washington's performance at Fort Necessity, and when the Virginia troops were reorganized Colonel Washington was reduced to captain. Washington resigned.

He admitted that he left only because his honor had been affronted and that he was still strongly drawn to the soldier's life. In spring 1755 he offered to join a new expedition against the French. It would be led by Edward Braddock, a blunt-tongued major general sent from London. Washington avoided the troublesome matter of rank by volunteering to serve as a civilian and to pay his own expenses. Again, Mary Washington insisted that George not leave her, and her pleas delayed him one day. But Washington believed he could endure any amount of abuse—even from his mother—as long as he acted from decency and principle. Before he rode to join Braddock at Fredericksburg, he paused to write a fond but decorous letter to Sally Fairfax, assuring her that none of his friends could bring him more real delight than she. Mrs. Fairfax replied that although she wanted news of him, he should send it through mutual friends and not write to her directly. Washington accepted that reproach—he called it a gentle rebuke—and wrote to her anyway.

At the end of May 1755, one year after he had surprised Jumonville at breakfast, Washington set out with Braddock and more than two thousand British regulars, volunteers and militia for the French fort of Duquesne, one hundred and fifty miles away. During the expedition, Washington was handed one of his mother's rare letters. She asked him to send her a supply of butter and a Dutchman to help on her farm. "Honoured Madam," Washington began dutifully and went on to explain that where he was traveling both commodities were in short supply.

As they drew within a few miles of Duquesne, Braddock's advance guard was attacked by a band of Indians and Frenchmen who picked them off from behind trees. Washington had dysentery and was trailing at the end of Braddock's column. He had been disappointed when Braddock ordered him to stay back, but the commander had promised to summon him when the attack began.

Although he could barely mount his horse, Washington heard the first shots and rode to join the fray. French bullets tore into his coat, he endured waves of nausea, and two horses were shot from under him. Through it all, Washington fought on. Before the firing ended, the attackers had killed or wounded almost a thousand of Braddock's men—two thirds of the force sent into battle. Still the British officers would not change their traditional tactics and fight the French and the Indians on their own terms. Edward Braddock was shot through the lungs as he was giving the order to withdraw, and Washington helped carry him off the field in a silk sash. Braddock died during the retreat. His men buried him secretly in a grove a mile and a half from Fort Necessity.

For Washington, it had been another failure. Yet this time he reaped only praise for his gallantry. To his brother John he wrote that when he got back to the British camp he had heard stories of his death and even of his deathbed speech: "I take this early opportunity of contradicting the first and of assuring you I have not composed the latter." The governor of North Carolina wrote to congratulate him on the honor he had gained, and he was commissioned a militia colonel once again and named commander in chief of Virginia's forces. At twenty-three, George Washington had come through three military engagements without even a flesh wound and had begun to seem equally adroit, or lucky, in surviving the political wars.

Despite his new prestige, George Washington was balked whenever he tried to turn Virginia's militia into soldiers capable of fighting the French. He complained to Dinwiddie that his authority was inadequate for coping with insolent soldiers and their indolent officers. Washington threatened to resign over the point, and this eventually led to a military code that permitted jailing, flogging, even death, for the militia. A man who lapsed into profanity could expect to be flogged twenty-five times with a cat-o'-nine-tails, and Washington justified to Dinwiddie the punishment he had meted out to serious offenders: "Your honor will, I hope, excuse my hanging, instead of shooting them. It conveyed much terror to others; and it was for example sake that we did it."

Washington was not good at recruiting, which made the persistent desertions even more disturbing. Though he could have deserters flogged until spectators wept at their suffering, men still ran away. He held rigidly to the British system that channeled all dealings with privates through their sergeant, which meant that he rarely came to know his soldiers individually. Just as he discouraged familiarity, Washington was slow to praise. No matter how long and industriously a man worked, he should not look for reward or acknowledgment.

Washington had pledged to his men that he would be absolutely fair, and—except for favors to two sons from the Fairfax family—he kept his promise. In time, that stern but impartial leadership won him loyalty and a measure of affection. But British regulars found Washington not especially personable, too blatantly ambitious and, at his best, merely competent.

In time of trouble, George Washington tended to solicit sympathy, but whenever he lamented his circumstances to Governor Dinwiddie or to Sally Fairfax's father-in-law, Colonel William Fairfax, he got few condolences. The colonel advised him to reflect on Caesar and Alexander and bear his difficulties with the same magnanimity. Writing to the governor, Washington covered himself with the kind of praise he withheld from his underlings. No man, he assured Dinwiddie in one letter, ever had endeavored to discharge the trust reposed in him with greater honesty and more zeal for his country's interest than he himself had done. But Washington complicated his relations with Dinwiddie by going around the governor to the Burgesses. When Dinwiddie's age, combined with a stroke, forced him from office, he wrote to Washington complaining that his many friendly gestures had been repaid by constant challenges to his authority. Washington denied the accusation, unless, he said, the governor was offended by "open, disinterested behavior." Washington sought in vain to call on the governor and clear up their last dispute, but Dinwiddie refused and sailed home to London convinced of Washington's ingratitude.

In March 1758, when Colonel Washington was twenty-six, he began to cough as persistently as Lawrence had done, and he traveled to Williamsburg for a medical diagnosis. The doctor gave him a reassuring report, and Washington left the capital in better spirits. On his return trip, he took advantage of the Virginia gentry's openhanded hospitality and spent the night at a large residence famous for its six chimneys. His hostess was Martha Dandridge Custis, who had been widowed for seven months.

Washington's feeling for Sally Fairfax clearly would come to nothing. On trips to New York he had paid court to a young heiress, Eliza Philipse, who was bright and spirited and considerably more sophisticated than her suitor. Martha Custis resembled Miss Philipse in only one way: she too was rich. Her late husband's father had been a cranky miser who kept his son a bachelor into his middle years. He had opposed Daniel Custis' engagement to Martha Dandridge because she wouldn't bring a sufficient dowry. But he had died before the wedding, and Daniel had inherited two fine estates and 17,500 acres of Virginia land. The bride had been nineteen, and in their seven years of marriage she had borne him four children. Two had survived. The widow Custis, now twenty-six, was tiny, barely five feet tall. She was only a few months older than George Washington, and she was modest. When she described herself, she settled for the word "healthy." Although she was plump, she danced nimbly, her smile reflected a sweet disposition, and she could afford any second husband she wanted.

Martha Custis had known Washington long before she was free to consider him for marriage. By now he had grown into a broad-shouldered, small-waisted man, a little thick at the hips from his constant riding. His eyes were gray and widely set, his abundant hair brown, his features regular. In conversation Washington was deferential; sitting silently, he was dignified; and he was graceful in the way he moved. He kept his mouth closed as much as he could. Martha Custis had beautiful teeth; his own were already going bad.

Washington's campaign was ardent and brief. Within a week of his first stay, he was back again, giving the Custis servants ten times his usual frugal tips and being amiable with Martha's two children, a boy four years old and a girl of two. Washington began to expand the simple farmhouse at Mount Vernon to prepare for a family and raised the roof to allow for a second story.

The couple were engaged within months, but Colonel Washington wanted one last chance at military glory before he resigned himself to life as a wealthy planter. William Pitt in London had ordered the British to drive the French from Fort Duquesne. Washington failed to get a commission with the regulars, but he decided to go along as a militia colonel. Besides putting together a fighting force three times the size of Braddock's expedition, Pitt had eased resentments among the militia by ruling that their officers could be commanded only by British regulars of a superior rank. That meant Washington would suffer no indignities from British majors and captains.

Before leaving for Ohio, Washington wrote two letters that mirrored the division in his heart. Placidly he reminded Martha Custis of the happy hour when they had made their pledges to each other and described himself as her faithful and affectionate

Martha Washington in a likeness her husband carried in a gold locket around
his neck throughout the Revolution

friend. But when Sally Fairfax wrote to tease Washington for becoming a "votary of love," he erupted with chagrin. Why, he demanded, did she write about his anxiety to possess Mrs. Custis
"when—I need not name it—guess yourself." He admitted that he
was a votary of love, but not for the reason she had given. "I acknowledge that a lady is in the case—and further confess that this
lady is known to you." To Sally Fairfax, Washington also recalled
their past times together—"the recollection of a thousand tender
passages." Then came a confession that caused Sally Fairfax to preserve a letter Washington must have expected her to burn: "You
have drawn me, my dear Madam, or rather have I drawn myself,
into an honest confession of a simple fact—misconstrue not my
meaning—'tis obvious—doubt it not, nor expose it—the World has
no business to know the object of my love—declared in this manner to you when I want to conceal it.

"I dare believe you are as happy as you say," wrote George
Washington, who had recently become engaged. "I wish I was
happy also."

The campaign at Duquesne ended in anticlimax. The French withdrew from the fort and set it on fire before the English could arrive. The only shots came when Washington and one of his junior officers got confused in the woods and fired on each other. He didn't record the episode, but British officers observed that Washington's sole enemy casualties had come from his own ranks.

Before he left Virginia, Washington had been elected to the House of Burgesses after two defeats. Returning home, he ignored the pleas of his loyal regiment, resigned his commission once more and took his seat in the legislature. On January 6, 1759, he married Martha Custis at her second estate, the White House on the York River. They spent their honeymoon at her Six Chimneys House in Williamsburg. Then Washington took his bride to Mount Vernon to begin their plantation life together.

Eleven years later, on a trip west, George Washington negotiated with the Commonwealth of Pennsylvania to buy the Great Meadows, including the site of Fort Necessity. Dear in blood, the property was cheap in money. Washington paid thirty pounds for it, which was less than what he spent that same year for a slave named Will.

As George Washington headed for Cambridge to forge a mass of men into the Continental Army, he was accompanied by four members of his new military family: a young man named Joseph Reed to serve as his secretary; Thomas Mifflin, a thirty-one-year-old aide-de-camp to write his speeches; and Philip Schuyler and Charles Lee, two major generals newly commissioned by the Congress. Along the way, Washington crossed the Rappahannock River to Fredericksburg to see his mother. Instead of going directly to Ferry Farm, he stopped at a nearby inn to send her a message that he was coming. The servants knew how Mary Washington would react if she saw her son in uniform and were afraid to deliver his note. But Mrs. Washington heard talk from her neighbors and sent for him. Washington went immediately. He hadn't yielded to her pleading twenty years ago and she couldn't dissuade him now. But, after some resistance, she agreed to move from Ferry Farm to a safer cottage at Fredericksburg.

As the third session of the Continental Congress opened in Philadelphia in mid-September 1775, an indiscretion by John Adams turned a political quarrel into a personal one. He had entrusted his letters, including the one with his exasperated remarks about John Dickinson, to a courier who was picked up by British sailors in Rhode Island. In a postscript to his wife, Adams had broadened the attack on his colleagues: "I wish I had given you a complete history from the beginnings to the end of the behavior of my compatriots. No equal to it. I will tell you in the future, but you shall keep it secret. The fidgets, the whims, the caprice, the vanity, the superstitions, the irritability of some of us is enough to—" Adams broke off there. General Gage got his letters and had them widely distributed. When Adams passed Dickinson for the first time on their way to the new session, he bowed and took off his hat. Dickinson cut him. From that time on, the men spoke only on the floor of the Congress.

John Adams had grown even closer to his cousin, and before leaving Massachusetts for their return to the third session he had persuaded Samuel Adams to take up horseback riding at the age of fifty-three. John found a very small and gentle horse and taught Samuel how to mount without two servants boosting him into the saddle—grasp the bridle with his right hand, place his left foot firmly in the stirrup, twist his left hand into the horse's mane halfway between his ears and shoulders and give a vigorous jump. The first day of riding was agony. Samuel Adams was able to continue only because his landlady that night sewed a pair of well-padded linen underdrawers for him so that his blister could heal. Now that he had been coaxed into it, Samuel's competitive spirit turned him into a good horseman. By the time they reached Philadelphia, on September 12, 1775, John Adams was writing in mock chagrin that men said Samuel rode fifty percent better than he did.

With Congress in session, Samuel Adams watched as John Hancock consorted with the Southerners who were most congenial to his nature. Adams' former protégé was becoming "King Hancock," traveling with twenty-five horsemen in front of his coach with their sabers drawn and another twenty-five behind. John Adams discovered that when Hancock dined at inns around Philadelphia the owners were expected to be grateful for the honor of serving him, and his entourage often rode off without paying their bills. John Adams mourned the example that Massachusetts was setting, and Samuel Adams was aghast that honest country folk enjoyed watching Hancock's display.

John Hancock's defenders, men like Benjamin Harrison of Virginia, liked him even better as he lost favor with his own radical delegation. But presiding over the Congress required work as well as pomp, and Hancock was soon complaining that he was worn out. His gout returned, and eye trouble drove him to buy glasses. During the six-week adjournment through August and early September 1775, Hancock had gone to claim his reward. Dorothy Quincy had not written often, not even when he had begged for letters or after he had sent gifts—hosiery, shoes, an airy summer cloak, a pretty hat. But she had agreed to marry the president of the Continental Congress. After a subdued ceremony that suited the times, Hancock returned to Philadelphia with his bride. Pleading ill-health, he missed the opening session.

The new Congress had to confront two procedural questions of a wide significance. For months some members had spoken of moving the Congress to Connecticut—either Hartford or New Haven—so that members would be closer to the fighting. They made their suggestions outdoors to keep them from being formal resolutions that would require a vote. So far, a majority was against the move, and Congress remained in Philadelphia. But with Washington's departure, it was clear that the center of America's crisis had shifted to the battleground. That was confirmed for John Adams when he traveled part of the way out of Philadelphia with the commander in chief and his two major generals. Watching the military display that accompanied them, Adams could see that their swords would soon be more acclaimed than his pen. "I, poor creature," he wrote to Abigail Adams, "worn out with scribbling for my liberty, low in spirits and weak in health, must leave others to wear the laurels which I have sown; others to eat the bread which I have earned. A common case."

Peyton Randolph's return to Philadelphia raised another question. Most members had assumed that John Hancock would occupy the president's chair only while Randolph was in Virginia. But the bridegroom on his working honeymoon showed no sign of stepping down. John Adams claimed to be particularly upset by Hancock's breach of good manners. Then, within six weeks, the issue was resolved without a vote. A stroke caused Randolph to choke over his dinner, and he died not long afterward.

Soon after George Washington's arrival in Cambridge on July 2, 1775, he had been decked with the laurels John Adams had predicted for him. Abigail Adams wrote to tell her husband how impressed she had been by the new commander. She summed him up as having "dignity with ease" and said that modesty marked every line and feature of his face. Washington reminded her of lines from Dryden, which she copied out for John Adams—"He's a temple sacred by birth" was one of them. If her rapture stirred a twinge of jealousy in her husband, Abigail Adams considered it his own fault. She had grown tired of the public quality to his letters and had warned him, "I want some sentimental effusions of the heart."

While he was making his social rounds, Washington also moved quickly to strengthen the army's defenses. It wasn't the first time he had been put in charge of undisciplined men, but he was forced to depend on them to prevent the British from breaking out of Boston and into the countryside. Washington estimated that the numbers favored him. General Gage's forces now totaled about twelve thousand against Washington's sixteen thousand, including the sick and the missing. But Washington had to maintain a circle around Boston of eight or nine miles, which the British could push and test at any weak point. He believed strongly in reliable intelligence reports and overcame his natural frugality to pay well for them. From agents he heard that the British were running out of food and were slaughtering their milk cows for beef. The number of Tories who had stayed in Boston or had taken refuge there was only about sixty-five hundred; fourteen thousand Bostonians had fled to the countryside. The Tories worried that as soon as the last patriot escaped from Boston the American Army would set fire to the town, and they persuaded Gage to go back on an earlier promise and stop anyone else from leaving.

George Robert Twelvetrees Hewes, the veteran of the Tea Party, had to go fishing for the British for several weeks before he and his friends could slip away to the town of Lynn and then to Cambridge. Washington came out to the yard of his headquarters to hear about their adventure. The men took off their hats in respect, but Washington told them to put them back. He was only a man, he said, smiling. When Hewes finished his rollicking story, he found that Washington "didn't laugh, to be sure, but looked amazing good natured."

Privately, the commander was less genial about the character of his New England soldiers. In a letter to Virginia, he described them as "exceedingly dirty and nasty people." Samuel Adams wouldn't have disagreed. He had heard that some of his colony's officers and men were disgracing the name of Massachusetts, and he wanted to improve the army's public reputation. He suggested that whenever a man of real merit appeared, every anecdote about him should be touched up and widely circulated. Any exaggerations, he added, should go only so far as decency permitted.

When Washington heard a full account of the battle of Breed's Hill, he sided with the survivors who claimed that the Americans might have won had the men been led properly. He authorized eight courts-martial for cowardice and corruption, and Samuel Gerrish was among those tried. Joseph Matthews, who was found guilty of selling a gun that his town had issued to him, was sentenced to ten lashes on his bare back. On Washington's order, Matthews was flogged in front of his company.

Over a lifetime of dealing with slaves, Washington had developed his own rules and penalties. He had encouraged them to marry, be faithful and attend church, although he expressed his own faith more comfortably out of doors. When slaves had become troublesome or run away, Washington sold or traded them, sometimes for rum or limes. He did not allow them to be whipped. Soldiers were treated differently. They were also expected to avoid profanity and drunkenness; Washington signed orders that any cider that came into the camp would be confiscated. His soldiers were not to be bawdy. A man named Daniel Davids was confined for the exhibition he had made while he was bathing.

"The general does not mean to discourage the practice of bathing while the weather is warm enough to continue it," one of Washington's orders explained, "but he expressly forbids it at or near the bridge in Cambridge, where it has been observed and complained of that many men, lost to all sense of decency and common modesty, are running about, naked, upon the bridge whilst passengers, and even ladies of the first fashion in the neighborhood, are passing over it, as if they meant to glory in their shame."

Washington believed that, by enlisting, the soldiers had made a commitment and should be held to it. He asked the Continental Congress for the same right to hang deserters that he had sought from the Burgesses twenty years before. Permission was slow in coming, and as he worked to improve discipline, Washington's aides told him that the men wanted the right to decide which officers to serve under and were insisting that the officers come from their own colony.

The Continental Congress had been sensitive to those regional loyalties and had been guided by political considerations in picking Washington's subordinates. Philip Schuyler, a delegate to the Congress from New York, was also a rich man with military experience. Artemas Ward and Israel Putnam were kept on to reassure New England. Charles Lee had become a favorite of both Samuel Adams and John Adams because he was a former British officer who had become fervent about America's cause. Lee delivered mesmerizing accounts of his past exploits and tended to behave rudely with civilians. James Warren had once met him in Massachusetts and had written to John Adams with misgivings. Adams reassured him that Lee's oddities were merely those of a great man. "He is a queer creature," Adams admitted, "but you must love his dogs if you love him, and forgive a thousand whims for the sake of the soldier and the scholar." One of those whims was that Charles Lee knew far more about waging war than George Washington did.

Washington's most pressing problem, however, was the shortage of supplies. He was consulting with his generals when aides interrupted with an urgent private message: Someone had miscalculated the army's reserve of gunpowder. Washington had been told there were four hundred and thirty barrels when there were only thirty-eight. Each of his men had fewer than nine rounds of ammunition to keep the British blockaded in Boston. When he had heard the report, Washington sat for half an hour without saying a word. Then he wrote immediately to the Congress appealing for more powder. But Washington didn't even tell his generals how desperate the situation was. He feared spies. Early in October 1775 one of those spies was unmasked, and his identity astonished everyone.

In Newport, Rhode Island, a woman called on a man named Wainwood shortly after the battle at Lexington. She had a letter addressed to a British major on General Gage's staff and asked

Wainwood to deliver it to friends who would then forward it to the major. Wainwood agreed, but he wanted no trouble. When the woman left, he opened her letter. It was written in code. He puzzled over the message and put it aside. But when the woman wrote asking anxiously whether Wainwood had delivered it, he went to Cambridge and requested a meeting with General Washington.

Washington heard the story and sent for the woman that same night. Although he coaxed and threatened her, she would say nothing until Washington ordered her confined to jail, when she broke down and told her story. She was being kept by Dr. Benjamin Church, the newly appointed surgeon general of the American Army, and now she was pregnant by him. Dr. Church had written the coded letter.

Because Washington was new to Massachusetts, the disclosure struck him as less preposterous than it did the many patriots who had served with Church for years on every crucial committee. To them, Church was the deacon's son who had studied medicine at the London Medical College and returned home to give free inoculations to the poor during the smallpox epidemics. Now in his early forties, Church had been a charter member of the Long Room Club over the Edes and Gill print shop and had written the scathing attack on Francis Bernard that began "Fop, witling, favorite stampman, tyrant tool . . ." Church had examined the bleeding body of Crispus Attucks, and he and Dr. Joseph Warren had been among Samuel Adams' favorite protégés. Adams had chosen him only two years earlier to speak at the anniversary of the Massacre.

Washington summoned Church and at the same time sent men to seize his papers. Church had given a decade of service to the patriots and believed that his explanation would be accepted. He admitted writing the letter but said it was meant for his brother. When it was deciphered, General Washington would see for himself that there was nothing criminal about it. Washington's aides returned to say they had found nothing incriminating at his house. Over and over, Dr. Church protested his innocence.

A clergyman and a militia colonel each tried to break the code by counting its symbols and assigning to each one the letter that turned up equally often in English. Both amateur cryptographers came up with the same result: the note was filled with valuable military data. Its last line read, "Make use of every precaution or I perish."

George Washington conducted Church's court-martial himself. Now patriots began to recall that Church had built a lavish country house at Raynham. How could he afford it? And his love affairs had been well known even before he took up with this latest expensive mistress. As another link, Church's sister was married to John Fleeming, the Tory bookseller who had been John Mein's partner. Paul Revere had watched disapprovingly as Church often dined with a British captain and one of the customs officials. But Revere felt he couldn't question Dr. Church about that peculiar friendship, and Church told other patriots that he was gleaning military intelligence the British unwittingly let drop. Now Revere understood Church's hasty flight into Boston immediately after the battle at Lexington. He felt he had been duped when the doctor pointed to the blood on his stockings. Revere had assumed that any man who would risk his life must be a friend to the cause. But a Boston clergyman told him that he had happened to see Church the day he left General Gage's house and that the doctor and the general had parted like old friends.

Whether he was driven by his debt or by doubt that the patriots could win, Church had apparently begun his spying in 1771, while Samuel Adams was struggling to keep the cause alive. The next year, Thomas Hutchinson had passed along gratifying news to Francis Bernard in London that the man who had written insultingly against Bernard had come over to the government's side. As a trusted member of the Provincial Congress and its Committee of Safety, Church had reported regularly to General Gage on the patriots' supply of powder and arms. When he had brought messages to the Continental Congress the previous spring, Church had lingered in Philadelphia to pick up information and had informed Gage about the debates over financing the new army.

Despite his protests that he loved America, the evidence against Church was too strong to doubt. Washington's court-martial found him guilty of holding criminal correspondence with the enemy. There were fewer supporting documents than the panel had expected, because a confederate had got to Church's papers before they could be confiscated. The court left the terms of Church's punishment to the provincial congress at Watertown, which ordered him confined to a jail in Connecticut. Washington had asked

Congress to let him hang men for far lesser offenses, but in jail Church was denied only the use of pen and paper. On pleasant evenings he was allowed to ride through the countryside with a trustworthy guard. That concession was one sign of New England's embarrassment that America's first convicted spy was also one of her most illustrious patriots.

With autumn ending, Washington faced a problem more grave than the lack of gunpowder. The men who had flocked to Cambridge after the excitement of Lexington had enlisted in the army for six months and now wanted to go home. Thomas Hutchinson had once predicted that the colonists would always be farmers before they were soldiers and would return to their land for planting and harvest. With the British poised to break through Washington's thin defensive line at any moment, he had to recruit a whole new army.

The money he could offer wasn't much inducement. Privates and drummers were given tents or barracks, their daily meals and a monthly pay of six and two thirds of a new currency called the American dollar. A civilian bachelor living simply would spend nine times that amount and not face British guns every day. All thirteen colonies had pledged to raise men, for his army. Yet he couldn't, with a total population of two and a half million, recruit fifteen thousand men. On the last day of December the old army disbanded, and fewer than ten thousand replacements had signed up for the new year. A thousand of them were holdovers away on the furlough they had demanded in exchange for reenlisting.

Every day Washington could expect the twenty British regiments to overrun his sparse defenses. But every day his luck held. The reason was that Thomas Gage's bloody victory at Breed's Hill had destroyed his career. Because of the stalemate in Boston, George III called him "the mild general," and in late September—about the time of the Benjamin Church scandal—Gage learned that he had been relieved of command. When he sailed from Boston two weeks later, few regretted his departure. The Tories were convinced that his replacement, General Howe, would strike where Gage had hesitated.

But something about Boston seemed to sap the spirit, and William Howe had never wanted to fight in America. In fact, he had written home to tell those Nottingham voters who had sent him to Parliament that moderate Americans were in the majority here and would drop their resistance and obey Britain's laws. And Howe had private reasons for lingering in Boston. He had taken a woman named Elizabeth Loring as his mistress. Her husband was a loyalist who cared nothing about being cuckolded so long as he was well paid, and Joshua Loring was assured his fortune when Howe named him to head Boston's prisons. Wives who lent themselves to enriching their husbands were not always condemned, but the affair had provoked a popular verse:

> *Sir William, he, snug as a flea,*
> *Lay all this time a-snoring*
> *Nor dreamed of harm, as he lay warm*
> *In bed with Mrs. ——.*

When General Howe heard that London was sending enough food and supplies for a proper campaign in the spring, he decided to stay warm in Boston and dream the winter away.

Charles Lee

Lee
1775

FOR BENEDICT ARNOLD, the weeks since his victory at Ticonderoga had been filled with humiliation and pain. He had pleaded with the Continental Congress to let him invade Canada. Instead, the Massachusetts Committee of Public Safety turned over the command at Ticonderoga to another Connecticut colonel. That rebuff led Arnold to resign his commission. He asked, however, that the Provincial Congress reimburse him for the money he had advanced for America's only victory. The legislature refused, advising Arnold to deal directly with the Continental Congress. When his unpaid soldiers heard that news, they mutinied, took Arnold prisoner and negotiated for themselves directly with Massachusetts. The men got their money, and Arnold was set free. He was ordered to report to Cambridge to settle his accounts.

He went instead to New Haven, where he learned that his wife had died. Although she had come to despise him, Peggy Arnold's death sent him into a depression that was complicated by a siege of gout. Then, while his sister Hannah tended to his three children, the eldest only seven, Arnold went to Cambridge to clear up the question of his expenses. There his figures were repeatedly challenged and disallowed. The board of examiners agreed to pay him one hundred and ninety-five pounds—less than half what he had spent to capture two forts and a wealth of armaments.

Arnold's one consolation was a meeting in Cambridge at which he was able to propose to General Washington his latest plan: Arnold would lead an expedition through the wilderness and mountains of Maine, take Quebec by surprise and capture it for America. Once again other men had anticipated him. George Washington, though he was hampered by a lack of supplies and manpower, had already explored the idea of a diversion in Canada and had picked General Schuyler to lead it. Very well, said Arnold, he would take his men north to support Schuyler.

The expedition was a belated attempt to enlist Canadians in America's revolution. France had ceded Canada to Britain under the 1763 treaty that ended the French and Indian War. Eleven years later, with the Quebec Act of 1774, Lord North's ministers tried to bind Canada closer to England by making concessions to its French Catholics. Even though Catholics already outnumbered British Protestants in Canada four hundred to one, the act brought in another eighty thousand French settlers by extending Canada's boundaries south to the Ohio River and west to the Mississippi. Lord North had promised the Canadians a legislature, but held off creating one because he wanted to keep the French Catholics in the minority and there was no way of guaranteeing that. But Catholics could practice their religion so long as their priests recognized the political supremacy of George III.

The Quebec Act had alarmed the American settlers who coveted the Ohio wilderness and had outraged New England Protestants with its leniency toward the Roman Catholic Church. Patriots like Samuel Adams traded on anti-Catholic sentiment as a tactic, but they also genuinely feared Rome's power. Whig speakers told their audiences that the Quebec Act would lead to a new Inquisition and the burning of heretics in Massachusetts and New York. In October 1774, during its first session, the Continental Congress had denounced the Quebec Act. Yet its members now assumed the Canadians would fight with them against British tyranny, even though George III was granting them more liberties than France's kings had ever done.

George Washington was prepared to test the Canadian response. A message was drafted for him and translated into French. Then, given Washington's past problem, General Charles Lee read it over for accuracy. "Let us run together to the same goal," Washington's appeal urged the Canadians. Because armed troops would be bearing the message, he tried to be reassuring: "The Great American Congress has sent an army into your province under the command of General Schuyler, not to plunder but to protect you."

The logistics behind Washington's plan were formidable. General Schuyler had ordered Brigadier General Richard Montgomery to leave Ticonderoga and march north. Schuyler would join Montgomery at Crown Point. Together they would have seventeen hundred men. Washington also authorized Benedict Arnold to lead another eleven hundred soldiers along the Atlantic coast to the Kennebec River. It would be a punishing trek, and Washington advised Arnold to recruit volunteers during a parade at headquarters on September 6. Arnold's own zeal and the promise of action after weeks of waiting in Cambridge contributed to the good response, and Washington also agreed to send several companies chosen by lot from the Pennsylvania and Virginia militia. A week later, Arnold's men were ready to march. According to the best information, the British had only one company at Quebec but could draw on eleven hundred more troops, some of them Indians, from Montreal and other forts.

General Washington told Arnold to send an express messenger back to Cambridge if problems arose during the march. When no messenger appeared, Washington was reassured rather than anxious. General Montgomery, who had served under James Wolfe during the successful British assault on Quebec in 1759, was indignant at the low quality of his American troops. He said that the brazen Yankees were all generals and not one a soldier. New Yorkers were worse. Their lax morals shocked Montgomery, and he found them "the sweepings of the streets." Yet he forged ahead, capturing two forts to the north of Lake Champlain—one at Chambly on October 20 and another at St. Johns two weeks later.

Benedict Arnold was paying the price for choosing the more rugged route. Aaron Burr, who had charmed Dorothy Quincy at his uncle's house, had been commissioned a captain and had joined

Arnold's expedition despite letters from home filled with such en-
couragements as "You will die, I know you will die." When a rider
caught up with the marching column to say that Burr's uncle had
ordered him home, Burr threatened to have the messenger hanged
if he bothered him again. But when the weather turned foul in October, it seemed likely Burr's family would be proved right. Benedict Arnold's men were slogging through rain and snow over half-
frozen swamps and were fording rivers so swollen and fast-running
that they whipped the army's supplies out of their canoes. Arnold's
only guide was his memories of a trip he had once made to Quebec
as a trader and the old journal of a British engineer.

The daily rations for Arnold's advance riflemen fell to half an
inch of raw pork and half a biscuit to last them from the Kennebec
River to the walls of Quebec, and they had no sure idea how far
that was. The brambles and the small firs had become so thick that
the men were scrambling along on all fours like dogs. They were
eating dog, too. A captain surrendered his great black Newfoundland, which had been a company favorite, and the men ate every
bit, including the entrails. They collected the bones, pounded them
to dust and brewed a greenish broth for the next day. Some men
tried to make soup from their deerskin moccasins, but no matter
how long they boiled them they were still leather. Starved men sat
down on the ground and were dead within minutes.

When one rifleman shot a duck, the others in his ten-man
party boiled it in a kettle along with their last bits of pork, each
marked with its owner's name. They drank the broth for supper,
ate the boiled pork for breakfast and cut the duck into ten parts.
As one man turned his back, the leader held up a portion—a wing,
a leg, the neck—and asked, "Whose shall this be?" The man called
out a soldier's name. For dinner the next day, they ate those shares
of duck. The day after that, they ate nothing.

When a man's boots wore out, he wrapped his sore feet in
flour bags and kept marching. For thread the men pulled up cedar
root, and during the portages they patched their dugouts with
pitch scraped from pine trees. Sickness cut the eleven hundred men
to nine hundred and fifty. The few women marching with their
husbands expected no favors. As the army moved across one frozen
pond, the ice broke and the men had to wade through the freezing
water with their rifles raised above their heads. When her turn
came, Mrs. Greer, a large and respectable sergeant's wife, hitched

up her skirts to the waist, and even the New Yorkers didn't make a joke about it.

By the time Colonel Arnold caught up with his forward companies their supplies were exhausted. He brought food, and men wept when they saw the cattle herded into camp. Arnold wrote optimistically to Washington that his provisions would last twenty-five days and that he expected to reach the waters of the Chaudière River in ten days, which would put him within striking distance of Quebec. At the Chaudière on October 27 Arnold received heartening political news. Two Indians brought him a letter saying that the people of Quebec rejoiced at his approach and would join the Americans in subduing the British forces.

From Arnold's positive report General Washington assumed that Arnold would be in Quebec on November 5, But when that day came, Arnold was facing new problems. He now had only six hundred and fifty men, many of them shivering in their shirts from the winter winds. French settlers told him that the British had burned all the boats on the St. Lawrence River to stop his troops from getting across. He ordered men to bring up the canoes from their last river crossing. In the past eight weeks, Arnold and his men had traveled nearly six hundred miles, through swampland one third of the way and carrying boats and baggage on their shoulders for forty miles. At times, one day's food had lasted a week. Now the men straggling to Arnold's side looked across the St. Lawrence to a disheartening sight.

In the harbor below the walled heights of Quebec was a British frigate with twenty-six guns and a warship, the *Hornet,* with another sixteen. The ships had arrived the day before, bringing five hundred men to reinforce the town. His informants continued to assure Arnold that all of the Canadians, except for a hundred staunch Tories, would greet his arrival by throwing down their weapons. Arnold needed the encouragement. On the same day, he discovered that all three companies of his rear detachment had decided that they didn't have enough provisions to continue and had headed back to Cambridge.

Arnold's shortage of boats was more critical now than it had been at Ticonderoga. For a week, he had to send men as far away as twenty miles to buy birchbark and canvas while every day the British went on improving their defenses. At last Arnold had enough boats for five hundred men, but a storm forced him to delay again.

It was 9 P.M. on November 13, 1775, before Arnold and his canoes slipped past the British ships on the river and landed at Wolfe's Cove. At daybreak, Arnold led the men up a steep path to an expanse of land called the Plains of Abraham. General James Wolfe had stood there sixteen years before, at the head of thousands of well-equipped British troops and with twenty-two ships to control the St. Lawrence. General Wolfe had taken Quebec from the French. But in the hour of his victory he had died, quoting from Thomas Gray, "The paths of glory lead but to the grave."

Arnold's several hundred ragged men compared with Wolfe's legions only in courage, and yet Arnold planned to use the same tactic that had succeeded before. Wolfe had provoked a skirmish outside the garrison's perimeter, and General Montcalm had let himself be drawn into it. Arnold intended to get the British out from behind their walls so that the Canadians and their militia could seize the town and turn it over to Arnold. That was his plan.

Benedict Arnold marched his band to the walls of Quebec and ordered them to give a cheer. The noise seemed to provoke curiosity inside the town, but nothing more. Britain's commander, Sir Guy Carleton, had served as a subaltern with Wolfe and wasn't going to be tricked by a stratagem the British had invented. Carleton had eighteen hundred men inside the fortress, but because he doubted the sympathies of the Canadians he kept his troops behind the walls. When Arnold sent a messenger to demand surrender, the British fired at the courier, who turned and ran back. Meanwhile, Arnold heard that even more British reinforcements were on the way. His men had ammunition for five rounds. Neither pride nor valor could argue against a timely retreat. Arnold took his men to a haven twenty miles above Quebec, set up camp at Pointe-aux-Trembles, and waited for General Montgomery to arrive. While there, Arnold received a message that General Washington had arrested the colonel who had given up the march and would try him for desertion. Washington believed that the Americans were now within the town walls, and he added that he hoped Arnold was enjoying the laurels that his hardships in taking Quebec had won for him.

The weeks during the autumn of 1775 when John Adams was away from home at the Continental Congress had been a melancholy time for his wife back in Braintree. On the first day of October, she lost her mother to an epidemic of dysentery. In November, she herself was struck by jaundice. She had expected her husband to return at any moment, but James Warren paid a call to tell her that the Congress would be staying in session another month. Abigail Adams resolved not to grieve.

She was troubled, though, by the secrecy imposed at Philadelphia, which prevented her husband from sharing with her the debates going on there. Her lonely waiting was making her pessimistic, and she confided her doubts in a letter to John: "I am more and more convinced that Man is a dangerous creature, and that power, whether vested in many or few, is ever grasping, and like the grave, cries, Give, give." She worried that Americans had grown so comfortable without a government that they wouldn't submit to any new order when it came. She was anxious about America's future, whether it was as a monarchy or as a democracy.

The Continental Congress was too distracted with logistics and finances to discuss the problems disturbing Abigail Adams. Members had just rejected giving a bonus to any soldier who enlisted in the winter army. But she was looking beyond the war's end and asking, "How shall we be governed so as to retain our liberties? Can any government be free which is not administered by general stated laws? Who shall frame these laws? Who will give them force and energy?"

At thirty-seven, General Richard Montgomery was three years older than Benedict Arnold and just as tough. He had swept over Montreal and brought his column within a day's march of Quebec, determined that soon he would join with Arnold and add the town to his conquests. His troops' enlistments expired at the end of the year, and they were homesick and mutinous. After Arnold's futile challenge at the walls, General Carleton had strengthened his forces to guarantee further that the Americans wouldn't take the town. Since Montgomery had left behind eight hundred men to hold Montreal, he arrived with only three hundred soldiers. Colonel Arnold sent Montgomery a letter extolling Aaron Burr's great spirit during the fatiguing march, and Montgomery accepted him on his staff. Burr spent his days drilling a unit of fifty men to climb ladders he intended to prop against the fortress walls.

As Arnold had done, General Montgomery sent a flag demanding that Guy Carleton surrender. When that was ignored, he sent a threatening letter, but Carleton refused to negotiate. He would not parley, he said, with rebels. With that, Montgomery told his men, "To the storming we must come at last." He would attack the lower town, and Arnold would lead an assault to the side. They would then join forces and assail the upper citadel while two sham attacks distracted Carleton elsewhere. Montgomery rejected Burr's idea of scaling the walls by ladder.

At two o'clock in the morning of the last day of 1775, the troops assembled in a blizzard and were issued bands of white paper to stick into their caps so that they would recognize one another through the darkness and the snow. Men printed fighting slogans on the cards. Those who had heard about Patrick Henry in Virginia wrote, "Liberty or death."

After a two-mile march, Montgomery approached Quebec's outer defenses from the west. Captain Burr had kept up with him, but most of the troops lagged behind and Montgomery sent back messengers to hurry them along. At a wood barrier he ordered his carpenters to saw off the pickets while he rushed ahead with two dozen men. They came to a log house with holes in its walls for muskets. Inside waited a guard of British soldiers and sailors. When the Americans came within range, the British fired their weapons and touched off cannon loaded with grapeshot.

Richard Montgomery was struck in the heart. In the first rank, only Aaron Burr and a French guide were left standing. The rest of the men ran for cover. With his last words General Montgomery tried to persuade his men to come back, and to Burr he said, "We shall be in the fort in two minutes." Burr tried to drag Montgomery away, but the general was burly, and, with the snowdrifts, he couldn't move him more than a few yards. The British found Montgomery's dead body at daybreak.

With Montgomery's charge on the lower town repelled, the entire British garrison was free to ward off Arnold's attack at the northeast. Arnold was again racing ahead, and his soldiers now knew that he would never say, "Go ahead, boys," but always "Come on, boys," called back to them over his shoulder. By the time he neared the Palace Gate, the storm was blowing more fiercely than ever. All of Quebec's bells were ringing, and on both sides of the walls drums were beating. The Americans ran along the wall in single file, ducking their heads against the snow and cradling their muskets under their coats to keep their powder dry. At a passageway, British soldiers began firing down at them from houses on either side. Arnold was struck by a musket ball that broke his leg and pitched him forward into the snow. Pulling himself up, he tried to lead the charge on one leg. Men wanted to carry him from the field, but he would not leave until the main body of his men arrived and he could urge them forward. But they were too few. At the next barricade, some retreated, others were forced to surrender. Arnold was led limping to a military surgeon a mile from the battle. Even there, he wouldn't let himself or the other wounded men be evacuated to the countryside. He called instead for his sword and two loaded pistols. If the British pursued him to his sickbed, Arnold vowed to kill as many as he could before they finished him off. As for retreat, he was adamant. "I have no thought of leaving this proud town until I first enter it in triumph."

Ethan Allen had also found that other forts weren't as vulnerable as Ticonderoga. Although he still held no commission from the Continental Congress, Allen had agreed to go north to recruit Canadians for General Montgomery. And by the time he got near Montreal, he had decided to assault the city on his own. On September 25 he had led a small band to its walls to demand surrender. As his troops got close they were struck by the absurdity of the challenge, and all but forty drifted away. When the British garrison opened fire, Allen and his men ran for nearly a mile before they were caught.

As Ethan Allen turned his sword over to a British officer, a painted and nearly naked Indian tried to shoot him, but Allen got the officer between them, and the Indian didn't fire. His escape left him content to be in custody, and he and his captors joked together as they escorted him to their barracks yard.

That good fellowship soon evaporated. A British general, Richard Prescott, demanded to know whether he was the same Colonel Allen who had taken Ticonderoga. When Allen said yes, Prescott swore, called him a rebel and shook his cane at him. Allen raised a fist and told the general to put his cane aside. At that, Prescott ordered his men to step forward with their bayonets drawn and stab to death the thirteen Canadians who had joined Allen in his raid. The prisoners had already begun to say their prayers when Allen bared his chest and told Prescott that since he was to blame for their mutiny, he should be the one to die.

Prescott thought for a moment. "I will not execute you now," he said, "but you shall grace a halter at Tyburn, God damn you." He ordered Allen bound hand and foot and taken to a schooner christened the *Gaspee* in honor of the ship burned in Rhode Island. Allen's leg irons weighed thirty pounds and were so tight around his ankles that he could lie only on his back with a sea chest as his bed. Each day the crew baited him and mocked his rage. Once, when he bit a nail off his handcuffs, Allen heard his jailor say, "Damn him, can he eat iron?" After that, a padlock was added to his chains. Six weeks passed before Allen was sent to England for trial.

Across the Channel from Ethan Allen's British prison, Louis XVI and his court in Versailles were intrigued by Britain's effort to crush the rebellion in America, but news reaching France was slow and unreliable. Since he was only twenty-one—about the age of George III when he had taken his throne—Louis relied heavily on his foreign minister, Charles Gravier, Comte de Vergennes. The count held no affection for the colonies. As a form of government, he admired pure despotism. But since France's defeat by the British in 1763 Vergennes had hated them. "I tremble, I shake," he told a friend, "I even turn purple at the very thought of England." Although the two nations were now at peace, Vergennes hoped to exploit Britain's troubles as long as it could be done discreetly. For that, he needed a spy.

The French ambassador in London came up with a candidate. The ambassador, the Comte de Guines, was no favorite of Vergennes and held his post because Queen Marie Antoinette found him amusing. Since Guines was both obese and a dandy, he had two sets of breeches—those for days he would be sitting down, and much snugger ones for days when protocol would keep him standing. Each morning, the count climbed onto two chairs and lowered himself into the appropriate breeches, held by two servants. Guines was an annoyance to a diplomat as shrewd and dedicated as Vergennes. But he agreed to the ambassador's choice, the Chevalier Julien Achard de Bonvouloir.

A childhood accident had lamed Bonvouloir, but that wouldn't hinder him in this assignment. Vergennes agreed to pay the twenty-six-year-old two hundred livres. That was no fortune when the queen had just spent two hundred and fifty thousand livres for two bracelets and dismissed the sum as trifling. But Bonvouloir would also receive a distinction he coveted: a commission in the infantry. He had once visited America. Now, upon his return to Philadelphia, he sought out a Frenchman who introduced him to Benjamin Franklin, and Franklin set up a meeting with the Congress's Committee of Secret Correspondence, which was entrusted with establishing a foreign policy for the colonies.

Franklin's lingering hesitation about breaking with England had vanished in the bloodshed at Breed's Hill. Three weeks after the battle, Franklin drafted a short note to one of his closest friends in London, the publisher William Straham:

> Mr. Straham,
>   You are a member of Parliament and one of that majority which has doomed my country to destruction. You have begun to burn our towns and murder our people. Look upon your hands! They are stained with the blood of your relations! You and I were long friends. You are now my enemy, and I am Yours,
>
>   B. Franklin

Even in outrage, Franklin was prudent. The note was not sent.

Because of his prestige, the Congress had named Franklin to several committees, including the Committee of Secret Correspondence. Its other members were more cautious men, including John Dickinson and John Jay of New York. Since meeting with Bonvouloir would be their first contact with a foreign agent, they took precautions against being found out by the British, and on the night of December 18, 1775, each of the five committee members went to Carpenters' Hall by a different route.

Before he left France, Bonvouloir had been told to claim that he was a private citizen with well-placed friends at court who would entertain any requests that the Congress might make. He also had been given clear limits to his authority. He was to gather as much military and political intelligence as possible. He was to let the Congress know that France sympathized with the American cause and would not intervene in Canada. And he was to offer the Americans, once they became independent, free use of French ships for their trading.

The game was delicate on both sides. Dickinson was one of those delegates resisting any rash claim of American independence, but even he admitted that the colonies could not win without aid from Europe, especially from France. And yet the French worried about committing themselves to the rebels, who might then give in and rejoin the mother country. If that happened, Louis XVI would be at war with both England and America.

The Americans doubted that this callow Frenchman carried much authority, but over the course of three meetings they probed for answers. Did the French court hold a favorable opinion of the American cause? George Washington required two competent French engineers. How could the colonies get them? Would France trade military supplies for products made in America? The colonies could already get French armaments by way of the West Indies, but the price was exorbitant. Cargo worth 90,000 dollars when it left a French port fetched 240,000 by the time it reached Boston.

Benjamin Franklin led the negotiations. Fifty years earlier, at the age of twenty, he had returned from his first trip to England with a set of rules to govern his life. He would live frugally and work industriously. He would speak truthfully, with one exception—he would never speak badly of any man, no matter how much the man deserved it. Instead, he would always try to excuse men's faults and speak of whatever good he knew about them. Franklin had held to those resolutions and become one of the celebrated men of his age. Under his spell, Bonvouloir went beyond his instructions and promised to send the French engineers, although he resisted committing France to an alliance.

But Bonvouloir's report after the final meeting on December 27 showed how thoroughly he had been captivated. He neglected to write his secret passages in milk as Guines had instructed him. Instead, his enthusiasm came tumbling out in the form of facts Franklin had supplied.

"Everyone here is a soldier," Bonvouloir wrote. "The troops are well clothed, well paid and well armed. They have more than fifty thousand regular soldiers, and an even larger number of volunteers who do not wish to be paid. Judge how men of this caliber will fight." He offered a prediction: "Independence is a certainty for 1776."

George Washington's army that December stood closer to five thousand than to fifty.

At Versailles, Vergennes called a meeting of the king's advisers to debate France's policy. The heads of both the army and the navy opposed any action that might draw France into another war with England. The comptroller of finances said he greatly admired the colonists—"America is the hope of the human race and can become its model"—but with France facing a deficit of twenty million livres that year, they couldn't afford to help finance the rebellion. All the same, Vergennes had been so impressed by Bonvouloir's statistics that in his report to the king he wrote, "England is the natural enemy of France; and she is an avid enemy, ambitious, unjust, brimming with bad faith." As the debate at the French court went on, Vergennes would try to persuade Louis XVI that England's goal was the humiliation and ruin of France.

In Cambridge, General Washington had no sympathy for men as rash or ambitious as Ethan Allen. He wrote to General Schuyler that he hoped Allen's capture would teach a lesson to any other officers who were tempted to try to outshine their generals. Washington's own inactivity was gnawing at him, but recruitment for the winter was slow and supplies were scarce. General Charles Lee tried his own method of coercing farmers and shopkeepers to remain with the army. He assembled the Connecticut militia at his door and asked those men who would not stay even four days past their enlistment to step forward. When three quarters of them did, General Lee formed them in a hollow square, moved into its center and addressed them: "Men, I do not know what to call you. You are the worst of all creatures."

Cursing, he threatened to run every one of them up Bunker Hill, which was now heavily fortified with British guns. If they refused to go, he would order them gunned down by his own riflemen. When Lee ran out of oaths, he left to draft a warning to innkeepers along the route to Connecticut not to feed or shelter the men as they made their way home. He posted a copy on his door.

During the night, someone took it down and put up another notice announcing that General Lee was a fool.

George Washington heard from a friend that some members of the Continental Congress, particularly New Englanders impatient to see the British run out of Boston, were criticizing him for passivity. But with no resources, Washington could take no action and could not defend himself without calling attention to the army's precarious situation. He was mortified and had to assure himself often of his integrity. He did have the encouragement of his wife, who had never before traveled outside Virginia but had come to Cambridge to pass the winter with him. By January 1776 the Washingtons had been married for seventeen companionable years. Three years earlier, Sally Fairfax had sailed for England with her husband to settle his estate. Whatever the outcome of the war, it was unlikely that Washington would see her again. Though he might never forget his days with Sally at Belvoir, he now had a wife who was willing to share the privations of camp life and who could disarm New England's wives. James Otis' sister, Mercy Warren, was often tart, but she praised Martha Washington's gentleness and candor and pronounced her exactly the woman to soften a hero's private hours.

A sergeant in Cambridge got a glimpse of that serenity when he delivered a report to Washington. He found the general sitting with his wife. After the young man repeated his message, Washington asked him what job he held. Assistant adjutant, the sergeant said.

"Indeed," said Washington. "You are very young to do that duty."

"I am young," the sergeant replied, "but I am growing older every day."

At that, he saw the general turn to Martha Washington and smile with her.

By the end of February 1776, Washington had set in motion a scheme to silence his critics. The young Boston bookseller who had been on the scene for the Massacre, Henry Knox, was portly and heavy-lidded, but he possessed great energy and had traveled to Fort Ticonderoga. Hiring carpenters, Knox built forty-two sleds, rounded up eighty yokes of oxen and dragged loads of British cannon and artillery back to Cambridge through the winter snow. Washington knew that General Howe was loading his own ordnance onto ships in Boston Harbor. He had received permission from London to abandon Boston and to set up a camp that would be easier to defend, perhaps near New York. Washington couldn't be sure whether the loading was a ruse to lull him or whether Howe was preparing to sail, but the promise of any action raised his spirits. He wrote to a friend that if he brought off his plan it would "bring on a rumpus between us and the enemy."

On the night of March 4, 1776, General Washington showed both the British and the Americans how the battle for Bunker Hill should have been waged. He had read newspaper accounts of General Burgoyne's letter to London about the earlier battle and paid attention to what Burgoyne said about the two heights that commanded all of Boston. Dorchester Heights east of Boston was the one elevation that Howe had neglected to fortify.

Washington now sent out enough men to build a massive breastwork overnight. By that time he knew about the disaster in Canada, and it reminded him of the traditional criticism of Americans as soldiers. They would not march boldly into a battle or keep shooting for long on an exposed plain, but they were good shots. Put them behind a parapet or a wall, and they would do the job.

Since the ground on Dorchester Heights was frozen two feet deep, Washington could not throw up earthen defenses as Colonel Prescott had done on Breed's Hill. Instead, he sent quantities of chandeliers, raw wooden frames that held bundles of fascines, the long cylinders of wood that stood upright and provided a solid defense. That would give his men their walls. Washington also agreed to a plan that a Boston merchant suggested. Barrels filled with dirt were brought to the hill and arranged in rows. If the British tried to climb up, the barrels could be rolled down on them.

In the morning, Howe found that Boston was now vulnerable to an attack from Dorchester Heights whenever Washington chose to fire Henry Knox's cannon. The March rains that drenched the town made Howe's muskets worthless. As he already had permission to withdraw his men, Howe decided to leave Boston as quickly as he could.

Washington watched the British make their undignified retreat—"in so much hurry, precipitation and confusion as ever troops did"—and shared his glee with his brother John, home in Virginia. Howe ordered his baggage wagons and artillery carts thrown off the docks, along with several hundred blankets. But in his haste he left behind mortars, cannon and shell. On Sunday, March 17, 1776, the British army and twelve hundred loyalists boarded ships to sail away from Boston.

George Washington won several awards for his victory without a casualty—a gold medal from the Continental Congress, an honorary doctor of laws degree from Harvard. But as he was being congratulated, the patriots returning to Boston were outraged at the way their town had suffered during the British occupation. The stately Old South had been turned into a stable for officers' horses. One deacon's pew had been chopped down to provide wood for a pigsty. General Washington spoke for his countrymen when he said of the Tory collaborators that "one or two have done what a great number ought to have done long ago, committed suicide."

Meanwhile, General Charles Lee had gone south to block an expected British assault in Virginia or the Carolinas. He set up headquarters in the Governor's Palace at Williamsburg even though he was not sure which target the British would strike. "I know not where to turn," Lee complained. "I am like a dog in a dancing school." At last the British fleet was sighted off Cape Fear, and Lee took two thousand men from Virginia and North Carolina to the broad harbor at Charleston, South Carolina.

The previous fall, Patrick Henry had taken command of the Virginia militia, but his longtime civilian opponents had thwarted every military move Henry proposed. In Cambridge, Washington thought that the Congress had made a grave mistake in letting Henry leave the legislature. He wished that Colonel Henry would see his unsuitability as an officer and resign voluntarily. By March 1, 1776, Henry had reached the same conclusion and he left the army.

The episode had been a bitter indignity for Henry, who at age forty was mourning the recent death of his troubled wife. Since military fame had been denied to him, Henry returned to politics. He began to discuss a new constitution for Virginia with George Mason and a young newcomer, James Madison. Charles

Lee would not have to contend with Henry's inexperience as a soldier combined with his immense popularity.

Lee had arrived in the South with his full complement of dogs; he said that dogs were faithful and men were not. Making his first tour of Charleston, he brought along a Pomeranian as big as a bear. But his passion for dogs was the least of Lee's oddities. A tall and skinny man of forty-four, he was strikingly ugly, with a bony nose so large that men called him "Naso." His nature was a jumble of contradictory quirks. He was vain enough to design his own uniform and have it expensively tailored but then wore it wrinkled and often filthy. He quoted from Plutarch and Shakespeare but as easily lapsed into a coarseness remarkable even in the army. He was an Irishman but had been born in England, sixteen days before George Washington in 1732.

Lee's father had been a colonel, and by the age of twelve the boy was studying in Switzerland and was already commissioned as an ensign in the British Army. Apart from a deep affection for his sister, Lee was as disillusioned with women as with men and seemed to prefer casual relations with those who followed an army camp. During the French and Indian War, Lee had served under Braddock in America and passed through Mohawk territory, where he married the daughter of a chief named White Thunder in a ceremony Lee did not regard as binding. The Mohawks observed the way Lee strode through their camp, always talking, and named him "Boiling Water."

Lee fought during the British siege of Montreal. When peace came in 1763, he went to Poland to become an aide to King Stanislas II, rising to the rank of Polish major general and watching and learning from the rebel brigades that were terrorizing Poland. He carried a message from Stanislas to George III in England and was granted an interview with the king. Lee expected to be rewarded for his services to a British ally. Instead, George began to apologize for having no military position to offer him.

Lee cut the monarch short. "Sir," he said, "I will never give Your Majesty an opportunity of breaking your promise to me again."

By that time, Lee was already allied with the British Whigs who opposed the king, and when he decided to settle in America he took up the patriot cause. Although he was not related directly to the Lees of Virginia, his political opinions endeared him to

Richard Henry Lee, and during a trip to New York he charmed the Northerners as well. John Adams decided that Lee was the only man he had met who had read more military history than he had. That was when he began cautioning friends that they must overlook Lee's dogs and his violent temper because of his attachment to liberty.

When war with Britain looked inevitable, Lee had traveled to Mount Vernon in December 1774 and spent five days as George Washington's house guest. Since they were comrades-in-arms from Braddock's campaign, Lee was not embarrassed to borrow fifteen pounds from Washington as his stay was ending.

The next year, when Lee's name was put forward for commission as a major general, John Hancock and other Massachusetts delegates strongly challenged his appointment. But both Adamses backed Lee, and George Washington personally requested the appointment. General Lee quickly justified the endorsements. Whenever British artillery probed Lee's position on the Charlestown peninsula, his men stood firm, and soon Nathanael Greene, the militant Quaker, was writing of Lee's genius. From Philadelphia, John Adams assured Lee, "We want you at N. York—We want you at Cambridge—We want you in Virginia—But Canada seems of more importance than any of those places, and therefore you are sent there." Lee had barely received that letter when Congress decided it wanted him most of all in the South, confronting Sir Henry Clinton, and he went to Charleston.

There he found a town panicked by the sight of the British armada on its horizon. Lee laughed at their fears, even as the local militia were desperately digging lead out of church windows to cast as musket balls. His officers soon came to accept Lee's rude manners as a fair trade for his apparent skill. He inspected a half-finished fort on Sullivan's Island fronting the Charleston harbor and found the same fault that had marred the redoubt on Breed's Hill—there was not space enough for retreat. "A slaughter pen," Lee called it, far too flimsy to withstand the guns of a British man-of-war.

As Sir Henry Clinton waited in the bay and weighed his next move, he also had reason to recall the day on the hills above Boston. Clinton was thought moody and suspicious, and his experiences in America hadn't improved his disposition. He had urged the British to pursue the Americans retreating from Breed's Hill.

When he had recommended fortifying Dorchester Heights, he had been ignored again. And yet Howe, not he, had been given the supreme command in Boston, and Howe had sent Clinton on this expedition, far away from the British headquarters.

For eight days in mid-June 1776, Clinton landed his troops at an undefended point near Charleston called Long Island. He took another twelve days to get his ships in place so that they could begin battering the fort on Sullivan's Island. On the morning of June 28, scouts in the harbor saw the British men-of-war unfurling their topsails and moving three miles in from where they had been anchored. The first to take up a position in front of the fort was a bomb ketch carrying mortars, the *Thunder*. Its crew threw their shells accurately, but the fort that Lee disparaged had been designed around a deep gorge, and most of the shells fell there and did little damage. Other ships joined the bombardment—the *Active*, the *Friendship*, the *Experiment*.

Months earlier, after John Adams had proposed an American navy, the colonies had amassed a haphazard collection of ships. To protect his fleet from any of them, Clinton directed three ships to sail out and cover his western flank, but the ships ran aground. And when Clinton tried to launch a ground attack on Sullivan's Island from Long Island, he was chagrined to find that an inlet between the two islands was much deeper than he had been told. He expected the water at low tide to drop to eighteen inches, which would let his men wade across. Instead, the water ran seven feet deep, preventing soldiers from reaching the fort. Without troops, Clinton had only his ships to pound Charleston into surrender, and they had to face the fort's twenty-six big guns.

But those guns were not always firing. The Americans had begun the siege with twenty-eight rounds for each gun. Although they were receiving more throughout the day, they often held their fire to conserve ammunition. As a boiling sun beat down on the fort, the men along the firing platform drank steadily from grog passed along to them in fire buckets. General Lee made only a brief appearance. The Americans were winning the battle and embarrassing the man who had urged that their fort be abandoned. Lee had clashed over that strategy with its commander, Colonel William Moultrie, and had tried to have Moultrie removed from his post. Now Lee simply said, "Colonel, I see you are doing very well here. You have no occasion for me. I will go up to town again."

Firing continued until 9:30 P.M., when silence fell across the harbor. General Clinton had ordered his commodore, Sir Peter Parker, to return the British frigates to anchor three miles away. For the next several days Clinton's troops were stranded on Long Island, short of supplies and prey to clouds of mosquitoes. General Lee upheld the civilities of war by sending General Clinton fresh supplies at his ship, and Clinton responded with drafts of porter and a good cheese for Lee. At last, Henry Clinton sailed north to rejoin General Howe.

Charles Lee's victory had not been as bloodless as George Washington's on Dorchester Heights. Ten men had been killed inside the fort and twenty-four wounded. But Charleston was another undeniable American victory and—to anyone who hadn't heard Lee's bad advice to Colonel Moultrie—another reason to forgive General Lee his peculiarities.

Thomas Jefferson in 1768

Jefferson
1775-76

EARLY IN the winter of 1776, John Adams read a new pamphlet
with a provocative title. He sent a copy to Abigail Adams and
predicted that its arguments would soon become common faith on
the American continent. The pamphlet, *Common Sense*, had been
published anonymously by a recent immigrant from England. Despite Adams' admiration, much about the essay irritated him, not
the least its phenomenal success. Already more than a hundred
thousand copies had been sold, and patriots everywhere were
praising it. Adams thought the author's reliance on the Old Testament as his authority was merely ridiculous, but the extreme democratic ideas in *Common Sense* were dangerous, and Adams wrote
an essay to refute them. His rebuttal led the author to call one
night on Adams at his Philadelphia lodgings.

Thomas Paine was thirty-eight, two years younger than Adams,
but his life had been equally eventful and considerably more raffish.

He had been raised in the Church of England, although his father, a corset-maker, was attracted to the Quakers. Thomas' sour mother was a trial to him. When he read *The Taming of the Shrew* he concluded that she might have provided the model. He also learned as a boy that the fine gentlemen in his town of Thetford had no scruples about sending hungry children to the gallows for stealing.

As his belief in British justice eroded, the Quakers caused Thomas to question God's divine plan with their belief that He was too good to permit His own son's death to save other men. In time, Thomas found the Quaker outlook too gray; he preferred the world in all its gaudy colors, but he retained a sympathy for the sect. He read a natural history of Virginia and, captivated by the lushness of its southern vistas, vowed that he would cross the Atlantic to the new world one day.

In the meantime, he took a wife and a badly paid job as a tax collector. His wife died in childbirth, and after he had been barely a year on the job the government removed him when he was caught out in a common ruse among the collectors: instead of traveling through the countryside collecting taxes, they had stayed home and simply issued stamps without checking inventories or assets. Paine could find no other work, and at the age of twenty-eight he was forced to beg for his job back.

By that time, Paine had become more aggressive. He had been driven to his past offense by low wages, and now he resolved to improve the pay of all excisemen. He was already proving that he had a gift for debating. A group of friends met regularly at the White Hart tavern to drink and wrangle, and the next morning they sent a prize—an old copy of Homer in Greek that they called the Headstrong Book—to the man who had been the most obstinate haranguer; usually the book went to Paine. The nights when Quakers joined the group, they sometimes supported his ideas: replacing war with international arbitration; rights for women; an end to slavery. Otherwise, he stood alone. Drawing on his debating practice, Paine wrote a pamphlet, "The Case of the Salary of the Officers of Excise and Thoughts on the Corruption Arising from the Poverty of Excise Officers." In it he argued that the collectors had not received a promised pay raise because toadies of George III had convinced Parliament to increase the king's salary by a hundred thousand pounds a year. Paine sent his essay to every member of Parliament, where it was greeted with indifference. Months passed with no redress. Paine began to shirk his duties and was removed from his job again. The charge was absent without leave.

His second marriage was going no more smoothly. Paine's long face was remarkable for his large and pendulous nose and the amused curve to his mouth. But what everyone remembered were his blue eyes. Men friends laughed at Paine's confidence that any woman who looked into those eyes fell in love with him. He might have sometimes deceived himself, but he hadn't been wrong about his landlord's daughter, Elizabeth, who was the sort of lovely blonde Paine preferred. Afterward none of his friends knew what went wrong with the marriage, and when they asked about his wife Paine was evasive. Certainly, when they married, Elizabeth had worshiped him. But Paine claimed he had never felt love for her, only pity. Elizabeth began flirting openly with other men, while Paine spent more nights at the White Hart. They separated formally in June 1774, and she went to live with her brother. Years later, his enemies ignored his first wife's pregnancy and spread the rumor that Paine was impotent.

Paine's appeal to the Parliament to increase the tax collectors' pay had opened one door to him. Oliver Goldsmith read the essay at the time he was writing *She Stoops to Conquer*, sought out its author and introduced him to his literary circle. Paine also met Benjamin Franklin, who remarked afterward on his wonderful eyes. When Paine, without job, wife or prospects, decided at the age of thirty-seven to see America, Franklin wrote a letter recommending him to his son-in-law in Philadelphia.

Paine arrived in America on the last day of November 1774, and his fortunes improved immediately. A bookseller who had just launched a magazine hired him as its editor. By the second issue, Paine could report to Franklin that he had doubled the circulation. He was learning that the ideas he had developed during the disputes at the White Hart were not widely shared in his adopted country. He wrote against cruelty to animals and cruelty to women. Man, he said, "in all climates and in all ages, has been either an insensible husband or an oppressor."

After Paine had been in America for some time, Benjamin Franklin, now back in Philadelphia, suggested that he write a history of the current upheaval against England. Paine took up the idea and wrote quickly in order to surprise Franklin with the result by New Year's Day 1776. When the manuscript was finished, Paine began looking for a printer. His forceful language frightened away several, but Benjamin Rush, a delegate to the Congress, put Paine in touch with a printer named Bell, who was also a patriot.

Paine felt little nostalgia for England and none for its king. He brought a passion to his pamphlet that had been missing from the writing of even the more fervent Americans. Paine was outraged over Lexington and Concord and claimed that his own rebellion had begun on that day. "I rejected the hardened, sullen-tempered Pharaoh of England forever," Paine wrote, adding that he felt disdain for "the wretch, with that pretended title of Father of His People, who can unfeelingly hear of their slaughter, and composedly sleep with their blood upon his soul." Few of the leading patriots—possibly Thomas Jefferson was one—felt that strongly about George III. And yet they found something heady, liberating, in hearing him called "the Royal Brute of Britain."

Paine's invective was stirring, but he had loftier aims for his essay. He wanted the Congress to draw up a charter for the united colonies that would guarantee the freedom and the property of all men, along with their right to worship according to their own conscience. He urged America to build a navy for its defense and calculated how it could be financed. "No country on the globe is so happily situated, or so internally capable of raising a fleet as America. Tar, timber, iron and cordage are her natural produce. We need go abroad for nothing." That spirit of optimism and pride coursed through Paine's essay. He longed to see the Americans declare themselves independent for one practical reason. He knew that America needed the support of France and Spain but that neither country would send aid so long as the struggle seemed to be a family matter between England and her colonies. Without a declaration of independence, the patriots were merely rebels. What European power would jeopardize its own empire by encouraging rebellion?

Paine's document would have excited its readers under any title, but *Common Sense* was rousing. Benjamin Rush, who had taken his medical degree in Edinburgh, had suggested the plain-spoken Scots title. After more than a decade of lawyerly appeals to the English constitution, here was someone urging the Americans to

Thomas Paine

COMMON SENSE:

ADDRESSED TO THE

INHABITANTS

OF

A M E R I C A.

On the following interesting

S U B J E C T S.

I. Of the Origin and Design of Government in general,
with concise Remarks on the English Constitution.

II. Of Monarchy and Hereditary Succession.

III. Thoughts on the present State of American Affairs.

IV. Of the present Ability of America, with some miscellaneous
Reflections.

Written by an ENGLISHMAN.

By Thomas Paine

Man knows no Master save creating HEAVEN,
Or those whom choice and common good ordain.
THOMSON.

PHILADELPHIA, Printed
And Sold by R. BELL, in Third-Street, 1776.

Common Sense, published in
1768

cut through history and tradition and rely on their intuition. Since every government's policies were based on economics, he reduced the question to whether America would prosper better with England or without her. Once Americans saw the answer as clearly as Paine did, why should old mythologies stop them from acting in their self-interest?

But the document was winning hearts across the continent less from pragmatic argument than from its pulsing excess: "O ye that love mankind! Ye that dare oppose, not only the tyranny, but the tyrant, stand forth! Every spot of the old world is overrun with oppression. Freedom hath been hunted round the globe. Asia and Africa have long expelled her—Europe regards her like a stranger, and England hath given her warning to depart. O! receive the fugitive, and prepare in time an asylum for mankind."

When John Adams met this brash recruit to the patriot ranks, he told Paine that his sketchy ideas for a new government lacked restraints and safeguards; Adams had never been as willing as his cousin to trust to the judgments of the masses. Adams also lectured Paine for claiming that the Jews had adopted the idea of monarchy from their heathen enemies. Those remarks about the Old Testament were so foolish, Adams added, that he had to question Paine's sincerity.

At that, Paine laughed and admitted that he had stolen his religious ideas from Milton. Paine clearly had contempt for the entire Bible, both the Old Testament and the New. Here in Philadelphia he had even lost his respect for the Quakers, because he thought their pacifism was a disguise for Tory sentiments. But when he saw that his free thinking irritated Adams, Paine backtracked and said blandly that he had decided not to publish his thoughts on religion until the latter part of his life.

The encounter ended amiably. Adams concluded that Paine was conceited but capable and a good writer. Adams was frank in a letter to his wife about his own more guarded approach to writing—"I could not have written anything in so manly and striking a style." Because John Adams was known to favor independence and because the pamphlet had been printed anonymously, men sometimes complimented him on *Common Sense*. But Adams knew that his own blueprint for the future was more clear-sighted. He told Abigail Adams that Paine was "a better hand in pulling down than building."

Paine's daring provoked an unprecedented response. By April, letters from Virginia convinced George Washington that a tide had turned. "I find *Common Sense* is working a powerful change in the minds of many men," he wrote. Thomas Jefferson, who had left Philadelphia and returned to his estate, Monticello, received a copy from a delegate, Thomas Nelson, who said he was offering a present of two shillings' worth of Common Sense. Conservative members of the Congress were still arguing against severing ties with England, but Thomas Paine's call resounded above all of them: "The blood of the slain, the weeping voice of nature cries, 'Tis time to part."

Paine had taken one other step to bring independence nearer, one that he did not announce. He had signed over the copyright of *Common Sense* to the Congress. At two shillings each, it went through edition after edition, until half a million copies had been sold. Penniless when he arrived from England, Thomas Paine had donated a fortune to the American cause.

For nearly a decade, North Carolina had been more contentious in the patriot cause than its neighbors, and its colonists had paid the price. At Alamance Creek in 1771, Governor William Tryon's troops had routed a group of farmers called the Regulators, who were protesting corruption among King George's appointees. Tryon ordered seven of the leaders executed. But a later British force was defeated by Carolina patriots in a battle at Moore's Creek, and, while the Continental Congress was still debating, the people of Mecklenburg, North Carolina, passed a resolution in May 1775 that severed their ties with England. On April 12, 1776, all of North Carolina declared itself completely independent.

Christopher Gadsden of South Carolina left Philadelphia to prod his colony's provincial congress at Charleston and arrived brandishing the first copy of *Common Sense* that the members had seen. They were thunderstruck at first by Gadsden's demand for independence, but when news reached them that Parliament had voted late in December 1775 to seize any American ships on the high seas, popular sentiment began to turn.

Before Thomas Jefferson returned to Philadelphia, he canvassed his neighbors and concluded that nine tenths of the people favored independence. On May 15, 1776, Virginians in Williamsburg instructed their delegates to present to the Continental Congress a resolution that the thirteen colonies be declared free and independent states. At the same time, John Adams had persuaded the Congress to recommend that each state form its own new government. Adams considered the action almost as good as a formal statement of independence. John Dickinson and his allies still thought that final step was hasty, and six colonies instructed their delegates to vote against separation. The same gallows humor that had once swept across Massachusetts had reached Pennsylvania, and as they debated separation the delegates joked morbidly about the consequences. Benjamin Harrison, who was six feet four inches and obese, boasted to slender Elbridge Gerry that when they were hanged his weight would guarantee him a shorter agony.

The debate seemed to be reaching its climax when a new disappointment arose for the delegates committed to independence. They had hoped that the Canadians would agree to become their fourteenth state, but word came in April that Benedict Arnold had given up his attempt to blockade Quebec and that American troops were retreating. Congress hadn't been able to supply its Canadian expedition with provisions, money or medicine, and smallpox had ravaged its ranks. "Defeated most ignominiously," John Adams wrote to James Warren in Massachusetts. "Where shall we lay the blame?" Benjamin Franklin had been a member of a commission to inspect the Canadian effort, and his group returned with a report of alarming mismanagement. John Hancock complained to George Washington that America's Northern troops had been ruined by a lack of discipline, and the colonies were desperately unprepared for any new British offensive.

But the Congress wasn't daunted. It authorized Washington to try to raise more militia—six thousand to send as reinforcements to Canada, thirteen thousand to station in New York, another ten thousand to keep in reserve. And on June 7, 1776, Richard Henry Lee took the floor to offer the resolution many delegates had been dreading. Lee was one of Samuel Adams' closest allies and had been criticized for representing Massachusetts more diligently than Virginia. That was why Adams could tell friends the evening before the speech that Lee's resolution would decide the most important question America had ever faced.

At forty-four, Richard Henry Lee was tall and lean, red-haired like Thomas Jefferson but with an aquiline nose and a profile described as Roman. He came from one of Virginia's most prominent families and in 1764 had applied for the job of stamp master but had quickly felt ashamed of that moment of greed and entered the ranks of the patriots. Lee felt a dislike for Virginia's slave economy, and long before independence became an issue he had reminded the House of Burgesses that Africans were their fellow creatures. They were "created as ourselves," Lee said, "and equally entitled to liberty and freedom by the great law of nature."

Richard Lee had blown off the fingers of one hand in a hunting accident, and whenever he rose to speak he would wrap the mutilated hand in a handkerchief. Before Patrick Henry arrived in the Burgesses, Lee had been its leading speaker, the sort of orator who moved himself deeply as he spoke. Now in Philadelphia he launched his three-part resolution with what he considered its least important point:

"That these United Colonies are, and of right ought to be, free and independent States, that they are absolved from all allegiance to the British Crown, and that all political connection between them and the State of Great Britain is, and ought to be, totally dissolved."

Lee went on to more vital matters: America should form foreign alliances, and the Congress should prepare a plan of confederation for the colonies. The Congress delayed debate on Lee's resolution until the following morning. Then, acting as a committee of the whole, the members began to debate whether or not America should declare herself free.

Even the conservatives did not complain about Lee's other two suggestions. Sending official delegates to France and drawing up a confederacy seemed sensible. But why declare independence before the colonies were sure they could achieve it? Why warn Britain of America's intentions? Wouldn't the colonies look ridiculous asking Europe's heads of state to support a union that didn't exist? Edward Rutledge of South Carolina—at twenty-seven, one of the youngest delegates—joined with John Dickinson to press those points. He hoped to postpone the discussion for three weeks, or for months if he could manage it.

By the following Monday, June 10, Rutledge seemed to have

prevailed. The Congress voted to postpone any decision until the first day of July. But Richard Lee's faction had a trick left to play. They won approval for appointing committees that would spend the next three weeks preparing drafts on each point of Lee's resolution. That way no more time would be lost if the Congress agreed to his recommendations. The next day, June 11, the Congress named those committees, drawing on the different talents of its members and balancing each committee politically.

Samuel Adams was appointed to the committee to prepare the draft of confederation, but he was not one of the five chosen to draw up a declaration of independence to be held in reserve. Two of the choices, John Adams and Benjamin Franklin, were almost inevitable. John Adams regretted that he had been talking too much these days; true respect, he concluded, went to men who were more aloof. But that was only Adams scourging himself. His passionate logic had, in fact, made him influential and widely trusted, and his fellow delegates named him both to the committee on the declaration and to the committee to draw up treaty plans for France. Nor would Congress pass over the talents of Franklin, its most celebrated author. Robert Livingston of New York had enough votes to join the committee, even though he had argued against Lee's resolutions. Roger Sherman of Connecticut was also chosen.

The fifth member won his place through compromise: some Northern delegates continued to believe that naming a Virginian to America's most visible positions was good strategy. Richard Henry Lee was not electable because he was considered too radical even within his own delegation. And Benjamin Harrison was too conservative for Lee's supporters, however much he might joke about being hanged. Both factions could agree, however, on Virginia's newest delegate. When Thomas Jefferson arrived at the Congress the year before, he had been preceded by a reputation in both literature and science. Many members had read his pamphlet *A Summary View of the Rights of British America*. Even those who thought his account of the Boston Tea Party sounded as though Samuel Adams had dictated it agreed that Jefferson wrote well. He seemed to shrink from public speaking, but in private his sentiments were everything the Adamses could hope for. John Adams lobbied for him to join the committee and was so persuasive that when the votes were counted Jefferson had received more than anyone else.

Jefferson was a modest man of thirty-two; John Adams was past forty. When the time came for one person to draw up a preliminary draft, Jefferson was ready to defer to his elders. He had just rejoined the Congress after an extended absence, but he remembered John Adams' need for respect. Seeking him out, Jefferson suggested that Adams be the one to draw up the declaration.

Adams was in a playful and self-deprecating mood when Jefferson offered him the assignment. "I will not," he said. Adams agreed with Richard Henry Lee that the declaration was only a formality and less important than the drafts to consolidate the colonies and enlist allies.

"You should do it," Jefferson said.

"Oh, no!"

"Why will you not?" Jefferson persisted. "You ought to do it."

"I will not."

"Why?"

"Reasons enough."

Jefferson indulged this antic mood. "What can be your reasons?"

John Adams began to tick them off: "Reason first, you are a Virginian, and a Virginian ought to appear at the head of this business. Reason second, I am obnoxious, suspected and unpopular. You are very much otherwise. Reason third, you can write ten times better than I can."

"Well," Jefferson said, "if you are decided, I will do as well as I can."

Thomas Jefferson's father had married well, possibly too well. Peter Jefferson became deeply enmeshed with his wife's family, the prosperous and prominent Randolphs of Virginia, and one cousin, William Randolph, was closer to him than a brother. William could afford to be generous to the rising young planter and once deeded Jefferson two hundred acres of undeveloped land. As payment, he asked for one bowl of arrack punch. William Randolph's wife died young, and when Randolph began to suspect that he was also dying he added a codicil to his will requesting that his loving friend move down to the Randolph plantation and remain there until Randolph's son was grown. Peter Jefferson— large, strong, scrupulous—mourned his friend by honoring his wish. Taking no pay, he moved his family from their modest home, Shadwell, to Tuckahoe, the imposing Randolph estate, where one story of the main house was set aside for visitors. That was why Thomas Jefferson's earliest memory, at two years old, was of being carried on a pillow by a slave as the Jeffersons moved downriver to Tuckahoe.

What his mother had thought of the move Thomas Jefferson never recorded. Her family may have felt that marrying Peter Jefferson had brought Jane Randolph down in the world; she may have agreed with them. As he grew up, the boy came to appreciate his father and admire him. Thomas himself would be tall, but never so burly or strong as Peter Jefferson. But whatever his parents told him about the move, Thomas was surrounded by reminders that he was being raised on the Randolph estate.

In 1752, when Thomas was nine years old, his parents re- turned to the plainer life of Shadwell, and five years later Peter Jefferson died. He left behind eight children, Thomas the oldest son. Jane Randolph Jefferson inherited the Shadwell house and its farmland, most of the slaves and all of the horses. When Thomas reached twenty-one he was to have his choice of lands on the Rivanna or Fluvanna River, along with a share of livestock and half the slaves. In the meantime, each child was left a personal servant. Peter Jefferson's own mulatto, Sawney, was considered the most valuable slave of the household staff, and he went to Thomas, along with books, mathematical instruments and a cherry- wood desk.

In later life, Thomas congratulated himself for having turned out as well as he had. He was only fourteen when he lost his father, and his mother had never been a source of guidance. His younger brother Randolph was slow-witted, and there was no strong bond between Thomas and his older sisters. Life in Virginia abounded with temptations for drinking and gambling, and if the colony's clergy couldn't resist them, why should a lusty young man? With his father gone, Thomas escaped the gentility at home by seeking out the neighborhood's rougher men and boys although he knew they were cardsharpers and wastrels for whom a fox hunt was life's highest aspiration. Even while they fed his rebellious side, he was being carried through adolescence by an inherent fastidiousness and an ardent love of books. He said later that if forced to choose between his father's estate and his classical education, he would always pick the education.

Thomas learned to ride and swim well, but it was through his mind that he intended to lift himself above the friends sunk in sport and pleasure. He had begun to judge his contemporaries and his elders harshly. Patrick Henry struck him as somewhat coarse and shallow, and when Thomas reached William and Mary, at the age of seventeen, he found his classmates even more disappointing. Low standards of admission had "filled the college with children," he complained, which made classes disagreeable, even degrading, to a properly prepared student like himself.

Instead of mixing with boys his own age, Thomas moved gratefully into a circle of cultured older men. Dr. William Small, a Scotsman who taught mathematics and philosophy, introduced Thomas to George Wythe, a distinguished lawyer, and to the colony's lieutenant governor, Francis Fauquier. That quartet, united by a love of music, often dined at the Governor's Palace. Fauquier had arrived in Virginia two years before Jefferson entered William and Mary. According to rumor, he had been given the post after an influential lord in London had won his entire inheritance at the gaming tables, felt sorry for him and helped him to a royal appointment in America. The story, true or not, may have contributed to Jefferson's lifelong dislike of cards; when he set up his own house, he did not allow them.

The governor may also have influenced Thomas to observe closely the world around him. During Fauquier's first year in Virginia, a freak hailstorm struck the capital and broke every window on the north side of the Governor's Palace. Fauquier used the ice to cool his wine and freeze his cream, but he also sent a precise report on the phenomenon to London, where it was delivered to the Royal Society.

Of his three older companions, Jefferson came to know George Wythe best, because Wythe agreed to tutor him when he decided to study law. Thomas was already measuring himself intellectually against every man he met, and although he considered his teacher a little slow in grasping an issue, Wythe always reached a sound conclusion. He also kept his religious creed, whatever it might be, out of their discussions, and Thomas found that reticence attractive.

Jefferson was now studying fifteen hours a day. He gave up riding and let his study of the violin lapse, though he had shown some talent. Rising at dawn, he stopped his studies only at twilight for a one-mile run out of Williamsburg and back. Progressing in the law, Jefferson cursed the impenetrable Coke as John Adams had done a decade before. "I do wish the devil had old Coke, for I am sure I never was so tired of an old dull scoundrel in my life."

Apart from musicales at the Governor's Palace, Thomas occasionally visited the Raleigh Tavern in Williamsburg and the surrounding plantations. Young women caught his eye regularly, and he traded gossip with his male friends, but he foundered in his mild attempts at courtship. As the years passed, Jefferson would grow into his large hands and feet, his ungainly height would come to seem imposing and his ginger-red hair a distinction, but in his youth he approached women with a diffidence that made him easy to refuse. Rebecca Burwell, the orphaned daughter of a past acting governor, was one favorite. Like John Adams courting Abigail Smith, Jefferson concocted a number of fanciful names for her. She was "Belinda" and, backward, "Adnileb." Jefferson was twenty and deep in his study of the law; Rebecca was sixteen. He considered himself profoundly in love, and yet he wanted to see the world before he settled down. He wrote to ask his friend John Page whether he would sail with him to Europe. They would go to Italy, where Jefferson could buy a good violin. Then they would move on to Egypt and finally travel home by way of Canada. Surely, he asked Page, the young lady would wait for him? After all, he wouldn't be gone forever—two or three years at the most. But Miss Burwell wasn't holding out much encouragement. What if he called his ship the *Rebecca?* His letters to Page were already suggesting Jefferson's lifelong battle between a warm heart and a cool head. He seemed to hope to watch from the sidelines, cheering on each part of himself impartially.

Jefferson began to see how his beloved might greet his travel plans and took refuge in youthful fatalism. "This should be a man's attitude: 'Few things will disturb him at all; nothing will disturb him much.' "

Throughout his young manhood, Jefferson's heart usually prevailed. When he was twenty-five and still not involved with a woman, another boyhood friend, John Walker, was called away on business to the Indian territories. Jefferson had been a member of Walker's wedding party, and it seemed natural for Walker to ask him to look after his young wife and infant daughter. Walker spent four months on the frontier. When he returned, he was puzzled that his wife kept asking him why he trusted his friend Jefferson.

A year or two later, the Walkers visited Shadwell, and Jefferson seized a few furtive opportunities to caress Mrs. Walker. He also slipped a note about the innocence of promiscuous love into the sleeve of her gown. Mrs. Walker destroyed it and told her husband nothing. Jefferson was as stirred by Mrs. Walker as George Washington had been over Sally Fairfax, though with perhaps less encouragement. One night when both Jefferson and the Walkers were staying at a militia colonel's house, he waited until the ladies had retired to bed, then claimed a headache and left Walker and the other men sitting over their drinks. He found the room where Mrs. Walker was undressing and slipped inside. Only her threat to scream sent him hurrying away.

Those escapades became known only much later, after Jefferson had learned to cope with desire more discreetly. "When young and single," he explained then, "I offered love to a handsome lady."

Jefferson had begun to settle into domesticity even before he found a wife to share it. On a slope across the Rivanna River from Shadwell he started grafting an orchard of cherry trees. He called the site by its Italian name—Monticello, little mountain. He was determined to put a mansion on top of his mountain, which meant setting himself dozens of technical problems. Simply getting water to the summit was a challenge. But from the crest the view of rolling woods across the lower hills would justify everything.

Excavation had already begun in February 1770, when the family house at Shadwell burned to the ground. A slave was sent to Jefferson, who was visiting in Charlottesville, to tell him of the disaster. The young lawyer asked, Did they save my books? "No, master," said the slave, "but we saved your fiddle." It was not the good instrument he had hoped to buy in Italy. Jefferson had not gone abroad, after all, and his violin had cost him only five pounds.

It was at this time that Jefferson provided rum and cakes for the voters and was elected to the Burgesses. A year later, he met a young and wealthy widow, Martha Wayles Skelton. During their courtship throughout 1771, Jefferson came to believe that he might be entitled to a coat of arms. When he investigated the possibility his inquiries were wry and offhand. He wrote to a London agent that if a family arms did exist he would buy it, since the novelist Laurence Sterne had assured the world that a coat of arms could be purchased as cheaply as any other coat.

On Christmas Eve 1771, Jefferson left the cottage that was the rough beginnings of his mansion and set off to be married. When he filled out his license form on the last day of the year, he wrote "spinster" in the space for designating his bride. Someone crossed that out and wrote "widow" instead. Martha Skelton had a four-year-old son, but she was only twenty-three and had been widowed for three years. She was small and pretty, with large brown eyes and dark-red hair, and she smiled and laughed in ways that complemented Jefferson's gravity. He had courted her by playing his violin to her harpsichord. In music or in language, he could release a sensuality that troubled him. Nine months after the wedding, Martha Jefferson gave birth to a daughter, also named Martha, and eighteen months after that to a second girl.

Jefferson devoted the first two years of his marriage to his family and his law practice. But by 1774 events were racing toward a break with England, and Jefferson was recruited into Patrick Henry's circle of patriots. He was thirty-one when he was elected to go to Philadelphia.

During one of his respites back in Virginia in August 1775, the Jeffersons lost their second daughter. The death caused Jefferson to linger at home, and for the moment his political sentiments were divided. He could see the desirability of reconciling with England, but the stories of British cruelty so outraged him that he felt willing to sink the whole island in the sea.

When he returned to Philadelphia in the fall of 1775, the other members of the Congress voted to sacrifice their December recess in order to cope with the crisis facing the Continental Army. Jefferson chose instead to ride home to Monticello, where he stayed, out of touch with public business, for four months. In Philadelphia, men who liked and admired him wondered whether he was being swayed by the Tories or by his wife. In February 1776 a fellow delegate urged Jefferson to bring his wife to the Congress if she was what was keeping him away. Jefferson also received the copy of *Common Sense*. It had moved a nation but it couldn't dislodge Jefferson from home.

Then, late in March 1776, Jefferson's mother died unexpectedly. Writing to relatives in England, Jefferson treated her death laconically—"We supposed it to have been apoplectic"—but he was struck down by a headache so severe that returning to Philadelphia was unthinkable. It was not the first time Jefferson had been afflicted; his head had ached for two days after he learned that Rebecca Burwell was marrying another man. But this was the worst attack, and it lasted six weeks. He described paroxysms of excruciating pain that reversed the pattern of the sun—they descended on him at dawn and lifted only with nightfall. After the ordeal had finally ended, Jefferson rode to Philadelphia in mid-May 1776, feeling almost like a new man.

It was in that spirit of deliverance that he began to compose the document Congress was expecting from him.

Independence

GIVEN A CHOICE, Thomas Jefferson would have joined John Adams in letting someone else draft a statement of independence. Delegates in Virginia had begun drawing up a new constitution, and Jefferson was alarmed that they were basing it closely on the existing one. Jefferson believed that building a proper foundation for his colony far outweighed drawing up another list of indictments against the king. He asked permission to return for the debate and

1776

mentioned his wife's uncertain health, but the leaders in Virginia directed him to stay in Philadelphia.

Jefferson was determined to be heard, however, and in less than two weeks he wrote three drafts of his own constitution for Virginia. Even that headlong dash came too late. Convention delegates had finished the bulk of their work before Jefferson's version reached Williamsburg. Debate was reopened to include a few of

Jefferson's points, but his most radical thinking was ignored.

Many of his proposals had stressed civil rights. He wanted to extend the right to vote; allow independent farmers to develop the West; guarantee decent treatment for Indians; reform the inheritance laws and provide for civilian control of the military. Jefferson's Virginia would have been a freer, fairer, more humane society, with full religious freedom and no capital punishment. He watched helplessly from Philadelphia as his colony turned away from those principles.

Jefferson did not intend his statement of independence to be original. He saw his assignment as setting down as clearly as possible the opinions commonly held by Americans and their Congress. The ideas he would be including had been in the air for many years, and he knew the arguments so well that he didn't need books or pamphlets in front of him as he wrote. His rivals would try much later to emphasize Jefferson's debt to other writers, especially John Locke. But as he began to write in June 1776, Jefferson borrowed most extensively from himself. As a preamble to his Virginia constitution, he had drawn up a list of King George's crimes, which he copied into this document.

Jefferson had rented a parlor and bedroom on the second floor of a new brick house on Market Street. There he set up a folding writing box that a cabinetmaker had built from his design. He made no claims for its beauty, but the box was plain and neat and took up no more room on the table in his parlor than any moderately sized book.

Jefferson wrote quickly in a small but legible hand, with no attempt at elegance. He made continual changes. First he wrote, "A declaration by the Representatives of the United States of America in General Congress Assembled." Then he went back and changed the phrase to "A declaration of . . ."

Next came "When in the course of human events . . ." That stately beginning survived all subsequent readings and drafts. He wrote that the people had to advance from subordination, then strengthened it to "dissolve the political bands which have connected them with another." But the document's purpose remained the same throughout the rewriting—to satisfy "a decent respect to the opinion of mankind" and declare the causes that were impelling the colonists to this separation.

Jefferson then produced language that justified the Congress in asking him to speak for America.

"We hold these truths to be sacred and undeniable," he wrote. Five years earlier, he had given a friend his list of essential books. Along with Locke, Jefferson had included *Inquiry into the Human Mind*, by Thomas Reid, who argued that moral truths were divided into those that were reached through reason and those that were self-evident to every man of understanding and morality. Jefferson struck out "sacred and undeniable" and wrote in "self evident." He continued through his draft, paring words away to make his language bolder. From "that all men are created equal and independent" he dropped "and independent." "Rights inherent and inalienable" became "unalienable rights." His next phrase came straight from his pen and could not be improved. Jefferson struck off those rights as "life, liberty and the pursuit of happiness."

Jefferson's third right represented his attempt to set the Continental Congress on a track that his own colony had rejected. Drawing from Locke, men had usually spoken of "life, liberty and property." But Jefferson recognized the way property reduced the power of men who didn't have it. If property was in fact power, couldn't it threaten liberty? Jefferson offered as his third unalienable right a substitute that provided a rhetorical flourish. By endorsing the pursuit of happiness, he wasn't lapsing into metaphysics or turning from political concerns to personal ones. His colleagues in the Congress would understand that Jefferson was speaking of the practice of happiness, not the questing after it. He used the phrase in the way that men spoke of pursuing law or pursuing medicine. Twelve years earlier, James Otis had argued in his *Rights of the British Colonies* that the duty of government was "to provide for the security, the quiet and happy enjoyment of life, liberty and property." At the time of the Stamp Act, New Yorkers had petitioned the king to protect the liberty that lay at the base of all their enjoyments. His subjects could be neither happy nor rich, they said, as long as there were restraints on their property. The patriots believed that men needn't seek happiness. If their government stopped abusing them, they would practice it.

Next, Jefferson made only slight revisions in seventy-five words that achieved what Samuel Adams and John Adams, the "Pennsylvania Farmer" and the *Boston Gazette*, Thomas Paine and the writers of a thousand patriot essays had been groping toward: "That, to secure these rights governments are instituted among men, deriving their just powers from the consent of the governed; that whenever any form of government becomes destructive of these ends, it is the right of the people to alter or to abolish it, and to institute new government, laying its foundations on such principles, and organizing its powers in such form, as to them shall seem most likely to effect their safety and happiness."

Jefferson passed to his indictment against George III, calling the king "his present majesty" and claiming that George was bent on establishing an absolute tyranny over America. As proof, Jefferson set down more than two dozen examples. For years America had been railing against Parliament, but Jefferson didn't mention either House. Although Thomas Paine had attacked the monarchy, many Americans still felt an allegiance to the throne and to the man who occupied it. Jefferson would prove to the world that George was not a fit king. His attack would be specific and personal. He would write nothing to alarm the other crowned heads of Europe.

The first dozen charges retraced the complaints common to most of the colonies: George III had refused to approve essential laws; had convened provincial legislatures at inconvenient sites and then dissolved them; had obstructed the nationalizing of foreigners; had made judges dependent on the crown; had kept standing armies in the colonies without the consent of their legislatures.

Some accusations were better founded than others, but they touched on grievances from every region. Over the last fifteen years Massachusetts had not been the only colony to have its legislature moved. During the rebellious days of the Stamp Act, South Carolina's assembly had been transferred from Charleston to Beaufort. Virginia, Massachusetts and South Carolina had all had their legislatures dissolved for refusing to rescind or ignore the Massachusetts circular letter. In 1771 North Carolina had passed a law exempting immigrants from all taxes for four years, but London had ruled that the measure might attract farmers from Scotland and damage agricultural production in Britain, and the act was disallowed.

In his next round of charges, Jefferson reminded the world of the cost to the colonies of quartering British troops, which long had been a sore point in New York. He denounced the act that permitted British appointees charged with crimes in America to be taken to England for trial "protecting them, by a mock trial, from punishment for any murders which they should commit on the inhabitants of these states." Reviewing his first draft, Jefferson remembered the way the Quebec Act had undercut revolutionary zeal in Canada and inserted a reference attacking George III for abolishing the system of English laws in a neighboring province. Occasionally, the logic behind a charge was specious. "He is, at this time, transporting large Armies of foreign mercenaries to complete the works of death, desolation and tyranny," Jefferson began one of his final accusations. But during the French and Indian War Americans had welcomed those same mercenaries as allies.

Jefferson's last indictments were also open to debate, although it was undeniable that the king's appointees had "excited domestic insurrection amongst us." As Virginia's royal governor, Lord Dunsmore had offered freedom to all slaves who would fight for Britain. And the king's agents were recruiting Indians—Jefferson called them "merciless Indian savages, whose known rule of warfare is an undistinguished destruction of all ages, sexes and conditions." But George Washington and John Adams, along with other patriots, wanted to win the Indians to America's cause.

Since his declaration had begun by proclaiming all men equal, Jefferson opened himself to charges of hypocrisy by raising the question of slavery. Now his last accusation against the king was also the strangest: "He has waged cruel war against human nature itself, violating its most sacred rights of life and liberty in the persons of a distant people who never offended him, captivating and carrying them into slavery, or to incur miserable death in their transportation thither." He contrasted King George's professed Christianity with his protection of a market where men could be bought and sold.

Jefferson himself was wholly the product of a slave society, and until he was nine years old blacks around him outnumbered whites by at least ten to one. As he drafted his statement, one third of Virginia's population of 400,000 were slaves. His father's will had bequeathed slaves to him, and when his wife's father died, some eighteen months after the wedding, Jefferson had inherited another 135 blacks. Included in that number was Elizabeth Hemings, whose mother had been African and whose father an English sea captain passing through Williamsburg. Jefferson's father-in-law had taken Elizabeth as his mistress after his wife died, and she bore him six children, all of them light-skinned. Virginians called them "bright mulattos." One of Martha Jefferson's unacknowledged half sisters was a girl called Sally, who promised to be as beautiful as her mother.

Jefferson's first legislation when he entered the Burgesses had been aimed at making it easier to free individual slaves. A slaveowner in North Carolina and Georgia could simply release a slave. Virginia law required that a slave be set free only for "meritorious service." Jefferson asked a relative, Richard Bland, to introduce a motion to give Virginians an unrestricted right to release their slaves, and Jefferson seconded the motion. But outrage swept through the House, Bland was denounced as an enemy of his county, and the bill was defeated.

Over the years, Jefferson had gone on deploring slavery and profiting from his slaves. He did not permit them to be whipped. But he advertised for a runaway he considered drunken and insolent and, after he got him back, sold him for a hundred pounds. Six years before he began drafting this declaration, Jefferson had argued as a lawyer for the freedom of a slave who claimed to have a white grandmother. In Virginia, with its gradations among mulattos, color counted less than the status of the mother. If she was free, her children were also free. Jefferson had argued then that under the law of nature all men were born free and that everyone came into the world with a right to his own person. The judge had interrupted his argument and held for the slave's owner.

His years of conflict now broke out across the page as Jefferson tried to blame Britain's king for what he considered an infamous practice among Americans. George III had "prostituted" his authority to keep alive the "execrable commerce" of slavery. Now the king was compounding this "assemblage of horrors" by inciting America's slaves "to purchase that liberty of which he deprived them, by murdering the people upon whom he also obtruded them; thus paying off former crimes committed against the *liberties* of the people with crimes which he urges them to commit against the *lives* of another."

Nothing had weighed heavier on Jefferson's conscience than being an accessory to the slave trade, and he hoped that the Congress would endorse his view of slavery. When John Adams read the draft, he objected privately to calling George III a tyrant, but he didn't protest because he assumed that the Congress would modify the phrase. Adams considered Jefferson's denunciations of slavery among the best parts of the declaration. Benjamin Franklin also read the draft before it went to the Congress and made only slight changes. Thomas Jefferson then wrote out a fair copy, and it was laid before the Congress on June 28, 1776.

On the first of July, with Jefferson's statement ready, delegates again took up Richard Henry Lee's resolution that the American states declare themselves independent.

Members from each faction rose and repeated their familiar positions. Some had labored long over their imagery. A Scottish preacher, Dr. John Witherspoon of New Jersey, said that the country was not only ripe for independence but in danger of becoming rotten for lack of it. John Dickinson had prepared one last protest. He argued that independence should be held up until the states were confederated, until the boundaries of the new nation had been fixed, until a pact could be reached with France. When he finished, John Adams waited for someone less partisan and less personally repugnant to Dickinson to answer him. When no one did, Adams rose once more.

He started humbly. For once in his life, Adams said, he wished he were as eloquent as the ancient orators of Greece and Rome, because he was sure that none of them had ever faced a question of more importance to his country and to the world. Speaking without notes, Adams went through his usual arguments. Then new delegates arrived and asked to hear what they had missed. Adams was urged to begin over. He protested that he felt like an actor or a gladiator brought out to entertain an audience, but he reviewed his position still another time.

At last even the latecomers were satisfied. With the Congress sitting as the committee of the whole, a vote was called. Nine of the thirteen colonies endorsed independence, but with the understanding that the final vote should come on the next day, the second of July. Before the session adjourned, however, a dispatch from General Washington arrived, which reported that the British seemed prepared to attack the American positions in New York. That alarm swayed the voters John Adams had not reached. The next day, South Carolina swung behind the resolution, along with

Delaware's delegates. John Dickinson and an ally stayed away from the hall so that Pennsylvania could also vote for independence. New York's delegation had not received authority to vote, but, with one exception, her delegates favored Lee's resolution.

On July 2, 1776, with no dissenting votes, the Congress at Philadelphia voted that the American colonies were henceforth free and independent states.

John Adams had never hesitated to remind his colleagues that their choice was momentous, perhaps the greatest decision that had ever faced mankind. The next evening he wrote home in triumph to Abigail Adams that the second day of July 1776 would "be celebrated by succeeding generations as the great anniversary festival." Adams knew how the day should be marked: "It ought to be commemorated as the day of deliverance by acts of devotion to God Almighty. It ought to be solemnized with pomp and parade, with shows, games, sports, guns, bells, bonfires and illuminations from one end of this continent to the other, from this time forward forever more."

Once again, John Adams was a little ahead of his countrymen. There was still Thomas Jefferson's declaration to approve. For three days, even before Lee's resolution was adopted, Jefferson had been mortified as delegates from South Carolina and Georgia tried to expunge his lines about slavery and leave that charge against the king bland and color blind—"He has excited domestic insurrections amongst us." The Southern colonies were joined by Northern delegates, and Jefferson observed that although Northerners might not have many slaves, their merchants had profited from shipping them.

The Congress struck down another paragraph that held great sentiment for Jefferson. He had wanted to express something of the loss Americans felt as they turned their faces away from their homeland. Because their brethren in Britain, Jefferson had written, were indifferent to the agonies the Americans were suffering, "we must endeavor to forget our former love for them, and to hold them as we hold the rest of mankind, enemies in war, and in peace friends." The Congress deleted the "love," retained the threat and went on to cut out the rest of Jefferson's wistful farewell:

"We might have been a free and a great people together; but a communication of grandeur and of freedom it seems is below their dignity. Be it so, since they will have it: The road to glory and happiness is open to us too; we will climb it in a separate state and acquiesce in the necessity which pronounces our everlasting Adieu!" Jefferson may have found the anguish of that ending too naked—or too Gallic—for in his final draft he had changed it to "our eternal separation."

Each cut in his prose was a mutilation for Jefferson. Sitting nearby, Benjamin Franklin observed his distress. Franklin's nature was at least as full-blooded as Jefferson's, but he was more than twice Jefferson's age. Over the years, he had imposed prudence and patience on himself and commended those virtues to readers of his popular *Poor Richard's Almanack*. Now he offered what consolation he could. He told Jefferson that he made it a rule not to draft any paper that had to be reviewed by a public body. He had learned his lesson from this incident:

When Franklin was a journeyman printer, one of his companions was an aspiring hatter who had served his apprenticeship and was about to open his own shop. He wanted a splendid sign for it with a proper inscription, and he wrote out: "John Thompson, Hatter, makes and sells hats for ready money." Below that he wanted a drawing of a hat. Before he had his sign painted, Thompson took his proposal to his friends for their suggestions.

The first man pointed out the redundancy of the word "Hatter," since it would be followed by the words "makes hats." Thompson struck it out.

Another friend said the word "makes" could be omitted since his customers wouldn't care who actually made the hats; if they were any good, they would buy them. Thompson took that out, too.

A third friend said that since it was not customary to sell on credit, the words "for ready money" were useless. By now the proposed sign read, "John Thompson sells hats."

"*Sells* hats?" said his next friend. "Nobody will expect you to give them away. What is the use of that word?" Thompson struck it out, and then he took out the "hats," since there was already a hat painted on the board. So his inscription ended up "John Thompson," with the drawing of a hat beneath it.

Franklin may have invented the story and very likely wasn't telling it for the first time, but Jefferson remembered for the rest of his life the genial attempt to ease his irritation.

When members of the Congress came to Jefferson's stirring conclusion, a majority thought it should include one last appeal to the power even greater than George III. Growing up among the abuses of the official church of Virginia had bred in Jefferson a hostility to state religions, and any cant came hard to him. But some of the men in the Congress were devout, and some were politicians who knew that a document intended as propaganda would be stronger with an allusion to God, and they added one. They did not, however, meddle with Jefferson's last oath, more solemn than anything they might devise:

"And for support of this Declaration, with a firm reliance on the protection of divine Providence, we mutually pledge to each other our lives, our fortunes and our sacred honor."

On July 4, 1776, independence was declared in language worthy of it.

That same day, across the ocean, Thomas Hutchinson, former governor of Massachusetts, was receiving a great honor. The previous April his son and his family and the Peter Olivers had arrived safely at Falmouth after General Howe's surrender of Boston to George Washington. The Hutchinson family was reunited—twenty-five people crowded into rooms on St. James's Street. On the fourth of July, Oxford University further eased the pain of exile by awarding Hutchinson and former Chief Justice Oliver honorary doctorates of civil laws; Francis Bernard had received the same honor four years earlier. Despite Hutchinson's volumes of history, the distinction was clearly political, not academic. Oxford's chancellor was Lord North.

The Continental Congress ordered a handsome copy of Jefferson's words prepared for the delegates to sign. While it was being lettered, the Declaration was read in the yard of Philadelphia's State House on July 8 to widespread cheering. Jefferson sent copies that same day to Richard Henry Lee, who had gone back to Virginia. One was the draft he had written, and the second was the version Congress had approved. Jefferson asked Lee to judge whether the Declaration was better or worse for the changes. Samuel Adams had been exhausted by the session, but he was gratified by the public response to independence. "The people seem to recognize this resolution," he wrote, "as though it were a decree promulgated from heaven." When New York formally adopted the Declaration on July 9, the state celebrated by releasing its debtors from prison. In Baltimore, Americans burned George III in effigy. In Savannah, they gave him an official burial. Virginia ruled that a sentence be deleted from all morning and evening church services—"O Lord, save the king and mercifully hear us when we call upon Thee."

Since proceedings of the Congress remained confidential, the names of the men signing the Declaration were withheld, and only Jefferson's fellow delegates knew he had written it. Entries in his journal for July 4 were sparse and uninformative. He noted that the day's temperature had gone from 68 degrees at 6 A.M. to a high of 76. He also recorded that he had bought seven pairs of women's gloves to take home.

But legends were already beginning to gather around the signing. One story was that John Hancock signed his name in a bold hand, rose from his chair and exclaimed, "There! John Bull can read my name without spectacles and may now double his reward of five hundred pounds for my head." Another account had Hancock turning to Charles Carroll of Maryland, the one delegate whose fortune dwarfed his own, and asking whether he would sign. "Most willingly," said Carroll, taking up the pen. Nearby somebody remarked, "There goes a few millions!"

Still another anecdote was accurate at least in conveying Franklin's wit. Hancock had cautioned the other delegates, "We must be unanimous. There must be no pulling different ways. We must all hang together."

To which Dr. Franklin replied, "Yes, we must indeed all hang together, or most assuredly we shall all hang separately."

On Saturday, August 10, 1776, the *Evening Post* in London scooped its competitors with the news of America's defiance. The following Monday, the *Morning Post* announced that the vote had been carried by only a small majority and had set off widespread desertions within the patriot camp. The following week, with a copy of the Declaration to work from, a contributor to the newspaper composed what the editor labeled "A reply to the declaration of the representatives of the Disunited States in American Congress assembled." The parody turned Jefferson's language on its head:

"When in the course of human events, pride, hypocrisy, dishonesty and ingratitude stimulate a subordinate community to shake off the duty and allegiances which in honor and in necessity they owe the superiority from whence they derive their existence; a fear of universal reprobation renders it necessary that they should declare causes to the world—no matter how ambiguous and falacious.

"It is a self-evident truth that all men, tho created equal, are not intended to remain so. That, without a resignation of part of our natural liberty, we should continue in a state of ignoble barbarism, unacquainted with that pure happiness, which flows from order."

Other news accounts declined to reprint the specific charges against George III. The *Gazetteer and New Daily Advertiser* broke off the text of the Declaration to say, "Here they enumerated their several grievances, the substance of which have repeatedly appeared in all the public prints." The *Morning Post's* satirist printed each charge but twisted it to his own loyalist slant—for example, "He has invariably treated the applications of insolent, factitious and weak men with a dignified contempt."

Not every newspaper was in the pay of the crown. The *Public Advertiser* wrote that the Declaration proved that "the despised Americans are manifestly not those cowards and poltroons which our over-hasty, ill-judging, wrong-headed Administration styled them." For the most part, though, reaction to the Declaration fell into two categories: editorial reassurances that the other European powers would not unite with the rebels against England, and attempts to demonstrate the patent absurdity of a paean to the equality of man from a continent where four hundred thousand black people, some seventeen percent of the population, were bound in slavery.

One London paper described a reading of the Declaration in Charleston, South Carolina, on an extremely hot July day. As a clergyman rose to speak, a black slave opened an umbrella and held it over his master's head. With his other hand the slave fanned the sweating patriot as he extolled the Declaration of Independence.

Lord Howe and the
British Fleet entering
the Narrows between
Long Island and
Staten Island

Long Island

AT THE AGE of fifty-four, Samuel Adams was working as hard as any delegate in Philadelphia. Men meeting him for the first time found that the perpetual tremor in his hands and the quaver in his voice gave his words a touching gravity, but the exertion was telling on him. Thomas Jefferson, more than two decades younger, watched him admiringly, but Adams made no efforts to recruit him as a protégé. Jefferson reflected a new spirit among the delegates,

1776

an indication that past strategies—caucuses, denunciations, even in-
timidation—might not be effective for the new nation. Pennsylvania had begun to draft a new state constitution, and conservatives
worried that its terms wouldn't allow enough protection for property and the state would succumb to a demagogue. Some Philadelphians blamed Samuel Adams for that democratic trend. They
were sure he was meddling behind the scenes, and as their resent-

ment rose, hints were dropped about the usefulness of an assassination.

Samuel Adams wasn't limiting himself to one state. He was named the Massachusetts representative to join with a member from each delegation in drawing up a form of government for America. Thomas Jefferson's committee had been amicable; Adams' was more rancorous and suspicious. During the month Jefferson had been preparing his Declaration, Samuel Adams, John Dickinson and the other eleven members were trying to patch together a plan for union.

Two other known opponents of independence served with Dickinson—Robert Livingston of New York and Edward Rutledge of South Carolina. Six others supported the idea of the Declaration but were conservative by temperament or wealth. Two more were simply cautious. As a result, Adams set out to shape the future with reliable support only from Stephen Hopkins of Rhode Island, who was even older than Adams and was impatient to leave the Congress.

Since Dickinson was representing Pennsylvania, there was no place on the committee for Benjamin Franklin. But Franklin's views were already on record; ten years before the Stamp Act, he had drawn up a plan to confederate the British colonies during a conference held in Albany in June 1754. Although the delegates had come to reach an alliance with the Iroquois, they also adopted the ideas Franklin had prepared for their consideration: Parliament would form one government for all of the colonies, with a legislature called the Grand Council and a President-General to supervise its laws. In England, the ministers of George II considered the Grand Council, elected by vote in each colony, too democratic and refused to submit the plan to the king. In America, the assemblies objected to a President-General appointed and paid by the crown and rejected Franklin's entire concept unanimously.

Franklin could be patient. Twenty-one years later, in the summer of 1775, he had drafted another version, "Articles of Confederation and Perpetual Union." Circulating it, Franklin said that his plan was meant merely to start the delegates thinking and that Congress would come up with a more perfect instrument.

His suggestions, however, were detailed, giving broad powers to an elected assembly from all the colonies. It could declare war and set terms for peace, conduct foreign affairs, operate a postal system. Each state would send delegates to the Congress based on its population of male citizens between the ages of sixteen and sixty, and all delegates would have equal votes. This central government's expenses would be prorated among the states on the same census of their male population.

Franklin took his plan from member to member, and Thomas Jefferson was one of those who were enthusiastic about it. But he also heard from those who were outraged. Although Franklin had provided for independence within the British Empire, the conservatives claimed that his plan proved that Franklin didn't want to reconcile with Britain on any terms. Franklin decided that his blueprint would only antagonize members and laid it aside.

But now another eleven months had passed, and the mood in Philadelphia was different. John Dickinson and his supporters were resigned to independence, and the objections to a confederation were coming from the other faction. Some delegates had transferred their fear and suspicion of England to their fellow Americans. They detested any central power, whether it was held by Parliament or by a new body created in Philadelphia. Samuel Adams was determined that each state should remain sovereign within its own boundaries. With the people of the states sharing neither a common history nor a common vision of the future, how could there be a strong union? Massachusetts had its own charter, which the patriots revered, and a crown-appointed governor they had despised and run out of the colony. In two neighboring states, Connecticut and Rhode Island, the authority had been less drastically split. They also had charters, but they controlled their own executive branches. Seven other provinces—New Hampshire, New York, New Jersey, North and South Carolina, Georgia and Virginia—had been guided only by traditions and customs rather than by formal constitutions, and they had been headed by governors appointed in England. Pennsylvania, Delaware and Maryland had been managed by families who held most of the rights and benefits.

Next came differences in religion and racial stock. Some of Massachusetts' three hundred thousand residents boasted that their bloodlines were more purely English than those in England itself. Virginia planters, who could not make that claim, wanted to exclude their blacks from any tax census and count them instead as property. The conflicting interests meant that nearly two years after Patrick Henry had proclaimed himself an American, the

Congress was again confronting questions of representation and voting.

John Dickinson drafted a confederation plan for the committee to work from, and the debate over each of its articles was angry and prolonged. After two and a half weeks, young Ned Rutledge was worried that Samuel Adams sought a government controlled by men who lacked a proper regard for money and position. To prevent any vast redistribution of property, Rutledge wanted the states to retain political control. Adams and Rutledge had opposing goals for their states, but they both hoped to keep the union weak and divided.

Other delegates on Dickinson's committee were as conservative as Rutledge but saw another danger. They were less worried about the bad example Massachusetts had set than about the democratic movements springing up within their own states. They believed that a strong central government would help to subdue uprisings at home. As the debate ground on, the issue became sharpened. Men who already controlled their states were fighting for a confederation that would perpetuate their control. That drive for power wasn't limited to the rich. Samuel Adams, who had given much of his life to deposing Bernard and Hutchinson, would never entrust his state's destiny to men who wanted George Washington as king of a new empire.

The draft that finally went before the Congress late in August reflected the strains between Samuel Adams and the conservatives and among the conservatives themselves. The first article ratified the title for the new nation: "The name of this confederacy shall be 'The United States of America.'" The second article described the colonies as entering into "a firm league of friendship with each other," one that would bind them all to join against attacks made on any one of them. That article mollified Samuel Adams by suggesting that the states were combining mainly because of outside threats to their security but remained sovereign powers.

The rest of Dickinson's draft ceded substantial power to the Congress. The third article read: "Each Colony shall retain and enjoy as much of its present laws, rights and customs, as it may think fit, and reserves to itself the sole and exclusive regulation and government of its internal police, in all matters that shall not interfere with the Articles of this Confederation." That language guaranteed a state control only over its own police—and then only if that control didn't obstruct the Articles. Every other power seemed to pass to the Congress. The one check on that power came in Article 18, but given the past dozen years, it was a potent and emotional one: The government of the United States could not impose or levy taxes on any state, except to support the Post Office.

Article 17 tersely disposed of the matter of representation: "In determining questions, each colony shall have one vote." But to protect the larger states, nine votes, not merely a majority of seven, would be required on broad matters of foreign affairs and economic policy—declaring war, entering into treaties, fixing the value of money and coining it, approving a budget for defense. Another source of contention couldn't be finessed so easily. Six states regarded themselves as "three-sided," which meant that their citizens considered their western boundaries still open. Basing claims on royal charters or on old Indian treaties, New York, Massachusetts, Connecticut, Virginia, North Carolina and Georgia all demanded the right to keep on expanding until they reached the Pacific Ocean. On competing maps, the state boundaries crossed and crisscrossed over the disputed territory. Virginia's northern line overlapped land claimed by four other states. It did no good for critics from the other states to point out that the impasse had arisen out of ignorance, that when some of the original charters were drawn, colonists had guessed that the Pacific Ocean was about a hundred miles from the Atlantic.

When the debate over the Articles of Confederation moved from committee to the floor of the Congress, John Adams joined those delegates who assailed Dickinson's one-state, one-vote provision. Now that his hard work had brought him wealth and eminence, he couldn't agree that property should count for nothing. But he also shared Samuel Adams' worries about a strong central government. Only the year before, John Adams had suggested that since uniting an enormous continent under one rule was impracticable, the Congress might consider a loose confederation, along the lines of ancient Greece or modern Switzerland.

John Adams was enough of a democrat that he regretted that these crucial deliberations were conducted in secret. He wanted galleries built and the doors opened so that people might understand the nature of the debate. When he was overruled, Adams acknowledged that some delegates had been reluctant to reveal how sharply divided they were on issues facing the newly united states.

But he was sure most of them simply didn't want the public to know what insignificant roles they were playing.

Adams had no such concern. He took on Samuel Chase of Maryland, who argued that slaves shouldn't be counted during any tax census. Northern farmers invested their profits in livestock, Southerners in slaves, which meant that slaves were simply property. Adams argued that because five hundred freemen produced no greater profit than five hundred slaves, freemen shouldn't be taxed, either. Benjamin Harrison of Virginia proposed a compromise. Because slaves did only half the work, count two slaves in the census for every freeman. A Pennsylvania delegate noted that while a freeman might work more, he also consumed more, since a slave wasn't fed or clothed as well, which left Northern colonies with no more surplus money for taxes than the Southerners had.

Benjamin Franklin, representing Pennsylvania's three hundred thousand residents, joined John Adams in opposing the one-voter-per-state provision and urged his earlier plan, in which voting, and taxing, would be based on population. The Reverend Witherspoon, who was the president of Princeton College and regularly wore his cap and gown to sessions, spoke for a population of only one hundred thirty thousand and took the other side.

Neither faction could be convinced, but the small states carried the vote with help from big-state delegates who feared a strong central power. The second article was strengthened to guarantee that the individual states retained all rights and powers not specifically delegated to the United States.

On the question of the Western claims, Dickinson's draft had authorized only the central government to deal with Indian tribes and buy land outside the existing state boundaries. John Adams listened disdainfully as Virginia's delegates opposed the measure; Adams was convinced that avarice for land was delaying any hope of union. Patrick Henry had been an early speculator, and Benjamin Franklin on his return from England had immediately involved himself in an ambitious land scheme.

The debate over confederation seemed to have no solution. At the end of August, the Congress agreed to put aside the whole question. Ned Rutledge reflected the frustration of most delegates that there was still no union six weeks after independence had been declared. "It is of little consequence if we never see it again," he wrote to a friend about confederation, "for we have made such a

Devil of it already that the colonies can never agree to it." But lately the delegates had been given a good excuse for deferring a showdown. A letter from George Washington shocked them into remembering that who might someday own the Pacific coast mattered very little compared with the fight for control of the Atlantic.

Long before the Declaration of Independence, Britain's commander in America had developed a simple strategy and made no secret of it. General Howe wanted to isolate the rebellious Yankees of New England by taking and holding the line along the Hudson River and Lake Champlain. That would allow the British to pacify the Southern colonies, where, Howe had been assured, most of the people were loyal to the king. He had recommended landing his entire force in New York, securing that town as his base, and then moving north. He had been overruled in London, and part of the British force had been diverted to Canada early in 1776 to meet the American threat there.

But the Congress in Philadelphia was learning that the British had arrived outside New York's harbor with warships and hundreds of transport vessels carrying thirty-two thousand professional soldiers. Their commander was General Howe's brother, Admiral Sir Richard Howe. Britain had sent powerful expeditionary forces in the past, but this was the greatest it had ever launched.

In the spring of 1776, George Washington had marched his troops down from Boston to meet the expected threat. By recruiting hard, he had scraped together 28,500 men, nineteen thousand fit for duty. His strategy called for a full defense of New York. Even if the British succeeded in taking the town, he hoped for another Breed's Hill, a victory bought at an exorbitant price. And Congress insisted that New York be defended. Some officers were annoyed that civilians safe in Philadelphia were staking so much on raw recruits of a new army. But John Adams was among those who had no doubts. "Let us drub Howe," he exhorted the generals, "and then we shall do very well."

How the drubbing was to be done was left to General Washington. Meanwhile, the commander had been beleaguered by more spies and traitors within his own ranks. In mid-June two American soldiers, Thomas Hickey and Michael Lynch, had been exposed as members of a secret cadre taking money from the British. Hickey had been jailed on a counterfeit charge, and during his confinement he and Lynch were overheard boasting that they would never fight again for America. They told other inmates that nearly seven hundred of General Washington's men had vowed to declare their allegiance to George III and turn their weapons on the Americans when the British arrived. The threat was more alarming because Hickey had served in Washington's personal guard and claimed that seven other guardsmen were conspiring in the plot.

A court-martial listened to four witnesses, whose testimony established that Hickey had been paid half a dollar for his treason to America. One rumor wasn't raised during the trial—that Hickey and Lynch intended to assassinate General Washington with the help of a woman. Mary Gibbons was said to be in the general's confidence—whatever that phrase might suggest. If she existed at all, Mrs. Gibbons had disappeared. Even without that charge, the court reached a unanimous guilty verdict. Punishment would be death by hanging. George Washington was proving scrupulous about consulting his fellow generals on policy matters. When he convened a council the next day to review the case, his six brigadiers advised him to uphold the sentence.

The Congress had authorized death for American soldiers who incited or joined a mutiny. The morning after Hickey's sentence was confirmed, a gallows was erected, and Washington ordered that all men who weren't on duty be marched out to watch the hanging. Altogether, twenty thousand people appeared. Hickey refused to see a chaplain because, he said, the clergy were all cutthroats. Shortly before noon he was hanged.

The next day, an American scanned the horizon at dawn and saw what looked like a forest of trimmed pine trees floating across the water toward New York. They were the masts of the British fleet Thomas Hickey had been waiting for.

For George Washington's first test as a tactician, he could hardly have been handed a worse battlefield. Everything about the New York harbor favored a navy, and Britain's oceangoing ships could navigate far enough up the Hudson River to carry out Howe's plan and cut the colonies in two. Between the Hudson and East Rivers lay Manhattan Island. Surveying it, Washington saw that it was too long for his troops to defend. But if he stationed men at its southern tip in New York, the Howe brothers could land their troops above the town and trap the American Army between British gunboats and British bayonets.

His victory on Dorchester Heights had convinced Washington to try for the high ground. Across the East River on Long Island, Brooklyn Heights rose up enough to command the southern tip of Manhattan. Washington made two major decisions: He would defend New York from positions nearest the enemy. And he would split his forces. Some would stay in Manhattan, others would be sent to hold Brooklyn Heights.

On July 3, 1776, more than nine thousand British soldiers were ferried from their ships and landed on Staten Island. On the day Congress was approving the Declaration, George Washington had waited tensely for General Howe to try to take New York. Twenty-four hours later, it had become clear that the British intended to dig in and wait. July 9 marked the anniversary of Washington's first council of war in Cambridge, and during that year he had not fought a single battle. Any day he expected General Howe to revenge himself for those lost twelve months.

Washington hoped that hearing the Declaration of Independence would give his men fresh incentive, and he ordered it read aloud on the ninth. That evening, local Sons of Liberty attacked the statue of George III in Bowling Green that John Adams had admired as he passed through New York two years earlier. The king had been portrayed as a Roman emperor and cast one-third larger than life from two tons of lead covered with gold leaf. Since its pedestal stood fifteen feet high, the Sons had to tie ropes to the king and his horse and pull the statue to the ground. The fall knocked off the king's head, which loyalists later obtained and shipped to London. The great mass of lead went to Connecticut, where munitions-makers calculated that it could be melted and molded into 42,088 bullets.

The Sons' riotous spirit in destroying the statue troubled General Washington. He knew the war had entered a new stage. The colonials were no longer a rebel force, free to harass the ruling powers. The Declaration had transferred those powers to the Americans, and he soon had the opportunity to impress that fact on the British.

On July 12, Admiral Howe sent two junior officers ashore with a letter. An American colonel realized when he saw the way it was addressed that Washington would refuse to accept it because it didn't recognize his military rank. The American adjutant general, Joseph Reed, went to deal with the messengers.

One of them, a Lieutenant Brown, rose, took off his hat and bowed. "I have a letter, sir, from Lord Howe to Mr. Washington."

Reed said, "Sir, we have no person here in our Army with that address."

Lieutenant Brown persisted. "Sir, will you look at that address."

The cover read, "George Washington, Esq."

"No, sir," said Colonel Reed, "I cannot receive that letter."

Brown seemed dismayed. Admiral Howe, he said, was only sorry he hadn't arrived a few days sooner, suggesting that the presence of his fleet might have forestalled the Declaration of Independence.

Brown withdrew. Four days later, Admiral Howe sent the letter back under a flag of truce. Now it was addressed to "George Washington, Esq., etc." This time Washington himself sent it back. The next day the admiral asked whether the American commander in chief would receive a visit from Howe's adjutant general. Washington agreed, and a meeting was set for July 20.

That conversation lasted almost half an hour, and the adjutant, Lieutenant Colonel James Patterson, was careful to address Washington by the title "Excellency." Surely, Patterson argued, the letter's salutation was proper. It was the same style of address used for ambassadors or plenipotentiaries whenever disputes arose over rank. Neither Admiral Howe nor his brother, the general, had meant to denigrate the rank of General Washington, whose character they held in the highest esteem.

Colonel Patterson then took out the letter. He did not presume to hand it to Washington directly. Instead, he laid it on the table between them and pointed out that although it was the earlier letter, it now had two additional "et ceteras."

Washington agreed that yes, the "et ceteras" could imply everything about his rank, but they could also imply anything. From its address, this could be a private letter. He must decline to accept it.

Colonel Patterson had anticipated that reply and proceeded to tell Washington what the letter said. The king had empowered the Howe brothers to settle the differences in America. Admiral Howe hoped this meeting would be the first of many. Washington suspected that the British had no desire for peace and were only marking time until they were ready to attack. He told Patterson that if Lord Howe had come to America with great powers to pardon, he had come to the wrong place. Not having been the ones to give offense, the Americans needed no pardon.

Patterson seemed confused by the dry jest. As he was leaving, he thanked Washington for not making him wear the customary blindfold during his trip to the American headquarters. Washington urged him to stay on for a light meal, but Patterson was eager to return to his commander and declined so much as a glass of water. Taking back the unopened letter, Colonel Patterson returned to the fleet. To America, George Washington was the patriotic commander of the nation's army. To the British, he was still a rebellious civilian planter from Virginia.

Every day that General Howe did not act allowed Washington to improve his fortifications and send for more arms and ammunition. By early August, the Americans were still bracing for an attack that did not come. Washington had always written candidly to his distant cousin Lund Washington, the caretaker at Mount Vernon, and by August 19 he was confessing that the delay was incomprehensible to him. Howe was apparently expecting another five thousand troops—German soldiers hired by George III. But even without them, Howe's troops already outnumbered the Americans. "There is," Washington confided, "something exceedingly mysterious in the conduct of the enemy."

Howe's delay may have been less mysterious than humane. Washington was prepared to make the British pay a steep price for New York. But William Howe had been present on Breed's Hill, as Washington had not, and had come away with a higher opinion than Washington's of American fighting spirit. Howe was not prepared to lose a thousand or fifteen hundred British troops. He had been schooled in his country's accepted military thinking, which made preserving his forces a commander's first obligation. Any other action would be, in Howe's word, "criminal."

Washington was making good use of the hiatus, but he faced a new crisis when his commander on Long Island came down with malaria. Washington tended to like men until they gave him reason to change his mind, and he had warmed to Nathanael Greene from the moment they met in Cambridge. Washington had decided that Greene would be his replacement should he be killed or captured. Greene had come to the war a thirty-three-year-old Quaker with no military experience. But from the time of the Boston Tea Party he had been preparing himself for the coming struggle, studying military manuals and reading the lives of history's great generals. He had also started to drill his neighborhood guard in Coventry, Rhode Island, so that by the time he presented himself to Washington he was already in charge of his colony's three Continental regiments. Greene had barely taken over his New York command when fever confined him to bed. Washington was forced to turn to a belligerent Irishman named John Sullivan.

New Hampshire had sent Sullivan to the First Continental Congress, where serving as a delegate had become a way for men with military ambitions to advance themselves. In 1775 Sullivan left the Congress with the rank of brigadier general. After the British evacuated Boston, Washington had sent him to lead reinforcements to Canada. When the Canadian campaign became a shambles, the Congress had considered replacing Sullivan. Washington signed an understated letter that praised Sullivan's spirit and dedication but noted that the general "has his foibles," which showed themselves "in a little tincture of vanity" and too great a desire to be popular. Congress took the hint and gave Horatio Gates the Northern command. The price Washington paid for his candor was finding Sullivan back at his side, convinced he had been ill-treated and burning to prove himself as Nathanael Greene's replacement on Long Island.

Sullivan knew nothing about the terrain he was supposed to defend. On August 20 he went to Long Island. The next day British ships began to move, but by nightfall Washington still couldn't be sure of their destination. A thunderstorm that night stopped the British advance. In the morning, Sullivan reported that British soldiers, including Henry Clinton's grenadiers back from Charleston, had landed on Long Island. The Americans estimated that eight thousand British soldiers had come ashore and were marching to Flatbush, only three miles from the outlying American positions.

General Washington sent immediate reinforcements to Sullivan. He couldn't be sure, however, that Howe wouldn't simultaneously attack New York. Throughout the morning of August

23, Washington stayed at his headquarters, assuring New Yorkers that he wouldn't burn the town to the ground and surrender it. When flood tide at 11 A.M. didn't bring British boats, Washington crossed to Long Island, checked Sullivan's deployment of his men and returned to New York. Later that day, Sullivan announced that the Americans had driven the British back by half a mile. But Sullivan was known to exaggerate.

The next day, still uncertain about where the British would strike, Washington again went to Long Island to inspect the defenses. He had named Israel Putnam as overall commander of the island's forces, and Sullivan remained in charge of the outer defenses. Riding along the front lines, Washington saw much that displeased him. American soldiers were shooting off their weapons aimlessly as they waited for the British attack. The stray bullets not only were a waste of ammunition but could defeat a propaganda tactic. Washington had ordered messages written in German for the Hessian mercenaries, urging them to defect. The leaflets were wrapped around plugs of tobacco and strewn where the German troops would be sure to find them. The idea had come from Benjamin Franklin, who recommended offering the Germans good pay and free farmland. Washington didn't want useless fire from the American lines to prevent any Hessian from deserting.

His years of overseeing an estate had made Washington attentive to detail, but one eluded him during his inspection of the defenses. Because American strategy was based upon holding Brooklyn Heights, the soldiers had built a string of forts over a distance of one mile. Between them and the British camp lay a five-mile stretch of heavily wooded hills that provided a natural defense. Over the years, farmers had beaten three main roads through the dense woods—the Gowanus road to the west, the Flatbush road running through them, and the Bedford road a mile to the east. There was a minor road even farther east, the road from the town of Jamaica, but John Sullivan wasn't concerned about it, nor was George Washington. Sullivan put his senior commander, Lord Stirling, in charge of the Gowanus road; it was nearest to the beaches and the British landing sites. General Sullivan took the command of the other two roads for himself.

His American colleagues had come to accept William Alexander's use of the title "Lord Stirling" as a harmless pretension. During a trip to England seventeen years earlier, Alexander had claimed the earldom of Stirling, disregarding the fact that it was extinct. The House of Lords ruled against him, but back home in New Jersey Alexander had begun to use his new name.

His lordship was no fool, and the unguarded road from Jamaica preyed on his mind. He learned that a Pennsylvania regiment was riding out along the road each day but withdrawing at night. Stirling came up with fifty dollars of his own money to pay five young officers to patrol the Jamaica road by night. There had been four hundred volunteer cavalrymen from Connecticut who could have performed that surveillance, but when the horsemen refused to dismount and fight on foot General Washington had ruled that cavalry were useless around these islands and sent them home.

His fellow generals regarded Lord Stirling's private guard as a waste of money. As they inspected American defenses on August 26, Israel Putnam and John Sullivan saw no cause for concern, and the Pennsylvania regiment returned at nightfall to say that there had been no movement among the British on the plain below. Secure in the sanctuary of the hills, the American Army went to sleep for the night.

As the battle for Long Island drew near, Henry Clinton, like John Sullivan, needed to vindicate himself for a previous failure. Clinton was back in New York fresh from his fiasco in Charleston, where he had expected troops to wade across a river seven feet deep. He was once again subordinate to William Howe, but Clinton was more familiar with the terrain around New York. His father had been governor of the colony, and young Henry had lived there until the age of nineteen. Now, riding out with other officers to scout a landscape he still remembered, Clinton saw where John Sullivan had positioned his troops. He returned to camp with a plan he was sure could destroy the American Army with one stroke.

William Howe rejected the plan out of hand. Clinton was not popular around the headquarters, and the other officers agreed that his tactic somehow smacked too much of the German school. By the next morning, that vague objection had faded, and General Howe announced that he would execute Clinton's plan after all. He would attack the Americans from the Jamaica road.

Throughout the day of August 26, 1776, Lieutenant General Charles Cornwallis moved his British troops near the beaches. But he left behind hundreds of pitched white tents to persuade American scouts that his men were still in camp. About 8 P.M., a British regiment went quietly through Jamaica Pass, taking prisoner any New Yorkers who might alert the American troops. Behind them came a thousand dragoons in red coats and helmets covered with black feathers. Leading the attack were Lord Cornwallis and Henry Clinton. Another two thousand grenadiers and infantrymen followed, dragging fourteen cannon. After midnight Howe planned to bring another seven thousand men. Despite his initial resistance, Howe was now committing two thirds of his total force on Long Island to the surprise attack. The rest would make diversions—one British unit along the Gowanus road, the Hessians at the American center.

At about 3 A.M., Clinton and Cornwallis seized the five mounted guards on the Jamaica road that Lord Stirling had posted with his own money. The march so far had been accomplished in complete secrecy. Clinton had insisted that his men saw down underbrush to make way for the cannon they were pulling rather than hack through it with axes that might ring out on the night air.

William Howe arrived with his men before dawn. He was still uneasy about the coming battle and demanded that Clinton prepare his troops to attack. Clinton refused. Since the Americans didn't stop us at the pass, Clinton explained, they can't take up a position here. The battle is over.

For Howe, that seemed far too easy, and he protested. "They'll open fire on us as soon as we reach Bedford."

"But we're here," Clinton told him. "We're in Bedford."

The British feint along the Gowanus road was turning out just as successfully. When John Sullivan was notified after midnight that the long-awaited British attack had begun there, he sent another battalion to support Lord Stirling. At the center stood a line of Germans, led by General Leopold von Heister, who weren't advancing but whose cannon could cover the two central passes. Neither General Sullivan nor Israel Putnam foresaw the calamity that awaited them. Putnam didn't order Stirling to draw back, and he sent no emergency message to George Washington.

About 8:30 A.M., Washington was rowed once again to Long Island to oversee his first battle. The bright sun promised a hot day after a chilly August night. To Washington, the situation looked serious but not hopeless. The British certainly wouldn't have launched so furious an attack against Lord Stirling unless they intended to make the Gowanus road their main arena, and Stirling seemed to be holding fast. The Hessians still weren't moving, and from their positions they seemed likely to stay in place for at least another hour. If the Americans showed any mettle, they would be slow in giving up the wooded hillside and could reach Brooklyn Heights with a minimum of losses.

Walking the lines, Washington was at his most imposing. He told his colonels that he had two loaded pistols and would shoot any man who turned his back this day. He reminded them that everything worth living for was at stake at this place. "I will not ask any man to go further than I do," Washington said. "I will fight as long as I have a leg or an arm."

At about nine o'clock, troops under John Sullivan and Lord Stirling saw soldiers coming down the road behind them. They assumed they were Americans sent as reinforcements. Then, from a mere fifty yards away, the British opened fire. Colonel Samuel Miles, whose Pennsylvania regiment had been patrolling the Jamaica road each day, found himself cut off from the American lines. He tried to fight, but when he saw the odds he released his men to run for their lives. Those familiar with the woods managed to reach the American base at Brooklyn. But by midafternoon, Hessian soldiers had found Miles and a few others hiding among the trees. A hundred and fifty-nine of his men were taken prisoner.

Once the Germans got their orders to join the battle, they were fearsome. British commanders told them that the Americans had vowed to be especially rough with any mercenary. As the Americans tried to reload their muskets, German soldiers rushed at them, caught them between the trees and stabbed bayonets through their chests. When John Sullivan's men tried to retreat to the fortress on Brooklyn Heights, the British cavalry barred their way and trapped them between Cornwallis' men and the roaring, charging Germans.

George Washington had reached Brooklyn before the battle began. Noticeably shaken, he watched the slaughter below him.

One soldier overheard him murmur, "Good God! What brave fellows I must lose this day!"

Along the wooded defenses, Lord Stirling had no choice but to fight on, even as the British trap was tightening around him. For nearly four hours, Stirling's men fought in close ranks. The British remained content to shell his position while their allies hurried around to cut off his retreat. After one last desperate charge, Stirling sent his men retreating through the deep marshes around Gowanus Creek. Many were shot as they slogged through the pond, and a dozen weak swimmers drowned in its depths. Stirling himself took two hundred and seventy Maryland soldiers and turned to confront Cornwallis. Men said afterward that he had fought like a wolf. But Stirling was as rigid about the rules of war as the British had been a year before. Instead of letting his men break ranks and take advantage of the woods and fences—the way the British and Germans had begun to do—he held them in a tight formation on exposed ground. Five times his band of Americans tried to cut through the British to safety in Brooklyn. Ten of them succeeded. The rest were killed or taken prisoner by the Germans closing in on them. Lord Stirling was reported missing. Then a dispatch reached George Washington that John Sullivan was lost as well.

Throughout the remainder of the afternoon, Washington waited at the Brooklyn fort while the few survivors of the frontline defense straggled back to safety. The British had been ordered not to storm the Heights. General Howe intended to take the hills in good time with an orderly strategy that would hold British casualties to what he termed "a very cheap rate." But Henry Clinton was delighted that his tactic had succeeded beyond his expectations. When he saw the Americans fleeing in panic, he couldn't bring himself to stop his men. Some of Clinton's assault columns chased the Americans right to their own trenches on the Heights.

Behind their earthworks, the Americans milled about. Their officers were missing, many in their ranks were dead or held prisoner in the woods below. George Washington tried to restore their spirit, shouting to them to remember what they were fighting for. Some troops obeyed and strengthened their defenses, particularly toward the Jamaica road. But when the British regrouped and charged, as they would, the American Army would be broken and the rebellion over.

Only one man could save them, and it was not the commander
in chief. From a hilltop, William Howe looked out over the day's
success and called on his grenadiers to halt. "Enough has been done
for one day," he said. His troops hardly agreed. Their blood was
running hot from the hours of fighting, and they wanted to charge
on and crush the enemy. Howe had to issue his order repeatedly
before he could convince them to stop in midvictory.

General Washington slept fitfully that night. He had assumed
at first that Howe was only pausing to regroup and would finish
the battle in the late afternoon. But as the hours stretched on toward night, Washington's men became less sure that this was America's last day of independence. His marksmen kept a steady barrage pouring down on the British camp, and by midnight it seemed
clear that this time there was no deception. Howe's army had
taken to its tents.

There were new fears of a British attack at dawn, and Washington was back at his post by 4 A.M. He had decided that he could
draw only limited reserves from New York. Though Howe had
committed a large part of his army to Long Island, he might still be
planning an attack against the town. Washington felt he must keep
men there to repel it. The morning passed. Howe remained silent.

A piercing rain began on the Heights, and Washington's men,
who had no tents, stood in their muddy trenches waist deep in water. They couldn't cook the pickled pork that was their only food.
Worse, the rain was soaking their powder and clogging their muskets. If Howe sent his Hessians to advance now, the Americans
would have no protection against their bayonets.

Washington couldn't depend forever on Howe's inertia.
Throughout the day he was developing a plan, which he kept
secret even from his aides-de-camp. When he found a moment to
send a report to the Congress in Philadelphia, he didn't mention his
hope for recovering from an unquestioned defeat. Washington told
the delegates that his army was almost broken. After the two nights
and a day since the battle had ended, he still could not estimate
American casualties, and both General Sullivan and Lord Stirling
were missing.

Later that afternoon, it was still raining when Washington
called his seven generals to a council of war at the country house

of Philip Livingston, one of New York's delegates to the Congress. Everyone understood how perilous their situation was. Washington's strategy had left them with fewer than ten thousand weary and disheartened men boxed into a narrow space about two miles square. Ahead were twice that number of British and German soldiers ready to finish off the job, and to the rear was the East River, a barrier one mile wide. Reports had arrived that Lord Stirling had surrendered to General von Heister and that General Sullivan had been caught in a cornfield and taken to a ship of Admiral Howe's fleet. The longer Washington and his staff delayed, the nearer they came to the same fate.

William Howe saw conditions the same way. The Americans were doomed. He would now bring up his cannon, his scaling ladders and the other tools his artillery would use to launch a methodical siege. His careful approach had saved fifteen hundred British lives. That was reason enough to forgo a premature rushing of an entrenched position. His brother's fleet was nearby to guarantee that Washington and his men would stay bottled up.

Throughout two rainy days, the British repaired the damage from the fighting on August 27. Then, on the morning of the thirtieth, Howe sent out a patrol. American sniping had continued throughout the night, and Howe wanted to know why there was now a lull in the fire.

The British scouts came back with an incredible answer. During the night, George Washington had disappeared with all of the American Army.

New York

IT WAS little consolation for George Washington, but, in its way, his retreat had been as skilled as the British attack. From the time his general staff approved the evacuation, he had moved with absolute secrecy. His troops were told only that the wounded men would be sent back across the river to Manhattan that night. Washington ordered every available vessel brought to the shore behind him, and swarms of barges, sailboats and punts collected there. Many

New York patriots
pulling down the statue
of George III

1776

of the sailors were fishermen from Marblehead, Massachusetts. By
10 P.M., Washington was ready to begin. Instead of facing the night
attack they had been dreading, the American soldiers were called
from their positions in the trenches. Their lines were so tightly organized that no gaps could be spotted by the British sentries. Campfires were kept burning while regiment after regiment left their sta-
tions and were replaced by the men behind them. Washington had

gone ahead to the river and was supervising the loading of the troops.

For three nights the men had barely slept, and they were past fatigue. The embarkation had begun smoothly, but when the men realized that they were being shipped out they were soon jostling and fighting for places in the first boats. Washington did his best to keep order, but frightened men at the back were trying to trample over the front ranks.

The noise and confusion awakened a woman who lived near the ferry point. She had no reason to support the rebels. Neighbors had reported her for still drinking English tea, and American soldiers had fired on her house. Now she sent a black servant to alert the British to the evacuation. The man worked his way through the lines until he came upon a German officer, but the German spoke no English and arrested the servant.

Even though soldiers were panicking along the shore, the rotation of troops through the lines facing the British had gone as ordered. Then one of Washington's aides made a near-fatal mistake. At 2 A.M. Washington was watching impatiently over the loadings when he was surprised to see Colonel Israel Hand riding toward the ferry. He had instructed Hand and his Pennsylvania troops to hold the American defenses to the very end.

Washington called to him through the darkness. "Isn't that Colonel Hand? You of all officers! I thought you would never abandon your post!"

Hand assured him that he had left only under orders from his immediate commander, General Thomas Mifflin.

"Impossible!" Washington said. Hand was trying to convince him when General Mifflin rode up and asked what was the matter.

Washington rounded on him. "Good God, General Mifflin! I'm afraid you have ruined us by so unseasonably withdrawing the troops from the lines."

Mifflin had slept no more than George Washington. He said angrily, "I did it by your order."

Washington said it couldn't be true.

"By God, I did!" Mifflin insisted. "Did Scammell act as aide-de-camp for the day or did he not?"

Washington acknowledged that Alexander Scammell had held that post.

"Then," said Mifflin, "I had orders through him."

Washington immediately became conciliatory. It had been a dreadful mistake, he said, but, with all of the confusion on the river-bank, if the British discovered that the front lines had been abandoned they could annihilate them. The common danger cooled tempers on both sides, and Colonel Hand led his men back to the trenches. They were reluctant, but they moved quickly and quietly, and the British didn't profit from the blunder.

As the night was ending, the last regiments who were left behind in the American lines became increasingly nervous. Then, just as dawn might have exposed their weakness, heavy billows of fog rose off the water and hid them in mist. The men blessed a cover so thick they couldn't see six yards in front of them. The fog persisted as they got their orders to head for the ferry. The last soldiers waiting to cross had one final scare: the boats had not returned from an earlier trip, and men huddled in the fog along the shore, fretting until they could be rowed to safety. General Washington waited with them and crossed with his gray charger in one of the last boats. He had left behind only a few old cannon sunk deep in mud.

When Washington reviewed the lessons of Long Island, he didn't dwell on the way he had overlooked the Jamaica road. And on the British side, General Howe's account of the triumphant battle filled three and a half columns in the London newspapers, while Washington's escape rated barely half a paragraph. Since Lord North's Ministry did not learn immediately about Howe's miscalculations and delay, George III rewarded Howe with a knighthood.

Washington knew he couldn't expect honorary degrees or gold medals this time. In his defense, he reminded one New York legislator that he had gone without sleep for forty-eight hours. Privately, he complained about the drawbacks in trying to fight a war with a militia rather than a standing army. Militia recruits had signed up for such short service that Washington's troops were usually preparing to go home before they had been properly trained. He had lost fifteen hundred men in combat on Long Island, and others were leaving the cause every day because they had crops to harvest or because they had been stricken with an illness their skeptical comrades called "cannon fever." The Connecticut militia dropped abruptly from eight thousand men to two thousand. Disembarking from the boats, Washington's survivors from Brooklyn limped into the town of New York sick, emaciated and, according to the Tories near their camp, smelling like pigs.

The disaster had also revealed the shortcomings of America's commander in chief. One of Lord Stirling's colonels wrote to a member of the Congress that he revered Washington, that the troops would always remember his patience and fortitude, but Washington had brought much of the calamity on himself. The colonel ended by reporting that officers and men were murmuring, "Would to Heaven General Lee were here!"

Washington hoped to recuperate from his losses by sending spies to find out where Sir William Howe would strike next. He was willing to spend lavishly for information, but money wasn't the motive for one of his first volunteers. Nathan Hale of Connecticult was twenty-four, a schoolteacher educated at Yale who had become a captain in a ranger company. Hale was also a poet, an expert at checkers and a football player with a powerful kick. So far he had not seen action, and although the penalty for spying was death, he wanted to serve his country. Posing as a schoolmaster in his civilian clothes, Hale made his way to Long Island and slipped behind the British defenses.

Soon after the American defeat, the Congress was distracted from General Washington's shortcomings by a dilemma that faced the delegates unexpectedly. Lord Stirling and General Sullivan had been passing the time more comfortably in captivity aboard Admiral Howe's flagship, the *Eagle*, than they would have done at Washington's side. The admiral, who was also a British lord, had decided that John Sullivan was probably less obdurate than his commander in chief. He had convinced Sullivan that they could end the war now and that the Parliament would ratify any treaty Howe made. The admiral had denounced the war as senseless and said that Britain must surrender all rights to tax the colonies. That at least was what Sullivan had thought the admiral was saying. After some hesitation, Sullivan had agreed to carry Howe's peace overtures to the Congress. Carrying a pass to get him through the British lines, Sullivan had reached New York on his way to Philadelphia hours before Washington completed his evacuation from Brooklyn.

George Washington was convinced that Howe's proposals would come to nothing. But after such a humbling defeat he was in no position to cancel Sullivan's mission. Three days later in Philadelphia, John Sullivan told the Congress about Lord Howe's generous terms. Sullivan's behavior in Canada had soured many delegates on him, and he had barely begun to speak when John Adams whispered to Benjamin Rush, "I wish that the first ball fired on Long Island had gone through his head."

Like Washington, John Adams distrusted Howe's overtures. Sullivan explained that the admiral proposed a meeting but could not deal with the Congress as an official body. He would be pleased to receive several members as private gentlemen for an hour or two of conversation. Adams spoke vigorously against any agreement with Howe and made no attempt to spare Sullivan's feelings. "A decoy duck," Adams called him, "whom Lord Howe has sent among us to seduce us into a renunciation of our independence."

But some delegates believed that spurning Howe's offer might suggest to people, at home and abroad, who were uncommitted to American independence that the British legitimately sought peace and that the Americans were protracting the war. After days of debate, the members decided to send an official delegation to New York, which Howe would probably refuse to receive. And if he did see the delegates, Howe would have no chance of working his wiles on them. Two of the three chosen to go were John Adams and Benjamin Franklin. Edward Rutledge of South Carolina was the third. The Congress also accepted Howe's offer to exchange Sullivan and Lord Stirling for two British prisoners.

When the delegates reached the town of Brunswick, New Jersey, all the inns were filled, and Adams and Franklin had to share a bed. Their tiny room had one small window. Adams closed it. He considered his health precarious and was wary of chills from the night air.

"Oh!" Franklin called to him. "Don't shut the window. We shall be suffocated."

Adams explained that he was afraid of catching cold.

Franklin assured him that with the window closed the air in their chamber would soon be worse than it was outside. "Come! Open the window and come to bed, and I will convince you. I believe you are not acquainted with my theory of colds."

Franklin was nearly thirty years older and one of the world's most distinguished men. Adams decided to risk a chill and hear the theory. He threw open the window and bounded back to bed.

Franklin began a detailed explanation. By respiration and per-spiration, the human body destroyed a gallon of air every minute. Two persons in this room would consume all of its air within an hour or two. Then they would begin breathing in the material thrown off by the lungs and the skin, and that was the true cause of colds. Adams thought that Dr. Franklin sounded more than half asleep as he spoke, and Adams himself dropped off before the ex-planation was over.

There had been no chance that Admiral Howe would refuse to see the Americans. Protocol would not deter him if he had a chance to persuade the Congress to give up its war. He agreed to meet the delegates on Staten Island at a house across from Perth Amboy and sent a barge to fetch them. He greeted the Americans with elaborate thanks for the honor they did him in coming and led them past ranks of grenadiers to the house, where they found, amid the military squalor, one large and handsome room spread with moss and green sprigs for a carpet. John Adams approved the effect—romantically elegant, he thought—and the fine dinner of cold ham, tongue and mutton, accompanied by a good claret.

Adams was somewhat relieved not to be overwhelmed by this titled Englishman. He calculated that Lord Howe was about fifty and certainly well-bred, but Adams had met many Americans around Boston who were more clever and articulate. Early on, Adams scored off the admiral when Howe said he was meeting with them not as members of Congress but only as gentlemen of great ability and influence. Adams replied that his lordship might consider him any way he pleased, except as a British subject.

Howe turned to the others with a smile and said, "Mr. Adams is a decided character."

After a few more exchanges, it was clear that Adams had been right in his suspicions. Richard Howe had no particular powers. Any peace depended on the colonies once again pledging their full allegiance to the throne. As for John Sullivan's assurances that Par-liament would give up its right of taxation—why, said Howe, Sul-livan had evidently misheard him.

At one point, Lord Howe insinuated a threat into his argu-ment. Ravaging and destroying America, he told his guests, would give him great pain.

Benjamin Franklin promptly replied that the Americans must take proper—and, he hoped, effective—care to spare his lordship's feelings.

The night with Howe ended as fruitlessly as John Adams might have wished, and the war remained George Washington's to lose or win.

Henry Clinton had another bold plan and, after his masterful strategy on Long Island, might have expected William Howe to embrace it. Clinton wanted the British to surround Washington again, this time on Manhattan. He wasn't satisfied with simply making the American Army run; he wanted to exterminate it. But Howe continued to have different ideas. For two weeks after the Americans crossed the river, he did nothing. Once more, Washington was waiting from night to night for an attack that didn't come. Israel Putnam summed up the American response to Howe's inaction: "General Howe is either our friend or no general."

Washington realized by now that he could not possibly hold New York. Nathanael Greene, recovering from malaria, had been reading military history and suggested a precedent that might be useful for the Americans. When France under Francis I had been invaded by the Germans, Francis had laid waste to vast territories, starving his enemies and defeating them without a battle. Why not burn New York? Tories owned two thirds of the town, and their hostility to the cause of freedom should cost them their property. The Congress had advised against that tactic, but John Hancock had written lately from Philadelphia that the army should not remain in New York a moment longer than the commander deemed safe. Washington's generals were divided on whether the army should stay or go, but Washington reminded himself that America's strategy had to be defensive. He must never let himself be drawn into a battle he could avoid. That was the advice of history, of his own experience, of friendly strategists visiting from Europe. The time had come to leave New York. Many citizens would welcome the British, and the town would provide excellent winter quarters for William Howe's army, but that couldn't be helped.

And yet Washington's pride was telling him not to give up New York without another fight. Once again, he split his already weakened and badly trained forces. Putnam's five thousand men were ordered to stay in the lower three miles of Manhattan that made up the town of New York. Another nine thousand soldiers would hold a section of Harlem Heights to the north. Their northern flank would reach to a new set of trenches and bulwarks called Fort Washington. Nathanael Greene would hold the territory in between with somewhat less than six thousand men, most of them militia. Washington's plan stretched the American Army over sixteen miles in a thin line that was particularly vulnerable at its center.

The British scheduled their attack for 4 A.M. on September 15. Henry Clinton argued to the last for a flanking movement rather than a frontal assault. He responded to William Howe's reasons for overriding him, "You may make every argument you wish. I will oppose you with all my might until four o'clock. But from that moment on, I will lead the attack as if I had planned it myself."

Howe ordered Clinton to land his men at Kips Bay, north of the town of New York, at the center where Washington's line was weakest. But as the British moved toward the riverbank in flat-bottomed boats, they confronted formidable-looking American defenses. Clinton thought the landing would be the most dangerous he had ever witnessed. The German troops in their open boats were singing hymns to keep up their spirits.

Their prayers were answered. The thunder from the eighty big guns of the British ships along the East River terrified the American soldiers waiting on the shore. Men thought that the sound alone would blow their heads off, and they leaped from their ditches to avoid being buried under sand and sods of earth. American officers saw that their lines could not hold. Without orders from General Washington, who was expecting the assault on Harlem Heights, they told their men to flee. The troops needed no urging. They broke and ran.

Waiting at the wrong place for the attack, George Washington heard guns, mounted his horse and galloped the four miles from the Heights to the riverbank where the British and the Germans had landed. Masses of terrified American soldiers poured toward him up the Post Road. Washington rode into their midst and cried out to them, "Take the walls!" as he pointed to fences where they could still mount a defense. Then, because they were clogging the road and blocking an orderly retreat, he shouted, "Take the cornfield!"

Some men ran off the road to do as Washington directed. Most surged forward blindly. At an orchard to their right, a few Americans moved toward the Germans with their arms raised in surrender. On Long Island, some of Howe's soldiers had pretended to give up, waited until the Americans drew close and then raised muskets and fired into their faces. This day the Germans were taking no chances. Despite the Americans' upraised hands, they shot them down and stabbed them with bayonets.

Washington was lashing out with his cane at the backs of the fleeing soldiers. He cursed them as "dastardly sons of cowardice" and threatened to run his sword through the next man who deserted. At one point he shamed a few hundred of the men into making a stand. But when a small unit of British soldiers appeared—no more than sixty or seventy—the Americans again turned and ran, leaving Washington and his aides unprotected. Nathanael Greene thought Washington was so angry over his men's conduct that he seemed more willing to die than to live. Other men said he threw down his hat in despair and cried, "Good God, have I got such troops as those?" But Washington's luck held, and he rode away unscathed.

New York was lost. With it went much of the American Army's baggage and tents and fifty or sixty cannon. Only three British soldiers had been killed, another eighteen wounded. As Washington retreated with his faltering troops to Harlem Heights, Israel Putnam was leading his men in the same direction. The British troops marched down Broadway in New York at 4 P.M., twelve hours after their landing, while Putnam's soldiers escaped along a parallel route next to the Hudson River. General Howe might have cut Putnam off with a rapid pursuit, but instead he was looking around town for rooms where he could be comfortable during the coming winter. When one of his officers pressed him to hurry after the retreating Americans, the general swore and said he would not be rushed. A conclusive victory was again within his reach, but Howe had decided that he could not crush George Washington this year.

The American Army was safe behind its ramparts on Harlem Heights, a rise four miles long and beyond the range of Admiral Howe's naval guns. The Americans now numbered about ten thousand. Their losses included a few dead, and twenty officers and three hundred men taken prisoner. In New York, Tory civilians came out of hiding to cheer loudly and carry British officers through the streets on their shoulders. The women were as wild with joy as the men, and one hoisted Britain's banner on a flagpole. Other loyalists guided the British soldiers from door to door as they placed a large "R" for "Rebel" on every patriot house.

During the night, one last skirmish was fought on the plains below Harlem Heights. A band of British infantrymen had tracked the Americans back to their redoubt, and in the gloom before dawn a British bugler blew "Gone to Earth." It was the hunter's call when the fox had found his hole. Joseph Reed, the American adjutant general, thought he had never felt such a sensation of shame. The jeering notes seemed to crown America's disgrace.

British soldiers inspected the elaborate trenches Washington's men had dug throughout New York and laughed over how quickly the Americans had deserted them. One officer noted that the rebel defenses "appear calculated more to amuse than for use." The morning after the battle, Washington was forced to report to the Congress from Harlem Heights on another disastrous rout. Given his position, he could hold the Heights, Washington said, if his troops would behave with a little resolution. But, he added, experience had taught him that he might wish for such behavior but could not expect it.

As if to prove him wrong, a sharp engagement broke out below the Heights before his letter was finished. American soldiers stood their ground, and for the first time in the war the British ran and the Americans chased after them. Washington feared a trap and recalled his men behind their defenses. But the brief exchange—in which the Americans suffered sixty casualties and the British lost a hundred more—cheered the American troops and even gave their commander a flicker of hope. Joseph Reed wrote to his wife, "You can hardly conceive the change it has made in our Army. The men have recovered their spirits and feel a confidence which before they had quite lost."

But during that invigorating exchange, Washington's orders had often been reversed or ignored, and although morale had risen briefly, he knew how wretched his prospects were. The two defeats had cut to the quick of Washington's pride. He even considered resigning his command, but his few confidants convinced him that the resulting confusion would doom the cause. His personal bravery had never been in doubt. From his time as a youthful commander, he had dared bullets and survived them so often that he may have believed he was indestructible. Washington's reputation as a strategist, however, was far more vulnerable, and every day it was assaulted. To Lund Washington he poured out his heart: He had never been so unhappy from the day he was born. If he wanted to wish the bitterest curse on an enemy this side of the grave, he would put the man in his place, with his feelings. He cautioned his cousin not to pass along any of this despair unless Washington fell in battle after all. Then the public should hear about militiamen who drew their provisions but never rendered an hour's service, about officers not worth the bread they ate.

Near midnight on September 20, 1776, General Washington was called from his quarters to watch the smoke from a fire as it spread over the southern tip of the island below him. Patriots who had hidden in New York after the British invasion had set three fires along the waterfront. From there they could trust the wind to spread the flames on flakes of burning shingle. The British could not ring the customary alarm, because the Americans had carted off the church bells to melt down for ammunition. Or so they had claimed. New York's fire engines also were out of commission, which led the British to conclude that the fires had been planned before the evacuation. William Howe suspected that the blaze meant a night attack and refused to let most of his men fight the fire until daylight. But a few British soldiers did patrol the streets, and when they found men in one house with firebrands the soldiers killed them and threw their bodies into the fire. The old and the sick, women and children, ran from house to house, thinking they were safe, and running out again, shrieking, as the fire spread. The tower of Trinity Church made a pyramid of flame, each timber burning separately until the whole spire came crashing down. At 2 A.M. the wind shifted and the fire stopped a little east of Broadway. By then, five hundred houses had been destroyed. Washington would neither take credit for the blaze nor deplore it. "Providence," he said, "or some good honest fellow, has done more for us than we were disposed to do for ourselves."

The next night the town was still in shock when British soldiers marched into General Howe's headquarters with a young man wearing the round broad-brimmed hat of a Dutch schoolmaster. His only identification was a Yale diploma, but the papers he was carrying proved what his mission had been. Nathan Hale had almost finished his drawings of British troop positions when a relative of his from New Hampshire recognized him at a tavern. Samuel Hale, a Tory, reported that Nathan was probably a spy, and the British made the arrest.

In the morning, Nathan Hale confessed frankly that he had been spying for General Washington. William Howe ordered him to be hanged without a trial, and the execution was set for 11 A.M. in front of the artillery park. A British officer who led Hale to his own tent to wait found the American calm and behaving with a gentle dignity. Asking for pen and paper, he wrote to his mother and to a fellow officer. Hale also asked to see a clergyman, but that request was denied.

When the hour came, Hale was taken to the gallows and the noose thrust around his neck. He addressed the spectators with great composure. It was the duty of every good soldier, Hale said, to obey any order from his commander in chief. He urged the British soldiers gathered around him to be ready to meet death in whatever shape it might appear.

Afterward, those who had heard him praised the way Nathan Hale had met his own death.

Trenton
1776

ON DECEMBER 11, 1776, the Congress in Philadelphia recommended that each of the United States set a day of solemn fasting and humiliation. They were instructed to implore the Almighty God to assist in the war against Britain. For George Washington and his men, the three months since the loss of New York had already provided humiliation enough. William Howe had allowed the Americans to dig in further on Harlem Heights until mid-October. Then, with four thousand troops, he had outflanked them and driven Washington and his army on a day-long march north to White Plains. After another delay of ten days, Howe attacked the extreme right of the American line, and Washington pulled the army back to North Castle. William Howe waited ten more days and surrounded Fort Washington on the east side of the Hudson. Nathanael Greene, who commanded the three thousand Americans stationed there, thought they could hold out, even though the British outnumbered them at least three to one. Washington was less sure, but he didn't overrule Greene.

On November 16 General Howe demanded that the fort surrender. An American colonel refused, reminding Howe that the Americans had joined "the most glorious cause that mankind ever fought in." The next day, British and German troops crushed the fort's defenses on three sides. They lost three hundred men but took the fort and 2,858 American prisoners of war. Four days later, Lord Cornwallis led four thousand men across the Hudson to New Jersey and tried to trap Washington and Greene between the Hudson and Hackensack Rivers. The Americans barely escaped. On November 30, two thousand militiamen from New Jersey and Maryland had come to the end of their enlistments and quit Washington's ranks as he was rushing his army away from the British advance through a cold rain. There was no question that Cornwallis had the Americans on the run, but Howe ordered him to pause, which gave Washington time to reach Trenton on December 3. When the British arrived five days later, Howe was with them. That same day in Rhode Island, Henry Clinton's men took possession of Newport unopposed.

George Washington had thrown out several false hints that he was preparing to turn and take a stand. That prospect had made the British cautious in their pursuit across New Jersey, and they had taken nineteen days to travel seventy-four miles. "They will neither fight nor totally run away," one of Howe's officers complained about the Americans. "But they keep at such a distance that we are always above a day's march from them. We seem to be playing at Bo-Peep."

By the time General Howe finally entered Trenton, the Americans once again had eluded him. Washington had collected every boat along the Delaware River for seventy miles and had rowed his shattered army across to Pennsylvania. The last of them had been shoving off from the riverbank as Howe and his army arrived on the scene.

For the moment, Washington had saved his troops, although their number had dwindled to five thousand. At any moment he expected another attack by twice that many British soldiers. Washington believed that if the residents of New Jersey had offered him any support he could have made a stand at Hackensack or Brunswick. But the militia had either disbanded officially or simply slunk away, leaving Washington with no choice but flight. Now Howe would certainly move against Philadelphia. Washington sent Israel Putnam there to fortify the town.

Members of the Congress were aghast that they might be forced to move their deliberations. Indignantly they called upon Washington to guarantee that they would be able to stay in Philadelphia. Until that moment, the Congress had tried not to admit how badly the war was going, but Washington could no longer encourage their optimism. He declined to predict the future, but said the Congress might have to leave. On December 12, 1776, members adjourned in Philadelphia and agreed to convene eight days later in Baltimore, Maryland. Samuel Adams was convinced the move was premature.

During those past three months, Thomas Paine had served in Nathanael Greene's command as a volunteer aide, amusing his commander by his willingness to debate any subject, even mathematics. But when General Horatio Gates probed tactlessly into Paine's marriage problems, Paine took his questions as an impertinence and broke off their friendship. After the British had taken the forts on the Hudson, Paine marched with the army on its retreat to Newark. He watched as enlistments expired and half the army deserted George Washington, but he never blamed the commander in chief for the dismal state of affairs. He considered Washington another Fabius, Hannibal's Roman opponent, who had been called the Delayer because of his tactics of waiting and patience. Paine predicted that one day, when the overwhelming odds against the Americans were fully understood, history would regard Washington's retreat through New Jersey as a glorious military maneuver.

During the day, Paine was consumed by his army work. But by the light of the campfire he began to write another pamphlet, which he called *The Crisis*. When it was done, Washington ordered bands of his downcast soldiers called together, and Paine's essay was read aloud to them.

"These are the times that try men's souls," Paine began. "The summer soldier and the sunshine patriot will, in this crisis, shrink from the service of his country; but he that stands it now, deserves the love and thanks of man and woman. Tyranny, like hell, is not easily conquered; yet we have this consolation with us, that the harder the conflict, the more glorious the triumph. What we obtain too cheap, we esteem too lightly: 'Tis dearness only that gives everything its value. Heaven knows how to put a proper price upon its goods; and it would be strange indeed if so celestial an article as Freedom should not be highly rated."

When the essay was published, it shamed some militiamen and made others bolder. Numbers of them returned to the fight. American morale badly needed a military victory, but for the moment *The Crisis* was all General Washington had.

Charles Lee was finding it impossible not to contrast his success at Charleston with his commander in chief's blunders and retreats. On his way to rejoin headquarters in October 1776, General Lee ignored the dire events at Harlem Heights and White Plains and stopped instead in Philadelphia. Before he had accepted his commission, Lee had informed the Congress that it must make good the large sums of money he was owed in England. Now, on the crest of his victory, Lee insisted on eleven thousand pounds sterling.

When he arrived finally in New York, Lee was received as something of a savior. His gritty assurance and his enthusiasm for the Continental Army gave the men confidence in their own capacity. For all of his eccentricities—men said he smelled more of the kennel than his hounds did—Lee had been right about George Washington's strategy on the Hudson. He had written to Joseph Reed, Washington's adjutant general, that he couldn't understand why Fort Washington wasn't evacuated when it clearly could not be held, no matter what Nathanael Greene had said.

But when the British overran the post, Lee was not smug. Instead, he lost all control, railing and shouting that had the wretched place been named for him and not for Washington, it would have been given up long ago. Reed had watched as Washington hesitated and debated with himself over the fort. Then, while Washington rushed through New Jersey, Reed had sent Lee a letter, suggesting that now was the time for a change in the high command. "I do not mean to flatter nor praise you at the expense of any other," Reed wrote, "but I confess I do think that it is entirely owing to you that this army, and the liberties of America so far as they are depending on it, are not totally cut off." Reed added that Lee could be decisive, a quality often lacking in minds that were otherwise valuable.

Lee had remained on the east side of the Hudson with about seven thousand troops from New York and New England when General Washington crossed the river with all of the Southern troops. As his situation worsened throughout November 1776, Washington had called upon Lee to join him, but Lee was reluctant to obey. If he went, he would be second in command. If he waited, the Congress might see Washington's obvious failures and do what it should have done in the first place—name an experienced British officer to replace an indecisive Virginia planter as commander in chief. Lee stalled and delayed as Washington grew more desperate. But Washington never became peremptory, even though he knew Lee's low opinion of him. Once, when Joseph Reed was away from headquarters, Washington opened one of Lee's letters addressed to the adjutant. He returned it to Lee with a mild note of apology for his mistake.

Now, with Philadelphia threatened in early December, Washington was reduced to begging. "Do come on," he wrote to General Lee. If Lee came quickly, he might save the town, with its symbolic meaning for America. Lee didn't believe that William Howe intended to attack Philadelphia, and though he consented to cross the Hudson he loitered along, making no determined effort to reach Washington's camp. The excuses he offered were ones Washington could also claim: Lee's roster of seven thousand men at White Plains had dropped to fewer than three thousand. With their enlistments about to expire, the troops of an entire New York unit went home just as Lee was preparing to cross into New Jersey. Like Washington's troops, Lee's men were badly clothed. Those without shoes were slaughtering cattle and wrapping their feet in the hides. And the people of New Jersey were as indifferent, even hostile, to Lee's army as they had been to Washington's. Despite strict orders, some of Lee's hungry troops had turned to looting. Whenever they came across a sheep, a goose or a turkey, they went through a charade of challenging it to give the day's countersign. When it didn't answer, they roasted it for its Tory sympathies.

By December 8, 1776, Lee's army had traveled fifty miles from its crossing on the Hudson, and he paused to rest at Morristown. He wrote to inform Washington that he could contribute more by raising a number of militia there than by hurrying to headquarters, and he made no attempt to conceal his disdain for the commander in chief. Lee had heard that Washington had towed along a fleet of heavy boats when he was forced across the Delaware, and he asked, "I am told you have the gondolas from Philadelphia with you; for Heaven's sake, what use can they be of?"

John Sullivan had been exchanged for a British officer and had joined Lee's troops. After a two-day rest at Morristown, General Lee moved his men eight miles to the village of Vealton. There he turned over the men to Sullivan and left camp for an evening of diversion. With a bodyguard of four officers and fifteen men, he rode to Basking Ridge, where an Irish widow named White kept a tavern. Mrs. White also had other women boarding at her establishment; during a long night, one of Lee's officers was awakened by female screaming.

The next morning, Friday the thirteenth, General Lee was late coming down for breakfast. In an old blue coat and greasy leather breeches, he sat at the table writing a letter to Horatio Gates, who he knew shared his opinion of George Washington.

"Entre nous, a certain great man is damnably difficult," Lee wrote. "He has thrown me into a situation where I may have my choice of difficulties. In short, unless something which I do not expect turns up, we are lost."

He was finishing his letter with "Adieu, my dear friend! God bless you!" when an aide rose from the breakfast table and told Lee he'd better look out the window.

Banastre Tarleton, aged twenty-two and lately of Oxford but now of the British Sixteenth Regiment of Light Dragoons, had come to the war with one purpose. Since Charles Lee had once been a British officer, Tarleton considered his treason the more damnable, and the dragoons felt doubly betrayed because Lee had once commanded their regiment in Portugal. Earlier in the year, while passing through London on his way to America, Tarleton had stopped by the Cocoa Tree Club in St. James's Street, where he had tapped his sword and vowed, "With this sword, I will cut off General Lee's head!"

During the night Lee spent at Mrs. White's tavern, Tarleton and thirty of the dragoons had been reconnoitering nearby for intelligence about Lee. The next morning they captured an American soldier, and, two miles farther on, some townspeople volunteered that General Lee was in the vicinity. Tarleton then picked up two of Lee's advance sentries. To save themselves, they told about Mrs. White's tavern and the general's guard, which wasn't large. Next the dragoons captured an American messenger carrying letters from Lee to John Sullivan, and he pointed out the tavern itself.

Reining up in front, Tarleton could see two American sentries standing at the tavern door. Shouting and waving their sabers, Tarleton and six dragoons rode at full speed up to the Americans, who panicked, dropped their weapons and ran off. Tarleton ordered his men to fire through every window and cut up the American troops inside. At that, an old woman appeared in the doorway and dropped to her knees. Begging for her life, she told Tarleton that General Lee was still there.

It was then that the aide had looked out the window and seen the rest of Tarleton's dragoons in their green uniforms charging down at the house from a nearby orchard.

"Here, sir," he told General Lee, "are the British cavalry!"

Lee asked, "Where?" He quickly signed his name at the bottom of his letter to Horatio Gates.

"Around the house."

Tarleton and the dragoons circled the inn and opened fire, hitting several of the guards. Lee watched in shock as a British soldier raised his saber and hacked through the arm of a sentry.

Tarleton shouted from outside that he knew General Lee was in the house. If he surrendered, he and his attendants would be safe. But if he didn't obey immediately, the tavern would be burned and every person in it, without exception, put to the sword.

Inside, Charles Lee couldn't believe that he had been captured. "For God's sake," he cried. "What shall I do?"

Mrs. White hustled him upstairs and tried to hide him in a nook between the chimney and the fireplace. But the space was small and Lee couldn't squeeze into it.

They heard Tarleton give orders to set the house on fire. Still Lee hesitated, pacing the chamber as he tried to think of an escape. At last he saw he had no chance and sent down word that he would surrender.

Lee's aide-de-camp, William Bradford, went to the front door. When he opened it, there was a fresh volley of shots. Bradford leaped back and shouted that his general was coming out. Charles Lee stepped forward and surrendered his sword. He said he trusted he would be treated like a gentleman. One of the dragoons agreed and ordered Lee to mount his horse. The British were far from their lines and eager to get their prize to headquarters. Lee asked for his hat and coat, and Captain Bradford went for them. Once inside, he snatched a servant's shirt and substituted it for his uniform jacket. The excited British soldiers had eyes only for General Lee and didn't notice the servant who handed over the general's coat. As Lee was being led away, Captain Bradford slipped back inside. An aide to Horatio Gates, who had been waiting to return with Lee's answer, escaped to a room that the British did not search, taking with him two pistols and the letter.

Tarleton's men rode rapidly for thirteen miles until they forded a river and considered themselves safe from American pursuit. Tarleton thought the entire affair seemed like a miracle. He and his men had taken prisoner America's most distinguished general and Britain's foremost traitor. Riding almost without stop, they covered the remaining sixty miles and turned Lee over to Lord Cornwallis. That night there was wild celebrating in the British camp. Military bands played until dawn, and officers toasted King George until they couldn't raise their glasses. From reports later, they fed so much alcohol to General Lee's horse that it got as drunk as they did.

John Honeyman, a butcher from Griggstown, New Jersey, had been hated by his neighbors for his Tory sympathies since the war began. Just before Christmas, 1776, he was foolish enough to leave the safety of the Hessian camp at Trenton, driving a single cow in front of him. American scouts seized him and took him across the Delaware to George Washington's headquarters.

Washington met alone with the prisoner for more than an hour. Then he ordered his cadre to lock up Honeyman in the log guardhouse. During the night, a fire broke out some distance from the guardhouse, and the sentries hurried there to put it out. When they returned to their posts, everything seemed quiet. In the morning, although the padlock was still secure on the cell, the prisoner was gone.

John Honeyman had been a spy, as his neighbors suspected, but for the Americans. A Scotch-Irish soldier who had been with Wolfe at Quebec, he had emigrated to Pennsylvania and enlisted in the Continental Army when war broke out. General Washington had heard his accent and decided it would get him into places where flatter American tones might be suspect. When Honeyman agreed to pose as a loyalist butcher, his disguise was so convincing that Washington issued an order protecting the wife and children of the man he described as a "notorious Tory."

On this night, Honeyman had brought the best news Washington could receive. With Philadelphia apparently in his grasp, William Howe was suspending military operations for the winter. Washington had heard that rumor but mistrusted it. He was sure that when the Delaware froze solid, Howe would march his troops across to fight in Pennsylvania. But Honeyman assured him that the British general was withdrawing his army to winter quarters on Staten Island and Manhattan, with some units going to Rhode Island. Howe's motives were mixed. He knew that enlisted men in a professional army were fighting less from zeal than to make a living and that few of his officers cared to wage war during the harsh Pennsylvania winter. Also, both General Howe and his brother the admiral disapproved of Lord North's policies. Howe thought a successful campaign of pacification might save thousands of British and American lives. He had asked for fifteen thousand more troops for a new campaign in 1777, and he expected loyalist sentiment to sweep across New Jersey and keep the state safe for the king. And, finally, it was hard to overestimate William Howe's craving for comfort.

Preparing to return to New York, Howe planned to leave a garrison of German soldiers behind at Trenton. Those soldiers had been sold into England's service by their princes and were commanded by a fifty-year-old colonel named Johann Gottlieb Rall. They were the first mercenaries to arrive in New York and had been in America only three months. Catherine of Russia had refused to sell Britain twenty thousand soldiers, as had Frederick the Great of Prussia. In England, Lord North's government cited precedents to show that in every war England had resorted to paying foreigners to fight for her. Lately, recruiting for the British Army had been slow, and conscripting civilians to fight in America would have inflamed the country.

The German nobility sold their subjects at different prices— the average ran to four shillings fourpence for each grenadier. A prince received that same amount whenever one of his soldiers was killed or when any three were wounded. The mercenaries came from various German principalities, but since the landgrave of Hesse-Cassel sent the bulk of them, all Germans became Hessians to the Americans. Colonel Rall's grenadiers wore dark-blue uniforms and bristled with mustaches stiffened with boot blacking. Working heavy tallow into their scalps, they gathered their long hair into queues that reached nearly to the waist. Johann Rall had proved his courage at the battle for Fort Washington, but he spoke no English and fellow officers found him flighty and self-pleased. He also drank.

William Howe thought that Trenton, which was spread across open country and easily reached by river, was vulnerable. One Hessian colonel urged him to treat the town merely as an outpost, with a guard of a hundred and fifty men. But Colonel Rall hungered for glory, and he arranged a meeting with General Howe and an interpreter. After a night of drinking, Rall usually lingered in his bath until 10 or 11 A.M., but that morning he was up early and persuaded Howe to leave three regiments in Trenton and put them all under his command. General Howe had directed Rall to dig in at Trenton and to set up artillery around the town, but Rall hadn't seemed to pay attention. "Let them come!" he answered when his lieutenants proposed building the fortifications. "We want no trenches! We'll at them with the bayonet!"

In place of trenches, Rall kept one regiment on alert each night and sent men to patrol the roads a mile into the countryside. What he had seen so far of the American rebels had invited contempt for them. Now, with Christmas approaching, he intended to celebrate with his troops in the traditional German way. He had never taken much interest in such details as whether the men kept their muskets clean, but he loved music and prided himself on his reputation as a fine host at a party. When Rall's best British spy showed up at camp a few hours after escaping from an American guardhouse, his information gave Rall no reason to reconsider his holiday plans. John Honeyman assured the colonel that in their present demoralized state Rall had nothing to fear from the Americans.

George Washington needed a victory. Thomas Paine had tried to soothe the nation by comparing Washington to Fabius the Delayer, but Washington's temperament was as bold and aggressive as ever, and he hated delay. The weaknesses that surrounded him—his troops, his shortages of supply—had led him to hesitate and had cost him Fort Washington. His troops were depressed by the months of disaster, and the calendar reminded them that time was running out. The enlistments of many of the militia would end on December 31, and few of them seemed willing to extend their service. But they still owed General Washington one more week.

On Christmas Eve, Washington called together his ranking officers at Lord Stirling's quarters. Washington's tactics had been criticized as too elaborate, and the new plan he was outlining seemed also to rely on an unrealistic degree of coordination. He proposed an ambitious variation on the Indian raids he had seen during his days with Braddock. He would ferry three elements of his army back across the Delaware River. They would march to Trenton, surround the two or three thousand Hessians, and attack them at three different points. The plan also resembled the strategy the British had used at Fort Washington. If everything went perfectly at Trenton, the haul of prisoners might match the American losses from that fiasco.

To Joseph Reed, his adjutant away in Philadelphia, General Washington wrote, "Christmas Day at night, one hour before day, is the time fixed for our attempt on Trenton." He added, "For Heaven's sake, keep this to yourself, as the discovery of it may prove fatal to us; our numbers, sorry I am to say, being less than I had any conception of: but necessity, dire necessity, will—nay, must—justify any attempt."

Reed answered from Philadelphia that Israel Putnam, the city's commander, could spare only five hundred militia to assist in the battle. Washington decided to go ahead all the same. On Christmas afternoon he sent twenty-four hundred men from his Continental regiments to McKonkey's Ferry, about nine miles upstream on the Delaware River from Trenton. Downstream, Colonel John Cadwalader of the Pennsylvania militia, with eighteen hundred men, and Brigadier General James Ewing, with another six or eight hundred, were ordered to time their crossings so that they could cut off any Hessian attempt to escape from Washington's main attack.

Late on Christmas Day, General Washington led his men along the west bank of the Delaware, following hills that would conceal their march from German scouts across the river. A cold and windy darkness fell as the men began preparing large cargo boats for the crossing. Washington was ready to mount his sorrel horse and supervise the embarking when a messenger arrived with a paper.

"What a time is this to hand me letters!" Washington said. By this time in his life, his self-control was so thorough that the messenger thought only that he sounded solemn. He had been sent by General Horatio Gates, he explained, to take charge of an American post at Bristol.

"By General Gates?" Washington asked. "Where is he?"

"I left him this morning in Philadelphia."

"What was he doing there?"

"I understood him that he was on his way to Congress."

"On his way to Congress!" Washington repeated.

Gates was claiming ill-health, but his absence was a reminder that, as Washington was launching his desperate gamble, intriguing among his fellow generals had moved from Philadelphia to Baltimore.

At 6 P.M. Washington paused to write a message from McKonkey's Ferry to Colonel Cadwalader downstream at Bristol. Despite the limited support he could expect, Washington told Cadwalader, "I am determined, as the night is favorable, to cross the river and make the attack upon Trenton in the morning. If you can do nothing real, at least create as great a diversion as possible."

The night before, Washington had spent Christmas Eve brooding over the state of an army dressed in tatters and preparing to leave him within the week. He had come up then with the countersign for tonight's attack on Trenton, and he issued it on the riverbank, to be passed along the ranks. It was "Victory or death."

The boats were ready. Washington began sending his troops across the Delaware. The current was rough, and ice crashing in the river made the crossing dangerous and slow. The campaign's logistics had been turned over again to Colonel Henry Knox, the Boston bookseller who had overseen the dragging of cannon from Fort Ticonderoga. Knox, who stood six foot three and weighed two hundred and eighty pounds, had a deep bass voice that carried over the roar of the Delaware. Amid fumbling and slips, he managed to get eighteen artillery fieldpieces aboard their carriers, most of them Durham boats used in peacetime to carry iron ore and grain into Philadelphia. Each boat was forty feet long and eight feet deep. With four or five men rowing and pushing them forward with poles, they could carry fifteen tons. Washington had hoped to have his men, artillery and horses across the Delaware by midnight, but it was becoming clear that the passage would take much longer. When his advance guard had reached the other bank and was holding the landing site, Washington boarded one of the boats. Soldiers were amused that the sharp wind had turned his nose bright red. Otherwise, the buoyant mood of the march had given way to foreboding. Few men were dressed for the bitter chill, and sleet was threatening to dampen their ammunition. But General Washington was determined to be cheerful.

He stepped over men to get to where Henry Knox was sitting and hailed him coarsely, at least in Knox's version. Few men ever penetrated Washington's careful reserve, and as his every word quickly went the rounds, it was usually touched up in the retelling. His troops enjoyed hearing that on this night Washington had nudged Knox with the toe of his boot and said, "Shift that fat ass, Harry. But slowly, or you'll swamp the damned boat!"

Though the river was only three hundred yards wide where the Americans were crossing, ice floes dashed against the oars and the poles and made progress slow. When Washington stepped out of the boat on the New Jersey side, he wrapped his cloak against the biting sleet and supervised the landing of the remaining troops. One officer thought he had never seen Washington as purposeful. His horse hadn't yet made the crossing, and when Washington wanted to sit an aide pulled up an empty box that had been used as a beehive.

The entire crossing took nine hours. It was 3 A.M. on Thursday, December 26, when the last American soldier stepped onto the New Jersey bank, and another hour before the army was ready to march and the order came, "Shoulder your firelocks." At the head of the line, a captain checked his priming powder and found that hail had saturated the handkerchief he was using to keep it dry. That news was conveyed to General Washington, who sent his answer ahead to John Sullivan: "Then tell the general to use the bayonet and penetrate into the town. For the town must be taken and I am resolved to take it."

Washington halted the column at the village of Birmingham to let the men eat a hurried meal. Washington's own plate was passed up to him on his horse. When the order was given to resume marching, many soldiers were found asleep in the snow. Rousing them was not easy, but when the men were on their feet Washington divided his column and sent them marching down two different roads that led the five miles to Trenton. John Sullivan took troops to the right, Nathanael Greene to the left. Night began to lift, and Washington saw that he would no longer be able to launch his surprise attack under a cover of darkness. Neither could he retreat. If the Hessians learned that the Americans were on this side of the Delaware, they could set upon them in full strength and trap them with the river to their backs. Men riding alongside General Washington thought he was weighing his options, but in fact he had left himself no choice.

Washington's horse lost its footing struggling up one icy slope, and he was nearly thrown. But he grabbed the horse's mane with both hands and saved himself the fall. To his cold and tired soldiers, he continued to call out, "Press on! Press on, boys!"

Near the front of the ranks, a young captain, Alexander Hamilton, was now getting the war he had prayed for in the West Indies. Hamilton's life since his days as a clerk had been a constant surprise. He was still a boy when he had experienced a hurricane in the islands and had written a vivid account of it. That had caused a group of wealthy men to seek him out and offer to send him to study in America. Hamilton had been enrolled at King's College in New York when a crowd of patriots gathered early in July 1774 for speeches about the crisis facing their colony. Near sunset, a pale youth with a high forehead and glittering eyes spoke so fervently against the British that when he was done men shouted approval. At nineteen, Alexander Hamilton had made himself celebrated.

Later, a company of artillery was raised in New York and Hamilton was chosen to command it. During the hectic retreat through New Jersey, Hamilton's energy and skill had impressed George Washington, who had invited him to his tent. By the end of their interview the young captain had become one of Washington's aides and soon afterward a favorite. On this morning, Hamilton had dismounted during the march and tethered his horse to one of the artillery pieces. He was slightly built but held himself very straight as he slogged along with his men. From time to time he reached out and patted the cannon rolling at his side as though it were a pet.

When Nathanael Greene's column came to an unexpected halt, Washington rode forward to find out why. Through the snow, he saw a group of American soldiers gathered in a lane off the main road. Washington rode to them and asked to see their commander. A captain came forward and identified himself as Richard Anderson of the Fifth Virginia, a brigade commanded by Brigadier General Adam Stephen III. Anderson said that General Stephen had sent him out to reconnoiter on Christmas Day. He had been ordered to spy out Hessian outposts as far as Trenton but was not to provoke an engagement. Anderson and his men had been returning from the town when they passed a German sentinel. Though the Hessian hadn't seen them through the heavy snow, they had shot him, along with five other guards, and left them wounded in the road. Now they were heading back to report to General Stephen.

All of Washington's meticulous planning was ruined. The gunfire must have alerted the Hessians and guaranteed that they would be waiting to cut down the Americans as they approached Trenton. As Anderson was reporting to Washington, General Stephen rode up. Washington had a low opinion of Stephen's military judgment from their time together in the French and Indian War, and they had been political rivals in Virginia. Washington turned on him with his full anger and frustration. Stephen had no authority to send a squad across the river the day before the assault, Washington said. How had he dared to do it? "You, sir," Washington concluded bitterly, "may have ruined all my plans by putting them on their guard."

Adam Stephen said nothing.

Washington quickly recovered himself. He turned back to Captain Anderson and became quiet and solicitous. Anderson was hardly to blame for the impending disaster.

Washington's fears seemed justified. At the sound of gunfire about 7 P.M. on Christmas Day, Colonel Rall had broken off a game of checkers and ordered the Hessians to fall out. The regiments waited in Trenton while scouting parties discovered the wounded men but no trace of their American attackers. Rall suspected that the incident had involved only a few local farmers trying to annoy him. Earlier that day, before the Christmas festivities, one of Rall's majors had suggested sending away all troop baggage since it would only encumber the Hessians if the Americans attacked. "Fiddlesticks!" Rall had replied. "Those clodhoppers will not attack us! And should they do so, we will simply fall on them and rout them."

Colonel Rall returned to the Trenton Tavern without leaving an outpost to guard the river. He switched from checkers to cards and prepared to go on drinking late into the night. When an officer recommended sending heavy patrols down all the roads and to every likely crossing on the Delaware, Rall said there would be time enough for all that in the morning. The Hessians blessed their luck in having such an unflappable commander and kept on celebrating.

Colonel Rall went for a late supper to the house of Abraham Hunt, a rich Trenton merchant who was trying to remain neutral in the struggle. While Rall was there, a loyalist farmer who had seen the American army on the New Jersey side of the Delaware rode into town and traced him to Hunt's house. It was already well past midnight, but Hunt didn't want to interrupt the drinking and the cards and told his servant not to let the farmer in.

The man scribbled out a note of warning, and the servant delivered it to Rall, who stuck it unread into a vest pocket.

At 4 A.M. on December 26, Lieutenant Friedrich Fischer of the German artillery, following his usual routine, ordered horses to be hitched to two brass guns in front of the guardhouse and went to inform Colonel Rall that his men were ready for their early patrol along the Delaware. Rall had gone to sleep, but the officer of the day told Fischer that the patrol was canceled because of the bad weather. The horses were untied and sent back to their stable.

At about 7:45 A.M., Andreas Wiederhold, another German lieutenant, was sitting in an outpost at Pennington Road that had once been a barrelmaker's shop. Throughout the night, small patrols had ventured out and returned to report that all was quiet. Now Wiederhold stepped out the shop door and spotted dark shapes moving toward him from the woods. When his men saw them, they shouted, "*Der Feind! Heraus! Heraus!*" The enemy! Turn out! Turn out!

As the Germans opened fire at the approaching figures, Jacob Piel in town ran to Rall's headquarters and found that the colonel was still sleeping deeply. Piel shook him, told him about the gunfire and went outside to help ready the troops. When Rall didn't come out, Piel rushed back to his bedroom and found him in his nightshirt.

"What's the matter?" Rall asked.

Piel asked whether he hadn't heard the shooting.

The colonel didn't answer, but he said, "I will be out in a minute."

The emergency seemed to sober him, and he was dressed and downstairs quickly. By then, American shells were exploding down his street.

It was already broad daylight when George Washington reached a house with a man chopping wood in front. Washington asked where the Hessian guards were posted. In these days of tangled loyalties, saying too much could mean death, and the man hesitated until one of Washington's aides said, "You need not be frightened. It is General Washington who asks the question."

With that, the man brightened and pointed up the road to the house the Germans were occupying.

Struggling through the blizzard on the road to Trenton had been an ordeal. Washington's men kept slipping on the ice, and soldiers marching barefoot or with old rags tied around their feet left trails of blood in the snow. During halts in the column, men sometimes sat on tree stumps and fell asleep. If they weren't shaken awake, they would freeze to death. Yet there had been no complaining, and a warming excitement was passing through the ranks as the men drew closer to Trenton. Washington heard a cannon shot in the distance and recognized it as coming from one of General Sullivan's guns. He began to think that the mission might succeed, after all.

As the Americans moved toward the center of town, they saw a confused rush of Hessian artillerymen trying to harness their horses and officers attempting to line up their troops. John Sullivan's men pushed into the town from one side while Nathanael Greene's forces entered from the other. The Hessians managed to fire off six shots from each of two cannon, but soon the crews were killed or wounded and the guns were in American hands. The Americans had also taken control of Trenton's main intersection, the crossing of King and Queen Streets, and by installing their own guns could rake relentlessly down the center of town. Captain Alexander Hamilton's company was sent to join the bombardment. Between firings, they held their hands over the touchholes of their weapons to keep out the freezing sleet.

The town was in turmoil. John Sullivan's troops were seizing the southern section, rushing with their bayonets upon the Germans so furiously that the Hessians ran at the sight of them. Some Americans shouted, "These are the times that try men's souls."

In the midst of the chaos, one Hessian major pressed the commander for any decisive action: "Colonel Rall, there is yet time to save the cannon!"

Rall didn't answer. Instead, hearing the shots coming from Sullivan's troops, he muttered, "Lord, Lord, what is it?"

His officers repeated that they could still save the cannon, but Rall was hardly listening.

"Never mind," he said. "We'll soon have them back."

The major urged Rall either to charge forward toward the center of town or permit a retreat. From atop his horse, Rall got elements of two regiments into line for a direct assault.

"Forward march!" he cried. "Attack them with the bayonets!"

The line moved out in good order, but sniping from neighboring houses and fences and the sharp fire from the American artillery cut the Hessians down in the street or sent them rushing to a nearby apple orchard. As their band began to play to encourage them, Colonel Rall took a slight wound. He assured his aides that he was more annoyed than disabled and urged the men to advance. "*Alle wer meine Grenadiere sind, vorwärts!*" he called to his men. All who are my grenadiers, forward! But Rall's loss of blood seemed to have weakened him.

The Americans were continuing their charge down King Street toward Colonel Rall's headquarters, though the storm made it hard for either side to tell friend from enemy. Rall's bravest men made a brief stand but took fifteen casualties without hitting a single American. The Hessian adjutant advised a retreat over the Assunpink Creek bridge, but by the time Rall authorized him to see whether the bridge was safe the Americans had captured it. Rall had no more ideas. When the Americans began firing from two cannon at the corner of Second Street, he decided that his men must rush down Third and Fourth Streets and head for cover in the orchard. He had barely given the command when he was directly hit, and two gaping wounds opened in his side. For a few minutes Rall lay on the ground. Then he rose with great effort. Supported by two Hessian soldiers, he walked slowly to the Methodist church at Fourth and Queen Streets.

Picking his way to shelter in the church, Rall found one of his lieutenants lying near a house. Rall asked whether the lieutenant was wounded. Yes, the man said. "I pity you," Rall said.

The surviving Hessian officers were divided over their next move. Some wanted to try to escape across a shallow spot in Assunpink Creek. Others wanted to surrender. A corporal tied a white handkerchief to a spontoon and led a badly wounded major to John Sullivan to give up his sword. Officers of a six-gun American battery at the head of Queen Street called to the two Hessian regiments trapped there to throw down their weapons or be shot to death.

Rall's adjutant had been learning English, and he interpreted the ultimatum for the others. The American line had moved within sixty feet of the Germans. A Hessian lieutenant colonel called out that they would surrender, and the Germans lowered their arms and their battle standards. Their officers put their hats on the points of their swords and held them aloft. The Hessians who were against surrendering threw their guns toward the woods instead of laying them down in front of them. Some managed to escape across the stream, but three were caught in the current and drowned.

When the commander of the third German regiment tried to hold out, Brigadier General Arthur St. Clair sent a message to him: "If you do not surrender immediately, I will blow you to pieces." The German captain asked that his officers be allowed to keep their swords and baggage, and he and St. Clair shook hands on it.

George Washington had been notified that the first two regiments had surrendered. Now St. Clair informed him that the last regiment had also given up. His messenger was Major James Wilkinson, the aide who had conveyed Horatio Gates's regrets to General Washington before the battle. Washington was in better spirits than he had been earlier, and he greeted Wilkinson with almost the same words that Samuel Adams had used in welcoming the sound of gunfire at Lexington. Pressing him by the hand, Washington said, "This is a glorious day for our country, Major Wilkinson."

Two of his generals were also exultant. John Sullivan and Lord Stirling had captured the same Hessian soldiers who had taken them prisoner during the battle for Long Island.

Colonel Rall was dying. He had been carried on a church bench back to his headquarters on King Street. As men cut away his clothes to treat his wounds, they found the note from the loyalist who had tried to warn him a few hours earlier. Rall looked over the message and said, *"Hätte ich dies zu Herrn Hunt gelesen, so wäre ich jezt nicht hier."* If I had read this at Mr. Hunt's, I would not be here.

Washington and Nathanael Greene sought out Colonel Rall at his headquarters and spoke briefly with him through an interpreter. Rall pleaded with the American commander to treat his men kindly, and Washington promised that he would. Colonel Rall endured another thirty hours of pain and died.

Rall was the highest-ranking casualty, but twenty-two other Hessian officers and men had been killed during the ninety-minute battle. Survivors hid in the houses of sympathetic Tories; most were soon discovered. By December 29, George Washington estimated that he had taken one thousand Hessians prisoner. Another four hundred had escaped because Washington's strategy had once again been overly ambitious. John Cadwalader had not been able to get his artillery across the rushing Delaware and had called back the infantrymen who had managed to make the crossing. James Ewing hadn't been able to launch a single boat.

Even so, the extent of Washington's success was evident in the small number of American losses—two officers wounded, along with two privates. Another two Americans may have frozen to death as they waited at the ferry for the last of the boats, but Washington's report to the Congress made no mention of them.

The American spoils included forty horses, six brass cannon, a thousand weapons, four wagons of baggage, three wagons of ammunition, and twelve drums. There were also twenty-one wagonloads of goods the Germans had looted from American homes. Washington invited the residents of Trenton to come and recover their property, but many civilians found that their mahogany furniture was missing because Rall had let his men heat their quarters by burning chairs and tables rather than tire them with cutting wood.

As word of the surrender spread through Trenton, American soldiers danced and yelled and threw their hats in the air. Some turned away sadly from the sight of Germans dead and dying. Others rifled the Hessian corpses; German swords were the most popular souvenirs. The Americans also discovered forty hogsheads of rum that the Germans had abandoned and were warming and rewarding themselves liberally before General Washington could stop them. Nathanael Greene and Henry Knox recommended chasing the Germans who had escaped, but when Washington convened his council of war the majority voted to return to Pennsylvania. Theirs had been a brilliant stroke, but Cadwalader and Ewing were still across the river, the enemy was strong both below Trenton and above it, the weather remained severe and the American army was drunk.

Battle of Princeton, by George Washington Parke Custis.

Princeton

DURING THE trip back to George Washington's headquarters on the
Pennsylvania side of the Delaware, the German prisoners cowered
in the boats. Had they shared a language with their captors, they
would have discovered that their backgrounds were not so different. In Germany, until their princes sold them into this distant war,
they had been weavers and tailors, shoemakers and carpenters,
butchers and bakers, masons and plasterers. To charge them up for

George Washington at left, General Hugh Mercer at right

1776-77

battle, British commanders had warned them that the American rebels were cannibals who would skin a Hessian with their tomahawks to make a cover for their drums or would roast his body on a spit and eat him like pork.

When they saw the Americans taking boyish pleasure in the brass caps they had plucked from Hessian corpses, the prisoners pulled off their own caps and began giving them away. One American guard smiled as he watched his friends, many shoeless and with the elbows out of their shirts, jamming the caps over their wet hair and capering and strutting on the way to camp.

General Washington had chosen a farmhouse five miles from the Delaware for his new headquarters. On the evening of December 28, he entertained twenty-eight Hessian officers, all in their dark-blue uniforms. The talk had to be conducted through interpreters, but as the evening wore on a frankness emerged between the fellow soldiers. Washington spoke with Lieutenant Andreas Wiederhold, who had been stationed at the guardhouse, and praised his conduct under fire. That emboldened Wiederhold to tell Washington how he would have conducted the battle if he had been in Rall's position. He claimed afterward that General Washington had commented favorably on his acumen, and Wiederhold decided that the American commander in chief was a fine, polite man. He hadn't said much, though, as he listened to Wiederhold outlining his strategy, and at times the lieutenant thought that Washington was looking rather sly.

George Washington usually communicated with his men through written orders read aloud to the ranks. But with less than forty-eight hours until their enlistments expired, he had the men lined up so that he could address them in person. The army was back in Trenton. After two days of rest and sobriety, time to wash and sleep, they had put on clean rags and been ferried once more across the Delaware. The second crossing had been worse than the first. Intense cold had frozen even more ice in the river, and moving the boats with poles and oars was exhausting.

When they reached the battle site, the Americans found that all was quiet. The British and the Germans had ceded the town and retreated—perhaps to Princeton, where General Howe kept large stores of munitions and supplies. This time, John Cadwalader had got his men across the river and was urging Washington to take advantage of the enemy's disarray and strike again. But the New England regiments were due to go home, and even with hundreds of militia volunteers coming from Philadelphia, Washington couldn't launch another attack without battle-tried veterans.

When the New England regiments were in place and ready to

hear him, General Washington rode to the center of their ranks and asked the men to give him six more weeks. Never again could they do more for their country, he said, than they could do now. Washington had cast off his normal austerity, and one sergeant found his tone warm, even affectionate. But Washington knew better than to trust to sentiment. He had sent an urgent note to Robert Morris, a Philadelphia banker, asking to borrow enough money to pay a ten-dollar bonus to each soldier who would extend his enlistment for six weeks. "Every lover of his country must strain his credit," Washington wrote. "No time, my dear sir, is to be lost."

To avoid any denial or delay, Washington told Morris to send the money back with the man who had brought his message. Morris met the challenge. Since the troops wanted hard money, not the Continental paper issued by the Congress, he filled two canvas bags with four hundred and ten Spanish silver dollars, along with a French half crown and ten and a half English shillings. Morris told Washington he would borrow the rest in silver, promise repayment in gold and then try to raise the gold as best he could. The banker had heard that Washington was low on wine and sent along a quarter cask of a good vintage.

In addition to those funds from Philadelphia, Washington had received copies of recent resolutions by the Congress in Baltimore that gave him sweeping emergency powers. Even Samuel Adams had agreed that the commander in chief must be entrusted with those powers, though they could make him a dictator. When Adams wrote home to Boston, he underlined that the authority had been granted for a limited time, no more than six months. Washington himself seemed disturbed that he might be accused of conniving for power and wrote reassuringly to the Congress that the sword, which was the last resort in preserving liberties, ought to be laid aside once those liberties were firmly established.

Now, as Washington finished his appeal to the New England regiments, their officers stepped forward to explain the terms of the bounty Robert Morris was providing. Next came a drum roll as volunteers were asked to step forward. No one moved. For weeks they had fixed their hearts on returning to their families. Only hours away from escape, they would not give up their dreams. Washington spoke a second time. Throughout his life he had nurtured his pride, but now he begged. My brave fellows, Washington said, you have done all I asked you to do and more than could reasonably be expected. But your country is at stake—your wives, your houses and all that you hold dear.

Again he asked that they give him a little longer, one more month. The drums beat again. Possibly because they had heard the general's pain, men were looking around at one another. Voices in the ranks said, We cannot go home now. Men told their friends, I will remain if you will.

They started to step forward until their numbers passed two hundred. Only men too weak to fight stayed behind. The officers asked whether they should sign up each man for his extended service.

No! said Washington. Men who volunteered at a time like this didn't need a piece of paper to hold them to their duty.

When the pleas and the bribes were over, between twelve and fourteen hundred men had agreed to stay with Washington for an extra six weeks—and an extra ten dollars. He also had the Pennsylvania militia to draw upon, its strength estimated from eighteen hundred men to twice that number. At the upper limits, the Americans would be pitting five thousand troops, most of them poorly trained, against an estimated eight thousand British and German professionals. Major James Wilkinson wrote bleakly, "How dreadful the odds."

To prevent those odds from getting worse, Washington had made the Hessian officers in his custody sign an oath that they would stay where he sent them and would not pass information to the British. The Hessians were then marched to Philadelphia and put on display to hearten the beleaguered residents. The Germans looked hearty and well dressed beside their barefoot American guards, and onlookers who didn't understand that the Hessians had been sold to the British were puzzled by their expression. They seemed, one elderly spectator remarked, satisfied.

The Hessians thought Philadelphia was big and beautiful, but once inside the town they found a mixed reception. Some sympathetic Americans approached them with bread and liquor, until clusters of old women stopped them and screamed that the Germans should be hanged for coming to America to deprive them of their freedom. Many spectators were hostile, but the old women were the most vengeful. Without protection from their American guards, the prisoners would have been killed. At the height of the furor, the American officer in charge said, "Dear Hessians, we will go to the barracks," and hurried them away. Once they were safe, General Washington issued a proclamation to be posted all over Philadelphia: The Hessians, who had been forced into this war, were blameless and should be treated not as enemies of the American people but as friends.

With that, the fury subsided. A stream of visitors, rich and poor, brought food to the Hessian barracks. A few days later the Hessian privates were marched off to work on Pennsylvania farms in Lancaster County; the officers were sent to Baltimore and then on to Virginia. Before they left, General Israel Putnam shook hands with several officers and insisted they share a glass of Madeira with him. During the ritual, one Hessian inspected Old Put, now in his forty-ninth year, and concluded that he might be an honorable man, but only the Americans would have made him a general.

With his Eton education and his military tutoring from a Prussian officer, Charles, Lord Cornwallis was closer to a Hessian's idea of a proper general. Cornwallis had justified that good opinion during the battle for Long Island the previous August and later at Fort Washington. When William Howe decided to put his army into winter quarters, he had given Cornwallis permission to return to England, where his wife was ailing. From the way Washington was fleeing through New Jersey, it looked as though the war might soon be over. If there was another campaign in the spring, Cornwallis could return for it. Then, suddenly, with the attack on Trenton Howe had to question his optimism. He canceled Cornwallis' leave just as he was about to sail, and on New Year's Day 1777 Cornwallis rode fifty miles through the rain in one day to arrive at Princeton after dark. He worked throughout the night to prepare his men to march against Washington's troops. At daybreak on January 2, Cornwallis left one brigade behind in Princeton and led seven thousand men down the main road to Trenton.

The Hessians in the British column were determined to make the Americans pay for their victory over Colonel Rall. Their commander went through the ranks telling the Germans that any man who took a prisoner would receive fifty stripes of the lash. They understood him. They were to kill any American who surrendered. When the British reached Trenton, near sunset, Cornwallis found George Washington in a worse predicament than he could have hoped. Washington's inexperience, coupled with his pride in the fluke he had brought off a week ago, had left his army with its back to the Delaware. But this time no boat could cross. The river was frozen, and yet not frozen solid enough to march men across it. From the outskirts of Trenton, Henry Knox's artillery was lobbing shells into the town, but that was merely to annoy the British upon their arrival. All that separated Cornwallis' men from the Americans was Assunpink Creek, and the Hessians escaping from the earlier battle had proved that it was possible to ford it.

From the British camp, Lord Cornwallis sent invitations to the ranking officers back at Princeton and at Maidenhead, off the Trenton road, to join him the next day and celebrate his victory over the Continental Army. An officer on his staff, Sir William Erskine, recommended not waiting until daylight but attacking across the Assunpink this same night.

"My lord," Erskine warned, "if Washington is the general I take him to be and you trust these people tonight, you will see nothing of them in the morning."

But the terrain was unfamiliar, and Cornwallis knew that his men were almost as tired as their commander. "Nonsense, my dear fellow," he said. "We've got the old fox safe now. We'll go over and bag him in the morning. The damned rebels are cornered at last!"

Erskine and the ranking Hessian colonel urged Cornwallis at least to send a patrol to the creek to keep watch over the American flank facing away from Trenton. Cornwallis didn't think that was necessary.

Cornwallis had not learned the lesson of Brooklyn Heights. Washington kept his campfires burning throughout the night while he led his men stealthily along an unobserved stretch of land well east of Trenton. Washington was going to confound every conventional expectation by not retreating but going on the offensive instead. His target was British supplies where they were now poorly defended, at Princeton. The weather relented and became Washington's ally. A thaw that day had threatened to leave the roads a mire of mud, but the night brought a freeze. The Quaker Road hardened, and Washington took his men and cannon, their wheels muffled with rags, north to Princeton.

At dawn, a cold sun revealed the branches of an orchard near the town. The trees were glistening with hoarfrost, and behind them were British scouts. As the Americans drew closer, the British opened fire. An early shot hit General Hugh Mercer as he was shouting for his men to retreat. When the Americans scattered, British soldiers ran after them and stabbed to death men who were trying to surrender. Mercer was wearing an overcoat that concealed his rank, and the British troops were sure they had captured George Washington. They jeered at Mercer, calling him a rebel and demanding he give up. Instead, he struck out with his sword. They overpowered him and stabbed him with their bayonets, seven times to the body, twice to the head. Mercer, mortally wounded, lay absolutely still. He heard one of his assailants say, "Damn him, he is dead. Let us leave him." But Mercer guessed from shouts in the far distance that the battle had turned. He died a few days later.

When Washington saw Mercer's men running away from the British, he galloped to the very front of his own ranks and cried out to the men to hold their ground. The new militia from Pennsylvania seemed to waver, but the Continental Army veterans from New England didn't break. With that shield, Washington could retrieve some of Mercer's soldiers and point them back to battle. Riding a white horse, he led the troops as they moved up a hill toward the British line. When they were within thirty yards, he called, "Halt!" and then "Fire!" Washington was so near the enemy guns that Colonel John Fitzgerald at his side pulled his hat down over his eyes so that he wouldn't see the general fall. The Americans fired, and the British began dropping back. As the smoke cleared, Fitzgerald looked to Washington's position. The general still sat unharmed on his white mount.

Fitzgerald broke into tears of relief and called to him, "Thank God, Your Excellency is safe!"

"Bring up your troops, my dear Colonel," Washington answered him. "The day is our own."

The victory was as sweet as it had been unorthodox. Writing to his wife, Henry Knox told of Washington's two daring strokes in language a civilian could understand: "The enemy were within nineteen miles of Philadelphia; they are now sixty miles. We have driven them almost the whole of West Jersey." Washington intended to march from Princeton to Brunswick, where General Howe maintained another supply depot and a reported seventy thousand pounds in cash. But his men were too fatigued to make the seventeen-mile march. At the first halt, soldiers dropped to the ground and refused to move. Washington instead took them north to an easily defended site in the hills near Morristown. A solar eclipse had been forecast, and Washington issued a warning so that his troops wouldn't become frightened when the sun vanished from the sky.

William Howe's army was only twenty-five miles away. But Howe himself, snug in New York with Elizabeth Loring, was done with fighting for the winter.

The hour's battle at Princeton had stirred Washington's blood. He had felt for a moment that he was back on the plantations of Virginia, and when the British began to run he had stood in his stirrups and shouted, "A fine fox chase, my boys!" Both he and Cornwallis had likened the struggle to a gentlemen's hunt, but the world quickly understood who had been run to earth.

General Howe wrote home to Lord George Germain, the secretary for America, that he couldn't see a way to end the war except with a major offensive. His previous tactic of attrition, accompanied by a campaign to win over the people of the conquered territories, was not working. Receiving news of the two American victories, Lord Germain thought he knew a better way to end the war. The Howe brothers had been soft on the rebels, he said. From now on, the Americans must feel the horror of warfare until "through a lively experience of loss and sufferings, they may be brought as soon as possible to a proper sense of their duty."

Before these last battles, America had respected George Washington because of the title that Congress had bestowed upon him. A few rival generals might have questioned his skill, but his men had responded to his imposing calm and a courage verging on recklessness. With these successes came a new reputation for the Continental Army, and for its commander. The troops noticed that the same residents of New Jersey who had been sullen and skeptical only a few weeks ago were cheering now as they marched through the countryside, and more civilians were coming forward to take up arms. As for George Washington, the new nation was ready to elevate him to the realm of folklore and myth. According to a letter in the *Pennsylvania Journal*, "If there are spots in his character, they are like spots in the sun, only discernible by the magnifying powers of a telescope. Had he lived in the days of idolatry, he would have been worshipped as a God."

Washington did not become intoxicated by the legends rising around him. When affairs had gone badly, he had let his friends and family know the degree to which others were to blame for each disaster. Even in victory he complained to Martha Washington's son, Jack Custis, about the "mixed, motley crew" of undependable men he had to rely upon as soldiers. After two battles already being hailed as classics in the history of warfare, Washington was telling his stepson, "In a word, I believe I may with truth add that I do not think any officer since the creation ever had such a variety of difficulties and perplexities to encounter as I have." He knew exactly how much of his recent success had been due to German sloth and British overconfidence, to turns in the weather, to luck or, as he preferred, to Providence.

Washington's mother in Fredericksburg agreed that George was receiving too much credit. When neighbors came to congratulate her on the outcome in New Jersey and to read aloud newspaper accounts of her son's genius, Mary Washington dismissed the reports as far too flattering. But she could assure her listeners that the American commander could withstand the excessive praise. "George," said his mother, "will not forget the lessons I have taught him."

Gates
1777

THOMAS JEFFERSON's behavior since he drafted the Declaration of Independence had exasperated even his closest allies. When the Congress asked him to go to France with Benjamin Franklin to urge the Comte de Vergennes to aid the beleaguered American Army, he refused. His colleagues accused him of preferring his comfortable life in Virginia to the hardships of serving his country. Jefferson tried to hint at his reasons for abandoning politics, but his explanation was couched so obliquely that he only angered the other delegates even more.

The month after the Declaration was approved, Jefferson had been worried about his wife's health. Martha Jefferson was apparently pregnant, and, given her history of childbearing, her husband knew she was going through a painful and dangerous time. But since he hadn't told his fellow representatives about his wife's distress, they were impatient when he resigned his seat in the Congress to be with her. That time the immediate crisis had subsided; Martha Jefferson seems to have suffered a miscarriage. By the time Jefferson was asked to travel to Paris in the fall of 1776, she was pregnant again. Jefferson thought that taking her with him on a rough ocean crossing was as unthinkable as spending months abroad without her. He tried then to make his reasons for refusing the assignment clearer. He wrote to Hancock, as president of the Congress, that "circumstances very peculiar in the situation of my family" dictated his refusal. But other delegates faced domestic crises and resented the implication that Jefferson's problems were more pressing. Richard Henry Lee, who was also concerned about an ailing wife, wrote to remind Jefferson that if everyone put his personal concerns above his country, the result would be slavery.

Not long after Jefferson had left the Congress, John Adams accepted another term. Following a brief respite in Braintree, he returned to his duty, leaving Abigail Adams pregnant for the sixth time. Adams, in lamenting Jefferson's absence, had expressed his own priorities when he wrote that their country was not yet secure enough "to excuse your retreat to the delights of domestic life."

The delegates were even more frustrated by Jefferson's refusal to go to France because his knowledge of French and his tact would have made him an admirable companion for Dr. Franklin. As for Franklin, he seemed to be taking the arduous new challenge in stride. He told Benjamin Rush, "I am old and good for nothing, but as storekeepers say of their remnants of cloth, I am but a fag end, and you may have me for what you are pleased to give."

When Jefferson remained adamant, the Congress asked Richard Henry Lee's brother Arthur, who was in London, to join Franklin in France. The third member of the delegation was Silas Deane, a former delegate to the Congress from Connecticut who had gone to Paris the previous March posing as a private merchant. Deane, thirty-eight, the son of a blacksmith, was a graduate of Yale, a successful merchant and an odd choice for any enterprise that required subtle judgment. He also had reasons to beg off from the assignment: his wife had been too frail to join him even in Philadelphia. In his role as a trader, Deane was authorized to buy goods from Frenchmen who sided with America. For that he would receive a five percent commission. No one in the Congress seemed troubled that Deane's profit-making activities might conflict with his duties as a secret agent.

Deane was still a novice at diplomacy, having been America's sole representative in France for only the last six months of 1776. He took his orders from the Committee of Secret Correspondence, which tried to lessen his distractions by forbidding him to sightsee around Paris "as so many foreigners are tempted to do." He also changed his lodgings often, partly because England had spies everywhere but also because the Congress was slow in forwarding his funds. Deane was not likely to be seduced by the Parisian salons; his wife had reproached him for being so indifferent to Philadelphia society that he had been unable to describe the latest fashions to her. And Deane was faring badly in other ways. Behind his back, Pierre-Augustin Caron de Beaumarchais called him the most silent man in Paris—he wouldn't open his mouth in front of Englishmen for fear of revealing his mission and he couldn't speak six consecutive words in French.

Even before Achard de Bonvouloir's mission to Philadelphia on behalf of the French court, Beaumarchais had taken up America's cause ebulliently. By the age of forty-three he had held many posts at King Louis's court, from royal watchmaker to music teacher for the king's daughters. He had married a rich, older widow and with her money bought himself the title of secretary to the king. It carried no duties but included a title of nobility. Beaumarchais could also pay his own way by writing successful plays, among them *Le Barbier de Séville* and *Le Mariage de Figaro*. When Vergennes wanted to support the American rebellion against Britain, he had turned to Beaumarchais. The playwright was authorized to set up a private company that could supply America with arms and material. Vergennes launched the firm—Roderigue, Hortalez et Compagnie— with a secret grant of a million French livres and persuaded the Spanish court to contribute the same.

Beaumarchais had met with Arthur Lee in London long before Silas Deane arrived in Paris. Lee assumed that the arms were a gift to America, and that was how he passed along the news to the Congress. But Vergennes had viewed the matter differently and told Beaumarchais that while there was no point in badgering the Americans for money, since they had none, he could ask the colonies for payment in products they manufactured. Beaumarchais asked the Committee of Secret Correspondence to send his company ten or twelve thousand hogsheads of the best American tobacco in return for his shipments of arms. Even after America began receiving the

French weapons, the committee neither replied nor sent the tobacco, and Arthur Lee continued to assure the Congress that no payment was expected. For months, Beaumarchais went on trusting to American integrity for his tobacco. The silence, he said, "is depressing, but depression is a long way from discouragement."

Silas Deane had been told very little about those tangled negotiations, but he soon found himself enmired in the affairs of Roderique, Hortalez and was authorizing the purchase of brass cannon and clothing for thousands of men. Still the French would not provoke London. When George Washington had been driven off Long Island, the British ambassador to France had sent a jubilant message to Vergennes, who had replied that he was deeply touched to be permitted to share the British joy over the American defeat. But Washington's early losses only made Vergennes more determined to speed supplies to America through the secret pipeline. For Beaumarchais, the adventure had become theater. "Unless a pistol stops me," he vowed, "those who stand in my way will find their match."

To mislead British spies, Benjamin Franklin hired a coach and rode off from Philadelphia as though he were going on a picnic. On the Delaware he boarded an American ship, the *Reprisal*. He took with him two grandchildren, William Temple Franklin, sixteen years old, and Benjamin Franklin Bache, seven. William's father, the governor of New Jersey, was now under house arrest there for his loyalty to the king. Benjamin Franklin hoped to brighten the boy's future by taking him to France as his clerk.

British agents in Paris tried to play down the sensation that Franklin's trip was provoking. When he arrived, they spread rumors that he knew the Revolution was lost, had turned his Continental paper bills into thirty thousand pounds of gold and was appealing to France for asylum. The French police were also watching Franklin. One police agent wrote a sketch of him for the files: "This Quaker wears the full costume of his sect. He has an agreeable physiognomy, spectacles always on his eyes; but little hair—a fur cap is always on his head. He wears no powder, but has a neat air, linen very white and a brown coat."

Lord Stormont, the British ambassador, tried to make a joke of Franklin's rustic fur hat. Franklin retaliated by coining a new French verb, *stormonter*, to lie, and the Parisians took it up over-

night. But there was nothing lighthearted in Stormont's warning
that Britain would consider Vergennes's receiving Franklin at Versailles an unfriendly act, one that could lead their countries into
open war.

The French knew that Stormont had a legion of paid informers and wouldn't be easily deceived about any dealings with the
Americans. Beaumarchais could leave Paris without telling even
his mistress where he was going, yet the British ambassador always
knew. Just before Christmas, 1776, Stormont had recruited his
most illustrious double agent. Dr. Edward Bancroft, who was born
in Springfield, Massachusetts, had known Silas Deane before going
to London to become a medical doctor. Bancroft had written several books, including a novel. An outspoken patriot, he was also
friendly with Benjamin Franklin, who regarded him as sensible and
highly intelligent. From the time Franklin arrived in France, he had
found Silas Deane entirely congenial, and when Dr. Bancroft appeared from London he became one more link between them.
Franklin and Deane hired Bancroft as a private secretary.

One of Franklin's admirers was allowing him to stay free of
charge in the Hôtel Valentinois, a large house with stately gardens
at Passy—one mile from Paris, seven from Versailles. The house became the informal headquarters of the American delegation, and
Bancroft also moved in. It was a period of watchful waiting, and
Franklin was circumspect as he met with French officials to ask for
more assistance than they were ready to give. Vergennes was equally
discreet; he had an aide refuse Franklin in person so that the Americans wouldn't have any written documents proving they had been
negotiating with France.

But Dr. Bancroft was rendering all of those precautions futile.
While professing loyalty to America, he had struck a deal with the
British to pass along everything he could learn about any future
treaty between France and America. His price was a down payment of five hundred pounds and another four hundred pounds
each year.

When Arthur Lee crossed the Channel to Paris and met Bancroft, he immediately distrusted him, but Lee's suspicions were
hard to take seriously. His years of living amid the intrigues of
London and a correspondence with Samuel Adams that fed their
mutual fears had made Arthur Lee moody and contentious. A man
had once observed to him that it was a very cloudy day. "It is a

cloudy day, sir," Lee had replied, "but not *very* cloudy." While in England, Lee had been sure that Benjamin Franklin was undermining the patriots. Now he was convinced that Deane and Beaumarchais were bilking Congress over the secret arms shipments. Lee's distaste for his new colleagues was not one-sided. Beaumarchais called him "the bilious Arthur Lee, with his yellow skin, green eyes, yellow teeth and hair always in disorder."

As it turned out, Lee wasn't suspicious enough. Because the British agents who controlled Bancroft distrusted his blatant greed, they wanted to have a second channel in case the Americans outbid them for his loyalties. As a safeguard, they enlisted John Thornton, Arthur Lee's secretary. British intelligence referred to Benjamin Franklin in its reports as "72" or as "Moses." Franklin claimed to be untroubled by spies and counterspies, and when a woman wrote to warn him not to trust supposed friends, Franklin answered that he was sure he was surrounded by such men, but one rule spared him any concern—he did nothing in private that a spy wasn't welcome to observe. If his valet was a spy, and he probably was, Franklin wouldn't discharge him as long as he gave good service.

The answer showed Franklin at his most disingenuous. He knew that his simplicity was part of his appeal and that his homely fur hat had enhanced his popularity. If the French regarded him as a Quaker, which he was not, let them. They took him for Rousseau's natural man, a brilliant philosopher who had arisen from the savage forests of the New World, a view that meant overlooking the twenty years Franklin had spent in European society. Whenever he ventured out from Passy, he was trailed by a curious but genteel crowd. People paid for places to stand to watch his coach pass, and Parisians hung engravings of him over their mantelpieces.

Franklin received the acclaim with open pleasure. He was sought after for his fame and wit, and although he suffered from gout he accepted invitations to dine every night of the week but Sunday. Franklin's French hostesses often had a sketchy knowledge of his past contributions, but they knew they had been substantial.

Franklin was no classic philosopher—metaphysical reasoning bored him—and the total of his writings on politics and government ran to a few pages. He went to church on occasion because he thought Christianity, while it might be untrue, was indispensable to the kind of society he preferred. His great renown had come as a self-taught scientist. Benjamin Franklin hadn't been the first man to suggest that lightning and electricity were the same force of nature, but he had been the first to offer proof.

Franklin had invited no onlookers for his first experiment in June 1752, because he didn't want witnesses if he failed. His son William, then twenty-two, had helped him raise a silken kite in the rain. Franklin had retreated to watch from a nearby shed while William ran with the kite across a cow pasture. A promising cloud passed with no effect, and father and son were disappointed. Then, at last, loose threads on the wet kite string stiffened and a spark flew off a metal key at the end of the string to William's knuckle.

For five months Franklin pondered the incident. Then he made a diffident announcement in the next edition of his *Poor Richard's Almanack* and also described his invention of the lightning rod. The experiments enhanced his reputation at home and overseas. Harvard College gave him the first honorary degree that had not gone to a member of its own faculty. The Royal Society of London sent its Copley Medal and the king of France his congratulations. Franklin said the honors made him feel like a little girl who holds her head higher because, unknown to anyone else, she is wearing a new pair of silk garters.

Readers on both sides of the ocean cherished Franklin's humor and the wisdom he wrapped in wit. In Braintree, Abigail Adams delivered a stillborn daughter and fought her way out of depression by recalling one of Franklin's most popular maxims: "That saying of Poor Richard often occurs to my mind: God helps them who help themselves."

But Franklin's experiments with the kite had come more than twenty years before this trip to France. He had broken with his son William when William suggested that the Bostonians had been wrong in their tea protest. Franklin had responded to his son's disloyalty by denouncing him: "But you, as a thorough courtier, see everything with government eyes." In France, Franklin was now the courtier, hoping to break through the timidity at Versailles and win the open support that America needed to win the war.

One night Franklin discovered that he was dining at the same inn as Edward Gibbon, whose first volume of *The History of the Decline and Fall of the Roman Empire* had been published the year before. Franklin delivered a note asking for the pleasure of his company. Gibbon replied that, much as he admired Mr. Franklin as a man and as a philosopher, as a loyal subject of his king he could not enter into conversation with a rebel. Franklin wrote again: He retained his high respect for the historian and would supply him with the many documents in his possession when Mr. Gibbon came to write his account of the decline and fall of the British Empire.

John Adams was visiting his cousin in his chambers one day during a recess when Samuel Adams took out a pair of scissors and began to cut up whole bundles of his letters into tiny scraps. Since the weather was mild and there was no fire, Samuel raised the window and threw out the bits for the wind to scatter. By this time, the two men were enough attuned in their politics that John felt he could twit his cousin for being so cautious. Samuel responded with a mild rebuke: "Whatever becomes of me, my friends shall never suffer by my negligence."

John Adams fretted later that his cousin's scruples would prevent history from ever understanding him. But his contemporaries sometimes seemed to know Samuel Adams too well. The depths of his Puritan fervor had been shown in his attempt to ban galas and dances in Philadelphia. When Martha Washington visited Philadelphia, a ball had been arranged in her honor at the City Tavern. After Adams called on her and explained that the Congress officially opposed "vain amusements," Mrs. Washington decided not to attend.

On matters of state, he could be equally inflexible. Men who sought to advance their relatives were reminded that Adams strongly disapproved of favoritism. He had been proud that Samuel Adams, Jr., was making his way as a surgeon in the army without assistance from his father. Adams' own willingness to sacrifice everything for his country had led to a detachment about other men's suffering that could seem unfeeling. Unless a memorial ceremony underscored a political point, Adams rarely paused to mourn. The death of his young friend Joseph Warren was "greatly afflicting," he had written to his wife, but it was man's duty to submit to the will of Heaven.

Although Samuel Adams freely confessed to his ignorance

about military matters, it didn't stop him from promoting the careers of certain generals, usually those whose outspoken patriotism had convinced him of their strategic genius. George Washington was far too composed, too little given to ardent rhetoric, to convince Adams he was trustworthy. With his own influence waning in the Congress and the nation, Adams watched disapprovingly as men began to worship General Washington. Adams considered Washington an imperfect idol. He had married wealth and he craved property. He owned slaves. He was not secure enough in his own righteousness to ignore his public reputation. He enjoyed the theater. He danced. But had the two men ever become intimates, Samuel Adams would have taken away a warmer impression of the commander in chief. Adams was a democrat before he was a Puritan, and he could have found no fault with Washington's belief that though a democratic nation might sometimes move slowly, the people would always be right.

Samuel Adams' ebbing authority in the Congress did not mean he was withdrawing from public life. Looking around the Congress early in 1777, John Adams saw that he and his cousin were among the few left from the first assembly. The rest had died, resigned or, like Patrick Henry and Christopher Gadsden, gone home to become governors or legislators in their state. Samuel Adams made occasional trips to Boston, where he reassured those friends who thought the war was causing a breakdown in society. As always, Adams believed the solution was to instill principles of morality in the young. Uncorrupted men whose love of country was their ruling passion would lead the state to purity and virtue.

In the meantime, the war must be won. By the time the Congress moved back to Philadelphia in March 1777, Adams was actively promoting the fortunes of a middle-aged major general, Horatio Gates.

Gates, the general who had not joined George Washington in his assault on Trenton, was the son of a duke's housekeeper in England. He had volunteered to fight with Braddock in the French and Indian War but had been badly wounded on his first day in battle. When the war ended, Gates had found that his lack of money and connections kept him from advancing in the British Army. He had retired and seemed destined to spend his days drinking and gambling. But his exposure to America had kindled a sympathy with the patriots' cause. In 1772 he wrote to George

Washington, whom he knew from the Braddock campaign, about buying an estate in Virginia. The next year Gates purchased a plantation he called Traveller's Rest. But when the Revolution began, he saw a chance to revive his military career. Stooped and gray, approaching fifty and looking older, he had become a valuable administrative aide to Washington in Cambridge during the first days of organizing the army. Gates was inclined to be cautious at strategy meetings and had recommended against seizing Dorchester Heights. His soldiers watched him move through camp with his spectacles perched low on his nose and called him "Granny Gates."

Samuel Adams detected a toughness in Gates's zeal for the patriot cause and had been impatiently trying, for months, to put him in charge of the Northern Army. The Congress had the power to make the highest appointments, and until the spring of 1777 members had continued to keep Philip Schuyler, the wealthy gentleman from Albany who had served as a delegate from New York at the first session, in charge of the Northern command. At one point, Gates had been sent north to lead the American retreat from the Canadian offensive, but he and Schuyler had wrangled over whose authority was greater, and the Congress had upheld Schuyler. Gates had stayed on to help rebuild an army shattered by defeat and devastated by smallpox. He chose Benedict Arnold to prepare American ships for fighting along Lake Champlain, and together they held off a British assault and held Fort Ticonderoga. While Washington was in his winter quarters, after the campaigns of Trenton and Princeton, Gates commanded the troops in Philadelphia, but when he was sent back to Ticonderoga in March 1777 he resumed his feud with Philip Schuyler. In July, British General John Burgoyne seized a peak named Mount Defiance above Ticonderoga, pointed his cannon down into the fort, and forced the Americans to evacuate without a fight. Schuyler had ignored Gates's repeated warnings about how vulnerable Defiance made Fort Ti. As a result, Congress finally replaced Schuyler with Gates as commander of the Northern Army and set the scene for a showdown between Granny Gates and Gentleman Johnny Burgoyne.

Both Adamses were pleased to see Schuyler removed. Samuel Adams had found his reports weak and contemptible, even though their pessimism was not much different from George Washington's own. John Adams wrote home that the only way to stiffen the army's spine was for the Congress to order that a losing general should be shot.

The year 1777 was proving no more successful for General Washington than for Philip Schuyler. William Howe had waited for reinforcements from Britain and delayed his campaign until September. Then, at Brandywine Creek southwest of Philadelphia, Howe and Washington restaged the battles of New York, with the same result. Washington had split his army in two, one unit under his own command, the other under John Sullivan. Washington again neglected the proper reconnaissance, and again the British, this time led by Cornwallis, marched upstream and almost succeeded in taking Sullivan's men from behind. Washington eluded the trap with some gallant rear-guard action and led an orderly retreat to Chester. Congress asked that John Sullivan be recalled, but Washington was opposed to punishing a general for his defeats and declined to take action. Howe marched at last on Philadelphia, and the Congress met for a day in Lancaster before moving to York, a small farming community across the Susquehanna River.

Howe met little opposition as he rode into Philadelphia on September 26, 1777. He had ignored the arguments against concentrating so much of his army in Pennsylvania, and in London Lord Germain supported him. Britain's colonial secretary believed that the nation's honor would not be redeemed until the British flag flew over Independence Hall. Punishing that seat of the Congress, Germain told Howe, would please the king and discourage the rebels. But as Howe's troops marched into Philadelphia, they were greeted not by despair but by the glee of those loyalists who had stayed behind. John Adams already held a low opinion of the Quakers who had settled in Pennsylvania, and he had expected no better of them now. He wrote to Abigail Adams that Quakers were as dull as beetles, "a kind of neutral tribe, or the race of the insipids." Thomas Paine urged patriots to raise up barricades and fight the British from house to house, but instead they followed the Congress into exile.

General Howe had returned successfully to his past strategy, and George Washington tried to do the same. Borrowing from his own tactics at Trenton, Washington sent out John Sullivan and Nathanael Greene at the head of columns of Continentals and militia, hoping to surprise the British forces north of Philadelphia at Germantown. But Washington also incorporated the worst aspect of his previous plans by depending on intricate coordination. The militia columns never reached the battle site, and although the British were unprepared for the attack, their officers were not recovering from nights of heavy drinking. By 9 A.M. they had formed their lines and routed the challenge. After that, Howe settled his men in Philadelphia, and George Washington looked around Pennsylvania for his own winter quarters.

When Lieutenant General Sir John Burgoyne returned to America from England for the 1777 campaign, he was ready to win a bet he had made the previous Christmas Day at Brooks's Club in London. There he had sworn an even rasher oath than Banastre Tarleton's threat to cut off Charles Lee's head. Burgoyne had gone to England to deal with personal affairs and take his seat in Parliament, but once there he had worked to ingratiate himself with the king, and his success was confirmed when George III took him riding in Hyde Park. During his stay, Burgoyne had also persuaded the Ministry to authorize one conclusive blow to end the war. When he met an opposition leader, Charles Fox, at Brooks's, he predicted, "Within a year I shall return from America victorious." The two men wagered fifty guineas, and the bet was recorded in the club's book.

Burgoyne's plan had sounded plausible in London and, even better, cheap. Throughout 1776, George Germain had become increasingly annoyed by William Howe's requests for more manpower. He bore a grudge against Howe that dated back to a military expedition nearly twenty years earlier, and he was not inclined to oblige him now. When Germain responded to Howe's call for reinforcements, he included every wounded soldier, deserter and prisoner as part of Howe's troop strength. And as a professional soldier, Howe resented having to take orders from George Germain. It was widely known that during the battle of Minden, in 1759, Germain had disregarded repeated orders to bring his cavalry into action. His disobedience smacked of cowardice and might have got him shot. Instead, he was court-martialed and cashiered from the army. Lord North had overlooked his past disgrace when he put Germain in charge of the war in America.

In theory, Britain's master strategy still called for its two armies to join at Albany—one from Montreal, the other from New York. The armies would set up a chain of forts from the St. Lawrence to the Atlantic that would cut off New England from the other colonies. But William Howe seemed content to conserve his men in Philadelphia, and Burgoyne had convinced Germain that he could hold Albany with only Britain's Northern forces while Howe kept George Washington tied down in Pennsylvania. Burgoyne's orders, however, were ambiguously written. He was "to force his way to Albany" and turn his troops over to William Howe. He was given latitude to act on his own "as exigencies may require." Was Germain insisting that Albany be taken at any cost? The imprecision scarcely mattered to Burgoyne. He knew he could take Albany, which would end the rebellion, win his wager with Charles Fox and earn him a place in British history. For John Burgoyne—rumored to be illegitimate, rumored to be a little sharp at cards, known to be socially ambitious and badly in debt—the gamble was irresistible.

Back in America, Burgoyne soon found that hacking his way south from Ticonderoga was harder than he had expected. He suffered eight hundred casualties—a seventh of his army—when his men were attacked at Bennington in the New Hampshire Grants by a troop of American farmers led by General John Stark. Now the British survivors were marching little more than a mile a day. Along their route, Americans whom Burgoyne had expected to be loyalists were proving hostile. And, despite what the Congress might believe, Philip Schuyler's retreat had been a courageous one. His men had scorched the crops and scattered the cattle, which delayed Burgoyne's advance. And yet Horatio Gates did not invite Schuyler to attend his first council of war in Albany. He did include Benedict Arnold, however, even though Arnold was known to be Schuyler's close ally.

Gates's arrival on August 19 had inspired his army. New Englanders had despised Schuyler for opposing them during the contest over the New Hampshire Grants and accused him of every wickedness: Schuyler embezzled funds and had taken a bribe to let the British capture Ticonderoga; the fort, they charged, had been won with silver bullets. Horatio Gates was a warmer man, less the autocratic disciplinarian.

Before Gates took command, the Americans had built their camp on flat land at the mouth of the Mohawk River. He insisted on another site sixteen miles north, on a high plateau above the Hudson. Gates didn't know how thoroughly committed John Burgoyne was to taking Albany, and he speculated about whether the British commander intended to fall back and entrench himself at Ticonderoga. That would be the sensible course, especially since Howe's troops were far away in Philadelphia. But to Burgoyne anything less than charging forward would be ignominious. Even before his easy defeat of Schuyler at Ticonderoga, Burgoyne had offered his troops a one-line summary of his strategy: "This army must not retreat."

The plateau Gates chose had been named Bemis Heights, after a man who kept the tavern on the road below. Gates installed his seven thousand men there and planned to stop Burgoyne on his march to Albany. He enlisted a young and clever Polish engineer, Colonel Thaddeus Kosciuzko, to lay out his defenses. Kosciuzko fortified the position with strong log breastworks and felled trees with their sharpened branches pointing outward.

An American reconnaissance party seized prisoners who told Gates that Burgoyne had severed his communication with Canada and seemed determined to take Albany. Since the town lay on the west bank of the Hudson, Burgoyne was forced to cross the river. He ordered a new bridge built and made his crossing into the village of Saratoga.

By now, Burgoyne's army had been reduced to less than six thousand—twenty-five hundred British and eighteen hundred German regulars; eleven hundred Canadians and Tory recruits; eighty Indians; and three hundred drivers, sailors and artillerymen. The officers' ladies were following in carriages one day's march to the rear. The expedition was exuberant, singing and laughing, eager for the victory at Albany. Burgoyne issued a standing order, however, that guards must be at their posts an hour before daylight and remain there until it was completely dark. His men knew that the enemy was waiting somewhere ahead and began sleeping in their uniforms.

Burgoyne had no way of knowing where the Americans would

attack. He had no dependable information about the size of Gates's force or how solidly the Americans were entrenched. But since the river lay to one side of the road and dense woods to the other, he saw that he would have to fight his way past any American fortress. On September 15, 1777, Burgoyne marched his troops in a magnificent parade, drums rolling and colors high, down the road toward Bemis Heights. Two days later they encamped only four miles from the American lines.

On the morning of September 19, scouts arrived at the cramped red house on Bemis Heights that General Gates had made his headquarters. The British had broken camp, they said, and were moving in three swerving columns, all headed toward a fifteen-acre clearing owned by a farmer named Freeman. At the news that the enemy was marching toward them, General Gates and Benedict Arnold began to quarrel over the proper response. With his usual caution, Gates hoped Burgoyne would try to dislodge the Americans from their impregnable stronghold. Spies confirmed that the British had crossed the Hudson with supplies for only one month and would soon collapse from their shortages. Benedict Arnold favored an aggressive response: Go out immediately and attack Burgoyne rather than wait passively for the British to haul up their large and punishing cannon and begin bombarding the fort.

Despite their differences, Gates had remained friendly with Arnold and had once saved him from a court-martial conviction provoked by his temper. But Gates resented the way Arnold was filling his staff with allies of Philip Schuyler, and he remembered that in a defensive action against the British on Lake Champlain, Arnold had disregarded his orders and engaged the enemy rashly. General Gates had faith in his troops so long as he kept them massed behind barricades; he wasn't sure how well they would fight in exposed lines down at Freeman's Farm. But Arnold kept pressing him, and Gates sent out units of riflemen and light infantry into the thick woods to keep the British from getting behind the American position.

It was past noon when riflemen wearing coonskin caps and led by Dan Morgan of Virginia reached Freeman's clearing. Morgan's men struck at a British advance guard and sent them running into the woods. Burgoyne set up battle lines in the pasture and easily repelled the Americans, who scattered during the retreat but regrouped when Morgan signaled with a turkey call, the pipe that hunters used to lure game.

Horatio Gates believed that a commander's place was at headquarters, where he could survey an entire operation and coordinate his instructions. Arnold stood at his side as Gates received couriers from the scene who reported troop movements that went back and forth. The engagement seemed headed for a stalemate. As the hours wore on, Benedict Arnold fed more men from his division into the battle—the Connecticut militia, three New Hampshire regiments, New Yorkers, the Massachusetts line. Gates told him that sending any more troops could jeopardize the post itself and insisted that Arnold remain at the headquarters. But when one messenger reported that the action had turned in the Americans' favor, Benedict Arnold rushed to his horse and shouted, "By God, I will soon put an end to it!"

Gates sent an aide to order him back to camp. Arnold obeyed, but in a furious temper. He was angrier still when sunset fell and the British still held on Freeman's Farm, where the fighting had begun. John Burgoyne was claiming that by holding the clearing he had won the day's victory, but his men knew otherwise. To those who had never fought the Americans before, the rebels had been astonishing. Burgoyne had ridiculed them after Ticonderoga, but on this day the Americans had held their ranks and fought for hours under a hot sun. Burgoyne had suffered two casualties for every American loss. He had lost a third of his forces in a single day and was hardly a step closer to Albany. That first night his men slept on the battlefield, and the next day they buried their dead. Some of the burial parties dug deep, others were slipshod in preparing the common graves and left arms and legs, even heads, above ground. In death, the one distinction accorded a British officer was being jammed into a hole by himself.

Over the next days, the enemy armies rested only two miles apart. Each night, Gates sent out raiding parties to harass the British and disturb their sleep. During the day, American sharpshooters climbed trees and sniped at any British soldier who came into view. Three days after the battle, as Congress was evacuating Philadelphia, General Gates wrote out an account of his contest on September 19. Even though Benedict Arnold's strategy and his troops had carried the day, Gates made no mention of Arnold in his dispatch. He wrote that the honors belonged instead entirely to Colonel Morgan, whose men had once been under Arnold's command but had been transferred lately to Gates's own.

When Arnold heard of the omission, he burst into Gates's headquarters and accused his commander of being jealous of his military talents. Gates would not back down. He told Arnold peremptorily to get rid of any aide who had remained loyal to Schuyler and who was hostile to Gates.

At that, Arnold demanded a pass that would let him join General Washington in Pennsylvania. Gates said he would be pleased to give him one but reminded Arnold that he had already resigned his commission the previous July in an earlier dispute with the Congress over seniority. When George Washington recommended him for the Northern Army, Arnold had tried to suspend that resignation, but his status was not clear. Very possibly, Gates suggested, Arnold no longer held the rank of major general at all. In any event, he would soon be relieved of command of the army's left wing, because Major General Benjamin Lincoln was arriving and his commission was dated earlier than Arnold's. Benedict Arnold stormed away and poured out his complaints to aides, who passed along their version to Philip Schuyler in Albany.

Back in his tent, Arnold hashed over his grievances in a letter to Gates that was half bluster and half a plea for reconciliation. But again he requested a pass. When Gates replied that he had never meant to be insulting, he also reminded Arnold of his threat to resign by enclosing a common pass that would let him go to Philadelphia. It was a pointed gesture. Most of Arnold's colleagues were sure that Burgoyne was growing weaker every day and that glory awaited the soldiers who defeated him. Benedict Arnold lingered at the camp with his pass in his pocket. Fellow officers circulated a petition entreating him to stay; the only men who refused to sign were those afraid of offending General Gates. With the quarrel now public, Gates looked for a new way to assert himself. On September 26, a civilian arrived at the camp seeking payment of a small bill Arnold had authorized months earlier when he was acting for General Schuyler. Gates refused payment and let Arnold understand that his authority didn't extend even to signing for fifty dollars.

On October 1, 1777, eight days after their quarrel, Arnold wrote again to Gates, repeating that he had been badly treated and not sufficiently consulted. He couldn't resist appealing to Gates once more to launch an immediate offensive. If they sat idly for another two weeks, Arnold was sure the Americans would lose four thousand men to sickness and desertion. That would also give Burgoyne time either to reinforce his position heavily or to stage a successful retreat. "I hope you will not impute this hint to a wish to command the army, or to outshine you," Arnold concluded, "when I assure you it proceeds from my zeal for the cause of my country, in which I expect to rise or fall."

Gates read John Burgoyne and his intentions differently. Burgoyne could not stay where he was. With his men already on half rations, it was his troops, not the Americans, who were suffering from disease and desertion. Sir Henry Clinton was reportedly pushing up from New York with reinforcements, but Burgoyne probably couldn't hold out long enough for them to reach Albany. As Arnold kept warning, it was certainly possible that Burgoyne would admit failure and retreat to Ticonderoga. But Gates doubted it. "He is an old gambler," he said. "Despair may dictate to him to risk all upon one throw."

General Gates would do what came naturally to him: wait behind his barricades and let John Burgoyne take up the dice.

Saratoga

AT 11 A.M. on Tuesday, October 7, 1777, General Burgoyne disregarded the advice of his generals and led out a reconnaissance force of fifteen hundred of his best men. He wanted to locate the position of the American line in the woods around Freeman's Farm. If the Americans looked vulnerable on their left, Burgoyne intended to return the next day with the rest of his men—the forty-

General Burgoyne
surrenders at Saratoga,
October 17, 1777

1777

five hundred he had left in camp. The British could then run
roughshod over the Americans and break free for Albany. As his
soldiers moved through a field of uncut wheat, Burgoyne climbed
onto a cabin roof for a better look at Gates's defenses. With the
British position so badly exposed, he couldn't advance farther.
While his officers continued to estimate the placement of the Amer-

ican left flank, some British soldiers ventured out to cut down wheat for bread. The rest formed double ranks in the field and sat down to await instructions.

On Bemis Heights, General Gates had been watching the activity through spyglasses. When a scout returned to headquarters, Gates asked him to describe the terrain and give his opinion about launching an attack. The British front was entirely open, the scout said. One flank bordered the woods and might be attacked from among the trees. On the right they were hemmed in by a high slope. Since the British seemed to be offering themselves so obligingly, the scout concluded, "I would indulge them."

With those odds, even Gates was willing to risk sending men outside his fortress. "Well, then," he said, "order Morgan to begin the game."

General Burgoyne's reconnaissance party had been lingering in the open field for an hour and a half when the Americans struck in three simultaneous assaults—right, left and straight ahead. Daniel Morgan had taken his hunters through the wooded rise on the British right and from there poured down torrents of fire. Gates's first instinct was to send only Morgan's riflemen, and he brushed away Benedict Arnold when he argued for a larger force: "General Arnold, I have nothing for you to do. You have no business here."

But General Lincoln persuaded Gates to send at least three regiments. In the end, he committed troops lavishly, holding back fewer than one thousand men to secure his base. When the battle was at its height, the Americans outnumbered the British and German soldiers six to one. Each of Burgoyne's men was determined to save only himself, and the entire British left wing charged into the brush.

For an hour, Benedict Arnold sat on a bay charger, seething that the assault was going forward without him. When he finally could stand it no longer, he spurred his horse toward the sound of gunfire. He knew Gates would again send an aide to order him back, but Arnold outrode him. At about 4 P.M. he arrived at the scene and spotted a British brigadier general, Simon Fraser, attempting to round up his men and lead them back to fight. Arnold pointed him out to Dan Morgan, who nodded and rode to a group of his riflemen. "That gallant officer is General Fraser," Morgan told them. "I admire him, but it is necessary that he should die. Do your duty."

Tim Murphy was renowned from his days as an Indian fighter, and he climbed a tree and took aim. His first shot cut the crupper of Fraser's horse, a second grazed its mane behind the ears. Fraser's men were calling to him to fall back out of range when a third bullet struck his heart. Two men led him back to his tent, still slumped over his horse. General Fraser asked a surgeon who was dressing his wounds, "Must I die?" The young doctor said yes, he would not live another day.

Fraser was taken to the house of a Hessian general's wife, who had been expecting him as a guest at dinner. Amid his dying groans, she heard Fraser call for his wife and then cry out, "Poor General Burgoyne! Oh, fatal ambition!"

As Fraser lay dying, Benedict Arnold was galloping across the lines so boldly that the troops were sure he was drunk. He made one wild thrust with his sword and struck an American infantry captain. The captain raised his musket and was going to demand an apology, but Arnold was already far across the field, charging into battle with a different company. With his former troops from Connecticut shouting encouragement, Arnold seemed to be dashing everywhere with commands for everyone. He dared one unit to overwhelm a Hessian redoubt, which was easily accomplished because the Germans hated their autocratic commander and shot him dead during the attack. Then a wounded German soldier on the ground raised his rifle and shot Arnold's charger as it was riding down on him. The horse stumbled and rolled over, and Arnold's leg was broken again, as it had been at Quebec. An American was about to strike the German with his bayonet, but Benedict Arnold stopped him. "Don't hurt him! He is a fine fellow! He only did his duty!"

A surgeon looked at Arnold's leg and said it might have to be amputated. "Damned nonsense," said Arnold. If that was all the doctors could do for him, they should hoist him back on another horse so that he could watch the battle end. As dusk fell on the field, Arnold was carried back to headquarters on a litter.

Horatio Gates sent down orders that overnight the Americans were to hold the ground they had taken. In the morning, during brisk exchanges of gunfire, Gates moved out enough men to keep the British trapped with the Hudson River at their backs. Burgoyne's decisive battle had come and gone the day before he had expected it. At sunset, as quiet in defeat as George Washington, Burgoyne buried Simon Fraser, struck the British tents, left his campfires burning and slipped north on the road away from Albany. He abandoned his field hospital and three hundred wounded men. By withdrawing in two stages, he came to rest in the hills above Saratoga. Burgoyne could have sunk his baggage and cannon and led a forced march to safety on Lake George. Instead, he gambled on digging in and waiting for an attack in which he would have the advantage of defending a raised position.

But General Gates was also content to wait. If Henry Clinton was coming up from New York, Gates didn't want to leave the American rear undefended. Burgoyne seemed to have lost half his men in the last engagement and had limited rations for the survivors. Gates dispatched artillery and marksmen to annoy the British but went on postponing a battle that was beginning to seem avoidable. By October 14, Burgoyne's army was surrounded, and he had provisions for only the next twenty-four hours. Oxen and horses had already died of starvation. The air over Saratoga was thick with the stench of their carcasses. By now it was too late even to jettison the artillery and break for Lake George.

Burgoyne convened his generals and put the question to them: Did national dignity and military honor ever justify an army of thirty-five hundred fighting men, who were well provided with artillery, in capitulating? His generals, British and German alike, agreed to offer their lives once more if Burgoyne saw an opportunity to attack. But if such a sacrifice would lead to nothing, it was wiser to conserve Britain's manpower and capitulate on honorable terms.

When the council adjourned, a British soldier carrying a flag of truce stepped from the tall pines along the American lines. He had come to say that Lieutenant General Burgoyne wanted to send a field officer to meet with Major General Gates "on a matter of high moment to both armies." What time tomorrow morning would the general be available? Gates pondered his response into the evening. Then he sent word that his aide would receive the British emissary at the American advance post the next morning at ten.

When the hour arrived, James Wilkinson went to Fishkill Creek, where he blindfolded the British officer and led him back to a room in Gates's headquarters. General Burgoyne, knowing that his letter would be read critically by George Germain in London, wrote that he had been determined to wage a third battle. Only the Americans' superior numbers and his own humanity were leading him to propose a cessation of fighting while terms could be established.

Colonel Wilkinson was surprised when General Gates fished in his pocket and took out terms he had already prepared. His note was short and brutal: "General Burgoyne's army being exceedingly reduced by repeated defeats, by desertion, sickness, etc., their provisions exhausted, their military horses, tents and baggage taken or destroyed, their retreat cut off, and their camp invested, they can only be allowed to surrender as prisoners of war."

Both sides agreed to an armistice until sunset while General Burgoyne and his council considered the demand for unconditional surrender. The British reply came with a flourish: "Lt. General Burgoyne's army, however reduced, will never admit that their retreat is cut off while they have arms in their hands."

Burgoyne was demanding that his defeated troops be allowed to surrender with full honors of war.

The next morning, Gates agreed to generous terms and spelled out the hour they should go into effect—3 P.M. that same day for the capitulation, 5 P.M. for the laying down of arms. The American generosity and haste made Burgoyne suspicious. Did Gates have better information than his own about Henry Clinton's progress to Albany? To delay the surrender, Burgoyne added new requirements: His men must be allowed to march out with their weapons and must be permitted to return to England; they would promise only that they would not come back to America to fight.

Again, Gates quickly agreed.

Burgoyne now demanded that the word "capitulation" in the surrender document be changed to a more neutral term.

Gates agreed.

Further stalling seemed impossible. On behalf of the British, a captain named Craig signed a letter accepting the terms. It was now 11 P.M. on Wednesday, October 15.

During the night, a British spy slipped into Burgoyne's camp to report that Henry Clinton's troops had reached the town of Esopus, which meant that even as Burgoyne was surrendering, his reinforcements might have entered Albany. The general reconvened his officers and put three new questions to them: Could they honorably break their treaty? Was the news of Clinton's approach reliable enough to justify sacrificing the advantageous terms they had negotiated? Was the army prepared to fight to the last man?

By a vote of fourteen to eight, Burgoyne's council advised him that he could not renege on the treaty and that even if the information about Esopus was accurate, the reserves might still be too far from Saratoga to save them. Two thirds of the officers also said they doubted that their troops, if forced into another battle, would fight with much spirit. Burgoyne couldn't accept that answer, and he went on inventing impediments to the signing. He informed Gates that he had heard that the Americans had broken the armistice by sending troops toward Albany, which meant he would be surrendering to a smaller army than the one that defeated him. He insisted that two British officers review the American ranks to determine whether the report was true.

Whether the rumor was correct hardly mattered to Burgoyne, but there was truth to it. A group of New York militia, whose term had expired, had packed their kit without Gates's permission and were headed home. By now, General Gates also knew that Clinton had taken Esopus and set fire to it. He wanted Burgoyne's surrender at once and sent Colonel Wilkinson to reject the latest demand about inspecting American troops. If the treaty was not signed at once, Wilkinson was to break off all further negotiation. But Burgoyne went on delaying, and Wilkinson was heading back to the American lines when a British officer overtook him and asked that he wait a little longer. General Burgoyne would deliver his final answer within two hours.

Wilkinson had waited those two hours and fifteen minutes more when he recognized a British lieutenant colonel named Sutherland across the creek and beckoned him over.

"Well," Sutherland said as he drew nearer, "our business will be knocked on the head after all."

Wilkinson asked why.

"The officers have got the devil in their heads and could not agree."

Wilkinson tried to act cheerful about the prospect of more fighting. Early in the negotiations, Colonel Sutherland had asked, as a favor, that he be allowed to keep a firing device he had owned for thirty-five years. "I am sorry for it," Wilkinson said now, "as you will not only lose your fusee but your whole baggage."

Sutherland was clearly downcast about John Burgoyne going back on his word, but he said there was nothing he could do about it. As they stood commiserating, Wilkinson remembered the letter that Captain Craig had signed the night before. He pulled it from his pocket and read it aloud to Sutherland.

Sutherland hadn't known about Craig's letter, but he understood that it pledged the British in writing to accept the surrender treaty. If the other officers could see Craig's signature, they would agree with him that Burgoyne must honor his commitment. Sutherland asked Wilkinson anxiously, "Will you give me that letter?"

Wilkinson said no, he would keep it as a demonstration of how much the good faith of a British commander was worth.

Sutherland grew excited. "Spare me that letter, sir, and I pledge you my honor I will return it in fifteen minutes."

Wilkinson knew what Sutherland hoped to accomplish and handed him Craig's letter. Sutherland ran the entire way to the British camp. As Wilkinson waited, a messenger from General Gates arrived with instructions to break off the negotiations if the treaty was not already ratified. Now it became Wilkinson's turn to stall. He sent back a message to his commander that he was doing his best and would see him within half an hour.

As he had promised, Colonel Sutherland came bounding back, bringing Captain Craig with him. Craig handed Wilkinson the treaty, signed by John Burgoyne.

Horatio Gates's first act after winning one of history's great military victories was to send quantities of meat across Fishkill Creek to feed his starving enemies. The next morning, General Burgoyne called his officers together for the last time. Although he was almost too overcome to speak, he justified the decision he had made and left them to judge its wisdom.

At 10 A.M. the British troops paraded out with drums beating and the full honors of war, as Burgoyne had insisted. But the inspiring marches sounded shamefaced, and men fought their tears. James Wilkinson was escorting Burgoyne to Horatio Gates, and as they reached the Fishkill Burgoyne looked down doubtfully and asked whether the creek could be forded.

Certainly, sir, Wilkinson replied. Don't you see the people on the opposite shore?

"Yes," Burgoyne said, with resignation. "I have seen them too long."

Accompanied by his adjutants and aides, Burgoyne crossed the creek and rode through the meadow to the front of the American camp, where General Gates was waiting for him. Burgoyne had not changed his clothes for more than two weeks before the armistice, even after bullets had torn his hat and waistcoat. But for today's ceremony he had put on his richest scarlet uniform. Horatio Gates wore a plain blue coat. When Wilkinson introduced the two generals, John Burgoyne raised his hat gracefully.

"The fortunes of war, General," he said, "have made me your prisoner."

Returning the courtly salute, Gates seemed to have prepared his remarks for the occasion. He said without hesitation, "I shall always be ready to bear testimony that it has not been through any fault of Your Excellency."

At that, one of Burgoyne's generals came forward. He had served with Gates in the British Army, and the two men saluted and shook hands warmly. The commanders then withdrew to Gates's hut on the front lines. During the negotiations, there had been nothing but a mattress in one corner, but now the Americans had made a table by laying bare planks across empty barrels. There were only four plates, but there was plenty of roast beef, and two glasses for the opposing generals to offer toasts in rum and water. Burgoyne raised his glass to George Washington, Gates to the British king. Quips and joking soon began among the other officers, and within minutes the entire party was laughing hilariously with exhaustion and relief. Philip Schuyler, who had ridden up from Albany for the occasion, escorted the wife of the ranking German general to a separate meal of smoked tongue and beefsteak. He explained that it might be embarrassing for her to dine with so many gentlemen.

One British artillery major was unsettled by the contrast between the carnage of the past weeks and the merriment today, and he turned to an American captain at his side to share his musing. Here they were, the best of friends, and only a fortnight ago they had been enemies trying to kill each other. It was, the major reflected, an odd old world.

General Gates had put his underlings in charge of taking the weapons of the British and German soldiers. That humiliation occurred in a meadow north of the creek, out of sight of the American soldiers. When the vanquished men had stacked their arms, they crossed the creek for their ritual march between the American ranks. The Americans were intensely curious about the British prisoners, who included the finest of Britain's fighting aristocracy. Besides Burgoyne, some dozen members of Parliament, English lords and Scottish knights had been taken, and, accompanying them, many of their ladies. In all, General Gates's Northern Army had captured seven generals and three hundred other officers, plus 3,379 British soldiers and 2,412 Germans. At Saratoga, John Burgoyne had lost everything, including 1,429 men either killed or wounded.

The defeated men marched with pets they had adopted during the long campaign—young foxes, a raccoon, a deer, even a bear. Among the camp followers at the rear came the three hundred women who had been entertaining the troops between engagements.

The British prisoners were impressed by the absolute stillness of their conquerors. The Americans said nothing and weren't leaning over to murmur to their neighbors. Certainly there were no jeers or gloating. When an American regimental band struck up a triumphant "Yankee Doodle," it was the one discordant note of a day almost religiously solemn.

After the last British troops reached General Gates's hut, Gates emerged with General Burgoyne. A new American flag of Grand Union had been pieced together from military coats and run up a pole. In view of both armies, John Burgoyne surrendered his ivory-handled sword to Horatio Gates, who took it with a courteous nod and instantly handed it back to him.

As the British captives were marched down the road to Albany, Burgoyne felt as though every American on the continent had turned out to witness his disgrace. From a doorway, one brazen Dutch woman shouted the crushing epitaph for his twenty-eight months in America. Above the crowd she kept crying, "Make elbow room for General Burgoyne!"

Valley Forge

HORATIO GATES may have been gracious and considerate to John Burgoyne, but he didn't extend the same courtesy to his own commander in chief. Gates announced his victory at Saratoga directly to the Congress at York and left George Washington to hear the news in a note from Israel Putnam. Washington rose above any annoyance and staged a fitting celebration for his cold and hungry men. They fired a thirteen-gun salute and listened to their chap-

George Washington
at Valley Forge

1777-78

lains praise the American triumph. But General Washington was aware of the contrast between Gates's fortunes and his own. After another small skirmish between Washington and Howe in Pennsylvania at White Marsh, the British general had returned to his winter of ease, while Washington was still shifting camp from place to place, looking for a site to house his men before a winter freeze overtook them.

General Gates had sent James Wilkinson to convey his message to the Congress, but along the way the colonel stopped off to spend some time with his sweetheart. When he finally got to York, the members had already known of Burgoyne's surrender for twelve days, and Samuel Adams made a motion that the Congress reward Colonel Wilkinson with a pair of spurs. But the delegates were euphoric about the American victory and named Wilkinson a brigadier general, jumping him ahead of colonels with greater battlefield experience.

The members couldn't know, as they bestowed that honor, that Wilkinson had made a blunder during his leisurely trip south that would convulse the American high command. Stopping at a tavern, Wilkinson had told an officer about a letter he had come upon to Horatio Gates from another general, Thomas Conway, that praised Gates at Washington's expense. Quoting from memory, Wilkinson repeated its gist—"Heaven has determined to save your country, or a weak general and bad counsellors would have ruined it."

The officer in whom Wilkinson confided hurried back to his own chief, Lord Stirling. Washington and Stirling had little in common other than the same enemies, including Conway and Benjamin Rush. Dr. Rush, the army's surgeon general, had told friends that the blunders Washington had been making "might have disgraced a soldier of three months' standing." And after an inspection tour that past autumn, Rush had denounced Stirling as "a proud, vain, ignorant drunkard." On the evening of November 8, 1777, while still at White Marsh, Washington received a letter from Stirling about a number of housekeeping matters. It concluded with an account of Wilkinson's version of General Conway's remark.

The disparagement didn't surprise Washington. He had first encountered Conway the preceding May and had written an amiable note of introduction for him to the Congress. Born in Ireland, Conway had joined the Americans by way of Paris, where he had served in the French Army. Silas Deane, who was constantly searching out military talent, had promised Conway a high rank if he went to America, and Conway had shown skill and courage while serving under John Sullivan at the battle of Brandywine. Within two weeks he was pressing John Hancock to upgrade his commission from brigadier to major general on the grounds that

Deane had guaranteed him the higher rank. Before the matter could be resolved, Conway had seen action at the battle of Germantown. He said afterward that George Washington had been befuddled and indecisive and had let junior officers overrule his orders. Then, when he came to York to argue for his promotion, Conway widened his criticism to include Lord Stirling, who, he said, was not only ignorant but no good to anyone after he had had his drinks at dinner. Dr. Rush and some members of the Congress saw in Conway a man of perception and integrity. They thought he embodied the military genius of Charles Lee, who remained a British prisoner, without Lee's vices or his dogs. "He is, moreover, the idol of the whole army," Rush assured his friends; if anyone deserved credit for the American showing at Germantown, it was Conway, not Washington.

In the past, Washington had been too busy and too proud to respond to gossip that he considered inevitable. The most he would do would be to write to a friend or relative that he at least knew the purity of his own heart. But even before the letter to Gates, Washington had realized he would have to take a stand on Conway. He wrote to Richard Henry Lee in the Congress that Conway's merit existed more in his imagination than in reality and that promoting him to major general would be "as unfortunate a measure as ever was adopted." Lee's answer was not reassuring. The Congress might not promote Conway but instead name him inspector general. In that role, as Washington knew, Conway could be a malignant nuisance. It was during that politicking at York that Washington got the news of Conway's letter to General Gates.

During the night, Washington considered his response. Then he sent Conway a cold but correct message. It simply said that Washington had received a letter that quoted General Conway to General Gates. Washington repeated the line about Heaven saving America from a weak general, added no further comment, and signed the note, "I am, Sir, Yr. Hble Servt."

Thomas Conway and Horatio Gates had clearly indicated what they thought of George Washington, but he remained the commander in chief. In his response, Conway denied that any such sentiment had appeared in his letter to Gates. "My opinion of you, Sir," said Conway, "without flattery or envy is as follows: You are a brave man, an honest man, a patriot and a man of good sense."

He added that, due to modesty, Washington sometimes let himself be influenced by men who were not his equals.

Horatio Gates took a different tack. Instead of simply disavowing the sentiment, Gates asked for Washington's help in unmasking the sneak who had been reading his letters.

Washington didn't reply to Conway, and for a time it looked as though he were rid of him, anyway. In mid-November, Conway submitted his resignation to Washington, citing the refusal of his request for promotion. Washington wrote back that since Congress had commissioned him, only Congress could accept his resignation. Washington's letter was a model of gracious restraint, ending with hopes for a favorable crossing to France and Conway's happy reunion with his family and friends. But the Board of War, a committee appointed by the Congress, refused to accept the resignation.

By that time, both John Adams and Samuel Adams were taking a respite in Massachusetts and weren't in the Congress to offer Conway their support. And yet each of them had welcomed a challenge to Washington. John Adams was still disturbed by America's veneration of the commander in chief he had nominated. He was almost superstitious about it, suggesting to Abigail that if Washington had been the man to defeat Burgoyne, the resulting idolatry might have jeopardized the nation's very liberty. "Now we can allow a certain citizen to be wise, virtuous and good without thinking him a deity or a savior," John Adams said.

Samuel Adams had spent a lifetime studying the vagaries of public opinion and had learned when to bow to its will. He knew that Washington was revered by much of the army, and that desertions would be even more widespread if he were replaced. Horatio Gates had sounded out Daniel Morgan on the subject before the first battle of Saratoga by saying that many officers seemed to want Washington removed. "I have one favor to ask of you," Morgan had answered, "which is, never to mention that detestable subject to me again; for under no other man but Washington will I ever serve."

Samuel Adams knew that civilians also idolized Washington in the way his cousin deplored. A politician had to be careful not even to insinuate that he didn't support the commander in chief, and lately that was the charge that John Hancock had been making against Samuel Adams. They had fallen out again, and this time their rift looked permanent. When Hancock stepped down as president of the Congress to return to Massachusetts, the Adamses had even tried to dissuade members from voting him a resolution of thanks. They argued unsuccessfully that a man need not be thanked for simply doing his duty.

Hancock coveted the governorship of Massachusetts and was hinting to Bostonians that Samuel Adams was scheming against General Washington. During his trip home Adams assured his comrades at the Green Dragon Tavern that he still supported Washington wholeheartedly.

As John Adams had observed, the Congress had changed drastically since George Washington left it for Cambridge. Only six remained of the members who had voted for him then. The current Congress was being criticized for its decline over the past three years in eloquence, wisdom and simple patriotism. Congress now seemed to be vacillating and wasting its energies on partisan feuds. Even so, Washington's opposition did not have the votes.

The Conway affair sputtered out over a period of weeks. Horatio Gates remained on the sidelines, ready to assume the high command should his supporters be able to install him. Washington treated Gates's letters scornfully, pointing out their errors in logic and coherence. Gates even tried to shift the blame entirely to Brigadier General Wilkinson. No one believed him, and Wilkinson challenged his former patron to a duel. He and Gates met on a field of honor behind the Episcopal church in York. Before the shooting could begin, General Gates took Wilkinson up a back street, burst into tears, called him his dear boy and denied ever speaking against him. The duel was called off, but Wilkinson wrote to the Congress accusing Gates of treachery and resigned his new post as secretary to the Board of War. Thomas Mifflin, a major general who had been a mediocre quartermaster general, also quit the board and departed indignantly from York, saying he was outraged by stories—possibly true—that he had been active in the cabal against Washington.

Dr. Rush tried to fan the dying embers in an unsigned letter to Governor Patrick Henry in Virginia, urging that General Gates be made supreme commander. Henry sent the letter at once to

George Washington, who recognized Rush's handwriting and rebuked him bitingly. Thomas Paine sprang to the defense of Washington's reputation and warned detractors that no slur to the commander in chief would escape his notice.

During the controversy, Thomas Conway was finally promoted and named inspector general. A majority of the Congress believed he was influential enough in France that any slight to him might stop Louis XVI from sending aid to America. As inspector general, he twice called on George Washington and complained to the Congress afterward that he had been coolly received. He was not exaggerating. As a leader of men, Washington had cultivated a certain reserve, and to that he now added an icy disdain. His officers did their best to emulate their general—until Conway told friends that the army couldn't bear the sight of him. In his own letter to the Congress, Washington explained that he had treated General Conway with the respect his title deserved but could hardly receive him as a warm and cordial friend. He was not capable, Washington added, of the arts of dissimulation.

Again Conway resigned, and this time the Congress accepted his resignation so enthusiastically that Gates chastised the members for not paying proper respect to Conway's service in America. Before he could return to France, Conway challenged General John Cadwalader to a duel over an insult to him. Cadwalader's shot struck Conway in the mouth. Thinking he was about to die, Conway wrote a letter of apology to Washington, assuring him, "You are in my eyes the great and good man." But Conway recovered and in time sailed for France. The halfhearted attempt to depose General Washington was over, but it was soon exaggerated by the title "the Conway Cabal." Thomas Conway always insisted afterward that until he came to America he hadn't even known what the word "cabal" meant.

George Washington had met duplicity and bad faith with anger and a gift for withering sarcasm. Men who had seen his fury were able to appreciate afterward the power of Washington's self-control.

The Congress sent Jonathan Austin of Boston to Versailles to tell the French about the victory at Saratoga. He sailed from Long

Wharf on the last day of October 1777 and landed in Nantes one month later. Benjamin Franklin had been waiting impatiently to know whether Philadelphia had been attacked, and Silas Deane was equally anxious for news from America, since he and Beaumarchais had slipped out seven shiploads of arms from Le Havre the previous year to aid in the campaign against Burgoyne. On Thursday, December 4, Austin arrived at Versailles, spent an hour there and, just before noon, rode to the Hôtel Valentinois at Passy. Silas Deane and Arthur Lee were now getting along so badly that they communicated only in writing. But all three American commissioners rushed into the mansion's courtyard to greet Austin as he stepped from his carriage.

Franklin was the first to speak. "Sir," he asked, "*is* Philadelphia taken?"

"It is, sir," Austin answered, and Franklin turned away to recover himself.

"But, sir," Jonathan Austin called after him, "I have greater news than that. General Burgoyne and his whole army are prisoners of war."

His listeners greeted Austin's news according to their temperaments. Beaumarchais had been visiting at Passy, and he raced off so hastily to spread the tidings in Paris that his carriage tipped over. He cut his arm and almost broke his neck but ignored the discomfort, saying, "The charming news from America is a balm to my wounds." The spy Dr. Edward Bancroft left for London, where he had investments; he suspected that Burgoyne's defeat would probably cause stocks in Britain to fall. Thomas Hutchinson heard the news in London, where he was in mourning for his daughter, Peggy, who had died at twenty-three after a long battle against consumption. Burgoyne's surrender ended Hutchinson's dream of returning to Massachusetts. "Everybody is in a gloom," he wrote of his fellow exiles. "Most of us expect to lay our bones here."

William Pitt, Lord Chatham, had been lecturing Parliament again, even before he heard of the surrender, "My lords, you *cannot conquer America*." If he were an American and foreign troops were in his country, Chatham said, "I would never lay down my arms! Never! Never! Never!" Hearing of Burgoyne's defeat, he urged Britain to make peace with America before France was drawn into the conflict. The Parliament's last motion on ending the war had been defeated 199 to 28, and members didn't seem more receptive to Chatham's advice now.

Yet across the Channel he was being proved right. Two days after Jonathan Austin's arrival, Count Vergennes sent his congratulations to Franklin, Deane and Lee and invited them to renew their request for a formal alliance. Franklin drafted a proposal on December 7 and had his grandson Temple deliver it the next day. On the twelfth, a coach called secretly for the Americans and took them to a house half a mile from Versailles, where Vergennes was waiting for them.

The count explained that France could join the war openly only if Spain agreed. Vergennes could have a courier to Madrid and back within three weeks. The Americans returned to their quarters prepared to wait. But five days later an official from the French Foreign Office came to Passy to report that the king's advisers had agreed to a formal alliance with America, though they wouldn't announce it until the Spanish court had sent its decision. With that assurance, Franklin was able to brush aside a British agent's appeals that the Americans travel to London to negotiate a cease-fire based on the status of the two countries before 1763. Franklin said America would never accept a truce without independence.

Spain declined to enter the alliance, but Louis XVI sent his word that he would still authorize a treaty between France and America. The king asked in return only that America pledge not to make a separate peace with England. The details of the pact took two weeks to work out, but on February 6, 1778, the parchment copies were ready for signing. America and France agreed mutually that neither would lay down arms until America's independence had been won. On the trip to Paris for the signing, Benjamin Franklin wore a blue coat that was noticeably old and worn. Silas Deane asked why he had chosen it.

"To give it a little revenge," Franklin said. "I wore this coat on the day Wedderburn abused me at Whitehall."

Word of America's treaty with France reached George Washington in April 1778, and he wrote to the Congress, "I believe no event was ever received with more heartfelt joy." The hard winter had tested Washington's spirit more than the months of scheming by his detractors. In the weeks after the fighting at Germantown, his army had been shifting position in the countryside around Philadelphia. Washington would not let his men go home for the winter. John Cadwalader, commanding the Pennsylvania militia, was even more adamant they should not. The people of his state had expected Washington to stop General Howe from taking Philadelphia. "They were disappointed!" Cadwalader wrote. Removing the American army from Pennsylvania would be taken as a proof of fatal weakness. When Washington met with his council late in November, Lord Stirling had recommended that the army move its base to the area around a village called Valley Forge. The community lay at the junction of the Schuylkill River and Valley Creek and consisted of a few houses and a forge the British had destroyed two months earlier.

A week before Christmas, 1777, Washington had notified his men that he expected them to hew a camp out of the wilderness. His order had assured them that he himself would "share in the hardship and partake of every inconvenience."

The two-mile site Washington chose was a sloping hill thick with the wood his troops could use to build their huts. It was protected by Valley Creek and by a peak called Mount Joy. The men chopped and sawed, their eyes smarting from the acrid fires, and when time came for supper, the hills echoed with voices shouting, "No meat! No meat!" They survived instead on damp masses of flour called "fire cake" because it could be baked on stones rather than in ovens. A young surgeon named Albigence Waldo got the same answer whenever he toured the camp. "What have you for your dinner, boys?" "Fire cake and water, sir."

When the Congress declared a day of thanksgiving, each soldier was given a treat—four ounces of rice and a tablespoon of vinegar. But amid the deprivation, farmers around Valley Forge were prospering by sending their meat and grain to Philadelphia, where they were purchased by the British, who paid in English pounds. Whenever Washington caught a man herding cattle to town for General Howe, he made use of the powers Congress had voted him, seized the herd and sent the farmer to jail. But Washington couldn't compete with the lure of hard money. He had only the paper scrip issued by the Congress, which was worthless in value and as an example of the printer's art. Counterfeit bills were always easily detected because they were better engraved than Congressional money, which was printed on cheaper paper and misspelled "Philadelpkia."

On Christmas Day the men were still in drafty tents. The number of sick increased, and they were treated more often with grog than with medicine. Some of the men did not have a single shirt or pair of breeches, and they went through camp wrapped in blankets and walked barefoot through the snow to haul water from the creek. For sentry duty they would stand with their naked feet inside their hats. Feet and legs froze, turned black and were amputated.

George Washington pleaded with the Congress for clothing and food. Even though his men were naked and starving, he said, they weren't deserting now and they didn't mutiny. When they could, they joked instead; one unit announced a dinner party limited to men without a whole pair of trousers. As the winter deepened and the cold increased, men were setting their tots of liquor on fire and swilling them down with the flame. A French volunteer was struck by the contrast between the men's attitude and their condition. So ragged, he said. And so merry.

An increasing number of volunteers began to arrive from European armies. Besides Thomas Conway, Silas Deane had recruited Colonel Johann Kalb, who called himself a baron with even less justification than William Alexander's in making himself Lord Stirling. Soon after his own interview, Kalb returned to Deane with a more legitimate nobleman. He was a short, slim, pale nineteen-year-old with reddish hair, a pointed nose and a shyly amiable expression. Kalb introduced him as Gilbert du Motier, the Marquis de Lafayette.

The boy had been two when his father was killed by a British bullet at the battle of Minden, and Gilbert had inherited a fortune along with his title. He grew up precocious—married at sixteen and a reserve captain in the French dragoons soon after. Now he made an irresistible proposition to Silas Deane. In exchange for the rank of major general in the American Army, Lafayette would serve for no pay, only expenses. He clinched the bargain by buying his own ship and slipping away from Le Havre before the official French embargo was lifted.

General Washington had a low opinion of many of the foreign adventurers Silas Deane was unloading on his army. And Lafayette also had reason to regret the bargain he had made. He had arrived in the American camp before General Howe took Philadelphia, and he was discouraged by the shacks and tents crowded with soldiers who were half naked or wearing faded hunting shirts. But Lafayette was tactful when the American commander in chief apologized to him. "We must be embarrassed," Washington said, "to show ourselves to an officer who has just left the French Army."

The marquis answered, "I am here to learn, not to teach."

George Washington had found a son. He invited Lafayette to join his military family and move into his headquarters, where the Frenchman quickly found that Washington embodied the ideals of nobility and majesty. At Brandywine, Lafayette fought courageously and took a bullet, and when Philadelphia fell to Howe he wrote to instruct his young wife, Adrienne, how to respond when French enemies of the American cause taunted her: "You will reply politely, 'You are all absolute idiots. Philadelphia is an uninteresting little town, open on all sides; its port was already blockaded; it was made famous, God knows why, because Congress resided there; that's what this famous city really is; and, by the way, we'll undoubtedly take it back sooner or later.'"

When the Congress granted Lafayette a command, he flattered Washington by requesting a division from Virginia. He proved his loyalty again during the Conway affair by turning down the leadership of a proposed expedition against Montreal that could have made him famous at twenty, because Thomas Conway would have been second in command. Writing home, Lafayette predicted of Washington, "His name will be revered throughout the centuries by all who love liberty and humanity."

The day the alliance between France and America was announced gave Lafayette a rare excuse to demonstrate his esteem. He ran to George Washington and kissed him on both cheeks. It was the day for such liberties. Washington's men said they had never seen such delight on his face as when he heard that France had become his ally.

Another foreigner who came to Valley Forge was less exuberant but equally welcome. Baron Friedrich Wilhelm von Steuben came recommended by both Silas Deane and Benjamin Franklin. The baron was about Washington's age, short and powerfully built, and spoke of his experience as a lieutenant general in the Prussian Army of Frederick the Great. Rather than cause resentment among the American officers by insisting on a generalship, he was offering himself as a volunteer without rank or pay. Steuben didn't want to command the troops, only to drill them. With Washington's blessing—and a sinking heart when he saw the condition of his students—Steuben conducted a training course for which he got up every morning at three. His goal was to turn half-clad men with rusty muskets into professional soldiers in time for the campaign of 1778. Steuben, who spoke no English, had to adapt his Old World methods to the character of these free men. Writing to a friend in Europe, he noted that with Prussians, Austrians or Frenchmen "you say to your soldier, 'Do this,' and he does it, but I am obliged to say, 'This is the reason you ought to do that.' And then he does it."

Because the Continentals lacked a set of written regulations, Steuben compiled the American Army's first manual. He wrote in French, an aide did the translation, and Alexander Hamilton smoothed out the English. Few of the men had even the most rudimentary knowledge of basic training, which meant that he had to define everything for them, including the position of a soldier at attention: "He is to stand straight and firm upon his legs, with his head turned to the right so far as to bring the left eye over the waistcoat buttons; the heels two inches apart; the toes turned out; the belly drawn in a little, but without constraint; the breast a little projected; the shoulders square to the front and kept back; the hands hanging down at the sides with the palms close to the thighs."

Steuben's manual broke down the procedure for firing a musket into eight counts and fifteen motions—from "Fire!" to "Return rammer!" His precision might have seemed pedantic, but he was simplifying European regulations and speeding up the firing. Steuben stressed that the war must be won with stand-up volleys from the American line, not by the wide-ranging but erratic riflemen. Bayonet fighting was barely treated.

Looking over his troops, the baron found companies with rolls of three hundred men that consisted of only thirty. One company was comprised of a single soldier. As a result, Steuben made the American companies more flexible than the British and formed them into two ranks rather than three—tallest men at the rear, shorter men toward the center. Officers tended the flanks and kept the line straight, and noncommissioned officers followed at the rear to prevent straggling.

Steuben became the army's first authority on hygiene. He stopped the men from stripping animals and leaving their carcasses to rot above ground. He explained why kitchens and latrines should be placed at opposite sides of the camp. He called on the soldiers to stop relieving themselves wherever they stood. Officers inspected the tents and huts daily to make sure that every utensil was clean and that on clear days the straw and the bedding were aired. Steuben required the men to wash their hands and faces once a day, more often when necessary, and to bathe whenever the creek was high.

Setting down his thoughts on leadership, Baron von Steuben listed as his first principle that an officer must try to gain the love of his men by treating them with every kindness and being alert to their complaints. But he appreciated the value of an occasional oath and was frustrated that the Americans only laughed when he exclaimed, "Sacre Goddam!" Once, he called to a translator, "These fellows won't do what I tell them! Come swear for me!"

By the time George Washington learned that his latest baron was another European fraud—a parson's son who had held no rank in Prussia higher than major—Steuben had made himself invaluable. Washington saw to it that the Congress rewarded his contribution with the rank of major general and the post of inspector general vacated by Thomas Conway.

Together with his foreign volunteers, Washington welcomed to Valley Forge in the spring of 1778 two of his former allies, one returning from the hospital, the other from captivity. Six weeks after he had fallen at Saratoga, the Congress had finally restored Benedict Arnold's rank and seniority, but he had spent that time, his wounded leg strapped to a board, brooding over the injustices he had suffered. One of his legs was now two inches shorter than the other, and when his coach drew up in front of Washington's headquarters it took four men to lift Arnold out. He dismissed them, took his crutches and prepared to hobble toward his commander. Instead Washington ran down the steps and embraced him.

Washington's greeting was equally warm for Charles Lee, who had been held prisoner in New York for fifteen months. The commander in chief personally led the welcome party out of camp to greet Lee. Martha Washington prepared as elegant a dinner as the camp could offer, and Lee stayed in a room next to her parlor. Even with those marks of favor, freedom was something of a comedown for Lee. The British had supplied a three-room suite in the New York City Hall, with rich food, fine wine and an Italian valet named Minghini. In return, Lee had told William Howe how the British might end the war.

General Lee was late to breakfast his first morning at Valley Forge. He had brought along a British sergeant's wife and had let her into his room by a back door. One of Washington's aides thought Lee looked dirty and disheveled at the breakfast table, as though he had spent the night rolling on the ground.

The Congress had watched Europeans flocking to Valley Forge and lately had ordered all officers to take an oath of allegiance before the next campaign. Washington called several together and directed them to place their hands on a Bible while he read out the oath. General Lee was among the group, and each time Washington began to read, Lee pulled his hand away. Washington stopped and asked why.

"As to King George," Lee said jauntily, "I am ready enough to absolve myself from all allegiance to him. But I have some scruples about the Prince of Wales."

When the laughter died down, the other men agreed that he was the same Charles Lee. Then Lee went ahead and took the oath.

No amount of mockery or bad manners, though, clouded Washington's evident relief in having Lee at his side as the year's campaign began. And, from conversations in New York, Lee was able to confirm what Washington's spies had only suspected: Lord North was dissatisfied with William Howe's inaction and had recalled him to England. North was turning over the command of Britain's army in America to Sir Henry Clinton.

Mary Hays (Molly Pitcher) replacing her fallen husband

Monmouth
1778

WILLIAM HOWE had wanted to resign his command soon after the British surrender at Saratoga. He was eager to get back to London and defend himself against growing criticism that he had been passive and inept. A London newspaper, commenting on the inconclusive battle at Germantown, had noted, "Any other general in the world than General Howe would have beaten General Washington, and any other general in the world than General Washington would have beaten General Howe."

As he waited for his resignation to be accepted, Howe indulged himself and his men with a winter given entirely to pleasure. He took a large mansion in Philadelphia, consorted openly with Mrs. Loring and was an indefatigable presence at the nightly concerts and balls. His officers took their cue from him, playing dice and piquet and pursuing the willing Tory daughters of the town. In London, George III railed that Howe had never been fierce enough in attack, that he had shown more cruelty by prolonging the war than if he had acted vigorously to end it. When Benjamin Franklin was asked in France whether it was true that General Howe had taken Philadelphia, he answered that it would be truer to say that Philadelphia had taken General Howe.

Howe's indifference to waging war had made him far more popular with his men than with the ministers in London, and when his orders to return home arrived his officers planned a farewell extravaganza worthy of his appetites. They called their fete the Mischianza—Italian for a medley. To make it truly spectacular, they turned to John André, a twenty-six-year-old British captain known for his talents in music, poetry and drama.

André had been born in London to a Swiss father. The boy had studied at the University of Geneva, where he mastered German, French and Italian and developed a flair for drawing. By the time his father died, André had grown into a handsome and charming youth, and he bought a commission in Britain's Seventh Foot Regiment. He had been captured in 1775 during the Canadian campaign, but, after fourteen months of house arrest, he was freed in a prisoner exchange and went to join William Howe at his headquarters.

There Captain André paid playful court to the young daughters of rich loyalists. He composed witty love poems and drew pencil sketches of them with their hair swept high. A favorite subject was Peggy Shippen, who was almost eighteen and the treasure of her Tory father. As the night of the Mischianza drew nearer, she and her sisters consulted often with André about her costume and coiffure.

There was, however, another side to John André that the society women of Philadelphia had not seen. He was an ambitious soldier who could be as ruthless as his ambition demanded. During his captivity, he had come to loathe the rebel soldiers and the civilian patriots who pelted British prisoners of war with filth from the streets and forced them to smell a hatchet that they promised would split their skulls the next day. Since his release, André had had a chance for revenge when he served as an aide to Major General Charles Grey. A ruthless professional with greater enthusiasm than William Howe's for blood and suffering, Grey had been ordered at Brandywine to exterminate a band of American snipers commanded by Anthony Wayne at a camp near Paoli, Pennsylvania. Before the attack, Grey told his soldiers to remove the flints from their muskets, which meant they couldn't fire but could only bayonet the Americans or club them to death with the butts of their weapons. Grey also warned his men that prisoners were only a burden. Captain André recorded in his journal the scene that followed. The British surprised Wayne's men, bayonetting them even as they surrendered and then striding through the wounded and stabbing them to death. There were also accounts of British officers slicing off the faces of the Americans with their swords. Wayne himself escaped.

At André's Mischianza, all memories of brutality would be banished. He had taken his theme from the *Arabian Nights*. Fourteen of Philadelphia's loveliest young women were to be dressed in white silk gowns with long sleeves. They would wear gauze turbans spangled and edged with gold or silver, and their veils would hang to the waist. Their sashes were being trimmed in colors to match those of the knights who would escort them. The Knights of the Blended Rose favored silver and pink satin, the Knights of the Burning Mountain orange and black. The competing knights would stage a joust to determine which of their ladies were fairer.

All went much as John André had planned it, except that at the last minute a delegation of Quakers convinced Edward Shippen that the ball was tasteless, even improper. Usually Peggy Shippen could depend on a tantrum to sway her father, but this time he couldn't be moved and withdrew his three daughters from the revels. A British officer called for the dresses so that other young women could wear them and preserve the symmetry of Captain André's vision.

Even without the Shippen girls, the ball was a triumph. After the mock joust fought on gray chargers, knights and their ladies adjourned to a hall for dancing. At 10 P.M. the windows were opened and the audience gasped at twenty firework displays designed by Captain Montresor, the chief British engineer. At midnight, supper was announced in a room set off by artificial flowers of green silk tied to a hundred branches, each lighted by three candles. Another three hundred candles lined the supper tables, where twelve courses were served by twenty-four marines, faces painted black and dressed as Nubian slaves. They wore silver collars and bracelets and bowed to the ground when William Howe approached.

In the midst of the dining and the toasts, an explosion echoed through the hall. Captain André reassured the guests that it had been more of Montresor's magic, a bit of thunder to trouble the sleep of the rebels at Valley Forge. In fact the blast had come from a supply depot at Germantown, where a few American raiders had slipped inside and blown up the ammunition. But in Philadelphia John André was letting nothing mar his Mischianza, and the dancing went on until 4 A.M.

William Howe, John Burgoyne and Henry Clinton had sailed across the Atlantic together to save America for England. Now, after delay and defeats, the job had fallen to Clinton alone. It was a responsibility he had tried to avoid; he considered it a hopeless command for a professional soldier. But London couldn't persuade any better-qualified general to take on the assignment.

Clinton's first order was to evacuate Philadelphia and return the army to New York. With France and her navy entering the war, London decided to protect Britain's lucrative trade with the West Indies. Clinton's new command would have to supply a third of the troops for that assignment, and he was ordered to consolidate his forces in New York by pulling out of Pennsylvania and Rhode Island. He was instructed to abandon New York if necessary and withdraw to Halifax, Nova Scotia, and ultimately even to Quebec. Those orders forced Henry Clinton into the same defensive posture he had deplored when he was urging action on William Howe.

Meanwhile, Britain had sent commissioners to America empowered to offer every concession short of independence. The British might have even accepted independence so long as the king could avoid the appearance of total capitulation. But the members of Congress didn't know that and refused to entertain the proposals. While the commissioners prepared to leave Philadelphia with Clinton's forces, they unwittingly alerted General Washington to the British timetable. A laundrywoman's son sneaked out to the American camp to say that some civilians had demanded that his mother have their laundry ready by June 16. Washington convened his council the next day to decide how to respond.

By spring, the men at Valley Forge were no longer a tattered camp in rags. Steuben had instilled discipline, and a successful raid on two British supply vessels had outfitted the American soldiers in woolen uniforms of red, gray and green. During the months of waiting, officers had opened a theater and put on classic dramas and light comedy; George and Martha Washington were its leading patrons. Life at Valley Forge was no Mischianza, but morale was high and the men were restless to break camp and get on with the fighting.

That mood did not extend to Charles Lee. His time with the British in New York had convinced him that the best solution was a prompt peace and reconciliation with England. He was the only one of Washington's generals to urge that Henry Clinton be allowed to retreat from Philadelphia unmolested. Both Lafayette and Anthony Wayne argued so vehemently against him that Washington had to calm their tempers by asking each council member to submit his opinion in writing.

But the British were moving too fast to permit more deliberation. Henry Clinton had only two choices. One was to send his troops to New York by ship. But that could be disastrous if the winds delayed him, because the Americans could march overland to New York and be there to greet him. Instead, Clinton decided to load his ships with American loyalists, who were clamoring to be saved from retribution when the patriots retook Philadelphia. Clinton also sent by ship the Hessians who might desert if he marched them through the countryside. Then he lined up everyone else with the baggage and set off on a march to New York. At midmorning on June 18, 1778, American horsemen rode into Valley Forge to say that the British were entirely gone from Philadelphia.

General Washington acted on impulse. Without consulting his council of war, he ordered his eleven thousand men to prepare at once for pursuit. Clinton had crossed the Delaware River below Camden and was marching north toward New York. Washington planned to cross the river at Coryell's Ferry, move directly east and cut off the British somewhere in New Jersey.

Washington left behind Benedict Arnold, who was still recovering from his wounds, as military governor of Philadelphia. Entering the town, American horsemen rode through in triumph, their swords drawn against the British soldiers who had decamped. Buildings in the center of town had not been badly damaged by the winter's occupation, although some had been turned into

stables and stank so badly that Henry Knox sent his wife back to
Valley Forge. The Congress returned from York and convened
in College Hall because the State House was too filthy to meet
there. The biggest change was the British styles adopted by the
loyalists—broad-brimmed hats for men, women's hair piled higher
than a neck seemed able to support. One prostitute known to have
slept with British soldiers still wore her hair in that upsweep—
perhaps three feet high—and she was paraded through the streets
in a parody of the Mischianza.

Henry Clinton and his troops were progressing so slowly that
Washington wondered whether he was being lured into a trap on
the high ground around Morristown. On June 24, with the sun
in another eclipse, Washington met with his council. Charles Lee,
who talked more than anyone else, argued that getting rid of the
British was so much in the American interest that the Continental
Army could justify building a bridge of gold to speed them along.
The majority of the generals agreed that Washington should avoid
a major battle, although his stalwarts—Wayne and Lafayette, Nathanael Greene and Henry Knox—voted to challenge Clinton's
forces before they reached New York. Young Alexander Hamilton, never one to favor caution, complained afterward that the
council's proceedings would have done honor to a group of mid-
wives.

Washington had been criticized for yielding to men less able
than he was, and now he seemed ready to do it again. He struck
a compromise. He would dispatch fifteen hundred men to annoy
the British during their retreat. Hamilton thought such a small
force could be only provocative; Lee opposed sending even that
many. When his fifteen hundred soldiers had barely gone, Washington, who had also been called indecisive, reinforced them with
another thousand men.

But Charles Lee was also being irresolute. His seniority ranked
second only to Washington, and military protocol demanded that
he be offered the honor of leading the charge, even though he had
strenuously opposed it. It looked at first as though Lee would ease
Washington's dilemma by agreeing that the command should go
to a young and eager officer like Lafayette. But before the orders
could be issued, Lee reconsidered. If the battle turned out to be

a major one, it might look odd that he had refused a role. Lee's argument with himself took hours, and Washington grew impatient. But Lee was worrying over his honor, and that was one consideration General Washington would not challenge. Washington patched together another compromise: Lafayette could strike first, then Lee would take charge as the senior major general. The best intelligence told him that Clinton had lengthened his lead in marching from Allentown to Monmouth Court House and might soon be out of reach.

The summer weather was sweltering, and mosquitoes swarmed over both armies. On Saturday, June 27, 1778, rain drenched the roads but didn't bring down the temperature from nearly 100 degrees. By now General Washington had split his forces—five thousand men were committed to the first attack under Lee, while Washington tried to bring up the main army to support Lee's charge. There was the usual welter of missed communications and vague instructions, but Lee's orders were clear: the minute Clinton moved his camp from Monmouth Court House, Lee was to attack the British rear guard.

The rear ranks ordinarily provided a tempting target. Although Clinton had sent much of his provisions by ship, his troops were encumbered by fifteen hundred wagons of equipment and boats, and goods looted along the route. The wagon train stretched out behind him twelve miles, and though Clinton had tried to limit camp followers to two for each company, scores of women had defied his orders and joined the march. When Clinton learned that the Americans were coming after him, he moved the baggage train to the center of the march and moved his best troops to the rear.

Such foresight was not typical of Charles Lee. Washington announced at noon on June 27 that the army would strike early the next morning. He then deferred modestly to his colleagues, asking all officers to waive any consideration of rank for this vital battle and put themselves entirely under the charge of General Lee. Washington also called on Lee to meet with his officers that afternoon to plan their attack. Lee held a meeting, but it was brief because, he said, he could have no plans when he didn't know General Clinton's intentions.

At midnight, a surgeon from a Virginia regiment asked to speak with General Washington. When Washington's officer of the guard refused to let him in, the doctor asked him to tell His Excellency that he had secret and important intelligence and craved only five minutes.

The doctor was allowed inside, and he told Washington, "I have come to warn you of Lee. That fellow is not to be trusted, Your Excellency. I know his breed too well. Pray be on your guard that he does the army no harm!"

The doctor didn't have proof, and the battle was set to begin in hours. Washington thanked the caller for his concern and showed him out.

On Sunday, June 28, 1778, at 4:30 A.M., an American scout saw the British forces begin to move away from their camp at the clapboard-and-shingle Monmouth Court House. General Washington sent word that Charles Lee and his five thousand men were to follow the enemy and force an engagement. Washington would lead the support team, and he had also sent out a thousand New Jersey militia and Daniel Morgan's six hundred riflemen. As the morning wore on, the temperature rose. Washington's men began collapsing from the heat, yet he kept urging them forward so that they would be in place when General Lee launched his offensive.

But the unfamiliar terrain was posing difficulties for Lee. He had not sent out his own scouts and now was cursing the conflicting information being brought to him. He didn't know whether the entire British army had left Monmouth Court House or whether some rear units had stayed behind. Time was running out. If Henry Clinton could get his men and baggage to Middletown, the surrounding hills would shelter them. Lee's route to Monmouth was blocked by three ravines and by rough woods and stretches of marsh. He had intended to keep the British engaged while he sent troops behind and to the left of them, cutting them off from their main force. But Henry Clinton had anticipated that tactic and, because he controlled the road, could send two divisions back quickly while Lee was still puzzling over the landscape. Trying to figure out where to cross one ravine, Lee led his troops back and forth across the same bridge until finally he cried out, "I am teased, mortified and chagrined by these little marches and countermarches."

Finally, Lafayette rode up and convinced Lee to disregard the conflicting intelligence and get on with the attack. Lee maneuvered his men over the second ravine and across open country toward the courthouse. But as the Americans approached, they caught a glimpse of Clinton's baggage train galloping away in the distance.

General David Forman of the New Jersey militia was on home ground and told Lee he knew a shortcut. Lee brushed him away. "I know my business," he said.

For a moment, it almost seemed he did. Lee sent troops around the courthouse and thought he was going to encircle the two thousand British soldiers who had remained there. He didn't seem bothered to be out of effective contact with most of his commanders, and he boasted to Lafayette, "My dear Marquis, I think those people are ours."

When a messenger rode up from George Washington, Lee assured him as well that he would cut off the British rear guard. "By God," Lee was exclaiming now, "I will take them all!"

Then, at about 10 A.M., Henry Clinton returned to Monmouth Court House with four thousand troops, and Lee's worst fears came flooding back. Lafayette wanted to begin a counterattack, but Lee forbade it. "Sir," he said, "you do not know the British soldiers. We cannot stand against them."

Some Americans were pressing forward to fight, others were falling away. Charles Lee first told officers to take their men into the woods to save their lives, then upbraided others for retreating without his order. "They are all in confusion, they are all in confusion," Lee kept repeating. His officers were appalled. A French captain of engineers, Pierre L'Enfant, demanded to know why the Americans were not attacking.

Lee said, "I have orders from Congress and the commander in chief not to engage."

At that moment, George Washington was five miles to the rear. He was riding a tall white horse at the side of his main army as it marched to back up Lee in his victory. An army doctor who was chatting with him remarked, "Looks like a Sunday battle, General Washington."

"Yes, it does. I don't feel much like fighting on the Sabbath," said Washington, who had waged his most successful attack on Christmas Day. "But I must yield to the good of the country."

They were interrupted by Thomas Henderson, a lieutenant

colonel in the militia from nearby Englishtown. Henderson called out that the American troops were retreating.

"Retreating?" Washington repeated. He asked where that information had come from. Henderson pointed to a fifer. Angrily, Washington hailed the boy and demanded to know what he had been saying.

It was true, the fifer insisted. Everybody was on the run.

Washington was sure the story must be false. He told a sergeant to put the boy under guard to stop him from spreading the damaging rumor.

Riding on, Washington came to American soldiers pulling their artillery back across a muddy brook, away from the courthouse.

"By whose orders are the troops retreating?" Washington asked their officer.

"By General Lee's," the man replied.

The aides watching him thought George Washington's passions were about to explode. "Damn him!" Washington said.

A little ahead, another aide, Colonel Robert Harrison, encountered one of General Lee's captains, John Mercer. For the love of God, Harrison shouted, why are you surrendering?

Agitated, Mercer shouted back that if Harrison went any farther he would meet columns of enemy foot and horse—

Colonel Harrison interrupted him. "Thank you, Captain, but we came to this place expressly to meet columns of enemy foot and horse!"

As Washington got closer to the scene, Alexander Hamilton rode up, jumped from his horse and ran to his side. "General!" Hamilton cried. "General! We are betrayed! General Lee has betrayed you and the army."

Washington said, "Colonel Hamilton, you will take your horse." He drew up his own reins and crossed the planks laid over a narrowing in the marsh. Two hundred yards farther on he met Charles Lee, who stopped his horse and was about to greet him when Washington blurted, "My God, General Lee! What are you about?"

Either Lee did not hear or the abrupt tone left him speechless. "Sir?" Lee said. "Sir?"

"I desire to know, sir, what is the reason for this disorder and confusion."

General Lee launched into various excuses: The intelligence had been contradictory. One unit had abandoned a favorable position. And, he concluded, the whole plan had been put into action against his advice.

"Whatever your opinions might have been," Washington replied, "I expected my orders would have been obeyed. The British at Monmouth were a covering party at most."

"Maybe so, sir," said Lee, "but it seemed stronger than that, and I did not think it proper to risk so much." He added that American troops could not stand up to British bayonets.

At that, Washington muttered something to himself, which his orderly overheard. Charles Lee may have heard him, too: "You've never tried them, you damned poltroon!"

Washington left Lee and rode forward to the front of the action. Colonel Harrison galloped up and reported that the British main force was barely fifteen minutes away and pressing hard. Washington had time only to act on reflex. He charged through the confusion, lining up the Americans behind a hedgerow. Alexander Hamilton watched admiringly as Washington, cool and firm, molded the soldiers back into a fighting force. Lafayette, who was also looking on, decided that he had never seen so superb a man as George Washington at that moment. Washington was still clearly angry, but calm as he rode effortlessly among the men, converting panic to enthusiasm.

General Wayne, who had survived the attack at Paoli, got his troops into position behind the hedge and waited for the British to charge. His men considered him a tyrant—Mad Anthony Wayne—but he could guarantee they would stand their ground. Charles Lee passed by and asked what he thought he was doing. Wayne said he was carrying out the express commands of General Washington.

At that, Lee made a ceremonial bow. "I have nothing further to say."

After Washington had stemmed the retreat and lined up the Americans for battle, General Lee rode to his side. "Will you take command," he asked, "or shall I?"

Washington, ready to put the last hour behind them, answered, "If you wish to take it, I will return to the main body and arrange them on the heights at the rear."

Lee said gravely, "I will take command here, Your Excellency, and check the enemy. Nor will I be the first to leave the field."

Alexander Hamilton was exalted by the impending battle. Joining them, he vowed, "I will stay with you, my dear General Lee, and will die with you here on the spot!"

Lee answered him dryly, "When I have taken the proper measures to get our main body in position, I will die here with you. On this spot, if you like."

Despite that pledge, Washington remained in control. Once Lee had restored order among his troops, Washington ordered him to march them as reserves to Englishtown. Within minutes, Alexander Hamilton fell in battle, but not as valiantly as he had promised. His horse rolled on him, and though Hamilton lived he was out of combat. The day was hard on horses. George Washington's white mount, a gift from the governor of New Jersey, collapsed of sunstroke, and Washington quickly switched to his favorite brown mare. Lieutenant Colonel Aaron Burr had a horse shot out from under him but freed himself unhurt. Colonel Burr was another officer who felt wronged over a slow promotion, for which he tended to blame Washington. Here at Monmouth, Burr was angered more when Washington stopped him from pursuing a host of British soldiers he was sure he could have captured.

Although the sun was sinking, heat still parched the soldiers' throats, and to slake their constant thirst a private's young wife had been fetching water from a nearby well for her husband and his fellow artillery gunners. She was Mrs. John Hays, but the men called her "Molly Pitcher." When her husband was shot dead, Mary Hays knew his job well enough to grab a rammer and keep the gun firing. Once, as she stretched to reach for a cartridge, a cannonball passed between her legs and tore away her petticoat. Mary Hays, who had chewed tobacco with these men and cursed with them, simply looked down and remarked that it was lucky the shot had not passed higher or it would have carried away something else.

At about 6 P.M. Washington wanted to launch a counterattack, but, under the hottest sun in recent memory, his men were as spent as they had been in the bitter cold at Princeton. Henry Clinton was vastly relieved for the respite. He was outnumbered, possibly by four thousand men, and described himself as ready to go raving mad from the heat. The British had suffered about twelve hundred casualties—four times the number of the American losses.

Clinton had already lost half that number in desertions; love-struck Hessians kept creeping back to sweethearts in Philadelphia. With the odds against him, Clinton quietly left Monmouth in an overnight retreat as skillful as any the Americans had made on the many occasions they had conceded a battlefield.

By midmorning on Monday, the British reached the safety of Middletown; two days later, Sandy Hook. There, on the fourth of July, 1778, Henry Clinton's men boarded Lord Howe's ships and sailed to New York. After more than three years of war and two years of embattled independence, the Americans had a reason to celebrate. This time it was their army that had chased the enemy across New Jersey.

George Washington had been content to let Charles Lee's erratic behavior be buried with the dead at Monmouth Court House. But Washington's momentary show of anger had affronted Lee. From the end of the battle and all through the next day, he awaited Washington's apology for his harsh remarks. When none came by Monday night, Lee was still seething and wrote his commander a letter:

Washington's manner of addressing him, Lee said, implied that he had disobeyed orders, failed in his conduct or showed cowardice. Lee asked Washington to tell him which of those charges he had made so that Lee could justify himself to the army, to the Congress, to America and to the world. Lee added that since the success at Monmouth had been due entirely to his maneuvers, "I have a right to demand some reparation." In conclusion, he attempted to be politic. Washington's cutting remarks could only have been prompted "by some of those dirty earwigs who will forever insinuate themselves near persons in high office."

Lee might have learned from Thomas Conway that Washington was slow to unleash his anger, but, once let free, it could be fierce. He began his response by pointing out that Lee had mis-dated his letter. Then Washington said he found General Lee's language highly improper but would soon give Lee the chance he was demanding. Lee could explain why he had not attacked but instead had made "an unnecessary, disorderly and shameful retreat."

Charles Lee exploded in fury. He wrote again, deliberately using the wrong date and claiming to welcome the opportunity for America to judge the respective virtues of her generals. Lee's talent for invective had always been highly developed, and now he indulged it fully. "I trust the temporary power of office, and the tinsel dignity attending to it, will not be able, by all the mists they can raise, to obfuscate the bright rays of truth." In yet another letter a few hours later, Lee called for a full court-martial, not merely a court of inquiry. Washington agreed immediately. The court began taking testimony on July 4.

Alexander Hamilton worried that Charles Lee's gift for language would affect the outcome of his trial, and it did, but not in the way Hamilton had feared. Lee was now denouncing his commander's behavior at Monmouth to anyone who would listen. "By all that's sacred," he wrote to Robert Morris, "General Washington had scarcely more to do in it than to strip the dead." Had Lee retreated? Only when a jealous Washington sent him from the field after victory was already assured. Lee claimed that twice in the past he had saved Washington and his whole army from perdition. And now at Monmouth he had given him the only victory Washington had ever tasted.

General Lee was forcing the country to choose between him and George Washington. He soon had his answer. By late July, Lee was complaining that any attack on Washington seemed to recoil against the attacker; Lee's fellow generals had begun to question his sanity. At the court-martial, three charges were considered: disobeying orders by not attacking, misbehavior in making a shameful retreat and, citing his letters of June 30, disrespect to the commander in chief. Lee conducted his own defense but could not salvage his reputation. When General David Forman was testifying, Lee challenged him to say whether other American retreats had been more or less disorderly than his own.

"I have seen retreats with more confusion and some with less," Forman answered.

Lee persisted: "Where did you see a retreat with less confusion in the face of the enemy?"

"At White Plains," Forman answered, reminding the court of Washington's skillful escape from New York.

Alexander Hamilton testified to Lee's instability during the battle, until Lee quoted back Hamilton's own overheated remarks.

General Lee, who was referring to his retreat as "retrograde maneuvers," called on the Marquis de Lafayette to speak for Lee's self-control as the fighting began. "Did you observe in my voice, manner, appearance, air or countenance that I was the least disconcerted, or whether, on the contrary, I was not tranquil and cheerful?"

The marquis had been studying English diligently and knew enough to avoid being helpful. "It seemed to me by your voice and features," he said, "you were then as you are in general."

The court found Charles Lee guilty on all three charges, although the word "shameful" was deleted from the description of his retreat. Fellow officers noted that of the three indictments, the disrespect to George Washington had been taken the most seriously. In pressing for a court-martial, Lee had exposed himself to a sentence of death. Instead, he was suspended from any command in the army for twelve months.

Like Conway, Lee had insulted George Washington and had paid the price. And, like the Conway affair, the incident ended in a duel. Both Baron von Steuben and General Anthony Wayne demanded satisfaction for aspersions they had detected in his letters and testimony. Lee apologized and turned away their challenges. But one of Washington's young aides, John Laurens, whose father had replaced John Hancock as president of the Congress, claimed that Lee had impugned Washington with the grossest abuse and insisted on dueling. Lee mocked him for taking it on himself to defend Washington's honor. He said Laurens was reviving the medieval custom that permitted any knight to champion "old women, widows and priests." But he agreed to the match.

Congress upheld the court-martial. Samuel Adams carried Massachusetts for Lee, but Georgia cast the only other vote for his acquittal. Two and a half weeks later, Charles Lee met Laurens in a wood four miles outside Philadelphia. The men fired from fifteen feet, and Lee received a slight wound. He said to Laurens, "You may fire at me all day, sir, if it will amuse you. What I have said I am not disposed to recall." Both men were preparing for a second shot when they were stopped by the protests of Laurens' second, Lieutenant Colonel Alexander Hamilton.

Benjamin Franklin welcomed at a French reception, 1778

Paris
1778-79

WHEN JOHN ADAMS found himself living in Paris in the spring of
1778, he was half thrilled and entirely censorious. He had been sent
to France to replace Silas Deane, whom the Congress had ordered
home for an accounting when Arthur Lee's vendetta against Deane.
became impossible to ignore. The members wanted a man of inflexible integrity to replace him and elected Adams while he was
on leave in Massachusetts. Abigail Adams bitterly lamented that
after being apart for three years they now faced another prolonged
separation. She worried about raising their four children alone,
especially since the three boys needed a father's example. John
Adams had his own qualms about making the trip. He assumed
that the British would find out about the appointment and try to
capture him on the seas and send him to Newgate Prison. He
would take whatever risk his country asked, but he would not

allow Abigail to go with him. As a compromise, he took their eldest son, John Quincy.

The six-week crossing was rough but not as daunting as the ordeal that introduced John Adams to Parisian society. On his second night off the boat, an elegant young married woman turned to him flirtatiously at a supper party. Adams spoke no French, so her remarks were put through an interpreter.

"Mr. Adams," she began, "by your name I conclude that you are descended from the first man and woman, and probably in your family may be preserved the tradition which may resolve a difficulty which I could never explain: I never could understand how the first couple found out the art of lying together."

That was how her pleasantry was translated to him, but Adams suspected that the phrase she had used for making love was a more energetic one. American women—modest, sensitive, dignified—would never have posed so indelicate a question. John Adams felt himself blushing. But he had come to France to represent America and he was determined to conceal his discomfort.

Through the interpreter, Adams replied that he thought the answer must be instinct. When a man and a woman came within striking distance, they flew together like the needle toward the pole—like two objects in an electrified experiment.

"Well," the woman replied, "I know not how it was, but this I know: it is a very happy shock."

Adams sat back satisfied with his performance, except he wished that after "striking distance," he had added "in a lawful way" to show her that he was speaking only about attraction within marriage.

He had come to France girded against any moral corruption. Although he admitted that the Paris Opéra was cheerful and sprightly, he refused to live in Silas Deane's house or to use his carriage; he found instead a modest apartment near Benjamin Franklin. Once they were alone, Franklin told Adams about the grievances that had split the American delegation. Franklin's version painted Arthur Lee as one of those men who went through life quarreling with one person after another until they went mad. Lee had been one of Samuel Adams' closest allies for most of the decade, and John Adams said only that he regretted the quarreling and was determined to stay aloof from it.

As Adams began his diplomatic rounds, he was repeatedly

dismayed when Frenchmen told him how honored they were to be meeting the famous Monsieur Adams. Each time, John scrupulously explained that he was not Samuel. He spent every spare moment studying the French language, but was torn between pride and mortification when John Quincy learned more French in a day at school than his father had learned in a week. Adams was comforted that Benjamin Franklin, for all of his social triumphs, spoke a most ungrammatical French. But the French seemed to forgive Franklin even that. When he made errors in gender, Franklin apologized by saying that for sixty years the matter of genders had been bothering him and he still found the French feminines a plague. Once, asked to attend a speech, Franklin thought he had devised a way to protect himself. He watched a Frenchwoman with similar political views, and every time she applauded he joined in. Afterward, his grandson informed him that whenever a speaker had praised the glories of Benjamin Franklin he had clapped longer and louder than anyone else.

By May, John Adams was finding that Franklin was far too occupied with his rounds of pleasure to bother with the tedious details of their assignment. Adams felt only compassion for Franklin's age—he was seventy-two—and he was perfectly content to take on all of the commission's drudgery if only Franklin would allot a few minutes each day for business. Adams began to keep a record of Franklin's indulgences. He noted that Franklin always slept late. Then, after breakfast, carriages began arriving at Passy filled with philosophers, scholars and economists. There were French translators at work on *Poor Richard*, and women and children who came to gape and boast of having seen the great man's bald head. By the time Franklin had obliged them all, it was time to dress for dinner. He had an invitation for every day and never turned one down. Adams was usually included but begged off, pleading business or his study of French. Franklin went nowhere without an appointment book in his pocket to keep track of his many engagements. Arthur Lee claimed—and Adams agreed—that the only job Franklin was punctual at was keeping the book up-to-date. After dinner, Franklin visited the French ladies who competed ruthlessly for his company, some so eager to impress him that they learned to make English tea. After tea came amusements. Ladies sang or played the piano while Franklin played checkers or chess. He usually went home anywhere from 9 P.M. to midnight.

Adams became irritated enough to set down the names of four of the French ladies pursuing Franklin, but he might have added many more. Franklin sent Madame Anne-Louise Brillon de Jouy, the wife of a treasury official, little stories that he called his bagatelles. He called her "my daughter," but she enjoyed the idea that they were provoking a scandal. "People have the audacity to criticize my pleasant habit of sitting on your knee," she wrote to him, "and yours of always asking me for what I always refuse." Franklin tried to make a match between his grandson Temple and her eldest daughter, Cunegonde, but Madame Brillon considered the boy too young and too poor.

One of Madame Brillon's leading rivals lived a few kilometers away. Madame Anne-Catherine Helvétius, still beautiful as she approached sixty, had once scolded Benjamin Franklin for not calling on an evening she expected him. Franklin had apologized, "Madame, I am waiting till the nights are longer." Adams was aghast to find that Madame Helvétius surrounded herself with three or four young priests, chosen more for their good looks than for their piety. At least one of them lived at her house. "Oh, mores!" Adams groaned to himself and vowed that such customs would never reach America.

There was one feminine heart Franklin did not flutter. Queen Marie Antoinette couldn't fathom why the young and pretty women of her court were drawn to him. One of them, the Duchesse Yolande de Polignac, had flaunted so often her medallion of Franklin wearing his fur hat that the king sent her another of Franklin's portraits, placed at the bottom of a Sèvres chamber pot.

Back in Philadelphia, Silas Deane's reception by the Congress was markedly hostile. Deane had John Hancock's support, which only damned him further in the eyes of Samuel Adams and his allies. Benjamin Franklin had written a letter of support for Deane, but Arthur Lee had insinuated that Franklin was Deane's partner in profiteering. John Adams sent a private letter from France saying that Deane was neither the savior of America nor a villain but had rendered useful service.

Deane's homecoming was more melancholy because his wife had died while he was abroad, and his personal finances were badly strained. He had also damaged his reputation by naively

Last page of Treaty of Alliance signed in Paris, February 1778 granting commissions in the American Army to many French and other European officers. For every Lafayette or Steuben, there had been many volunteers who made extravagant demands for rank and salary and yet brought none of the skills General Washington required. Worst of all, Deane had left France so hurriedly that he had neglected to bring the vouchers to substantiate his claims.

The Congress kept Deane waiting a month before permitting him to report in mid-August 1778. He spoke and answered questions for four days. Another month passed, and Deane was informed that he had been charged publicly in France with the misapplication of public money. Arthur Lee wrote that he and John Adams had tried to make sense out of the accounts that Deane left behind, which Lee called "studied confusion." He added, "All we can find is, that millions have been expended, and almost everything remains to be paid for."

By November 20 the Congress still had not acted on Deane's detailed defense. In desperation, he took his case "to the free and virtuous citizens of America" with a letter published in early December in the *Pennsylvania Packet*. Deane not only attacked the Lee brothers but also accused Arthur Lee of revealing American secrets to an English earl and other British agents. Thomas Paine sided with Arthur Lee and under the pen name "Common Sense" argued that Deane's attacks on the Lee brothers had disqualified him from public service. Paine's choice of pseudonym was not much of a disguise, and after the article appeared one of Deane's supporters caught and whipped him on a Pennsylvania street.

The controversy continued into the new year. France's recently appointed minister to the United States criticized Paine's article for revealing that Vergennes had been secretly supplying America with war materials long before a treaty was signed. The French protest resulted in Paine's dismissal as secretary of the Committee for Foreign Affairs. It was not until August 6, 1779, that Congress voted on the Deane affair, and then the members neither cleared nor censured him. They awarded Deane $10,500 for the thirteen months he had spent waiting for resolution of the charges and permitted him to return to France as a private citizen to tend to his business affairs. Deane sailed from America resentful that, despite his many services to America, Arthur Lee had succeeded in tarnishing his name.

During his unhappy stay in Philadelphia, Silas Deane had spent evenings at the mansion of the town's military commander, Benedict Arnold. Civilians on the town council had warned Deane not to be associated with Arnold, who they were convinced was corrupt. Their most serious charge was profiteering in wartime, but the prevailing customs tended to be lax. Arnold undeniably had used army wagons to carry goods that he later sold for profit in Philadelphia. But since he reimbursed the army, the offense might seem a lapse in judgment rather than a criminal act. The civilians were also indignant about a pass that General Arnold had issued for a private cargo ship, the *Charming Nancy*. The circumstances suggested he might have been bribed. Arnold was giving passes for shipments from Philadelphia to New York so freely that the Congress voted to take away his right to issue them. George Washington was not likely to discipline General Arnold, even though controversies over his handling of funds went back to the Ticonderoga and Quebec expeditions. His generals were so often accused of wrongdoing by civilian authorities that Washington investigated only when the charges became official.

Washington had not prospered militarily since the battle at Monmouth Court House. Continuing his march north, he had circled New York and set up camp forty miles away, with bases stretching in an arc from Middlebrook in New Jersey through West Point in New York and Danbury in Connecticut. The Continental Army had returned to the neighborhood of White Plains, where Colonel Johann Rall's Hessians had overwhelmed the militias of Massachusetts and New York two years earlier. Washington waited during the winter and through the spring of 1779 for Henry Clinton to attack, as he had once waited for General Gage and General Howe. It took him a while to discover that the British strategy had shifted to the South, where the ministers in London believed more Americans remained loyal to the throne. When Clinton didn't attack, Washington considered him indecisive and foolish.

As he was waiting, Washington was not heartened by the first engagements of his new French allies. When the French fleet arrived off Sandy Hook in New Jersey, Washington hoped they would attack the British ships in New York Harbor. But the French commander, the Comte d'Estaing, decided that his ships were too heavy for an engagement there and sailed toward Newport instead. Washington's alternative plan was to drive the British out of Rhode Island. He put General John Sullivan in charge of all the militia Sullivan could raise and sent more men commanded by Lafayette and Nathanael Greene. John Hancock went south, making his debut as an army officer, along with Lieutenant Colonel Paul Revere and his son, Captain Paul Revere, Jr. Despite Revere's value as a messenger, the Congress had never commissioned him in the Continental Army, and he was serving now only in a Massachusetts artillery unit.

The early stages of the maneuver went according to Washington's plan. The French fleet landed four thousand troops for a joint assault on Newport. But when Admiral Howe's ships appeared, d'Estaing called his men back to help him engage the British at sea. John Sullivan took his troops forward alone, expecting the French to return soon to the mainland. Instead, a storm at sea badly damaged both fleets. Howe took the British ships back to New York for repair, and despite the pleas of Lafayette and Greene, d'Estaing set sail for Boston to rebuild and refit his navy. Sullivan was left alone and, when the British mounted an offensive, was forced to escape to Providence. America's defeat was undeniable, but there were some conspicuous examples of bravery. One Rhode Island regiment made up entirely of black soldiers—slaves fighting in exchange for their freedom—withstood three ferocious charges by Hessian troops.

George Washington tried to make Sullivan understand that blaming the French publicly for the campaign's failure would jeopardize an essential alliance. All the same, Sullivan and his officers published an attack on d'Estaing that reached Boston before the French fleet arrived. A melee broke out between Frenchmen and Americans, and a French lieutenant was killed. Boston's politicians had been managing public opinion for years, and they reacted promptly. The Massachusetts Assembly voted money to raise a statue to the Frenchman's memory. John Hancock, home again in Boston, feted d'Estaing and his officers at his mansion. And a rumor was spread throughout the town that the riot had been started by the British soldiers taken prisoner at Saratoga.

The Americans began a military campaign in May 1779, but their victories were sharply limited. Soldiers under Anthony Wayne took a British fort at Stony Point, on the Hudson, which Washington decided not to hold. A young major from Virginia, Lighthorse Harry Lee, successfully raided a British post in New Jersey across from the lower end of Manhattan Island. Washington also sent John Sullivan out along the northern frontier to raze the villages of Indians who had been attacking white settlers.

In December 1779 Washington took his army to winter quarters in a mountainous area called Jockey Hollow, three miles southwest of Morristown. In January a storm broke over the camp, and snows six feet deep ended the supply of food. For a week the men lived like Benedict Arnold's soldiers on their doomed drive to the north—eating black birchbark, roasting old shoes, killing and eating a favorite dog. Life at Morristown became even harsher than at Valley Forge two winters before. Desertions ran high, but General Washington held to his strict discipline. To stop their screams, men who were being whipped until their wounds bled bit down on a lead bullet. After the beating stopped, they spit it out, crushed flat. For the worst offenses, men were flogged over a number of days, so that their newly inflamed skin would be more tender and they would have two or three nights to dread what was in store.

The spring brought no relief to the shortages. When all the meat was gone and the officers had put themselves on bread and water, two Connecticut regiments broke into open mutiny. Colonel Walter Steward tried to shame them out of the rebellion. The ladies of Philadelphia called young Steward "the Irish beauty," but he was grim as he faced the men and said, "You Connecticut troops have won immortal honor to yourselves the winter past by your performance, patience and bravery. And now you are shaking it off at your heels." The uprising died away, but, because of the number of men involved, Washington had no choice but to pardon everyone except the few men who had actually left camp.

Just when General Washington's fortunes seemed at their lowest, he heard that Henry Clinton had once again tried to take Charleston and this time had succeeded.

Whenever the army was in winter quarters, Martha Washington came north to pass the idle months with her husband—"the old man," she called him. At Morristown she too had been distressed by the cold temperatures that brought Washington's cadre of eighteen officers and servants into the warmth of her small kitchen. She was also troubled by the anxieties gnawing away at her husband more persistently than ever before. And lately he had been without the consolation of Lafayette's company. The marquis had returned to France on indefinite leave after the debacle at Newport. He had begun to question America's future, but never the grandeur of her commander in chief. From France, Lafayette assured Washington that he had "a wife who is in love with you" and invited Washington to visit them whenever the war was ended.

Lafayette's letter was one that Washington didn't turn over to Alexander Hamilton or the other aides who lightened his load of correspondence. Going to France in peacetime would be the greatest pleasure, Washington responded. "But remember, my good friend, that I am unacquainted with your language, that I am too far advanced in years to acquire a knowledge of it, and that to converse through the medium of an interpreter upon common occasions, especially with the *ladies*"—Washington underlined the word—"must appear so extremely awkward, insipid and uncouth that I can scarce bear it in idea."

As a Virginian, General Washington loved to dance, and he put together a dancing assembly with thirty-four other officers. They persuaded girls from the neighboring farms to struggle out through the snow, and, with the women there, the officers danced night after night until 2 A.M. Washington often sought out pretty Kitty Greene, her husband Nathanael watching complacently with Martha Washington as the couple danced three hours at a time without sitting down.

Occasionally the merriment could threaten the commander's dignity. One night several officers decided that a civilian named George Olney was sneering at them for drinking so much. In return, they set out to get him as drunk as they were. Olney tried to escape by joining the ladies. When the officers voted to pursue him, Washington volunteered to lead a raid to bring him back, by force if necessary. It all seemed to be a good-natured scuffle, until Olney's wife screamed at Washington, "If you do not let go my hand, I will tear out your eyes or the hair from your head." Washington might be a general, she added, but he was still a man.

Kitty Greene sprang furiously to Washington's defense. It

took her husband to separate the two women. By that time, General Washington had disappeared, leaving his aides to smooth things over. Nathanael Greene took the Olneys into another room and explained that the whole fracas had really been George Olney's fault. In the future, Olney should be less blunt in refusing to drink with the commander in chief.

Betrayal
1780

IN AUGUST 1780, General Washington learned that English ships had blockaded the French fleet at Brest, which meant that the French wouldn't be reaching America in time for a further offensive that year. Also, Horatio Gates had not been able to repeat his spectacular triumph at Saratoga and had been beaten decisively by Lord Cornwallis at Camden, South Carolina. Charles Lee had jeered from the sidelines when his friend Gates first took on the Southern mission: "Take care lest your Northern laurels turn to Southern willows." The defeat had been total and humiliating, possibly the worst of the war.

Alexander Hamilton hoped that the disaster might finally convince the Congress to replace Gates in the South. And for God's sake, he added, let the replacement be Nathanael Greene.

Benedict Arnold's life in recent months had been a mix of pleasure and anxiety. In an army court-martial early in the year, the court had cleared him of the charges that civilians in Philadelphia had first brought against him, but found him guilty of improperly issuing a pass for the *Charming Nancy* and of an imprudent use of army wagons for his own commercial trade. His punishment was to be a reprimand from His Excellency the commander in chief, who had lately found Arnold overbearing and presumptuous. But Washington respected his courage as a soldier and phrased his reproach tactfully. The affair of the wagons, Washington wrote, was indeed improper, and he would rather have bestowed "commendations on an officer who has rendered such distinguished service to his country."

While serving as military commander of Philadelphia, Arnold had cut a dashing figure despite lingering pain from his injured leg. He spent money extravagantly and took over Mount Pleasant, the mansion William Howe had occupied. Arnold drove through the streets in a fine carriage with attendants wearing livery and bought wine at a thousand pounds a pipe. After the death of his estranged wife, Arnold had married another Margaret, the beautiful eighteen-year-old blond daughter of the loyalist Edward Shippen. As her father knew, Peggy Shippen was not a girl to let war interfere with pleasure. Arnold's marriage to a girl almost twenty years younger had caused his expenses to mount still higher. His spinster sister came to live with the couple and look after Arnold's three sons. Hannah Arnold's disapproval of her new sister-in-law had less to do with Peggy's taste for luxuries than with her susceptibility to any attentive man.

Washington had been forced to reprimand Arnold, but he regarded him as toughened and tested in battle. When Arnold asked urgently to be named commander of a critical fort at West Point, New York, Washington had accepted Arnold's argument that his crippling wounds fitted him for the less strenuous duty there. Before she joined him at West Point, Peggy Shippen Arnold wrote her husband amusingly malicious letters about Philadelphia's social life, and what she didn't tell Benedict Arnold his sister filled in. Hannah Arnold wrote that if she were more inclined to mischief, she could tell him about his bride's many assignations and billets doux. But Hannah eventually accepted Arnold's devotion to his wife. With the child Peggy Arnold gave him and his new post at West Point, Benedict Arnold's happiness seemed complete.

There was one brief tremor. A report reached Philadelphia that Washington had offered General Arnold command of the army's left wing in the coming military campaign. When Peggy Arnold heard the news, she went into one of her fits of hysteria, even though friends explained that the offer represented a promotion. Arnold managed to stay on in command of West Point, and his wife joined him in a house across the river from the fort.

Washington was looking forward to a stopover there in September on his way back from a conference in Connecticut. Food and lodging at West Point would be especially welcome, since currency these days was so debased. The eight thousand dollars Washington's entourage had raised for the trip would barely pay for rooms at an inn for two nights. In Connecticut the night before, the party had been relieved when a tavern owner told them that the governor had ordered the state to pay their expenses.

As he neared West Point, Washington sent Major James McHenry and another aide ahead to tell the Arnolds that his party would be arriving soon and, if it was convenient, would appreciate being offered breakfast, a prospect that brightened Washington's spirits. Riding with him was the Marquis de Lafayette, who had returned from France. At one point Washington turned off the direct road to inspect a fortification, and Lafayette called to him that he was heading the wrong way. Washington replied that he knew all young men were in love with Mrs. Arnold and wanted to get to her as quickly as possible. If Lafayette wished, he could go ahead with Major McHenry. Lafayette smiled and stayed with Washington.

They reached the Arnolds' house at about 10:30 A.M., but neither the general nor his wife was there to greet them. An aide apologized on behalf of General Arnold, who, he said, had been called across the river to the fort after receiving Washington's advance party. Arnold had promised to be back in an hour to meet with His Excellency. Mrs. Arnold was still in her room. Lieutenant Colonel Richard Varick, Benedict Arnold's chief aide, had been confined to bed with a fever, but he got up briefly to welcome the visitors. Washington's immediate concern was breakfast. After they ate, he announced, they would inspect the fort. If General Arnold had not returned, they would see him there.

Only after Washington and his officers had finished their meal and been rowed across the Hudson were they puzzled by Arnold's absence. At the fort, they were told that he hadn't been seen all morning. Washington was nettled by Arnold's apparent lack of respect, and his inspection of the fort did not improve his disposition. The entire outpost was in appalling disrepair and suffered from many evidences of bad judgment. One section of the fort had been so crudely built of dry wood that the first British shells would ignite it. Another position had been left nakedly vulnerable to attack from a nearby hill. It would take months of work to make West Point an effective fortress.

The inspection lasted two hours. Washington returned to the Arnold house with vague misgivings. Dinner had been delayed until 4 P.M., and there was still no sign of General Arnold. As Washington prepared for dinner, Alexander Hamilton, who had stayed behind at the house during Washington's inspection, came to his room and handed him a packet of letters. Washington skimmed through them, cried out and immediately sent Hamilton to ride at full speed down the river.

As he waited for Hamilton's return, Washington was told that Mrs. Arnold had gone berserk. She had been shrieking in her bedroom all morning that her husband was gone, gone forever! Now she was raving about a hot iron burning into her head. She claimed that only General Washington could lift it from her. He must come at once.

Hamilton had returned with another letter for the commander. He joined Washington and Lafayette as they went to see their hostess. They found her with her blond hair uncombed and streaming down her back. The nightgown she wore was so sheer she was almost nude. Wailing, Mrs. Arnold strode back and forth, sometimes clutching up her baby to her breast. When Washington was announced, she screamed that the man in front of her was not the general but instead was the man who had come to kill her baby. Peggy Shippen Arnold had become hysterical before when thwarted, but Washington had no way of knowing this, and in any event he had reason to trust her mad ranting. Benedict Arnold was gone forever.

The papers Alexander Hamilton had passed to Washington that afternoon had been pried the previous day from the boot of a man traveling as John Anderson. He had been riding south on the east side of the Hudson toward Tarrytown when he was accosted by three men playing cards as they loitered by a stream. Gangs of highwaymen had begun roaming the neutral ground in Westchester County between the two armies, confiscating the property of any enemy they captured; the patriot bands were called "Skinners," the loyalist bands "Cowboys." One of these groups had stopped aristocratic John Anderson in his wine-colored coat and civilian's beaver hat.

Since one man wore a British Army coat, Anderson addressed the group confidently. "I hope, gentlemen, you belong to the lower party"—a reference to the British-occupied southern area, Manhattan and Long Island.

"We do," said one of the men.

"So do I," Anderson said with relief. "I am a British officer on business of importance and must not be detained."

But one of the men was already taking Anderson's watch, brandishing a musket and telling him to get down from his horse. Apparently the gang had deceived him—they were patriotic Skinners. The supposed loyalist was wearing a coat he had stolen from a British corpse.

Anderson tried another approach. "I am happy, gentlemen, to find I am mistaken. You belong to the upper party and so do I." He reminded them that these days a man had to use any tactic to get through no-man's-land. To prove he was genuinely on the American side, he pulled out a pass signed by General Benedict Arnold.

The men—John Paulding, Isaac Van Wart and David Williams—thought of themselves as members of the militia when it didn't interfere with extortion. "Damn Arnold's pass," one of them said. "You said you was a British officer. Where is your money?"

"Gentlemen, I have none about me."

"You a British officer and no money!" a man repeated incredulously. "Let's search him."

They led their prisoner to a wood off the highway to avoid having their prize plucked off by a larger gang. They emptied his pockets and found nothing. "He has got his money in his boots," one man said. Between his stocking and his bare foot they found a wad of papers, but they paid no attention to them and went on looking for money hidden in his saddle.

Anderson decided these men were neither loyalists nor patriots but simple thieves, and he asked them to name their price for taking him to King's Bridge at the southern end of no-man's-land. His captors thought it was a trick. If we take you there, they said, you will turn us in to the authorities, and we'll end up in prison.

"If you will not trust my honor," Anderson said, growing edgier as the minutes passed, "two of you may stay with me, and one shall go with a letter which I shall write. Name your sum."

They set a price, but then decided the risk was too great and they might all be seized by the British. They would take the prisoner instead to the commander on the American lines.

That was how three Skinners captured Major John André, Sir Henry Clinton's adjutant general, Peggy Shippen's former dancing partner and Benedict Arnold's accomplice in his plot to betray America.

The papers in Major André's boot could not have damned him more clearly. They included a plan of the fortifications at West Point, an American engineer's analysis of how to defend the fort and a copy of the secret minutes of General Washington's last council of war. By the time the papers reached Washington, André had realized that concealment was hopeless and admitted his identity to Washington in a letter. André claimed that, despite appearances, he had not gone behind American lines as a spy. General Clinton had warned him not to disguise himself but to act as though he were traveling under a flag of truce. The mission had been marred by blunders, however, and André had been forced against his will to wear civilian clothes and use a false name.

As the significance of the capture struck George Washington, he confronted more urgent problems than André's military honor. Washington had endured dinner at the Arnold table with his customary reserve, not mentioning Arnold's flight to Richard Varick. But to Lafayette he had cried out when he first received the messages from Hamilton, "My God! Arnold has gone over to the British. Whom can we trust now?" Washington's shoulders had slumped and, impossible as it seemed, the American commander in chief had looked close to tears.

West Point's neglected defenses, along with André's papers,

suggested that Benedict Arnold had intended to stage a sham resistance and then surrender the fort to the British. Now that the plot was exposed, Henry Clinton might strike at once. The fort was put on alert, André was placed under close guard, and Nathanael Greene and Anthony Wayne were told to rush reinforcements to West Point. Wayne got the word at 1 A.M. and within an hour was moving his Pennsylvania troops north. They marched sixteen miles in the dark for four hours without halting and reached the fort by sunrise. The night had been tense and discouraging for Washington, and he could hardly believe that relief had come so fast. He greeted the troops with an effusiveness that Wayne said made him feel like a god. "All is safe," Washington told him, "and again I am happy."

Washington's precautions had been wise, but Henry Clinton didn't yet know that André had been captured and he had no plan to attack so quickly. When Clinton had been advising Gage and Howe, he had pressed for lightning action, but now that he was in charge he was as wary and cautious as his predecessors. Days passed and the attack did not come. General Washington was left to deal with John André and with Benedict Arnold's young wife.

Arnold was safely beyond Washington's reach. When Washington first read the captured documents, he had sent Hamilton to try to head Arnold off before he could reach sanctuary on a British sloop, the *Vulture*, at anchor in the Hudson. Arnold had been negotiating with Henry Clinton for more than a year over the terms for his betrayal. André had been their go-between. Arnold had first asked for twenty thousand British pounds but settled for a cash payment of six thousand pounds sterling and a commission in the British Army. Once the deal was struck, Arnold had to persuade General Washington to appoint him commander at West Point. Except when Washington had seemed to prefer putting Arnold on the battlefield, that part of the conspiracy had gone smoothly.

Benedict Arnold had not been the only American officer the British had approached. John Sullivan, Daniel Morgan, Philip Schuyler, even Israel Putnam, had all been sounded out and all had rejected the overture indignantly. The same was true of the coxswain on Arnold's barge the morning of his escape. As commander of the fort, Arnold had been told of John Anderson's arrest at the time he was greeting Washington's advance party. After a brief farewell with his wife, he had rushed to the barge and ordered its crew to take him to the *Vulture*. He announced his switch in allegiance during the trip and promised crew members promotions in the British Army if they would join him.

"No, sir!" said the coxswain, Corporal James Larvey. "One coat is enough for me to wear at a time."

The rest of the crew agreed. When they reached the *Vulture*, Arnold had them taken prisoner by the British sailors. From the sloop, he had sent the message to Washington that Hamilton delivered: "The heart which is conscious of its own rectitude cannot attempt to palliate a step which the world may censure as wrong. . . ." Arnold's letter revealed a sense of injustice that had been festering longer than his war wounds. "I have no favor to ask for myself," he continued—although he did request that his clothes and baggage be sent after him. "I have too often experienced the ingratitude of my country to attempt it." But, he said, because of General Washington's well-known humanity, he was asking protection for Mrs. Arnold. "She is as good and as innocent as an angel, and is incapable of doing wrong."

George Washington's entourage had the same opinion. The night the Americans worked to strengthen their fortifications, Alexander Hamilton, only five years older than the bereft woman, had tried to comfort her. Peggy Arnold received him and his fellow officers from bed. She had recovered from her apparent madness and said she remembered nothing about burning irons or plots to kill her baby. But she was so overcome by the prospect of the hostility she would soon face that Colonel Hamilton wished he were her brother and entitled to defend her honor. He might have been less sympathetic had he known about the letters that had passed between John André and Mrs. Arnold. On their surface, André had merely offered to become Peggy Arnold's milliner, but the correspondence had been intended to determine the price of her husband's loyalty. Whether or not General Washington was equally convinced of Mrs. Arnold's innocence, he sent her and her infant home to Philadelphia, and Lafayette wrote ahead to say that it would be exceedingly painful to Washington if Mrs. Arnold were not received with the greatest kindness.

Washington would not extend the same charity to John André. The major considered himself a legitimate wartime emissary and still hoped he would be exchanged again as a prisoner of war.

Riding downriver to be put on trial at Washington's headquarters in Tappan, New York, André had tried to draw some comforting words from his escort, Major Benjamin Tallmadge. But he had chosen the wrong man.

Surely, André asked, he would not be treated as a spy?

His guard evaded the question. When André persisted, Tallmadge told him about a classmate from Yale, a friend he had loved, who had joined the American Army and then served General Washington by entering New York in civilian clothes and gathering information about British installations. The young man was Nathan Hale.

"Do you remember the sequel of this story?" Tallmadge asked.

"Yes," said André. "He was hanged as a spy, but you surely do not consider his case and mine alike?"

"Precisely similar," said Tallmadge, "and similar will be your fate."

For the first time, André understood the enormity of his offense. Benjamin Tallmadge had reason to gloat over André's obvious agitation, but he had been as charmed by him as men and women always were, and he watched with nothing but sympathy.

General Washington selected Nathanael Greene to preside over André's trial. Greene had been a Quaker once, but that was many battles ago. If John André was a spy—and he freely admitted that he had not gone to West Point under any legal protection—he must pay with his life. That was the finding of the board. The next day, October 1, 1780, George Washington endorsed it: "The commander-in-chief directs the execution of the above sentence in the usual way this afternoon at 5 o'clock precisely." The usual way was hanging.

In New York, Henry Clinton threatened to execute American prisoners of war if André was hanged, but Washington remained unmoved. He knew that his army held too many British prisoners for Clinton to embark on bloody reprisals. Alexander Hamilton, who felt sympathy for the prisoner, wrote an anonymous letter to Clinton suggesting that André be traded for Benedict Arnold. Since Hamilton regularly wrote George Washington's letters, Clinton recognized his handwriting and assumed he was speaking on Washington's behalf. Even so, Arnold was too great a prize to surrender. Other American officers also fell under André's spell and suggested that Hamilton ask André to make the plea himself. Surely Clinton would not refuse an appeal from his favorite young officer. But Hamilton refused even to pass along the idea, because he was sure André's high sense of honor would force him to reject it.

When André saw that nothing would save him and that he would die before nightfall, he sent General Washington a message asking to be shot as a soldier rather than hanged as a spy. Washington did not reply. He had decided not to honor the request and thought it was a kindness to let André go on hoping until the final moment. When Hamilton made the same plea on André's behalf, Washington continued to resist it. John André, for all his charm and good manners, had been convicted of spying, and spies were hanged.

As the hour approached, a vast crowd gathered at the field behind Maybie's Tavern where the gibbet had been built. Then, at the last minute, Henry Clinton caused a cruel delay. In exchange for André's life, Clinton offered any American prisoner he held. By the time Washington had rejected the proposal, the hanging had been delayed until noon of the next day.

As his admirers expected, John André behaved impeccably on the last day of his life. A servant was allowed through the lines to bring him a dress uniform, but when the man entered the room in tears André sent him away, saying, "Leave me until you show yourself more manly."

Each morning since his arrest, André's breakfast had come from George Washington's own table, and this day was no different. After André ate, he was shaved and dressed in full uniform. Seated before a mirror, he made a pen-and-ink sketch of himself as a memento for one of his guards. He then rose and linked arms with the two men who were to escort him. "I am ready at any moment, gentlemen, to wait on you," André said. The guards thought his mood seemed cheerful.

Again a crowd had turned out. Only General Washington and his staff were absent. Washington had ordered his shutters drawn against the sight of the execution. There was no glee in carrying out the sentence, only sadness. André walked out from his quarters, arm in arm with the American officers. He smiled as he bowed to members of the court that had condemned him, and he complimented the fifers of the military band on the excellence of their music. André expected to face a firing squad, and when he saw the gallows he gave a start and held back.

"Why this emotion, sir?" one of the guards chided him.

André recovered and continued walking. "I am reconciled to my death," he said, "but I detest the mode."

A wagon with his coffin had been drawn up directly under the gallows. André stepped upon the back of the wagon and, hands on hips, paced up and down the length of his coffin as he surveyed the audience that had come to see him die. Those nearby watched him look to the top of the gallows and say, "It will be but a momentary pang."

The executioner appeared, his face and arms smeared with black grease. He was a Tory prisoner named Strickland, who would be paid for the day's work with his freedom. When he tried to put the noose around André's neck, André pulled back and said, "Take your black hands off me." Instead he did it himself, drawing the rope up snugly, with the knot under his right ear. He took a handkerchief from his pocket and tied it over his eyes. The commanding officer announced that his arms must also be bound, and André produced a second handkerchief and let himself be tied behind his back, just above the elbows.

The commander asked if he had any last words. Major André said, "Only bear witness that I died like a brave man."

The rope was long, and when the wagon was suddenly pulled away John André's body swung in a great arc. Gradually, the movement slowed until he hung still. The commander ordered a soldier to shorten André's misery by pressing down hard on his shoulders. For almost half an hour, his body hung from the gallows amid silence from the crowd.

America was avenged, but George Washington had lost twice in the affair. Benedict Arnold, once his bravest general, was now his enemy. And Alexander Hamilton could not forgive Washington for his hardness of heart and began to look less worshipfully at his commander.

The battle of Yorktown, painted by an eyewitness, Louis van Blarenberghe

Yorktown

THOMAS JEFFERSON had suffered a series of political defeats over the five years since the bright days of his Declaration of Independence. Serving in the Virginia assembly until June 1779, he had proposed a host of reform measures to redistribute the privileges held by the plantation owners and the Anglican clergy. Jefferson believed that for a strong society to arise, the community should consist of many farmers with small holdings, perhaps fifty acres,

1781

rather than the same men working vast estates as tenants. Jefferson had also proposed tax-supported schools to give both boys and girls at least three years of education. He advocated revising the penal code so that only murder and treason remained punishable by death and argued for absolute separation of state and church. But after three years he had succeeded in passing only one major reform—a bill abolishing primogeniture, which had required that upon a man's death the bulk of his property go to his oldest son. For all his influence in Philadelphia, Jefferson had been no match for the conservative faction in the Virginia legislature. When he ran for the speaker's post in 1778, he had been defeated by better than two to one.

Patrick Henry had nominated Jefferson as governor, a post Henry had held for three one-year terms. The Virginia assembly elected Jefferson by a six-vote margin in June 1779, but by the time he took office Virginia had become all but ungovernable. Henry, unable to curb his need for applause, had worked harder at being popular than at preparing Virginia for the war that was moving steadily south. And Jefferson, devoted to liberty and the virtue of reason, lacked the imperial qualities of a war governor. Behind the scenes, he and Patrick Henry often differed, and Jefferson suspected that Henry wanted to return to office, not as Virginia's governor but as her despot. Both men still supported having a militia over the standing army that Washington considered essential. Yet Jefferson's stewardship of the militia was uncertain. Troops would be called to duty to find that their arms and equipment had been sent halfway across the state. When the Congress gave the Continental Army's quartermaster the right to confiscate provisions for the soldiers, Jefferson worked to limit his authority.

As governor, Jefferson did not always bring the full power of his unquestioned intellect to his public duty. Frail as she was, his wife continued to conceive, but the infants did not live. In their most recent loss, the boy died even before he could be given a name. Two of five children had survived, both daughters. During Jefferson's second year as governor another baby daughter died in her fifth month, but by that time he had already decided to resign. Other politicians had been suggesting for years that Jefferson was on the easy path to premature retirement. They did not know how mortified Jefferson became whenever he faced a greater challenge than he thought he could meet. When, in the face of increasing threats from the British, the seat of government moved from Williamsburg to Richmond, Jefferson announced that he would quit the governorship on July 2, 1781.

His decision became unshakable when Britain's newest general, Benedict Arnold, made an unexpected assault on Richmond. Although Arnold had failed to deliver West Point, Henry Clinton had paid him the full six thousand pounds John André had promised, plus three hundred and fifteen pounds in expenses. Arnold was also commissioned as a provisional brigadier general, which gave him an annual salary of six hundred and fifty pounds, far more than his former pay in devalued Continental currency. Despite Clinton's patronage, General Arnold quickly made himself so unpopular that many younger British officers refused to serve under him. Changing allegiances had left him neither less rough-edged and graceless nor less audacious. Burning and pillaging his way through Virginia, he showed his contempt for the state's militia. Jefferson had ignored warnings of the coming attack and only at the last minute had appointed Baron von Steuben to defend Richmond. Finally Jefferson himself rode his horse to exhaustion as he tried to raise a resistance. His effort was ineffectual, and although he was not captured, Jefferson wrote candidly about the debacle to George Washington. The general sent back his sympathy, along with Lafayette and twelve hundred Continental troops to keep Benedict Arnold at bay.

It had seemed unlikely that there could be worse humiliation in store for Governor Jefferson, but in April Arnold returned as part of a new force led by Major General William Phillips, commander of the artillery at the battle of Minden, where Lafayette's father had been killed. Avid for revenge but badly outnumbered, Lafayette protected Richmond and gave Jefferson the chance to move the capital again, this time to Charlottesville. Jefferson wrote another letter to Washington, pleading with him to come and save his native state. But Washington was developing a broader strategy, and though he answered Jefferson kindly, he stayed in the North.

Despair was leading Jefferson to a hatred of Benedict Arnold that calm reason could not purge. He hoped Arnold would be kidnapped and hauled around America, exhibited as a public display of infamy. Arnold knew how deeply his former countrymen longed for revenge. During this Virginia campaign, he had amused himself by asking a captured American officer what would happen to him if he were captured. The American said that Arnold's left leg, wounded at Quebec and Saratoga, would be cut off and buried with full military honors. The rest of him would be hanged.

On July 1, 1781, the night before Jefferson was due to leave the governorship, a hulking American captain named Jack Jouett rode out on a mission that would have challenged the stamina of Paul Revere. Jouett left the Cuckoo Tavern, forty miles outside Charlottesville, with the same purpose for which Revere had ridden six years before—to warn a prominent patriot that the British were coming to seize him. This time their target was Thomas Jefferson. Jouett had stopped at the Cuckoo and found two hundred and fifty British dragoons and mounted infantrymen there. They were led by Banastre Tarleton, who had once vowed to cut off Charles Lee's head. Earlier in the year, Tarleton had been defeated by Daniel Morgan in a South Carolina pasture called Hannah's Cowpens. Now he was headed for Monticello to restore his reputation by taking Jefferson prisoner.

Jouett was a first-class horseman. Wrapped in a scarlet cloak, he rode over paths so thick with brush that when he reached Jefferson's mansion before dawn his face was cut and bleeding. Governor Jefferson revived him with a glass of Madeira and told him to alert Virginia's other officials in town.

Jefferson sent his wife, his daughters and their house guests to a neighboring estate. Building his mansion on a hill had seemed an impractical fancy during construction, but now its view of the surrounding countryside gave him a good start on any British soldiers coming to capture him.

Many stories sprang up later about Jefferson's behavior in the face of the enemy. One of the few favorable ones had Jefferson riding up the slope behind Monticello until he reached Carter's Mountain and turned a telescope toward Charlottesville. He saw no trace of the green-and-white uniforms worn by Tarleton's men and decided that Jouett's alarm had been mistaken and that he would not have to abandon his house. George Washington's concern for Mount Vernon was evident in the long letters he wrote home, but when he heard that his caretaker had given food to a band of British troops to prevent them from destroying his house, Washington had sent a reprimand: Never again yield to blackmail. Jefferson's feelings for his home were even more profound than Washington's and now, with no enemy in sight, he turned his horse back to Monticello.

At that moment, the story continued, Jefferson noticed that his light walking sword had slipped from its sheath while he was kneeling on a rock to adjust his lens. Going back for the sword, he raised the telescope once more, and this time he found Charlottesville buried under a blizzard of green and white. Jefferson saw nothing logical about confronting the foe like Don Quixote; these were not windmills but prime British troops. He mounted his horse and, avoiding the road, headed to the safety of the next hill. From there he rode to the house where he had sent his family.

At Monticello, Jefferson's slaves were doing their best to protect his property. Martin Hemings, Jefferson's valet, had also done the household shopping during Martha Jefferson's frequent confinements. As the British approached, Hemings gathered the family silver and began handing it to another slave in a hiding place under a plank of the front portico. When Tarleton's dragoons rushed up, Martin Hemings dropped the board over the slave and the silver and stood on it. A British officer pressed the barrel of his pistol to Hemings' chest and threatened to fire unless he told them where Jefferson had gone.

"Fire away, then," Hemings said.

Instead, the unit's commander inspected the mansion and ordered that nothing be touched. The British withdrew that same night, and Monticello's slaves became its caretakers.

Lord Cornwallis made his headquarters at the Elkhill plantation that had come to Jefferson through marriage. There the British showed no restraint. They burned barns filled with corn and tobacco, carried off cattle and sheep and cut the throat of every horse too young to be ridden. They also induced Elkhill's thirty slaves to desert their master and come away with them. Jefferson said afterward that had Cornwallis freed them he would have done the right thing. But Jefferson spoke of the runaways as though they had been abducted, even though they had left willingly. Most of them lost their chance for freedom when they died of smallpox in the British camp. Even after their defection, Thomas Jefferson owned two hundred slaves.

Jefferson remained in hiding over the next weeks and then crowned his luck by falling off his horse. The accident happened long after the danger had passed, but his detractors sneered that he had injured himself during an unbecoming flight from Monticello. In the bitterest moment of Jefferson's career, a young political opponent demanded that the legislature investigate Governor Jefferson's conduct over the past twelve months. Jefferson was convinced Patrick Henry was behind the move and never forgave him. The legislature eventually endorsed Jefferson's ability, rectitude and integrity, and a friend consoled him for the indignities he had suffered by reminding him that "the envious only hate the excellence they cannot reach."

Virginia's politicians knew that Thomas Jefferson and Patrick Henry were estranged, but the marauding British troops still thought of them as partners in treason. Henry had fled as hastily as the governor, yet the difference in their popularity was reflected in a story about his flight from Charlottesville at about the time Jefferson was riding to Carter's Mountain. Tarleton's dragoons had already captured seven legislators, and other British soldiers were chasing down the road behind Jack Jouett's bright cloak. Patrick Henry was trying to escape with a group that included the assembly speaker, Benjamin Harrison, and John Tyler, who had stood in the Burgesses' doorway with Thomas Jefferson as a student and listened to Henry threaten George III with the fate of Caesar and Cromwell. As the fugitives struggled through the hills, they grew tired and hungry and stopped at a cabin for shelter. The woman who came to the door demanded to know who they were.

"We are members of the legislature," said Henry, "and have just been compelled to leave Charlottesville on account of the approach of the enemy."

"Ride on, then, you cowardly knaves!" the woman said indignantly. "Here my husband and sons have just gone to Charlottesville to fight for you, and you running away with all your might! Clear out! You shall have nothing here!"

Patrick Henry persisted. "But we were obliged to fly. It would not do for the legislature to be broken up by the enemy. Here is Mr. Speaker Harrison. You don't think he would have fled if it had not been necessary?"

The woman did not give way. "I always thought a good deal of Mr. Harrison till now," she said. "But he'd no business to run from the enemy." She began to shut the door.

"Wait a moment, my good woman," said Patrick Henry, and he named the other members of the party.

"They here?" said the woman dubiously. "Well, I never would have thought it." She seemed to weaken, then recovered. "No matter. We love those gentlemen, and I didn't suppose they would ever run from the British, but since they have, they shall have nothing to eat in my house. You may ride along."

As a final plea, John Tyler stepped forward. "What would you say, my good woman, if I were to tell you that Patrick Henry fled with the rest of us?"

"Patrick Henry! I would tell you there wasn't a word of truth in it. Patrick Henry would never do such a cowardly thing."

"But," said Tyler, pointing to him, "this is Mr. Henry."

The woman looked astonished and tugged at her apron as she considered the news. "Well, then, if that is Patrick Henry, it must be all right."

She showed them into her cabin and went off to fix their meal.

Although Alexander Hamilton was still writing George Washington's confidential military correspondence, his indignation over the hanging of John André continued to boil. Colonel Hamilton had changed somewhat since his impetuous outbursts at Monmouth Court House. During the winter of 1780 he had courted Philip Schuyler's daughter Elizabeth. General Schuyler had endorsed the match, but Hamilton had been concerned about the difference between their fortunes and asked his fiancée, "Do you soberly relish the pleasure of being a poor man's wife?" The couple had married after Benedict Arnold's defection and spent their honeymoon in the Schuyler mansion at Albany. By February 1781, Hamilton was back as Washington's aide in the American headquarters at New Windsor, New York, and working until midnight on dispatches for the French allies at Newport. But secretarial duty was palling on Hamilton. He had applied twice for a field command and had been turned down each time.

One day after Hamilton and Washington had stayed up late the previous night drafting messages, both were weary and strained. Hamilton was going down from the second floor of the headquarters building on an errand when he passed General Washington climbing the stairs. "I would like to speak with you, Colonel Hamilton," Washington said.

"I will wait upon you immediately, sir," Hamilton replied.

He delivered his papers to another aide, Tench Tilghman, and was heading back upstairs when he met Lafayette in the hall. They had been hoping for permission to attack New York with Hamilton leading the light infantry, but lately their plan seemed to have been jettisoned. After some moments of talk, Hamilton pulled himself away and hurried up the staircase.

Washington stood at the top, wearing his coldest face. "Colonel Hamilton," he said, "you have kept me waiting at the head of these stairs these ten minutes. I must tell you, sir, you treat me with disrespect."

"I am not conscious of it, sir," said Hamilton, "but since you have thought it necessary to tell me so, we part."

It was not the response the commander in chief had expected. After a moment, Washington said, "Very well, sir, if it be your choice."

Hamilton retired to his quarters. Within the hour, Colonel Tilghman brought him a message from Washington, assuring Hamilton of his great confidence in his abilities and integrity and inviting him for a candid conversation to heal their differences.

Hamilton had spent years with Washington and knew how hard humble appeals were for him. But he sent back a message asking to be excused from meeting with the general; he would stay on only until other aides could assume his duties. Hamilton wrote to his father-in-law that Washington was indeed an honest man and his popularity was essential to America's safety, but "for three years past I have felt no friendship for him and have professed none."

Hamilton kept his vow to leave and throughout the spring of 1781 wrote articles for the *New York Packet* on the new nation's problems, especially in its economy. Congress had at last hammered out the Articles of Confederation, and after a long delay Virginia had ceded her claims to the Northwest. Maryland accepted the Articles and a national government could be organized, five years after independence.

Taxation remained a dilemma, however. Since only the states could levy taxes, the Congress was printing paper money that it could not back with gold. At last, in spring 1780, the members had voted to declare forty paper dollars worth one gold dollar. That devaluation cut the national debt from two hundred million to five million, but it did not produce more money for the hard-pressed Continental Army. To solve the problem, Hamilton urged Robert Morris, the Philadelphia banker, to accept the new federal office of financier. Hamilton also argued vigorously for a stronger central government that would enlarge the powers of Congress.

Publicly, Hamilton remained correct and formal with George Washington and even returned briefly to help extricate Washington from a rare indiscretion. In a letter to Mount Vernon, Washington had criticized the French for sending fewer ships to a maneuver in Chesapeake Bay than he had requested. British soldiers had intercepted the letter and printed it in a Tory newspaper. Washington needed the French as never before, and he personally oversaw the revisions of the apology that Hamilton drafted for him. When Washington's French colleague, the Comte de Rochambeau, received the letter, he declared the incident closed.

As Hamilton was preparing to leave the staff again, he wrote to General Washington requesting a battlefield assignment. Washington responded the same day, embarrassed that he couldn't oblige him and concerned that Hamilton might link his refusal to their past friction. With that, Hamilton took his wife, three months pregnant, home to the Schuyler estate in Albany and resigned his commission. Once more, Colonel Tilghman came to him on Washington's behalf and urged him not to leave the army. Three weeks later Colonel Hamilton was named to lead two New York regiments. But the question remained, where would he lead them? Did Washington intend to attack Henry Clinton's forces on Manhattan?

Nathanael Greene's tough and clever campaign had been picking off exposed British outposts in the Carolinas, but Lord Cornwallis went on sweeping and burning through the South. His successes had no great strategic value, and a victory he claimed at Guilford in North Carolina cost him nearly forty percent of his army. Cornwallis' constant motion perplexed the Americans and their allies. "These English are mad," Lafayette said. "They march through a country and think they have conquered it." All the same, Lafayette wrote to Hamilton that his Virginia troops were so badly outnumbered by Cornwallis' men that he had to stay in camp and resist the urge to fight.

With the war in its seventh inconclusive year, every strategic decision was overshadowed by the question of what support the French would provide before the 1781 campaign ended. General Rochambeau, who commanded the five thousand French troops in Rhode Island, claimed he had forgiven Washington's tactless letter, but he seemed so evasive in discussing France's plans that Washington was becoming resentful. Rochambeau had good reason, however, to question American security. General Washington had developed no code for letters to his commanders in the

South. On the last day of May 1781 he wrote openly to Lafayette in Virginia that French and American troops would launch a joint attack against New York. An alert British patrol got hold of the letter and brought it to Henry Clinton. Initially, the British commander was dubious. Couldn't the letter be a ruse planted to deceive him? But the intercepted pouch also contained a letter from Martha Washington to Mount Vernon filled with domestic details, and another from Washington to his dentist, requesting a pair of pliers for repairing his teeth. All those homely touches guaranteed that the letter to Lafayette was legitimate. Knowing Washington's intentions was invaluable to Sir Henry, and he willingly paid two hundred guineas to the man who had seized the pouch.

The proof that Manhattan would be America's target was particularly welcome to Henry Clinton because he was locked with Lord Cornwallis in a test of wills and ambition much like the one that George Washington had faced from Charles Lee.

Clinton was now beginning his fourth year as commander in chief of Britain's forces yet had little to show for his exertions. Lord Cornwallis, like Burgoyne before him, had used the excuse of his wife's illness for a trip to England, where he spent his time ingratiating himself with George Germain. He returned to America with a document naming him Clinton's replacement should the commander be killed or incapacitated. Cornwallis—and apparently Germain as well—wanted to win the war in the South, even if that meant evacuating New York. Henry Clinton had rejected that strategy, and now Washington's intercepted letter proved him right. The major engagement of 1781 would come in the North, and to prepare for it Clinton ordered Cornwallis to gather up his men and secure a base for the British Navy in Chesapeake Bay. Cornwallis suggested a site in Virginia near the settlement of Yorktown. Because the post would be only defensive, Clinton also directed Cornwallis to send two thousand troops to bolster New York's defenses against an attack that might involve twenty thousand French and American soldiers. Cornwallis first stalled and then announced with bad grace that he would march his men away from Yorktown and put the requested troops on ships bound for New York. To do that, however, Cornwallis would have to give up Chesapeake Bay altogether.

That blackmail succeeded. George Germain was insisting on the bay's importance, and Clinton, who already felt himself slipping in favor, did not want to cross the Ministry. Clinton was less lax about security than the Americans and wrote his revised orders to Cornwallis in cipher. But the decoding at Lord Cornwallis' headquarters was somehow delayed, and it was a week before Cornwallis read the latest directive: he must stay at Yorktown and keep as many men as he needed to fortify that installation. Cornwallis was already grumbling about the difficulties in defending the site, although he had chosen it himself. He decided that to make Yorktown secure, he couldn't spare any men for Henry Clinton.

George Washington's letter about the coming campaign hadn't been an example of guile but of something more characteristic in his life—a calamity shot through with luck. Early in July 1781, Washington did indeed meet with General Rochambeau at White Plains to plan a joint attack on New York. But soon afterward American advance parties trying to land secretly on Staten Island ran into British troops foraging for food. Washington cherished the weapon of surprise, and now that it was denied him he began to rethink his campaign.

In mid-August, Washington received news that his most fervent dream was about to come true, but with one significant change. Admiral François-Joseph-Paul Comte de Grasses was on his way to America with more than thirty ships of the French fleet and with thirty-two hundred fresh troops. Instead of coming as far north as New York, however, de Grasse was sailing for Chesapeake Bay, where he could stay only until the middle of October. If Washington wanted to launch an offensive supported by the French Navy, he had two months to do it. And he and Rochambeau would have to march their armies four hundred and fifty miles south.

Later, Washington learned that General Rochambeau had been planning a Southern campaign all along. At fifty-six, Jean-Baptiste-Donatien de Vimeur, Comte de Rochambeau, was seven years older than Washington and much his senior in warfare. Rochambeau had put himself nominally under American command, but when he thought Washington was mistaken, he felt no obligation to abet him. He had written secretly to Admiral de Grasse urging him to sail directly from the West Indies to Chesapeake Bay. A Southern campaign had never appealed to Washington, and he wasn't at all sure it would work. He knew that if Cornwallis stayed where he was, he could hold off Lafayette's troops. But if he heard that Washington and Rochambeau planned to move south, Cornwallis could march his forces inland to North Carolina, away from the French Navy's damaging guns. And if Henry Clinton in New York learned of such a plan, he could put his men on ships, sail them down the coast and reinforce Cornwallis long before the Americans could get to Virginia on foot. Those were the obstacles Washington foresaw. When he realized that Rochambeau had forced the change on him, Washington had gone into a rage. Oblivious to the others in his headquarters room, he strode back and forth, crying out that his hopes were blasted and his country lost. That went on for half an hour, until Washington regained himself and apologized to a group of civilian visitors who had witnessed the scene. But then Washington burst out again: If only the French would either fulfill his expectations or not raise them at all. Washington had wanted desperately to retake New York. Now that would have to wait still another year.

Once he was resigned to the new strategy, General Washington took it as his own and became sly. On the morning of August 19, 1781, he moved advance troops into New Jersey in what appeared to be preparations for an attack on New York. Men suspected of being spies were allowed to glimpse secret reports that Admiral de Grasse was coming north to join the assault on Staten Island. American engineers laid down the outlines of a major camp in New Jersey so authentic that the ovens could bake thousands of loaves of bread.

Washington ordered that his own troops be told nothing. "If we do not deceive our own men," he instructed his staff, "we will never deceive the enemy." He had determined that he could take twenty-five hundred of his own troops to Virginia, along with all five thousand of Rochambeau's soldiers. As a line officer, Hamilton was now one of those kept mystified. He was heard complaining that the Great Man had set off on a wild goose chase.

Henry Clinton watched the preparations for an attack on Staten Island without surprise or suspicion, although he had heard rumors from his network of spies that the Americans might actually be moving south. Benedict Arnold recommended that the British assault the troops that were left behind in order to force Washington to fight in the North. But Clinton hesitated. He had heard contradictory stories and for ten weeks had been relying on Washington's captured letter to justify a defense of Staten Island. Clinton might have ventured out to see for himself, but he had always preferred to command—and quarrel—by letter. "I'm a shy bitch," he had once confessed unhappily, and he detested any sort of confrontation.

At the moment, everything seemed to be conspiring against Clinton. His housekeeper, a British captain's wife, was pregnant with his child, and he was feuding with an ancient British general, James Robertson, whom Clinton accused of thievery and of roaming the countryside "smelling after every giddy girl." As pressure mounted for Clinton to make a decision, he was supplied with an unassailable excuse for not leaving his headquarters. Twice, he went temporarily blind. When he recovered, he continued to draft elaborate, even persuasive, plans on paper. He kept a meticulous record of how his own officers and the Ministry in London were failing him. But Clinton did not act.

In Virginia, Lord Cornwallis was being just as sluggish. He had begun his fortification of Yorktown on August 1, but the weather was scorching hot, and many of the blacks he had persuaded or compelled to serve the British were dying every day working on the walls and the trenches. Cornwallis usually would not force his soldiers to make that same exertion under the broiling sun. Even allowing for the heat, though, Cornwallis had arrived at a puzzling decision: in order to control Chesapeake Bay against the French fleet, he would fortify one town on each bank of the York River. Of the two sites, Yorktown was more essential, but Cornwallis ordered his men to build defenses first across the river at Gloucester. Because he had refused Henry Clinton's call to send troops north, Cornwallis retained five thousand British regulars and eighteen hundred Hessians to hold the two defensive positions. But as he turned to fortify Yorktown, Cornwallis was having increasing doubts about the position he had chosen. It was not, he feared, very strong.

On the last Saturday in August 1781, as General Clinton waited in New York, three columns of the American and French armies began their long march south. George Washington worked to the last moment to keep his ruse alive. His orders to the men covered only their route for a few days and gave no confirmation of their final destination. He was pleased to hear that soldiers in his own camp were betting over whether they would be fighting in New York or Virginia.

On August 29, Washington had dinner with Rochambeau at Princeton before riding on to Trenton and then to Philadelphia. After four days Washington had established the lead over Henry Clinton he had hoped for, but he was receiving only unreliable information about the size and location of the French and British fleets. Washington knew the British had squadrons in the West Indies under Admirals Sir George Rodney and Sir Samuel Hood, and he hoped that they hadn't intercepted Admiral de Grasse's French fleet. One promising rumor had de Grasse defeating Hood's large navy. If the French ships at Newport could link with those coming up from the Caribbean, Washington's forces might possibly command Chesapeake Bay.

On Monday, September 3, 1781, members of the Continental Congress stood outside the State House in Philadelphia to accept a tribute from their army. Years earlier, Samuel Adams had warned Boston's Town Meetings against the papist French. Now Adams was back home, and his colleagues were taking their hats off to General Rochambeau's men. The French soldiers marched past in gleaming white broadcloth uniforms with pink and white plumes in their hats. Their commander had ordered his officers to salute the Congress as though it were, collectively, a crowned head.

As their allies paraded by, the delegates were hopeful that America's ordeal was moving toward a climax, but George Washington was plagued by doubts which he confided only to the few men closest to him. He wrote to Lafayette that he was distressed beyond words that he didn't know the whereabouts of the French ships that were essential to his campaign. Whatever happened, Lafayette was to keep Cornwallis from retreating inland until Washington and Rochambeau arrived. "Adieu, my dear Marquis!" Washington concluded. "If you get anything new from any quarter, send it, I pray you, on the spur of speed, for I am almost all impatience and anxiety . . ."

Washington's admirers like Thomas Paine had painted him as a modern Fabius, a conservative general fighting a canny defensive war. But, from the first, Washington had been suppressing a gambler's instinct as strong as John Burgoyne's. Defeat had provoked him at Trenton and Princeton into making gallant, foolish gestures, and he had won those rolls of the dice. More often he had been forced to rely on elements outside his control—disobedient or traitorous generals, independent French admirals, hostile weather, botched communications. His need was greater this time than ever before that all the pieces of the mechanism mesh and turn together, and this time even more of the pieces lay beyond his reach. Washington was no longer the inexperienced and overwhelmed commander William Howe had driven from New York. He had learned from his blunders and found confidence in his own decisions. Less than a month before, he had been determined to conquer New York. Now he was in the South, risking everything on speed and intuition. But this was another intricate strategy, perhaps as overly complicated as his worst failures, and again he had left himself at the mercy of events he could not control.

On the afternoon of September 5, Washington was riding south from Chester, Pennsylvania, when a horseman came galloping down the road toward him. Washington read through the dispatches the messenger brought and ordered his advance party to turn and go back to Chester. General Rochambeau was heading there by water from Philadelphia, inspecting river forts along the way, and Washington wanted to greet him with the news he had just received.

As Rochambeau's boat approached the dock, General Washington was waiting for him. There was no mistaking Washington's excitement. He was waving his hat to Rochambeau in great sweeps with one hand and waving his handkerchief with the other. When Rochambeau landed, Washington embraced him and explained his uncontrollable joy. On August 29 Admiral de Grasse had reached Chesapeake Bay from Santo Domingo in the West Indies and had brought three thousand French troops. Now there could be no more excuses. Washington laid out the alternatives starkly to Lafayette: "We must take Cornwallis or be all dishonored." Providence, and His Most Christian Majesty the king of France, had given George Washington the chance to save his country and to enter history as one of its greatest generals.

The British surrender at Yorktown,
October 18, 1781

Victory

LORD CORNWALLIS could not see the entrance to Chesapeake Bay
from his fort at Yorktown. He had to be told by a British naval
lieutenant that the French fleet, led by Admiral de Grasse's huge
flagship, the 104-gun *Ville-de-Paris*, had arrived. Cornwallis urgently sent a message in code to General Henry Clinton: "There are
between thirty and forty sail within the capes, mostly ships of war
and some of them very large."

1781

Before his message reached Clinton's headquarters, the British fleet under Rear Admiral Thomas Graves had sailed from New York, heading for the Chesapeake. Graves knew only that de Grasse was somewhere on the seas and that Admiral Louis de Barras might have taken his ships away from Newport. But Graves, like Clinton, thought the Americans were preparing to strike at Staten Island, and he expected no opposition to his fleet at Chesapeake Bay.

Graves's progress was leisurely, a mere three miles per hour. At dawn on September 5 he came in sight of the Chesapeake capes and planned to enter the channel by noon and contact Lord Cornwallis the next day. Then, at 9:30 A.M., a lookout on the admiral's frigate sighted what looked like the masts of ships anchored in the bay ten miles away. A veteran navy captain assured the lookout that they couldn't be ships but might be the trunks of charred pines. Virginians often burned them for their tar, he said, and left them standing.

Admiral de Grasse was dismayed to find the British advancing. His scouts had first thought that the approaching fleet was Barras's ships from Rhode Island. As they drew nearer, however, de Grasse was about to be forced into a sea battle he had not expected. He had just sent nearly two thousand officers and men ashore inside the bay to gather water and firewood. That meant he had twenty-four ships moored within the bay that must be readied for the attack. The gunships of both navies were designed to carry only their cannon; they were simply broad platforms, with masts and canvas sails that rose a hundred, even two hundred, feet, and were hard to move and turn. In battle, their crews were shut up with the cannon in narrow cells, where they shot off a thousand pounds of metal ball in each broadside. Their position left them exposed to enemy shells hurtling toward them, and before an engagement sailors scattered sand over the decks to keep from slipping on the blood that would soon flood over them.

Admiral de Grasse stood six feet two inches, and until his waist thickened with the years he had been considered one of his navy's most handsome officers. His men were proud of his arrogance and temper. They boasted that during battle he grew another four inches. Now he moved his fleet far enough out of the bay to give him sea room for the coming engagement. But the British had the advantage of coming with the wind in compact formation while de Grasse was still struggling to get his fleet out of the harbor.

With the delay Admiral Graves might have picked off the French ships one by one as they struggled out toward the open sea. But de Grasse had put his fastest ships in front, and before

Graves grasped his advantage the French had pulled into a ragged fighting formation. When de Grasse saw a gap at the center of his own line, Admiral Graves surprised him—and infuriated his fellow British officers—by dropping his sails and waiting for de Grasse to shore up his ships. Graves had legitimate reasons for the delay. He was having problems with some of the ships Admiral Hood had brought up from the West Indies. The *Terrible* had been crippled long before it reached the Chesapeake; five pumps were barely keeping her afloat, and she lagged behind Graves's fighting line.

It was past 4 P.M. before the two admirals decided that they were in a position to fight. And then Admiral Graves mixed up his signal flags and ran up the pennant that told his fleet to bear down and engage with the enemy before he had taken down the previous signal. The error puzzled Admiral Hood at the rear, and he was late in bringing up his ship. When the firing began, the lines were still not perfectly matched despite all the delay. But the aim from both sides was deadly, and each crew suffered more than two hundred casualties. The British ships were the worse damaged. After ninety minutes of cannon fire, three of them, in addition to the *Terrible*, were leaking from shots through their hulls. As night fell, the enemy fleets rolled on the waves across from each other while men patched up the day's wounds.

At a council of war the next morning, Admiral Graves and Admiral Hood quarreled over the previous day's perplexing signals. For the next forty-eight hours the fleets drifted seven or eight miles apart, until they were nearly a hundred miles from the mouth of the Chesapeake. Admiral Graves was unaware that Lord Cornwallis was bottled up at Yorktown. He knew only that de Grasse was avoiding another engagement at sea, and he would do the same. On September 9, though he had the wind with him, Graves didn't strike.

Each side began to worry that the other might sail back to the mainland and take command of Chesapeake Bay, and on the night of September 9 de Grasse made that decisive move. Admiral Hood watched in alarm as French sails billowed up and the ships sailed off. Hood grew angrier when he learned that Admiral Graves had no idea where the French fleet was heading. Graves waited until September 11, trying to salvage the *Terrible*, before he ordered her evacuated and set on fire. Then he too set off for Chesapeake Bay. What met him there was the worst possible development: Admiral de Barras had sailed eight ships down the Atlantic coast from Newport to North Carolina, then doubled back, slipped past the British patrols and entered the bay. When de Grasse's ships joined those of de Barras, Chesapeake Bay became impenetrable to the British.

Admiral Graves sought the advice of his second in command. Admiral Hood wrote back: "Sir Samuel would be very glad to send an opinion, but he really knows not what to say in the truly lamentable state we have brought ourselves."

Graves had no course left except to sail back to New York. He would repair his ships, return to the Chesapeake and try again. And Lord Cornwallis would have to defend Yorktown alone for another month.

While Admiral Graves was hesitating outside the bay, George Washington had ridden sixty miles to prepare Mount Vernon for a visit by his French allies. He hadn't returned to his estate in more than six years, and he found that the roads around the plantation had been badly neglected. Even though it was dusk when Washington arrived, he dictated a letter directing the Fairfax militia to begin work on repairs. At the plantation, Washington was greeted by his stepson, Jack Custis. Washington agreed with Custis' former schoolmaster who had said the young man was remarkably spoiled even by the standards of the Virginia gentry, so exceedingly indolent and surprisingly voluptuous that nature must have intended him to be an Asiatic prince. Custis, now twenty-eight and father of four children, wanted to go to Yorktown for a taste of the war, and Washington took him on as a civilian aide.

On September 10, General Washington received his staff for dinner. Seeing their commander at home for the first time, the Americans were impressed by his opulent hospitality. That evening General Rochambeau and his entourage arrived at Mount Vernon, and the next day Washington resumed his ride south, hoping to find that Admiral de Barras had succeeded in joining de Grasse. In the first report, Washington was told about the battle at sea but nothing about its outcome. The suspense persisted when he reached Williamsburg two days later. A fervent Lafayette threw open his arms and kissed Washington from ear to ear, but Lafayette also had been without news for the past eight days. Then, early on the morning of September 15, Washington got a letter from de Grasse announcing that he was again in possession of Chesapeake Bay and that Barras's squadron had arrived from Newport without a loss. Two days later, de Grasse sent a cutter for Washington and Rochambeau, who sailed through the muggy September heat to see the thirty-two French ships massed in the bay. Afterward Washington's aides told how de Grasse had pulled himself to his full height, kissed Washington on both cheeks and cried, "My dear little General!"

But the admiral's embrace was genuine, and Washington was given the assurance he had come for. Even though de Grasse's orders were to depart Chesapeake Bay on October 15, he took it upon himself to guarantee that the fleet would stay until the end of October. Near sunset Washington left the *Ville-de-Paris* amid a salute of guns from the flagship while thousands of French sailors crowded the decks for a glimpse of America's most famous man.

On his return aboard the cutter, squalls kept Washington at sea for four days. Finally he became so impatient to get back to headquarters that he climbed into a small open boat and was rowed thirty miles up the James River. The delay hardly mattered, because at Yorktown Lord Cornwallis was only continuing to dig in. Washington assumed from the British preparations that Cornwallis was preparing to defend his position to the end. Washington himself had a despairing moment when Admiral de Grasse sent a message that because British ships were reportedly on their way he was going to leave the bay after all. Washington wrote a heated protest—"Your leaving the Bay ruins the cause to all intents and purposes"—and the admiral answered cheerfully that, although his plan to leave had been brilliant, his officers had overruled him. The French fleet would stay on to keep Cornwallis trapped at Yorktown.

At 5 A.M. on Friday, September 28, 1781, the drums in General Washington's camp at Williamsburg struck the tattoo to march. The American officers wanted their men to begin this crucial campaign as freshly groomed as their French allies and ordered them to be well shaved. One brigade commander issued each regiment twelve pounds of flour so that his troops could powder their hair. American riflemen and cavalry, interspersed with cannon, moved along the sandy road that would take them through a dozen miles of pine and black cedar to Yorktown. General Rochambeau's French troops followed them, also with their artillery mixed into the column and not dragged along at the rear. They passed the spot across the river where the Indian princess Pocahontas was said to have saved the life of Captain John Smith nearly a hundred and seventy-five years before.

After the first five miles, the troops reached a fork in the road. The Americans swung left, the French took the more direct path on the right. General Washington rode near the front of the American line on a new light sorrel horse with a white face, named Nelson. By evening the two columns had come within sight of the battlements at Yorktown.

Because the headquarters tents had not arrived, General Washington spent the first night under a mulberry tree. When a few of Cornwallis' dragoons were spotted scouting around the American camp, two companies of American grenadiers easily chased them back to their lines. Cornwallis had built his inner ring of defenses—with seven redoubts for guns—on a rise overlooking a sandy plain. Washington pitched camp there, amid cactus and dried grass and out of range of the British artillery. He was waiting for his own heavy guns, which the French were supplying and bringing up from the banks of the James River six miles away.

On the morning of September 30, Washington discovered that overnight the British had evacuated three of their forward works. It gave the Americans such a critical advantage Washington had to wonder what Cornwallis was thinking. He immediately moved French and American troops into those defenses and turned them toward Yorktown rather than away. Both sides were firing only sporadically, and, though his aides tried to discourage him, Washington made his own reconnaissance just three hundred yards from the British advance posts. He assumed that Cornwallis intended to round up boats along the York River one night and rely on his artillery to hold off the French fleet while he evacuated his men. To frustrate that escape, Washington asked de Grasse to send up several frigates and block the river. The admiral replied that the risk to his ships would be too great. Besides, de Grasse assured Washington, Cornwallis would never try anything so foolish.

Behind his barricades at Yorktown, Lord Cornwallis appeared unperturbed by the mounting crisis. His insouciance did not calm his officers but only spurred them to try to puncture it. Cornwallis was doling out provisions sparingly and seemed convinced they would outlast the siege. Hessians in the camp found the meat putrid and the biscuits wormy, but their complaints didn't reach Cornwallis. He seemed to be relying on his threat to Henry Clinton that he must send aid or "be prepared to hear the worst." Clinton had promised that Admiral Graves's ships would be repaired quickly and would leave New York no later than October 5. But Cornwallis was unaware of the shortage of lumber that was delaying Graves or that Prince William, King George's third son, had arrived in New York. Parades and parties in the sixteen-year-old prince's honor had set back work two days. Even without knowing that, Banastre Tarleton warned Cornwallis not to depend on Clinton's assurances. As soon as the French and the Americans first arrived, Colonel Tarleton had wanted Cornwallis to attack them before they could get their guns in place. Cornwallis had paid as little heed to that advice as Horatio Gates had given to Benedict Arnold at Saratoga. In one argument, Tarleton's brother showed Cornwallis how inadequate his earthworks were by nimbly leaping over one of them. Cornwallis was not shaken. "In that case," he said, "the blame will fall on Clinton, and not on me."

General Washington had hoped for a dark night for his men to begin digging a trench opposite Cornwallis' main defenses where they would station the French and American cannon. But it was still early autumn—the Virginians called the season Indian Summer—and the moon was barely starting to wane. Washington had to send workmen out with only an occasional cloud to protect them. As the digging continued, the weather turned and the nights were rainy. Washington and the French engineers worked to position their cannon as the mire spread across the plain. He walked out on the line with a cloak disguising his rank, and those watching him stand exposed wished they had the nerve to scold him and pull him back to safety. On the night of October 6, Washington returned to the line with a pickax and struck a few ritual blows to indicate that the siege of Yorktown would soon begin. While the trench was being dug, British guns kept up a steady fire against the Americans. At one point, a cannonball landed close to Washington's party and sprayed sand over the hat of his chaplain, Israel Evans. The clergyman took off his hat to brush it, but Washington stopped him. "Mr. Evans, you had better carry that home and show it to your wife and children."

By the dawn of October 7, the Americans had moved their trenches close enough that they could see the British flag fluttering over Yorktown.

Two days later, when the French completed their batteries, the American line was secure on its extreme right, and General Washington was ready to launch his siege. At three o'clock on an afternoon of brilliant sunshine, Washington told the French that they would have the honor of beginning the bombardment. Two hours later, American soldiers ran their flag, which they called the Star-Spangled Banner, up its pole, and Washington came forward to fire the first shot from the American lines. He was led to a newly developed French gun with fitted ammunition and a precision greater than anything he had ever seen. A French adviser pointed to a target on the British walls, and Washington fired and hit that spot. Henry Knox, the bookseller who had made himself an artillery expert, repeated a British deserter's story that Cornwallis, trying to raise his men's morale, had assured them that neither the French nor the Americans had brought any heavy artillery.

After those first shells, the British troops knew better. Over the next twenty-four hours, Yorktown and its harbor took more than thirty-six hundred shots. Shells flew across the night sky in bright arcs, trailing long streams of fire, and the Americans thought the display was the most brilliant they had ever seen. Across the barricades, a Hessian soldier watched the shells hurtle toward him and said they shook the ground like earthquakes.

Cornwallis wrote despondently to Henry Clinton at midnight

on October 11, 1781, that the enemy batteries had been firing without pause for two days, and he estimated that the barrage was coming from forty pieces of cannon and sixteen mortars of eight to sixteen inches. Cornwallis had already lost seventy men. He concluded, "Against so powerful an attack, we cannot hope to make a very long resistance."

Each day Washington's guns got closer to the town. They had been six hundred yards away when Cornwallis wrote his letter. The next day the Americans opened a second parallel and cut the distance in half. The American troops expected that this development would compel Cornwallis to venture out from behind his defenses and fight. But Cornwallis had built a bunker in the grotto of his headquarters and was living underground.

On October 14, a Sunday, the Americans trained their fire on two advance British redoubts near the river. That night General Washington granted Alexander Hamilton's request to lead the attack on one of them. Colonel Hamilton had chosen as his password "Rochambeau," which, said quickly with an American accent, sounded like "Rush on, boys." Hamilton ordered his men to unload their muskets to avoid accidental shots that would alert the British. They were to charge with bayonets. French soldiers would storm the second redoubt, and before the two parties set out each commander addressed them. Washington spoke briefly and simply, urging the Americans to be brave. General Rochambeau pitched his appeal in a higher key. "My children," he began, "I have great need of you tonight." When he finished, a French soldier called from the darkness, "We will fight like lions. Until the last man is killed."

The assault began and it looked as though the volunteers had chosen suicide. As they stormed barricades of felled trees under intense British fire, the soldiers sometimes stumbled into holes blasted in the ground by their own artillery—holes deep enough, one American sergeant thought, for burying an ox. American sappers and miners ran ahead with axes to cut a way past the British defenses, but the troops jammed up and blocked their way. Alexander Hamilton was too short to climb over the wall, but he ordered one of his men to kneel, hopped up on his back and leaped over. As the British gave up their position they threw in crackling grenades, and taking the redoubt cost the Americans nine dead and twenty-four wounded. Lafayette, directing the operation from the rear, was glad to see his American friends performing well in the eyes of the French. He entered the redoubt with Hamilton's forces and sent a teasing message to the French officer charged with taking the other position: "I am in my redoubt. Where are you?"

The French had been assigned the larger of the two positions, and their commander sent back a message: "Tell the marquis I am not in mine but will be in five minutes."

After the British had been driven from both outposts, the nightly rains began, but the American troops waded willingly through the mud to secure the captured redoubts. Now no section of Yorktown was safe from enemy fire. George Washington praised Hamilton, Lafayette and the others for intrepidity and coolness and awarded one of the wounded, Sergeant William Brown of Connecticut, a new medal for valor called the Purple Heart.

Cornwallis inspected his losses on the morning of October 15 and wrote to General Clinton that his position had become so precarious that he couldn't recommend either the British army or navy risking an attempt to save him. But Cornwallis was being driven to the desperate measures the Americans had been expecting. The night of his report to Clinton, he ordered a heavy barrage of artillery down from his walls and sent out three hundred and fifty men to penetrate the enemy lines and silence their guns. One British unit, pretending to be an American relief party, succeeded in getting inside the second parallel. As several British soldiers stabbed the French sentries, others broke off their bayonets in the touchholes of the cannon. Before they were discovered and driven back, they had killed or wounded seventeen French and American soldiers. But they had disabled only six guns, which were repaired before sunup.

The next afternoon Lord Cornwallis gathered all the small craft on the riverbank and had some of his wounded rowed to safety on Gloucester Point. That night, he ordered Banastre Tarleton to prepare to break out from Gloucester and lead a forced march to New York. Though many of their boats had been damaged by the constant shelling, Cornwallis thought he could get his able-bodied troops over the river in three crossings. He would travel with the second and leave behind a letter for George Washington, asking mercy for the sick and wounded he would have to abandon at Yorktown. It was the maneuver Washington had predicted, the one Admiral de Grasse had shrugged away.

Cornwallis' entire first division reached Gloucester before midnight. But then rain and squalls scattered the boats and blew two of them downstream, where they were captured by the Americans. The storm went on until 2 A.M., and Cornwallis gave up all hope of escaping. At noon the next day, the men who had made the first crossing returned to Yorktown, amid a severe barrage from the French. On October 17, French and American commanders celebrated the fourth anniversary of John Burgoyne's surrender at Saratoga with the heaviest thunder of shell they could muster. This was also the day Henry Clinton received Cornwallis' dispatch warning him that Yorktown was probably past saving. All the same, Clinton went ahead with his preparations. He signed a new will and got ready to sail to Virginia to snatch victory away from George Washington.

The October 17 bombardment had begun at daybreak. Before 10 A.M., a young boy wearing a red coat and carrying a drum climbed up on a British parapet and beat the signal for a parley. Immediately, an officer appeared behind him holding a white flag on a standard. He moved outside the British fortification with the drummer at his side. The boy's drum couldn't be heard above the cannon roar, but American soldiers saw the two figures moving toward them and gradually stopped firing. An American officer sprang forward, ran to meet the British soldier, tied a handkerchief over his eyes and led him to a house at the rear of the American parallels. The drummer boy was sent back to Yorktown.

Cornwallis' white flag of truce came a week earlier than George Washington had expected. He knew that British provisions at Yorktown were scarce, but he thought Cornwallis could feed his troops for seven more days and would hold out in hopes that the British Navy would save him. Instead, Cornwallis proposed that hostilities cease for twenty-four hours while representatives drew up the terms for a British surrender. General Washington ordered that the siege continue until an aide drafted a reply for his approval. The answer was ready at 2 P.M.

"An ardent desire to spare the further effusion of blood will readily incline me to listen to such terms for the surrender of your post and garrisons of York and Gloucester as are admissible," was Washington's message. But before scheduling a conference, he demanded the British terms on paper and would permit only a two-hour cease-fire while Lord Cornwallis wrote them out.

Late that afternoon, the proposals arrived in the American camp, along with Cornwallis' complaint that Washington had not given him time to go into proper detail. Cornwallis asked for the same generous terms Horatio Gates had given John Burgoyne at Saratoga. Before the siege had begun, Cornwallis had been adamant about never surrendering as cravenly as Burgoyne had done. Now, without a single British cannon to fire, he had to trust Washington for favorable concessions. He asked specifically that his surrendering troops be returned to Britain or Germany if they pledged not to rejoin the fighting. Gates had been severely criticized for that same provision; even if these same soldiers didn't return to America, they eased Britain's military burden by relieving her forces elsewhere. After Saratoga, the Congress had discovered a lapse in the agreement by Burgoyne and had declared the entire treaty void. Most of his troops were still prisoners in Virginia. George Washington had no intention of being as lenient in victory as General Gates, and he rejected the British terms. But he extended the cease-fire for the night.

The silence of that cold October night was solemn for the Americans. Meteors streaking through the sky reminded them of trailing bombs but without the same horror. The next morning, the British stood along their battlements and serenaded the peaceful dawn with bagpipes. The French responded with their regimental band. As the sun rose, officers and men from each side lined up along their parapets to study their foe across two hundred yards.

Washington had never been in the position to dictate peace terms, and, like Cornwallis, he relied on a recent precedent. When Henry Clinton had taken Charleston, General Benjamin Lincoln of Massachusetts was among the prisoners. He had been exchanged later and had joined Washington at Yorktown. General Washington now extended the British conditions at Charleston to Cornwallis. The harshest was a point of honor. Clinton had forbidden General

Lincoln to march out his vanquished men with drums beating and flags unfurled. Now Washington denied Cornwallis the same courtesies and gave the British commander two hours to agree. After that, the music would stop and the artillery would resume.

Even with all of Washington's planning and nerve, he could not have succeeded without the French Navy. He invited Admiral de Grasse to come ashore and join him at a ceremony that was beginning to look certain, but the admiral was confined to his ship with asthma and sent Barras in his place. Despite the American deadline, negotiations continued throughout the night of October 18 while the British representative tried to ease the terms by pointing out that Lord Cornwallis hadn't been responsible for Henry Clinton's harshness at Charleston. Early the next morning, Washington approved an overnight compromise that gave way on the music. The British army could come out from behind their walls playing a marching tune, but it had to be one of their own melodies, not a mocking rendition of "Yankee Doodle." Washington refused, however, to grant immunity to the Tory civilians at Yorktown or to his own deserters.

Lafayette's brother-in-law, heir to one of France's great fortunes, had served as the French delegate during the talks and protested that, since Cornwallis' war chest held only eighteen hundred pounds sterling, it was undignified to worry about what became of it. America's negotiator replied that to a new country with a devalued currency the money meant a good deal, and the chest must become the property of the United States. General Washington informed Cornwallis that he was to sign the surrender by 11 A.M. and be ready to turn over his troops three hours later.

Washington chose a field between the American camp and the trenches for the ceremony and sent Pennsylvania troops with spades to fill in earth that had been dug from the Yorktown road. Riding on a white horse, Washington led his army onto the plain. He was accompanied by General Rochambeau at the head of the French troops, who wore bright coats with black gaiters setting off white broadcloth trousers. The Americans lined up across from them in hunting shirts and faded Continental uniforms. After the cold nights, the sun warmed the soldiers' backs as they waited past the agreed time for the British to appear.

Five hundred miles north, Henry Clinton's ships had lifted

anchor and were sailing to the Chesapeake. Clinton estimated that in five days he could assist Cornwallis in repelling the enemy.

At the moment, Lord Cornwallis was claiming an indisposition and staying behind his lines. He sent General Charles O'Hara to surrender for him. Count Mathieu Dumas cantered up from the French line and offered to lead O'Hara to General Washington. O'Hara smiled broadly and asked instead for General Rochambeau. Count Dumas had ridden with Washington from New Jersey and had watched worshipful Americans turn out simply to touch their commander in chief's boots. He was not going to let the British cheat Washington of this moment. Dumas pressed his horse forward, putting himself between O'Hara and Rochambeau. Even so, O'Hara held out his sword to the French commander.

Rochambeau shook his head and gestured to Washington. "We are subordinate to the Americans," he said. "General Washington will give you your orders."

O'Hara swung around and approached Washington. Once again he extended his sword, but Washington had given Benjamin Lincoln the honor of conducting the surrender. As he declined to take the sword himself, Washington spoke a consoling word: "Never from such a good hand."

After their insistence on marching out to music, the British had chosen a glum song. The drummer beat to it indifferently as the fifers piped the melancholy tune to its words:

If ponies rode men and if grass ate cows,
And cats should be chased into holes by the mouse . . .

Benjamin Lincoln explained to General O'Hara that the British were to enter a large circle formed by mounted French hussars. About half of Cornwallis' men had come out for the surrender; the rest, the wounded, had been left behind at Yorktown. Within the circle, soldiers from each British regiment were ordered to lay down their arms and march back between the French and American lines. The British soldiers seemed far more shaken than their Hessian allies. Among the thirty-five hundred men, many seemed drunk, and others bit their lips to keep from weeping. Still others gave up and cried out loud. When they were commanded to give up their arms, the men hurled down their weapons to damage them or hugged them in a last embrace and crooned words of farewell. Through it all, the band played on:

If summer were spring and the other way round,
Then all the world would be upside down.

Farewell

A FEW WEEKS before the siege of Yorktown, Horace Walpole in London had been complaining that no significant battles were being fought in America. Walpole, who had served in Parliament during the Stamp Act riots, added that the war was not even entertaining; it would bore more people to death than it killed. Then, on November 26, 1781, London's newspapers carried the terms of Lord Cornwallis' surrender, and the public impatience

General Washington resigning
his commission as
Commander in Chief before
the Continental Congress,
Annapolis, December 23, 1783,
by John Trumbull

1781-83

and indifference turned to a disgust with the war and its leaders.
As Cornwallis had predicted, most of the scorn fell on Henry
Clinton, who was blamed for letting George Washington march
secretly on Yorktown and for not reinforcing Cornwallis in time.
The nation's editors largely spared Cornwallis. His misfortune
seemed even to rehabilitate John Burgoyne's reputation four years
after Saratoga. Editors granted that since Cornwallis, a hero to the

British press, had been forced to surrender, perhaps other men of courage sometimes had to do the same.

In Virginia, General Washington hadn't yet taken in the full meaning of his victory. During the first days, he was distracted by the illness of his stepson, who had developed the fever that had swept both the American and British camps. But Jack Custis had insisted on traveling in a carriage to watch Britain's soldiers give up their weapons. Soon afterward he died, and his stepfather was occupied with comforting Custis' young widow and worrying over Martha Washington's response to her loss.

Washington had not written to his mother throughout the war. Now, after Yorktown, he received a letter from Mary Washington. She didn't mention the war or his victory, but she thanked him for five guineas he had sent, asked him to build her a house on his property near the Blue Ridge and indicated that her health was so poor she might never see him again.

After one week at Mount Vernon coping with family affairs, Washington was ready to strike again. He proposed sending militia from three states to Nathanael Greene, along with the available cavalry. Washington would lead the army to South Carolina personally, and he wrote to Admiral de Grasse, asking for French support in a campaign to retake Charleston. De Grasse, however, was far more interested in chasing a British squadron from the West Indies, and he pulled out his fleet and headed south. Washington was sufficiently annoyed to berate Lafayette for the admiral's defection.

Washington considered America still at war, and George III was under that same misapprehension. Early in November 1781 the king had been momentarily buoyed by reports that Henry Clinton had sailed to Yorktown to reinforce Cornwallis. Otherwise, George had little reason to be encouraged. John Adams, who had returned home from Paris to help draft a constitution for Massachusetts, had then gone to Holland as an emissary in the summer of 1780. The result had been that the Dutch declared war on Britain and were adding their substantial fleet to the American cause. Catherine II of Russia was still operating under a cloak of neutrality, but she had engineered a pact with Sweden and Denmark closing the Baltic to warships, which hampered Britain from boarding vessels at sea and searching them for arms headed to America. Spain had entered the war and, with the French, was picking off valuable British cargo ships around the Caribbean. The Earl of Pembroke, who had once served in King George's household, wrote that everyone now pitied the king as they saw his vast powers crumbling away.

Parliament met two days after the stories of Cornwallis' defeat appeared in the British newspapers. The speech Lord North had prepared for the king made only a passing reference to the American war, but North knew that the surrender had been disastrous for Britain. When he read the first dispatch, he had staggered around his chambers as though a musket ball had pierced his heart, crying, "Oh, God! It is all over!" King George took the news more stoically and called for a new speech urging his subjects to redouble their efforts. The king told North that the war could still be won but if his ministers were despondent it was surely lost.

Within two weeks, hard political questions in the Commons were forcing North to admit that the war had become too expensive for Britain to send its soldiers deeper into the colonies. London seemed headed back to an earlier strategy, a naval blockade of the American coast, which had not succeeded even before the French Navy entered the war. Nonetheless, the king wanted to persist. Henry Clinton clearly couldn't stay on as commander, and the man George wanted to replace him with, the hero of the Canadian campaign, Sir Guy Carleton, refused to serve under George Germain. That impasse was resolved when Germain resigned from the government. But by that time it was too late for another shift of command. On February 25, 1782, the king's ministers, drawing on all of their authority, narrowly defeated—by a margin of one vote—a resolution in Parliament that would have ended the war.

George III felt that the House of Commons was running amok. He told Lord North that he would go on ruling even if the Parliament voted no confidence in his ministers. North was appalled and tried to resign, but George bullied him into staying. "Remember, my lord," the king said, "it is you who desert me, not I you!" Very soon it became clear that the opposition had the votes to unseat North, and he took the floor in Parliament to announce that his Ministry was disbanded.

"At last," the king wrote to him, "the fatal day has come."

In his depression, King George drafted a message of abdication: ". . . His Majesty therefore with much sorrow finds He can be of no further utility to his native country, which drives him to the painful step of quitting it forever." The letter was never delivered to Parliament. Instead, the king turned briefly to Benedict Arnold, who had come to England full of assurances that the war could still be won. But by then the House of Commons was on record that any Briton who advised continuing the war in America would be considered an enemy to his country.

Early in 1782, the British sent Richard Osborne, a retired merchant, to open negotiations with the Americans and, if possible, to separate them from France. But when Sir Guy Carleton wrote to General Washington that summer to assure him that George III had agreed to America's independence, Washington suspected a trick and warned his countrymen not to lower their guard. "The readiest way to procure a lasting and honorable peace," he wrote, "is to be fully prepared vigorously to prosecute war."

John Adams had enjoyed serving as America's sole minister in the Netherlands far more than reflecting Benjamin Franklin's celebrity in France. He had pressed successfully for diplomatic recognition at The Hague and had asked bankers in Amsterdam for a loan for America. By June 1782 he had overcome the initial resistance and had arranged for a Dutch syndicate to advance the United States five million guilders. In case his countrymen failed to appreciate the magnitude of his achievement, Adams was prepared to tell them. His success in Holland, he wrote, "was the greatest blow that has been struck in the American cause, and the most decisive." When he returned to France someone remarked, "Sir, you are the Washington of negotiation," and John Adams recorded the compliment in his diary just as he had heard it— "*Monsieur, vous êtes le Washington de la négotiation.*" He decided that the praise was "the finishing stroke. It is impossible to exceed this."

Adams might have suspended his practice of reassuring himself about his reputation had he known that, in a shipment of state papers to America, pages from his diary would be mingled with the official documents and his private thoughts would be read aloud on the floor of the Congress to hoots of derision. As the laughter continued, delegates from Massachusetts protested that the entries obviously hadn't been intended for Congress to hear, and the diary was reluctantly laid aside.

In fall 1782, Adams returned to Paris to join the peace negotiations. He had been away from America for almost three years. His eldest son, fifteen-year-old John Quincy Adams, had gone the previous year to St. Petersburg as the private secretary to Francis Dana, who was trying to negotiate a treaty between America and Russia. Adams' younger son Charles had come to Holland to stay a few months but had grown homesick and returned to Braintree. "He is a delightful child," his father had written to Abigail Adams, "but has too exquisite sensibility for Europe."

Even before Yorktown, the Congress had named a five-man committee to go to Paris and wait there until Britain was ready to negotiate peace terms, possibly after the next military campaign. Besides Benjamin Franklin and John Adams, the list included John Jay, America's representative in Spain, and Thomas Jefferson. Though Jefferson's political fortunes might be low in Virginia, he was still admired in the Congress and was nominated for the delegation by a young member named James Madison. The prospect appealed to Jefferson because, after a prolonged illness, his wife had died, leaving him to a lonely exile at Monticello. He planned to take his two daughters with him to France, but first his ship was delayed and then the British would not guarantee him safe passage across the Atlantic, and it was too dangerous to go without such a pass. The commission's fifth member, Henry Laurens, had been seized during his crossing and confined to the Tower of London. When Laurens was released, he went to Paris but sailed home soon after. Jefferson did not go at all.

That left America's future to Franklin, Adams and Jay, who in June 1781 had been granted powers by the Congress that ran broad but not deep. They were to demand independence and sovereignty and to trust their own discretion on the details. In January 1782, with independence looking certain, Congress told them that any pact should spell out boundaries and fishing rights. But they were under specific orders to consult with the French and not to enter into an agreement without informing Vergennes and his ministers. Benjamin Franklin was amenable to that restriction because he knew that America's victory would have been impossible without French money, ships and soldiers. But John

Adams had been in Holland during the climactic months of the war, and John Jay had been in Spain; both had distrusted France for much of their lives and felt that Franklin's close ties to the French court made him suspect.

Franklin was aware that he would be criticized for favoring the French whatever terms he extracted from the English. Vergennes had already achieved one goal by opening American markets to French ships. But the French also wanted control restored to them over the port of Dunkirk, which the British had not let them fortify for seventy years, and Vergennes was committed to helping Spain regain Gibraltar, held by the British since 1704. Franklin drew up an eight-point treaty that dealt only with American issues. Four of the points he deemed essential: complete independence; settling boundaries for the colonies; moving the Canadian border north to its position before the Quebec Act of 1774, which had extended the line south to the Ohio River and west to the Mississippi; and freedom for American fishermen to catch both fish and whales in the waters off Newfoundland. Franklin termed four other conditions advisable: the British should pay reparations for burning American towns; Parliament should openly confess to its error in waging the war; each country should extend trading privileges to the other; and England should cede all of Canada to America.

John Jay had left his long and barren negotiations in Spain convinced that France had never truly promoted America's cause with her Spanish ally. Vergennes in fact resisted the idea that the United States should totally control the American continent, and he backed Spain's claim to territory between the Alleghenies and the Mississippi. In Paris, Jay did not accept the restrictions Congress had laid upon him and his fellow commissioners, and he was determined that America, not Spain, would have all land to the Mississippi's eastern bank. Jay couldn't justify that claim by population, however. The new nation of the United States of America had only three million people, and France's population ran to twenty-six million. Vergennes was not likely to regard Jay's demand as growing out of an urgent need to expand to the center of an immense continent.

Vergennes began private negotiations with the English to protect France's interests. John Jay did the same to argue for

America's expansion. Spain had been violating a secret treaty with France and carrying on her own clandestine peace talks with England. Control of Gibraltar, at the tip of Spain and western entrance to the Mediterranean, was a high Spanish priority but so were West Florida and Louisiana and land along the Mississippi. Lord Shelburne, England's new and unsteady colonial minister, decided the best safeguard for Gibraltar would be quick and secret dealings with America. He accepted Franklin's first four points, plus one of Jay's—both England and America would keep Spain out of the area east of the Mississippi by sharing unrestricted navigation along the river.

John Adams agreed with Jay about disregarding Congress's instructions to include France in all negotiations. "It is a glory," he wrote, "to have broken such infamous orders." When Adams first returned to Paris, nursing his old resentments against Franklin, he would not even pay him a courtesy call. Franklin had summed up his feelings about Adams during the Silas Deane affair: "John Adams is always an honest man, often a wise one, but sometimes and in some things absolutely out of his senses." When the three delegates met with a British agent, Franklin declared common cause with the others and agreed to bypass the French. "I am of your opinion," he said, nodding toward Adams and Jay, "and will go on with these gentlemen in the business without consulting the Court."

Although Vergennes was being subverted, even betrayed, he was not expected to raise the sort of moral objection that came naturally to John Adams. France had entered the war only to distress England. America's liberty had been incidental, and possibly not even desirable. As Vergennes once said, relations between nations should never be governed by gratitude.

When the Americans excluded their French allies, the negotiations with England progressed rapidly. A preliminary draft of the peace agreement was signed on November 30, 1782. John Adams had argued fervently to protect America's fishing rights in order to save the livelihood of many fellow Yankees. He warned the British that if they did not permit Americans to fish off the coasts of Newfoundland and Nova Scotia, and to dry their fish along those shores, America would wage another war and seize that territory. Faced with his obstinacy, the British gave way. Indeed, Lord Shelburne made so many concessions to the Americans that when Vergennes finally heard the terms he said the British had not made a peace but bought one.

John Jay, in his haste to get a treaty, ignored Franklin's recommendation that Canada be ceded to the United States. Jay said his country would not hold up peace by haggling over what he termed a few acres. The most sensitive issue of the negotiations for England involved the fate of the loyalists. Parliament was determined to safeguard those subjects who had remained loyal to the king, and Shelburne's representatives demanded that their confiscated property be returned to them. The issue jeopardized the treaty until Benjamin Franklin asked that the British pay damages for all destruction wrought by either the king's soldiers or his loyalists. He claimed to have prepared an estimate of those costs but added that mutual recriminations would delay reconciliation between Britain and America for generations.

At last the British accepted a hollow compromise. The Congress would simply recommend—"earnestly"—that the individual states return Tory land and goods to their owners. The Americans explained that with Congress as weak and divided as it was, they could promise no more.

With the preliminary treaty signed, it fell to France's staunchest American friend to inform Vergennes that the Americans had made their own peace without regard to French interests. Benjamin Franklin delivered the news, and Vergennes responded with a letter asking how Franklin could justify his incivility toward Louis XVI. Franklin replied that France should ignore the little misunderstanding and not allow the English to believe they had divided America from France. In the same letter, Franklin ignored France's severe economic problems and asked for the loan of another six million livres.

Vergennes saw the value of France's future relations with America and put aside his pique, even though he suspected that the ties between America and England were so strong, despite the bloodshed, that no other country could ever come between them. Benjamin Franklin got the money he requested and remained on good terms with the Comte de Vergennes.

On the morning of September 3, 1783, the three American negotiators met in Paris to sign the definitive treaty. The Congress had approved it, but not without the grumbling that Franklin had anticipated. Charles Fox had replaced Shelburne as secretary of state for foreign affairs, and George III liked Fox even less than his predecessor. According to custom, gifts were to be exchanged at a signing, but when Fox asked the king what to give the Americans, George said only, "Give them whatever the French do." Since the French usually offered a portrait of their king studded with diamonds, Fox decided that a purse of one thousand pounds sterling would be more appropriate.

Vergennes waited until after the American ceremony ended to sign France's treaty with England. Then he entertained Franklin, Adams and Jay at dinner in his residence at Versailles. Lafayette was also invited; John Adams found the marquis overly ambitious and insecure. At the close of the day, John Jay retired to his room and speculated on America's future.

"If we are not a happy people," he wrote, "it will be our own fault."

For Samuel Adams, happiness had never been the supreme goal. He preferred virtue. While other men in the Congress and the army had found ways to improve their fortunes, Adams had returned to Boston in spring 1781 even poorer than when he had left for the First Continental Congress. Since his own house had been damaged during the British occupation, the state allowed him to occupy, at nominal rent, a house once owned by a British ports commissioner. He used money due to him as clerk of the Massachusetts assembly to pay for bits of furniture confiscated from the Tories. As the peace negotiations went forward in France, Samuel Adams was elected president of his state's senate and again aroused his countrymen by vowing to oppose any treaty that did not protect New England's fishing rights. "No peace without the fisheries!" became the cry.

Many of Adams' followers had dropped away, and John Hancock was swept into the governor's mansion in an outpouring of popular affection. Once installed, he hosted night after night of lavish fetes and balls. James Warren, married to James Otis' sister, called them "more suitable to the effeminacy and ridiculous manners of Asiatic slavery than to the hardy and sober manners of a New England public." In 1782 Adams ran against Hancock for governor, but the Adams campaign was desultory, and he finished a distant second. By now his tremors would disappear for long periods but return even more violently. As styles in dress grew opulent, he went on wearing the coats and breeches from the days when his revolution was young. Again Samuel Adams was standing alone, but this time the past seemed to hold more promise than the future. "I love the people of Boston," he wrote to a friend. "I once thought the city would be the Christian Sparta. But alas! Will men never be free?"

Samuel Adams' first ally was spared the disillusionments of peace. James Otis had lived for years on farms outside Boston, sometimes under restraint. Other times he was lucid, and he even ventured into Boston occasionally to plead a case in court. After many invitations, Governor Hancock persuaded Otis to come to dinner, but the evening proved too stimulating for him, and the family had to send him back to his retreat at Andover. Otis had become enormously fat on a diet of bread and honey, and although he wasn't yet sixty he began to have premonitions of death. He was still fascinated by perishing in fire and told visitors he would like to be struck by a bolt of lightning. In March 1783, Otis drew up a will; to his daughter who had married a British officer he left only five shillings.

Eight weeks later, when Otis' family was visiting him at the farm, a heavy cloud arose in the spring sky. As the storm broke, the others ran inside the house, but Otis took his cane and went to stand in the open door and lean against the doorpost. First there was a glare, then a crash as lightning struck the chimney. It followed a rafter in the roof and grounded at a timber in the door. The casing of the door split apart, and Otis fell down dead.

Paul Revere's rides had become legend, but his service as a lieutenant colonel in the militia had threatened to tarnish their luster. Once, when British ships arrived off the shore at Penobscot, Revere had led out a band of raw troops. America's ships, commanded by Dudley Saltonstall, had refused to engage the enemy, so Revere had marched his men back to Boston. In order to absolve themselves of blame for the defeat, each commander had blamed the other. Captain Saltonstall was court-martialed. Paul

Revere was accused of disobedience and cowardice and relieved of his command. Revere sought a court-martial to clear himself, but his request was not granted. Now in his midforties and angered by the slur to his name, he returned to silver engraving. After six petitions, Revere was given a trial in 1782. The court acquitted him on each count and ruled that Colonel Revere should be accorded "equal honor" with the other officers of the confused and failed expedition.

The peace had left John Hancock with little to complain about. As governor of Massachusetts, he reveled in his title, his entertainments, his independence from King George and from Samuel Adams. Hancock was the first citizen of the "mushroom gentry," the new class of profiteers and speculators who had turned a profit from the war. Whenever he appeared in public, admirers ran beside his carriage to cheer, gape at his mink coat and scramble for the coins he tossed out to them. As the governor's wife, Dorothy Quincy Hancock served so many rich sauces to visiting French nobility that she instructed her servants to milk every cow on the Boston Common, no matter who owned it. Before the war's end, Dolly Hancock had completed her husband's happiness by giving him a son; an infant daughter had died before she was a year old. Hancock used his son's birth to demonstrate that he held no grudge from the day John Adams had risen in Philadelphia and nominated a commander in chief. He named the new heir John George Washington Hancock.

In Virginia, Patrick Henry had continued to surprise politicians who thought they could predict him. When Horatio Gates was defeated at Camden, Henry forgave Gates his role in the Conway Cabal and pushed through the Virginia legislature a tribute to the general's past glories. Thomas Jefferson watched scornfully as Henry bought a ten-thousand-acre plantation and paid for it in depreciated paper money that Jefferson claimed was not worth oak leaves.

Yet even his enemies acknowledged that the size of Patrick Henry's family gave him unusual responsibilities. After his first wife died, he married the daughter of the Colonel Dandridge who had long ago introduced Henry and Jefferson at a house party. Dorothea, a cousin of Martha Washington, had been four years old at the time of the party. Henry's first wife left him with six children. In time, Dorothea Henry would provide him with another eleven.

While tending his financial interests, Henry did not lose his political touch. Thomas Jefferson might deplore his rapacity, but he never underestimated Henry's hold over the state. The introduction of any legislation was hopeless if Henry opposed it. As the war ended, Henry tried to help Virginians avoid paying their outstanding debts to the British. At the same time, he also urged his state to permit the loyalists to return from abroad. Henry argued that Virginia's prosperity depended on greater population, and he was willing to set aside personal resentments. For that matter, he hoped the merchants and farmers and artisans of the Old World would join the Tories. "Open your doors," Henry preached to America. "Tell them to come and bid them welcome."

After leaving the governorship, Thomas Jefferson found happiness most often in his library. Ever since the fire at Shadwell thirteen years before, Jefferson had been collecting books assiduously and, by the time of the peace treaty, had acquired more than twenty-six hundred volumes. He was also producing a book of his own. He had begun his *Notes on the State of Virginia* in the unhappy days after the fall from his horse had left him incapacitated. On behalf of the French government, the Marquis de Barbé-Marbois had sent Jefferson twenty-three questions about Virginia. Jefferson's answers grew into essays that ranged from natural history to moral philosophy. One quarter of the manuscript was devoted to detailed analyses of the vegetable, mineral and animal resources of his state. Jefferson wanted to refute charges that European wildlife had degenerated in America, and he wrote to experts for information on the weight of every animal from—as he put it—the mouse to the mammoth.

Jefferson attempted the same dispassionate observation of social questions. When he began, he didn't expect to publish the results and gave little effort to being politic. He once again exposed his anguished conflict over the question of slaves and slavery, deploring the way white children first witnessed despotism on a plantation and then grew up to imitate it. He thought only the rarest man could remain undepraved. But although Jefferson considered himself one of those rare men, he wrote about blacks as if they were another variation on the mammoth or the mouse. According to Jefferson, black people seemed to require less sleep than whites. He offered as proof the fact that after a day's hard labor the slightest amusement could keep blacks up past midnight. Because black people secreted less by their kidneys than through their glands, he added, they could have a very strong and disagreeable odor. Blacks seemed to him more ardent, but he believed their love was more often an eager desire instead of the tender mixture of sentiment and sensation he defined as love. That was the romantic love Jefferson had lost—he thought forever—when his wife died. But after compiling his observations, his biases, his keen interest and his ignorance, Jefferson knew, as he had always known, the final truth about slavery:

"Indeed, I tremble for my country when I reflect that God is just."

In Britain, Sir Henry Clinton had begun a long and fruitless attempt to explain his failure as a commander. He wrote a massive reconstruction of the war that blamed Britain's loss on the king's ministers and his fellow generals, especially Lord Cornwallis. By that time, the public had moved beyond excuses. Sir Guy Carleton agreed to assume command in America, but only to oversee the British evacuation of New York. John Burgoyne and William Howe had both joined the opposition faction in Parliament, and in 1782 Burgoyne had been named commander in chief in Ireland. General Howe lost his seat in Parliament, but with the king's personal support he had been appointed Britain's lieutenant general of ordnance after Lord North left the government. Charles, Earl Cornwallis, did better still. Sent to India, he ran up a list of accomplishments that reduced Yorktown to a stumble in his long career.

Benedict Arnold had not convinced Britain to pursue the war, but when peace came the king liberally rewarded Arnold's family with an annual pension of five hundred pounds for Peggy Shippen Arnold and a hundred pounds each for their present and future children. Arnold's three sons by his first marriage were given commissions in the British Army and lifetime pensions at half pay.

The king eventually gave the Arnold family more than thirteen thousand acres of crown land in Canada.

The American generals who had crossed George Washington politically did not prosper as well as their British counterparts. When the peace treaty was nearly completed in Paris, Charles Lee died in a squalid Pennsylvania tavern. In his will, Lee requested that he not be buried near any churchyard. In America, he explained, "I have kept so much bad company when living that I do not choose to continue it when dead." His last estimate of George Washington described him as a "puffed up charlatan." All the same, Lee's estate repaid the money Lee had borrowed at Mount Vernon before the two generals set out for Cambridge in 1775.

Horatio Gates's disgrace at Camden had endured for two years before the Congress repealed its call for an official inquiry and reinstated him as the second-ranking officer of the Continental Army. The same year the peace treaty was signed, Gates left military service to attend to his dying wife at Traveller's Rest.

General Washington's indispensable partner at Yorktown, Admiral de Grasse, was defeated in American waters only six months later. In April 1782 the British Navy bested him in a battle off Saints Passage in the West Indies, and de Grasse was taken prisoner.

Silas Deane had helped bring de Grasse's fleet to America, but with one action he ensured that his country would never honor him for it. In March 1781 Deane had offered his services to Lord North's government and written letters from London urging Americans to end the war and to stop insisting on independence. His letters were printed in New York while the nation was celebrating Cornwallis' surrender at Yorktown. By 1783 Deane had moved on to Belgium, where he was living in cheap hotels and avoiding any face from home.

Thomas Paine had been second only to Arthur Lee in attacking Deane, and Paine had also gone to Europe in 1781 to secure aid from the French court. He returned with a gift for America of two and a half million silver livres but reaped nothing from his achievement. After Yorktown, he had to remind George Washington that "the country which ought to have been a home has scarcely afforded me an asylum." Washington contacted Robert Morris, America's superintendent of finance, and arranged for Paine secretly to be paid eight hundred dollars a year for his future writings.

Paine had planned to write the history of the American Revolution as Benjamin Franklin had once urged him to do, but the closest he got was reviewing a book on the war by Abbé Raynal in France. When the peace treaty was signed, Paine's clandestine salary ended. He wrote one final *Crisis:* "The times that tried men's souls are over—and the greatest and completest revolution the world ever knew, gloriously and happily accomplished." Over the following months, General Washington continued to solicit money for Paine—"He is poor! He is chagrined!" Washington wrote—but a bill in the Virginia legislature that would have awarded him a grant of land lost on its third reading. The Treaty of Paris was a year old before the state of Pennsylvania voted Paine a generous payment for his past services.

Francis Bernard had died of an epileptic seizure long before Yorktown, and Thomas Hutchinson had died of a stroke. Hutchinson's last act was to reject a shirt that his servant had brought him. It was soiled, Hutchinson said, and he was determined to "die clean." He didn't live to hear that James Warren and his wife bought his estate in Milton and took delight, as Hutchinson had, in its lovely vistas. John Adams heard of Hutchinson's death while in Europe and sent a letter to the Boston press that became the former governor's obituary. Adams did not feel obliged to temper his judgment, and the words "ambition" and "avarice" figured prominently. But in his hatred Adams endowed Thomas Hutchinson with a sort of grandeur: "He was, perhaps, the only man in the world who could have brought on the controversy between Great Britain and America . . ."

As America had waited anxiously for peace, General Washington was still doing battle once more but this time with the officers and men of his own army. In January 1783 a committee of Continental Army officers went to Philadelphia to demand that the Congress release the soldiers' back pay and benefits for the wounded. Their claims went back at least three years. Washington warned a member of Congress, "The temper of the army is much soured and has become more irritable than at any period since the commencement of the war." But Congress lacked the necessary funds. Unless the states amended the Articles of Confederation to allow Congress to collect its own taxes, the members could not meet the army's demands.

Some men hoped to use the discontent to shape a future government they preferred. Alexander Hamilton had been elected to the Congress from New York, and, along with such allies as Robert Morris, Horatio Gates and Henry Knox, he was pressing for a strong central government. Hamilton wanted the army to state that it would not fight again even if treaty negotiations failed and the war resumed, but that it would not disband if there was a peace. Washington suspected who was fomenting the army's discord, although some participants, like Henry Knox, denied their role and seemed to agree when Washington called the army "a dangerous instrument to play with."

The plotters had first tried to enlist the commander in chief as the head of their movement. The previous year, a colonel had urged Washington to resolve the delays and frustrations of civilian politics by declaring himself king, but Washington viewed that idea with abhorrence. Now, because Alexander Hamilton had remained a colonel in the army, he felt he could lecture Washington on the mood within the general's ranks. He wrote that if the army was not properly compensated after peace was declared, the soldiers would use their bayonets to procure justice, with or without General Washington.

Washington contemplated his decision for days before responding to Hamilton that he could not accept actions that would disrupt society and end in blood. He would trust the more discerning officers to remember his past conduct and endorse his resistance to any armed rebellion. To succeed, the leaders of the revolt would have to remove or discredit him.

Early in March 1783, an unsigned leaflet passed among the officers at Newburgh, New York, where Washington was waiting for Britain to withdraw her troops. The circular, written by an aide to Horatio Gates, attacked the Congress for its coldness and severity to the army and urged officers to suspect any man who advised them to be more patient or moderate. General Washington responded immediately with an order forbidding his men to meet secretly, and he scheduled an open discussion for March 15. Washington wasn't going to attend, but when a second leaflet claimed that he had endorsed the rebel officers' demands by calling the meeting, Washington changed his mind and went.

The confrontation was held in a new wooden hall built for both chapel services and dancing. George Washington had relied throughout his public career on other men to voice his sentiments and write his speeches. He arrived visibly nervous, with a paper prepared by an aide. He briefly rebutted the anonymous writer of the leaflets. "Can he be a friend to the army?" Washington asked. "Can he be a friend to this country?"

As the officers listened, they showed no emotion. They seemed to treat Washington as a stranger who had to win them over on the strength of his arguments.

Washington ended his prepared remarks with fine, flattering cadences: "You will, by the dignity of your conduct, afford occasion for posterity to say, when speaking of the glorious example you have exhibited to mankind, 'Had this day been wanting, the world would never have seen the last stage of perfection to which human nature is capable of attaining.' "

His speech was finished, but Washington was not. He had brought a letter from a Virginia congressman who spoke forcefully of the nation's debt to the army and promised to redeem it. As Washington began to read, he faltered. After the first paragraph, he stopped, fished in a pocket and took out a new pair of spectacles.

"Gentlemen," Washington said, "you must pardon me. I have grown gray in your service and now I find myself growing blind."

Tears welled up in the eyes of many of the men. Washington finished reading the letter and left the hall. When he had gone, the assembled officers voted unanimously to express their confidence in the Congress and to ask George Washington to continue as their spokesman.

On April 19, 1783, eight years to the day since General Gage's troops fired on Lexington Green, the cessation of hostilities between Great Britain and the United States of America was announced. At Continental Army headquarters, the men gave three huzzahs and sang a song called "Independence."

In June, General Washington wrote the last of his circular letters—appeals he had made regularly to the governors of all thirteen states asking them for recruits and provisions. The tone was different this time, and men were soon calling it "Washington's Legacy." The commander in chief reminded the states that they were entering a time of political probation. Washington named four things that would be necessary to preserve American independence: an indissoluble union of states under one federal head; a sacred regard for public justice; the adoption of a proper peace establishment, which meant an army scaled down and disciplined to America's new needs; and a friendly willingness of the people of the United States to forget their local prejudices and, when called upon, to sacrifice their individual advantages to the good of the community.

Before the month was out, the country learned the urgency of what Washington called "a proper peace establishment" when eighty soldiers in Lancaster, Pennsylvania, mutinied over their grievances. Less portentous than the insurrection Washington had faced down at Newburgh, this one had more immediate impact. When the rebels marched on the capital, soldiers in Philadelphia joined them and increased their number to five hundred. They surrounded the Congress, shouting and pointing their muskets at the windows.

The revolt was soon over, and its two ringleaders escaped on a ship just leaving for Europe. But during the threatening hours members of the Congress had fled to Princeton, New Jersey. When calm was restored, Philadelphians asked them to return, but the delegates were tired of being abused and mocked there and voted not to go back. After several months in Princeton, they moved on to Annapolis. The members decided to build two federal towns—one on the banks of the Delaware, another, to mollify the Southern states, on the Potomac River.

In rueful letters to friends and family throughout the years he had been away from home, General Washington had repeated a Biblical phrase: he longed for the day when he could repose again under his own vine and fig tree. Now, in the autumn of 1783, he judged that the time had come. On November 25 the last British soldiers were evacuated from New York, and Washington returned there for the first time in seven years. He held up his procession through the streets for an hour because he wanted the American flag flying before he started down Broadway, but the departing British troops had greased the flagpole and the Americans couldn't shinny up it. At last a young man borrowed cleats from an ironmonger and climbed to the top.

At noon on Tuesday, December 4, Washington's officers in New York held a farewell dinner for him at Fraunces Tavern in Pearl Street. When the general arrived, his men seemed to hold their breath. No one spoke. Washington filled his glass with wine and raised it.

"With a heart full of love and gratitude," he began, "I now take leave of you."

Washington wished for them that their days ahead would be as prosperous and happy as the days behind them had been glorious and honorable.

His officers took up their glasses. Then Washington said, "I cannot come to each of you, but I shall feel obliged if each of you come and take me by the hand."

Henry Knox was nearest. As he grasped the general's hand, Washington's face was bathed in tears and they embraced silently. After that, each officer came forward and kissed Washington on the cheek. The only sound was weeping. George Washington would return to Mount Vernon, and his officers felt they would never see him again.

Washington's leavetaking continued through tumultuous receptions in Philadelphia, Wilmington and Baltimore. At Philadelphia, Washington left an accounting of his expenses since 1775. He included the cost of bringing his wife to headquarters between campaigns, along with his supplies, travel, pay for secret intelligence and the entertainment necessary for a man in his position. The eight-year total was 1,972 pounds, nine shillings and fourpence. When auditors went over the accounts, they found that Washington's figures were off by less than one American dollar.

At Annapolis, although many delegates had already left the Congress to attend to business at home, more than two hundred men turned out for a dinner in Washington's honor. As one guest observed, the mood of the affair was so elevated that not a soul got drunk. Washington attended a ball that evening at the State House, where he danced every set—he still loved to dance—because he owed it to the ladies to give each that memory.

On Tuesday, December 23, 1783, General Washington entered the congressional chamber of the Maryland State House precisely at noon. He left his horses waiting at the door. When the ceremony was over, Washington planned to set out on the fifty-mile ride that would have him at Mount Vernon in time for Christmas. He would take with him trunks of official papers and two young former officers who would help him sort and arrange them.

Washington had been yearning to retire to his plantation, and now he was almost free and on his way. He had no reason to think that his countrymen would ever demand that he asssume new burdens for America. Yet Washington made two changes in the draft of his farewell to the Congress before he delivered it. In his "affectionate and final farewell" to the Congress, he removed the words "and final." And when he spoke of taking his "ultimate leave" of public life, Washington struck the word "ultimate."

Charles Thomson, the first secretary of the Congress, escorted General Washington to his seat. Thomas Mifflin, once suspected of plotting in the Conway Cabal, was the presiding officer. "Sir," said President Mifflin as the galleries quieted, "the United States in Congress assembled are prepared to receive your communications."

General Washington stood and bowed to the twenty members. As he pulled out his farewell remarks, the general's hands trembled. He congratulated the Congress on the nation's independence and said that he was resigning "with satisfaction the appointment I accepted with diffidence—a diffidence in my abilities to accomplish so arduous a task, which however was superseded by a confidence in the rectitude of our cause, the support of the supreme power of the union and the patronage of Heaven."

Washington asked for Congress's patronage for his family of officers and commended his country to the protection of Almighty God. Then his voice broke, and everyone in the State House felt his agitation. He recovered, reached into his coat, and brought out his commission as commander in chief. With a few words, he handed it back to Thomas Mifflin.

In his tribute to the retiring commander, President Mifflin

praised George Washington, not only for his wisdom and fortitude but for always protecting the nation's civil rights through
every change and disaster. Many found Mifflin's reading of his
remarks dry and uninspired, but no one complained about the
words themselves, which had been written for the occasion by
Thomas Jefferson.

Acknowledgments

Writing the story of the American Revolution first occurred to me more than twenty years ago when I was reporting from Saigon on the war in Vietnam. The unconventional tactics of the National Liberation Front as its soldiers fought the world's most powerful nation brought back memories of the battle of Lexington and Concord from high-school history class. From time to time after that, I tested the parallel by reading histories of the American Revolution, and I found that they fell into two categories. Those surveys that were intended as textbooks were often blandly neutral and heavy with dates. Books by such writers as Susan Alsop, Bernard Bailyn, Fawn Brodie, Marcus Cunliffe, Burke Davis, Pauline Maier, Edmund Morgan, Gary Nash, Arthur Tourtellot and Hiller Zobel were vivid and exciting, but they usually treated a single life or event—Thomas Hutchinson or Thomas Jefferson, the Stamp Act congress or the Boston Massacre. There seemed to be a place for a book that approached the revolution as a story, focusing on the principal actors as they moved from the writs-of-assistance trial in 1761 to General Washington's resignation from the Continental Army in 1783. The book would be meant for readers who knew that Washington had crossed the Delaware, but didn't know why; that Benedict Arnold had betrayed his country, but didn't know how. The research taught me that after two centuries few facts or interpretations were beyond dispute. Parson Weems's anecdote of George Washington and the cherry tree appeared only in the fifth edition of his imaginative biography. Other inventions and errors were harder to detect and, sometimes, to give up. Modern historians do not believe, for example, that Nathan Hale said he regretted having but one life to give for his country. Many of them also question whether Patrick Henry had the presence of mind to conclude his challenge to George III with "If this be treason, make the most of it." In their old age, Thomas Jefferson and John Adams each gave slightly different answers to historians who were asking about events already fifty years past. A writer today can only sift the evidence and make judgments, aware that Samuel Adams would probably repudiate every line that has ever been written about him.

No pleasure quite compares with reading original letters and diaries in their own faded ink. But if a writer ignored the modern scholarship available to him, he might labor a lifetime and still not grasp the whole epic story. I have drawn on the writers I've mentioned, as well as the multivolume works of James Thomas Flexner, Dumas Malone, Douglas Southall Freeman, G. O. Trevelyan and William V. Wells, among others. Sometimes the most valuable insights have come from the shortest studies. Professor Bailyn's essay on John Adams succinctly revealed Adams' admirable, contradictory character; and Arthur M. Schlesinger's article on the phrase "the pursuit of happiness" convinced me that he had penetrated its significance. Two other unusually valuable guides have been George F. Scheer and Hugh F. Rankin's *Rebels and Redcoats* and the monumental bibliography of the Revolution completed in 1984 by Ronald Gephart for the Library of Congress.

I have had kind and knowledgeable assistance from staff members at the British Library in London, the Doheny Library of the University of Southern California, Harvard University's Houghton Library, the Massachusetts Historical Society, the New York Public Library, the New-York Historical Society and the Swem library, William and Mary College. I would like to mention especially Virginia Renner and Leona Schonfeld at the Henry E. Huntington Library in San Marino, California, and Judith Farley at the Library of Congress in Washington, D.C. Professors Larry Ceplair and Pauline Maier undertook careful readings of the manuscript, and their suggestions were extremely helpful.

Among other friends and colleagues who aided and encouraged me were Norman Corwin, Peter Craske, Ed Cray, William X. Dunne, Charles Fleming, Karl and Anne Taylor Fleming, Donald and Patty Freed, Betty Friedan, Albert B. Friedman, Lew Grimes, David Halberstam, Denton Holland, Sue Horton, Richard Houdek, Leonard Leader, Irwin C. Lieb, Luther Leudtke, Ethel Narvid, Bryce Nelson, Lynn O'Leary-Archer, Frances Ring, Joe Saltzman, Sebastião Santos, Jorge Schement, Robert J. Schoenberg,

Clancy Sigal, Ronald Steel, Peter Virgadamo, Franklin Woodson, Paul Zall and the late Jon Bradshaw.

Lynn Nesbit at International Creative Management brought an enthusiasm for the project that has been heartening throughout the years of research and writing. The skill and dedication of Alice E. Mayhew and Henry Ferris in their editing at Simon and Schuster, and of Vera Schneider in her copyediting and indexing, have been unique in my experience. I thank them most gratefully.

Notes

OTIS: 1761–62

Page 13
Adams in Town House: Hosmer, 56–57; Tudor, 60; Francis Bowen, 63–64;
Wells, I, 44; John Adams, *Works*, X, 245; John Adams, *Statesman*, 126–28.
14
Molasses: Galvin, 69.
Boston's unemployed: Benjamin Labaree, *Colonial*, 218.
15
Hutchinson supported writs: *Old South*, 4.
Hutchinson family deaths: Bailyn, *Ordeal*, 22.
16
". . . *te expectare*": Hutchinson, *Diary*, I, 46.
"Depend on it": Sibley, VIII, 152–53.
Hutchinson's style: Bailyn, *Ordeal*, 20.
Hutchinson and silver: Warden, 139.
17
Hutchinson in Milton: Hutchinson, *Diary*, I, 164.
Peggy Hutchinson dies: Bailyn, *Ordeal*, 29.
"Summa Potestatis": Galvin, 18. "Potestas": M. H. Smith, 227.
Otis calls on Hutchinson: Hosmer, 47; Waters, 119.

Otis sees Hutchinson on Boston Neck: Galvin, 20.

18

threw out votes: Waters, 82.

Indian scalps: Ibid., 89.

Speaker Otis as shoemaker: Oliver, 27.

19

"little low dirty things": Waters, 105.

Bernard offers justiceship: Hutchinson, *History*, III, 63; Hosmer, 47.

Montesquieu: Hosmer, 67–68.

province in flames: Oliver, 36.

". . . hell I'll stir.": Francis Bowen, 45.

20

". . . danced the brutes!": Ibid., 10.

pregnant nanny: Waters, 75.

Otis' largest fees: Francis Bowen, 16.

"Powder plot . . .": Forbes, 89.

21

Otis refused a fee: Francis Bowen, 18.

". . . despise all fees.": Tudor, 57.

Gridley's arguments: Waters, 22.

Ware anecdote: Francis Bowen, 60; Adams, *Works*, II, 525.

22

Thacher's voice: Tudor, 58.

Hutchinson on Thacher: Sibley, X, 325.

Otis as flame of fire: Francis Bowen, 58.

23

Parliament's power: Bailyn, ed., *Pamphlets*, I, 100–102.

Otis warns king: Bancroft, IV, 415; Hosmer, 58.

"A man's house is his castle": M. H. Smith, 554.

Adams' attitude toward Britain: Ibid., 254–56; John Adams, *Spur*, 34n.

Adams on taking up arms: Wells, I, 44; John Adams, *Statesman*, 132.

24

London Magazine: Hutchinson, *History*, III, 68.

Otis elected to House: Ibid., 69.

"a damned faction": John Adams, *Works*, X, 248.

Otis' temper in House: Francis Bowen, 67–68.

25

"Bedlamism": Sibley, XI, 254.

". . . beings called devils.": John Adams, *Diary*, I, 346.

Otis would take revenge on Hutchinson: Waters, 148.

26

". . . live half well enough.": *Boston Gazette*, Jan. 11, 1761.

". . . ill-gotten gain and power.": Sibley, XI, 256.

27

House drops Otis' language: Francis Bowen, 84–85.

ADAMS: 1762–63

28
"is very obstinate": Bancroft, IV, 386.
29
"reading the Bible": Guedalla, 23.
George's sexual desires: Guttmacher, 32–33.
". . . according to his deserts.": George III, *Letters to Bute*, Dec. 8, 1758.
"Be a King!": Guttmacher, 25.
30
Hutchinson's lecture: Miller, *Adams*, 41.
"Esquire Bluster": Waters, 130.
"Furio": John Adams, *Diary*, I, 237.
Otis threatens to resign: Waters, 148.
Deacon Adams: Wells, III, 427.
Land Bank: Miller, *Adams*, 9–11.
31
"the idle and the extravagant": Young, 15.
32
Adams' thesis at Harvard: Wells, I, 10.
Adams' indifference to money: Ibid., 54.
Adams saves his house: Ibid., 28; Sibley, X, 422–23.
33
tyranny by the few: Becker, *Eve*, 166.
34
America's area: Morison, *History*, I, 1.
". . . greasy, shining head.": Sibley, XIII, 380.
35
gentlemen outvoted in Town Meetings: Young, 22.
"a filthy skunk": *Boston Evening Post*, Mar. 28, 1763.
Hutchinson's history: Bailyn, *Ordeal*, 19.
Hutchinson on Whigs: Hutchinson, *History*, III, 75.
36
Bernard's background: Higgins, I, 174–82.
Bernard's son: Ibid., 219.
37
". . . spread with brass.": Harlow, 21.
". . . an hour more.": Ayling, 328.
". . . Mr. Greenville.": Bancroft, V, 145.

HENRY: 1763–64

39
meetings broken up: Willison, 62.
40
Virginia games: George Morgan, 55.

Maury's slaves' names: Willison, 73.
tobacco laws: Tyler, 36.

41
Peter Lyons: Willison, 78.
Henry accepts fifteen shillings: Meade, 126.
Jefferson on Henry: Jefferson, *Works*, XII, 388n.

42
Henry's preparation for law: George Morgan, 44.
Henry's hunting: Meade, 52–53.
"sold the last peck": George Morgan, 38.
Peyton Randolph's education: Willison, 53.

43
Henry with John Randolph: George Morgan, 47.

44
man of genius: Jefferson, *Works*, XI, 228.
Virginia considers barring lawyers: Meade, 95.
tobacco rates: Tyler, 38.

45
". . . vulgar herd": Mayer, 63.
Henry's jurors: Willison, 77.

46
first reaction to Henry: Tyler, 45.
Lyons objects: Willison, 80.

47
". . . the lying-in woman!": George Morgan, 68–72.
one-penny award: Willison, 81.
Maury's reaction: George Morgan, 72.

48
220,000 pounds: Green, 227.
Pitt dropped the idea: Willison, 111.
Walpole bequeaths tax plan: George Morgan, 88.
"This is taxing them": Willison, 110.

49
Mauduit's prediction: Edmund Morgan, *Crisis*, 42.
past taxes only to regulate trade: Otis, *Rights*.
Samuel Adams' instructions: Wells, I, 46–48.

50
"Perhaps I may be too suspicious.": Harlow, 34.
Rhode Island's letter: Hutchinson, *History*, III, 83.

51
Grenville on tax: Hosmer, 80.
"the easiest, the most equal . . .": Green, 230.
items taxed: Charles Andrews, 245.
Isaac Barré: Page Smith, *New Age*, I, 192–93.
"Sons of liberty" as familiar term: Maier, *Resistance*, 82.

Riots: 1765

52
Liberty Tree: Forbes, 97.
53
". . . hanging on a tree": Sibley, VII, 394.
54
". . . set people a-thinking . . .": Otis, *Rights*, 73.
flop down before the tree: *Boston Gazette*, Aug. 19, 1765.
Samuel Adams wants to inquire further: Miller, *Adams*, 61.
55
cheers sounded defiant: Bernard, letter to Halifax, Aug. 15, 1765, Sparks Collection.
56
destroying Oliver's building: *Boston Gazette*, Aug. 19, 1765.
patriots deny stealing valuables: Ibid.
57
Gazette treats lightheartedly: Ibid.
100 pounds reward: Ibid., Sept. 2, 1765.
58
previous rioting: Maier, *Resistance*, 4.
burned private barn: Edmund Morgan, *Crisis*, 159.
"a single man . . .": Sibley, VIII, cites Andrew Oliver to John Spooner.
Hutchinson seen heading for country: Hutchinson, *History*, III, 88.
59
"black regiment": Oliver, 29.
Mayhew background: Sibley, XI, 465.
Bernard on mob: Bernard to Halifax, Aug. 31, 1765, Sparks Collection.
Boston merchants as smugglers: Hutchinson, *History*, III, 89.
Hallowell's house: Miller, *Origins*, 243.
cellar drunk dry: Morgan, *Crisis*, 166.
60
greatest civil violence: Bailyn, *Ordeal*, 35.
destruction of Hutchinson's house: Hosmer, 92.
61
". . . anguish of his soul": Ibid., 95.
Hutchinson address: *Proceedings, Mass. Hist. Soc.*, IV, April 1858.
62
Mayhew's response: Wells, I, 62.
63
Hutchinson on same villains: Miller, *Adams*, 67.
"rude fellows," "hellish fury": *Boston Gazette*, Sept. 2, 1765.
Mackintosh background: Anderson, "Mackintosh," 15.
64
grudging admiration: Oliver, 54.
set Mackintosh free: Hutchinson, *Diary*, I, 71.
". . . Mackintosh has the credit . . .": Harlow, 50.

65
"very tame apes, too.": Maier, *Resistance*, 62.

POLITICS: 1765

66
"Orator of Nature": George Morgan, 75.
67
candidate too stingy: Willison, 87–92.
Washington's defeat: Ibid., 93.
68
Burgesses on horseback: Hodges, 15.
". . . filling his pockets with money?": Edmund Morgan, *Crisis*, 120.
69
Henry's apology: Beeman, 38.
70
". . . for a single vote": Jefferson, *Works*, XI, 229n.
Hutchinson softened letter: Galvin, 93.
71
". . . They are men! . . .": John Adams, *Works*, X, 287.
Bernard as good-natured man: *Barrington–Bernard Corresp.*, 32.
Bernard sure all would be well: Ibid., 53.
Bernard's spies: Bernard, letter to Pownall, Aug. 23, 1765, Sparks Collection.
72
"The dignity of Great Britain . . .": Ibid., to Jackson, Aug. 24, 1765, Sparks.
troops would inflame the mob: Ibid., to Lords of Trade, undated (September 1765), Sparks.
Description of stamp: Anderson, "Mackintosh," 14–15.
Cost for bail bond: Force, 4th series, 40.
73
New Hampshire volunteered to sign: Tudor, 225.
74
South Carolina felt isolated: Andrews, 205–6.
". . . all of us Americans.": Goodloe, 7–10.
Otis wouldn't sign: Gordon, I, 174.
75
"Young man . . .": Weslager, 154.
"cutting one another's throats . . .": Ibid.
no house left to destroy: Miller, *Adams*, 96.
76
"a perpetual itching . . .": Hooker, 65.
Blacks kept out of march: Miller, *Adams*, 69.
Samuel Adams frees slave: Wells, II, 20.
77
Adams' tax deficits: Goodell, 213–26.
Hutchinson blamed Adams: Miller, *Adams*, 61.
"Massah Tamp Act . . .": Oliver, 65.

78
John Adams' diary entry: Adams, *Diary,* I, 264-65.
". . . they smoke tobacco . . .": Wells, I, 86-87.
drank flip: Peladeau, 5.
Samuel Adams' radical love of liberty: Wells, I, 86-87.
"If not . . . !": *Boston Gazette,* Dec. 23, 1765.
79
Oliver's remarks: Sibley, VIII, 159.
Sons' strategy: Edmund Morgan, *Crisis,* 174.
Attorney general's rheumatism: Ibid., 179.
80
Bernard's "total languor . . .": *Barrington-Bernard Corresp.,* 240-41.
". . . some emphasis behind it.": Hancock, 100-101.
John Adams' arguments: Adams, *Diary,* I, 267.
81
Hutchinson thought his life in danger: Hutchinson, *History,* III, 103.

HANCOCK: 1765-68

83
Grenville suffered defeat: Green, 233-34.
84
"These yellow shades of men . . .": Edmund Morgan, *Birth,* 21.
no right to retaliate: Page Smith, *New Age,* I, 237.
Pitt's speaking style: Butler, 17-18.
Pitt's speech: Green, 253-54.
85
". . . I only finish.": Ayling, 341.
". . . totally and immediately.": Green, 258-59.
86
". . . forfeit the name of Pitt . . .": Bancroft, VI, 24.
Franklin's testimony: Force, 80-81.
87
Hancock's fireworks: Goss, I, 36.
"Every dirty fellow . . .": Frothingham, *Warren,* 73.
maddened with loyalty: Wells, I, 115.
88
ought to be beheaded: John Adams, *Diary,* I, 280.
". . . John that may do better?": Francis Drake, lxiii n.
Hancock background: Allan, 23-30.
89
slave made drunk: Morison, *Harvard,* 115.
". . . as possible to her size": Allan, 34.
Thomas Hancock's smuggling: Ibid., 45-47.
90
". . . that young man's fortune their own.": Tudor, 262.

92

losses of 2500 pounds: Hutchinson, *Diary*, 70.

rabble and scum: Miller, *Adams*, 113.

Townshend found distinction ridiculous: Ibid., 115.

93

he knew "the mode . . .": Beach, 128.

94

knew the tactic was extortion: Edmund Morgan, *Birth*, 37–38.

"the greatest political curses . . .": Miller, *Adams*, 118.

Hulton laughs at parade: Beach, 136.

95

". . . lick the dust . . .": Miller, *Adams*, 140.

". . . directly to his kennel.": Ibid., 98.

"defalcation": Hutchinson, *History*, III, 212.

". . . tail of the rattle snake.": Oliver, 40.

forgave Adams' debt: Miller, *Adams*, 101.

"His power over weak minds . . .": Oliver, 41.

96

Captain Marshall incident: Zobel, 73.

H.M.S. *Romney* arrives: Beach, 146.

impressed men held: *Boston Gazette*, June 20, 1768.

"a blackguard town . . .": Beach, 150.

Madeira disappeared: Hancock, 157.

97

Englishwoman's response: Beach, 147.

". . . To your tents, O Israel.": Ibid.

Tory dinner guests: Beach, 154.

John Adams' calculation: John Adams, *Works*, X, 260.

98

". . . even unto blood": Harlow, 123.

"If you are men . . .": Ibid.

threatening them with famine: Beach, 148.

Bernard was self-impressed: Tudor, 330.

". . . enjoy it a week.": Ibid.

99

circular letter: Beach, 140.

". . . the whole Empire.": Miller, *Adams*, 125.

". . . to quieuvicue them": Tudor, 317.

100

". . . the contempt it deserves.": Edmund Morgan, *Birth*, 41.

dissolve the House: Beach, 145.

Otis' remarks: Tudor, 325.

". . . pimps and whoremasters.": Miller, *Adams*, 143.

101

". . . like a horned snake.": Adam, 17.

". . . by dividing we fall.": Tudor, 502.

"Poor Paxton's usual . . .": Bailyn, *Ordeal*, 25.

102
"bad thing for Boston . . .": Miller, *Adams,* 120.
"popish" towns: Ibid., 129.
103
Washington welcomed ban: Maier, *Resistance,* 119.
Bernard's fears about troops: *Barrington–Bernard Corresp.,* 113–14.
Adams reassures Hillsborough: Harlow, 128.
104
Warren's attack: *Boston Gazette,* Feb. 29, 1768.
". . . punish such lying.": Baldwin, 58–59.
"behaves like a madman . . .": Bernard to Shelburne, Mar. 5, 1768, Sparks Collection.
105
humoring a willful child: *Barrington–Bernard Corresp.,* 126.
Isaiah quotation: Hutchinson, *Diary,* frontispiece.
". . . authority over his children.": Hosmer, 137.
". . . America prostrate at our feet.": Frothingham, *Warren,* 95n.

OCCUPATION: 1768–69

108
"for obvious reasons": Bernard to General Gage, July 2, 1768, Sparks Collection.
Council advising Bernard: Ibid., to Col. Dalrymple, July 3, 1768, Sparks.
Adams–Otis exchange: Ibid., to Hillsborough, July 9, 1768, Sparks.
109
False report about Adams: Frothingham, 80.
110
". . . they will be delivered.": Miller, *Adams,* 151.
". . . as foreign enemies": Harlow, 133.
". . . lives and fortunes.": Maier, *Resistance,* 82.
". . . violent designs of others.": Miller, *Adams,* 159.
111
"a fresh token . . .": *Boston Chronicle,* Oct. 3, 1768.
". . . scalded hogs.": Miller, *Adams,* 161.
"Yankee Doodle" background: Maverick, 106–35.
112
British parade: Zobel, 100.
113
people would not be awed: *Boston Gazette,* Oct. 3, 1768.
". . . I will stand alone.": Williams, "Samuel Adams," 47.
Samuel Adams and child: Wells, III, 220.
". . . feats of action.": Miller, *Adams,* 162–63.
". . . red-dressed": John Quincy Adams, 121.
"the ridiculous puff . . .": Miller, *Adams,* 163.

114
Otis about British stench: Tudor, 338.
Dalrymple reward: Beach, 161.
". . . cut your masters' throats": Zobel, 102.
blown off course: Beach, 168.
Molineux letting property: Zobel, 104.

115
". . . spend our last drop of blood . . .": Ibid., 171.
". . . thou fool!": Sibley, XIII, 382.
". . . give laws to England.": Bailyn, *Ordeal*, 127.

116
"shuddered at the sight of hemp": Miller, *Adams*, 167.
"within a hair's breadth": Ibid.
make the Council more responsive: Walett, 205–22.

117
". . . worst effects.": Ibid.
". . . great contempt.": Miller, *Adams*, 171.
cut the heart out of portrait: Ibid.
". . . black eye.": Harlow, 135.

118
canoe: *Barrington–Bernard Corresp.*, Oct. 12, 1769, p. 207.

119
". . . independent we shall be.": Hutchinson, *History*, III, 190.
"Journal of the Times": Miller, *Adams*, 174.
"working the political engine": John Adams, *Diary*, I, 432–33.
war producing more births than deaths: Miller, *Adams*, 175.
". . . favorite grand-daughter": Ibid.
gunfire and horseraces: Lemisch, 492.

120
"They stick at nothing.": Bailyn, *Ordeal*, 125.
traditional password: Samuel Adams, *Writings*, I, 255.
dig in ribs: Miller, *Adams*, 176.
change parade schedule: Frothingham, *Rise*, 117–18.
ear-piercing fife: John Adams, *Diary*, III, 289–90.
Britain's determination: Beach, 165.

121
"cool, abstemious, polished": Miller, *Adams*, 94.
". . . loved good cheer.": Ibid.
noblest of duties: Tudor, 356.
". . . or any of his cabal.": *Boston Gazette*, Sept. 4, 1769.
". . . to break his head.": Ibid.

122
brawl in tavern: Ibid., Sept. 18, 1769.

123
assassination attempt: Ibid., Sept. 11, 1769.
"very unfair play": Bailyn, *Ordeal*, 137.
Robinson to pay costs: Tudor, 366.

smeared Mein's signs: Zobel, 151.
124
had her jailed: Mitchell, I, 2.
careless about spelling: Schachner, 5.
divorce in England: Ibid., 8.
Decalogue in Hebrew: John Hamilton, 3.
". . . wish there was a war": Ibid., 4–5.

MASSACRE: 1770

125
". . . rest of the people never could.": Zobel, 153.
126
Hutchinson wrote to London in code: Bailyn, *Ordeal*, 154.
Mein's attacks: Zobel, 156.
Molineux and Adams get warrant: Ibid., 158.
128
"Stop, Mr. Molineux! . . .": Ibid., 166–67.
". . . treating my person.": Ibid., 167.
Hutchinson's distress: Hutchinson, *History*, III, 192.
129
". . . able to please him.": Zobel, 173.
make a lane through them: *Boston Gazette*, Feb. 26, 1770.
". . . Your liver out!": Zobel, 174.
130
". . . son of a poor German.": Hutchinson, *History*, III, 194.
Bostonians resented the competition: Lemisch, 485–504.
exchange at Gray's ropeworks: John Adams, *Legal*, III, 134; Samuel Drake,
273.
131
Burdick episode: Page Smith, *New Age*, I, 332.
132
small boy rings bells: Francis Bowen, 350.
133
Private White and Garrick: Zobel, 186.
136
Preston background: Higgins, II, 221.
138
Firing on King Street: Zobel: 195–200.
". . . they will not fire.": Kidder, 6.
139
Crispus Attucks: Ibid., 29–30n.
140
"You are only frightened.": Ibid., 287.
141
"Perhaps, sir, you may.": Zobel, 200.

Trial: 1770

142
Adams after shootings: John Adams, *Diary*, III, 292.
144
John Adams as boy: Chinard, 12.
Adams mourns end of Harvard days: Sibley, XIII, 514–15.
infant petticoats: John Adams, *Diary*, I, 13.
Adams weighs career: Ibid., III, 264.
145
Adams on suffrage: Ibid., 265.
Adams as dramatist: Bailyn, *Butterfield's*, 243–45.
Franklin considered genius: John Adams, *Diary*, I, 13.
Gridley–Adams exchange: Ibid., 272.
146
"no friends": Bailyn, *Butterfield's*, 244.
Paine–Adams exchange: John Adams, *Diary*, I, 59.
Adams about Hannah Quincy: Ibid., 67.
". . . gain a reputation!": Ibid., 78.
147
Adams considers proposing to Hannah: Shaw, 30.
". . . obliging, active.": John Adams, *Diary*, I, 234.
". . . legs of a lady": Page Smith, *Adams*, I, 68.
Adams' mortification: Shaw, 53.
148
path to madness: Frothingham, *Warren*, 51.
declined Admiralty Court: Trevelyan, I, 72.
". . . not get her with child": Page Smith, *Adams*, I, 109.
". . . rational amusements or inquiries.": Ibid., 110.
fame and power: Rossiter, *Legacy*, 528–50.
James Forrest: John Adams, *Diary*, III, 292.
150
". . . die by the law!": Bailyn, *Ordeal*, 158.
Preston led to jail: John Quincy Adams, 138–39.
". . . without hesitation he shall have it": John Adams, *Diary*, III, 293.
151
delegates call on Hutchinson: Wells, I, 323.
152
"Both regiments or none!": Ibid.
guilty of high treason: Bailyn, *Ordeal*, 159.
"I can do nothing further.": Zobel, 207.
153
Hutchinson's knees trembling: Warren and Adams, I, 9.
Hutchinson sees proof of plot: Bailyn, *Ordeal*, 161.
"And take the troops with you.": Zobel, 209.
154
common grave: Kidder, 30.
". . . tyrants not one mile away?": Ibid., 215.

no excuse for delay: Samuel Adams, II, 18.
"Sam Adams's two regiments": Beach, 196.
Revere's engraving: Forbes, 154–55.
155
"God send thee a good deliverance.": Zobel, 239.
never convict Preston: Ibid., 245.
156
". . . harken to your evidence": John Adams, *Legal*, I, 123.
157
". . . we must conform to the times.": Kidder, 20.
Jack's testimony: Zobel, 258.
Preston didn't thank Adams: Forbes, 170.
Quincy background: Ibid., 157–58.
158
Samuel Adams on servant and master: Samuel Adams, II, 132.
Carr's testimony: Forbes, 160; Zobel, 286.
159
Samuel Adams on Carr's reliability: Forbes, 160.
John Adams on mob: Zobel, 292.
160
three brawlers at the ropeworks: Lemisch, 485.
". . . guilty of manslaughter.": Wemms, 207–9.
161
benefit of clergy: Burleigh, 95n.
Montgomery confessed: Mayo, 33.
". . . a little more significant": Hosmer, 192.
patriots accused of plunder: Samuel Adams, II, 15–16.
Samuel Adams on red cloak: Ibid., 124.
162
Hutchinson accepts the governorship: Bailyn, *Ordeal*, 167.

Tea: 1771–73

163
". . . Cursed be the day I was born.": Miller, *Adams*, 219.
164
Abigail Adams burst into tears: John Adams, *Diary*, III, 294.
"Never in more misery . . .": Ibid., II, 6.
Samuel Adams letter to Hancock: Samuel Adams, II, 9.
165
". . . hope to see a good effect.": Frothingham, *Warren*, 102.
Hancock and cadets: Fowler, 136.
promote Hancock to Council: Bailyn, *Ordeal*, 178.
Hutchinson warns against Adams' cunning: Fowler, 141; Wells, II, 12.
166
tried where goods were confiscated: Bartlett, 7.
hanged as pirates: Staples, 5.

167
aboard the *Gaspee:* Bartlett, 15-24.
169
Dudingston refuses to testify: Ibid., 25.
Hutchinson's response: Bailyn, *Ordeal,* 194; Wells, II, 14.
burning five times as serious: K. G. Davis, 6.
". . . wash her hands in innocence.": Wells, II, 16.
170
Dudingston sends gold buckle: Bartlett, 24-45.
". . . make themselves ridiculous.": Wells, II, 2.
Adams–Warren exchange: Warren and Adams, I, 14, Dec. 9, 1772; Frothingham, *Warren,* 212.
towns' endorsements: Wells, II, 3.
172
Adams didn't believe letters useful: Ibid., 318.
tyrants tremble: Bailyn, *Ordeal,* 240.
Hancock swore: Miller, *Adams,* 280.
Franklin on ruse: Bailyn, *Ordeal,* 240n.
Adams as "Novanglus": Ibid., 243.
173
". . . cries from the ground.": Ibid., 249.
Hutchinson on King David: Ibid., 251.
Adams on Hancock's tea: John Adams, *Diary,* II, 5.
174
bribes for customs officers: Schlesinger, "Uprising," 62.
legal tea cost less: Ibid., 63.
East India Co. second to Bank of England: Fowler, 154.
Hutchinson's sons licensed: Bailyn, *Ordeal,* 259.
175
". . . sake of gain.": Dickinson, *Writings,* I, 459.
first shipment from China: Labaree, *Tea Party,* 4.
rheumatism and nervous fevers: Schlesinger, "Uprising," 78.
". . . shall not be landed": Frothingham, *Warren,* 240.
Faneuil threatened: Francis Drake, xxix.
". . . trifling subject.": Frothingham, *Warren,* 247.
Dartmouth arrives: Goss, I, 120.
176
". . . stares you in the face.": Newell, 217.
Hutchinson on Adams: Frothingham, *Warren,* 258.
"that the tea should be returned . . .": "Minutes of the Tea Meetings," 10–11.
watch committee appointed: Ibid., 11.
". . . representative of *majesty?*": Bailyn, *Ordeal,* 261.
Hutchinson's response: Francis Drake, liv.
177
"The ship must go . . .": Ibid., lv.
178
Hutchinson's research: Labaree, *Tea Party,* 139.

179
towns advised to appoint inspectors: Francis Drake, lix.
Meeting agreed to extension: Ibid., lxvi.
"A mob! A mob!": Labaree, *Tea Party*, 141.
". . . to save the country.": Goss, I, 127; Wells, II, 122.
"Boston harbor a teapot tonight!": Francis Drake, lxiv.
". . . do what is right in his own eyes.": Forbes, 189.
Edes and Mohawks: Francis Drake, lxxviii.
180
Hewes: Thatcher, 61–112.
Rhode Island crew: Maier, *Resistance*, 7.
"The path is wide enough . . .": Francis Drake, lxxx.
181
"What a cup of tea . . .": Ibid., lxxxii.
onlookers underfoot: Labaree, *Tea Party*, 145.
182
tea falling back on deck: Francis Drake, lxxxviii.
"You had better make your will first!": Thatcher, *Hewes*, 183.
Montagu–Pitts exchange: Ibid., 185.
"Well, George . . .": Ibid., 187.
wife more tea-drinker: Forbes, 192.
183
"a little saltwater tea": Ibid., 191–92.
Sessions left town: Francis Drake, lxxx.
Mackintosh: Anderson, 60–64.
Hancock's undisclosed interest: Hancock, 178n.
184
"We are in perfect jubilee . . .": Goss, I, 131.
New York pact: Jensen, *Founding*, 446.
"There is a dignity, a majesty . . .": John Adams, *Diary*, II, 86.
"Rally, Mohawks!": Goss, I, 128.
Dartmouth not informed: Labaree, *Tea Party*, 174.
185
". . . wild pretensions": Channing, III, 133.
Philadelphia throng: Wells, II, 129.
". . . bungling politician.": Ibid., 43n.
Hillsborough and Franklin: Bailyn, *Ordeal*, 232; Fennelly, 363.
Dartmouth and Franklin: Bailyn, *Ordeal*, 254.
186
". . . a hundred grievances . . .": Morison and Commager, 159.
Wedderburn in Edinburgh: Mumby, 314.
Wedderburn's attack: Van Doren, *Franklin*, 469.
187
Whatley sues Franklin: Bailyn, *Ordeal*, 257.
Franklin on prison: Mumby, 317–18.

Port Act: 1774

188
Gage in London: George III, *Correspondence with North*, 164.
Gage's dull conversation: Miller, *Origins*, 398.
Gage resembled Adams: Samuel Drake, 243.
189
Gage had recommended troops for two years: Nichols, 140–44.
Boston would be destroyed: Labaree, *Tea Party*, 183.
Debate in Parliament: Bancroft, VI, 514; Channing, III, 135.
190
colonies more a burden: Becker, *Eve*, 208.
Gibbon on Port Act: Channing, III, 135.
George III jeered: Bancroft, VI, 514.
". . . submit or triumph.": Becker, *Eve*, 208.
Merchants and North: Labaree, *Tea Party*, 193.
another load of tea dumped: Bailyn, *Ordeal*, 270.
Tory bills affecting Boston: Labaree, *Tea Party*, 195–96.
191
Barré opposition: Ibid., 200.
Gage could restore privileges: Mumby, 342.
Gage's reception in Boston: Leonard Larabee, 125.
Hancock delivers Adams' speech: Wells, II, 138.
192
Hutchinson prepares to leave: Bailyn, *Ordeal*, 264–65.
Oliver's death: Ibid., 269.
men overheard at funeral: Mumby, 329.
Hutchinson's tributes: Bailyn, *Ordeal*, 273.
Adams' disparagement: Miller, *Adams*, 301.
Hutchinsons seasick: Bailyn, *Ordeal*, 274.
193
Hutchinson's interview with George III: Hutchinson, "Interview," 326ff.
197
Hutchinson hissed: Fowler, 173.
hangmen with Port Act: Fiske, "Eve," 359.
Samuel Adams' response to Port Act: Wells, II, 147.
Adams solicited food: Ibid., 181.
Committees pledged support: Ibid., 159.
198
Adams reassured about break: Mumby, 319.
Adams and Tories in House: Wells, II, 173–78.
199
Gage and Boston strengths: Forbes, 213; Tourtellot, 86.
200
farmers and fishermen send food: Fiske, "Eve," 359.
committee should be annihilated: Wells, II, 182.
Adams' fable: Ibid., 184.

201
Gage to Dartmouth: Ibid., 186.
"A guinea never glistened . . .": Umbreit, 176–77.
Fenton's bribe: Wells, II, 195.
202
"Tell General Gage . . .": Fiske, "Eve," 366.
"United we stand . . .": Meade, 311.
A Summary View . . . : Jefferson, *Jefferson*, ed. Peterson, 105–22.
203
tobacco exports to stop: Meade, 312.
". . . I know George will.": Ibid., 315.

CONGRESS: 1774–75

204
Samuel Adams' wardrobe: Wells, II, 208.
205
coach and four: *Boston Gazette*, Aug. 15, 1774.
John Adams' reflections: John Adams, *Diary*, II, 100.
206
watermelon: Ibid., 101.
brick buildings: Ibid., 104.
sumptuous breakfast: Ibid., 105.
logic to avalanche: Ibid., 107.
207
". . . and talk away.": Ibid., 109.
Samuel Adams dangerous: Wells, II, 219.
John Adams cold: John Adams, *Diary*, II, 115n.
208
Lynch on Washington: Ibid., 117; III, 308.
"We have not men fit for the times. . . .": Ibid., II, 97.
Randolph admired: Meade, 318.
Henry's reputation: John Adams, *Diary*, II, 113.
Silas Deane wrote home: Burnett, *Letters*, I, 4.
209
first vote: John Adams, *Diary*, II, 122.
Thomson seemed to faint: Meade, 322.
John Adams on quibbling: Ibid., 319.
210
". . . difficulty and distress.": Ibid., 323.
". . . not a Virginian but an American.": John Adams, *Diary*, II, 125.
211
no man could speak twice: Burnett, *Letters*, I, 13.
Duché praying: John and Abigail Adams, 76.
212
"Power results from the real property . . .": Burnett, *Letters*, I, 22.
made Adams blush: John and Abigail Adams, 71.

John Adams eating: Ibid., 78.
213
Galloway's plan: Miller, *Adams*, 322.
Henry's objection: Burnett, *Letters*, I, 53.
Galloway fears mob: Miller, *Adams*, 323.
Washington writes home: Burnett, *Letters*, I, 54n.
Galloway on Samuel Adams: Ibid., 55.
214
John Adams' complaint: John and Abigail Adams, 78.
Elizabeth Adams on Tories: Samuel Adams, Papers, Box 2, Sept. 12, 1774, Bancroft Collection.
Dr. Benjamin Church wrote: Ibid., Sept. 29, 1774.
Suffolk Resolves: Miller, *Adams*, 324.
Henry and John Adams: John Adams, *Diary*, II, 151; Meade, 333.
215
Gage discredited: Shy, *Toward Lexington*, 411.
farmers march to Boston: Channing, III, 155–56.
troops dissatisfied with Gage: Tourtellot, 86.
troops caught in market: John Andrews, Letters, Aug. 20, 1774.
cannon as signal: Ibid., Jan. 4, 1775.
216
". . . wish to make it your own.": Mumby, 373.
Burke's argument: Fiske, "Eve," 363.
"We shall be forced . . .": Pitt, *Correspondence*, IV, 379.
Never! said Montagu: Lecky, 190.
217
Dartmouth's orders: Mumby, 376.
Lydia Hancock and Dorothy Quincy: Fowler, 177.
". . . plunder the effects!": *Boston Evening Post*, Sept. 19, 1774.
218
Warren's oration: Wells, II, 278–80.
219
D'Bernicre and Brown's mission: D'Bernicre, *Instructions*, 5–6.
220
Hancock and British: Hancock, 191.
Corps disbanded: Ibid., 185.
Lydia Hancock leaves: Ibid., 182.
221
complaint about chambermaid: Fowler, 168.
Dorcas Griffith: Tourtellot, 62; Fowler, 169.
Sally Jackson: Forbes, 73.
Dorothy Quincy: Woodbury, 81.
222
Jefferson on Henry's nerve: George Morgan, 185.
Henry's speech: Ibid., 191–95.

LEXINGTON: 1775

225
Isaiah Thomas: Forbes, 236.
226
". . . die up to my knees in blood.": Tudor, 466.
Revere remarries: Farrington, 10.
". . . the bumpkins pronounce it easier.": Forbes, 11.
Revere advertises teeth: Dallas, 20.
Revere didn't powder hair: Forbes, 85.
227
Concord hides cannon: Ibid., 237–38.
228
Gage sends six hundred: Murdock, "British," 71n.
Smith's spying mission: Forbes, 233.
answer, "Patrol.": Mackenzie, I, 18.
229
matron informs Church: Forbes, 242.
"You are the third person . . .": Ibid.
"The people here are a set . . .": Murdock, Nineteenth, 18.
"Why, the cannon at Concord.": Forbes, 243.
Robert Newman: Ibid., 244–45.
230
flannel still warm: Ibid., 246.
231
William Dawes: Tourtellot, 93.
Revere's ride to Lexington: Revere, Own Story and Three Accounts.
232
Revere at parsonage: Farrington, 42–43.
233
British uniforms: Ketchum, Decisive, 123.
British throw away rations: Murdock, "British," 73.
Lexington Minute Men: Tourtellot, 129–30.
234
men vote to disband: Ibid., 21–29.
". . . that hill called Beacon.": Samuel Drake, 340.
chaise prepared: Revere, Own Story, 19.
235
Hancock–Quincy exchange: Woodbury, 68; Forbes, 255.
Revere captured: Revere, Three Accounts.
237
Minute Men reassembled: Narrative, 9.
238
"If I had my musket . . .": Tourtellot, 111.
Revere and trunk: Forbes, 256–57.
239
Pitcairn had no intention: Tourtellot, 127.

"Disperse, ye villains . . .": *Narrative*, 6; Murdock, *Nineteenth*, 27.
". . . Form and surround them.": Tourtellot, 131.
Samuel Adams hears gunfire: Warren and Adams, 54.
240
". . . glorious morning for America.": Wells, II, 294.
"Do you know where a drummer is?": Tourtellot, 137.
"What's that?": Forbes, 258.
hiding valuables: Fowler, 185
241
fine salmon: Revere, *Own Story*, 19–20.
Adams and Hancock in wood: Hancock, 194.
salt pork and potatoes: Woodbury, 67.
Marine sealed orders: Tourtellot, 182–83.
"War's begun . . .": Allan, 33.
242
Buttrick leads march: Tourtellot, 152.
". . . let us die here.": Murdock, "British," 78.
243
"This is the price of blood.": Tourtellot, 157.
Pitcairn hopes to stir blood: Forbes, 260.
244
Description of Brown Bess: Ketchum, *Decisive*, 125.
245
Guns used for duck hunting: Mackenzie, I, 27.
246
Joseph Palmer: Forbes, 261.
". . . I shall call you a coward.": Tourtellot, 219.
head split with tomahawk: Murdock, "British," 88, 93.
248
Deacon Haynes killed: Tourtellot, 219.
249
infantrymen panting: Wells, II, 295.
British shot any man: Tourtellot, 196.
skulking like dastards: Waitt, 96.
"King Hancock forever!": Mackenzie, I, 21.
252
"Old Put": Forbes, 261.
254
London *Chronicle:* Waitt, 94–95.
George III's ultimatum: Channing, III, 159–60.

ARNOLD: 1775

255
Benedict's teachers remembered: Decker, 11.
256
stole birds, strewed glass: Sparks, 5–6.

Arnold deserted: Sellers, 14.
Arnold's trade: Boylan, 36.
Hannah Arnold's suitor: Decker, 21.
257
Arnold's duel: Sellers, 6.
Peter Boole: Boylan, 39.
258
Arnold's disease: Ibid., 37.
"None but Almighty God . . .": Arnold, 36.
259
Arnold commissioned: Ibid., 38.
260
"Carillon": Jellison, 106.
"noisy": De Puy, 79n.
"Huzzah for the Green Mountains!": Ibid., 159.
262
"Come out, you old rat!": Tourtellot, 251.
". . . what—what—does this mean?": Forbes, 278.
Boys spat at Arnold's feet: Boylan, 43.
Stores at Fort Ti: Arnold, 40.
263
"Boston *must* be entered . . .": Hancock, 197.
264
Dolly Quincy knew whom to blame: Woodbury, 91.
"in short, no person . . .": Hancock, 198-99.
Adams objected to men pulling carriage: Wells, II, 30-31.
Massachusetts paid for Adams' clothes: Ibid.
265
Franklin slept in chair: John Adams, *Works*, I, 663-64.
Congress told Allen to inventory British artillery: Boylan, 45-46.
266
"Johnny, you will be hanged . . .": Ibid., 316.
"What is the reason . . .": Miller, *Adams*, 339-40.
"one of the grandest revolutions . . .": Ibid., 340.
"a great fortune and piddling genius . . .": John Adams, *Diary*, II, 174n.
267
". . . first politician in the world.": Wells, II, 304.
"We will show Britain . . .": Hancock, 201.
Adams confessed knew nothing of military: Miller, *Adams*, 346.
268
three parties at Congress: John Adams, *Diary*, III, 321.
269
Adams nominates Washington: Ibid., 323.

BUNKER HILL: 1775

271
". . . soon find elbow room.": Ketchum, *Decisive*, 2.
272
"an impotent general . . .": Ibid., 25.
choice of Breed's Hill: Fleming, 349.
275
narrow entrance on north side: Ketchum, *Decisive*, 111.
ditch might protect them: Coffin, 12.
276
knapsacks loaded down: Lecky, 204.
". . . gates of hell": Ketchum, *Decisive*, 127.
Not one came back: Coffin, 16.
277
Stark's men prepare: Ibid., 18.
"carcasses": Fleming, 240.
278
"Remember, gentlemen . . .": Clark, *Diary*.
279
Stark posted men: Coffin, 12.
". . . you will be slain.": Forbes, 279.
280
"I have no command . . .": Coffin, 15.
281
". . . whites of their eyes": Fleming, 245.
dead thick as sheep: Coffin, 13.
282
Howe's deployment: Ibid., 9–17.
284
Putnam and Gerrish: Ketchum, *Decisive*, 165.
". . . let me die in peace.": Ibid., 172.
285
Pitcairn speaking about duty: John Clarke, 18.
286
". . . might have *led* them up.": Coffin, 33.
Warren's death: Frothingham, *Warren*, 517; Cary, 221.
287
John Dutton's death: John Clarke, 8.
Otis at battle: Starrett, 154; Fiske, "Eve," 376.

WASHINGTON: 1775

289
"A few such victories . . .": Ketchum, *Decisive*, 209.
". . . sell them another hill . . .": Fiske, "Eve," 377.

losses: Forbes, 281; Murdock, *Bunker Hill*, 32.

290
". . . seven times seven years.": Washington, *Writings*, ed. Fitzpatrick, III, 294.
". . . embarked on a wide ocean . . .": Ibid., 30 June 1775.

291
Washington named for Eskridge: Cunliffe, 23–24.

292
Washington description: Hodges, 18.
Washington copied rules: Cunliffe, 26n.; Hughes, 29.
verses on true happiness: Haworth, 5–7.
Mary Washington: Flexner, *Forge*, 19.

293
blanket with fleas: Whipple, 785.
romped with neighborhood girl: Hodges, 15.
Sally Fairfax: Cunliffe, 30.

294
wrote four times: Fleming, *Yours*, 16.

295
Mary Washington objects to military service: Turner, 184.
"As to the summons . . .": Freeman, II, 368.
French assured Washington privately: Cunliffe, 35.

296
pay of eightpence a day: Alberts, 5.

297
". . . charming in the sound": Fleming, *Yours*, 18.

298
Washington signs confession: Flexner, *Forge*, 104.
Indians joining French or neutral: Alberts, 44.
"He would not say so . . .": Cunliffe, 37.
Washington famous for incompetence: Flexner, *Forge*, 108.
Washington exceeded authority: Alberts, 25.

299
Sally Fairfax asks Washington not write: Flexner, *Forge*, 123.
a gentle rebuke: Fleming, *Yours*, 27.
"Honoured Madam": Bellamy, 19.
Washington at end of column: Cunliffe, 39.

300
"I take this early opportunity . . .": Whipple, 786.
"Your honor will, I hope . . .": Cunliffe, 42.
Washington slow to praise: Freeman, I, 370–71.

301
favors to Fairfax sons: Ibid., III, Appendix II.

302
Washington's teeth: Haworth, 13–14.
Washington to Martha: Fleming, *Yours*, 32.

303
". . . this lady is known to you.": Ibid., 33.

304
confused firing in woods: Freeman, II, 357–58.
price of Fort Necessity: Alberts, 57.
slave named Will: Kitman, 155.
servants afraid to deliver note: Turner, 220.
305
". . . the irritability of some of us is enough to—": John and Abigail
Adams, 106.
Dickinson cuts Adams: John Adams, *Diary*, II, 173.
Samuel Adams taught to mount: Warren, I, 110–11.
306
country folk gape at Hancock: Fowler, 194.
Hancock's gifts to Dorothy Quincy: Hancock, 203.
Congress debates move: Burnett, *Letters*, I, 113.
"I, poor creature . . .": John and Abigail Adams, 92.
307
Randolph's death: Fowler, 199.
". . . sentimental effusions . . .": John and Abigail Adams, 100–101.
British slaughtering cows: Fleming, *Yours*, 58–59.
308
". . . amazing good natured.": Thatcher, *Hewes*.
"exceedingly dirty and nasty people": Washington, *Writings*, ed. Fitz-
patrick, III, 433.
Washington did not whip slaves: Kitman, 54.
cider confiscated: "Orderly Book of Camp at Cambridge."
"The general does not mean . . .": Ibid., 6.
309
"He is a queer creature . . .": Willard, 46.
310
Church's treason: Freeman, III, 545–48.
Church examines Attucks: Sibley, XIII.
311
". . . or I perish.": Freeman, III, 548.
Church's sister: French, 151.
Church claims to be gleaning information: Goss, I, 207–8.
Revere saw Church: Tourtellot, 227–28.
Hutchinson's report on Church: Sibley, XIII, 384.
312
Church allowed to ride: Forbes, 285.
Army pay: Kitman, 29.
holdovers away on furlough: Lecky, 232.
"the mild general": Ketchum, *Decisive*, 213.
Howe had written home: George III, *Correspondence with North*, II, 13.
"Sir William, he . . .": Ketchum, *Decisive*, 36.

Lee: 1775

314
Arnold's expenses disallowed: Boylan, 46–47.
315
Catholic population: Pemberton, 233.
a new Inquisition: Wandell, 42.
316
"Let us run together . . .": Freeman, III, 536.
"The Great American Congress . . .": Ibid., 533.
"the sweepings of the streets": Wandell, 44.
317
"You will die . . .": Ibid., 45.
eating dog: Arnold, 67.
eating duck: Ibid., 57.
Greer's wife: Ibid., 66.
318
sickness drops men to 650: Ibid., 60.
320
". . . force and energy?": John and Abigail Adams, 113.
321
"To the storming . . .": Arnold, 80.
"We shall be in the fort . . .": Wandell, 50.
Burr tries to drag Montgomery: Lomask, 41.
322
". . . enter it in triumph.": Arnold, 84.
323
"I will not execute you now.": Dorson, 46.
"I tremble . . .": Alsop, 32.
324
Bonvouloir: Ibid., 14–24.
"Mr. Straham . . .": Ronald Clark, 276.
325
"Everyone here is a soldier. . . .": Alsop, 31.
326
"America is the hope . . .": Ibid., 35.
"England is the natural enemy . . .": Ibid., 32.
Washington on Ethan Allen: Scheer and Rankin, 127.
"Men, I do not know . . .": Ibid., 113.
328
"bring on a rumpus . . .": Fleming, *Affectionately Yours*, 80.
Washington had read Burgoyne's letter: Ibid., March 31, 1776.
Washington writing about parapets: Ibid., Feb. 1, 1776.
Barrels filled with dirt: Heath, 32–33.
329
". . . committed suicide.": Montross, 134.
". . . dog in a dancing school.": Scheer and Rankin, 194.

330
"Naso": Burke Davis, *Washington*, 18.
"Boiling Water": Patterson, 40.
"Sir, I will never give Your Majesty . . .": Walpole, I, 404–5.
331
John Adams on Lee: Miller, *Triumph*, 70.
Lee borrows 15 pounds: Alden, 73.
"We want you at N. York . . .": Lee, *Papers*, I, 312.
332
"Colonel, I see . . .": Ibid., 154.

JEFFERSON: 1775–76

336
Paine's mother a shrew: Edwards, 5.
God was too good: Conway, I, 11.
the Headstrong Book: Connell, 18.
337
Paine's eyes and women: Hawke, *Paine*, 14.
Elizabeth Paine: Edwards, 16.
". . . husband or an oppressor": Conway, I, 45–46.
338
"I rejected . . .": Paine, 44.
Paine longed for independence: Wills, 330.
340
"O ye that love mankind! . . .": Paine, 50.
Paine and John Adams: John Adams, *Diary*, III, 333–34.
"a better hand . . .": Scheer and Rankin, 168.
341
Jefferson receives *Common Sense:* Malone, I, 217.
"The blood of the slain . . .": Paine, 40.
Paine donates royalties: Conway, I, 69.
Regulators: Montross, 134.
South Carolina sentiment turns: Conway, I, 78.
342
Virginia instructions: Malone, I, 217.
Harrison's joke: Montross, 131.
"Defeated most ignominously. . . .": Ibid., 139.
343
"created as ourselves": Maier, *Old*, 189.
Lee's mutilated hand: Wills, 3.
Rutledge hoped for delay: Burnett, *Letters*, I, 476–77.
345
Adams–Jefferson exchange: Ibid., 541n.
346
Jefferson carried by slave: Randall, I, 11.
Jefferson's inheritance: Malone, I, 32; Page Smith, *Jefferson*, 9.

"filled the college with children": Ibid., 15.
Jefferson did not allow cards: Randolph, 30.
347
Fauquier used ice: Malone, I, 77.
348
"I do wish the devil . . .": Nock, 19.
Jefferson's travel plans: Ibid., 21.
"This should be . . .": Ibid., 22.
349
"When young and single . . .": Malone, I, 449.
350
coat of arms: Ibid., 156.
Jefferson wrote "spinster": Curtis, 32.
Jefferson willing to sink island: Brodie, 130.

INDEPENDENCE: 1776

353
Jefferson's Virginia draft: Jefferson, *Papers*, I, 33ff.
355
Jefferson wrote in "self evident": Wills, 181–82.
Jefferson on property: Page Smith, *Jefferson*, 96–97.
meaning of "pursuit": Schlesinger, "Lost Meaning," 323–25.
New Yorkers had petitioned: Force, 24.
356
South Carolina's assembly moved: Fisher, 274.
357
blacks outnumbered whites ten to one: Brodie, 41.
one third of Virginia was black: George Howard, 20.
358
Bland was denounced: Brodie, 103.
Jefferson did not permit whipping: Ibid., 22.
Jefferson advertised and sold slave: Ibid., 104.
Jefferson as lawyer: Ibid.
John Adams objected: Meigs, 233.
359
Adams considered denunciation best part: Becker, *Declaration*, 213.
Witherspoon on ripeness: Trevelyan, II, 158.
Dickinson on delay: Wells, II, 432.
Adams felt like actor: John Adams, *Diary*, III, 397.
360
"It ought to be commemorated . . .": John and Abigail Adams, 142.
Jefferson on Northern merchants: Brodie, 144.
361
Franklin's hatter anecdote: Jefferson, *Works*, X, 120.
362
Hutchinson degree: Bailyn, *Ordeal*, 356.

chancellor was North: Malone, I, 229.
363
Jefferson asked Lee to judge: Burnett, *Letters*, II, 2.
George III buried in Savannah: Brodie, 146.
Virginia's deletions: Frank Moore, I, 266.
Jefferson's journal: Brodie, 148.
"There! John Bull . . .": Hazelton, 210.
"Most willingly . . .": Chamberlain, 277n.
". . . all hang separately": Van Doren, *Franklin*, 551.
Evening Post: Bond, Aug. 10, 1776.
Morning Post: Aug. 12, 1776.
364
"A reply . . .": *Morning Post*, Aug. 20, 1776.
"Here they enumerated . . .": *Gazetteer*, Aug. 17, 1776.
". . . a dignified contempt.": *Morning Post*, Aug. 20, 1776.
"the despised Americans . . .": Bond, *Public Advertiser*, Sept. 11, 1776.
400,000 blacks: Middlekauff, 28.
365
slave fans speaker: Hazelton, 277.

LONG ISLAND: 1776

368
usefulness of assassination: Wells, II, 438.
Hopkins impatient to leave: Burnett, *Letters*, II, 78.
Franklin's plan rejected: Pleasants, 5–6.
369
Samuel Adams on state sovereignty: Miller, *Triumph*, 426.
governments of colonies: Nevins, 2.
Massachusetts bloodlines: Ibid.
Virginia on excluding blacks: Jensen, *Making*, 25.
370
Rutledge's goals: Jensen, *Articles*, 128.
George Washington as king: Ibid., 112.
371
Pacific 100 miles from Atlantic: Ibid., 154.
John Adams on Swiss model: Montross, 182.
372
no Northern surpluses: Ibid.
"It is of little consequence . . .": Burnett, *Letters*, II, 56.
373
Britain's greatest force: Ketchum, *Decisive*, 126.
"Let us drub Howe . . .": Miller, *Triumph*, 118.
Hickey and Lynch: Freeman, IV, 115.
374
Mary Gibbons: Ross, I, 197.
all clergy cutthroats: Freeman, IV, 120.

forest of trimmed pine trees: Burke Davis, *Washington*, 87.
375
Washington's deployment: Coakley, 46.
George III statue: Freeman, IV, 134.
molded into 42,088 bullets: Ketchum, *Decisive*, 127.
Washington and Howe letter: Freeman, IV, 140; Brooks, 59.
377
". . . something exceedingly mysterious . . .": Washington, Aug. 19, 1776,
in *Writings*, ed. Fitzpatrick, V, 458.
Howe on "criminal" action: Maldwyn A. Jones, "Sir William Howe," in
Billias, *Opponents*, 53.
378
Greene's background: Theodore Thayer, "Nathanael Greene," in Billias,
Generals, 109.
379
Franklin's propaganda: Burke Davis, *Washington*, 97.
"Lord Stirling": Trevelyan, III, 177.
380
Washington rejected cavalry: Burke Davis, *Washington*, 100.
Clinton had lived in New York: William B. Willcox, "Sir Henry Clinton,"
in Billias, *Opponents*, 74.
381
Jamaica road guards seized: Irving, 216.
"But we're here . . .": Burke Davis, *Washington*, 102.
382
"I will not ask . . .": Scheer and Rankin, 186.
383
"Good God! . . .": Burke Davis, *Washington*, 105.
Stirling fought like a wolf: Trevelyan, II, 280.

NEW YORK: 1776

389
Scammel's blunder: Scheer and Rankin, 193.
Washington left old cannon: Trevelyan, II, 290.
George III knighted Howe: Maldwyn Jones, "Sir William Howe," in Billias,
Opponents, 52.
Connecticut militia drops: Flexner, *Indispensable Man*, 83.
390
"Would to Heaven . . .": Rodney, 112.
391
"I wish that the first ball . . .": Charles P. Whittemore, "John Sullivan," in
Billias, *Generals*, 145.
"A decoy duck . . .": Burnett, *Letters*, II, 70n.
Franklin on colds: John Adams, *Autobiography*, III, 418.
392
Adams approved of meeting site: Ibid., 420.

Adams' impression of Lord Howe: Ketchum, *Winter*, 117.
"Mr. Adams is a decided character.": Burke Davis, *Washington*, 122.
393
"General Howe is either . . .": Ibid., 117.
Greene on Francis I: Trevelyan, II, 295.
394
Germans sang hymns: Burke Davis, *Washington*, 124.
"Take the walls!": Freeman, IV, 193.
395
Germans stabbed Americans: Ibid.
"dastardly sons of cowardice": Miller, *Triumph*, 134.
Greene thought Washington willing to die: Trevelyan, II, 300n.
"Good God, have I got . . . ?": Freeman, IV, 194n.
396
woman hoisted Britain's banner: Serle, 104–5.
"You can hardly conceive . . .": Freeman, IV, 203.
397
Washington to Lund Washington: Washington, Sept. 30, 1776, in *Writings*, ed. Fitzpatrick, VI, 138.
"Providence or some good honest fellow . . .": Scheer and Rankin, 212.
398
Hale hanged: Mackenzie, I, 62–63.

TRENTON: 1776

399
Howe outflanked Americans: Middlekauff, 350.
400
British took 19 days for 74 miles: Miller, *Triumph*, 142.
"They will neither fight . . .": Scheer and Rankin, 231.
Washington complains about New Jersey support: Washington, Dec. 18, 1776, in *Writings*, ed. Fitzpatrick.
401
Paine and Gates: Patterson, 65.
"These are the times . . .": Paine, 75.
402
Lee is paid 11,000 pounds: Miller, *Triumph*, 70.
"I do not mean to flatter . . .": John Shy, "Charles Lee," in Billias, *Generals*, 35.
403
Lee's troops looting: Dwyer, 131.
404
"I am told . . .": Burke Davis, *Washington*, 153.
female screaming: Ibid.
"Entre nous . . .": Lee, *Papers*, II, 345.
"With this sword . . .": John Shy, "Charles Lee," in Billias, *Generals*, 40.

405
"Here, sir, are the British cavalry!": Dwyer, 145.
406
Honeyman escape: Keller, 18–19.
407
Howe's officers not enthusiastic about winter campaign: Channing, III, 232.
Catherine of Russia refused soldiers: Bolkhovitinov, 6.
Prices of mercenaries: Lowell, 5.
408
Hessians described: Azoy, "Merry," 484–85.
Rall drank: Miller, *Triumph*, 155.
Rall persuades Howe: Dwyer, 151.
Rall doesn't build defenses: Channing, III, 233.
"Let them come! . . .": Burke Davis, *Washington*, 161.
409
"Christmas Day at night . . .": Patterson, 110.
Washington's plan: Freeman, IV, 308.
410
"What a time . . . !": Ibid., 309.
Gates does not join: Stryker, 131.
"I am determined . . .": Ibid., 132.
411
"Shift that fat ass . . .": Fast, 120.
"Then tell the general . . .": Stryker, 140.
412
Washington's near-fall: Dwyer, 248; Burke Davis, *Washington*, 166.
"Press on! . . .": Stryker, 143.
Hamilton's speech: Baldwin, 29–30.
Hamilton pats cannon: Burke Davis, *Washington*, 165.
413
"You, sir . . .": Freeman, IV, 313.
"Fiddlesticks! . . .": Dwyer, 221.
414
Rall is warned: Stryker, 123–25.
415
"What's the matter": Ibid., 154.
"You need not be frightened. . . .": Ibid., 162.
soldiers' hands over touchholes: Keller, 22.
416
"Colonel Rall, there is yet . . .": Burke Davis, *Washington*, 171.
"*Alle wer meine Grenadiere* . . .": Stryker, 173.
417
"I pity you.": Ibid., 174.
". . . I will blow you to pieces.": Ibid., 184.
"This is a glorious day . . .": Dwyer, 263.
418
"*Hätte ich dies* . . .": Stryker, 192.
Hessians burned furniture: Dwyer, 262.

PRINCETON: 1776–77

420
Occupations of Hessians: Stryker, 196.
422
Washington looking sly: Ibid., 210.
424
I will remain if you will: Sergeant R——, 515.
"How dreadful the odds.": Dwyer, 294.
Hessians seemed satisfied: Stryker, 213.
425
Hessian evaluation of Putnam: Dwyer, 298.
426
Assunpink Creek possible to ford: Custis, 179–80.
". . . We've got the old fox . . .": Azoy, "Happy," 225.
427
"Damn him, he is dead. . . .": Dwyer, 342.
"Bring up your troops . . .": Freeman, IV, 354.
428
"The enemy were within nineteen miles . . .": Stryker, 451.
"through a lively experience . . .": Miller, *Triumph*, 161.
429
"If there are spots . . .": Freeman, IV, 359.
"In a word . . .": Washington, Jan. 22, 1777, in *Writings*, ed. Fitzpatrick, VII, 53.
"George will not forget . . .": Stryker, 306–7.

GATES: 1777

431
"circumstances very peculiar . . .": Brodie, 152.
"to excuse your retreat . . .": Ibid., 154.
"I am old . . .": Parton, II, 166.
Deane background: James, 5–6.
432
"as so many foreigners . . .": Alsop, 45.
Beaumarchais on Deane: George Clark, 44.
433
The silence "is depressing . . .": Ibid., 65.
"Unless a pistol stops me . . .": Miller, *Triumph*, 279.
hired a coach: Schoenbrun, 50.
stormonter: Alsop, 68.
434
"It is a cloudy day . . .": Curtis, 27.
435
"the bilious Arthur Lee . . .": Alsop, 82.

Franklin would not discharge valet: Van Doren, *Franklin*, 569.
436
Franklin on Christianity: Rossiter, 269.
Franklin feels like little girl: Ibid., 47–48.
"That saying of Poor Richard . . .": Ford, 227.
"But you, as a thorough courtier . . .": Willard Randall, 286.
Franklin and Gibbon: Van Doren, *Franklin*, 577–78.
437
"Whatever becomes of me . . .": Beach, 11–12.
No favoritism for Samuel Adams, Jr.: Maier, *Old*, 34.
"greatly afflicting": Ibid., 46.
438
Washington's belief in democracy: Washington, *Writings*, ed. Sparks, VII, 267.
John and Samuel Adams among few left in Congress: Burnett, *Letters*, II, 260.
Gates wounded on first day: Billias, "Horatio Gates," in his *Generals*, 81.
439
"Granny Gates": Ibid., 80.
John Adams on shooting generals: John Adams, *Familiar*, 292.
440
Germain on Independence Hall: Miller, *Triumph*, 197.
"a kind of neutral tribe": John Adams, *Familiar*, 249.
Paine urged barricades: Miller, *Triumph*, 204.
441
"Within a year . . .": Furneaux, 23.
442
Burgoyne's character: Billias, "John Burgoyne," in his *Opponents*, 145.
443
"This army must not retreat.": Ibid., 174.
Kosciuzko's fort: Higginbotham, 187.
445
"By God, I will soon . . .": Boylan, 110.
British graves: Furneaux, 187.
446
Gates refuses payment of bill: Nelson, 248.
447
"I hope you will not impute . . .": Furneaux, 205.
"He is an old gambler . . .": Patterson, 167.

SARATOGA: 1777

450
"I would indulge them.": Furneaux, 224.
"That gallant officer . . .": Ibid., 235.
451
"Must I die?": Patterson, 169.

"Poor General Burgoyne! . . .": Furneaux, 236.
"Don't hurt him! . . .": Ibid., 239.
"Damned nonsense.": Johnson, 85.
Arnold asks to watch battle end: Trevelyan, IV, 181.
452
"on a matter of high moment . . .": Patterson, 175.
453
"General Burgoyne's army . . .": Furneaux, 261.
454
Wilkinson and Sutherland: Ibid., 265–66.
455
Gates sends meat: Trevelyan, IV, 193.
456
"Yes, I have seen them . . .": Wilkinson, I, 321.
"The fortunes of war . . .": Ibid., 322.
"I shall always be ready . . .": Ibid.
toasts in rum and water: Trevelyan, IV, 194.
major reflected on contrast: Patterson, 183.
457
casualties: Furneaux, 273.
"Make elbow room . . . !": Patterson, 183.

VALLEY FORGE: 1777–78

460
Samuel Adams suggests spurs: Wells, II, 494.
"Heaven has determined . . .": Washington, *Writings*, ed. Fitzpatrick, X, 29.
Rush about Washington's blunders: Miller, *Triumph*, 247.
"a proud, vain, ignorant drunkard": Ibid.
461
"as unfortunate a measure . . .": Freeman, IV, 548.
"I am, Sir . . .": Patterson, 222.
"My opinion of you . . .": Freeman, IV, 556.
462
Gates denounces sneak: Higginbotham, 218.
"Now we can allow . . .": John Adams, *Familiar*, 322.
"I have one favor . . .": Burke Davis, *Washington*, 247.
463
Adamses tried to block thanks for Hancock: Wells, II, 504.
Gates and Wilkinson meet to duel: Trevelyan, IV, 314.
464
Paine defends Washington: Miller, *Triumph*, 257.
Conway received coldly: Ibid., 258.
"You are in my eyes . . .": Washington, *Writings*, ed. Sparks, V, 517.
465
Deane shipped arms: James, 20.
"Sir, *is* Philadelphia taken?": Ronald Clark, 1983.

Bancroft left for London: Van Doren, *Franklin*, 588.
"Everybody is in a gloom. . . .": Bailyn, *Ordeal*, 365.
"My lords, you *cannot* . . .": Chatham, *Oratory*, 36.
466
Parliament's last vote: Montross, 231.
"To give it a little revenge. . . .": Van Doren, *Franklin*, 594.
"I believe no event . . .": Cunliffe, 86.
467
"They were disappointed!": Cadwalader, 468.
"share in the hardship . . .": Washington, *Writings*, ed. Fitzpatrick, X, 167.
"What have you for your dinner, boys?": Scheer and Rankin, 334.
468
Counterfeit money: Ibid., 349.
So ragged and so merry: Flexner, *Indispensable Man*, 117.
Deane meets Lafayette: Howard H. Peckham, "Marquis de Lafayette," in Billias, *Generals*, 213.
469
"We must be embarrassed . . .": Bernier, 48.
"You will reply politely . . .": Ibid., 52.
"His name will be revered . . .": Ibid., 58.
470
"you say to your soldier . . .": Miller, *Triumph*, 231.
"He is to stand . . .": Wilkens, 8.
471
Steuben on hygiene: Ibid., 11.
"Sacre Goddam!": Burke Davis, *Washington*, 270.
472
Lee's appearance at breakfast: Ibid., 273.
"As to King George . . .": Lossing, 34.

Monmouth: 1778

473
"Any other general . . .": Maldwyn A. Jones, "Sir William Howe," in Billias, *Opponents*, 61.
George III railed: Miller, *Triumph*, 229.
474
Franklin on Howe: Lossing, 32.
475
André and Wayne: Boylan, 130.
Mischianza: Bland, I, 92–94.
476
American raiders: Boylan, 147.
laundrywoman's son: Burke Davis, *Washington*, 279.
478
Washington feared trap: Freeman, V, 16.
Hamilton's complaint: Hamilton, *Papers*, I, 510.

479
Lee had no plans: Azoy, "Monmouth," 572.
480
"I have come to warn you . . .": Ibid.
"I am teased, mortified . . .": Ibid., 573.
481
Forman knew a shortcut: Ibid.
"My dear Marquis . . .": Burke Davis, *Washington*, 286.
"I have orders . . .": Ibid., 287.
"Yes, it does. . . .": Azoy, "Monmouth," 576.
482
"Retreating?": Martin, 96–97.
"Colonel Hamilton, you will take . . .": Custis, 219.
"My God, General Lee! . . .": Azoy, "Monmouth," 576.
483
"You've never tried them . . . !": Ibid., 577.
484
Burr blames Washington: Lomask, 57.
"Molly Pitcher": Lossing, 45; Burke Davis, *Washington*, 293.
485
Lee awaits apology: Stryker, 98.
"I have a right . . .": Lee, *Papers*, II, 435.
486
"an unnecessary, disorderly . . .": Washington, *Writings*, ed. Fitzpatrick, XII, 132.
"I trust the temporary power": Lee, *Papers*, II, 439.
Lee was complaining: Freeman, V, 57.
"I have seen retreats . . .": Lee, *Proceedings*, 32.
487
"Did you observe . . . ?": Ibid., 17–18.
"old women, widows . . .": Theodore Thayer, "Nathanael Greene," in Billias, *Generals*, 82.
"You may fire at me . . .": Ibid.
Hamilton stops duel: Mitchell, 256n.

PARIS: 1778–79

488
Abigail Adams lamented separation: John and Abigail Adams, 202.
489
"Mr. Adams, by your name . . .": John Adams, *Diary*, IV, 37.
Franklin's version of Lee: Ibid., 43.
490
Franklin about French feminines: Van Doren, *Franklin*, 693.
Franklin clapping: Ibid., 650.
Franklin's schedule: John Adams, *Diary*, IV, 118–19.

491
"People have the audacity . . .": Van Doren, *Franklin*, 641.
"Madame, I am waiting . . .": Ibid., 647.
"Oh, mores!": John Adams, *Diary*, IV, 59.
Sèvres chamber pot: Alsop, 112.
Adams sent letter for Deane: James, 63.
493
"All we can find . . .": Ibid., 74–75.
Paine whipped: Ibid., 80.
494
Deane and Arnold: Decker, 321.
495
Paul Revere and son: Scheer and Rankin, 390.
Riot instigated by British prisoners: Ibid., 392.
496
men whipped: Thacher, 181.
497
"But remember, my good friend . . .": Washington, *Writings*, ed. Fitzpatrick, XVI, 372.
"If you do not let go . . .": Flexner, *Indispensable Man*, 136.

BETRAYAL: 1780

499
"Take care lest . . .": Billias, "Horatio Gates," in his *Generals*, 99.
Hamilton calls for Greene: Burke Davis, *Washington*, 332.
500
bestowed "commendations . . .": Boylan, 161.
501
Lafayette stayed with Washington: Freeman, V, 197.
502
Peggy Arnold shrieking: Ibid., 202.
503
"I hope, gentlemen . . .": Benson, 14; King, 294.
504
André's papers: Hamilton, 12.
"My God! Arnold has gone over . . .": Flexner, *Traitor*, 372.
505
"All is safe . . .": Boylan, 225.
Arnold's payment: Higginbotham, 403.
506
"No, sir! One coat . . .": Boylan, 219.
Lafayette wrote on behalf of Peggy Arnold: Burke Davis, *Washington*, 341.
507
Tallmadge and André: Tallmadge, 756.
"The commander-in-chief directs . . .": Scheer and Rankin, 444.

508
André asks to be shot: Boylan, 232.

509
"Take your black hands . . .": Burke Davis, *Washington*, 346.
Hamilton looks differently at Washington: Tansill, 185.

YORKTOWN: 1781

512
arms and equipment missent: Miller, *Triumph*, 557.
Jefferson mortified by obligations: Brodie, 163.

513
Arnold's pay: Willard M. Wallace, "Benedict Arnold," in Billias, *Generals*,
187.
Jefferson's hatred of Arnold: Brodie, 164.
Arnold's leg would be buried: Boylan, 239.
Jack Jouett: Malone, I, 356.

515
"Fire away, then.": Brodie, 180.
Jefferson's slaves desert: Malone, I, 391.

516
"the envious only hate": Ibid., 367.
"We are members . . .": George Morgan, 305–6.

517
"Do you soberly relish . . . ?": Mitchell, 77.
"I would like to speak with you": Ibid., 89.

518
"for three years past . . .": Ibid., 91.

519
Washington's indiscretion: Freeman, V, 281.
Hamilton asks for battlefield assignment: Mitchell, 96.
"These English are mad. . . .": Burke Davis, *Campaign*, 107.

520
Washington's intercepted letter: Randolph Adams, 28.
Cornwallis wanted to win in South: Clinton, I, viii.

522
"If we do not deceive . . .": Burke Davis, *Campaign*, 19.

523
"I'm a shy bitch.": William B. Willcox, "Sir Henry Clinton," in Billias, *Opponents*, 96.
"smelling after every giddy girl": Burke Davis, *Washington*, 389.

524
soldiers making bets on destination: Freeman, V, 314.
Washington knew British squadrons were in Indies: Eckenrode, 28.
"Adieu, my dear Marquis! . . .": Washington, *Writings*, ed. Fitzpatrick,
XXIII, 7.

525
"We must take Cornwallis . . .": Burke Davis, *Campaign*, 67.

VICTORY: 1781

526
"There are between thirty and forty . . .": Pearson, 380.
528
trunks of charred pines: Burke Davis, *Campaign*, 149.
530
"Sir Samuel would be very glad": Pearson, 386.
Washington dictated letter on road repair: Freeman, V, 326.
531
"My dear little General!": Burke Davis, *Campaign*, 180.
533
"be prepared to hear the worst": Hugh F. Rankin, "Charles Lord Corn-
wallis," in Billias, *Opponents*, 218.
Prince William's visit to New York: Miller, *Triumph*, 608.
"In that case, the blame . . .": Burke Davis, *Washington*, 412.
534
"Mr. Evans, you had better . . .": Freeman, V, 356.
535
"Against so powerful an attack . . .": Clinton, *Letters*, Oct. 11, 1781.
"Rush on, boys.": Scheer and Rankin, 563.
"My children, I have great need . . .": Burke Davis, *Washington*, 423.
536
"I am in my redoubt. . . .": Ibid., 424.
538
"An ardent desire to spare . . .": Freeman, V, 378.
539
British forbidden "Yankee Doodle": Burke Davis, *Washington*, 433.
540
"Never from such a good hand.": Denny, 44.
"*If ponies rode men . . .*": Pearson, 398.

FAREWELL: 1781–83

542
Horace Walpole's complaint: Miller, *Triumph*, 612.
543
Burgoyne's reputation rehabilitated: Lutnick, 475.
544
Mary Washington's letter: Burke Davis, *Washington*, 447.
545
Pembroke's letter: Long, 286.

"Oh, God! . . .": Miller, *Triumph*, 612.
king warns North: Long, 288.
"Remember, my lord . . .": Guttmacher, 135.
"At last, the fatal day . . .": Long, 295.
546
House of Commons on record: Bolton, 70.
"The readiest way to procure a lasting . . .": Freeman, V, 421.
"was the greatest blow . . .": Alsop, 224.
547
"He is a delightful child . . .": John and Abigail Adams, 291.
549
"It is a glory . . .": Bailey, 30.
"John Adams is always . . .": Corbin, 141.
"I am of your opinion . . .": Van Doren, *Franklin*, 690.
551
John Adams on Lafayette: Bernier, 141.
"If we are not a happy people . . .": Morris, 580.
"more suitable to the effeminancy . . .": Harlow, 301.
552
"I love the people of Boston. . . .": Wells, III, 158.
Otis struck by lightning: Tudor, 486.
553
Revere's "equal honor": Forbes, 351.
John George Washington Hancock: Fowler, 229.
554
hopeless to introduce measure Henry opposes: Meade, 251.
"Open your doors. . . .": Wirt, 253.
white children witness despotism: Jefferson, *Jefferson*, ed. Peterson, 288.
555
"Indeed, I tremble . . .": Ibid., 289.
556
"puffed up charlatan": Burke Davis, *Washington*, 299.
557
"The times that tried . . .": Paine, 113.
"He is poor! . . .": Conway, 207.
Bernard dies of seizure: Bailyn, *Ordeal*, 373.
"die clean": Forbes, 349.
"He was, perhaps, the only man . . .": Bailyn, *Ordeal*, 375.
558
Army would not disband: Jensen, *Making*, 31.
"a dangerous instrument . . .": Mitchell, 79.
559
"Can he be a friend . . . ?": Washington, *Writings*, ed. Fitzpatrick, XXVI, 226–27.
"Gentlemen, you must pardon me. . . .": Shaw, 103–5.
560
"Washington's Legacy": Washington, *Writings*, ed. Fitzpatrick, XXVI, 487.

561
"With a heart full of love . . .": Tallmadge, 95–98.
Washington's expenses: Manuscript, Swem Library, William and Mary College.
562
Washington changes draft: Freeman, V, 474.
"with satisfaction . . .": Washington, *Writings,* ed. Fitzpatrick, XXVII, 284.
563
Jefferson wrote remarks: Freeman, V, 477n.

Bibliography

Adam, G. Mercer. *Samuel Adams*. Milwaukee, 1903.
Adams, Abigail. *Letters of Mrs. Adams*, Charles Francis Adams, ed. Boston, 1841.
Adams, Charles Francis. *Studies Military and Diplomatic*. New York, 1911.
Adams, James T. *Revolutionary New England*. Boston, 1923.
Adams, John. *Diary and Autobiography*, L. H. Butterfield, ed., 4 vols. Cambridge, Mass., 1961.
———. *Familiar Letters*. Freeport, N.Y., 1970.
———. *Legal Papers of John Adams*, L. Kinvin Wroth and Hiller B. Zobel, eds., 3 vols. Cambridge, Mass., 1965.
———. *The Spur of Fame: Dialogues of John Adams and Benjamin Rush*, John A. Schutz and Douglass Adair, eds. San Marino, Calif., 1966.
———. *Statesman and Friend: Correspondence with Benjamin Waterhouse*, Worthington Chauncey Ford, ed. Boston, 1927.
———. *Works*, Charles Francis Adams, ed., 10 vols. Boston, 1856.
———, and Abigail Adams. *The Book of Abigail and John: Selected Letters of the Adams Family, 1762–1784*, L. H. Butterfield, Marc Friedlaender and Mary-Jo Kline, eds. Cambridge, Mass., 1975.

Adams, John Quincy. *The Life of John Adams*, 2 vols. Philadelphia, 1871.

Adams, Randolph G. "A View of Cornwallis's Surrender," *American Historical Review*, Vol. 37 (October 1931–July 1932).

Adams, Samuel. Papers. Bancroft Collection, New York Public Library.

———. *The Writings of Samuel Adams*, Harry Alonzo Cushing, ed., 4 vols. New York, 1904–8.

Akers, Charles W. *The Divine Politician*. Boston, 1982.

Alberts, Robert C. *A Charming Field for an Encounter*. Washington, D.C., 1975.

Alden, John Richard. *General Charles Lee*. Baton Rouge, La., 1951.

Allan, Herbert S. *John Hancock*. New York, 1948.

Allen, Ethan. *Reason: The Only Oracle of Man*. Bennington, Vt., 1784.

Allison, John Murray. *Adams and Jefferson*. Norman, Okla., 1966.

Alsop, Susan Mary. *Yankees at the Court*. New York, 1985.

Anderson, George Pomeroy. "Ebenezer Mackintosh," *Publications of the Colonial Society of Massachusetts*, Vol. XXVI, *Transactions, 1924–26*. Boston, 1927.

André, John. *Journal*, Henry Cabot Lodge, ed., 2 vols. Boston, 1903.

Andrews, Charles M. *The Colonial Period*. New York, 1912.

Andrews, John. Letters, Winthrop Sargent, ed., *Proceedings, Massachusetts Historical Society*, Vol. 8, July 1865.

Aptheker, Herbert. *The American Revolution*. New York, 1960.

Arnold, Isaac N. *The Life of Benedict Arnold*. Chicago, 1867.

Aspinall, A. *Politics and the Press*. London, 1949.

Ayling, Stanley. *The Elder Pitt*. New York, 1976.

Azoy, A. C. M. "Happy New Year 1777," *Infantry Journal*, May–June, 1938.

———. "Merry Christmas 1776," *Infantry Journal*, November–December 1938.

———. "Monmouth," *Infantry Journal*, November–December 1939.

Bailey, Thomas A. *A Diplomatic History of the American People*. Palo Alto, Calif., 1945.

Bailyn, Bernard. "Boyd's Jefferson," *New England Quarterly*, Vol. 3 (1960).

———. "Butterfield's Adams," *William and Mary Quarterly*, 3rd ser., Vol. 19, April 1962.

———. *The Ideological Origins of the American Revolution*. Cambridge, Mass., 1967.

———. *The Ordeal of Thomas Hutchinson*. Cambridge, Mass., 1974.

———, ed. *Pamphlets of the American Revolution, 1750–76*. Cambridge, Mass., 1965.

Baldwin, Jo. G. *Party Leaders*. New York, 1855.

Bancroft, George. *History of the United States*. Boston, 1858.

Barrington-Bernard Correspondence, ed. Edward Channing. Cambridge, Mass., 1912.

Bartlett, John Russell. *A History of the Destruction of His Britannic Majesty's Schooner Gaspee*. Providence, 1861.

Beach, Stewart. *Samuel Adams*. New York, 1965.

Becker, Carl. *The Declaration of Independence*. New York, 1922.

———. *The Eve of the Revolution*. New Haven, 1918.

Beeman, Richard. *Patrick Henry.* New York, 1974.

Belcher, Henry. *The First American Civil War,* 2 vols. London, 1911.

Bellamy, Francis Rufus. *The Private Life of George Washington.* New York, 1951.

Benson, Egbert. *Vindication of the Captors of Major André.* New York, 1865.

Bernard, Francis. Letters. Sparks Collection, Houghton Library, Harvard University, Cambridge, Mass.

Bernier, Olivier. *Lafayette.* New York, 1983.

Billias, George Athan, ed. *George Washington's Generals.* New York, 1964.

———. *George Washington's Opponents.* New York, 1969.

Birnbaum, Louis. *Red Dawn at Lexington.* Boston, 1986.

Bland, Theodorick. *Papers,* Charles Campbell, ed., 2 vols. in 1. Petersburg, Va., 1840–43.

Bolkhovitinov, Nikolai. *The Beginnings of Russian–American Relations, 1775–1815.* Cambridge, Mass., 1975.

Bolton, Charles K. *The Private Soldier Under Washington.* New York, 1902.

Bond, Donovan H., and W. Reynolds McLeod, eds. *Newsletters to Newspapers.* Morgantown, W. Va., 1977.

Bowen, Catherine Drinker. *John Adams and the American Revolution.* Boston, 1950.

Bowen, Francis. *Life of James Otis.* Boston, 1884.

Boylan, Brian Richard. *Benedict Arnold.* New York, 1973.

Brennan, Ellen E. "James Otis," *New England Quarterly,* December 1939.

Brodie, Fawn M. *Thomas Jefferson.* New York, 1985.

Brooks, Noah. *Henry Knox.* New York, 1900.

Brown, Richard D. *Revolutionary Politics in Massachusetts.* Cambridge, Mass., 1970.

Brown, Robert E. *Middle-Class Democracy and the Revolution in Massachusetts, 1691–1780.* Ithaca, N.Y., 1955.

Burgoyne, John. "Surrender to Gates," *New-York Historical Society Quarterly,* Vol. 3, October 1919.

Burleigh, Anne Husted. *John Adams.* New Rochelle, N.Y., 1969.

Burnett, Edmund C. *The Continental Congress.* New York, 1941.

———. *Letters of Members of the Continental Congress,* 6 vols. Washington, D.C., 1963.

———. "The Name 'United States of America,'" *American Historical Review,* October 1925.

Burr, Aaron. *Memoirs,* 2 vols. New York, 1836.

Burr, Samuel E., Jr. *Colonel Aaron Burr.* New York, 1964.

Butler, Henry Montagu. *Lord Chatham as Orator.* Oxford, 1912.

Cadwalader, John. "Letter," *Pennsylvania Magazine of History and Biography,* Vol. 82 (1958).

Callahan, North. *Henry Knox.* New York, 1958.

Cary, John. *Joseph Warren.* Urbana, Ill., 1964.

Chamberlain, Mellen. "The Authentication of the Declaration of Independence," *Proceedings, Massachusetts Historical Society,* 2d ser., Vol. 1 (1884–85).

Channing, Edward. *A History of the United States*, Vol. III, *The American Revolution*. New York, 1920.

Chatham, Lord. *Masterpieces of English Oratory*. Philadelphia, 1885.

Chinard, Gilbert. *Honest John Adams*. Boston, 1933.

Clark, George L. *Silas Deane*. New York, 1913.

Clark, Ronald W. *Benjamin Franklin*. New York, 1983.

Clarke, John. *An Impartial and Authentic Narrative of the Battle Fought on the 17th of June, 1775*. London, 1775.

Clarke, Joseph. "Diary," *New Jersey Historical Society Proceedings, 1854*.

Clinton, Henry. *Cornwallis Letters*, Benjamin F. Stevens, ed., 2 vols. London, 1888.

———. *Narrative Relative to His Conduct*. London, 1783.

Coakley, Robert W., and Stetson Conn. *The War of the American Revolution*. Washington, D.C., 1975.

Coffin, Charles, ed. *History of the Battle of Breed's Hill*. Select Pamphlets, Vol. 117. New York, 1831.

Collins, Paul V. "Disbanding the Revolutionary Army," *Daughters of the American Revolution Magazine*, July 1930.

Connell, J. M. *Thomas Paine*. London, 1939.

Conway, Moncure D. *The Life of Thomas Paine*, 2 vols. New York, 1893.

Corbin, John. *The Unknown Washington*. New York, 1930.

Cunliffe, Marcus. *George Washington*. New York, 1982.

Curtis, William Eleroy. *The True Thomas Jefferson*. New York, undated.

Custis, George Washington Parke. *Recollections and Private Memoirs of Washington*. Philadelphia, 1859.

Dallas, C. Donald. *The Spirit of Paul Revere*. Princeton, N.J., 1944.

Davis, Burke. *The Campaign That Won America*. New York, 1970.

———. *George Washington and the American Revolution*. New York, 1975.

Davis, K. G., ed. *Documents of the American Revolution*, Vol. 5, *Transcripts, 1772*. Dublin, 1974.

D'Bernicre, Henry. *General Gage's Instructions*. Boston, 1779.

Decker, Malcolm. *Benedict Arnold*. Tarrytown, N.Y., 1932.

Denny, Ebenezer. *Military Journal*. Philadelphia, 1859.

De Puy, Henry W. *Ethan Allen and the Green-Mountain Heroes of '76*. New York, 1970.

Dickerson, Oliver M. *The Navigation Acts and the American Revolution*. Philadelphia, 1951.

Dickinson, John. *Writings*, Paul Leicester Ford, ed., 2 vols. Philadelphia, 1895.

Donovan, Frank. *The Women in Their Lives*. New York, 1966.

Dorson, Richard M. *America Rebels*. New York, 1953.

Drake, Francis S. *Tea Leaves*. Boston, 1884.

Drake, Samuel Adams. *Old Boston Taverns and Tavern Clubs*. Boston, 1917.

———. *Old Landmarks and Historic Personages of Boston*. Boston, 1883.

Dull, Jonathan R. *A Diplomatic History of the American Revolution*. New Haven, 1985.

Dwyer, William M. *The Day Is Ours!* New York, 1983.

Eckenrode, H. J. *The Story of the Campaign and Siege of Yorktown.* Washington, D.C., 1931.

Edwards, Samuel. *Rebel!* New York, 1974.

Ellet, Elizabeth. *The Women of the American Revolution,* 3 vols. New York, 1852.

Farrington, Charles C. *Paul Revere and His Famous Ride.* Bedford, Mass., 1923.

Fast, Howard. *The Crossing.* New York, 1971.

Fennelly, Catherine. "William Franklin of New Jersey," *William and Mary Quarterly,* 3rd ser., Vol. VI (1949).

Fiore, Jordan D. "Governor Bernard for an American Nobility," *Boston Public Library Quarterly,* Vol. 4, July 1952.

Fisher, Sydney G. "The Twenty-eight Charges Against the King in the Declaration of Independence," *Pennsylvania Magazine of History and Biography,* Vol. 31, July 1907.

Fiske, John. "The Eve of Independence," *The Atlantic Monthly,* November 1888.

———. "The Temple–Bernard Affair," *The Essex Institute Historical Collections,* Salem, Mass., Vol. XC (1954).

Fleming, Thomas J. *Affectionately Yours, George Washington.* New York, 1967.

———. *Now We Are Enemies.* New York, 1960.

Flexner, James Thomas. *George Washington: The Forge of Experience, 1732–1775.* Boston, 1965.

———. *The Traitor and the Spy.* New York, 1953.

———. *Washington: The Indispensable Man.* Boston, 1974.

Fliegelman, Jay. *Prodigals and Pilgrims.* Cambridge, Mass., 1982.

Flower, Milton E. *John Dickinson.* Charlottesville, Va., 1983.

Forbes, Esther. *Paul Revere and the World He Lived In.* Boston, 1942.

Force, Peter, compiler. *American Archives.* Washington, D.C., 1840.

Ford, Paul Leicester. *The Many-Sided Franklin.* New York, 1899.

Fowler, William M., Jr. *The Baron of Beacon Hill.* Boston, 1980.

Freeman, Douglas Southall. *George Washington,* 7 vols. New York, 1948–57.

French, Allen. *General Gage's Informers.* Ann Arbor, Mich., 1932.

Friedenwald, Herbert. *The Declaration of Independence.* New York, 1904.

Frothingham, Richard. *Life and Times of Joseph Warren.* Boston, 1865.

———. *The Rise of the Republic of the United States.* Boston, 1872.

Furneaux, Rupert. *The Battle of Saratoga.* New York, 1971.

Galvin, John R. *Three Men of Boston.* New York, 1976.

George III. *Correspondence,* Sir John Fortescue, ed., 6 vols. London, 1967.

———. *The Correspondence of King George the Third with Lord North,* 2 vols. London, 1867.

———. *Letters to Lord Bute, 1756–66,* Romney Sedgwick, ed. London, 1939.

Gephart, Ronald M. *Revolutionary America,* 2 vols. Washington, D.C., 1984.

Goodell, A. C., Jr. "Charges Against Samuel Adams," *Proceedings, Massachusetts Historical Society,* Vol. XX, May 1883.

Goodloe, Daniel R. *The Birth of the Republic.* Chicago, 1889.

Gordon, William. *History of the Rise . . . of the United States.* London, 1788.

Goss, Elbridge Henry. *The Life of Colonel Paul Revere,* 2 vols. Boston, 1891.

Green, Walford Davis. *William Pitt.* New York, 1901.

Guedalla, Philip. *Fathers of the Revolution.* New York, 1926.

Guttmacher, Manfred S. *America's Last King.* New York, 1941.

Hamilton, Alexander. *Letter: The Fate of Major André.* New York, 1916.

———. *Papers,* Harold C. Syrett, ed. New York, 1961.

Hamilton, John C. *The Life of Alexander Hamilton.* New York, 1840.

Hancock, John. *John Hancock: His Book,* Abram English Brown, ed. Boston, 1898.

Haraszti, Zoltan. *John Adams and the Prophets of Progress.* Cambridge, Mass., 1952.

Harlow, Ralph Volney. *Samuel Adams.* New York, 1923.

Harrison, Frederic. *Chatham.* London, 1905.

Hatch, Charles E., Jr. *Guilford Courthouse and Its Environs.* Washington, D.C., 1970.

Hawke, David Freeman. *Honorable Treason.* New York, 1976.

———. *Paine.* New York, 1974.

Haworth, Paul Leland. *George Washington: Country Gentleman.* Indianapolis, 1915.

Hazelton, John H. *The Declaration of Independence.* New York, 1906.

Heath, William. *Memoirs,* William Abbatt, ed. New York, 1901.

Hensel, W. U. *Major John André as a Prisoner of War.* Lancaster, Pa., 1904.

Higginbotham, Don. *The War of American Independence.* New York, 1971.

Higgins, Sophia E. *The Bernards of Abington and Nether Winchendon,* 4 vols. London, 1903-4.

Hodges, George. *The Apprenticeship of Washington.* New York, 1909.

Homans, Isaac Smith. *Sketches of Boston.* Boston, 1851.

Hooker, Richard J. "The American Revolution Seen Through a Wine Glass," *William and Mary Quarterly,* 3rd ser., Vol. 11, January 1954.

Hosmer, James K. *The Life of Thomas Hutchinson.* Boston, 1896.

Howard, Brett. *Boston: A Social History.* New York, 1976.

Howard, George Elliott. *Preliminaries of the Revolution.* New York, 1905.

Howe, M. A. De Wolfe. *Boston.* New York, 1903.

Hutchinson, Thomas. *Diary and Letters,* Peter Orland Hutchinson, ed., 2 vols. Boston, 1883-86.

———. *The History of the Province of Massachusetts Bay,* Lawrence Shaw Mayo, ed., 3 vols. Cambridge, Mass., 1936.

———. "Interview with George III," *Proceedings, Massachusetts Historical Society,* October 1877.

Irving, Washington. *Life of George Washington.* Tarrytown, N.Y., 1975.

James, Coy H. *Silas Deane.* East Lansing, Mich., 1975.

Jameson, J. Franklin. *The American Revolution Considered as a Social Movement.* Princeton, N.J., 1926.

Jefferson, Thomas. *Jefferson,* ed. Merrill D. Peterson. New York, 1984.

———. *Papers,* Julian P. Boyd, ed. Princeton, N.J., 1950.

———. *Works,* Paul Leicester Ford, ed., 12 vols. New York, 1905.

Jellison, Charles A. *Ethan Allen.* Syracuse, N.Y., 1969.

Jensen, Merrill. *The Articles of Confederation.* Madison, Wis., 1970.

———. *The Founding of a Nation.* London, 1968.

———. *The Making of the American Constitution.* Princeton, N.J., 1964.

———. *The New Nation.* New York, 1950.

Johnson, Curt. *Battles of the American Revolution.* New York, 1975.

Jones, Howard Mumford, and Bessie Zaban Jones, eds. *The Many Voices of Boston.* Boston, 1975.

Journals of Congress, From Sept. 5, 1774 to Jan. 1, 1776. Philadelphia, 1777.

Keller, Allan. "Washington's Crossing," *American History Illustrated,* February 1972.

Ketchum, Richard M. *Decisive Day: The Battle for Bunker Hill.* Garden City, N.Y., 1974.

———. *The Winter Soldiers.* Garden City, N.Y., 1973.

Kidder, Frederic. *The History of the Boston Massacre.* Albany, N.Y., 1870.

King, Joshua. "Letter," *Historical Magazine,* Vol. 1, October 1857.

Kitman, Marvin. *George Washington's Expense Account.* New York, 1972.

Knollenberg, Bernhard. "Benjamin Franklin and the Hutchinson and Oliver Letters," *Yale University Library Gazette,* July 1972.

———. *Washington and the Revolution.* New York, 1940.

Labaree, Benjamin W. *The Boston Tea Party.* New York, 1964.

———. *Colonial Massachusetts.* Millwood, N.Y., 1979.

Larabee, Leonard W. *Royal Government in America.* New Haven, 1930.

Lecky, William E. H. *The American Revolution.* New York, 1898.

Lee, Charles. *Proceedings of a General Court-Martial.* New York, 1864.

———. *Papers,* 4 vols. New York, 1871–74.

Lemisch, Jesse. "Radical Plot in Boston (1770)," *Harvard Law Review,* December 1970.

Locke, John. *Selections from Second Treatise of Government.* Boston, 1773.

Lomask, Milton. *Aaron Burr: The Years from Princeton to Vice President, 1756–1805.* New York, 1979.

Long, J. C. *George III.* Boston, 1960.

Lopez, Claude-Anne, and Eugenia W. Herbert. *The Private Franklin.* New York, 1975.

Lossing, Benson J. "The Battle of Monmouth Courthouse," *Harper's,* Vol. 27, June 1878.

Lowell, Edward J. *The Hessians.* New York, 1884.

Lutnick, Solomon. "The Defeat at Yorktown," *Virginia Magazine of History and Biography,* October 1964.

Luzader, John. *The Saratoga Campaign of 1777.* Washington, D.C., 1975.

Mackenzie, Frederick. *Diary,* 2 vols. Cambridge, Mass., 1930.

Maier, Pauline. *From Resistance to Revolution.* New York, 1972.

———. *The Old Revolutionaries.* New York, 1980.

Main, Jackson Turner. *The Anti-Federalists.* New York, 1974.

Malone, Dumas. *Jefferson and His Times,* 6 vols. New York, 1948–81.

Martin, Joseph P. *Narrative.* Hallowell, Me., 1830.

Maseres, Francis. *A Fair Account of the Late Unhappy Disturbance at Boston in New England*. London, 1770.

Maverick, Lewis A. "Yankee Doodle," *American Neptune*, April 1962.

Mayer, Henry. *A Son of Thunder*. New York, 1986.

Mayo, Catherine. "Additions to Thomas Hutchinson's History of Massachusetts Bay," *American Antiquarian Society, Proceedings*, Vol. 59 (1949), No. 11.

Meade, Robert D. *Patrick Henry: Patriot in the Making*. Philadelphia, 1957.

Meigs, Cornelia L. *The Violent Men*. New York, 1949.

Middlekauff, Robert. *The Glorious Cause*. Oxford, 1982.

Miers, Earl Schenck. *Crossroads of Freedom*. New Brunswick, N.J., 1971.

Miller, John C. *Origins of the American Revolution*. Boston, 1943.

———. *Sam Adams, Pioneer in Propaganda*. Boston, 1936.

———. *Triumph of Freedom*. Boston, 1948.

"Minutes of the Tea Meetings, 1773," *Proceedings, Massachusetts Historical Society*, Vol. XX, November 1882.

Mitchell, Broadus. *Alexander Hamilton*, 1 vol. New York, 1976.

Montross, Lynn. *The Reluctant Rebels*. New York, 1950.

Moore, Frank. *Diary of the American Revolution*, 2 vols. New York, 1860.

Moore, George H. *The Treason of Charles Lee*. Port Washington, N.Y., 1976.

Morgan, Edmund S. *Birth of the Republic*. Chicago, 1977.

———. *The Genius of George Washington*. New York, 1980.

———, and Helen M. Morgan. *The Stamp Act Crisis*. New York, 1953.

Morgan, George. *The True Patrick Henry*. Philadelphia, 1929.

Morison, Samuel Eliot. *The Oxford History of the United States*, 2 vols. London, 1927.

———. *Three Centuries of Harvard*. Cambridge, Mass., 1936.

———, and Henry Steele Commager. *The Growth of the American Republic*. London, 1942.

Morley, John. *Burke*. New York, undated.

Morris, Richard B. *John Jay*, 2 vols. New York, 1980.

Mumby, Frank Arthur. *George III and the American Revolution*. London, 1924.

Murdock, Harold. "The British at Concord," *Proceedings, Massachusetts Historical Society*, Vol. 56 (1922–23).

———. *Bunker Hill*. Boston, 1927.

———. *The Nineteenth of April*. Boston, 1923.

Namier, Sir Lewis, and John Brooke. *Charles Townshend*. London, 1964.

Narrative, Excursions and Ravages of the King's Troops. Worcester: Isaiah Thomas, 1775. Reprinted, New York, 1968.

Nash, Gary B. *Race, Class and Politics*. Urbana, Ill., 1986.

Nelson, Paul David. "The Gates-Arnold Quarrel," *New-York Historical Society Quarterly*, Vol. LV, July 1971.

———. *General Horatio Gates*. Baton Rouge, La., 1976.

Nevins, Allan. *American States*. New York, 1969.

Newell, Thomas. "Diary," *Proceedings, Massachusetts Historical Society*, Vol. IV.

Nichols, Franklin Thayer. Review of Alden's *General Gage in America*, in *William and Mary Quarterly*, 3rd ser., Vol. VI, January 1949.

Nock, Albert Jay. *Jefferson*. New York, 1926.

Old South Leaflets. Boston, 1920.

Oliver, Peter. *Origin and Progress of the American Revolution*, Douglass Adair, ed. Stanford, Calif., 1967.

"Orderly Book of Camp at Cambridge," manuscript, Swem Library, William and Mary College, Williamsburg, Va.

Otis, James. *Rights of the Colonies Asserted and Proved*. Boston, 1764.

———. *A Vindication of the Conduct of the House of Representatives of the Province of the Massachusetts-Bay*. Boston, 1762.

Paine, Thomas. *Common Sense, The Rights of Man and Other Essential Writings*, Sidney Hook, ed. New York, 1969.

Parton, James. *Life and Times of Benjamin Franklin*, 2 vols. New York, 1864.

Patterson, Samuel W. *Horatio Gates*. New York, 1941.

Pearson, Michael. *Those Damned Rebels*. New York, 1972.

Peladeau, Marius B. *The Verse of Royall Tyler*. Charlottesville, Va., 1968.

Pemberton, W. Baring. *Lord North*. London, 1938.

Pencak, William. *America's Burke*. Washington, D.C., 1982.

Pettengill, Ray W., trans. *Letters from America*. Boston, 1924.

Pitt, William. *Correspondence*, 4 vols. London, 1838–40.

Pleasants, Samuel A. III. *The Articles of Confederation*. Columbus, Ohio, 1968.

Plumb, J. H. *Chatham*. Hamden, Conn., 1965.

Pryor, Mrs. Roger A. *The Mother of Washington and Her Times*. New York, 1903.

Randall, Henry S. *The Life of Thomas Jefferson*, 3 vols. New York, 1858.

Randall, Willard. *A Little Revenge*. Boston, 1984.

Randolph, Sarah N. *The Domestic Life of Thomas Jefferson*. Cambridge, Mass., 1939.

Revere, Paul. *Three Accounts of His Famous Ride*, Edmund S. Morgan, ed. Boston, 1961.

———. *Paul Revere's Own Story*, Harriet E. O'Brien, ed. Boston, 1929.

Rodney, Caesar. *Letters*, George H. Ryden, ed. Philadelphia, 1933.

Rosebery, Lord. *Lord Chatham*. New York, 1910.

Ross, Peter. *A History of Long Island*, 3 vols. New York, 1902.

Rossiter, Clinton. "The Legacy of John Adams," *Yale Review*, Summer 1957.

———. "The Political Theory of Benjamin Franklin," *Pennsylvania Magazine of History and Biography*, July 1952.

Rush, Benjamin. *Autobiography*, George W. Corner, ed. Princeton, 1948.

Schachner, Nathan. *Alexander Hamilton*. New York, 1946.

Scheer, George F., and Hugh F. Rankin. *Rebels and Redcoats*. New York, 1963.

Schlesinger, Arthur M. "The Lost Meaning of 'the pursuit of happiness,' " *William and Mary Quarterly*, 3rd ser., Vol. 21, July 1964.

———. "The Uprising Against the East India Co.," *Political Science Quarterly*, Vol. 32, March 1917.

Schoenbrun, David. *Triumph in Paris*. New York, 1976.

Sellers, Charles C. *Benedict Arnold*. New York, 1930.
Sergeant R——. "Battle of Princeton," *Pennsylvania Magazine of History*, Vol. XX (1896).
Serle, Ambrose. *American Journal*, Edward H. Tatum, Jr., ed. San Marino, Calif., 1940.
Shaw, Peter. *The Character of John Adams*. Chapel Hill, N.C., 1976.
Shaw, Samuel. *Journals*. Boston, 1847.
Sherrard, O. A. *Lord Chatham*. London, 1952.
Shy, John. *Toward Lexington*. Princeton, N.J., 1965.
Sibley, John Langdon (and Clifford K. Shipton). *Biographical Sketches of Graduates of Harvard University in Cambridge, Massachusetts*. Cambridge, Mass., 1873–.
Smith, Frank. *Thomas Paine, Liberator*. New York, 1938.
Smith, M. H. *The Writs of Assistance Case*. Berkeley, Calif., 1978.
Smith, Page. *John Adams*, 2 vols. Garden City, N.Y., 1962.
——. *Jefferson*. New York, 1976.
——. *A New Age Now Begins*, 2 vols. New York, 1976.
Sparks, Jared. *The Life and Treason of Benedict Arnold*. Boston, 1835.
Stamp Act Congress. *Proceedings*. New York, 1765.
Staples, William R. *Documentary History of the Destruction of the Gaspee*. Providence, R.I., 1845.
Starrett, Vincent. "Otis at Bunker Hill," *American Book Collector*, Vol. 6, April 1935.
Stryker, William S. *The Battles of Trenton and Princeton*. Boston, 1898.
Tallmadge, Benjamin. *Memoir*. New York, 1858.
Tansill, Charles Callan. *The Secret Loves of the Founding Fathers*. New York, 1964.
Taylor, Joseph. *Relics of Royalty*. London, 1820.
Thacher, James. *A Military Journal*, 2nd ed. Boston, 1827.
Thane, Elswyth. *The Fighting Quaker*. New York, 1972.
Thatcher, Benjamin B. *A Memoir of George R. T. Hewes*. New York, 1835.
——. *The Making of a Scapegoat*. Port Washington, N.Y., 1976.
Tillotson, Harry Stanton. *The Beloved Spy*. Caldwell, Idaho, 1948.
Todd, Charles Burr. *The Real Benedict Arnold*. New York, 1903.
Tourtellot, Arthur Bernon. *William Diamond's Drum*. Garden City, N.Y., 1959.
Trevelyan, George Otto. *The American Revolution*. New York, 1899.
——. *George the Third and Charles Fox*, 2 vols. New York, 1927.
Tudor, William. *Life of James Otis of Massachusetts*. Boston, 1823.
Turner, Nancy Byrd. *The Mother of Washington*. New York, 1930.
Tyler, Moses Coit. *Patrick Henry*. Boston, 1887.
Umbreit, Kenneth. *Founding Fathers*. Port Washington, N.Y., 1941.
Van Doren, Carl. *Benjamin Franklin*. New York, 1938.
——. *Secret History of the American Revolution*. New York, 1941.
Waitt, Ernest L. "How the News of the Battle of Lexington Reached England," *New England Magazine*, March 1909.
Walett, Francis G. "The Massachusetts Council, 1766–1774," *William and Mary Quarterly*, October 1949.

Walpole, Horace. *Last Journals*, A. Francis Steuart, ed., 2 vols. London, 1910.

Wandell, Samuel H., and Meade Minnigerode. *Aaron Burr*. New York, 1925.

Warden, G. B. *Boston, 1689–1776*. Boston, 1970.

Warren, James, and Samuel Adams. *Warren–Adams Letters*. Boston, 1925.

Washington, George. *Diaries*, John C. Fitzpatrick, ed., 4 vols. Boston, 1925.

———. *Diaries*, Donald Jackson, ed. Charlottesville, Va., 1978.

———. *Writings*, Jared Sparks, ed., 12 vols. Boston, 1834–37.

———. *Writings*, Worthington Chauncey Ford, ed., 14 vols. New York, 1889–93.

———. *Writings*, John C. Fitzpatrick, ed., 39 vols. Washington, D.C., 1931–44.

Waters, John J., Jr., *The Otis Family in Provincial and Revolutionary Massachusetts*. Chapel Hill, N.C., 1968.

Wells, William V. *The Life and Public Services of Samuel Adams*, 3 vols. Boston, 1865.

Wemms, William. *The Trial of Wemms et al*. Boston, 1770.

Weslager, C. A. *The Stamp Act Congress*. Newark, N.J., 1976.

Wharton, Anne Hollingsworth. *Martha Washington*. New York, 1897.

Whipple, Wayne. "The Humor of George Washington," *Century Magazine*, Vol. 81, March 1911.

Wilkens, Fred J. "Steuben Screamed," *Picket Post*, 1948.

Wilkinson, James. *Memoirs of My Own Times*, 4 vols. Philadelphia, 1816.

Williams, William Appleman. "Samuel Adams," *Studies on the Left*, Winter 1969.

Willison, George F. *Patrick Henry and His World*. Garden City, N.Y., 1969.

Wills, Gary. *Inventing America*. Garden City, N.Y., 1978.

Wilson, Woodrow. *George Washington*. New York, 1897.

Wirt, William. *Sketches of the Life and Character of Patrick Henry*. New York, 1859.

Woodbury, Ellen C. D. Q. *Dorothy Quincy*. Washington, D.C., 1901.

Young, Alfred F., ed. *The American Revolution*. De Kalb, Ill., 1976.

Zall, P. M. *Benjamin Franklin Laughing*. Berkeley, Calif., 1980.

Zobel, Hiller B. *The Boston Massacre*. New York, 1971.

Index